Culturally Competent Practice

A Framework for Understanding Diverse Groups and Justice Issues

Third Edition

DOMAN LUM, EDITOR

California State University, Sacramento

THOMSON

BROOKS/COLE

Australia • Brazil • Canada • Mexico • Singapore • Spain
United Kingdom • United States

THOMSON

BROOKS/COLE

***Culturally Competent Practice*: A Framework for *Understanding Diverse Groups and Justice* Issues, Third Edition**
Doman Lum, Editor

Acquisitions Editor: *Dan Alpert*
Assistant Editor: *Alma Dea Michelena*
Editorial Assistant: *Sheila Walsh*
Technology Project Manager: *Julie Aguilar*
Marketing Manager: *Meghan McCullough*
Senior Marketing Communications Manager:
  Tami Strang
Project Manager, Editorial Production: *Christy Krueger*
Creative Director: *Rob Hugel*
Art Director: *Vernon Boes*

Print Buyer: *Linda Hsu*
Permissions Editor: *Roberta Broyer*
Production Service: *Buuji, Inc.*
Production Editor: *Sara Dovre Wudali*
Copy Editor: *Kristina McComas*
Cover Image: © *Geoffrey Clements*/CORBIS
Cover Designer: *Roger Knox*
Cover Printer: *Courier Corporation/Stoughton*
Compositor: *International Typesetting and Composition*
Printer: *Courier Corporation/Stoughton*

Printed in the United States of America
1 2 3 4 5 6 7 10 09 08 07 06

Library of Congress Control Number: 2006925077

Student Edition: ISBN 0-495-18978-2

Thomson Higher Education
10 Davis Drive
Belmont, CA 94002-3098
USA

For more information about our products, contact us at:
Thomson Learning Academic Resource Center
1-800-423-0563

For permission to use material from this text or product, submit a request online at **http://www.thomsonrights.com.** Any additional questions about permissions can be submitted by e-mail to **thomsonrights@thomson.com.**

To the persons and groups who have influenced the development of this book:
Herbert Aptekar and Herman Stein, who brought me into social work education
The Cultural Diversity Committee of the Board of Directors, Council on Social Work Education, who have been advocates of cultural competence programs
The social work educators who have written in the area of culturally competent practice
My wife, Joyce, and children: Lori, Jonathan, Amy, and Matthew Lum
And above all to Dr. Nancy Nystrom for her willingness and her perseverance in proofreading, researching, and correcting this entire manuscript.

Brief Contents

Contents

CHAPTER THREE

Advancing Social and Economic Justice   73

Dorothy Van Soest

Part Two: A Cultural Competence Framework 109

CHAPTER SEVEN

Skill Development   185

Doman Lum and Yuhwa Eva Lu

CHAPTER EIGHT

Inductive Learning   226

Francis K. O. Yuen, Andrew Bein, and Doman Lum

Part Three: Culturally and Ethnically Diverse Groups 253

CHAPTER NINE

Cultural Competence with First Nations Peoples 254

Hilary N. Weaver

CHAPTER TEN

Cultural Competence with African Americans 276

Ruth G. McRoy

CHAPTER ELEVEN

Cultural Competence with Latino Americans 299

Betty Garcia and Maria E. Zuniga

Foreword

Doman Lum has achieved the next level of advancement in cross-cultural social work education. Our field has moved these issues forward—sometimes in tiny increments, sometimes in quantum leaps. This work is one of those quantum leaps forward. It not only represents an advancement in how to think about cultural competence but also brings the field of social work home to its roots and brings the dialogue about cultural content to the heart of our profession where it belongs.

This work moves social work closer to what it should be. It is about the complex interplay between individual and environment, and for the first time, a textbook challenges the social work student to understand his or her own behavior culturally as a prerequisite to effective practice. Past social work education has focused so heavily on the self that it has frequently short-changed learning about the impact of the societal forces that shape and limit the expression of the self. Cultural competence as described in this work holds the promise of solving social work's existential dilemma: Who are we as social workers? We are social beings, individuals with good intent and free will yet limited by our capacity to see beyond our own experience, caught up in a world of asymmetrical power and resource relationships, working to help others resolve the challenges of life in a complex environment. As beings in this context, we are at risk of not seeing the true implications of our actions. It is not enough to be of good intent, as our own history teaches us. We must be able to step back and examine ourselves, and our profession, from a cultural self-assessment point of view if we are to truly honor our own values. This gives a framework for that self-examination and overcomes many of the barriers to effective cultural competence education and training.

In over 25 years of providing training, graduate-level education, and supervision in cross-cultural social work practice, I have found this area of practice to be one of the most challenging to teach. I believe it is challenging due to the nature of the subject matter and the fact that few topics in social work education are more emotionally charged or shaped by the vulnerability and fears of the learner. Few students in social work enter the field with openly racist sentiments. Some are adult children of racist families who have chosen a different path. Most are under the false impression that ignoring differences is sufficient to deal with diversity. Others overidentify with people who are different. As a trainer, I have yet to encounter a group of white supremacists wanting my training. Overall, the social work profession attracts people who want to help people and who define their own identity via the good they do. This is the basis of the fear that I often see in people confronting professional development in cultural competence. Most abhor the idea that they might be unintentionally biased or be seen as the problem. To teach in this area, we must help students confront the demons of oppression within, in such a way as to encourage safe dialogue and self-disclosure and at the same time face the hard truth. We must help students gain insight into the danger that confronts every social worker—the unexamined cultural being and especially the unexplored internal capacity for tolerance—and the danger of doing harm out of good intent.

Social work is a profession that people enter out of identifying themselves as a helper. It is not a profession that people enter for the prestige, power, or money. A social work identity is associated with "doing good." In cultural competence education and training, we confront the learner with a high-risk learning challenge. If the learner does not have cultural knowledge, if the comfort level with a different group is not high, if she or he harbors stereotypes or bias, maybe what the learner "does" is not good. Cultural competence education or training, if not presented with attention to this internal process, is at risk of attacking the very core identity of the would-be social worker, shutting off learning rather than enhancing development. This book makes an important contribution to the field by addressing these issues intentionally and respectfully.

This is the most comprehensive look at cultural competence yet written. The reader will examine why to do it, what it is, and how to do it. This book begins to touch on the advanced issues in culturally competent practice as well. For example, the complex interplay between personality and culture is presented with depth and clarity. The book also reveals the paradox of social work's competing agendas. When is self-determination a priority over consciousness-raising? When does advocacy for a particular social justice cause become activism against difference? As cultural competence continues to evolve in the future, these and other issues will be better understood and confronted ethically and openly.

The real danger in cross-cultural social work is doing harm out of good intent. Social work's history is full of examples of this. In the 1950s, social work was largely responsible for inappropriate removal of Native American children from their families on reservations and placement in non-Native homes. By 1976, one in four Native American children was in out-of-home care or institutions. The passage of the Indian Child Welfare Act of 1978 was designed to stop the practice and protect the rights of Native American children, families, and tribes. Social work participated in sterilization programs in the Indian Health Service as late as the 1970s. Many in our profession at the time thought this policy was warranted given the poverty they saw yet could not change. Other cultures, other groups, have their own stories, just as troubling.

We must ask ourselves, What are the actions of policies of today that we are implementing out of good intent but that may be mechanisms of harm? Is the headlong rush of our field toward evidence-based practice one more wave of oppression that will harm populations and agencies unable to verify their cultural helping practices as evidence based? Will we one day see the disproportionality in today's juvenile justice and child welfare systems as inflicting harm out of good intent? The self-examination encouraged by this book will help us turn the lens inward and hopefully understand these dynamics and begin to avoid the mistakes of the past.

Yet untouched in cultural competence literature is the need to move toward the principles of reconciliation in cross-cultural social work practice. Participants in the 2005 conference *Reconciliation: Looking Back, Reaching Forward—Indigenous Peoples and Child Welfare*, held in Niagara Falls, Canada, came up with the following framework to guide the work of reconciliation between those harmed by the good intentions of others and those of good intent today. The event resulted in forming a concept of reconciliation as engaging both parties in a process that is comprised of four phases[1]:

1. Truth Telling: The process of open exchange (listening and sharing) regarding child welfare's past
2. Acknowledging: Affirming and learning from the past and embracing new possibilities for the future
3. Restoring: Addressing the problems of the past and creating a better path for the future
4. Relating: Having recognized that indigenous peoples are in the best position to make decisions about indigenous children and youth, we move forward together in a respectful way, along a new path to achieve better outcomes for indigenous children and youth

As social work continues to grow in its ability to work effectively in the context of cultural differences we will learn more and more about how to respect each other. As we engage in dialogue, we will learn more about how to reconcile the tensions held over from the past and how to relate in new ways. As we build a framework for dialogue, self-examination, knowledge development, and skill building, we will take the profession to new levels of awareness and competence. I am pleased and honored to offer these words as the foreword for such an accomplished work. It is clear from this text that cultural competence has come of age. And, most exciting of all, we have only just begun!

Terry L. Cross, MSW,
Executive Director,
National Indian Child Welfare Association,
Portland, Oregon

1 C. Blackstock, T. Cross, J. George, I. Brown, & J. Formsma. (2006). *Reconciliation in child welfare: Touchstones of hope for indigenous children, youth, and families.* Ottawa, ON, Canada: First Nations Child & Family Caring Society of Canada / Portland, OR: National Indian Child Welfare Association.

Preface

As we are in the midst of the 21st century, the theme of culturally competent practice in social work education has become a part of the discussion in culturally diverse social work. Indeed, cultural competence has been recognized as an essential element in dealing with clients as patients in medicine, nursing, psychology, social work, and related helping disciplines and in federal and state government programs in health care, mental health, education, social services, and related fields. For social work education, cultural competence became a reality in the late 1990s. The 1998 University of Michigan, Ann Arbor, conference devoted time to integrate cultural competence into eight social work curriculum areas, and the 2001 University of Texas, Austin, conference furthered the integration of cultural competence into child welfare as it pertained to family violence and substance abuse. These two events were indicators of the vision and leadership of the board of directors of the Council on Social Work Education in this area. I want to thank the Council on Social Work Education, the University of Michigan School of Social Work, the University of Texas at Austin School of Social Work, and the Casey Family Foundation for funding them.

In 2001, three major texts appeared with references to cultural competence in a social work context. One is a whole text (in addition to mine), *Culturally Competent Practice: Skills, Interventions, and Evaluations*, edited by Rowena Fong and Sharlene Furuto (fellow colleagues of the Asian American Social Work Educators caucus, Council on Social Work Education). Major references to cultural competence also appear in Joe M. Schriver's *Human Behavior and the Social Environment: Shifting Paradigms in Esssential Knowledge for Social Work Practice* (third edition) and in Shulamith Lala Ashenberg Straussner's *Ethnocultural Factors in Substance Abuse Treatment* (she uses the term *ethnocultural competency*). This was followed by a succession of social work books that have influenced the profession toward cultural competence: in 2004, *Culturally Competent Practice with Immigrant and Refugee Children and Families* (edited by Rowena Fong) and *Education for Multicultural Social Work Practice: Critical Viewpoints and Future Directions* (edited by Lorraine Gutierrez, Maria Zuniga, and Doman Lum); and in 2005, *Cultural Competence, Practice Stages, and Client Systems: A Case Study Approach* (edited by Doman Lum) and *Multidimensional Contextual Practice: Diversity and Transcendence* (edited by Krishna L. Guadalupe and Doman Lum). These texts demonstrate encouraging signs of major shifts to this new theme.

THE DEVELOPMENT OF THIS TEXT

Cultural competence is an important innovation in social work practice because it challenges us to ask to what extent we are competent about our own culture and the cultures of others in our community. In the field of multicultural social work we want to craft our cultural abilities with clients and measure our effectiveness in terms of behavioral learning outcomes. The development of cultural competence began with social work, which introduced the themes of empowerment, ethnic sensitivity, cultural awareness, and related people of color, gender, and sexual orientation issues. Along the way, a mutual helping discipline, multicultural counseling psychology, shaped a competence framework and a system of competencies or performance characteristics during the early 1990s. Social work likewise incorporated its previous cultural and ethnic diversity concerns and its commitment to client outcomes into a culturally competent perspective. The 1999 NASW (National Association of Social Workers) Code of Ethics with a section on cultural competence and the 2001 NASW *Standards for Cultural Competence in Social Work Practice* are the strongest criteria for any helping profession in the United States.

This text builds on my earlier book, *Social Work Practice and People of Color: A Process-Stage Approach*, as a companion text. Running throughout both books is a case study that views the Hernandez family through the lens of generalist and advanced practice. This case follows the social worker as he or she masters the knowledge and skills necessary to lead the clients through the process stages (contact, problem identification, assessment, intervention, and termination) and develops cultural competence (cultural awareness, knowledge theory, skill development, and inductive learning).

Along with the Hernandez family case study are special sections throughout the text entitled "Competency Study" and "Tools for Student Learning." These sections are strategically placed to assist the reader in the development of cultural competence and are springboards for small-group discussion in the classroom. In many instances there are questionnaires designed to help students with the application of concepts in their personal and professional lives.

CHANGES TO THIS EDITION

The third edition of this book has a number of new features that add to the knowledge and understanding of culturally competent practice in social work and which will hopefully delight the readers of this text:

- New sections on the ethics of cultural competence, ageism, intergenerational acculturation, cultural communication contact skills, and the Abdullah family
- Updates on the cultural competence literature and trends in the last three years
- New conceptual definitions of cultural competence and the federal and state government programs related to cultural competence
- Research findings of the pretest and posttest instrument on ethnic and cultural groups (First Nations Peoples, African Americans, Latino Americans, Asian Americans, women of color, and gay and lesbian persons of color) and on social and economic justice covering content material in these areas by guest contributors to this third edition, along with the existing pretest and posttest measuring cultural competence (cultural awareness, knowledge acquisition, skill development, and inductive learning), which has been slightly revised from the first edition of this text. These two pretest and posttest research instruments allow us to measure student learning in a social work diversity, populations-at-risk, and social and economic justice course; I know of no other existing social work education

text that offers multiple research outcome measures for the social work educator in a single book.
- Updated guest contributory chapters on inductive learning, diverse groups (called populations-at-risk by the Council on Social Work Education), and on social and economic justice

The contributory chapters were written by a talented and nationally recognized group of social work educators and scholars from across the country:

Chapter Three, Advancing Social and Economic Justice, by Dorothy Van Soest, University of Washington

Chapter Nine, Cultural Competence with First Nations Peoples, by Hilary N. Weaver, State University of New York at Buffalo

Chapter Ten, Cultural Competence with African Americans, by Ruth McRoy, University of Texas at Austin

Chapter Eleven, Cultural Competence with Latino Americans, by Betty Garcia, California State University, Fresno, and Maria E. Zuniga, San Diego State University

Chapter Twelve, Cultural Competence with Asian Americans, by Rowena Fong, University of Texas at Austin

Chapter Thirteen, Cultural Competence with Women of Color, by Gwat-Yong Lie and Christine T. Lowery, University of Wisconsin–Milwaukee

Chapter Fourteen, Cultural Competence with Gay and Lesbian Persons of Color, by Karina L. Walters and John F. Longres of the University of Washington, Seattle, and Chong-suk Han and Larry D. Icard, Temple University

The contributory chapters were written from a common detailed outline, which helped to conduct cross-comparison of conceptual themes.

Additional new and revised material in this second edition includes:

- Updated chapters: Chapter Seven: Skill Development, by Doman Lum and Yuhwa Eva Lu, New York University; and Chapter Eight: Inductive Learning, by Francis K. O. Yuen, Andrew Bein, and Doman Lum, California State University, Sacramento

ACKNOWLEDGMENTS

Terry L. Cross, executive director of the National Indian Child Welfare Association, has graciously written the foreword of this book. Mr. Cross, an MSW social worker, is the father of the cultural competence movement in the United States. His 1989 text, *Towards a Culturally Competent System of Care*, written with Mr. Cross as the lead coauthor with B. J. Bazron, K. W. Dennis, and M. R. Isaacs, is the beginning point of reference for those who write about the historical development of cultural competence. My congratulations to a First Nations Peoples social work practitioner/social activist who started the cultural competence movement even before multicultural psychology took up the cause.

I want to thank Larry Ortiz, Professor of Social Work, University of Maryland, who invited me to give the workshop on cultural competence in Chicago and started me on the road to writing this book in the fall of 1996; Moses Newsome, Jr., former President of the Council on Social Work Education, former dean of the Ethelyn R. Strong School of Social Work, Norfolk State University, and now vice president of research, planning, community, and economic development at Mississippi Valley State University, for his encouragement in pursuing this area of study; the late Howard J. Clinebell, Jr., Professor Emeritus of Pastoral Counseling, Claremont School of Theology, who was my teaching, writing, and clinical counseling mentor; Ronald Boltz, Professor Emeritus of Social Work, California State University, Sacramento, who helped me with the data analysis for the preliminary research findings of the pretest and posttest instruments; and Stacy Fekkers and Pauline McNabney, my research assistants and social work undergraduate majors, California State University, Sacramento, for their many hours of accurate data entry of material, especially entering questionnaire items into the computer. I also want to thank the manuscript reviewers:

Ruth Bounous, Our Lady of the Lake University
J. Camille Hall, The University of Tennessee
Anita Jones Thomas, Loyola University Chicago
Munira Merchant, Walden University
Miriam Potocky-Tripodi, Florida International University
Carol Tully, University of Louisville

Special thanks are due to Lisa Gebo, social work editor at Brooks/Cole, who recognized the importance of this book and willingly advocated for the third edition of the book; to Alma Dea Michelena, Assistant Editor at Brooks/Cole, who worked with me in the fine details, practical decision making, and general supervision of this new edition; and to the staff at Brooks/Cole: Project Manager, Editorial Production, Christy Krueger; Permissions Editor, Roberta Broyer; Assistant Editor; Caroline Concilla; and Production Editor, Sara Dovre Wudali, of Buuji, Inc.

Above all, a special word of thanks and gratitude goes to my family: my wife, Joyce, who is a first-grade teacher at Mary Tsukamoto Elementary School, Elk Grove, California, School District; my daughter Lori, who is with the Pfizer Pharmaceutical Company, Los Angeles, California, and her husband, Noel; my son Jonathan, who is an occupational therapist with the University of Southern California–Los Angeles County Medical Center; my daughter Amy, who recently graduated with her Master of Business Administration from San Francisco State University and is a market analyst for the Safeway Stores, Inc. in Pleasanton, California; and my son Matthew, who worked for the Jet Propulsion Laboratory, Pasadena, California, and has enrolled in the UCLA graduate program in urban planning and community development. My competence work as a husband and a father never ends and is a great challenge and joy.

A special word of thanks goes to Dr. Nancy M. Nystrom, lecturer at the University of Washington School of Social Work, who took on the enormous task of editing the final version of this text. Thank you, Nancy, for your willingness to work on this unselfishly.

Doman Lum, PhD, ThD
Professor Emeritus of Social Work
California State University, Sacramento

Contributors

Andrew Bein. Dr. Andrew Bein is Professor of Social Work at California State University, Sacramento, Division of Social Work. Dr. Bein has 15 years' experience as a social work practitioner in a variety of settings: Latino social service agencies, schools, counseling agencies, and youth agencies. In addition to teaching social work practice from an inductive and ethnographic perspective, he is exploring how these perspectives are enriched through a spiritual approach.

Rowena Fong. Dr. Rowena Fong is Professor of Social Work at the University of Texas at Austin. She is coauthor or co-editor of *Culturally Competent Practice: Skills, Intervention, and Evaluation*, (with Sharlene Furuto, Allyn & Bacon Publications, 2001); *Culturally Competent Practice with Immigrant Children and Families* (Guilford Publications, 2004); *Children of Neglect: When No One Cares* (with Margaret Smith, Brunner-Routledge, 2004); and *Intersection of Child Welfare, Substance Abuse, and Family Violence: Culturally Competent Approaches* (with Ruth McRoy and Carmen Ortiz Hendricks, Council on Social Work Education Publications, in press). Dr. Fong's teaching, research, and publications concentrate on Asian American, immigrant, and refugee children and families; child welfare; and culturally competent practice. Widely published, she has done consultation and training in the People's Republic of China on foster care, adoptions, and social work curricula.

Betty Garcia. Dr. Betty Garcia is Professor of Social Work in the Department of Social Work Education at California State University, Fresno. She is a clinical social worker and obtained her Ph.D in social psychology from Boston University. Dr. Garcia has an extensive background in mental health practice and advocacy. She teaches in direct practice with individuals, families, and groups, including children. Her research and publications have addressed Latino dropouts in higher education, atomic veterans, and diversity teaching and social justice.

Chong-suk Han. Mr. Chong-suk Han is a dean's appointment lecturer in sociology at Temple University, Department of Sociology, Philadephia, and a Ph.D degree candidate in social welfare at the University of Washington, Seattle. His dissertation is entitled *Geisha of a Different Kind: Negotiating Gay Asian Male Identity*. He has also been a teaching assistant in the Department of American Ethnic Studies at the University of Washington and the editor of the *International Examiner*, the oldest pan–Asian American newspaper in the United States.

Larry D. Icard. Dr. Larry Icard is Professor and Dean of the School of Social Administration at Temple University, where he also serves as director of the Center for Intervention and Practice Research. He received his doctorate from the School of Social Work at Columbia University, New York City. He has published numerous articles on African American gay and racial sexual minorities. Dr. Icard's empirical research focuses on developing and testing family-based interventions to reduce health problems experienced by at-risk populations in the United States and in South Africa.

Gwat-Yong Lie. Dr. Gwat-Yong Lie is Associate Dean for Academic Programs and Student Services at the University of Wisconsin–Milwaukee. Her tenure home is the Department of Social Work in the Helen Bader School of Social Welfare, University of Wisconsin–Milwaukee. She has taught courses in social work methods and intimate partner violence. She has done research and published in the areas of intimate partner violence, multicultural social work practice, and women's issues, including those concerning Asian American women.

John F. Longres. Dr. John F. Longres is Professor Emeritus of Social Work at the University of Washington, Seattle. He has published extensively in the areas of adolescence, aging, and mental health, especially as these are influenced by class, race, and ethnicity. His recent interests have focused on homosexually active men of color. He served as editor-in-chief of *The Journal of Social Work Education*, is a senior consulting editor of *The Journal of Gay and Lesbian Social Services*, and is a consulting editor for *The Journal of Ethnic and Cultural Diversity in Social Work*. Throughout his career he has been active in the Latino community, sitting on boards of grassroots agencies.

Christine T. Lowery. Dr. Christine T. Lowery (Laguna/Hopi) teaches at the University of Wisconsin–Milwaukee and serves as the coordinator for the undergraduate social work program. Currently she is working on a longitudinal, ethnographic study of aging and cultural change at the Pueblo of Laguna in New Mexico. Dr. Lowery was the keynote speaker at the Cultural Competency in Child Welfare: Substance Abuse and Family Violence conference at the University of Texas at Austin held in February 2001.

Yuhwa Eva Lu. Dr. Eva Lu is Associate Professor of Social Work at New York University, Ehrenkranz School of Social Work, where she teaches courses on social work direct practice, ethnocultural issues, and working with Asian and Asian American clients. She also directs the Summer International Training Institute for cross-cultural trauma training and is a consultant for the development of a National Trauma Studies Center at Tzu-Chi University, Taiwan. She is the founding president of the PEARL Institute (Pacific Education, Advocacy, Research, and Learning Institute), established since 1993, and has been a Chinese bilingual/bicultural practicing psychotherapist for the past 20 years.

Doman Lum. Dr. Doman Lum is Professor Emeritus of Social Work at California State University, Sacramento. His previous books have been in the areas of cultural competence and practice and client systems, social work practice and people of color, health care policy and social work, and suicidal crisis intervention. He has written articles on Asian Americans, health care delivery and health maintenance organizations, culturally diverse social work practice, suicide prevention, and pastoral counseling. He has been on the board of directors and the Commission on Accreditation of the Council on Social Work Education, was the 2000 recipient of the Distinguished Recent Contributions in Social Work Education award from the Council on Social Work Education, and received the 2004 Lifetime Achievement award from the Asian Pacific Islanders Social Work Educators of the Council on Social Work Education. Dr. Lum is an ordained minister of the United Church of Christ, Northern California Conference.

Ruth McRoy. Dr. Ruth McRoy is the Ruby Lee Piester Centennial Professor Emeritus at the University of Texas at Austin School of Social Work. During her 26 years as a faculty member at UT, she held a joint appointment with the Center for African and African American Studies, and for 12 years, she served as the Associate Dean for Research and Director of the Center for Social Work Research at the University of Texas. She was a member of the University of Texas Academy of Distinguished Professors and Director of the Diversity Institute at the UT School of Social Work. At the university, she taught many courses, including Social Work Practice with African American Families. Dr. McRoy's research interests include racial identity development, transracial adoptions, cross-cultural relationships, cultural diversity, African American families, African American adoptions, and the disproportionate representation of African American children in the foster care system. Dr. McRoy is currently a Research Professor at UT and a consultant on diversity and child welfare issues.

Dorothy Van Soest. Dr. Dorothy Van Soest is Professor of Social Work and former Dean at the University of Washington, School of Social Work. She previously was Associate Dean and Professor at the University of Texas at Austin, School of Social Work, and has also been on the faculty at the University of Minnesota, St. Thomas University, Smith College, and The Catholic University of America. Dr. Van Soest has made numerous contributions to social work education in relation to preparing professionals who are culturally competent practitioners with a commitment to social justice advocacy and violence prevention and has written six books and numerous articles on oppression, social justice, violence, and empowerment.

Karina L. Walters. Dr. Karina Walters is Associate Professor of Social Work at the University of Washington School of Social Work and an MSW and Ph.D. graduate of the University of California, Los Angeles School of Social Welfare. She is an enrolled citizen of the Choctaw Nation of Oklahoma. Dr. Walters was a clinical social worker in Los Angeles County and has served as an American Indian Commissioner in Los Angeles County. Currently she is on several national Native boards of directors and is preparing to start a six-site national study on American Indian Two-Spirit health.

Hilary N. Weaver. Dr. Hilary N. Weaver (Lakota) is Associate Professor of Social Work at the State University of New York at Buffalo. Her work focuses on cultural issues in the helping process with a particular emphasis on indigenous populations. She currently serves as president of the American Indian Alaska Native Social Work Educators Association and as president of the Native American Community Services of Erie and Niagara Counties, a human service agency serving the off-reservation Native American population in western New York state. She regularly publishes on cross-cultural and indigenous issues.

Francis K. O. Yuen. Dr. Francis K. O. Yuen is Professor of Social Work at California State University, Sacramento Division of Social Work. His practice and research interests are in the areas of family health social work practice, children and families, disability, human diversity, refugees and immigrants, grant writing, and program evaluation. He has published widely and is an editor for a refereed journal on disability and a social workbook series on children and families. Among his publications is a Brooks/Cole book, *Practical Grant Writing and Program Evaluation.*

Maria E. Zuniga. Dr. Maria E. Zuniga is Professor Emerita of Social Work at San Diego State University. She has focused on cultural competence for the past 25 years of her teaching, both in practice and human behavior courses. She has written extensively on the immigration experiencees of Latinos, noting the vulnerabilities of those who are not documented. She has served on local and national boards, notably the board of directors of the Council on Social Work Education, representing the concerns of diverse populations. In 1998 she cochaired the Cultural Competency in Social Work Education Curriculum Conference held at the University of Michigan School of Social Work and coedited a book on the conference that was published by the Council on Social Work Education. She received the 2005 Council on Social Work Education Feminist Scholarship Award from the Commission on the Role and Status of Women.

PART ONE

Culturally Competent Practice

Part One lays a foundation for culturally competent practice by introducing the meaning and dimensions of cultural competence so that the reader has an adequate background for understanding the role of cultural competence in effective practice. Next, human diversity is explained, with an emphasis on explaining how each person is both unique and part of a particular social context that interacts with racism, sexism, homophobia, discrimination, and oppression. The key is to determine how one can maintain and foster cultural competence in this social environmental context where diversity interacts with the social realities facing ethnic, gender, and sexual orientation groups.

Knowledge and understanding of culturally competent practice and the social context must be tempered with a passion and commitment for social and economic justice. We are reminded that social problems are rooted in economic cause factors and that economic issues take their toll on the lives of people in society. It is important to raise these issues early in this text so that the reader can reflect on the meaning of social and economic justice and their effects on ethnic and cultural groups. Distributive justice, corrective justice, and political justice are the essential characteristics for understanding social, economic, legal, and democratic justice in our society. We must constantly strive for the ideal, social and economic justice, in light of the real shortcomings that we experience in the world.

The diversity standards from the 2002 Council on Social Work Education *Educational Policy and Accreditation Standards* serve as guidelines for the content in Part One. They include the following areas:

- Content that promotes understanding, affirmation, and respect for people from diverse backgrounds
- Content that emphasizes the interlocking and complex nature of culture and personal identity
- Social services that are culturally relevant and able to meet the needs of groups served
- Diversity within and between groups that may influence assessment, planning, intervention, and research
- Skills on how to define, design, and implement strategies for effective practice with persons from diverse backgrounds

1

The current social and economic justice guidelines of the Council of Social Work Education are as follows:

- Content grounded in an understanding of distributive justice, human and civil rights, and the global interconnections of oppression
- Content related to implementing strategies to combat discrimination, oppression, and economic deprivation and to promote social and economic justice
- Preparation to advocate for nondiscriminatory social and economic systems

CHAPTER ONE

Culturally Competent Practice

DOMAN LUM

This book is an introduction to cultural competence, which is an interest area for exploration. We begin by discussing the context and meanings of culture, competence, and cultural competence. In doing so, we trace the growth of cultural competence as an organizing theme, pose some questions and beliefs about this area, and ask you to take two cultural competence pretests that measure your present baseline knowledge. We hope that you will, as a part of your social work education, prepare yourself to be competent and effective professionals who are able to integrate the knowledge, values, and skills for competent practice, particularly with culturally and ethnically diverse clients. The emphasis is not so much on how to be culturally competent with clients, as that outcome will occur in the course of working with culturally diverse people, but rather on developing an awareness of your own understanding of yourself as a cultural person and on gaining competencies in helping others.

A panoramic view of this book is provided in Figure 1.1. In following the culturally competent practice model shown in the figure, this book begins with the social context of diversity in society and the realities of racism, sexism, homophobia, discrimination, and oppression. It moves to a cultural competence framework that provides the tools of cultural awareness, knowledge acquisition, skill development, and inductive learning. This book then offers chapters on a number of cultural and ethnic groups that are least advantaged, known, and understood, and ends with the goal outcome for which we constantly strive: social and economic justice. The 2002 Council on Social Work Education's *Educational Policy and Accreditation Standards* on diversity, populations-at-risk, and social and economic justice serve as points of orientation for the model.

THE CONTEXT FOR CULTURAL COMPETENCE

As we are in the midst of the 21st century, we are faced with a rich ethnic and cultural diversity context. The 2000 U.S. Census presents fresh data on the changing ethnic and cultural diversity that can serve as a starting point for understanding the present context and for our discussions of cultural competence. Between 1980 and 2000, there was a marked increase in minority populations as compared to the White non-Hispanic population. In 1980, out of a total population of 226.5 million, the minority population was

FIGURE 1.1 *Culturally Competent Practice Model*

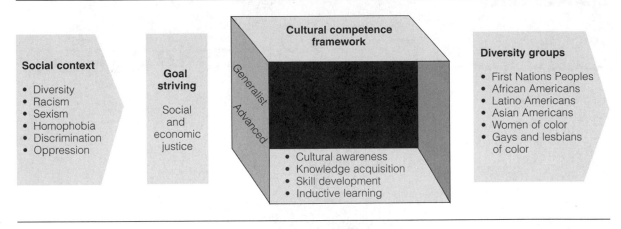

45.6 million. By 1990, the total population of 248.7 million was composed of 60.6 million minority and 188.1 million White non-Hispanic. In 2000, however, the total population reached 281.5 million with a minority population of 86.9 million and a White non-Hispanic population of 194.6 million.

The significance of this 20-year growth was the doubling of the minority population, which increased by 41.3 million, whereas the White non-Hispanic population in the same period increased by only 13.7 million persons ("A Rapid Move to Diversity," 2001). Moreover, two groups emerged as the most rapid growth groups in the United States: Hispanic or Latino, and Asian. Hispanics or Latinos moved from 22,354,059 in 1990 to 35,305,818 in 2000, an increase of 12,951,759 persons or a 57.2 percent growth. Asians went from 6,908,638 in 1990 to 10,242,998 (race alone, a 3,334,360 increase or a 48.3 percent growth) or to 11,898,828 (race alone or in combination, a 4,990,190 increase or a 72.2 percent growth). (The 2000 U.S. Census allowed persons to indicate a single ethnic group [race alone] or combinations of ethnic groups [in combination].)

By July 1, 2004, the total population of the United States was 293.6 million with Whites (236 million), Hispanics or Latinos (41.3 million), Blacks (37.5 million), Asians (12.3 million), and American Indian and Alaska Natives (2.8 million) (U.S. Census Bureau, 2004). The Latino population has exceeded the Black population and is over three times the number of Asians. These demographics are compelling data for the case for cultural competence as we tune into the history of oppression of these groups, reflect on service delivery programs that will meet social needs, and shape effective ways to build relationships and intervention strategies.

THE MEANING OF CULTURE

A starting point in our understanding of cultural competence is the concept of *culture*. What is culture? Culture is the way of life of multiple groups in a society and consists of prescribed ways of behaving or norms of conduct, beliefs, values, and skills (Gordon, 1978). Culture is the sum total of life patterns passed on from generation to generation within a group of people and includes institutions, language, religious ideals, habits of thinking, artistic expressions, and patterns of social and interpersonal relationships (Hodge, Struckmann, & Trost, 1975). Recently culture has been broadened to be inclusive of many groups. Culture "implies the integrated pattern of human behavior that includes the thoughts, communications, actions, customs, beliefs, values, and institutions of a racial, ethnic, religious, or social group"; refers to "the totality of ways being passed on from generation to generation"; and "includes ways in which people with disabilities or people from various religious backgrounds or people who are gay, lesbian, or transgender experience the world around them" (National Association of Social Workers [NASW], 2001, p. 4). Culture, in short, encompasses behavioral patterns, intergenerational passages, and particular group life experiences.

Many dimensions of culture add to the fascinating and complex understanding of this rich concept. Hall (1976) describes a high/low cultural context approach that should be determined by the worker and the client at the beginning of the helping relationship. Individualistic-oriented cultures tend toward the low-context approach, whereas collective-oriented cultures lean toward the high-context approach. James and Gilliland (2005, p. 542) explain low-context and high-context cultural differences:

> In low-context cultures, one's self-image and worth are defined in personal, individual terms. In high-context cultures, one's self-worth and esteem are tied to the group. In low-context cultures, information is generally transmitted explicitly and concretely through the language; in high-context cultures, information is transmitted in the physical context of the interaction or internalized in the person. In high-context cultures, facial expressions, gestures, and tone of voice are as important as the meaning of words that are said. Thus, in high-context cultures, the individual will expect the other person to know what is bothering him or her so he or she does not have to be specific and become embarrassed and lose face talking directly about the issue.

Awareness of these cultural contextual orientations is an important part of grasping cultural differences that result in distinct and varying behavioral responses. This reading of culture reflects the multiplicity of cultures in the United States and is part of the following dimensions of culture involving pluralism, behavioral responses, and spirituality.

Cultural pluralism is a reality confronting our current society. It involves the coexistence of multicultural communities that tolerate and acknowledge each other's styles, customs, languages, and values (Pantoja & Perry, 1976). At times, bicultural tension and conflict occur when there are differences between the values and behavior of an individual's family and those of the society at large (Galan, 1992).

A number of related cultural behavioral responses may be familiar to you. Culture shock (Draguns, 1996) involves cognitive disorientation and personal helplessness due to an abrupt immersion in a different cultural environment, particularly when there is minimal or no preparation. Culture shock, which occurs when a group or individual confronts a physically and otherwise dramatically different culture, was experienced by rural Hmong refugees of the Laos highlands who relocated to metropolitan areas of the United States. Culture accommodation (Higginbotham, West, & Forsyth, 1988) is a process that involves social workers in exploration, data gathering, and negotiations before developing culturally appropriate programs in new cultural settings. Local needs expressed by indigenous leaders and conflicts, insecurities, and preferences are taken into account in the process, prior to the introduction of new services in an ethnic community. Cultural empathy (Ridley & Lingle, 1996) involves the learned ability of social workers to gain an accurate understanding of the self-experience of clients from other cultures based on the interpretation of cultural data. It involves culturally empathic understanding and responsiveness based on cultural perception, sensitivity, and interpretation along with cognitive, affective, and communicative processes between workers and client communities.

Van Hook and Aguilar (2001) describe the link between religion and culture:

> All religion is practiced in a cultural context, and one's culture defines one's beliefs about the relationship of healing to the supernatural. Religion is often a conduit for spirituality, because it provides the cultural structure in which a person can grow spiritually. Culture and ethnicity inform religion and spirituality and influence the expression and practices of religion. (p. 282)

A broadening of culture should include all aspects of life that are meaningful to the client. Spiritual faith is a powerful expression of culture for many persons.

Culture is a key factor in the social work helping process. Pinderhughes (1989) asserts that culture defines the problem perspective, the expression of the problem, the treatment provider, and the treatment options. Social work practice must be culturally relevant to clients. Cultural factors may contribute to the problem situation, affect the interaction between the worker and the client, and influence cultural interventions related to the extended family, the ethnic church, and ethnic community resources.

THE MEANING OF COMPETENCE

The word *competence* means sufficiency, adequacy, and capability. Competence may vary from person to person. The concept implies a striving toward mastery of a particular ability or area of expertise. Competence "implies having the capacity to function effectively within the context of culturally integrated patterns of human behavior defined by the group" (NASW, 2001, p. 4). The NASW Code of Ethics (1996) views competence in terms of a value of the social work profession that develops and enhances professional expertise through knowledge and skills applied to practice. The Code also understands that competence is an ethical standard under which social workers are to provide competent services within the boundaries of their professional education, licensing, and certification—with appropriate study, training, consultation, and supervision from competent persons—and to take responsible steps to ensure the competence of their work and to protect clients from harm.

THE MEANING OF CULTURAL COMPETENCE

The field of social work and related applied social sciences disciplines, as well as various federal organizations, have produced a number of working definitions of cultural competence. A comprehensive definition of cultural competence is as follows:

> [A] set of congruent practice skills, behaviors, attitudes, and policies that come together in a system, agency, or among professionals and enables that system, agency, or those professionals to work effectively in cross-cultural situations.

It is the ability to demonstrate skills and knowledge which enable a person to work effectively across cultures; the ability to provide mental health treatment within the cultural framework of the consumer; the ability to provide effective services to people of a specific cultural background, including one different from the provider. (Substance Abuse and Mental Health Services Administration, 1997)

Orlandi (1992) defined cultural competence:

[Cultural competence is] a set of academic and interpersonal skills that allow individuals to increase their understanding and appreciation of cultural differences and similarities, within, among, and between groups. This requires a willingness and ability to draw on community-based values, traditions, and customs and to work with knowledgeable persons of and from the community in developing focused interventions, communications, and other supports. (pp. 3–4)

The Oregon Department of Education (2004) based on a cultural competency summit of 100 education stakeholders offers a wider and more comprehensive definition:

Cultural competence is based on a commitment to social justice and equity. Cultural competence is a developmental process occurring at individual and system levels that evolves and is sustained over time. [It] requires that individuals and organizations:

1. Have a defined set of values and principles, demonstrated behaviors, attitudes, policies and structures that enable them to work effectively in a cross-cultural manner
2. Demonstrate the capacity to (a) value diversity, (b) engage in self-reflection, (c) facilitate effectively (manage) the dynamics of difference, (d) acquire and institutional cultural knowledge, (e) adapt to the diversity and the cultural contexts of the students, families, and communities they serve, and (f) support actions which foster equity of opportunity and services
3. Institutionalize, incorporate, evaluate, and advocate the above in all aspects of leadership, policy-making, administration, practice, and service delivery while systematically involving staff, students, families, key stakeholders, and communities

A reading of these three definitions underscores a number of skills related to individuals, groups, agencies, and communities.

Prior and current understandings of cultural competence have focused on the individual, professional education, practice model, and system levels. LaFromboise, Coleman, and Gerton (1993) suggest that a culturally competent individual possesses a strong personal identity, has knowledge of the beliefs and values of the culture, and displays sensitivity to the affective processes of the culture. In a cultural setting, this person communicates clearly in the language of the cultural group, performs socially sanctioned behavior, maintains active social relations within the cultural group, and negotiates the institutional structures of that culture. Cultural competence is part of a continuum of social skill and personality development. This concept addresses an individual's sense of self-sufficiency and ego strength; cultural identity related to culture of origin and cultural context; and knowledge, appreciation, and internalization of basic beliefs of a culture. Externally this translates into positive attitudes about a cultural group; bicultural efficacy, or the ability to live effectively within two groups without compromising one's sense of cultural identity; the ability to communicate, verbally and nonverbally, ideas and feelings to members of one's own or another culture; possession of a role repertoire or range of culturally appropriate behaviors or roles; and belonging to stable social networks in more than one culture.

From an education and training perspective, cultural competence may also be understood as the development of academic and professional expertise and skills in the area of working with culturally diverse clients. A starting point is the fostering of cultural self-awareness. The social worker becomes culturally effective with the client when the worker develops cultural awareness through an exploration of his or her own ethnic identity, cultural background, and contact with ethnic others. Next, the social worker must develop a knowledge acquisition perspective and a set of skills in order to work with multicultural clients. Knowledge acquisition provides a body of facts and principles that serve as boundary guidelines. Skill development applies knowledge acquisition to actual practice with clients from a culturally competent perspective. It also addresses the service delivery structure that ought to be in place for client services. Finally, cultural competence must constantly uncover new facts about multicultural clients through an inductive learning process.

So, cultural competence involves the areas of cultural awareness, knowledge acquisition, skill development, and continuous inductive learning. The social work student reaches a point of comprehension and relative mastery of multicultural knowledge and skills in the classroom, the field placement, and the research project. Cultural competence is a learning outcome that integrates cultural dimensions of social work. It is a continuous, lifelong process that involves new learning to maintain.

Manoleas (1994) presents a preliminary social work cultural competence model that categorizes cultural competence according to three dimensions: knowledge base, skill base, and value base. The knowledge base for cultural competence explains how culture affects basic developmental events, such as gender role development, rites of passage, sexuality development, mate selection, child-rearing practices, development of social networks, aging, and mourning; different cultural caregiving patterns within families, kinship networks, and communities, such as caring for the young, infirm, aged, and mentally ill; non-European ways of relating to nature, metaphysical harmony, time, and spirituality; and patterns of interdependency, mutuality, and obligations between individuals, their families, and their communities that exist in various cultures.

According to Manoleas, the skill base necessary for cultural competence includes assessment of health, illness, functional and dysfunctional behavior, and psychopathology, taking into account the cultural relativity of categories and modes of expression; culturally appropriate interviewing techniques that consider level of intrusiveness, directness, social distance, formality, and forms of address; evaluation of the client family's worldview and level of acculturation or biculturality; cultural self-assessment on how the worker's cultural amalgam complements or contrasts with the client's cultural modes of expression; and development of professional relationships across cultures with the appropriate level of intimacy and proper timing. The values necessary for cultural competence involve acknowledgment and acceptance of the following: cultural differences and their impact on service delivery and utilization; heterogeneity within and diversity between cultures; cultural relativism or different ways of viewing and interpreting phenomena, particularly non-Western and traditional as well as neo-European views; and the clash and complementary nature of professional social work and client cultural values.

In Competency Study 1.1, Jenkins (2001, p. 79) presents a contextual definition of cultural competence that broadens the interconnectiveness of this term with a number of multidimensional environmental elements of culture.

The Contextual Definition of Cultural Competence

COMPETENCY STUDY 1.1

Cultural competence (Greene & Hucles-Sanchez, 1994) is a measurable professional standard that evaluates the incorporation of the differential historical, political, socioeconomic, psychophysical, spiritual, and ecological realities, their interaction, and its impact on individuals or groups. Here culture is used in its broadest sense to include race, ethnicity, gender, and sexual orientation and considers other dimensions of individual or group experiences that are salient to their understanding of the world and of themselves. This definition also suggests that factors that are prominent in contextualizing the identity and relational development of one racial/ethnocultural group may differ significantly from those of another. For example, Jenkins, De La Cancela, and Chin (1993) contend that culture, inclusive of customs, traditions, and language of origin, is the most prominent determinant of Asian Americans' experience while race, gender, and social class are most prominent for African American women.

THE LEVELS AND DIMENSIONS OF CULTURAL COMPETENCE

Miley and colleagues (1998) view cultural competence on three levels: practitioner, agency, and community. On the *practitioner level,* the worker must know about self-awareness in terms of his or her own personal values and cultural heritage, values differences and conflicts regarding assimilation and cultural pluralism, and awareness of the cultures of others, especially clients. The authors suggest that the social worker take a cultural self-inventory on personal identity, spiritual beliefs, knowledge of others, and cross-cultural skills, and study cultural groups through observational community research. They state:

> In summary, learning to be a competent cross-cultural practitioner is an evolutionary process that begins with awareness and increases with each interaction with clients. Workers first attempt to understand their own cultural filters. Next, they build a knowledge base of other perspectives through literature reviews and field research. Third, workers analyze the impact of cultural identities on the power dynamics of the worker–client partnership. Finally, practitioners continue to fine tune their cultural sensitivity through their ongoing practice experiences with unique client systems. (Miley, O'Melia, & DuBois, 1998, pp. 72–73)

In terms of *agency-level* cultural competence, workers are trained in the skills necessary for diversity-sensitive practice, and multicultural awareness and functioning are promoted in organizational structure and program delivery. Cultural competence permeates agency policies on hiring and training staff, program evaluation, and criteria for eligibility, and it involves: programs and procedures that focus on client strengths; culturally sensitive assessment instruments; culture as a resource; and ethnically oriented indigenous helping networks. Structures are designed for multicultural interchanges between agency, worker, and client; worker control over practice; and client influence on services. For example, in the field of health care, Kaiser Permanente (2004) has published an educational monograph on cultural competence and has established Centers of Excellence in Cultural Competence targeting specific populations. BlueCross BlueShield of Florida (2004) has instituted internal diversity training and cultural competence education for providers. These health care agency efforts have created a favorable atmosphere for cultural competence to flourish as providers consider how best to deliver services. The desired physical environment is an accessible neighborhood location, outreach services, and cultural decor and setting. Culturally competent agencies have resource networks that include institutions and individuals in the ethnic community such as churches, schools, clubs, local healers, neighborhood leaders, and culturally oriented media.

The third level of cultural competence discussed by Miley and colleagues (1998) is the *community level*, which replaces the context for discrimination, segregation, and distinct boundaries with a context of pluralism, celebration of diversity, promotion of cross-cultural interaction, and social justice. The model for practitioner, agency, and community cultural competence sets a new benchmark for this field. An increasing area of cultural competence has been the health care of persons with chronic conditions and medical care in general.

The Center on an Aging Society (2004) reports:

> If the providers, organizations, and systems are not working together to provide culturally competent care, patients are at higher risk of having negative health consequences, receiving poor quality care, or being dissatisfied with their care. African Americans and other ethnic minorities report less partnership with physicians, less participation in medical decisions, and lower levels of satisfaction with care. The quality of patient–physician interaction is lower among non-White patients, particularly Latinos and Asian Americans. Lower quality patient–physician interactions are associated with lower overall satisfaction with health care. African Americans are more likely than other minority groups to feel that they were treated disrespectfully during a health care visit (e.g., they were spoken to rudely, talked down to, or ignored). Compared to other minority groups, Asian Americans are least likely to feel that their doctor understood their background and values and are most likely to report that their doctor looked down on them. (p. 5)

As a result on the community level, cultural competence in health care services has sought to provide interpreter services; recruit and retain minority staff; provide training to increase cultural awareness, knowledge, and skills; coordinate with traditional healers; use community health workers; incorporate culture-specific attitudes and values into health promotion tools; include family and community members in health care decision making; locate clinics in geographic areas that are easily accessible for certain populations; expand hours of operation; and provide linguistic competency beyond the clinical encounter to the appointment desk, advice lines, medical billing, and other written materials.

The Liaison Committee on Medical Education (LCME), the national accreditation body for medical schools in the United States and Canada, has mandated higher standards for curriculum material on cultural competence. Medical schools must provide students with skills to understand how people of diverse cultures and belief systems perceive health and illness and respond to various symptoms, diseases, and treatment, as well as explore their own racial and gender biases in themselves, others, and in the delivery of health care. Harvard Medical School (2005) reported on the use of the Association of American Medical Colleges (AAMC) Tool for Assessing Cultural Competence Education (TACCT), which has created a map of the knowledge, skills, and attitudes of students and faculty for the Harvard medical curriculum. It depicts current cultural competence training efforts and identifies gaps where further integration of cultural issues is needed. Harvard Medical School has sponsored a session on Developing Culturally Competent Care Faculty and offers an elective course called "Emerging a Culturally Competent Physician," using case-based learning to teach cultural competence. In addition, there is a coordinator for the Harvard Medical School Culturally Competent Care Education Committee. These community thrusts in cultural competence and health care are encouraging signs of growth and development.

Likewise, we can view cultural competence on the micro, meso, and macro levels. *Micro cultural competence* involves the client and the social worker. The client acquires cultural competence from personal background and development. The client has the task of sorting his or her culture of origin and elements of the dominant culture to achieve bicultural integration and bicultural competence. Likewise, the worker develops expertise and skills through education and through working with culturally diverse clients. It is "the process by which individuals and systems respond respectfully and effectively to people of all cultures, languages, classes, races, ethnic backgrounds, religions, and other diversity factors in a manner that recognizes, affirms, and values the worth of individuals, families, and communities and protects and preserves the dignity of each" (NASW, 2001, p. 5). This client system is broad and comprehensive in scope and outreach.

Meso cultural competence addresses the organizational level to determine whether an institution has a culturally competent system of care. Cross, Bazron, Dennis, and Isaacs (1989) explain six anchor points along a cultural competence continuum with regard to an organizational system of care:

1. *Cultural destructiveness* describes attitudes, practices, and policies that promote the superiority of the dominant culture and attempts to eradicate the inferior and different culture.
2. *Cultural incapacity* refers to attitudes, practices, and policies that adhere to separate but equal treatment and tend toward segregated institutional practices.
3. *Cultural blindness* refers to attitudes, practices, and policies that have an unbiased view of undifferentiated elements of culture and people and treat all people as assimilated.
4. The *culturally open organization* has attitudes, practices, and policies that are receptive to the improvement of cultural services through staff hiring practices, training on cultural sensitivity, and minority board representation.
5. The *culturally competent agency* has attitudes, practices, and policies that demonstrate respect for different cultures and people by seeking advice and consultation from ethnic and racial communities and by being committed to incorporating these practices into the organization.
6. *Cultural proficiency* describes attitudes, practices, and policies that are sensitive to cultural differences and diversity, improve cultural quality of services through cultural research, disseminate research findings, and promote diverse group cultural relations.

On the meso level, cultural competence is "a set of congruent behaviors, attitudes, and policies that come together in a system or agency or among professionals and enable the system, agency, or professionals to work effectively in cross-cultural situations" (NASW, 2001, p. 5). A culturally competent service delivery system should value diversity, have the capacity for cultural self-assessment, be conscious of the dynamics of cultural interaction, institutionalize cultural knowledge, and develop programs and services that promote diversity between and within cultures.

However, Nybell and Gray (2004) underscore the conflictual nature of organizational change rather than a unified, linear development continuum as previously depicted by Cross and others (1989). In terms of cultural competence and multicultural organizational development, in an organizational case study of three child and family agencies, Nybell and Gray found that ". . . achieving cultural competence in a predominantly

White social services agency requires redistributing power toward clients, toward programs that disproportionately serve the most disenfranchised clients, to workers of color, and to representatives of communities of color" (p. 25). Nybell and Gray emphasize the conflictual nature of cultural competence change and redistribution of power in organizations and communities as realities that we must confront.

The National Center for Cultural Competence (NCCC) has a number of useful steps for Organizational Self-Assessment in order to build cultural competence on a meso organization level:

- Cultivate leadership: Identify members from all strata of an organization to fulfill leadership roles and to share power in the self-assessment process.
- Buy in: Establish a shared vision of the self-assessment process to the organization, its personnel, and the families/consumers/communities served in order to act collectively based on informed decisions of a coalition of stakeholders.
- Assure community collaboration and partnerships: Work in conjunction with natural, informal, support, and helping networks within diverse communities, which involves developing a shared vision, identifying leadership roles and responsibilities, distributing tasks equitably based on capacity, and allocating resources among community partners who are valued and respected.
- Structure support for the process: Convene a work group from policy making, administration, service delivery, consumers, and other community stakeholders who will assume responsibility for the self-assessment process and who will have access to decision makers or have the ability to make decisions.
- Allocate personnel and fiscal resources: Determine a budget and level of effort for organizational personnel, which include subcontracts for consultants/facilitators, meeting or conference facilities, interpretation and translation services, and other associated costs that delineate the duration and intensity of time required for personnel.
- Manage logistics: Provide sufficient time for planning and preparation, dissemination of information, and the development of a calendar and schedule of activities.
- Analyze and disseminate data: Plan for task force and workgroup members involvement in data collection (census and program needs assessment data blended with data from the self-assessment), analysis, interpretation, presentation, and dissemination of culturally competent and participatory action designs.
- Take the next steps: Establish organizational priorities, develop a strategic plan, allocate necessary resources, maintain community stakeholder partnerships, and incorporate self-assessment results into the state block grant planning and development process (see http://gucchd.georgetown.edu/nccc/orgselfassess.html).

Meso organizational steps to ensure cultural competence are imperative in a collective community effort.

Macro cultural competence refers to large system efforts to address cultural competence issues and programs. On the national level, the NCCC has been a leadership force at the Georgetown University Child Development Center. The mission of the NCCC is to increase the capacity of health care programs to design, implement, and evaluate culturally competent service delivery systems. It is a funded project of the Health Resources and Services Administration (HRSA), Department of Health and Human Services

(DHHS). The center serves as the clearinghouse for planning, policy, and programs related to cultural competence (see http://gucchd.georgetown.edu/nccc/pa.html).

Among the current 2005 projects of the NCCC are the following:

- The Children and Youth with Special Health Care Needs Project to assist Title V Maternal and Child Health and Children with Special Health Care Needs programs in the design, implementation, and evaluation of culturally and linguistically competent service delivery and support system. The intent is to develop access to comprehensive, family-centered care; affordable insurance; early and continuous screening for special health care needs; and transition services to adulthood within a service delivery and support systems that are culturally and linguistically competent (see http://gucchd.georgetown.edu/nccc/nccc4.html).

- The Sudden Infant Death Syndrome/Other Infant Death Project to increase culturally and linguistically competent service delivery systems to address the disparities in infant mortality outcomes where significant racial and ethnic disparities in the rate of infant deaths still exist. Among the activities are the dissemination of cultural and linguistic competence information, national conferences and a pool of consultants on cultural and linguistic competence and SID/ID programs, and technical assistance and collaboration (see http://gucchd.georgetown.edu/nccc/nccc5.html).

- The Bureau of Primary Health Care Project to provide high-quality primary health care services that are culturally and linguistically competent to community health centers, migrant health centers, Health Care for the Homeless grantees, Healthy Schools, Healthy Communities grantees, Health Care for Residents of Public Housing grantees, primary care associations, and primary care offices. The project provides culturally competent organizational self-assessment for selected community health centers and health care practitioners; training, technical assistance, and consultation and dissemination of products to promote culturally and linguistically competent systems of care and service delivery (see http://gucchd. georgetown.edu/nccc/nccc.html).

A number of major texts address cultural competence issues on a macro professional level (see Ponterotto, Casas, Suzuki, & Alexander, 1995; Pope-Davis & Coleman, 1997; Fong & Furuto, 2001; Fong, 2004; Constantine & Sue, 2005b). The U.S. Public Health Service's Office for Substance Abuse Prevention launched a series of monographs that integrated cultural competence, alcohol and drug abuse treatment programs, and ethnic groups and community (Orlandi, Weston, & Epstein, 1992). This interface between ethnic target groups, major problem areas, and cultural competence for treatment workers further illustrates how macro cultural competency can be expressed. Macro-level efforts have resulted in statewide cultural competence programs in mental health and health care in such states as California, New York, and South Carolina.

Several social work educators have offered related cultural competence dimensions that can add to our discussion. Straussner (2001, pp. 7–8) introduced the related term *ethnocultural competency* and emphasized the following characteristics:

- The ability of a clinician to function effectively in the context of ethnocultural differences, particularly the influence of client–clinician communication and trust, effective provision of services, and the retention of clients

- An awareness and acceptance of differences that need to be explored respectfully, nonjudgmentally, and with curiosity
- A move beyond cultural sensitivity to include cognitive, affective, and skill dimensions
- An understanding of one's own ethnocultural background and values
- A basic knowledge about the ethnoculture of clients with whom one is working
- A commitment to working with diverse clients
- An ability to adapt practice skills to fit the client's ethnocultural background, including flexibility to reach out to appropriate cultural resources in an ethnic community
- An enhancement of the agency setting with recognition and celebration of ethnocultural holidays, customs, and rituals of diverse ethnic client groups; hiring of professional and paraprofessional staff who reflect the ethnic and linguistic diversity of clients; and ongoing training and supervision of staff to help them understand their clients
- The establishment of close linkages with ethnocultural community groups
- Computerized management information systems to record data on client ethnicity, migration and immigration, religious and spiritual beliefs, and languages and interpreters
- Treatment outcome research to identify ethnoculturally competent treatment services

Schriver (2001) recognized the importance of cultural competence when he observed: Culturally competent social work practice—its meaning and its application—is emerging as one of the most critical aspects of social work practice. It is especially important as the diversity of the U.S. population continues to increase. Culturally competent practice is also increasingly important as we become more and more interrelated with other people in the world as a result of the rapid shifts toward ever more global economics, communication, and transportation. (p. 26)

Fong and Furuto (2001) focused on values and ethics, knowledge, and skills, particularly related to assessment, intervention, and evaluation for individuals, families, communities, and organizations. Fong (2004) specialized in cultural competence pertaining to immigrant and refugee children and families, providing an overview, theoretical perspectives, contexts and environments, and 13 Asian, Latino, and Eastern European ethnic groups. Delgado, Jones, and Rohani (2005) wrote about social work practice with refugee and immigrant youth and its relationship to cultural competence. The themes of cultural competence and culturally competent social work practice continue to unfold and grow as we move into the 21st century.

THE HISTORY OF THE CULTURAL COMPETENCE MOVEMENT

The Civil Rights Act of 1964 set in motion legal protection based on nondiscrimination of persons on the basis of race, sex, color, national origin, disability, age, and religion. In the early 1970s, when social work educators began to study a number of ethnic groups, Solomon (1976) published her landmark book on African American powerlessness and empowerment. Green (1982) and Pinderhughes (1989) introduced the concept of cultural competence to social work. Pinderhughes explained:

"Cultural competence" demands that clinicians develop flexibility in thinking and behavior, because they must learn to adapt professional tasks and work styles to the values, expectations, and preferences of specific clients. This means that practitioners must choose from a variety of strategies that are useful for the range of cultural groups and social classes, levels of education, and levels of acculturation that exist among clients. (p. 163)

These social work educators pioneered the theme of cultural competence.

The field of psychology also has shown concern in the area of cultural competence. The American Psychological Association (APA) in 1980 adopted a professional competence practice requirement and recognized cultural competence as an essential element of competent practice (APA, 1980). In 1982, a major position paper on cross-cultural counseling competencies asked that there be specified multicultural knowledge, awareness, and skill areas in counseling psychology (Casas, Ponterotto, & Gutierrez, 1986; Ibrahim & Arredondo, 1986).

In 1989, Terry Cross, a First Nations Peoples social worker, took the leadership in composing a monograph (Cross et al., 1989) and formulated six anchor points along a cultural competence continuum regarding an organizational system of care (see the previous discussion of meso-level cultural competence). Those of us who write about cultural competence point to this publication as the first systematic treatment of this topic.

In April 1992, the Association for Multicultural Counseling and Development (AMCD), a group of counseling psychologists who were committed to infusing the profession with multicultural content, approved a document that emphasized the need and the rationale for a multicultural perspective in counseling. This document covered such areas as counseling psychology doctoral education and training internships, professional standards and practices, and research and publication. As a result of this effort, the Professional Standards Committee of the American Association for Counseling and Development proposed 31 multicultural counseling competencies to the APA and recommended that the APA adopt these competencies in its accreditation criteria (Sue, Arredondo, & McDavis, 1992).

In 1992, a paradigm model of the characteristics of a culturally competent counselor and the dimensions of cultural competence was constructed. This model gave the movement a conceptual framework. According to this model, a culturally competent counselor is aware of his or her own values, understands the worldview of his or her culturally different clients, and uses sensitive intervention strategies and skills with clients. Dimensions of cultural competence entail beliefs and attitudes about racial and ethnic minorities, knowledge and understanding of the counselor's own worldview, and intervention strategy skills that can be used with minority groups (Sue et al., 1992). By 1993, the APA had committed itself to multicultural competence with ethnically, linguistically, and culturally diverse populations (APA, 1993).

Another useful description of cultural competence has been provided by Zayas, Evans, Mejia, and Rodriguez (1997). According to these authors, cultural competence includes knowledge and interpersonal skills to understand, appreciate, and work with individuals and families from cultures other than one's own; the use of knowledge and skills effectively to employ therapeutic techniques in achieving behavioral and emotional change; the awareness of critical cultural values, beliefs, behaviors, and interactions that structure social and family life and psychological functioning; and self-awareness, acceptance of differences, knowledge of a client's culture, and adaptation of helping skills to the client's culture (Zayas et al., 1997).

The cultural competence movement has grown in two related directions. On the clinical level, it has provided the helping professions (psychiatry, psychology, and social work) with a culturally focused theme. LaFromboise and colleagues (1993) described the client from a culturally competent perspective. Cultural competence has provided an education and training perspective by which to develop academic and professional expertise and skills in working with culturally diverse clients. Social work education has fostered cultural competence in child welfare and social work practice. The Title IV-E child welfare training grant under the auspices of the California Social Work Education Center at the University of California at Berkeley (1996) identified 14 cultural competencies according to population groups, child welfare knowledge, and practice skills. Population groups competencies recognized cultural and ethnic differences, ethnic group dynamics, cultural influence on behavior, socioeconomic and psychosocial issues facing immigrants and refugees, and the importance of client language. Child welfare knowledge competencies involved knowledge of child welfare services to cultural and ethnic populations and knowledge of relevant ethnic child welfare legislation. Practice skills competencies dealt with relationship information and communication development, ethnic sensitivity assessment, evaluation of intervention models, community outreach collaboration, and resource and service advocacy.

On the community level, efforts have been made to place cultural competence on the national public health and mental health agendas. As mentioned earlier, the U.S. Public Health Service's Office for Substance Abuse Prevention launched a series of monographs that integrated cultural competence, alcohol and drug abuse treatment programs, and ethnic groups and community (Orlandi et al., 1992)—a match between ethnic target groups, major problem areas, and cultural competence for treatment workers that illustrated how macro cultural competence can be expressed. By 1997, cultural competence guidelines for managed care and mental health were identified for Asian and Pacific Islanders and Native Americans (Substance Abuse and Mental Health Services Administration, 1997a & b). The guidelines for Asian and Pacific Islander populations (1997a) offered a provider network plan for public and private sectors that set the standards for cultural competence and service delivery, including overall system standards and guidelines specifying cultural competence planning, ongoing program development, governance, benefit design, quality monitoring and improvement, decision support and management information systems, and human resource development; provider competencies addressing knowledge and understanding, skills, and attitudes as well as prevention, education, and outreach; and clinical standards and guidelines covering access and service authorization, triage and assessment, care planning, plan of treatment, treatment services, case management, communication styles and cross-cultural communication support, communication styles and linguistic support, self help, and discharge planning.

States such as California (1997) and New York (1998) were in the midst of articulating cultural competence plans on the state and county levels. California was concerned about planning culturally competent mental health services, particularly through population assessment of county geographic and socioeconomic profiles, demographics (ethnicity, age and gender, primary language), and Medi-Cal mental health services utilization (ethnicity, age and gender, primary language), as well as through organizational and service provider assessment of mental health plans policy and administrative direction, human resources, location, quality of care and competency, and quality assurance. New York developed cultural competence performance measures for managed behavioral health care programs to identify methodology and data collection strategies. It formulated a conceptual framework for domains of cultural competence in mental health service delivery. Domain areas were needs assessment, information exchange, services, human resources, policies and plans, and cultural competencies outcomes. Related areas in which to implement these domains were the administrative managed care organization and state mental health authority, provider network, and individual staff members.

South Carolina has a cultural competence plan for 2003–2005 (Office of Multicultural Services, 2005), which addresses governance and administration (the support of the leadership of the South Carolina Department of Mental Health (SCDMH) to develop a system of culturally and linguistically competent care), human resources (the workforce of SCDMH to reflect the diversity of their communities), education and training (programs to promote and assure cultural competence among staff), clinical services (culturally and linguistically appropriate clinical care and services), consumers' families, the community (the involvement of advocacy groups, consumers and their families in participatory, collaborative partnerships to design and implement cultural and linguistically appropriate services) and outcomes, data, and information management (statewide performance indicators reflecting cultural competence in the care of children and adults). New Jersey (Adams, 2005) has passed a 2005 law requiring physicians to take cultural competency training as part of licensure. It is the first state to require physicians to learn how to culturally attune to patients in order to practice medicine. The intent of this law is to help reduce health care disparities among racial and ethnic minorities and to ensure that physicians become more responsive to cultural and language differences among their patients. Approximately 30,000 physicians who already have a license will have to complete cultural competency training to renew their licenses every two years.

A group of 10 multicultural counseling psychologists (Derald Wing Sue, Robert T. Carter, J. Manuel Casas, Nadya A. Fouad, Allen E. Ivey, Margaret Jensen, Teresa LaFromboise, Jeanne E. Manese, Joseph G. Ponterotto, and Ena Vazquez-Nutall; see Sue et al., 1998) has provided an ideological worldview perspective of multicultural counseling competencies at the micro, meso, and macro levels. The objectives of multicultural competence include cultural awareness of values, biases, and assumptions about human behavior; knowledge and understanding of minority or culturally different worldviews of groups and clients; appropriate and effective intervention strategies for working with culturally different clients; and awareness of organizational and institutional forces that enhance or negate multicultural competence. There are four major areas of multicultural competence: awareness of one's own worldview, awareness of the worldview of the culturally different client, the use of culturally appropriate intervention strategies, and the development of multicultural organizations.

In 2003, the APA adopted Guidelines on Multicultural Education, Training, Research, Practice, and Organizational Psychology (Constantine & Sue, 2005b) that are grounded in six principles and five guidelines:

Principle 1: Ethnical conduct of psychologists is enhanced by knowledge of differences in beliefs and practices that emerge from socialization through racial and ethnic group affiliation and membership and how those beliefs and practices will necessarily affect the education, training, research, and practice of psychology.

Principle 2: Understanding and recognizing the interface between individuals' socialization experiences based on ethnic and racial heritage can enhance the quality of education, training, practice, and research in the field of psychology.

Principle 3: Recognition of the ways in which the intersection of racial and ethnic group membership with other dimensions of identity (e.g., gender, age, sexual orientation, disability, religion/spiritual orientation, educational attainment/experiences, and socioeconomic status) enhances the understanding and treatment of all people.

Principle 4: Knowledge of historically derived approaches that have viewed cultural differences as deficits and have not valued certain social identities helps psychologists to understand the underrepresentation of ethnic minorities in the profession and affirms and values the role of ethnicity and race in developing personal identity.

Principle 5: Psychologists are uniquely able to promote racial equity and social justice. This is aided by their awareness of their impact on others and the influence of their personal and professional roles in society.

Principle 6: Psychologists' knowledge about the roles of organizations, including employers and professional psychological associations, are potential sources of behavioral practices that encourage discourse, education and training, institutional change, and research and policy development that reflect rather than neglect cultural differences. Psychologists recognize that organizations can be gatekeepers or agents of the status quo, rather than leaders in a changing society with respect to multiculturalism.

Guideline 1: Psychologists are encouraged to recognize that, as cultural beings, they may hold attitudes and beliefs that can detrimentally influence their perceptions of and interactions with individuals who are ethnically and racially different from themselves.

Guideline 2: Psychologists are encouraged to recognize the importance of multicultural sensitivity/responsiveness to, knowledge of, and understanding about ethnically and racially different individuals.

Guideline 3: As educators, psychologists are encouraged to employ the constructs of multiculturalism and diversity in psychological education.

Guideline 4: Culturally sensitive psychological researchers are encouraged to recognize the importance of conducting culture-centered and ethical psychological research among persons from ethnic, linguistic, and racial minority backgrounds.

Guideline 5: Psychologists are encouraged to apply culturally appropriate skills in clinical and other applied psychological practices.

Cultural competence as a movement has made major strides. Medicine, psychology, and social work have established national cultural competence standards in their academic and professional disciplines. Social work education has begun to apply this theme to its curriculum structure (social work clinical, community, and organizational practice; human behavior and the social environment; social welfare policy; human diversity, and populations-at-risk; social research; and social work fieldwork). Cultural competence needs to be applied to such social problem areas as family violence and substance abuse, mental health and health care practice, and related issues. Cultural competence is the theme of a movement that can be carried in multiple directions as social work educators continue to apply the concept to the client populations confronting them.

MY BELIEFS ABOUT CULTURAL COMPETENCE

I hope that as you read this book, you will formulate some strong convictions and beliefs about cultural competence as part of your knowledge and skill base for being a practitioner. Here I share some of my beliefs about cultural competence in the hope that they will prompt creative discussions among social workers in both classrooms and agencies.

Belief 1: Culturally competent practice is a major subject area for culturally diverse social work practice and a process of individual educational and professional growth.

Cultural competence is the subject area that relates to the social worker's experiential awareness of culture, ethnicity, and racism. Cultural competence is the result of a number of processes: individual and social reflection, academic education, career development, skill mastery, and continued contributions in multicultural practice. As a social work student, you will go through a reflection process that involves you as learner and thinker in the social environment of the classroom, in the field agency, and in life events and experiences. Acquiring a degree of cultural competence through an academic education will be an asset in the development of your career as a social worker. However, skill mastery, like an exercise program, involves a continuous learning process. Just as you must have regular exercise in order to maintain a fit and healthy body, so should you continue a cultural competence learning program with other social workers in your community in order to master cultural competence skills. The outgrowth of cultural competence is the continued contribution, in papers and articles, of new information and conceptual understanding acquired through working on client cases.

Belief 2: We can trace a historical progression of related multicultural themes such as ethnic sensitivity, cultural awareness, cultural diversity, and now cultural competence. These concepts are not mutually exclusive. Rather, cultural competence serves as a rubric that embraces these areas of concern.

Social workers often use such terms as *cultural sensitivity*, *cultural awareness*, and *cultural diversity* interchangeably when they discuss cultural competence. Devore and Schlesinger (1981) began culturally diverse social work practice with an emphasis on ethnic sensitivity. The main thrust of their work was to provide a practice structure for working with all ethnic groups. Green and associates (1982) introduced cultural awareness with an ethnographic approach to offering help. These authors wrote about the common and specific patterns of four major ethnic minority groups.

By the middle of the 1990s, multiculturalism and diversity were key concepts in ethnic studies literature. Lum (1996) conceptualized culturally diverse social work practice. About the same time, the Council on Social Work Education revised its evaluative standards to include the emphasis on outcome measurements. Social work educators began to speak about cultural competence, which influenced Lum and Lu (1997) to devise a social work cultural competence framework.

Hodge (2004, p. 39) has made the case for evangelicals in social work and spiritual competency as an integral part of cultural competence. As a form of cultural competency, spiritual competency consists of knowledge of one's own spiritual worldview and associated biases, an empathetic understanding of the client's spiritual worldview, and the ability to develop intervention strategies that are appropriate, relevant, and sensitive to the client's spiritual worldview. This may be another development in the ongoing application of cultural competence to related areas of concern for social work.

Belief 3: There is a concern about evaluating the competence of students through measurement instruments. Cultural competencies are outcome characteristics that can be measured to determine the extent to which social work students have attained teaching/learning objectives.

Students evaluate the teaching performance of instructors, while social work educators grade student performance in midterms and final examinations, term papers, and individual or group presentations. Now social work education is seeking to measure student acquisition of knowledge and skills. The competence movement is a reflection of this effort to measure individual student outcomes.

Social work programs may eventually devise outcome course competence instruments. Social work practice, behavior, research, and policy courses may follow the same evaluation format reflected in the field evaluation instrument that measures placement performance.

Belief 4: The applications of cultural competence to culturally diverse social work are legion and raise some interesting issues of how to foster the growth of cultural competence on the community practice level, with fields of practice, populations-at-risk, and particular ethnic groups.

The application of cultural competence to various settings should be a priority for us. How does cultural competence apply to indigenous community front-line paraprofessionals? These community outreach workers are a part of the team with BSW and MSW practitioners (that is, those with bachelor's and master's degrees in social work). Are there levels of cultural competence for various staff? A related question is how field placements can build cultural competence into helping structures. Should there be specific cultural competencies for social work education field experiences? A particular concern of social service agencies is the need to define cultural competencies as a part of their philosophy of services, program components, and program evaluation. On the job, a social worker could be evaluated according to culturally competent criteria based on some continued education training in cultural competence.

At the state level, the state of Washington requires human service workers to complete training in multicultural practice with a cultural competence certificate as a part of the licensing process. The NASW should work toward such a requirement in every state of the union. This requirement would guarantee minimum standards for any mental health worker who works with a multicultural client and provide social work programs with continuing education workshops in multicultural social work for certification purposes.

Multicultural clients and communities should be brought into the discussion on cultural competence. These persons should advocate for culturally competent workers to ensure that the services they receive will be ethnically sensitive and culturally effective. There should be multicultural advisory consumer boards and consumer interns who graduate from client to paraprofessional helpers in social service agencies. These groups should have strong ethnic community and culturally oriented perspectives and seek to have agency directors incorporate recommendations into the daily functioning of the agency.

Belief 5: Social work faculty members should become culturally competent. Many social work educators have been self-learners of multicultural social work practice. They toiled by themselves or in groups, taught themselves culturally diverse practice principles, and singularly conducted multicultural research-oriented practices. It is time to formulate theory and concepts based on culturally sensitive research as part of a national social work education effort.

In 1996, the Council on Social Work Education Board of Directors, Cultural Diversity Subcommittee, presented a proposal for a multicultural social work curriculum conference that would assess past and present contributions and plan 10-year multicultural curriculum projects in practice, behavior, policy, research, field, and international social work. The result was a conference entitled "Culturally Competent Social Work Education in the 21st Century" that was held in December 1998 at the University of Michigan, with the purpose of laying a foundation for developing a multicultural approach to practice that can more effectively address the social context of the 21st century. Selected social work educators who had made particular contributions in the culturally competent social work field were invited to present position papers, participate on response panels, and collaborate on five-year developmental plans for culturally competent social work theory and practice as a future blueprint for social work educators and practitioners.

The next step was a follow-up conference, "Cultural Competence in Child Welfare Practice: A Collaboration Between Practitioners and Academics," that focused on substance abuse and family violence among African American, Latino, Asian and Pacific Islander, and Native American/First Nations Peoples families. The objective was to apply cultural competence to two problem areas and to use the concept to direct practice, community organizing, and field practicum. This conference was held at the University of Texas at Austin during February 2001.

A growing debate exists among helping professionals about whether our knowledge and skills about cultural competence apply to treating clients of any cultural background, which includes racial and ethnic as well as gender, social class, and sexual orientation, or whether cultural competence should be particularized to cultural and ethnic groups. How broad a term is *culture?* Does culture extend beyond ethnicity to encompass the culture of women, the poor, and gays and lesbians (Ridley, 2005, pp. 183–184)? Culturally competent practice in social work started with a cultural and ethnic perspective but has moved to a discussion of women, gays and lesbians, immigrants and refugees, and spiritual persons. As long as there are advocates for these groups who make a case for cultural competence, there will be a broad application of this theme to multiple populations.

TOOLS FOR STUDENT LEARNING 1.1

Preliminary Thoughts on Cultural Competence, Questions, and Beliefs

We have covered the various facets of cultural competence and shared some beliefs about cultural competence. Now you have the opportunity to write down your preliminary thoughts about what you have read so far. Your instructor may wish you to share these thoughts in small groups as part of the classroom activities.

1. What are your understandings of cultural competence?

2. What are some questions that you have about cultural competence?

3. What are your preliminary notions about cultural competence that may later become beliefs and convictions?

THE ETHICS OF CULTURAL COMPETENCE

Social work ethics has a connection to cultural competence. *Ethics* are based on the values that we have as individuals and as professionals, which guide our choices based on our sense of right and wrong and on ideals such as the highest good, the promotion of fairness, or the moral duty and obligation that we have to ourselves, others, our profession, our community, and to a higher being. At times, our ethical guidelines force us to make a tragic moral choice where we must choose the lesser of the two evils because the two or more available selections are less than ideal. In short, Leppien-Christensen (Nebraska Prevention, n.d.) states: "The field of ethics involves systematizing, defending, and recommending concepts of right and wrong behavior." Social work has a tradition of a professional code of ethics.

The NASW's 1999 Code of Ethics has a section on cultural competence:

1.05(a) Social workers should understand culture and its function in human behavior and society, recognizing the strengths that exist in all cultures.

1.05(b) Social workers should have a knowledge base of their clients' cultures and be able to demonstrate competence in the provision of services that are sensitive to clients' culture and to differences among people and cultural groups.

1.05(c) Social workers should obtain education about and seek to understand the nature of social diversity and oppression with respect to race, ethnicity, national origin, sex, sexual orientation, age, marital status, political belief, religion and mental or physical development

Interestingly, the Standards for Cultural Competence in Social Work Practice, which we will cover in the next section, and the NASW Code of Ethics charge the social worker with the ethical responsibility to be culturally competent. Both go hand in hand to delineate ethical and professional standards for culturally competent social work practice. Social work has adopted a broad meaning for culture ". . . to include sociocultural experiences of people of different genders, social classes, religious and spiritual beliefs, sexual orientations, ages, and physical and mental abilities" (NASW Standards for Cultural Competence in Social Work Practice, 2001). Our task in this section is to blend this understanding of culture with the values, beliefs, and guidelines of ethics in order to address the ethics of cultural competence.

There has been increasing interest in the ethics of cultural competence. Among the ethical moral guidelines and the cultural beliefs and practices are the following principles that comprise an ethical notion of cultural competence:

- The acknowledgement of the importance of culture in people's lives
- The respect for cultural differences
- The minimization of any negative consequences of cultural differences, which has a discriminatory effect on persons and/or groups
- The assessment of personal cultural values, acknowledging the existence of a cultural lens that shapes our interpretations of the world
- The understanding and acknowledgement of the historical relationship between your own culture and other cultural groups
- The creation and dissemination of institutional culture knowledge, which recognizes and honors diversity
- The development of policies and ethical guidelines, which implements service delivery reflecting an understanding of cultural diversity (Cross et al., 1989; Paasche-Orlow, 2004; Nebraska Prevention, n.d.)

The ethics of cultural competence ought to sensitize social workers, clients, and community to cultural similarities and differences that are the essence of diversity. It should allow us the freedom to use cultural symbols and practices in communication and daily living. It should guide us in the development of policies and practices that seek the input of community members of various cultures. It should encourage agencies and professional bodies to develop written ethical guidelines and practices that guide the infusion of cultural competence into staff selection and development, as well as strategies, policies, procedures, and practices for cultural competence. In short, it is the underpinnings for evaluating the relationship between the ethics of cultural competence and the ethics of social work.

SOCIAL WORK AND CULTURAL COMPETENCIES

Social work has done considerable work with professional standards of cultural competence. These cultural competence guidelines, which could be called *cultural competencies*, are statements that focus on specific behavioral cultural competence criteria. They describe culturally competent activities of the professional practitioner.

The NASW (2001) has also issued *Standards for Cultural Competence in Social Work Practice*. Ten standards provide guidelines, goals, and objectives of cultural competence; these standards can be considered cultural competencies:

Standard 1. Ethics and Values: *Social workers shall function in accordance with the values, ethics, and standards of the profession, recognizing how personal and professional values may conflict with or accommodate the needs of diverse clients.*

Among the major ethical and value areas is a sensitivity to cultural and ethnic diversity. Cultural and ethnic sensitivity extends to behavior appropriate to a culture based on cultural traditions and norms, client cultural background, the planning of social services, a recognition of cultural strengths, and ethnical and cultural value conflict dilemmas.

Standard 2. Self-Awareness: *Social workers shall develop an understanding of their own personal and cultural values and beliefs as a first step in appreciating the importance of multicultural identities in the lives of people.*

Social workers should examine their own cultural backgrounds and identities, become culturally aware of their own heritage as well as those of others, and move from cultural awareness through cultural sensitivity to cultural competence.

Standard 3. Cross-Cultural Knowledge: *Social workers shall have and continue to develop specialized knowledge and understanding about the history, traditions, values, family systems, and artistic expression of major client groups served.*

Social workers are challenged to expand their knowledge about culture, behavior, language, social service policy impacts, resources, and power relationships; particular providers and client groups; social, cultural, and political systems in the United States; and the limitations and strengths of current and relevant theories and principles.

Standard 4. Cross-Cultural Skills: *Social workers shall use appropriate methodological approaches, skills, and techniques that reflect the workers' understanding of the role of culture in the helping process.*

Among the personal attributes and qualities of a culturally competent social worker is an acceptance and openness to differences among people, an understanding of the role of language in the client's culture, an assessment of cultural norms and behaviors as strengths rather than problematic or symptomatic behaviors, and advocacy and empowerment skills.

Standard 5. Service Delivery: *Social workers shall be knowledgeable about and skillful in the use of services available in the community and broader society and be able to make appropriate referrals for their diverse clients.*

Among the specific ways of implementing culturally competent service delivery are recruiting multiethnic staff and including cultural competence job requirements, reviewing demographic trends to determine interpretation and translation services, having program décor and design that reflect the cultural heritage of clients, and developing culturally competent performance measures.

Standard 6. Empowerment and Advocacy: *Social workers shall be aware of the effect of social policies and programs on diverse client populations, advocating for and with clients whenever appropriate.*

Empowerment involves consciousness raising, the development of personal power, and skills for social change. Advocacy involves a client's understanding of what it means to advocate based on respectful collaboration and mutually agreed-on goals for change.

Standard 7. Diverse Workforce: *Social workers shall support and advocate for recruitment, admissions and hiring, and retention efforts in social work programs and agencies that ensure diversity within the profession.*

This implies the recruitment and retention of a diverse cadre of social workers who have some indigenous sense of cultural competence and make efforts to increase culturally competent skills.

Standard 8. Professional Education: *Social workers shall advocate for and participate in educational and training programs that help advance cultural competence within the profession.*

Social work needs to keep up with the changing needs of diverse client populations. There should be continuing education offers in culturally competent practice. Above all, it is important to provide culturally sensitive supervision and field instruction.

Standard 9. Language Diversity: *Social workers shall seek to provide and advocate for the provision of information, referrals, and services in the language appropriate to the client, which may include the use of interpreters.*

Agencies and providers should take reasonable steps to provide services and information in appropriate languages for clients who speak limited English. Language interpreters and translation are important, and persons engaging in these services should be trained in the ethics and linguistics of interpreting in an effective and confidential manner.

Standard 10. Cross-Cultural Leadership: *Social workers shall be able to communicate information about diverse client groups to other professionals.*

Leadership entails empowering diverse client populations, disseminating information about these groups, and advocating for fair and equitable treatment at the interpersonal and institutional levels.

NASW cultural competence standards are the benchmarks for the social work profession. But how does one turn these standards into culturally competent statements, or *cultural competencies*, and measure them to determine to what extent a social worker has accomplished them? The NASW *Standards for Cultural Competence in Social Work Practice* (2001) states: "As the social work profession develops cultural competencies, then the profession must have the ability to measure those competencies. The development of outcome measures needs to go hand in hand with the development of those standards" (p. 14).

Fortunately, the Council on Social Work Education (CSWE) has been concerned about outcome measures and measurement methods for the past decade and has developed accreditation standards (CSWE, 2003). Accreditation Standard 1—Program Mission, Goals, and Objectives—emphasizes the relationship between mission, goals, and objectives. The purpose of this standard is to help the program, the faculty, and the student in their quest to determine whether adequate linkage has occurred in a course area. Regarding outcome measures and measurement methods, Accreditation Standard 8—Program Assessment and Continuous Improvement—states:

> 8.0 The program has an assessment plan and procedures for evaluating the outcome of each program objective. The plan specifies the measurement procedures and methods used to evaluate the outcome of each program objective. 8.1 The program implements its plan to evaluate the outcome of each program objective and shows evidence that the analysis is used continuously to affirm and improve the educational program. (CSWE, 2003)

The emphasis is on the achievement of objectives, measurement instruments and statistical procedures, and program and curriculum evaluation. Examples of measurement instruments include pre- and posttests of knowledge and/or skill, student self-reports, evidence of contribution to professional knowledge building, and student evaluations of courses and instructor performance.

Accreditation Standard 8 has created interest in measuring course learning, which in turn has led to a discussion of cultural competencies. As noted, cultural competencies are a series of behavioral outcomes related to multicultural social work learning and professional practice. Cultural competencies are identified in a culturally competent framework that provides a basis for measuring the development and inclusion of abilities in the person. The framework could be used to translate the components of cultural competence into clear, measurable statements in a research instrument. Such an instrument could measure the degree of cultural competence before a multicultural social work course and on completion of the course in order to determine whether the knowledge and skills taught during the course have had an effect on the student.

As an example of cultural competencies, let us consider some competence statements developed in the field of child welfare. The Title IV-E child welfare training grant heightened interest in the child welfare curriculum and social work graduate-level education for child welfare specialists. The California Social Work Education Center (CalSWEC) at the University of California at Berkeley became the focal point for a statewide system of MSW child welfare training in all the California graduate social work programs. Recently, the California graduate schools of social work have made new thrusts in the field of mental health with state mental health funding available through Proposition 63, a statewide tax initiative designed to obtain mental health revenue funds from those who earn $1 million or more per year. CalSWEC (2005) has expanded its role in graduate mental health social work education.

The 2005 CalSWEC II Mental Health Initiative identified two sets of mental health competencies at the foundational and advanced levels in accordance with the 2004 California Mental Health Services Act and the 2003 California Mental Health Master Plan: A Vision for California. The following culturally and linguistically competent generalist practice foundation competencies were identified:

1. Student understands the impact of the role of racial, ethnic, age, class, multiple cultural identities, gender identities, and sexual orientation identity on interpersonal encounters in community mental health practice relationships.

2. Student demonstrates knowledge of immigration, migration, resettlement, and relocation patterns of the major ethnic groups in the United States in the context of both historical and current manifestations of oppression, racism, prejudice, discrimination, bias, and privilege.

3. Student demonstrates knowledge of differences between the experiences of immigrants and refugees and the different impact those experiences have on individuals and families.

4. Student demonstrates awareness of the effects of acute and accumulative trauma on the health status; health beliefs; help-seeking behaviors; and health practices, customs and traditions of diverse clients and communities.

5. Student demonstrates knowledge of the unique legal, historical, and current relationships with the U.S. government that American Indian/Alaska Native nations possess and the effect these relationships have on the health status; health beliefs; help-seeking behaviors; and health practices, customs, and traditions within and among their diverse tribal communities.

6. Student understands the influence and value of traditional ethnic and culturally based practices, which impact the mental health of the individual or family, and uses this knowledge in working with clients, families, and the community.

7. Student demonstrates knowledge of legal, social, political, economic, and psychological issues facing immigrants and their families in a new and different environment. The student uses this knowledge to better understand client's choices/decisions related to mental health care, health care, and so on.

8. Student demonstrates an understanding of the impact and importance of assimilation and acculturation processes in order to work effectively with culturally diverse individuals, families, and communities.

9. Student understands the background and applicability of theories of practice to various ethnic and cultural groups, as well as other diverse groups.

10. Student shows respect for professional social work values and demonstrates a commitment to cultural competence by demonstrating an ongoing self-evaluation process with regard to his or her own multicultural awareness and perceptions of difference.

11. Student understands the importance of the client and community's native language, how it reflects and influences identity, meaning, and worldview, as well as its importance in mental health treatment and its necessity in all communication with clients and the community (signs, forms, receptionist, media, etc.).

12. Student understands the full range of implications for assessment and diagnosis, including the danger of misdiagnosis when English is not the client's primary language and professional translation services are not utilized.

13. Student understands that variance in a client's language can impact the expression and understanding of symptoms and attributions of illness.

14. Student understands and is aware how his or her own cultural values, beliefs, norms, and worldview influence perception and interpretation of events and can influence relationships with clients.

15. Student respects religion and/or spiritual beliefs and values about physical and mental functioning that are different from his or her own.

16. Student understands how biases, prejudices, and beliefs are formed about poverty, gender identities, sexual orientation, homelessness, substance abuse, and mental illness and understands the effect on his or her relationship with clients.
17. Student demonstrates understanding and awareness of disparities for racial and ethnic minorities and other culturally diverse groups in terms of access, appropriateness, availability, and quality of mental health services.

Likewise, the following set of advanced competencies relates to culturally and linguistically competent mental health practice:

1. Student can apply knowledge and appreciation of his or her own culture and the cultural differences of others, being able to identify the strengths of diverse populations. Student is able to identify how his or her culture may impact positively or negatively on provision of services.
2. Student demonstrates knowledge of diversity within ethnic and cultural groups in terms of social class, assimilation, acculturation, and his or her particular way of being.
3. Student is able to develop treatment goals and interventions that are congruent with cultural perspectives across diverse groups.
4. Student can critically evaluate how to use or set aside his or her own cultural values and norms in transcultural social work mental health practice and demonstrates skill in understanding and using his or her own identity and sense of self in same culture as well as cross-cultural interpersonal encounters.
5. Student demonstrates flexibility and uses an array of culturally sensitive and relevant clinical skills in the teaching, advocacy, treatment, healing, and case management roles.
6. Student is knowledgeable about the common elements of practice (e.g. making eye contact, initiating a handshake, etc.) and how they may clash with the cultural values of various ethnic and cultural groups.
7. Student demonstrates knowledge about (1) specific cultural features that may be present in various disorders, (2) culture-bound syndromes, (3) cultural explanations of illness, (4) help-seeking behaviors in diverse populations, and (5) appreciation for traditional ethnic and cultural healing practices.
8. Student demonstrates knowledge and ability to work with interpreters in ongoing treatment and in long-term treatment relationships.
9. Student can apply awareness of the effects of acute and accumulative trauma on the health status; health beliefs; help-seeking behaviors; and health practices, customs, and traditions of diverse clients and communities.
10. Student can work through differences sensitively in community mental health practice relationships with clients, their families, colleagues, other professionals, and the community.
11. Student is able to critically evaluate the relevance of intervention models to be applied with diverse ethnic and cultural populations and other special needs groups.
12. Student can apply knowledge of immigration, migration, resettlement, and relocation patterns of the major ethnic groups in the United States in the context of both historical and current manifestations of oppression, racism, prejudice, discrimination, bias, and privilege.

13. Student works to remove institutional barriers that prevent ethnic and cultural groups from using mental health services and can identify appropriate macro-level interventions.
14. Student is knowledgeable about the potential bias present in clinical assessment instruments and critically interprets findings within the appropriate cultural, linguistic, and life experience context of the client.
15. Student engages in efforts to systematically collect and organize observations, knowledge, and experience that will advocate for improved policies and delivery of services in the community.

Each competency statement is related to the practice of mental health and reflects a comprehensive understanding and social work diversity content. Although there is a strong emphasis on immigrants and refugees, these competencies cover the broad range of practice concerns and skills that are necessary in working with ethnic population groups who are in socioeconomic need. The foundational competencies emphasize knowledge and understanding, whereas the advanced competencies focus on knowledge application and the development of skills. There is a strong case for the worker to practice linguistically competent practice.

Furthermore, Sue and Sue (2003, pp. 18–23) delineate 3 major competency sets with 14 competencies:

Competency One: Therapist Awareness of One's Own Assumptions, Values, and Biases
1. The culturally competent mental health professional is one who has moved from being culturally unaware to being aware and sensitive to his or her own cultural heritage and to valuing and respecting differences.
2. The culturally competent mental health professional is aware of his or her own values and biases and of how they may affect minority clients.
3. Culturally competent mental health professionals are comfortable with differences that exist between themselves and their clients in terms of race, gender, sexual orientation, and other sociodemographic variables. Differences are not seen as being deviant.
4. The culturally competent mental health practitioner is sensitive to circumstances (personal biases; stage of racial, gender, and sexual orientation identity; sociopolitical influences; etc.) that may dictate referral of the client to a member of his or her own sociodemographic group or to another therapist in general.
5. The culturally competent mental health professional acknowledges and is aware of his or her own racist, sexist, heterosexist, or other detrimental attitudes, beliefs, and feelings.

Competency Two: Understanding the Worldview of Culturally Diverse Clients
1. The culturally competent mental health professional must possess specific knowledge and information about the particular group with which he or she is working.
2. The culturally competent mental health professional will have a good understanding of the sociopolitical system's operation in the United States with respect to its treatment of marginalized groups in our society.

3. The culturally competent mental health professional must have a clear and explicit knowledge and understanding of the generic characteristics of counseling and therapy.
4. The culturally competent mental health professional is aware of institutional barriers that prevent some diverse clients from using mental health services.

Competency Three: Developing Appropriate Intervention Strategies and Techniques

1. At the skills level, the culturally competent mental health professional must be able to generate a wide variety of verbal and nonverbal responses.
2. The culturally competent mental health professional must be able to send and receive both verbal and nonverbal messages accurately and appropriately.
3. The culturally competent mental health professional is able to exercise institutional intervention skills on behalf of his or her client when appropriate.
4. The culturally competent mental health professional is aware of his or her helping style, recognizes the limitations that he or she possesses, and can anticipate the impact on the culturally different client.
5. The culturally competent mental health professional is able to play helping roles characterized by an active systemic focus, which leads to environmental interventions. Such a mental health professional is not trapped into the conventional counselor/therapist mode of operation.

The preceding competency statements are important indicators to measure cultural competence and could be translated into items on assessing cultural competent performance.

Social work has also begun to apply cultural competence to various populations at risk. Teasley (2005) presents cultural competence research regarding school social workers and African American children. In a sample of 247 school social workers in Atlanta, Philadelphia, Cleveland, and Baltimore, Teasley found that perceived levels of cultural competence were associated with postgraduate professional development and that African American school social workers scored higher on overall perceived levels of cultural competence in urban schools than their White counterparts. He suggested that many practitioners gain advanced knowledge of their service population after completing their formal education and that school systems may require and design professional development programs relevant to such populations as urban African American youth. Van Den Bergh and Crisp (2004) make the case for cultural competence with gay, lesbian, bisexual, and transgendered clients and conceptualize around attitudes, knowledge, and skills. At the same time, there is increasing concern about adequate assessment instruments to measure cultural competence. Teasley (2005) advocates the development of reliable and valid measures of assessing levels of cultural competence, and Green and colleagues (2005) share extensive research on the Multicultural Counseling Inventory surveying 344 social workers on their multicultural awareness, multicultural relationships, knowledge, and counseling skill. Cultural competence and social work practice and research are currently of great interest.

In Competency Study 1.2, Hepworth, Rooney, and Larsen (1997) underscore the need for students to develop and update competent social work practice.

By now you should understand the importance of translating cultural competence standards into cultural competencies that can be measured in a questionnaire. We have

COMPETENCY STUDY 1.2

Competent Practice

Competent practice is defined as "fitting, suitable for the purpose; adequate; properly qualified; having legal capacity or qualification." To assess professional competency, however, is far from simple because competency in practice embodies knowledge, values, skills, and attitudes essential to fulfill one's professional role skillfully. Ingredients essential to perform one's role adequately vary according to the demands of each situation. A practitioner may thus be competent in providing certain types of service, such as marital or family therapy, and not in others, such as correctional services or protective services to children who have been abused or neglected. Furthermore, the elements of competent practice in various settings evolve as a result of expanding knowledge, emerging skills, and the changing demands of practice. Competency must thus be viewed within a temporal context, for a practitioner may achieve competence at one time only to suffer steady erosion of that competence by failing to keep abreast of ever-expanding knowledge and skills. (p. 16)

operationalized a series of cultural competencies based on the content of this text into pretest and posttest instruments (see the Tools for Student Learning sections that follow). The instruments included here are the Social Work Cultural Competencies Self-Assessment instrument and the Social Work Cultural Competencies with Diverse Groups of Color and Social and Economic Justice instrument.

The Social Work Cultural Competencies Self-Assessment instrument (Tools for Student Learning 1.2) is a 44-item Likert-type scale that measures your level of cultural competence. It is based on the framework in Chapter 2 and covers four competence areas (cultural awareness, knowledge acquisition, skill development, and inductive learning) and two levels (generalist and advanced). It is designed to satisfy the cultural diversity curriculum outcome requirement of the CSWE's Accreditation Standard 1. You are invited to take the self-assessment instrument as a pretest now. At this point, you should be familiar with the idea of cultural competency, although you may have minimal comprehension of this field.

Your score on the self-assessment instrument is determined by counting the numbers you have circled and adding them together (see scoring information at end of instrument). You will score the instrument yourself and need not disclose the results to anyone else. Your scores at the beginning and at the end of the course will not affect your grade. There are four possible levels; you are expected to score in the Level 1 or 2 range on the pretest unless you have had a strong multicultural life experience or extensive course work in ethnic studies, or both. It is normal to score at the lower levels when you are just beginning the course. You will master knowledge and skills during the semester. At the last class session, you will be asked to take the test again as a posttest outcome measurement and to score yourself. There should be a significant difference between your pretest and posttest scores. You should move into the Level 3 or 4 categories.

I suggest that you write a two-page analysis comparing the results of the test before and after the course and sharing areas of growth and inquiry. The results provide excellent feedback for your instructor, who is concerned about teaching effectiveness in a culturally diverse practice course. These results will help your instructor determine which themes require more explanation in the next class.

A companion instrument is the new Social Work Cultural Competencies with Diverse Groups of Color and Social and Economic Justice instrument (Tools for Student

Learning 1.3), which measures the knowledge and skills of students concerning six diverse populations-at-risk groups and the theme of social and economic justice, both of which are a part of the CSWE's *Educational Policy and Accreditation Standards*. Whereas the first pretest measures generalist cultural competence, this pretest covers cultural competence with First Nations Peoples, African Americans, Latino Americans, Asian Americans, women of color, and gay and lesbian persons of color, as well as social and economic justice. Statements relating to particular diverse groups measure diversity, oppression, cultural awareness, social service needs, knowledge acquisition, practice skill development, inductive learning, and social and economic justice. You are invited to take this pretest now. As with the first pretest, scoring information is presented at the end of the instrument.

Chapter 15 contains some posttests that are related to both of the pretests presented here.

TOOLS FOR STUDENT LEARNING 1.2

Social Work Cultural Competencies Self-Assessment Pretest

Written by Doman Lum, Ph.D (all rights reserved)

Introduction

This instrument measures your level of cultural competence at the beginning and end of the semester. The results of this self-assessment will be evaluated by your social work instructor. Strict confidentiality is observed regarding the results of the self-assessment.

Rate yourself on your level of competency on a scale of 1–4: 1 = Unlikely; 2 = Not very likely; 3 = Likely; and 4 = Definitely. Circle the appropriate number.

Social Security # (last four digits):   *Course:*   *Instructor:*   *Campus:*

Background Information

1. Age: _____   2. Sex: Male _____ Female _____

3. Ethnicity (please check all that apply):
   African American _____   Asian American _____   European American _____
   Jewish American _____   Latino American _____   Middle Eastern _____
   First Nations Peoples _____ Other (please specify) _____

4. Years of education (e.g., 12 = high school graduate) (circle correct number):
   12 13 14 15 16 17 18 19 20 21 or more

5. Highest degree earned/major:

6. Years of previous social service volunteer experience:
   None ___ 1–3 years ___ 4–6 years ___ 7–9 years ___ 10 years or more ___

7. Years of previous social work employment:
   None ___ 1–3 years ___ 4–6 years ___ 7–9 years ___ 10 years or more ___

8. Prior courses on cultural diversity:
   None ___ 1 course ___ 2 courses ___ 3 or more courses ___

Cultural Awareness

1. I am aware of my life experiences as a person related to a culture (e.g., family heritage, household and community events, beliefs, and practices).

   1–Unlikely   *2–Not very likely*   *3–Likely*   *4–Definitely*

2. I have contact with other cultural and ethnic individuals, families, and groups.

   1–Unlikely   *2–Not very likely*   *3–Likely*   *4–Definitely*

3. I am aware of positive and negative experiences with cultural and ethnic persons and events.

   1–Unlikely   *2–Not very likely*   *3–Likely*   *4–Definitely*

4. I know how to evaluate my cognitive, affective, and behavioral experiences and reactions to racism, prejudice, and discrimination.

   1–Unlikely   *2–Not very likely*   *3–Likely*   *4–Definitely*

5. I have assessed my involvement with cultural and ethnic people of color in childhood, adolescence, young adulthood, and adulthood.

   1–Unlikely   *2–Not very likely*   *3–Likely*   *4–Definitely*

6. I have had or plan to have academic course work, fieldwork experiences, and research projects on culturally diverse clients and groups.

   1–Unlikely   *2–Not very likely*   *3–Likely*   *4–Definitely*

7. I have had or plan to have professional employment experiences with culturally diverse clients and programs.

   1–Unlikely   *2–Not very likely*   *3–Likely*   *4–Definitely*

8. I have assessed or plan to assess my academic and professional work experiences with cultural diversity and culturally diverse client.

   1–Unlikely   *2–Not very likely*   *3–Likely*   *4–Definitely*

Knowledge Acquisition

9. I understand the following terms: *ethnic minority, multiculturalism, diversity,* and *people of color.*

   1–Unlikely   *2–Not very likely*   *3–Likely*   *4–Definitely*

10. I have knowledge of demographic profiles of some culturally diverse populations.

    1–Unlikely   *2–Not very likely*   *3–Likely*   *4–Definitely*

11. I have developed a critical thinking perspective on cultural diversity.

    1–Unlikely   *2–Not very likely*   *3–Likely*   *4–Definitely*

12. I understand the history of oppression and multicultural social group history.

    1–Unlikely   *2–Not very likely*   *3–Likely*   *4–Definitely*

13. I know information about men, women, and children of color.

    1–Unlikely   *2–Not very likely*   *3–Likely*   *4–Definitely*

14. I know about culturally diverse values.

    1–Unlikely   *2–Not very likely*   *3–Likely*   *4–Definitely*

15. I know how to apply systems theory and psychosocial theory to multicultural social work.

    1–Unlikely   *2–Not very likely*   *3–Likely*   *4–Definitely*

16. I have knowledge of theories on ethnicity, culture, minority identity, and social class.

    1–Unlikely   *2–Not very likely*   *3–Likely*   *4–Definitely*

17. I know how to draw on a range of social science theory from cross-cultural psychology, multicultural counseling and therapy, and cultural anthropology.

    1–Unlikely   *2–Not very likely*   *3–Likely*   *4–Definitely*

Skill Development

18. I understand how to overcome the resistance and lower the communication barriers of a multicultural client.

    1–Unlikely   *2–Not very likely*   *3–Likely*   *4–Definitely*

19. I know how to obtain personal and family background information from a multicultural client and determine the client's ethnic/community sense of identity.

    1–Unlikely   *2–Not very likely*   *3–Likely*   *4–Definitely*

20. I understand the concepts of ethnic community and practice relationship protocols with a multicultural client.

    1–Unlikely   *2–Not very likely*   *3–Likely*   *4–Definitely*

21. I use professional self-disclosure with a multicultural client.

    1–Unlikely   *2–Not very likely*   *3–Likely*   *4–Definitely*

22. I have a positive and open communication style and use open-ended listening responses.

    1–Unlikely   *2–Not very likely*   *3–Likely*   *4–Definitely*

23. I know how to obtain problem information, facilitate problem area disclosure, and promote problem understanding.

    1–Unlikely   *2–Not very likely*   *3–Likely*   *4–Definitely*

24. I view a problem as an unsatisfied want or an unfulfilled need.

    1–Unlikely   *2–Not very likely*   *3–Likely*   *4–Definitely*

25. I know how to explain problems on micro, meso, and macro levels.

    1–Unlikely   *2–Not very likely*   *3–Likely*   *4–Definitely*

26. I know how to explain problem themes (racism, prejudice, discrimination) and expressions (oppression, powerlessness, stereotyping, acculturation, and exploitation).

    1–Unlikely   *2–Not very likely*   *3–Likely*   *4 Definitely*

27. I know how to find out about problem details.

    1–Unlikely   *2–Not very likely*   *3–Likely*   *4–Definitely*

28. I know how to assess socioenvironmental impacts, psychoindividual reactions, and cultural strengths.

    1–Unlikely   *2–Not very likely*   *3–Likely*   *4–Definitely*

29. I know how to assess the biological, psychological, social, cultural, and spiritual dimensions of the multicultural client.

    1–Unlikely   *2–Not very likely*   *3–Likely*   *4–Definitely*

30. I know how to establish joint goals and agreements with the client that are culturally acceptable.

    1–Unlikely   *2–Not very likely*   *3–Likely*   *4–Definitely*

31. I know how to formulate micro, meso, and macro intervention strategies that address the cultural needs of the client and special needs populations such as immigrants and refugees.

    1–Unlikely   *2–Not very likely*   *3–Likely*   *4–Definitely*

32. I know how to initiate termination in a way that links the client to an ethnic community resource, reviews significant progress and growth development, evaluates goal outcomes, and establishes a follow-up strategy.

    1–Unlikely   *2–Not very likely*   *3–Likely*   *4–Definitely*

33. I know how to design a service delivery and agency linkage and culturally effective social service programs in ethnic communities.

    1–Unlikely   *2–Not very likely*   *3–Likely*   *4–Definitely*

34. I have been involved in services that have been accessible to the ethnic community.

    1–Unlikely   *2–Not very likely*   *3–Likely*   *4–Definitely*

35. I have participated in delivering pragmatic and positive services that meet the tangible needs of the ethnic community.

    1–Unlikely   *2–Not very likely*   *3–Likely*   *4–Definitely*

36. I have observed the effectiveness of bilingual/bicultural workers who reflect the ethnic composition of the clientele.

    1–Unlikely   *2–Not very likely*   *3–Likely*   *4–Definitely*

37. I have participated in community outreach education and prevention that establish visible services, provide culturally sensitive programs, and employ credible staff.

    1–Unlikely   *2–Not very likely*   *3–Likely*   *4–Definitely*

38. I have been involved in a service linkage network to related social agencies that ensures rapid referral and program collaboration.

    1–Unlikely   *2–Not very likely*   *3–Likely*   *4–Definitely*

39. I have participated as a staff member in fostering a conducive agency setting with an atmosphere that is friendly and helpful to multicultural clients.

    1–Unlikely   *2–Not very likely*   *3–Likely*   *4–Definitely*

40. I am involved or plan to be involved with cultural skill development research in areas related to cultural empathy, clinical alliance, goal-obtaining styles, achieving styles, practice skills, and outcome research.

    1–Unlikely   *2–Not very likely*   *3–Likely*   *4–Definitely*

Inductive Learning

41. I have participated or plan to participate in a study discussion group with culturally diverse social work educators, practitioners, students, and clients on cultural competence issues, emerging cultural trends, and future directions for multicultural social work.

    1–Unlikely   *2–Not very likely*   *3–Likely*   *4–Definitely*

42. I have found or am seeking new journal articles and textbook material about cultural competence and culturally diverse practice.

    1–Unlikely   *2–Not very likely*   *3–Likely*   *4–Definitely*

43. I have conducted or plan to conduct inductive research on cultural competence and culturally diverse practice, using survey, oral history, and/or participatory observation research methods.

    1–Unlikely   *2–Not very likely*   *3–Likely*   *4–Definitely*

44. I have participated or will participate in the writing of articles and texts on cultural competence and culturally diverse practice.

    1–Unlikely   *2–Not very likely*   *3–Likely*   *4–Definitely*

What are your questions and views on cultural competence and cultural competencies?

What are your reactions to this self-assessment instrument?

Please count your scores on the 44 self-assessment items and rate your level of cultural competence. Circle the appropriate level and write your raw score in one of the following levels:

Level 1: Unlikely (scores 44–77)
Level 2: Not very likely (scores 78–101)
Level 3: Likely (scores 102–135)
Level 4: Definitely (scores 136–176)

Thank you for your cooperation on this self-assessment instrument. You have made a significant contribution to our research on social work cultural competence.

TOOLS FOR STUDENT LEARNING 1.3

Social Work Cultural Competencies with Diverse Groups of Color and Social and Economic Justice Pretest

Written by Doman Lum, Ph.D (all rights reserved)

Introduction

This instrument measures your level of cultural competence with diverse groups of color and social and economic justice at the beginning and end of the semester. The results of this test will be evaluated by your social work instructor. Strict confidentiality is observed regarding the results of this instrument.

Rate yourself on your level of competence on a scale of 1–4: 1 = Unlikely; 2 = Not very likely; 3 = Likely; and 4 = Definitely. Circle the appropriate number.

Social Security # (last four digits):   *Course:*   *Instructor:*   *Campus:*

First Nations Peoples

1. I know about the diversity of Native nations, which differ in terms of language, religion, social structure, political structure, and many aspects of culture.

   1–Unlikely   *2–Not very likely*   *3–Likely*   *4–Definitely*

2. I understand the concept of Seven Generations, which provides a historical and current perspective on oppression experiences.

   1–Unlikely   *2–Not very likely*   *3–Likely*   *4–Definitely*

3. It is important to choose interventions and design programs that accurately target the needs of First Nations Peoples, which may be different for each community.

   1–Unlikely   *2–Not very likely*   *3–Likely*   *4–Definitely*

4. Knowledge about First Nations Peoples requires an understanding of sovereignty issues and policies that apply to indigenous people.

   1–Unlikely   *2–Not very likely*   *3–Likely*   *4–Definitely*

5. Patience, listening, and silence are important skills to practice when working with First Nations Peoples clients.

   1–Unlikely   *2–Not very likely*   *3–Likely*   *4–Definitely*

6. I know about First Nations Peoples community immersion projects to increase inductive learning.

   1–Unlikely   *2–Not very likely*   *3–Likely*   *4–Definitely*

7. The Supreme Court has consistently ruled against the rights of First Nations Peoples.

   1–Unlikely   *2–Not very likely*   *3–Likely*   *4–Definitely*

African Americans

8. Diversity among African Americans involves such factors as physical characteristics, residential patterns, marital status, education, income, age, social class, and employment.

   1–Unlikely   *2–Not very likely*   *3–Likely*   *4–Definitely*

9. I understand the unique historical background of African Americans regarding involuntary migration, slavery, segregation, and continued oppression.

   1–Unlikely   *2–Not very likely*   *3–Likely*   *4–Definitely*

10. I am able to explain the four stages of the helping process that African American clients may go through with a practitioner.

    1–Unlikely   *2–Not very likely*   *3–Likely*   *4–Definitely*

11. I can identify several knowledge areas about the African American population and about the African American client.

    1–Unlikely   *2–Not very likely*   *3–Likely*   *4–Definitely*

12. I understand Afrocentric practice approaches, which are based on the Nguzo Saba value system.

    1–Unlikely   *2–Not very likely*   *3–Likely*   *4–Definitely*

13. I can explain the inductive learning strengths perspective approach for African American clients.

    1–Unlikely   *2–Not very likely*   *3–Likely*   *4–Definitely*

14. I comprehend the internalization of oppression that leads to disempowerment as a starting point for understanding how to achieve social and economic justice.

    1–Unlikely   *2–Not very likely*   *3–Likely*   *4–Definitely*

Latino Americans

15. I know the distinctions in Latino diversity pertaining to language differences, immigration history and patterns, and traditional and intergenerational acculturation.

    1–Unlikely   *2–Not very likely*   *3–Likely*   *4–Definitely*

16. I understand the historical and current oppression experiences of Mexican, Puerto Rican, Cuban, and Central American Latinos.

    1–Unlikely   *2–Not very likely*   *3–Likely*   *4–Definitely*

17. The religion of a Latino client is important because Catholic and Protestant denominations often establish social service outreach resources for the Latino community.

    1–Unlikely   *2–Not very likely*   *3–Likely*   *4–Definitely*

18. Knowledge of children and youth from war-torn countries such as El Salvador and Nicaragua indicates that exposure to violence may result in suicidal behaviors, serious antisocial acts, insomnia, and other physical, psychological, and social problems.

    1–Unlikely   *2–Not very likely*   *3–Likely*   *4–Definitely*

19. In social work practice with Latinos, it is important to use a "dicho" to create a cultural ambience.

    1–Unlikely   *2–Not very likely*   *3–Likely*   *4–Definitely*

20. It is important to cover legal documentation with Latino clients in order to seek, in an inductive nonthreatening manner, services that will not endanger them.

    1–Unlikely   *2–Not very likely*   *3–Likely*   *4–Definitely*

21. I understand the dynamics of Latino immigrant exploitation in employment and housing as issues of social and economic justice.

    1–Unlikely   *2–Not very likely*   *3–Likely*   *4–Definitely*

Asian Americans

22. I know about the diversity between Asians and Pacific Islanders, among different ethnic groups of Asian Americans, and between Asian immigrants and refugees.

    1–Unlikely   *2–Not very likely*   *3–Likely*   *4–Definitely*

23. I am aware of the discriminatory experiences of Asian immigrants, the racist attitudes and behaviors toward American-born Asians, and the colonialist practices toward Pacific Islanders, particularly Native Hawaiians.

    1–Unlikely   *2–Not very likely*   *3–Likely*   *4–Definitely*

24. I understand the broad and varied social service needs of specific Asian American and Pacific Islander groups.

    1–Unlikely   *2–Not very likely*   *3–Likely*   *4–Definitely*

25. I know that Asian American and Pacific Islander knowledge acquisition consists of knowing the ethnic culture and using the cultural values to explain ways of thinking and behaving.

    1–Unlikely   *2–Not very likely*   *3–Likely*   *4–Definitely*

26. I understand that in developing treatment planning with Asian and Pacific Islanders, traditional ways of healing should be matched with Western interventions, and Western interventions should be evaluated to determine whether they foster the cultural values of the ethnic community.

    1–Unlikely   *2–Not very likely*   *3–Likely*   *4–Definitely*

27. I am aware of the need to discuss Asian Americans and Pacific Islanders by lifespan development, gender, and sexual orientation issues and needs in order to create an intersection of inductive learning themes.

    1–Unlikely   *2–Not very likely*   *3–Likely*   *4–Definitely*

28. I understand the social and economic issues of land rights and welfare reform for Asian and Pacific Islander immigrants.

    1–Unlikely   *2–Not very likely*   *3–Likely*   *4–Definitely*

Women of Color

29. I can explain several of the multiple identifying characteristics of diversity among the 42 million women of color in the United States.

    1–Unlikely   *2–Not very likely*   *3–Likely*   *4–Definitely*

30. I am able to explain the meanings of structural intersectionality and political intersectionality and relate these concepts to oppression among women of color.

    1–Unlikely   *2–Not very likely*   *3–Likely*   *4–Definitely*

31. I am aware of the specific health and mental health needs of women of color.

    1–Unlikely   *2–Not very likely*   *3–Likely*   *4–Definitely*

32. I am knowledgeable of the issues facing immigrant women of color.

    1–Unlikely   *2–Not very likely*   *3–Likely*   *4–Definitely*

33. I know the principles related to the practice skills of rapport development/engagement, assessment, and intervention pertaining to women of color.

    1–Unlikely   *2–Not very likely*   *3–Likely*   *4–Definitely*

34. I have a strong notion of new inductive learning areas about women of color.

    1–Unlikely   *2–Not very likely*   *3–Likely*   *4–Definitely*

35. I understand the areas for advocating social and economic justice for women of color.

    1–Unlikely   *2–Not very likely*   *3 Likely*   *4–Definitely*

Gay and Lesbian Persons of Color

36. I understand the different meanings of the terms *sexual orientation* and *homosexual*.

    1–Unlikely   *2–Not very likely*   *3–Likely*   *4–Definitely*

37. I am aware of the issues of gays and lesbians of color in terms of their negotiating and reconciling competing demands from the dominant society, their own ethnic/racial community, and the gay and lesbian community.

    1–Unlikely   *2–Not very likely*   *3–Likely*   *4–Definitely*

38. I can explain the meaning of women–men, men–women, and two-spirited people from an First Nations Peoples perspective.

    1–Unlikely   *2–Not very likely*   *3–Likely*   *4–Definitely*

39. I understand the effects of HIV/AIDS on the African American community in general and on the African American gay and lesbian community in particular.

    1–Unlikely   *2–Not very likely*   *3–Likely*   *4–Definitely*

40. I am aware of the dilemmas that many gay Asian men face in their ethnic community and the larger gay community.

    1–Unlikely   *2–Not very likely*   *3–Likely*   *4–Definitely*

41. I am aware that in some instances Latino men can engage in same-sex sexual behavior without threatening their heterosexual masculine identity.

    1–Unlikely   2–Not very likely   3–Likely   4–Definitely

42. I understand the gay and lesbian of color sense of bicultural competence that integrates positive aspects of gay/lesbian and racial/cultural perspectives without losing cultural values or internalizing heterosexist biases.

    1–Unlikely   2–Not very likely   3–Likely   4–Definitely

Social and Economic Justice

43. I understand the relationship between cultural diversity and social justice in terms of historical and ongoing oppression and privilege that different social identity groups experience in our society.

    1–Unlikely   2–Not very likely   3–Likely   4–Definitely

44. I understand the meaning of economic class as a prime indicator of oppression and the creation of a class system based on difference as a function of oppression.

    1–Unlikely   2–Not very likely   3–Likely   4–Definitely

45. I can explain the concept and perspectives of distributive justice and their implications for social and economic justice.

    1–Unlikely   2–Not very likely   3–Likely   4–Definitely

46. I can connect the concepts of moral exclusion and fairness.

    1–Unlikely   2–Not very likely   3–Likely   4–Definitely

47. I understand the human rights and oppression concepts of the United Nations Universal Declaration of Human Rights.

    1–Unlikely   2–Not very likely   3–Likely   4–Definitely

48. I am aware of the United Nations materials on human rights for social work.

    1–Unlikely   2–Not very likely   3–Likely   4–Definitely

49. I understand the meaning of and the connection between empowerment and social and economic justice.

    1–Unlikely   2–Not very likely   3–Likely   4–Definitely

50. I understand how the grieving cycle is related to how a person feels about oppression and injustice.

    1–Unlikely   2–Not very likely   3–Likely   4–Definitely

Please count your scores on the 50 items and rate your level of cultural competency. Circle the appropriate level and write your raw score in one of the following levels:

Level 1: Unlikely (scores 50–89)
Level 2: Not very likely (scores 90–129)

Level 3: Likely (scores 130–169)
Level 4: Definitely (scores 170–200)

Thank you for your cooperation on this self-assessment instrument. You have made a significant contribution to our research on social work cultural competence.

SUMMARY

This chapter has presented the case for cultural competence for social work students. We have underscored the growing development of this emerging area. We have defined the crucial concepts, analyzed trends influencing cultural competence, posed questions about cultural competence/competencies, and shared a number of beliefs about this new theme.

Central to this book are the Social Work Cultural Competencies Self-Assessment instrument and the Social Work Cultural Competencies with Diverse Groups of Color and Social and Economic Justice Test instrument. These self-assessment instruments, which are unique features of this text, aid the social work student in the measurement of competencies at the beginning and the end of the semester. In the next chapter of this book, the social contexts of diversity, racism, sexism, homophobia, discrimination, and oppression are presented with the understanding that social workers must grapple with these issues in order to maintain cultural competence with self and others.

CHAPTER TWO

Social Context

DOMAN LUM

The social context of a person describes the essential elements of the individual and his or her particular environment. It is what makes a person understandable as, in part, a product of one's environment. In Chapter 1 we explained the meaning and dimensions of cultural competence. In this chapter we are concerned about the unique characteristics of diverse people, that is, what makes a person similar to and different from another person. We want to cover the aspects of diversity, building an understanding of the elements of a person. This is an important *person-centered context* for understanding and interaction.

We also want to look at the *environmental-centered context*, particularly at racism, sexism, homophobia, discrimination, and oppression. We recognize that there are other related issues such as social classism, ageism, and religious intolerance that are a part of social problems. But we select the areas of diversity; ethnic, gender, and sexual orientation issues; and discrimination and oppression as the major arenas of concern in this chapter. We believe that as we understand our own diversity as people and experiences of oppression, there is an opportunity to build bridges of understanding across differences based on an acceptance and appreciation of what it means to be unique human beings. Certainly this attitude and approach to people as particular persons is the beginning of cultural competence.

In this chapter we seek to be inclusive about the multiple factors of diversity; the problems and potential solutions related to racism, sexism, and homophobia; and the dynamics of discrimination and oppression. We recognize that these social realities will be present in our social context as long as there are living human beings. But this is the social context in which we must live and cope as well as survive and endure. Therefore, our starting point in this chapter is a discussion of social context as a backdrop for understanding.

THE MEANING OF SOCIAL CONTEXT

The term *context* implies the "joining and weaving together" of textures that are surrounding or immediately next to parts that create how a situation, background, or environment is structured or put together. In social work we discuss the social context in terms of the person and the environment or the psychosocial perspective. That is, we are concerned about understanding the important characteristics of the person and the environment as well as the interaction between the person and the environment. This is the core meaning of social context.

In order to fully understand a person, one must take into account the total context of how the texture of the person has been woven together to form a unique being. What pieces or ingredients have been put together to form a mosaic or detailed pattern? What is the total context that transcends the person and the environment and must be understood for helping to proceed? We are concerned about such diverse ingredients as ethnicity, gender, sexual orientation, ability/disability, social class, age, religion, and related areas important to understanding the person. Often social environmental issues are uncovered as we explain how a trait of diversity affects a person. For example, a discussion of ethnicity may mean explaining the ethnic background and identity of a person as well as the involvement of ethnic family, cultural traditions, and community practices and activities. Aspects of the person and the environment interact with each other to portray the unique meaning of ethnicity for an individual.

Social context is increasingly a crucial theme in the worker–client relationship. A number of social science clinicians view the context as the overarching theme—as a major part of the sum total of the scope of understanding the client and the situation. *Context* has a broad inclusive meaning. Rose (1990) speaks of context in terms of contextualization. For Rose, this involves a focus on the client's own understanding of him- or herself that allows a dialogue between the worker and client to occur based on the client's reality. In the dialogue, the client is enabled to express, elaborate, and reflect upon his or her feelings and understanding about life. This reaching into the client and for the client's context is an important conception in comprehending a contextual practice perspective. Ragg (2001, pp. 13–18) identifies a number of contextual environmental influences that encompass the family and the broader social environment: family rules; family problem solving; emotional expression; family roles; and relating to others, neighborhood, culture, and institutions.

In particular, the life stories of the person are the basis for comprehending contextual behavior. The assumption is that life stories are recollections of the important behavioral events that have occurred in the human context of living. Murphy and Dillon (1998) articulate a pragmatic understanding of the context of behavior. By *context*, they mean "when, with whom, and under what circumstances the target behaviors occur" (p. 183). Furthermore, Murphy and Dillon (1998, p. 68) explain that context is important for understanding the client's stories. The immediate context refers to the client's personal circumstances where there are happenings pertaining to current living arrangements, family and social relationships, economic status, personal history, health, and the particulars of daily life. However, the immediate context is often embedded in a larger system context where economic, social, political, and religious forces and institutions affect global relationships and developments. Often, connective and mutual influences relate to immediate and larger contexts. These spheres of context are broad ranging and get at the dimensions of context that are a part of our perspectives. In this sense we can never understand the context of an individual without comprehending the context of the larger system that forms the playing field of human interaction and drama.

We may also move social context into the areas of assessment and intervention. Contextual assessment focuses on the construction of both personal and environmental interaction; issues of concern and available resources; personal social networks for active consultation, collective exchanges, and empowerment; and the partnership of worker and client in the process of knowledge development. Contextual intervention should critically analyze the impact of environmental conditions, particularly power relationships; offer effective action to oppressive social and environmental conditions; and make connections between individual experiences and collective issues, such as linking different communities of interest and larger coalitions and efforts.

Kemp, Whittaker, and Tracy (2002) bring together the themes of environment and empowerment. They point out that social life is spatial and contextual; that empowerment practice is contextualized in the sense that there is an emphasis on the importance of external circumstances and conditions in client concerns; and that changes in personal and interpersonal resources and aspirations must be supported and reinforced in external contexts. For them, contextual social work practice involves *person–environment practice*. There are links between people's issues and the challenges and resources in daily life contexts. Among the dimensions of environment are the physical environment (natural and built), the social/interactional environment, the institutional/organizational environment, the cultural and sociopolitical environment, the experienced environment, and environmental strengths and resources. These person and environment transactions are apparent in the areas of contextual assessment and contextual intervention.

Our concern in this section is a basic understanding of human diversity as part of the social context of the person and the environment. Although we must leave for another time the rest of how context and contextual social work practice have emerged, it is important to understand how much social work is interested in the concept of context.

PERSON-CENTERED CONTEXT: THE MEANING OF DIVERSITY

The person-centered context is concerned about the setting and characteristics of the individual. The unique diversity of people is our focus in this section. Human diversity involves the recognition of differences and similarities in the experiences, needs, and beliefs of people. *Diversity* focuses on the differences that make a person distinct and unique from another person. It offers an opportunity for a person to name these distinctions and invites another person to discover those particular qualities about that particular individual. It is an inclusive term that encompasses groups distinguished by race, ethnicity, culture, class, gender, sexual orientation, religion, physical or mental ability, age, and national origin. Diversity tends toward these distinctive categorical differences (Greene, Watkins, McNutt, & Lopez, 1998).

Yet diversity recognizes that there are similarities between persons that bind people together as part of our common humanity. There may be common and uncommon experiences, needs, and beliefs that cause bonding and distinctiveness. Human diversity calls for discovery, learning, and understanding of each other.

Schriver (2001) covers four categories of diversity that contribute to our understanding:

1. *Diversities and worldviews:* the values and perspectives that shape the worldview of a person who is part of an ethnic/cultural group; emphasis varies from collective and corporate family and society to values as a response to oppression over a

period of time; biculturality may be a part of functioning in two related societies such as the heterosexual and gay/lesbian worlds; alternative cultures offer a strength perspective in diversity such as the acceptance of gay and lesbian members in some Native American communities as seers, shamans, full of wisdom; belief systems about the harmony of humans and the natural world; and the role of the elders and their contributions to the common good

2. *Diversity within diversity:* the movement away from viewing the world in terms of binary White and Black people and toward multiple racial realities of many diverse groups with diverse characteristics and qualities within and between the ethnic categories and subcategories

3. *Multiple diversities:* considerable variability of an individual who may simultaneously have membership in multiple diverse groups in terms of ethnicity, genetics, gender, sexual orientation; emphasis is upon the need to understand the full background and perception of identities of the client; multidimensionality stresses multiple fluid identities with various groups that offer differing and rich understanding of individuals

4. *Interrelatedness and interconnectedness of human beings:* a holistic perspective that shares a sense of interrelatedness of humans with all elements of environment; mutuality or partnership in a process of seeking meaning and understanding that results in mutual help to reach our potentials as persons; sharing of our personal experiences with those around us in order to recognize similarities and differences about ourselves and others, which helps in joining together

Schriver makes the case that diversity means inclusion of worldviews and mutual perspectives and interrelatedness and interconnectedness, which reiterates the concept of similarities. At the same time diversity reminds us that differences and distinctions are important in terms of diversity within diversity (inter- and intragroup diversity) and multiple diversities (often called multiple identities).

On a practical level, it is difficult to work through diversity issues. Armour, Bain, and Rubio (2004) conducted a cultural competence diversity training workshop for field instructors and focused on the issue of difference. The content of the training consisted of exploring relationship with self and normalizing discomfort between field instructors and students, relationship with the supervisee and being direct and engaging personally, and relationship with the agency and challenging disempowerment. Attendees were asked to address issues of difference with others, to identify their memberships in various groups and to "pool" the stereotypes that oppressed them, and to deal with the discomfort of differences. Next, they focused on interpersonal differences to help them experience the directness, honesty, and quality of connection necessary to explore diversity in supervision with students. They were asked to identify common fears that prohibit candidness and authenticity in supervision. Finally, they were asked to look at the negative messages that they give to themselves that result in feelings of disempowerment and were asked how to challenge disempowering beliefs and establish trust-based relationships. The focus on avoidance behaviors in relationship to diversity issues and developing cultural competence was a major result of the workshop. In the next section of this chapter, we will pursue some of these concepts.

TOOLS FOR STUDENT LEARNING 2.1

Understanding Your Diversity

The preceding categories of diversity provide an opportunity for you to explore your understanding of diversity. Please look over the major categories of diversity with their specific characteristics and relate them to your own diversity (what makes you a unique person).

1. Describe yourself from a diversity and worldview perspective (e.g., values and beliefs, culture and ethnicity, family, gender, sexual orientation, significant others, and other areas that are applicable to you).

2. How would you identify your ethnic diversity? How would you apply the concept of diversity within diversity (multiple realities between and within your own ethnic group) to your situation?

3. How would you describe your multiple diversities (e.g., self-identification and membership in multiple groups, your own background and perception of identities, the multiple stressors that have shaped your life)?

4. How are you interrelated and interconnected to other people (e.g., how are you similar to and different from others)?

Social work education has fostered the concept of diversity in its curriculum. The 2002 *Educational Policy and Accreditation Standards* (EPAS) of the Council on Social Work Education addresses the spirit of positive understanding, affirmation, and respect; the complexity of culture and identity; the planning of social services for diverse groups; diversity between and within groups; and diversity-focused practice in recommending that social work education:

- Integrate content that promotes understanding, affirmation, and respect for people from diverse backgrounds
- Emphasize the interlocking and complex nature of culture and personal identity
- Ensure that social services meet the needs of groups served and are culturally relevant
- Educate students to recognize diversity within and between groups that may influence assessment, planning, intervention, and research
- Learn how to define, design, and implement strategies for effective practice with persons from diverse backgrounds

Garcia and Van Soest (2000) link cultural competence and diversity in relationship to a number of issues:

In order to adequately prepare students to become multiculturally competent professionals, diversity content taught in schools of social work must include content on oppression, privilege, social identity, and racism. This requires that students engage in a demanding experience that involves both learning about diverse populations and confronting their own personal experience related to difference and privilege within the dominant culture. Such learning, by necessity, rests on examination of the consequences of injustice, inequity and oppression. Exploration of one's experiences, values and perspectives about social justice can threaten core belief systems, leaving students feeling devastated. Focusing the learning on individual concerns within a context of social power places enormous demands on both faculty and students that exceed intellectual and emotional expectations ordinarily found in other curricula. (pp. 21–22)

Learning about diversity from a personal and professional perspective as person, student, and social worker is basic for the individual.

We now turn to several new concepts that are related to diversity and are the basis for discussion in this area.

NEW DIMENSIONS OF DIVERSITY: CRITICAL CONSCIOUSNESS, POSITIONALITY, AND INTERSECTIONALITY

An emerging way to understand diversity arises from the work of Reed, Newman, Suarez, and Lewis (1997) and Spencer, Lewis, and Gutierrez (2000). Together they provide new insights and avenues of dialogue in our understanding of various dimensions of diversity. Reed and colleagues make the case for moving interpersonal practice beyond diversity and toward social justice. In one sense they recognize the reality of diversity in terms of addressing similarities and differences among people. Yet they argue for the need to reinsert the value perspective of social justice into the discussion. The question becomes: How can we retain the need to address diversity and yet maintain social justice as part of the dialogue in multicultural practice? Three concepts (critical consciousness, positionality, and intersectionality) are introduced to move the concept of diversity beyond the general discussion.

Critical Consciousness

What is critical consciousness? Critical consciousness is a concept that was introduced by Freire (1970) in his book *Pedagogy of the Oppressed*. Freire speaks of *conscientizacao*, or the awakening of critical consciousness. Developing critical consciousness is a two-step process that involves learning to perceive social, political, and economic contradictions and taking action against oppressive elements. It is a process through which people come to an understanding of power, empowerment, and oppression. One develops greater critical consciousness through approaching, equalizing, and finding out about situations. It is developed through praxis (the exercise or practice of a skill) or a combination of action and reflection.

Reed and others (1997) use the concept of critical consciousness to apply the concept of power to relationships and multiple identities. This does not distort the reflective nature of Freire's insights on oppression but further advances the discussion on critical consciousness to include the concept of micro and macro aspects of multiple identities. Reed and others explain:

Critical consciousness incorporates and gives us a greater understanding of power relationships and commonalities and differences among and within people. People create multiple identities based on their life experiences that are shaped by these forces. We need to work to understand people through *their* construction and enactment of their multiple identities. That is, people must be understood in terms of the social/political/historical macro forces influencing their lives and the meaning they as individuals make of these forces. We can also apply our critical skills to understand the social environments around us—our families, organizations, communities, and governments. (pp. 46–47)

That is, the various identities of people (gender, age, ethnicity, social class, and other primary ways of self-definition) are socially constructed or built as people interact with various larger macro systems that affect their lives. Ridley (2005) observes:

The notion that any given person has only one racial or cultural identity overlooks the fact that each unique person has multiple identities. A minority client is not merely a representative of a single racial or ethnic group. He or she is a member of a variety of groups, with group identities overlapping to create a blend that is unique and special to that individual. (p. 88)

Or as Keenan (2004) observes:

These multiple cultural group memberships and one's relations in those groups provide the lens of beliefs, expectations, and meanings as well as specific types of status and material resources. People, therefore, are composed of varying combinations of privileged and oppressed social statuses that operate in a fluid manner, changing over time and with various contexts. (p. 542)

An example might be that in the midwestern United States, a White male may feel a sense of privilege and access in the dominant majority, whereas the same person may feel like an oppressed minority in some parts of Hawaii where there is a majority Asian and Pacific Islander population.

Finding out about these multiple identities that shape the critical consciousness of an individual is part of understanding the unique diversity of a person. The implications for understanding diversity and shaping culturally competent practice according to a critical consciousness are applicable to the social worker. Among the guidelines for developing a sense of critical consciousness in a helping relationship are the following:

- Approach every interpersonal helping practice relationship with an awareness of who you are as a cultural self and what you have to offer as a helping person.
- Equalize the power relationship between you as the professional worker and the client as the vulnerable individual so that you both become persons in the eyes of the other.
- Find out what is similar and common between you as the worker and the person as the client and affirm the similarities and commonalities.
- Explore the differences between the worker and the client, respecting and learning from them, and incorporate these unique features in the relationship.
- Address the multiple identities of the client and relate them to your multiple identities as the worker, understanding where they came from and how they are formed in the beings of two people.
- Understand and respect how each of you constructed and shaped your multiple identities and how this sense of self works for each of you.

- Draw a time line showing how social, political, and historical forces have had an impact on your ethnic group, your family, and yourself and have caused you to be who you are today.
- Critically examine the client's social environment (family, friends, school/work, community) and its effect on the person and on the helping relationship.

Notice that there are critical consciousness areas of concern for the worker and the client. Critical consciousness is an attitudinal approach that you consciously take regarding yourself and others, particularly clients. Implementing these recommendations based on a critical consciousness perspective into a helping relationship translates the concept of diversity into practical action steps.

TOOLS FOR STUDENT LEARNING 2.2

A Case Study on Critical Consciousness

Tabitha, a 16-year-old African American teenager, is a client of a large residential facility for girls. She has a number of strengths: her enjoyment of reading, her leadership, her verbal communication with other residents and with staff, and her survival knowledge. She was raised by her extended family, which has a chronic history of unstable relationships. Her grandmother has been her point of reference and is a spiritual woman.

Tabitha missed high school for a year and a half and was a runaway on the streets selling drugs, but she claims that she did not use drugs. She was involved in physical assault toward her mother and verbal threats and vandalism with her aunt. There is a history of child abuse and neglect on the part of her family. She is in a nonpublic school, and her academic performance has been inconsistent. She is currently employed in a part-time job after school and would like to finish public high school.

You are a social work intern in her residential facility and are working with Tabitha on a one-to-one basis.

Based on the principles of critical consciousness, discuss the following questions in your class:

1. As you begin this helping relationship with Tabitha, how could you increase your awareness as a cultural person (cultural self-awareness) and become aware of Tabitha as an African American young woman (cultural other-awareness)? What do you think you have to offer her?

2. How would you equalize the power differences between you as the worker and Tabitha as the client so that you both become persons in the eyes of the other?

3. How could you find out what is similar between both of you in order to build a bridge between you and Tabitha?

4. How would you discover your differences and communicate respect of these uniquenesses?

5. How would you communicate and interpret your multiple identities as a person and find out about Tabitha's multiple identities?

6. What are particular social, political, and historical forces that have had an impact on your ethnic identity and family group and affect who you are today? How would you find out about Tabitha in these areas?

7. What is Tabitha's social environment (family, friends, school/work, community) and its effect on her and on the helping relationship you have with her?

Positionality

Related to critical consciousness is the concept of positionality. Similarities with people as well as those differences that foster uniqueness assist us in the sorting out of our multiple identities and establish our position as a person in relations to others. Reed and colleagues (1997) explain the characteristics of positionality:

- An inward process of self-examination and self-exploration and an outward process of understanding and situating one's self in the world
- A dialogue between thinking and action, knowledge and experience, where there is a joining of critical reflection and an engagement that leads to involvement and commitment
- A different position involving a different standpoint from which one develops a level of awareness about one's social location
- A connection between positionality and worldview

In one sense, positionality is self-reflection on who you are, where you have come from, and where you are heading as a diverse person. It is *the continuous discovery and rediscovery of your place in life and how you want to position yourself in relation to self and significant others.* Keenan (2004) encourages us to take an informed not-knowing stance in the worker–client relationship: "This stance is based on an assumption in critical theories that knowledge is always partial, perspectival, and constructed through the lens of understanding, meaning, and interests of one's social position" (p. 543). Later she explains:

A stance of informed not-knowing assumes a perspectival relation with knowledge, focusing on skills of questioning and listening to obtain understanding and knowledge (otherwise experienced as 'how to function in a rapidly changing global world where it is impossible to know everything'). (p. 544)

It is an existential journey into yourself to find out who you are, and a simple declaration of your emerging self to others. It involves self-appraisal and reflection that bring the strength of becoming involved with other persons and issues.

The psychological and social location of a person is constantly changing based on the interactions occurring in life. One must constantly take a social location contextual reading of the situation. Keenan (2004) points out:

Social workers can move out of a center-margin dichotomy by shifting to a description of social location that provides greater complexity (i.e., naming the context in which services are being provided, describing relations between the groups of people present in that context, describing culture–power relations between people and the social structures, and describing the meanings these relations have for the client and the worker. (p. 542)

There is a constant reinventing of self that results in positioning and repositioning. Where is an individual as a growing, emerging person who is changing according to the new experiences encountered in life? How does one explain and interpret what happens in the past, present, and future of a person?

Diversity recognizes the need to understand where the client and the worker are coming from. There are at least two different positions in the relationship: the perspectives of the worker and those of the client. Furthermore, there are complex intersections of past, present, and future positions that influence what positions a person takes in life interactions.

TOOLS FOR STUDENT LEARNING 2.3

Questions about Positionality

One's diversity is a composite of all that has taken place, is happening now, and will occur in the immediate future. Putting the pieces of the past, present, and future together is a part of understanding the diversity of an individual. Please answer the following questions taken from the characteristics of positionality:

1. How would you answer the following: Who am I? Where did I come from? Where am I? Where am I going?

2. Share a conversation you recently had with yourself about an important issue related to a major decision you made (e.g., a dialogue of thinking and action, knowledge and experience, reflection and engagement).

3. In thinking about where you are and where you are going, have you ever gotten a different and new perspective about your life that has caused you to make a major change in a new direction? If you have, describe the incident. If you have not, explain why this has not happened.

4. How would you connect where you are in your life with your view of the world?

Intersectionality

Intersectionality is those multiple intersections and crossroads in our lives that are replete with multiple social group memberships that are interconnected and interrelated. Collins (1990) introduced the concept of intersections of race, class, and gender and coined the term, *a matrix of domination,* based on the societal configuration of race, class, and gender relations. For Collins, this structural pattern affected individual consciousness, group interaction, and group access to institutional power and privileges. However, others used the concept of intersectionality to describe the various connecting points that converge in their lives.

According to Spencer and colleagues (2000), intersectionality involves three factors: (1) we all have multiple group memberships and identities, (2) the impact of these factors on our daily lives is not simply additive, and (3) each social group membership cannot be completely extracted from all others. Intersectionality is concerned with the uniqueness of the individual's family and groups and with types of social group memberships such as age, physical or mental ability, and economic class, as well as larger constructs of ethnicity, gender, and sexual orientation. These various combinations affect the allocation of resources and power for individuals, families, and groups.

Multiculturalism and social justice issues are related to intersectionality in terms of target groups influencing change, structural changes in organizations, and a greater participation of people of color in agency governance. Three forces are at work resulting in change: (1) ethnoconsciousness based on an appreciation and celebration of the strengths existing in communities of color; (2) ethnic sensitivity fostering partnership, participation, and advocacy where people of color are active agents in individual and social transformation; and (3) empowerment or the process of gaining personal, interpersonal, and political power where social and individual changes occur through active engagement of community members in change efforts at all levels. Intersectionality begins with an understanding of diversity, particularly multiple identities, and utilizes various intersecting combinations to mobilize people of color toward empowerment and social change in their communities.

Intersectionality focuses on our multiple identities that intersect our life, shape our personalities, and influence us. What are the multiple identities that are a part of our life? How do these identities intersect? I offer two terms to help us in understanding our diversity on external and internal levels. *External intersections* are outward and external characteristics of a person that we can readily observe, while *internal intersections* are those that are not readily observable and must be shared, discovered, and appreciated. At a particular point in time, a number of external and internal intersectional factors may converge and mark a crucial crossroad for a person.

For example, three weeks after my 60th birthday *(age/life span)*, I suddenly had pain in my chest and underwent a quadruple heart bypass operation that incapacitated me for six weeks *(temporary disability)*. I was worried that I would not be able fully to resume my teaching and writing at the university *(career)*. I focused on the scars on my chest, arm, and leg from the open heart surgery and felt self-conscious about showing them (*personal appearance*). I was so weak that I could hardly walk outdoors or drive a car, and lay on the family room couch watching TV, unable to concentrate and read a book. During the time I could not work and was confined to my home *(residence)*, I felt the support of my wife who nursed me back to health (*partnership status*), of my family who called and cheered me (*family background*), and of friends and colleagues around the country who demonstrated care for me through visits and get-well cards. These external and internal intersections marked a significant crossroad in my life at a crucial time.

External Intersections.   Among the external intersections that may be obvious and overt to you and others are the following categories.

Age/life span. Age is a particular factor in a larger understanding of life-span development. Life-span development is concerned about the "behaviors, dispositions, skills, and traits over a substantial period of the life span" and "age-related biological, psychological, and behavioral changes from birth to death" (Ashford, LeCroy, & Lortie, 2001, p. 24). The life-span perspective is concerned about growth in every period of life, the interrelationships of the parts of the whole person, and contextual behavior in settings and relationships. Ageism should not be confused with age. The former involves prejudices and stereotypes applied to older persons on the basis of their age, while the latter is seen as chronological age in the midst of life-span interaction and change.

Ethnicity. Ethnicity is identity based on ancestry and nationality (a group's sense of commonality) that is transmitted from one generation to another by the family, which is part of a larger community of similar persons. In the present there is interaction between family and community ethnic groups as well as interaction with other ethnically diverse people. Ethnicity is passed on in future generations in terms of historical continuity. Language, customs, traditions, beliefs, food, and other related ethnic traits are useful indicators of ethnicity.

Language. Language is related to ethnicity. It is the primary means of communication. We often notice the regional accents of English and the accents of people speaking foreign languages.

Gender. Gender refers to the social structural relationships of male and female. It is a social construct and includes the social processes of how men and women are to behave in their social life. Behind the gender sex roles of men and women are the power differentials and conflict associated with change when these role expectations are challenged. Gender must be differentiated from biological sexual differences of male and female.

Social class. Social class involves the relative wealth and access to power that differentiate people into socioeconomic classes and social stratification. The term *social stratification* refers to a hierarchy of prestige ranking based on money earned or otherwise acquired, level of occupation, and prestige of occupation. Social classism pits the privileged wealthy with high status against the poor and working class who are stigmatized and disadvantaged based on relative wealth. Power and domination due to social and economic resources become the basis for social class conflict.

Disability. A disability involves a physical and/or mental impairment that hinders the major activities of an individual. A functional disability deals with the inability to perform certain tasks and the impairment of mobile functions such as walking, eating, sight, and hearing. A socially imposed disability refers to the person's perception of his or her interaction with and adaptation to an environment in which society may impose discrimination and isolation on the person.

Size. Height, weight, and body proportion are important to the self-image of a person. The average height of a person is often determined by genetics of the parents. Women generally prefer men to be taller than them. For some, height is an important factor in the selection of a mate or partner. Taller persons have a more commanding effect over an audience compared to shorter persons. Height, weight, and body size are an integral part of a person's persona.

Personal appearance. Personal appearance is often an indicator of social acceptance. Our hairstyle, selection of clothes for the occasion, jewelry, and demeanor communicate a message about our external persona. Well-dressed people with a current hairstyle and a confident and friendly demeanor make a positive and lasting impression on others.

Others. Think about other primary external characteristics that you would consider important that are not included on this list.

Internal Intersections.   Among the internal intersections that are not obvious about you and others and may have to be explored and uncovered through questions and inquiry are the following.

Culture. Culture is the way of life of a society and life patterns related to conduct or ways of behavior, beliefs, traditions, values, art, skills, and social relationships. Culture perpetuates the sharing of ideas, attitudes, values, and beliefs among individuals of that culture.

Sexual Orientation. Sexual orientation "refers to a characteristic of an individual that describes the people he or she is drawn to for satisfying intimate affectional and sexual needs—people of the same gender, the opposite gender or of both genders" (Appleby and Anastas, 1998, p. 49). Sexual orientation, that is, sexual identity, is an important part of one's personal self.

Education. The extent of education (high school, undergraduate, and/or graduate university) and the major field of study are important aspects for every individual. Education provides the academic background that prepares one for a professional career.

Career. Employment and professional lifetime work may change as we move through our adult years. We may make a series of career choices, or we may pursue multiple careers at the same time. Our sense of self-worth as adult workers is wrapped up in our career.

Family background. Our father, mother, brothers, and sisters are important persons in our lives. The family is our first group and a constant point of reference as we move through the stages of life. Losses of family members, the changing nature of our family, and other family issues affect us.

Partnership status. Our partner (the person with whom we share intimate contact and relationship) is the major social being in our lives. Partnership status involves: being single, living with another person(s), being married, or other relationship arrangements.

Residency. Our home is a source of familiarity and comfort. Where we live in terms of geographic region or section of the city/town may be an indicator of socioeconomic class, personal preference, and employment proximity.

Faith and religion. Our sense of spirituality may be expressed in terms of a personal philosophy of life or faith as well as participation or nonparticipation with a religious community (church, synagogue, or mosque).

Others. Think about other important internal person/self traits that have not been covered but are meaningful for you.

TOOLS FOR STUDENT LEARNING 2.4

Multiple Identities and Intersectionality

1. Using the previous discussion of external and internal intersections, *list the important areas related to external and internal intersections that pertain to your life now.* Explain how and why you selected these areas.

External Intersections	Internal Intersections
a.	*a.*
b.	*b.*
c.	*c.*
d.	*d.*

2. Using these external and internal intersections, connect them to a *personal life story* about yourself that reflects a *major crossroads* you are now facing.

ENVIRONMENTAL-CENTERED CONTEXT: RACISM, SEXISM, HOMOPHOBIA, AND AGEISM

Along with an understanding of the person-centered context of diversity must be a discussion on the environmental-centered context of racism, sexism, homophobia, and ageism. These "isms" interact in such a way as to compound their impact on the person. That is, racism, sexism, homophobia, and ageism configure various actions and reactions—both negative and positive in terms of resolution—between the person and the environment.

Racism is a belief about the superior/inferiority of ethnic groups. One cannot discuss racism without relating it to sexism, homophobia, and agesim. *Sexism* deals with gender superiority and inferiority, dominance and submission. *Homophobia* underscores the reaction of society (fear of same-sex persons). *Ageism* involves the prejudice and discrimination against a particular age group, particularly the elderly. Racism, sexism, homophobia, and ageism are historical and societal beliefs and reactions to persons of color, women, gays and lesbians, and the elderly in a predominantly White male heterosexual society that claims that identity as the rule and standard of being. A man of color may face single jeopardy due to his ethnicity; a woman of color may encounter double jeopardy because of her ethnicity and gender; gay or lesbian persons of color may confront triple jeopardy due to their ethnicity, gender, and sexual orientation; and an elderly person may experience discrimination based on the age factor. An elderly and lesbian woman of color may be the recipient of all three -isms reactions from the broad society.

Racism

Racism is the cognitive belief that one ethnic group is superior to and dominant over another inferior and subjugated group, supposedly because of genetic composition, intelligence, skin color, character, or related rationale. Racism is a bias that is learned from individuals, the family, groups, and/or society and is perpetuated through the negative affective feelings of prejudice and the behavioral action/reaction of discrimination on the personal, institutional or organizational, and cultural and societal levels. Ridley (2005) states: "Racism is any behavior or pattern of behavior that tends to systematically deny access to opportunities or privileges to members of one racial group while allowing members of another racial group to enjoy those opportunities or privileges" (p. 29). Carter and Jones (1996) underscore the inferiority and majority themes of racism when they state: "Racism results from the transformation of race prejudice and/or ethnocentrism through the exercise of power against a racial group defined as inferior, by individuals and institutions with the intentional or unintentional support of the entire (race or) culture" (p. 2). In particular, institutional forms of racism erect structural barriers that exclude certain groups from social resource access and power.

From a historical perspective, the opportunity to own land and cultivate the resources of America has been the privilege of a dominant White class and involved the disenfranchisement of non-White people of color from economic, political, and social rights. In short, racism pervades our social system and emerges and submerges, depending on the series of social events that activate and deactivate it.

Several social science writers have described the theme of modern racism. The emphasis is on racism as a system of power and privilege that is seen in the attitudes, actions, and institutional structures based on exclusion. Modern racists oppose issues that promote equality for all ethnic groups and defend practices that maintain social privilege (Andersen & Collins, 1998; Deaux, Dane, & Wrightsman, 1993).

Dominelli (1997) views the dynamic interaction of three main dimensions of racism: individual or personal racism, institutional racism, and cultural racism. *Individual racism* consists of those attitudes and behaviors that depict a negative prejudgment of racial groups. It must be seen in connection with *institutional racism*, which excludes from resources and power those groups that are defined as racially inferior and then pathologizes the members of those groups for their failure in the system and blames them for their predicament. *Cultural racism* reinforces individual and institutional racism. It promotes values, beliefs, and ideas endorsing the superiority of the dominant culture. These three entities (individual, institutional, and cultural racism) feed on each other and permeate everyday life.

Ridley (2005) talks about *unintentional racism*, where a person denies his or her racism overtly but covertly exhibits racist behavior:

> Unintentional racists perpetuate racism not because they are prejudiced but because they deny that they are racists. Denial—the refusal to recognize the reality of external threats— is the essence of the unintentional racist's mind-set. For an unintentional racist, admitting to racism is a threat to the individual's conception of him- or herself as a nonracist person. (p. 161)

Ridley is concerned about covert racism that is unacknowledged by the person.

I would add that there is *professional racism*, where stereotypes and related forms of racism surface in academic and clinical settings among peers and colleagues in the helping professions. In Competency Study 2.1, Daniel (2000, p. 130) shares a revealing incident that occurred between two women scholars, one White and one Black. It is interesting that in this report, the Black woman scholar did not call the White woman scholar a racist or point out that the White woman held a distorted stereotype of Black women's hair. The Black scholar kept the discussion going at a professional level while still holding her ground and communicating a covert message that she understood where the White woman scholar was coming from in her biased comment.

COMPETENCY STUDY 2.1

Professional Racism

At a professional symposium on women, I heard a prominent White female scholar make the statement that all Black women wear their hair straight because "they want to be White and hate their blackness." Sitting at the same table was a Black woman scholar with straight hair. The White woman's assumption was outrageously ethnocentric, and could be regarded as a racialized assault on a fellow professional. The perceived intent was to silence the Black woman scholar with straight hair, that is, to score a scholarly knockout. Despite this assault, the Black woman scholar took the opportunity to point out that one cannot determine the politics or the state of racial identity of a Black woman by her hairstyle alone. Although the Black woman responded quickly and appropriately to her attacker, the disparaging personal statement that was made about her hair, in an open professional forum, constituted a form of racial assault. Once the generalization was made, she was forced to negotiate it on both conscious and unconscious levels. The Black scholar could have added that some Black women have naturally straight hair because of mixed European American and Native American ancestry.

Ridley (2005) describes the need for *antiracism assertion:*

[T]he use of behaviors that protect one's own rights without interfering with the rights of others [which mean] . . . (a) refusals to acquiesce to the requests of others, (b) expressions of opinions and feelings, and (c) expressions of one's own requests. (p. 120)

Ridley also states: "Assertive people express their feelings and thoughts honestly, make socially appropriate responses, and consider the feelings of others at the same time" (p. 120). Ridley champions an honest integrity that stands up to racism.

Sue (2006) advocates for antiracism as a social justice agenda. He believes that racial stereotypes and racism are formed from three main sources: schooling and education, mass media, and peers and social groups. I may add that parents and the family environment play an important part in early formation of racial beliefs, practices, and behavior. He suggests that social workers work toward the construction of a multicultural curriculum in society that stresses social justice in the forms of equity and antiracism.

Sue argues that on a community level, racism is most likely to diminish under the following conditions:

- Have intimate and close contact with others
- Cooperate rather than compete with each other
- Share mutual goals
- Exchange accurate information
- Share an equal relationship
- Support racial equity by leaders and groups in authority
- Feel connected and experience a strong sense of belonging

Sue (2006) urges that ". . . social workers must use their knowledge and skills to (a) impact the channels of socialization (education, media, groups/organizations) to spread a curriculum of multiculturalism, and (b) translate the seven antiracism principles to help guide social work policy and practice" (p. 253). Sue breaks some new ground in the antiracism principles that seem to emphasize interpersonal relations on the micro, meso, and macro levels. However, a step-by-step way of practically implementing these seven areas is missing along with tighter social work practice principles.

Sexism

According to Longres (1995), sexism is "those norms and expectations existing in law, in religious dogma, or in kinship relations that assign women a subordinate place with regard to men" (p. 57). Sexism is the cognitive belief that one gender, generally male, is superior to and dominant over the other gender, female, because of intelligence, physical strength, education and career status, and related factors.

Related to sexism are the concepts of gender stratification and male dominance. Stockard and Johnson (1992) define gender stratification as "hierarchical ranking of the sex groups that involves their differential access to both resources and rewards," while male dominance is "the beliefs and cultural meanings that give higher value and prestige to masculinity than to femininity, and that value males over females, men over women" (pp. 3, 4). These conceptual dynamics express how sexism is played out in society. Worden (2001) argues that gender difference is a social construct of a society that perpetuates sexism:

> Social constructionism views people as active participants in perceiving and making sense of their surrounding environments. In this perspective, there are no universal truths about *innate* differences, which are socially constructed, consensually held, and reinforced. These beliefs become our definitions of reality. (p. 71)

If a social constructionist view of gender differences is correct, we must deconstruct this concept and in its place reconstruct a reality where men and women are equal persons in rights, privilege, and opportunities.

From a conceptual perspective, sexism along with racism is a form of colonization. It reiterates the subjugation and exploitation of one party over another. Comas-Diaz (1994) states:

> For women of color, the status of being colonized involves the added negation of their individuality by their being subjected to sexual-racial objectification. Women of color are stripped of their humanity, denied their individuality, and devalued. As female colonized entities, women of color are often perceived as part of the bounty conquered by the colonizer. Historically, conquered males have been killed while conquered females have been raped, enslaved, and sexually subjugated. (pp. 289–290)

The colonization motif illustrates the historical oppression of women as sexual objects. As a result, women of color experience low social status and limited access to power (Gutierrez & Lewis, 1999) due to racism, sexism, and classism.

Related to this understanding are a number of levels where sexism is expressed in terms of interactive factors. For example, Bradshaw (1994) identifies several related variables: "[s]exism in the culture, power differentials between men and women, women's access to alternatives and self-sufficiency, cultural views of physical violence, racism extant in the culture, attitudes toward marriage or partnership" (p. 106). These are related to individual and cultural perspectives of domestic violence, which is a major focus of how sexism is expressed between women and men.

Furthermore racism, sexism, and homophobia are related to each other in a dynamic interaction. Bradshaw (1994) observes:

> The 'triple jeopardy' of racism, sexism, and homophobia that faces lesbians of color essentially means there is no safe place, no place to belong, whether in the majority or minority community. Often as a result of this condition, violence occurs, further complicating the feelings of shame, guilt, and fear. (p. 109)

Uncovering the dynamics of sexism means interconnecting the specific factors that comprise the sexist experience of a particular client. Therefore, it is important to delineate an accurate and detailed statement of what constitutes sexism as part of the problem dynamics.

Sexism is a systemic institutional problem that is played out in labeling of and blaming the victim. Greene (1994) states:

> Additionally, racism and sexism come together in attempts to present African American women as the cause of failures in family functioning, suggesting that a lack of male dominance and female subordination has prevented African Americans from being truly emancipated. Males in

the culture are encouraged to believe that strong women are responsible for their oppression, and not racist institutions. Many African American women, including those who are lesbians, have internalized these myths. (p. 398)

Ethnic gender blaming is a trap that people want to avoid as not being healthy and helpful.

In Competency Study 2.2, Reid (2000, xiii) reiterates the racism and sexism of stereotypes with which African American women must cope.

COMPETENCY STUDY 2.2

The Myths of African American Women

There exist at least two myths of African American women; they are either "good" or "bad." The "good" African American woman is strong, maternal, hard-working, devoted to family, and quiet. (Note that quietness is traditionally considered a virtue in children, Blacks, and women.) The "bad" African American woman is ugly, lascivious, lazy, negligent, emasculating, and loud. Both views are based on stereotypes born of a need to justify public policies or societal treatment of African American women; they do not come from data or any close investigation of reality. Thus, when psychologists attempt to address therapeutic needs, obvious anxieties, or behavioral problems, they must ask, "What do we know about African American women?" Too often the answers have been couched in terms of these myths as well as other mistaken notions that may abound.

How does a client, particularly a woman of color, cope with sexism and racism? Gutierrez and Lewis (1999) offer an empowerment strategy:

- Developing a specific focus on the details of how individual women have been affected by racism, ethnocentrism, and sexism and on which particular social structures might be challenged
- Assisting the client to gain a sense of personal, interpersonal, and political empowerment with the ultimate goal of changing oppressive structures
- Tracing the strengths of ethnic women in history and in contemporary society to forge ahead in the face of obstacles and using these stories as a road map for similar journeys
- Recognizing that ethnic women have worked with their male counterparts to foster change because racism and sexism have affected both equally in terms of acts of violence against people
- Breaking the cycle of male domination and the gender division of labor to free men and women to participate equally in their ethnic community

Implementing these principles helps the client to combat sexism and racism by analyzing the situation, devising an empowerment plan, drawing on the strengths of role models, and freeing men and women so that they are able to work on these problems together.

Moreover, Stockard and Johnson (1992) argue for economic, legislative, and social egalitarianism on behalf of women:

Women's greater participation in the labor force, the passing of legislation that requires equality in the economy, and the increasing acceptance of egalitarian roles for men and women are certainly important steps toward a more egalitarian society. As feminists work toward additional changes that focus not just on increasing women's representation at all levels of the occupational world, but also on support for families and children and the specific concerns of working class and poor women, we may be able to move closer to a society in which greater equity exists for women and men in all areas of society. (p. 255)

Working toward eliminating sexism frees both men and women in the end.

Homophobia

Weinberg (1972) first used the term *homophobia* to describe prejudice against homosexuality. Appleby and Anastas (1998) assert that one must understand homophobia as the result of heterosexism. That is, heterosexism is an ideological system that denies, denigrates, and stigmatizes any nonheterosexual form of behavior, identity, relationship, or community, whereas homophobia is the fear and hatred of those who love and sexually desire those of the same sex. The implication is that heterosexuals have the responsibility to change their sexual orientation perspective to include the acceptance of same-sex persons as equal members of society.

Tully (2000) explains that homophobia has three components: institutional, individual, and internalized. *Institutional homophobia* is the heterosexual macro-cultural structural barriers against gays and lesbians that are manifested in public policy initiatives (e.g., U.S. Armed Forces policy of "don't ask; don't tell" and the ban on gay and lesbian marriage). Tully cites the following examples:

[T]he criminalization of same-sex sexual activities; the refusal by most businesses, communities, and states to acknowledge same-sex partners; the lack of support for same-sex marriage; the difficulty faced by gays and lesbians who want to have or adopt children; and the generalized lack of support in the nongay community for gay families. (p. 157)

These institutional policies fail to provide for the equal rights of gays and lesbians who are excluded from the Civil Rights Act of 1964, which does not include sexual orientation in its nondiscrimination policy statement. Recent attempts to reverse institutional homophobia include protection of gay and lesbian students against sexual harassment in California schools and the inclusion of civil and legal rights of gay and lesbian partners in the state of Vermont.

Individual homophobia manifests itself in singular acts of overt and covert hostility and violence against gay and lesbian persons on a continuum ranging from hate crimes, such as murder, rape, and physical assaults, to threats, ridicule, and related forms of verbal harassment. The murder of Matthew Shepherd in Laramie, Wyoming, and the murders of a gay couple in Redding, California, by the Williams brothers are examples of individual homophobic homicidal responses.

Institutionalized and structural homophobia is where public law on the state or federal level excludes gay and lesbian persons from such institutional practices as legally recognized marriages and where institutional policies exclude gay and lesbian persons from institutional recognition, as in the case of the ordination of seminary-trained ministers. Generally, gay and lesbian marriages are prohibited by law (with the exception of Vermont) and in the major Protestant denominations (with the exception of the United Church of Christ and other individual instances of Protestant clergy performing such ceremonies). Many major Protestant denominations such as the Presbyterian Church in the United States, the United Methodist Church, and the Southern Baptist Convention have rejected or are deeply divided over clergy ordination and gay and lesbian church marriages.

Internalized homophobia is where the gay or lesbian person introjects society's view or his or her own negative feelings about his or her sexuality. It results in self-hatred and loathing and a learned fear of his or her sexual orientation, which may result in a personal and unhealthy crisis situation. Greene (1994) observes:

> When passing is accompanied by the belief that being gay or lesbian is a sign of inferiority or pathology, it represents an expression of internalized homophobia. Lesbians and gay men who pass, particularly when it is dangerous not to do so, are confronted with stressors that can leave them at risk for negative psychological outcomes. (p. 5)

Undoing the psychological damage is a major task for a person who has suffered internalized homophobia.

We may add to these categories *professional homophobia*. Health and mental health providers may have to cope with medical psychopathology biases learned before 1973 when the category of homosexuality was removed from the list of mental disorders recognized by the American Psychiatric Association. Appleby (2001) observes:

> Health and mental health professionals, including social workers, are not immune from the negative attitudes toward gay, lesbian, and bisexual people that other Americans share. Their attitudes are especially significant in that these are the professionals who have responsibility for assisting gay, lesbian, and bisexual clients to cope with the personal and social consequences of homophobia, to work through the shame and guilt imposed by a homophobic and heterosexist society, to develop a positive lesbian or gay identity, and to help with the management of stigma and stress. Nonjudgmental attitudes are necessary to support social change and to end individual and organizational prejudice. Gay men and lesbians have not always been well served by the health, mental health, and social service professions. (pp. 163–164)

Messinger (2004) conducted an exploratory study of the experiences of lesbian and gay social work students in field placement and identified problems as well as supports and resources. There were 11 sexual orientation issues: managing disclosure of sexual orientation, homophobic attitudes and behaviors, heterosexist attitudes and behaviors, absence and dismissal of gay and lesbian issues, unfriendly climate of placement, professionalism as a gay or lesbian person, identity development concerns, conflicts in intimate relationships, pressures associated with hiding one's sexual orientation, conflicts with field instructors, and general feelings of lack of safety or anxiety. A number of interpersonal supports and institutional resources were suggested: faculty support and mentoring, supportive field education staff, gay and lesbian social work professionals as mentors, field instructors educated about sexual orientation issues, out gay and lesbian agency staff, educated and supportive heterosexual coworkers, resource information for lesbian and gay students, information about sexual orientation issues in placement, a list of gay-friendly agencies, gay and lesbian agencies as placement sites, and resources for gay and lesbian clients.

It is hoped that social work builds on social work education diversity courses where gay and lesbian content is covered as a foundation for continuing investigation into homophobic stereotypes and related biases of social workers. However, in many social work classes there are religiously oriented students who have religious and moral beliefs against homosexuality. Despite NASW Code of Ethics and CSWE Accreditation Standards forbidding discrimination based on sexual orientation, some social work students struggle with their social work professional self and their religious personal self and convictions. Van Den Bergh and Crisp (2004) have a number of suggestions:

> Consequently, practitioners who hold such beliefs should be required to address their beliefs in supervision and to attend trainings that will increase their knowledge and understanding of GLBT clients. When practitioners feel that their beliefs preclude sensitive treatment with GLBT clients, they should refrain from working with these clients until their attitudes have changed and they feel they can work with GLBT clients in identity-affirming ways. (p. 228)

Social work programs are constantly struggling with this issue among their student bodies.

Homophobia is manifested in many families. Heterosexual parents often are horrified or deny that their adolescent is gay or lesbian when they find out about it, either accidentally or because their child tells them (Tully, 2000). Mothers tend to be more accepting than fathers, and gay and lesbian youth seem to find it easier to tell their siblings than their parents.

Greene (2000, p. 117) offers observations in Competency Study 2.3 on racism, sexism, and homophobia pertaining to African American women.

COMPETENCY STUDY 2.3

African American Lesbian and Bisexual Women

For African American lesbian and bisexual women, the effects of racism, sexism, and heterosexism (among other forms of discrimination) cannot be neatly separated from one another. Sexism and heterosexism affect African American and White women differently. Racism affects African American heterosexual and lesbian and bisexual women differently. Being an African American shapes the construction and understanding of the client's sexuality in a reciprocal fashion. It also shapes the construction and manifestations of heterosexism and internalized homophobia as well. Gender, race, and sexual orientation oppression interact with one another in particular ways, and all shape and interact with the personality dynamics of each individual. Any analysis that fails to take this complex interaction of experiences and their effects into account can neither sensitively nor appropriately address the treatment of African American lesbian and bisexual women.

How does one bring an empowerment perspective to working with gays and lesbians? Tully (2000) offers some excellent suggestions:

- Establish an egalitarian relationship where the worker demonstrates concern for the client and creates a safe, homosocial environment where a relationship can develop and flourish.
- Assume a nonjudgmental approach where the client is able to disclose his or her own particular situation, sort through available resources, master the immediate crisis, and make a positive resolution of the issues.

- Start with the client's narrative of what has happened and evolve in a nonthreatening way through a respect for the client's rights and responsibilities.
- Strengthen adaptive potentials (internalized and environmental resources), work for gradual social and economic justice for gays and lesbians (equal rights, protection, nondiscrimination in all aspects of living), and believe that all disenfranchised groups should be permitted the opportunity to succeed.

Ageism

The term *ageism* originated with Butler (1969) and describes negative attitudes and stereotypes experienced by older persons as a form of bigotry and prejudice. Yet, according to Friedman (2004), older adults are the fastest-growing population group in this country and will increase from 35 million to 70 million between 2000 and 2030, or from 13 percent to 20 percent during this time period. The areas of mental health and health care are of most concern regarding the elderly. The number of older adults with mental illnesses will grow from 7 million to 14 million between 2000 and 2030. Adequate health care for the minority elderly is a major national concern. It is estimated that older minority adults are more likely to be living in poverty: White elderly (10 percent), Native American elderly (20 percent), Latino American elderly (25 percent), and African American elderly (30–50 percent).

There is a growing body of literature on ageism and cultural competence, particularly in the fields of health care and mental health. Fain (2005) observes that our health care system remains largely separate and unequal in the field of minority geriatrics. There is unequal treatment for racial and ethnic minority elderly, where minorities are less likely than Whites to receive needed services even when controlling for access to care. Black patients in the United States generally receive lower quality health care than White patients. To a large extent, Black and White patients are treated by different physicians. The physicians treating Black patients may be clinically less well trained and may have less access to important clinical resources than do physicians treating White patients. Specifically, ageism in medical practice occurs to minority elderly in the following ways:

- Five minutes less time per visit
- Fewer tests
- Fewer treatment responses
- Fewer referrals
- Fewer responses to pain symptoms
- Less effort to save life
- Negative response to caregiver

Fain (2005) advocates cultural competence in geriatrics, where physicians and other providers will provide health care in ways that are acceptable and useful to elders and congruent with their cultural background and expectations. Health providers need to be aware of their personal biases and their impact on professional behavior. They should have knowledge of health-related cultural values, beliefs, and behaviors; disease incidence, prevalence and mortality rates; population-specific treatment outcomes; and skills in working with culturally diverse populations.

In the New York State Mental Health 5-Year Plan for older adults (Friedman, 2004), there are 10 areas of concern that address ageism and cultural competence: (1) diverse population recognition in terms of severity, isolation, and potential prevention of mental illnesses; (2) community support to help elderly with mental illness live in the community and modification of community support concepts and models; (3) appropriate housing availability with particular concerns regarding the adult home scandal and adequate mental health services in nursing homes; (4) family support in terms of addressing the needs of family members and caregivers to reduce stress and provide needed treatment when family members develop mental disorders; (5) integrated services to build linkages between mental health and health services and to design new integrated structures of services; (6) access and utilization in terms of widespread public education about geriatric mental health and to address issues of capacity, mobility, access to medication, and affordability; (7) workforce issues in terms of an initiative to promote careers in geriatric mental health and to develop new roles for mental health professionals, paraprofessionals, volunteers, and older adult peer workers; (8) clinical and cultural competence promotion and evidence-based mental health practices for older adults; (9) finance for models that support integrated health, mental health, and aging services; reimbursement for mobile services, outreach, preventive services, and services in medical and geriatric social services settings; adequate Medicare financing for mental health; and (10) leadership to create a bureau on the mental health of older adults, planning preparation for the mental health system for the elder boom, and the development of interagency planning for the mental health needs of older adults.

Working to cope with racism, sexism, homophobia, and ageism are constant struggles that test the rule of law and the values of corrective justice and social and economic justice. Working with individuals, groups, and communities who are oppressed victims and social oppressors is a challenge that faces us all.

TOOLS FOR STUDENT LEARNING 2.5

Insights into Racism, Sexism, Homophobia, and Ageism

Answer the following statements by circling the appropriate answer that best describes you. Discuss the 10 statements and your answers in class.

1. I do not consider myself a racist because I believe that everyone is equal and should be treated with respect and dignity.

   1–True   *2–Somewhat true*   *3–Somewhat false*   *4–False*

2. I would consider myself somewhat of a racist because I believe that my children should marry within their own ethnic group.

   1–True   *2–Somewhat true*   *3–Somewhat false*   *4–False*

3. I would consider myself a racist because I would not live next to a house or apartment inhabited by a person or family of color.

   1–True   *2–Somewhat true*   *3–Somewhat false*   *4–False*

4. I would not consider myself a sexist because I believe that women should be able to work in any organization, providing that they have the qualifications and skills necessary to do the required work.

   1–True   *2–Somewhat true*   *3–Somewhat false*   *4–False*

5. I would consider myself a sexist sometimes because I would like my wife or husband to stay home, keep house, and take care of the kids while I work and earn the living for my family.

   1–True   *2–Somewhat true*   *3–Somewhat false*   *4–False*

6. I would consider myself a sexist because I enjoy having sexual affairs with several different women or men at the same time without making a commitment to any of them.

   1–True   *2–Somewhat true*   *3–Somewhat false*   *4–False*

7. I do not consider myself homophobic because I support equal rights for gay and lesbian persons as far as military service, employment, and marriage are concerned.

   1–True   *2–Somewhat true*   *3–Somewhat false*   *4–False*

8. I would consider myself somewhat homophobic because I feel uncomfortable as a heterosexual person relating to a gay or lesbian person.

   1–True   *2–Somewhat true*   *3–Somewhat false*   *4–False*

9. I would consider myself homophobic because I would be very upset and angry if my son told me that he was gay or my daughter indicated that she was a lesbian.

   1–True   *2–Somewhat true*   *3–Somewhat false*   *4–False*

10. I believe that racism, sexism, and homophobia will always be a part of human nature and that people who are racist, sexist, or homophobic will remain so.

    1–True   *2–Somewhat true*   *3–Somewhat false*   *4–False*

DISCRIMINATION AND OPPRESSION

Discrimination is a behavioral response that is unfavorable to members of an ethnic, gender, sexual orientation, or related out-group. It is preceded by prejudice, which is a negative affective attitude and a learned condition. A person discriminates against others because of a cognitive belief (e.g., racism, sexism, homophobia, ageism) and an affective attitude (e.g., prejudice).

There are several theories related to discrimination. First, discrimination occurs because of situational pressures. For example, a person may not associate with another person because of peer reaction in a wider group that pressures the person not to relate to another and because of the social sanctions that may occur as a result of the relationship. Situational peer pressure that goes against the majority population or against the will of an influential group is a strong force reinforcing discrimination. A specific example might be a situation in which associating with a gay or lesbian person would provoke a strong reprimand from a person's family, church, or community that is extremely homophobic. Second, discrimination may occur as a reaction to group gain. That is, competition for scarce resources and ethnocentrism may result in ethnic domination and subordination, particularly when there is the possibility for economic loss of jobs or a downturn in the economy. A scapegoat group may be blamed when jobs are scarce or there is a threat of losing employment to a group that will work for lower wages. Third, institutional discrimination occurs in employment, education, housing, and other life-sustaining areas where marginal and fringe outgroups are unable to secure resources due to dominant social majority locks on unionized jobs, schools and housing in desirable neighborhoods, and other amenities.

McAleavy (2002) reports on a national survey study of 1,003 workers interviewed between September 28 and October 18, 2000, by Rutgers University and the University of Connecticut under the auspices of the John J. Heldrich Center for Workforce Development. Reporting on what minority and White employees experience on the job, 28 percent of African Americans and 22 percent of Latinos stated that they have personally experienced unfair treatment at work, compared with 6 percent of White employees. Fifty percent of African American employees believe that they are the most likely racial group to be treated unfairly at work compared with 10 percent of Whites and 13 percent of other races. When discrimination was reported, 57 percent of minorities said that their employer did not respond promptly or satisfactorily to complaints (e.g., being passed over for promotion, being assigned undesirable tasks, or hearing racist remarks). Ethnic discrimination on the job remains a primary issue.

Bonacich and Goodman (1972) identify a number of social conditions that heighten discrimination in a community:

1. Biologically, culturally, and socially distinct populations that are present in a social system and do not allow other groups outside these perimeters to enter their geographical location
2. A segment of the population that is threatened by another group over competition for scarce resources and that believes these resources will be lost as a result of the entrance of the outside group
3. A group that is stereotyped and perceived as the common enemy of other groups so that the label of enemy unifies the other groups regardless of whether the group in question is a threat or whether there is an irrational reaction formation on the part of the majority population
4. Unequal degrees of power in populations so that the haves with power over access to resources react against the have-nots without power, goods, and services
5. Institutional discriminatory actions that are legitimated in social structures and cultural beliefs such as religious institutional sanctions, ethnic exclusion, and negative community practices

The Nature of Oppression

Oppression occurs when a segment of the population, systematically and over a period of time, prevents another segment from attaining access to scarce and valued resources. Oppression is a process whereby specific acts are designed to place others in the lower ranks of society and is also a structure that creates a bottom rank in a hierarchical system of ranks.

There are interlocking systems of oppression—that is, institutions and systems in society interrelate and interconnect with each other to form oppression. An interplay of oppression exists among different systems (Collins, 1990). Schriver (2001) states:

> We . . . recognize that oppression in any institution directed toward any individual or group is connected with and results in oppression in other institutions and of many other individuals and groups. This interrelated or interlocking quality gives oppression its systemic nature. (p. 97)

The emphasis should be to focus on the links among the systems of oppression. In this sense, the discussion is on the structural nature of oppression. Young (1990) states:

> Oppression in this sense is structural, rather than the result of a few people's choices or policies. Its causes are embedded in unquestioned norms, habits, and symbols, in the assumptions underlying institutional rules and the collective consequences of following those rules. (p. 41)

In brief, institutional oppression results in the oppression of groups and individuals.

Freire has done the pioneer thinking about the nature and dynamics of oppression. Having worked with poor peasant people in South America in the 1960s and 1970s, he has reflected on his experiences. Freire (1970), in *Pedagogy of the Oppressed*, defines oppression in the following terms:

> Any situation in which "A" objectively exploits "B" or hinders his pursuit of self-affirmation as a responsible person is one of oppression. Such a situation in itself constitutes violence, even when sweetened by false generosity, because it interferes with man's ontological and historical vocation to be more fully human. With the establishment of a relationship of oppression, violence has *already* begun. (pp. 40–41)

Critical consciousness leads to the expression of social discontents, which are components of an oppressive situation. The problem of humanization leads to the recognition of dehumanization as a historical reality. Freire (1970) teaches:

> As the oppressors dehumanize others and violate their rights, they themselves also become dehumanized. As the oppressed, fighting to be human, take away the oppressors' power to dominate and suppress, they restore to the oppressors the humanity they had lost in the exercise of oppression. (p. 42)

Dehumanization is a distortion of what it means to be fully human.

The historical task of the oppressed is to liberate themselves and their oppressors. According to Freire, to restore the humanity of the oppressed and the oppressors is to restore true generosity. However, the oppressed, instead of striving for liberation, find in their oppressor their model of manhood because the oppressed have internalized the image of the oppressor and are fearful of freedom, which includes autonomy and responsibility. The oppressed must not fall into this trap. They must liberate themselves from becoming the oppressors. To be free is human completion.

Oppression is dehumanization. The oppressed have been unjustly dealt with, deprived of their voice, and cheated in the sale of their labor. The oppressed must develop the pedagogy of their liberation. They must affirm that they are persons and, as persons, they should be free. Liberating education carries out the pedagogy of the oppressed through educational projects to organize the oppressed and systematic education that can be changed by political power. There are two stages of the pedagogy of the oppressed, according to Freire: The first stage is where the oppressed unveil the world of oppression and commit themselves to its transformation, while the second stage is the reality of the oppressed transformed and the pedagogy becomes a pedagogy of all in the process of permanent liberation. The oppressed go from self-depreciation ("we don't know anything") to realization ("we were exploited"). The oppressed must engage in critical and liberating dialogue and reflection on their concrete situation. The oppressed have the ability to reason. Libertarian action must transform dependence into independence. The oppressed must intervene critically in the situation that surrounds them and must be subjects, not objects, and fight in the revolutionary process. The oppressed must learn this perspective, which serves as a guideline.

Having reviewed the nature and dynamics of oppression, we now turn to the major categories of oppression.

Types of Oppression

Young (1990) discusses five faces of oppression that will add to our understanding: exploitation, marginalization, powerlessness, cultural imperialism, and violence. These types of oppression are played out in the social and economic order of society and are directed against vulnerable populations-at-risk.

Exploitation. This form of oppression occurs when the results of the labor of one social group are transferred to benefit another group. The energies of the have-nots are expended to maintain the power, status, and wealth of the haves. Gender oppression is a case in point. Not only is there an inequality of status, power, and wealth between women and men but women also are excluded from privileged activities. Women work in jobs that enhance the pleasure and comfort of others, usually men. Solutions to economic and status oppression involve the reorganization of institutions, the revamping of existing practices of decision making, and alteration of the division of labor.

Marginalization. This is the most dangerous form of oppression because it sets aside people that the labor system cannot and will not use as workers. This results in severe material deprivation and social dependency. A major concern is to restructure productivity to address the right of participation and to include marginalized people in a public works or self-employed economic effort.

Powerlessness. This form of oppression involves persons who are powerless or who lack the authority to develop and exercise skills in work. Young (1990) observes: "The powerless have little or no work autonomy, exercise little creativity or judgment in their work, have no technical expertise or authority, express themselves awkwardly, especially in public or bureaucratic settings, and do not command respect" (pp. 56–57). They are inhibited in the development of their capacities, lack decision making in their work life, and are exposed to disrespectful treatment due to their lack of status.

Cultural Imperialism. This involves the establishment of a dominant group's experience and culture as the norm to the exclusion of other groups that are rendered invisible and stereotyped. Women, Jews, First Nations Peoples, African Americans, and gays and lesbians are prime examples of excluded groups. Cultural imperialism results in the experience of *double consciousness*, a term coined by Du Bois (1903/1969). Young (1990) explains:

> Double consciousness arises when the oppressed subject refuses to coincide with these devalued, objectified, stereotyped visions of herself or himself. While the subject desires recognition as human, capable of activity, full of hope and possibility, she receives from the dominant culture only the judgment that she is different, marked, or inferior. (p. 60)

Such a person experiences a sense of worthlessness and subjugation.

Violence. In this form of oppression, violence is directed at certain persons because they are members of vulnerable groups that are liable to violation. Violence against others is perpetual, tolerated, and irrational and is based on fear and hatred of these groups. Violence may be an expression of the will to power, marked by the insecurities of the violators, and is a form of injustice (humans' inhumanity to humans).

Coping with Oppression

Can we cope with oppression? Several answers have been proposed. Freire (1970) provides solutions that involve community organizing based on dialogical action and education. Action to overcome oppression begins with the oppressed and the leaders dialoguing and communicating with each other. People in communion liberate each other, according to Freire. Antidialogical action consists of conquest, divide and rule, manipulation, and cultural invasion. First Nations Peoples identify with this pattern, as leaders often took such actions against them. Dialogical cultural action consists of cooperation based on a critical analysis of a problematic reality, unity for liberation growing out of communion with the united people from a consciousness of being an oppressed class, organization based on authentic and critical witness (consistency between words and actions, boldness to confront existence, radicalization leading to increasing action, courage to love, and faith in the people), and cultural synthesis from the oppressed people's own values and world ideology, which are guidelines for mutual support and action.

Freire (1970) offers an existential analysis of the nature of oppression and an educational dialogue that leads to action overcoming oppression. He lays the foundation for later discussions on oppression and liberation.

Internalized oppression has been explained in terms of stigmatization. Appleby (2001) explains:

> Oppression is an institutional process that is experienced personally as stigma, stress, guilt, and shame. Stigma significantly influences identity development. It is stigma that results in internalized oppression, which every minority person must learn to manage in the process of developing a healthy identity. (pp. 45–46)

Being oppressed and stigmatized have grave psychological effects that must be dealt with and resolved.

Gil (1998) broadens the discussion on oppression to the concerns of social work. Oppression is "a mode of human relations involving domination and exploitation—economic, social, and psychologic—between individuals; between social groups and classes within and beyond societies; and, globally, between entire societies" (p. 10). Dominion, exploitation, and oppression are related, according to Gil (1998), as follows: "Domination is the *means* to enforce exploitation toward the *end* of attaining and maintaining privileged conditions of living for certain social groups relative to some other groups" (p. 10). Gil also observes that oppression is fluid and changing in a society:

> Societies whose internal and external relations involve oppressive tendencies are usually not divided simply into oppressors and oppressed people. Rather, people in such societies tend to be oppressed in some relations and oppressors in others, while some relations may involve mutual oppression. Oppression is not a static context but a dynamic process. (p. 11)

At the same time, a nonoppressive society is one in which people are treated as equals, have equal rights and responsibilities, and are subject to the same level of expectations and constraints about work and other aspects of life. Gil advocates that social workers follow these radical practice principles of social change:

- Reject political neutrality and affirm politics of social justice and human liberation.
- Affirm values of equality, liberty, cooperation, and affirmation of individual and social development.
- Transcend technical/professional approaches in favor of helping people trace the links between their problems and ways of life.
- Facilitate critical consciousness through dialogue leading to insights into human nature, shaping social realities, and changing and reshaping these realities.
- Advocate human rights to which people are entitled, such as equal rights, responsibilities, and opportunities.
- Confront obstacles to needs fulfillment of human needs and people's capacities for a just and free society.
- Gain insight into personal oppression that will transcend divisions and identify with human liberation and social equality.
- Prefigure future possibilities toward participatory democratic egalitarian forms of human liberation.
- Spread critical consciousness and build social movements that promote political action.

Gil follows in the tradition of Freire and makes a case for social work involvement in dealing with oppression and liberation on a political societal level.

Violence as an Oppression Theme

A current oppression theme is portrayed in the violence against women. Women as victims, the battered woman syndrome, and women's experience of domestic violence are major concerns that relate violence and oppression. Mahoney (1994) explains the interrelationship between violence and oppression:

> The long struggle to reveal the prevalence and harm of domestic violence often emphasized incidents of violence, however, rather than placing the woman's experience in the

context of her life in an oppressive society, or emphasizing the abusive patterns of the batterer's quest for control. Inquiry focuses on particular incidents of violence and the woman's response to them. When battering is seen only as discrete episodes of physical assault, this facilitates the position that leaving the relationship is the sole appropriate form of self-assertion. But battering reflects a quest for control that goes beyond separate incidents of physical violence and that does not stop when the woman attempts to leave. A focus on control reveals the danger that violence will continue as part of the attempt to reassert power over the woman. (p. 75)

In other words, unless we move beyond the acts of physical violence against women to focus on the issues of power and control in an oppressive society, we miss the whole point, namely, that violence is an expression of societal oppression.

The power and control wheel developed by Ellen Pence (n.d.) and the Duluth Domestic Abuse Intervention Project illustrates oppression as physical and sexual violence. Power and control are at the hub of the wheel, with spokes emphasizing the use of economic abuse, coercion and threats, intimidation, emotional abuse, male privilege, children, isolation, and minimizing, denying, and blaming. Under each of these headings are details of oppressive behavior:

- *Economic abuse:* preventing her from getting or keeping a job; making her ask for money; giving her an allowance; taking her money; not letting her know about or have access to family income
- *Coercion and threats:* making and/or carrying out threats to do something to hurt her; threatening to leave her, to commit suicide, or to report her to welfare; making her drop charges; making her do illegal things
- *Intimidation:* making her afraid by using looks, actions, gestures; smashing things; destroying her property; abusing pets; displaying weapons
- *Emotional abuse:* putting her down; making her feel bad about herself; calling her names; making her think she's crazy; playing mind games; humiliating her; making her feel guilty
- *Male privilege:* treating her like a servant; making all the big decisions; acting like the "master of the castle"; being the one to define men's and women's roles
- *Children:* making her feel guilty about the children; using the children to relay messages; using visitation to harass her; threatening to take the children away
- *Isolation*: controlling what she does, who she sees and talks to, what she reads, and where she goes; limiting her outside involvement; using jealousy to justify actions
- *Minimizing, denying, and blaming:* making light of the abuse and not taking her concerns about it seriously; saying the abuse does not happen; shifting responsibility for abusive behavior; saying she caused it

These categories are areas of assessment that can be used to determine the specific incidents of violent oppression against women.

Crenshaw (1994) uses the concept of intersectionality discussed earlier as an aspect of diversity to explain violence against women of color. Her task is to trace how racism and sexism have intersected the experiences of women of color, particularly male violence against women expressed in battering and rape. She distinguishes between structural intersectionality and political intersectionality. The former focuses on the economic social class structures (lack of access to employment, housing, and wealth) that form the experiences of a battered woman of color, while the latter refers to the subordination and marginalization of women of color that racially stratify and disempower them. Intersecting these barriers and dilemmas are ways of understanding differences among us, which are also the means of constructing new groups and alliances to overcome the differences. The task is to create new and positive intersections where people can meet, draw strength and courage from each other, and build new roads that lead to liberating and healthy lives.

A tragedy of monumental national importance was the September 11, 2001, hijacking of the four U.S. commercial airliners that resulted in the loss of more than 3,000 lives in New York City, Washington, DC, and Pennsylvania. From a U.S. history perspective, these events were the primary example of oppression as violence perpetuated by Middle Eastern terrorists who, in turn, have felt national, ethnic, and religious oppression and displaced their anger and hostility onto the United States.

In one of the many articles that appeared in the days following the September 11 tragedies, Wilgoren (2001) identifies the profile of the suspected hijackers: adults with education and skill, middle class, ages ranging from 20s to 40s, years of studying and training in the United States with valuable commercial skills, and working in a small group with a platoon-type fighting mentality. One hijacker had a wife and four children. In the article, Stuart Grassian, a psychiatrist at Harvard Medical School, states:

> The kind of horrifying prospect is that Osama bin Laden and what he represents has sort of crystallized a moment in history that has an evil and a horror to it that's sort of akin to what Hitler was able to crystallize around him.

This national loss of life is another example of humans' inhumanity to humans and the most severe illustration of oppression as violence.

SUMMARY

The social context of diversity, racism, sexism, homophobia, discrimination, and oppression is with us as we help people with problems. This chapter has presented these themes along with solutions and strategies for immediate action. The message is that these social contextual factors must be confronted and dealt with on a constant basis. It is hoped that the reader will return to these sections with possible answers to these perennial problems.

In the subsequent chapters of this book, we make the case for a culturally competent framework and for the culturally competent themes of cultural awareness, knowledge acquisition, skill development, and inductive learning. Being a culturally competent practitioner in the midst of the social context described in this chapter is the way that we must point social work students and practice providers.

CHAPTER THREE

Advancing Social and Economic Justice

Dorothy Van Soest

Considerable attention has been paid during the past decade to the increasingly diverse appearance of the United States. Much of the attention has focused on the significant increase in non-White populations and projections of increasing numbers of "minority majority" cities, regions, and states. Two prevailing responses exist. First, dominant White America clearly shows signs of being threatened, as evidenced by increased use of institutional and individual violence to maintain dominance and oppression over people of color. Some examples are widespread anti-immigrant and anti–affirmative action sentiment and political action, growing numbers of hate crimes, and a proliferation of White hate groups and on-campus accusations of balkanization of student bodies. The intensity of the anti-immigrant sentiment has even spilled over to include immigrants with European backgrounds.

A second predominant response is an attempt to successfully prepare for a significantly more diverse workplace. A proliferation of education and training efforts aimed at cultural awareness and multicultural competence in the workplace characterizes this response. For social work and other helping professions, this translates into a focus on preparing professionals to effectively serve clients from diverse cultures. The notion of cultural competence has become the center of this response; it is defined by Cross and others (1989) as a "set of congruent behaviors, attitudes, and policies that come together in a system, agency, or among professionals and enable that system, agency, or those professionals to work effectively in cross-cultural situations" (p. 13).

Although the two predominant responses to changing demographics represent either a stance of resistance or a stance of working together to strengthen the economy, this chapter proposes a third response. The fundamental premise of this chapter is that, in order to be truly culturally competent, it is necessary to understand the meaning of diverse cultures and difference. And, the experience of difference means both culture as a source of strength (i.e., capacity to overcome life circumstances and mobilize social movements) and group membership as a basis of inequity, injustice, and oppression. The threat many people feel in the face of an increasingly diverse U.S. society is related to fear of losing their position of dominance and privilege over those who are assigned a subordinate status primarily because they are perceived as "different."

Thus, successfully navigating the new multicultural terrain not only requires an understanding and appreciation of diverse cultures but also requires an equal understanding of the sources and dynamics of injustice and oppression that are inextricably connected with cultural difference. Although social workers, in particular, have professional responsibilities to provide culturally competent services, they have additional mandates to challenge social injustice and to promote social and economic justice. These mandates are expressed in the National Association of Social Workers Code of Ethics (NASW, 1996a), the *International Declaration of Ethical Principles of Social Work* of the International Federation of Social Workers (IFSW, 1994), and the *Educational Policy and Accreditation Standards* of the Council on Social Work Education (CSWE, 2002).

For almost three decades, social work education has increasingly addressed the need to develop social justice practitioners who are culturally competent. Beginning in the early 1970s, the inclusion of diversity has been mandated by social work curriculum standards for purposes of accrediting educational programs. In 1992, the Council on Social Work Education's curriculum requirements for accreditation specifically mandated content on women, people of color, gay men, and lesbian women; on the patterns, dynamics, and consequences of oppression related to these and other vulnerable groups; and on skills to promote change for social and economic justice (CSWE, 1992).

In CSWE's (2002) most recent *Educational Policy and Accreditation Standards*, the purposes of social work as a profession are delineated and include the following two purposes related to this chapter:

- To enhance human well-being and alleviate poverty, oppression, and other forms of social injustice
- To develop and apply practice in the context of diverse cultures

The standards go on to state that in order to achieve these purposes, social work education prepares social workers to alleviate poverty, oppression, and other forms of social injustice; to practice without discrimination, with respect, and with knowledge and skills related to clients' age, class, color, culture, disability, ethnicity, family structure, gender, marital status, national origin, race, religion, sex, and sexual orientation; and to recognize the global context of social work practice. The standards clearly delineate that the foundation curriculum content in all social work education programs must be consistent with these purposes of the profession and social work education by integrating content on diversity and cultural competence; social and economic justice content grounded in an understanding of distributive justice, human and civil rights, and the global interconnections of oppression; and implementation strategies for combating discrimination, oppression, and economic deprivation and for promoting social and economic justice so that students are prepared to advocate for nondiscriminatory social and economic systems.

This chapter addresses issues related to these professional mandates and connects the themes of the other chapters in this book with the concepts of social and economic justice: The dimensions of cultural competence must be understood within the social context of an environment of social and economic injustice that is inextricably interconnected with discrimination and oppression based on race, ethnicity, gender, sexual orientation, age, ability, and so on; one's own determination of who is entitled to social justice rests in understanding one's own personal and professional cultural awareness as well as one's acquisition of knowledge about diverse populations and how they are subjected to social injustice and the development of skills necessary for restoring social and economic justice; and, finally, learning to advance social and economic justice in one's social work practice, which requires a learning process characterized by empowerment.

In this chapter, the first section briefly discusses definitions of social justice. The second section argues that culturally competent practice insists on a commitment to promoting social and economic justice. The role of social justice advocate requires that social workers engage in critical thinking that begins with serious reflection, awareness, and analysis of their own personal beliefs about what is fair and just. Thus, the third section suggests some exercises as a place to begin that work. This is followed by a section of social justice theory that presents perspectives against which one's personal perspectives can be critically assessed. The connections between social justice and oppression are then presented, followed by a section that makes global connections between human rights and oppression. The chapter ends with a discussion of and exercises aimed at increasing understanding and practice of social change strategies.

DEFINING SOCIAL JUSTICE

NASW clearly mandates in its Code of Ethics that "social workers promote social justice" and "challenge social injustice" (NASW, 1996a, p. 1, 5), yet it leaves social workers to face the immediate difficulty of understanding what social justice and social injustice mean. Throughout history, social justice as an idea has been highly contested, and it has taken on various meanings. As will be discussed later in this chapter, social justice is often seen through the eye of the beholder, based on his or her position in society. As Reisch (2002) points out, people march under the banner of social justice while promoting radically different ideas of what it is, with "liberals and conservatives, religious fundamentalists, and radical secularists all regard[ing] their causes as socially just" (p. 343).

Although there is not yet one common, universally accepted definition of social justice and social workers are challenged to engage in their best critical thinking in order to determine its meaning in practice, several related definitions in the social work literature guide our thinking. The *Encyclopedia of Social Work* (Flynn, 1995) defines it as the embodiment of fairness (reasonable treatment), equity (similar situations dealt with similarly), and equality in the distribution of societal resources. *The Social Work Dictionary* (Barker, 2003) defines social justice as follows:

> An ideal condition in which all members of a society have the same basic rights, protection, opportunities, obligations, and social benefits. Implicit in this concept is the notion that historical inequalities should be acknowledged and remedied through specific measures. A key social work value, social justice entails advocacy to confront discrimination, oppression, and institutional inequities. (pp. 404–405)

Lum (personal communication, May 9, 2005) provides definitions of both social justice and economic justice:

> Social justice governs how social institutions deal fairly or justly with the social needs of people as far as opening access to what is good for individuals and groups. It also secures social rights and benefits in terms of such social provisions of well-being such as nutrition,

housing, employment, education, and health care. Social justice also addresses historical and current forms of oppression and seeks legal and societal means to correct such abuses and establish an equal playing field for all regardless of ethnicity, gender, sexual orientation, social and economic class, age, and other related areas.

Economic justice encompasses moral principles of how to design economic institutions so that a person can earn a living, enter into social and economic contracts (monetary agreements to buy a car, house; obtain assets; e.g., stocks), exchange goods and services in order to produce an independent material foundation for economic sustenance. It also ensures education and employment to nurture people in learning and career development and, when a person is unable to provide for him/herself, economic justice fosters temporary welfare assistance until a person can function in a work environment.

In this chapter, three types of social justice are recognized—distributive, legal, and commutative—with distributive justice having been a longstanding concern of social work. Wakefield (1988) favors it as the organizing value of social work, a position that is taken in this chapter as well. However, if we are to connect the dots between social work's traditional notion that citizens have a right to have their needs met and the issues of multiculturalism, cultural competence, and oppression—a main contention of this chapter—then the distributive paradigm is not sufficient to encapsulate the complexities of injustice (Young, 1990). The concept of social justice needs to be about more than the distribution of income and other goods and services; "a concept of justice should begin with the concepts of domination and oppression" and should seek institutional remedies for "cultural sources of oppression, the manifestations of which are seen in racism, sexism, homophobia, ableism, etc." (van Wormer, 2004, p. 12).

CULTURAL COMPETENCE MEANS PROMOTING SOCIAL AND ECONOMIC JUSTICE

The definition of *cultural diversity*, as that term is used in this chapter, refers to differences between groups with distinctive characteristics and social identities based on culture, ethnicity, gender, age, sexual orientation, religion, ability, and class. Diversity is seen as inseparable from issues of oppression and social and economic justice. The integration of cultural diversity and social justice recognizes the historical and ongoing oppression and privilege that different social identity groups experience in our society. It recognizes economic class as a prime indicator of oppression and, in fact, sees the creation of a class system based on difference as a function of oppression. It further recognizes the intersection and complex interaction of multiple social identities and a continuum of harm and privilege that these identities confer.

Multiculturalism thus refers to issues of representation and democratic inclusiveness with its roots in the relationship between politics and power, within the context of a historical past and a living present where racist exclusions were "calculated, brutally rational, and profitable" (Goldberg, 1993, p. 105). Thus, in order to be culturally competent, social workers need to learn how to "interrogate, challenge, and transform those cultural practices that sustain racism" and to "link the struggle for inclusion with relations of power in the broader society" (Giroux, 2000, p. 499). In sum, the definition of *culturally competent social work*, as that term is used in this chapter, begins with Lum's

(1999) definition as "the set of knowledge and skills that a social worker must develop in order to be effective with multicultural clients" (p. 3) and includes as a requirement a commitment to promote social justice arising from a clear understanding of the impact of oppressive systems on individuals and families. Ultimately, the goal of culturally competent practice is to transform oppressive and unjust systems into nonoppressive and just alternatives (Gil, 1998). This means that, in an increasingly diverse and inequitable society, social workers face the challenge of not only understanding societal oppression but also translating that understanding into actions designed to facilitate social change for social justice. The challenges are daunting and require careful study, reflection, and action.

In a book called *Teaching/Learning Anti-Racism: A Developmental Approach* by Louise Derman-Sparks and Carol Brunson Phillips (1997), the authors provide the following parable:

> Once upon a time a woman, strolling along a riverbank, hears a cry for help and, seeing a drowning person, rescues him. She no sooner finishes administering artificial respiration when another cry requires another rescue. Again, she has only just helped the second person when a third call for help is heard. After a number of rescues, she begins to realize that she is pulling some people out of the river more than once. By this time the rescuer is exhausted and resentful, feeling that if people are stupid or careless enough to keep landing in the river, they can rescue themselves. She is too annoyed, tired, and frustrated to look around her.
>
> Shortly after, another woman walking along the river hears the cries for help and begins rescuing people. She, however, wonders why so many people are drowning in this river. Looking around her, she sees a hill where something seems to be pushing people off. Realizing this as the source of the drowning problem, she is faced with a difficult dilemma: If she rushes uphill, people presently in the river will drown; if she stays at the river pulling them out, more people will be pushed in. What can she do? (pp. 1–2)

The second woman's thoughts suggest that she may be questioning why the people in the river share particular characteristics and if a selection process is underway. Consider that both women who witnessed people drowning in the river are social workers who want to help. If we define racism, sexism, heterosexism, classism, and other forms of oppression as the force on the hill, then this metaphor suggests three alternative solutions for social workers: (1) rescue people in trouble and return them to the oppressive conditions that caused the problem; (2) after rescuing people, teach them how to manage their problems so that if they "get pushed into the river again," they at least will not drown; and (3) organize with people to destroy the source of the problem (Derman-Sparks & Phillips, 1997, p. 2).

As stated in the introduction to this chapter, there is an inextricable connection between diversity and social justice. Thus, culturally competent practice requires choosing the third position. Social workers need to do more than respond to the symptoms or consequences of oppressive conditions. They need to develop strategies for responding to the sources of oppression. Further, they must be willing to reevaluate their own role, on both personal and professional levels, in the continuation of that oppression. Social work must ultimately be about recognizing the problem and learning to understand and to eliminate it.

The metaphor presented in the story of the two women at the river raises several questions:

- If the river represents a situation of oppression or disadvantage, what is it like to be in the river? In other words, what are the conditions and processes of oppression, and how do they affect people's lives and life chances?
- Who are the people being pushed into the river? What characteristics do they have in common? What is the singular facet of their experience that puts them at risk?
- What people are *not* being pushed into the river? What are their common characteristics? How do they benefit from having others pushed into the river?
- If the force on the hill that is pushing people into the river represents racism, sexism, classism, heterosexism, ageism, and other systems of advantage, how does the force operate? How much of this is to be understood in individual, psychological terms, and how much as a "business-as-usual" patterning of institutional practices? What is the mix of factors that keep the force on the hill operating?
- What happens so that people who used to be in the river get out and then go up the hill to push people who look like them into the river?
- What role can social workers learn to take in helping the people pushed into the river?
- What organizational, collaborative, and advocative skills can social workers develop in order to eliminate the force that is pushing them into the river? How can social workers differentiate business-as-usual discrimination from behavior motivated out of personal bias?

In order to address these questions, social workers need to understand the centrality of race and racism as "a mode of human relations involving domination and exploitation" that, on an economic level, creates a class system (Gil, 1998, p. 103). They must further understand the complex interaction of racism with the systemic dynamics of oppressions based on gender, class, sexual orientation, age, ability, and the concept of multiple identities. Striving for such understandings is not easy. Gil also asserts the following:

> Understanding injustice and oppression and their sources—domination and exploitation— tends to be fraught with multidimensional existential dilemmas and emotional stress, for it implies the need for people to make significant changes in their ways of life, work, and patterns of social relations. It means therefore exchanging the "bliss of ignorance" for the burden of holistic social knowledge along with difficult new choices, conflicts, and fears. (p. 130)

A PLACE TO BEGIN: AWARENESS, REFLECTION, CRITICAL THINKING

In our efforts to understand diversity and social justice issues and to develop cultural competence aimed at social change, we must start with ourselves. Social workers need to conscientiously engage in a process of becoming aware of their personal values and beliefs about social justice, reflect on where those values and beliefs originated, and engage in critical thinking about the implications of their current perspective.

We often hear the expression "life is not fair," especially when something bad has happened to us or to someone we care about. The expression is perhaps a manifestation of a belief that life is, indeed, not fair. Is it fair that our destinies are often shaped and determined by accident of birth (i.e., by race, gender, class, abilities, country of origin, etc.)? A more relevant question, when considering issues of social justice, might be: Is life *just?* The exercises in Tools for Student Learning 3.1 are aimed at individual and small-group exploration of issues related to those questions.

TOOLS FOR STUDENT LEARNING 3.1

Reflection Exercises

Take some time to answer the following questions. Write down your thoughts so you can look at them later and also discuss them with others.

1. What are rights? What do people have a right to (i.e., what should people get just because they are human beings)?

2. What are privileges (i.e., what do people deserve because they have earned it)?

Now consider the following more focused questions.

3. Is it fair to take (e.g., through taxes) from one group and give to another group? When is it fair and when is it not fair? Does it have to do with rights or privileges? When is it a form of justice, and when is it an infringement on people's freedom?

4. If there is a situation in which the goods and services produced are inadequate to satisfy everyone's desire for them, on what basis or according to what principles can these goods and services be distributed justly? For example, if you believe that everyone has a right to food and there is an inadequate supply, how do you distribute it? If you believe that having food is a privilege, then what do people have to do to earn it? And what should be done when people who have not earned it get it and those who earn it do not get it?

5. If there is a situation in which the goods and services produced are adequate to satisfy everyone's desire for them, on what basis or according to what principles can they be distributed justly?

Reflection and Discussion

Now take a moment to read your responses and reflect on them. Do any themes emerge? Are you surprised by any of your responses? What beliefs do you think underlie your answers? Where do those beliefs come from? How comfortable are you with your responses?

In a small group of three to four of your peers, discuss each of the questions. Hear how others responded, and compare their responses with yours. Be sure to talk about where your beliefs come from.

Classroom Exercises

After reflecting on and discussing the previous questions, use the following two exercises to help you think further about your perspectives on justice and to identify the principles upon which you judge whether or not a situation is fair.

Exercise 1. Provide a bag of small candy bars such as those you can buy at Halloween (or you might just imagine that you have a bag of candy bars). Small groups of four to six students, depending on class size, meet to discuss how to distribute the candy to the class according to what they think is just. Each group presents their proposal (if the candy is imaginary) or actually distributes the candy according to the distributive system they have developed. If the candy is actually distributed, it will need to be collected for the next group to implement their distribution plan. After each group has presented their method of distribution, discuss the following questions:

1. On what was your distribution system based (e.g., everyone should get an equal amount)? Should distribution be based on need—like who did not eat breakfast this morning? Should distribution be based on what people deserve according to a merit system?

2. Which system would you consider to be the most fair?

3. Which system would you consider to be the most just?

4. Might there be a situation when one system would be more fair and just than in another situation? How do you decide?

Exercise 2. Read the following case scenario and then discuss the questions that follow.

A staff association at a major university is calling for a "sick out" to call attention to a number of their demands. One of the demands is that all staff getting salaries up to $60,000 should get an increase of $321 per month. Discuss the following questions about their demand.

1. Would you consider this to be a just demand? Would you consider it to be fair? Why or why not?

2. Would it be just (fair) to give the same amount to a person who has been working at the university for a short time (say 1 year) at a salary of $59,500 as to a person who has been working for more than 10 years and still only makes $15,000 a year?

3. On what basis do you think the cutoff point (in this case, $60,000) should be set? Why not set it at $30,000 or $35,000? On what basis would you make such a decision?

4. What do you think about demanding a monthly increase for workers earning salaries in the bottom quintile?

FIGURE 3.1 *Fairness from Different Perspectives*

The intent of the discussion exercises in Tools for Learning 3.1 is to stimulate awareness of your own perspective and the diverse meanings of social justice. The point is that, when discussing issues and strategies related to promoting social and economic justice, it is important to understand how the term *justice* is being used and to have guiding principles from which to make decisions about justice claims. We need to struggle with the question of justice. What is it? Is justice equality? Is justice having freedom? Whether we are aware of them or not, each of us believes in certain principles about and theories of justice. And, as Figure 3.1 illustrates, our perspective on what is just and fair is often related to our own position in society.

SOCIAL JUSTICE THEORY

As the previous section aimed to illustrate, we need to be rigorous in our thinking about what social justice means and how to go about achieving it if we are to take the social work mission seriously. Many of us have experienced the phenomenon of finger-pointing, both within the profession and with our student peers, with some people claiming to be *for* social justice while others accuse them of *not* being for social justice. A misperception or myth exists among social workers that we all mean the same thing when we use the term *social justice*. Social workers need to develop a knowledge base and framework for understanding social justice as an organizing value of our profession. We must begin by examining and critically challenging our personal perspectives about justice, developing a knowledge base about social justice perspectives and principles that are coherent and congruent with social work values, and translating these understandings into effective strategies and actions to promote justice and fairness.

FIGURE 3.2 *Three Types of Justice*

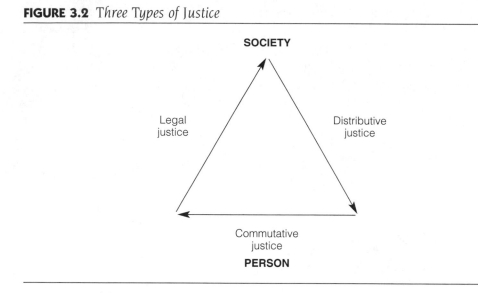

What follows is a brief review of a few principles and contemporary social justice theories that are prevalent in the literature, with a focus on the different types of social justice and different perspectives about the type of justice called distributive justice. This section aims to highlight the complexities of social justice issues that point to the need for critical thinking and continuous knowledge development as professionals.

Types of Social Justice

First, when we speak about social justice, it is important to recognize that conceptually there are different types of justice: distributive, legal, and commutative. The types are based on the social contract tradition that has prevailed among political philosophers from Hobbes, Locke, Kant, and Rousseau to John Rawls and Robert Nozick. The three types of justice are illustrated in Figure 3.2. When looking at the contract involving what society owes the person, we are talking about the type of justice called distributive justice. When looking at the contract involving what the person owes to society, we are talking about the type of justice called legal justice. When we look at the contract between persons—what we owe each other—we are talking about the type of justice categorized as commutative justice.

Distributive Justice as an Organizing Framework for Social Work

Although social work is concerned about all three types of social justice, Wakefield (1988) argues that the organizing value of social work is distributive justice and that Rawls's particular perspective (described later in this section) on distributive justice provides the most coherent framework for our profession. Distributive justice has particular relevance for the professional role of advocating for social and economic justice. The following definition of justice for social work, proposed by Beverly and McSweeney (1987), emphasizes its distributive quality:

> Justice . . . means fairness in the relationships between people as these relate to the possession and/or acquisition of resources based on some kind of valid claim to a share of those resources. . . . [T]he justice or injustice of a particular policy or situation is determined by looking at the fairness of the distribution of resources in relation to the claims or demands made for those resources. (p. 5)

For social workers, the distribution of goods other than political or economic resources, such as health services, education, and leisure, is within the realm of social justice. To begin thinking about distributive justice, do the exercise in Tools for Student Learning 3.2.

TOOLS FOR STUDENT LEARNING 3.2

A *Beginning Exercise*

These statistics were taken from Quadrini, V. and Rios-Rull, J.-V. (1997, Spring). Understanding the U.S. Distribution of Wealth. Federal Reserve Bank of Minneapolis Quarterly Review, 21(2), 22–36.

Read the following statistics and then reflect on the questions that follow. It is suggested that you write your reactions on paper before engaging in classroom discussion.

Imagine a society in which the top .5 percent of the population owned 55 percent of the wealth and the top 10 percent owned 80 percent of the wealth while 80 percent of the population scrambled over the remaining 20 percent of the wealth.[1]

1. Is such disparity just or unjust?

2. Can you think of any situation or condition in which this kind of disparity might be just?

3. What principles would be used to conclude that such disparities are, in fact, just?

Whereas most social workers would jump to the quick conclusion that the disparities given in the exercise are definitely unjust, others might consider that their justness or unjustness could depend on certain qualifying conditions, and still others might even say that they are actually just. How do we account for such differences of perspectives, even among social workers? The following brief overview of four theories of distributive justice will illustrate how each would judge the justness of disparities in wealth differently. The first three perspectives—utilitarian, libertarian, and egalitarian—are *prescriptive*, not descriptive; that is, they present a case for what social justice *should* be or how each theorist would want us to define social justice. They do not describe the situation as it is now; that is, they do not discuss what the state of our society and the world is in relation to achieving any semblance of social justice as they define it. The fourth theory, called

FIGURE 3.3 *Distribution of Goods Based on Utilitarian Justice*

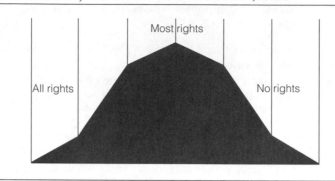

the racial contract, is critical to understanding social work's role of promoting social and economic justice. The racial contract perspective of distributive justice is *descriptive*, in that it explains the inequities of the actual social contract, and normative, in that analysis of the way things actually are is used normatively to point to reform.

Utilitarian Perspective. The major proponent of the utilitarian theory was John Stuart Mill (1863, as reprinted in Sterba, 1992). The key question from the utilitarian perspective is "What distribution of goods, what principles of justice, what ascription of rights are such that their acceptance is in the general interest?" Justice is arrived at by weighing the relative benefits and harms of a situation or condition and determining what maximizes the greatest good for the greatest number of people.

So, from a utilitarian perspective, it may be determined that social justice exists even if some people have no rights met while others have all their rights met as long as it is determined that it is for the common good. Utilitarian justice would tend to produce a distribution of goods and services similar to a Bell curve (Figure 3.3).

The "common good," however, is open to varied definitions, and the definition determines whether one believes a situation is just or not. For example, some people believe that it would not serve the common good if some people are provided for when they can provide for themselves; on the other hand, others argue that when some people are not provided for, the common good is not served because there may be unrest or because it harms us morally as individuals and as a society.

Libertarian Perspective. In contrast to the utilitarian perspective, the libertarian position advanced by Robert Nozick (1974) is based on the principle that the distribution of resources occurs by means of a natural and social lottery. Thus, this theory is considered to be basically amoral and based on a description of the social contract as it occurs naturally. According to the libertarian perspective, people hold certain rights by entitlement, and justice consists in the widest possible latitude of freedom from coercion in what they accumulate and what they dispose of and when. From this perspective, it is good to give to others, and charity is considered a virtue. However, in a just society each person has total freedom to determine how much, to whom, and when to give. No institution or person should interfere with that freedom.

When a segment of the population appears to be unjustly treated and lacking in access to goods and services, the libertarian perspective argues that we are only looking at one slice of history and that the long-term historical picture would reveal that that same population, at another point in time, may have occupied a privileged position. In other words, the natural social lottery is at work, and there is an inherent justice to it over the long term.

Egalitarian Perspective. Egalitarianism, developed by John Rawls (1971) and based on Locke's theory of the social contract, maintains that designing a just society needs to be done under a veil of ignorance—that is, with the sense that none of us would know in advance what our position in that society would be, and thus we would all have a stake in avoiding extreme inequalities at the outset.

Rawls developed two egalitarian principles upon which a just society would be based. His principles rule out justifying inequalities in order to achieve a greater common good (utilitarianism) or to maintain individual freedom (libertarianism). The first principle requires that basic liberties must be equal because citizens of a just society have the same basic rights to freedom, to fair equality of opportunity, to access to goods and services, and to self-respect. The second principle asserts that although the distribution of income and wealth need not be *equal*, any inequalities in power, wealth, and other resources must not exist *unless* they work to the absolute benefit of the worst-off members of society.

Thus, from an egalitarian perspective, in contrast to the libertarian view, redistribution of resources is a moral obligation. The unmet needs that should be redressed first are those of the least-well-off people. This means that, in order to provide genuine equality of opportunity, society must give more attention to those with fewer native assets and to those born into the less favorable social positions. According to egalitarian principles, then, greater resources might be spent, for example, on the education of the less- rather than the more-intelligent students in our schools, at least in the earlier years, in order to ensure equality of opportunity in life.

The Racial Contract. Although the three contemporary distributive justice theories discussed so far serve as useful tools for social work, they have serious limitations in terms of explaining why certain groups of people consistently get less justice, and they do not explain the phenomenon of oppression. *The Racial Contract* (Mills, 1997) is a perspective that provides a way of making a connection between contemporary mainstream theories and the injustices prevalent in our society and the world. The racial contract perspective is based on the social contract tradition, as are the others. However, Mills' viewpoint is different in that he sees the notion of the social contract as being the basis of Western democratic societies as, in fact, a myth. He contends that the real basis of Western societies is a "racial contract." The basic difference between Mills' perspective of social justice and the other perspectives is that the peculiar social contract to which Mills refers is not a contract between everybody (as in "we the people"), but between just the people who count, the people who really are people (i.e., were considered to be fully human when the United States was founded—"we the White people").

Utilitarians, libertarians, and egalitarians use the social contract as a normative tool—to present an *ideal* social contract that explains how a just society *would* be formed, ruled by a moral government, and regulated by a defensible moral code. Mills' usage of the social contract is again different: he uses it not merely normatively but descriptively to explain the actual genesis of the society, how government functions, and people's moral psychology. The racial contract thus explains how an unjust, exploitative society, ruled by an oppressive government and regulated by an immoral code, came into existence.

According to this perspective, it is crucial to understand what the original and continuing social contract actually was and is, so that we can correct for it in constructing the ideal contract toward which social work can then strive. Mills points out that the social contract has always consisted of formal and informal agreements between the members of one subset of humans who are designated as White and are thus considered to be full persons. The remaining subset of humans who are designated as "non-White" and of a different and inferior moral status of subpersons are not a consenting party to the contract but are the objects rather than the subjects of the agreement. The moral and legal rules normally regulating the behavior of Whites in their dealings with one another do not apply in dealings with non-Whites or apply only in a qualified form. Mills' main point is that the general purpose of the social contract, as it has been and is, is always the differential privileging of Whites as a group with respect to non-Whites as a group. From the beginning, then, race is in no way an "afterthought" or a "deviation" from ostensibly raceless Western ideals of the social contract but rather a central shaping constituent of those ideals.

The racial contract makes a strong claim to being an actual historical fact as Mills describes specific subsidiary contracts designed for different modes of exploiting the resources and peoples of the rest of the world for Europe, including the expropriation contract (which granted Europeans dominion over all territories of the world, not by virtue of any conquest of them, but as a right acquired simply by "discovery"), the slavery contract, and the colonial contract.

The racial contract is a conceptual bridge between two areas now largely segregated from each other. On the one hand, there is the world of mainstream philosophy (including the utilitarian, libertarian, and egalitarian theories of social justice) that focuses discussions of justice and rights in the abstract. On the other hand, there is the world of First Nations Peoples, African Americans, and political thought of the global South that has historically focused on issues of conquest, imperialism, colonialism, race and racism, slavery, jim crow, reparations, apartheid, Afrocentrism, and so on.

In order to endorse or emulate an *ideal* social contract, the *nonideal* contract as it exists needs to be demystified and condemned. So, the point of analyzing the injustices as they exist both historically and in the present—predominantly along race and gender lines—is to explain and expose the inequities of the social contract as it actually is in order to see through the theories and moral justifications offered in defense of them. Just as Mills provides a framework for analyzing the social contract related to race, Carole Pateman's (1988) book, *The Sexual Contract*, provides a similar analysis of how the social contract has been based on gender. The point is that analysis of the way things *are* does normative work for us by enabling us to understand the social contract's actual history and how its values and concepts have functioned to rationalize oppression, in order to reform them.

Differing Perspectives and Social Work. Differing popular perspectives exist about what social justice is or should be. So, when we say that social workers need to see social problems and individual troubles through a social justice lens, it is important to recognize that there are different lenses that provide differing views on what is just. It is often proposed that the egalitarian theory of justice is closest to traditional values and ethics of social work. Wakefield (1988) supports that view by arguing that "social work strives to ensure that no person is deprived of a fair minimum level of those basic social goods to which everyone is entitled," and supports Rawls's inclusion of self-respect in the list of social goods (p. 187). Yet, there is some empirical evidence that social workers, perhaps holding to egalitarian principles as the ideal, may tend to operate from a utilitarian perspective (Conrad, 1988; Reisch & Taylor, 1983). Terms such as *cost-benefit analysis* and "triage" strategies related to managed care realities might point to a utilitarian approach in practice. The racial contract perspective provides a conceptual tool for the integration of diversity, social and economic justice, and the impact of oppression.

The social work profession continues to struggle with the following questions: Which perspectives are compatible with what social work is about? Which justice principles should be adopted to provide guidance for our profession? The combination of the racial contract and the egalitarian perspective merits serious consideration for the profession. Whereas the racial contract explains and describes injustice, the egalitarian perspective can point the way for reform.

SOCIAL JUSTICE AND OPPRESSION: MAKING THE CONNECTIONS

The social justice theories briefly described in the previous section provide a foundation for understanding the complexity of our notions about what social justice *is* and what social justice *should be*. Analysis of notions about social justice point to their race- and gender-based nature. The questions posed about social justice at the beginning of this chapter were, "Is life fair?" "Is life just?" In this section, we turn to the related question: Justice and fairness . . . for whom? As we examine the meaning of social justice for the profession and social workers struggle to promote social and economic justice in everyday practice, it is important to analyze the differing views and make explicit the connections between these concepts and oppression. We now turn to a discussion of those connections.

Who Is Entitled to Justice? The Concept of Moral Exclusion

At the beginning of this chapter, some exercises were suggested to promote self-reflection and examination of our personal beliefs about social justice and a critical assessment of them within the context of contemporary theories. Grounded in the notion of racial (and sexual) exclusion as the basis of Western society's social contract, we can now look at how we also have beliefs about which people should be treated justly. The concept of moral exclusion (Opotow, 1990) provides a useful framework for understanding personal beliefs in relation to different groups in society.

Moral exclusion occurs when persons or groups are perceived as being outside the boundary in which values, rules, and considerations of fairness apply—that is, outside the boundaries of social justice. Persons outside our moral boundaries appear expendable or undeserving, and thus harming them appears acceptable, appropriate, or just. The process of categorizing groups negatively and excluding them from the realm of acceptable norms or values is linked to stereotypes and prejudicial attitudes related to ethnocentrism. It is linked to the notion that the social contract has always been and is an exclusionary one.

Although seldom conscious of them, we all have beliefs about which people should be treated justly, and the broadness or narrowness of our moral boundaries is influenced by prevailing cultural norms (e.g., it is no longer considered acceptable in the United States to own people as slaves or to make interracial marriages illegal, but it is generally considered acceptable to exclude gay men and lesbians from certain benefits such as partner benefits and the right to marry).

The exclusion of an out-group from the norms of fairness is a cognitive, affective, and behavioral phenomenon that enables otherwise considerate people to engage in self-serving behavior or inaction in everyday situations in order to gain benefits to themselves even though at injurious costs to others. We live in a world where certain groups of people benefit from an implicit and explicit contract that disadvantages other groups. At the same time, most people who benefit from the contract do not think about it or, if they do think about it, consider it to be just the way things are rather than as the outcome of a history of political oppression (Mills, 1997).

The concept of moral exclusion provides a tool for making obvious one's own personal processes of excluding certain people from the boundaries of fairness. A considerable body of research exists on moral exclusion, disengagement practices that make it possible to justify exclusion, and antidotes to exclusion. Analyzing one's own moral boundaries within the context of oppression theory, along with research evidence of antidotes to marginalization, suggest strategies for change.

Oppression and Its Common Elements

The racial contract perspective reveals that some people are seen as expendable or undeserving and are thus excluded from the realm of social justice. The process of categorizing groups negatively, and thus justifying their exclusion, is linked to stereotypes and prejudicial attitudes related to ethnocentrism. The result is a condition of oppression, which is defined as a situation in which one segment of the population acts to prevent another segment of the population from attaining access to resources or that acts to inhibit or make them *less than* in some way in order to dominate them (Bulhan, 1985).

Persons who have been and are excluded from the realm of the norms and values of social justice include people of color; women; gay, lesbian, bisexual, and transgendered persons; elderly people; and people with disabilities. Although the conditions and manifestations of oppression may vary, as well as each person's unique experiences of its effects, common elements characterize all oppression. The definition in the previous paragraph, for example, is one that fits all oppressions. In addition, the condition of oppression always involves power and advantage, which are granted to certain people and denied to others based on the notion of the "other" that is different from what is considered to be the *norm*. The defined norm (White, male, heterosexual) is the standard of *rightness* wherein all others are judged in relation to it. The "other" is not only different from the norm, however; the "other" is also believed to be inferior and deviant, which justifies advantage for those who fit the norm and disadvantage for the "other."

Power is an essential factor in all oppression. Racism, sexism, and heterosexism are not personal prejudices based on stereotypes; they include social and economic power as an essential part of the equation that makes the difference between talking about prejudices and discrimination (which we all engage in) and a *system* of advantage that confers economic, social, judicial, and political power on people who fit the "norm." To understand oppression, we can look at indicators in any of those areas. For example, in the political arena, how many senators are black, women, or openly homosexual?

Another common element of oppression is that all oppressions are held in place by ideology and the use or threat of violence. The ideology on which Mills (1997) contends that the racial oppression is based is that of racial superiority (i.e., White supremacy); the ideology on which sexual oppression is based is that of gender superiority; and the basis for homosexual oppression is an ideology of heterosexual superiority and morality. With an ideology of superiority as its foundation, violence is used to enforce and maintain all oppressions. The violence may be physical and direct (lynching, rape and battering, gay bashing), or it may be personal and psychological, such as name calling. It may be indirect, or it may be institutionalized and characterized by indicators such as differential poverty rates, the predominance of men of color in the criminal justice system and on death row, and the reality of police brutality.

Another element that is common to all oppressions is that they are *institutionalized*, which means that racism, sexism, and heterosexism are built into the norms, traditions, laws, and policies of a society so that even those who have nonracist, nonsexist, and nonheterosexist beliefs are compelled to act otherwise. Institutionalized racism ensures that Whites, males, and heterosexuals benefit regardless of the intentions of individuals in those institutions. Pinderhughes (1989) writes about how institutional racism ensures that Whites benefit *and* exonerates them from responsibility while at the same time blaming people of color. She points out that there is considerable resistance against comprehending the institutional aspect of racism and that the process of understanding its systemic nature can be very painful, especially for Whites who have seen themselves as different from Whites whom they view as racists. She further writes about how it is particularly devastating for White people who have been involved in civil rights activities to face the implication that they, along with other Whites, could be the beneficiaries of racism. There is a sense of injury that stems not only from recognition of themselves as trapped in the systemic process of racism that benefits them and exploits people of color but also from the realization that, although for many people of color this reality has been obvious, for them it has heretofore been obscure.

Implications for Social Workers

If the mission of social work is truly to promote social and economic justice, we must translate that commitment into culturally relevant and nonoppressive social work practice. Social workers need to do their own work in relation to understanding their own boundaries of moral exclusion and developing a stance of inclusion, in which all people are entitled to the same values, rules, and considerations of fairness. Further, social workers need to understand the elements of oppression and how they operate and translate that understanding into antioppression practice. Van Voorhis (1998) suggests that practitioners need to integrate the following elements into their direct practice with clients: knowledge about oppression; self-awareness and acceptance of one's own multiple identities and position in relation to power and privilege; knowledge about the psychosocial effects of oppression for people in all marginalized groups; and skills in listening to clients' stories, assessing the psychosocial effects of oppression on clients, intervening to enhance identity and change oppressive social conditions, and evaluating practice interventions by monitoring client progress related to empowerment outcomes.

HUMAN RIGHTS AND OPPRESSION: MAKING GLOBAL CONNECTIONS

The NASW Code of Ethics (1996a) mandates that social workers promote social and economic justice not only in the United States but globally. In Ethical Standard 6, the Code clearly states that "social workers should promote the general welfare of society, from local to global levels, and the development of people, their communities, and their environments" (Standard 6.01) and, further, that "social workers should promote conditions that encourage respect for cultural and social diversity within the United States and globally" (Standard 6.04c).

Social work as a profession is grounded on humanitarian and democratic ideals with a focus on meeting human needs and developing human potential and resources. This focus on human needs shapes a professional conviction that the fundamental nature of these needs means that their being met is not a matter of choice but an imperative of basic justice. This imperative of basic justice applies to all humanity. A 1992 United Nations publication, *Teaching and Learning about Human Rights: A Manual for Schools of Social Work and the Social Work Profession*, moves the discussion of diversity and social justice to a consideration of human rights as the organizing principle for professional practice (p. 9). A transition from an orientation of meeting human needs to one of affirming human rights is necessary because substantive needs must be met. Thus, the idea of human rights has become a powerful social construct to fulfill human needs (Wronka, 1998). In this section, the discussion revolves around the connections between affirming human rights and promoting social and economic justice from a global perspective.

What Rights Are Human Rights?

The United Nations (1987) defines human rights as those rights that are inherent in our nature and without which we cannot live as human beings. Human rights are basic for a life in which the inherent dignity and work of each person receives respect and protection. Human rights are universal and apply to every person without discrimination. Three generations of human rights are set forth in the Universal Declaration of Human Rights, which was adopted and proclaimed by the United Nations General Assembly in December 1948. The first generation, labeled "negative rights," represents civil and political rights as set forth in articles 2–21. These are rights devised to ensure freedom from any curtailment of individual liberty. The second generation, labeled "positive rights," is aimed at ensuring social justice, freedom from want, and participation in the social, economic, and cultural aspects of life as set forth in articles 22–27 of the Declaration. The third, "collective rights" (article 28), sets forth that everyone is entitled to a social and international order in which the rights and freedoms set forth in the Declaration can be fully realized. The Universal Declaration of Human Rights, with its three generations, combines the antioppression social work imperative with its calling to promote social and economic justice. In an increasingly interdependent world, recognition of the interdependence of the three human rights generations is increasing, and the struggle for social and economic justice is being seen as one of international solidarity. The 1992 United Nations manual for social workers advises the following:

> The evolution from a defensive stand against oppression to an affirmation of the right to satisfaction of material and non-material human needs and equitable participation in the production and distribution of resources is the logical outcome of an increasing socio-political consciousness and economic development mainly, but not exclusively, in industrialized nations. In developing countries the sheer proportion of need, and possibly of exploitation, lead to the collective vision of the right to social and economic development beyond the personal level to the national and regional levels, with a system of international solidarity for development as its ultimate aim. (p. 6)

Social Work and Human Rights

The social work profession's focus on substantive human needs that must be met is inseparable from the search for and realization of positive rights and entitlements. Working within different political systems, social workers around the globe uphold and defend the rights of their clients while attempting to meet their needs. Because social workers are often employed as agents of powerful institutions or agencies, many are placed in a precarious role due to their duty to be a loyal employee and their duty to serve their clients. Culturally competent social workers, as they strive to eliminate oppression and promote social justice, are often required

> [T]o mediate between the people and state and other authorities, to champion particular causes, and to provide protection when state action for the public good threatens the rights and freedoms of particular persons or groups. . . . [A]s a bridging profession, social work has to be conscious of its values and possess a solid knowledge base, not least in the field of human rights, to guide it in many conflicting situations throughout its practice. While social workers through their actions may well reinforce the rights of clients, faulty judgment can lead them to jeopardize those rights. Viewing its work from a global human rights perspective helps the profession by providing a sense of unity and solidarity, without losing sight of the local perspectives, conditions and needs which constitute the framework within which social workers operate. (United Nations, 1992, p. 9)

Human rights are inseparable from social work theory, values and ethics, and practice. They are inseparable from culturally competent practice. Rights corresponding to human needs have to be upheld and fostered. Advocacy for such rights must therefore be an integral part of social work. In countries under authoritative regimes, such advocacy can have serious consequences for social work professionals.

The direct knowledge that social workers have of the conditions of vulnerable populations makes them more conscious than other professionals that their concerns are closely linked to respect for human rights. Social workers understand that the full realization of civil and political rights is not possible without enjoyment of economic, social, and cultural rights. And, in order to achieve lasting progress in the implementation of human rights, there must be effective national and international policies of economic and social development.

The Global Context in Which Social Workers Advocate for Human Rights and Social Justice

The United Nations (1992) manual for social workers emphasizes that human rights and social work have to be considered within the context faced by the majority of people in the world. The manual offers the following poignant contextual conditions (pp. 10–11):

- It is estimated that in the 1980s alone, more human beings lost their lives as a result of economic and social deprivation than those who perished in World War II.
- Countless people have been killed and tortured or have disappeared in a world subjected to domination and oppression. Exploitative and oppressive systems and structures give rise to dictatorships and authoritarian regimes under which millions become victims of human rights violations as the price of their struggle for freedom and survival.
- Each day, 40,000 children die from malnutrition and diseases including AIDS, lack of clean water, and inadequate sanitation.[2]
- Of a population of about 6 billion, 900 million adults are illiterate, 10 million are homeless, and 15 million are refugees. Of the 15 million refugees, at least 75 percent are women and children. In some developing countries, women and children constitute 90 percent of the refugee population.[3]
- Women are prominent in the statistics of poverty and deprivation. Two-thirds of the world's illiterate people are women.[4] Maternal mortality rates are high in most developing countries. An African woman, for example, has 1 chance in 21 of dying in childbirth; an Asian woman, 1 chance in 51; and a South American woman, 1 chance in 73. In contrast, a North American woman has 1 chance in over 6,000.[5]
- The crisis is deepening. Military spending is about 15 percent of gross national product in industrial as well as developing countries. In the early 1990s, the World Bank estimated that the staggering debt burden of the developing countries (including the debts of Eastern Europe) amounting to $1.3 trillion was estimated to increase substantially in the near future.[6]

Hope exists for improvement in the implementation of the human rights instruments that guide global human rights and an ever-growing international consciousness and solidarity. Social workers have a role to play in strengthening such solidarity and ensuring that the principles preserved in the international human rights instruments are "gradually translated into reality, paving the way for a world in which people's most urgent and legitimate needs are satisfied" (United Nations, 1992, p. 11).

It has been argued that social work has been a human rights profession from its conception due to its basic tenet that every human being has intrinsic value and its mission to promote equitable social structures. Yet, the International Federation of Social Workers and the International Association of Schools of Social Work believe that greater knowledge and understanding of human rights is needed to improve the actions and interventions of social work professionals in advancing social and economic justice and eliminating oppression. As these two bodies state:

[S]ocial workers work with their clients on a variety of levels: the micro level of individual and family; the meso level of community; and the macro level of society—nationally and internationally. Concern for human rights must be manifested by social workers at all levels and at all times. (United Nations, 1992, p. 3)

The following short summary of the basic instruments concerning human rights, with the dates of adoption by the United Nations General Assembly, illustrates the connection between culturally competent social work practice and its requisite commitment to promote social justice and human rights.[7] Social workers need to become familiar with the documents and the specialized agencies, United Nations bodies, and mechanisms for implementing the human rights mandates.

Instruments Providing General Protection:
- The Universal Declaration of Human Rights (1948)
- The Covenants on Human Rights (1966)
- The International Covenant on Civil and Political Rights
- Right to life, liberty, and security
- Right not to be subjected to torture and cruel, inhuman, or degrading treatment or punishment
- Prohibition of slavery
- Right not to be arbitrarily detained
- Rights to freedom of expression, religion, assembly, and association, including trade union membership
- Right to freedom of movement and residence
- Right to vote through universal suffrage
- Right to a fair trial
- Rights of minorities to protection
- The International Covenant on Economic, Social, and Cultural Rights
- Right to work
- Right to social security
- Right to protection of the family
- Right to an adequate standard of living
- Right to education
- Right to health
- Right to join trade unions

Instruments Providing Particular Protection
- International Convention on the Elimination of All Forms of Racial Discrimination (1965)
- Convention on the Elimination of All Forms of Discrimination against Women (1979)
- Convention against Torture and Other Cruel, Inhuman, and Degrading Treatment or Punishment (1987)
- Convention on the Rights of the Child (1989)
- International Convention on the Protection of the Rights of All Migrant Workers and Members of Their Families (1990)

Rules Regarding Detention and Treatment of Offenders
- Standard Minimum Rules for the Treatment of Prisoners (1955)
- Principles of Medical Ethics (1982)
- Standard Minimum Rules for the Administration of Juvenile Justice (1985)

Other Human Rights Instruments
- Declaration on the Rights of Mentally Retarded Persons (1971)
- Declaration on the Protection of Women and Children in Armed Conflicts (1974)
- Declaration on the Elimination of All Forms of Religious Intolerance (1981)
- Declaration on the Right to Development (1986)

BECOMING EMPOWERED TO UNDERSTAND AND PRACTICE CHANGE STRATEGIES AND SKILLS

In order to fulfill our mission of promoting social and economic justice, eliminating oppression, and promoting human rights, we must translate the knowledge and understanding we gain about injustice into effective strategies for social change. Empowerment theory and the empowerment process help in our work with clients who have been marginalized and excluded from the boundaries of fairness and justice. Social workers also need to engage in an empowerment journey for themselves. Thus, this section discusses the issue of empowering ourselves for social justice advocacy.

Empowerment Process[8]

Dictionary definitions of *empowerment* include phrases such as "to give power or authority to," "to authorize," "to enable or permit," and "to license." When social workers become empowered to advocate for social justice, they affirm the authority that already belongs to them as human beings and as citizens. This power is both internal, in terms of how they experience their own efficacy, and external, in terms of the power they have to persuade others in interpersonal encounters and relationships. This power enables them to protest injustice and to seek alternatives to oppression at the levels of organization, community, country, and world.

Empowerment is a process of discovering within ourselves and in others the capacity to bring about change. Empowerment means accepting personal responsibility to act. As social workers realize their power, they become free to transform themselves and to discover untapped strengths. Their individual actions of protest and creativity create a ripple effect that empowers others. At the heart of the empowerment process is the phenomenon of helping someone to see something that he or she has not seen before and, subsequently, to act upon that insight. It is a power to help others see new things as possible.

In the model proposed in this section, social workers are encouraged to see the empowerment process as beginning with the smallest of individual actions. When joined with others, these efforts create a chain reaction that releases human energy. Over time, this energy can build to become a critical mass that results in social change. Each person's awareness and actions will increase the likelihood that a critical mass will accumulate and that ultimately change will take place.

Creating a just society and world is a global issue of overwhelming proportion. A transformation from injustice and oppression to just alternatives will not come about easily or quickly. Giving birth to social justice will be a long and painful process. It requires personal commitment and social transformation on a massive scale. Despite the magnitude of the problem, if social change for social justice is to take place, it will grow from the grassroots—at the level of the individual, the small group, local organizations, and communities. By starting at this level, the empowerment process provides a bridge that connects the person and the smaller group with the larger social change movement. This bridge becomes a vehicle for change as students join with others in crossing over to yet uncharted terrain. If we trust the process, empowerment will provide the energy needed for creating a just society.

Personal Transformation and Connections

In the 1980s it became clear that if social movements were to grow, organizations needed to focus on the individual. Individual needs must be met if the larger cause is to flourish. In *The Aquarian Conspiracy*, Marilyn Ferguson (1980) describes how social activism stems from personal transformation. In the empowerment process, first steps toward such personal transformation take place when social workers acknowledge their deep feelings about injustice and oppression and the role they play as privileged or oppressed based on their social identities. Personal connections are critical, and they can be painful. However, once we begin to accept feelings of shame, guilt, anger, and other feelings of distress as normal human reactions to the horrors of injustice, we can become free to see ways in which we are all personally connected to the issue.

Personal connections can be many and varied. Awareness and acknowledgment of their own feelings about racism in the United States begins the change process for many people, who may begin to feel personally involved with racism in a variety of ways. Perhaps the most basic connection comes from personal fears about being victimized by racism and other forms of oppression. For those who have benefited from an oppressive system based on race, concerns about being viewed as a racist can cause some people to take action. Although some of those actions might take the form of defensiveness and attempts to prove they are not racist, connecting with the issue of racism in such a personal way opens the door to exploring new ways of thinking. Some people become enraged when they learn about historical events of which they had previously been unaware, and they make new connections through those feelings of anger at not having been taught all aspects of their country's history. Some become outraged at the lack of vital human service programs for certain populations in the United States. Others make a connection to the issue of social justice in a more direct, political way through an analysis of how economic and political interests operate to ensure inequities. Some people begin to question laws that sanction and create oppressive conditions and realize that horrors can be unleashed legally as, for example, when slavery in the United States was legal. They realize that everything done by the Nazis in Germany, based on creating a superior race, was done legally and with the approval of citizens and the establishment. Such questioning compels some people to begin to respond to higher principles. Some people feel a deep sense of commitment based on a moral or philosophical principle regarding the value of human life, a perspective that transcends traditional differences between people based on race, ethnicity, religion, and so on.

Educating ourselves about cultural diversity for social justice calls upon us to look within to identify connections such as those described earlier. By making connections between injustice and oppression and our personal lives, we begin to consider ways to respond. Thus, the empowerment process starts with where each of us is at on the issues and the personal connections that create feelings of conflict and distress.

During the process of exploring diversity and oppression, some people make a profoundly personal connection when they discover a gap between what they want to see in themselves and what they actually find in themselves. We may experience a loss of or threat to self-respect and question the self-image we want to hold as we struggle to come to terms with effects that privilege and oppression have had in our own lives (Pinderhughes, 1989). Marris (1974) proposes that such a sense of loss is triggered by a "discrediting of familiar assumptions" that creates a "crisis of discontinuity" (p. 21). Thus, learning about social justice and injustice often involves a process similar to the grieving process. By understanding the grieving process and appreciating it as a normal response, we can support and validate each person's personal journey toward change. The following discussion demonstrates how the process of transformative learning to become social change advocates relates to issues of loss and grief.

The Grieving Cycle

As we begin to share our experiences and reactions to injustice and oppression, we may experience a process that is similar to the grieving cycle described by Elisabeth Kubler-Ross (1975) and others in relation to death and other losses. The following summaries of the five stages of grieving contain examples of how each may be experienced in relation to racism and other forms of oppression.

1. Denial.　Although many social workers believe there is injustice in the United States and the world, they deal with their feelings by denying that a problem exists at this stage of the process. This protects them from making personal connections that thus do not need to be felt. It is a state of "psychic numbness." In this state, we are protected against a feeling of being out of control and against feeling responsible. The denial stage helps cushion the impact of the horrors of injustice and oppression under which we all live. We are resistant to information about injustice. Our response is automatic and unemotional. For example, upon hearing about racism as an institutionalized phenomenon, some people may experience confusion and be incapable of comprehending what that means. They may consider such ideas to be propaganda. There is a desire to hold on to a belief that the world as they perceive it is a just place and to maintain faith in our "experts" and leaders to uphold justice.

2. Anger/Rage.　In reaction to loss—whether it is loss of innocence, of belief that the world is just, or of self-image—denial is often followed by anger or rage. At this stage, we react with intense feelings, for instance, as we share stories about a racial profiling incident, a hate crime, an innocent black man living on death row for decades before his innocence is proved, or any number of stories of oppression. As one social worker expressed:

> I am angry when I realize that I have always lived in a racist and sexist society and that everyone lied to me about it. . . . I am furious when I discover that our country was founded on violence, slavery, and annihilation of indigenous people when I have always been taught that

it was founded on truth and justice. . . . I am angry when I consider that some people are considered to be expendable by the powers that be.

A student of color in a social work class expressed his anger when he wrote:

I could strangle some of the privileged white students in this program and in this class! They don't *know* about police brutality? What in the world do they think slavery was about? Are they stupid or do they just choose to put their heads in the sand? I am so sick of hearing them be shocked about injustice that I want to scream!

This stage of the grieving cycle is perhaps the most uncomfortable for many, especially those of us who have been taught that it is not polite to be angry and who may cringe at the expression of anger by others.

3. Bargaining. In the bargaining stage, we may be aware of the seriousness of injustice and oppression and at the same time try to protect ourselves from understanding the full impact on both ourselves and other people. A desire to strike a bargain to minimize pain and sense of responsibility might be expressed in words such as the following:

I understand that the world is unjust and that there is work to do. Yet, it is important that we understand that things are not anywhere near as serious now as they used to be. We no longer enslave people, for example, and everyone has the right to vote. While there are still problems with some people accessing what they need, there are laws that now protect people from unfair and unequal treatment.

4. Depression. The magnitude and ramifications of oppression, when truly faced directly, can be so overwhelming that thinking about it can produce feelings of extreme helplessness and even despair. Social workers sometimes describe their dismay at recognizing the disparity between personal anguish over the realities of oppression and injustice and the social reality of "business as usual." Some people express feelings of self-blame, suggesting that it is they who are insane and overreacting rather than society perpetuating and allowing such injustices. When we begin to experience such feelings, we often retreat to a state of denial in which we may refuse to acknowledge the problems and resist becoming involved in change actions.

Apathy characterizes the depression stage of the grieving cycle. Social workers who observe the consequences of oppression on a regular basis may report withdrawal symptoms and feel that they have no energy left to hear anything else about injustice. They feel hopeless, helpless, and alone. It is a state of despair. Optimism vanishes, and all that remains are pain, separation between all human beings, and ignorance and prejudice. There is little or no hope for changing conditions.

5. Acceptance and Reorganization. At this stage, social workers refuse to accept the inevitability of injustice. Instead, they accept responsibility to act and are able to reorganize their behavior and purposefully work toward finding solutions. They have an increased awareness of reality. They are empowered to bring about change. They have hope in the possibility of change.

The grieving cycle, as described here, can provide a useful guide for understanding what we may go through as we face the realities of racism, injustice, and oppression.

The cycle is not absolute—not everyone goes through every stage in the exact sequence or at the same predictable pace. Yet the model can help us comprehend our own feelings and behavior and those of others. It is important to also recognize that the cycle, as applied to our reactions to learning about cultural diversity and oppression, differs from other types of grieving in that we cannot foresee a final resolution of the problem, nor of our grieving, in the immediate future. As long as problems of injustice are ongoing, we may find ourselves repeating stages. In other words, the feelings of denial, apathy, despair, anger, and helplessness may return when we learn of a new situation of injustice. Social workers need to be prepared for that eventuality and to understand that, although feelings of grief can be overwhelming at times, hope cannot be bought with a refusal to feel.

The empowerment process helps us to accept the fact that experiencing the feelings in the grieving cycle is a sane reaction to facing the realities of an unjust world. It helps us to know that we are not alone in our feelings. Whether in the classroom or in a social service agency, social workers can help each other by acknowledging their mutual feelings and by talking about the problems. It is important to discover that we are all in this together. The fact that our situation is a collective one, bearing on us all, albeit in different ways depending on the status conferred by our social identities, has tremendous implications. It means that in facing oppression together, openly and deeply, people can rediscover their interconnectedness in the web of life, and this brings personal power and resilience (Macy, 1983).

The Necessity of Actions

Actions give social workers the energy to work through the grieving cycle. Callahan (1982) writes about the effectiveness of actions:

> New and different actions can change thought and feeling just as new and different thoughts can change behavior. Taking even one small step on a journey changes one's perspective on the landscape, as well as changing one's self definition to that of a person who is able to move out toward new goals. Action, either practical or symbolic, overcomes the learned helplessness, inertia and apathy correlated with the absence of hope. (p. 1)

By taking action, commitment to effecting change is strengthened, and so are the chances for making social change possible.

Actions become the steps on the empowerment journey. Often the first steps are the most difficult. To act in response to social injustice is an evolutionary process. What we are able to do today may be radically different from what we may be doing next month or next year. It is important to learn that small steps lead to larger actions in a natural progression. As a first step, we may think more about racism and other forms of oppression and begin to talk about it with our families, friends, and others in our immediate circles. Gradually, we may move to reading more about the subject on our own, to speaking out at public gatherings, to writing letters, to educating others, to wearing a button, to circulating and signing petitions, to lobbying our political representatives, to advocating for agency policy changes, to peaceful demonstrations, to organizing actions with others. It is important that all efforts are acknowledged, including the smallest effort, because social justice is accomplished by laying one brick at a time, taking one step at a time.

In order to be advocates for social justice, we can weave the issues into our daily lives and work. We can be most effective by bringing our advocacy work with us wherever we go—in our own families, neighborhoods, workplaces, social gatherings, and agencies. Everyone has a skill or talent that can be used in the empowerment process. By focusing on the present, asking ourselves what it is we do in our clients' daily lives, and then doing it for social justice, our lives are changed but not rearranged.

Each action becomes the impetus for growth. The more we do, the greater our desire to learn and to share what we have learned. Because we choose our actions, we can set our own limits and control our rate of change. In order to get started, all that is needed is a strong commitment to work for an end to racism and other forms of oppression and injustice. We learn from the examples of others. When we begin to act, our actions join with the actions of others to provide the energy for the journey.

Barriers to Change

Part of the process of change in this area involves looking at the barriers that keep us from being advocates for social justice. A common block for many is personal fear: of taking risks, of standing out by making a personal statement, of being embarrassed in public, of losing security or the respect of people they had thought were friends, of being alienated from family or friends or peers.

Social workers are often deterred from social justice advocacy actions by a fear of stepping outside their personal safety zones. We all have spheres of operation in which we feel safe. Stepping outside this area is risky, for when we confront issues in a public way, we may be subjected to the ridicule, misunderstanding, and anger of others. For example, interrupting a racist joke or challenging an oppressive agency policy can be a terrifying and thus courageous action to take when the response could quite possibly be ostracism from others for doing so. The empowerment process, however, generates confidence and courage. As we become more involved and are sustained by the support of others, we discover that our safety zones expand.

Another significant barrier for many is the fear of creating communication gaps, tensions, and conflict within our own agencies if we identify the prejudice and discrimination within that system. Applying the process of empowerment to that of agency change can be helpful in this regard. Students can be encouraged to be sensitive to each person's attitude toward the issues. Unrealistic expectations about the others' responses usually increase the tension. Communicating consideration for others while respecting one's own stage of involvement can help reduce resistance to open discussion about the issues and help one stay in the struggle.

Some people speak quite honestly about another barrier: that of losing the privileges conferred on them based on their own social identities in an oppressive system. As one social work student wrote in his journal:

> I feel terrible about the inequities I am learning about and I want to work to change the system. I must admit, though, that I am quite ambivalent about what I might have to give up in terms of the privileges and benefits I currently get from the system as it is since I am a white, heterosexual male. It is easy to think theoretically about social justice but when I think in practical terms—like maybe I wouldn't get preferential treatment in a job application situation if there were truly equal opportunity—I am ashamed to say that I have to think twice.

We need to acknowledge the courage it takes to be honest about this and challenge each other to face our cognitive dissonance rather than slipping back into denial. Positive role models of people throughout history who were advocates for social justice can help in this regard as well.

Two additional barriers frequently impede progress in becoming social justice advocates: the fear of speaking out in public, and the fear of not being sufficiently informed. By encouraging small steps, the empowerment process can be used to overcome these fears.

Speaking out in public will seem less frightening if we first talk to those with whom we feel most comfortable. Then, when we are ready, we can begin to speak to other people in small groups and at public meetings. It can be very rewarding to find that acquaintances and even strangers are willing to talk about issues of racism, poverty, and oppression of other kinds. Often the message on a pin or button (e.g., "Stop Racism," "A Social Worker for Justice") will help begin a conversation. Speaking out is a natural outgrowth of increased commitment and involvement.

To reduce the fear of being uninformed, it is helpful to understand that we can never have enough information or remember all the facts. Statistics change, and one fact can counteract another. What is most important is an understanding of underlying concepts. If we develop a point of view as a framework for our own thinking, the facts will fall into place. A preponderance of information exists in books, articles, and videotapes. To make sense out of the facts, it is helpful to absorb only small amounts of information at one time and take time to process it. We will soon be surprised by how much we know.

Benefits of Empowerment

As advocates for social justice, social workers are enriched and strengthened by the friendships that are made with others who share common goals. We get to know and appreciate others whose backgrounds and lifestyles may be quite different from our own. People who work for social justice are old and young, rich and poor, religious and non-religious, heterosexual and homosexual and bisexual and transsexual, and come from a variety of cultural and ethnic backgrounds. Our strength grows as we celebrate this diversity and face our differences honestly. In the process, we learn to trust each other enough to live justly on a personal level.

Throughout the empowerment process, our actions become seeds that germinate best within a supportive environment. As the seeds grow, we discover that we have developed previously untapped strengths and talents. We find ourselves taking actions that we thought we could never take when the opportunity to act presented itself. Like wild-flowers, our actions spread, affecting those in the world around us. Thus, the circle continues to grow. As personal transformations become interwoven with social change, lives take on new meaning and deeper purpose.

What sustains us in our social justice advocacy work is the belief that our actions can and will make a difference. Although individual acts may seem insignificant, they have tremendous power when joined with the efforts of countless others. Historically, we know that social and political changes have always stemmed from the grassroots. The abolition of slavery, the right to unionize, women's rights, and civil rights, to name a few, all came about as a result of grassroots efforts. If social justice is to become a reality, a collective commitment to change must be made at the local level. As more and more people unite, we gain the strength to change both the world and ourselves.

> Actions are clearly effective when those involved in them experience their capabilities and their strength. That exciting feeling of empowerment is something that cannot be taken away. It becomes part of how we think about ourselves, as purposeful, effective people who can express ourselves clearly on an issue of vital importance.[9]

SOCIAL AND ECONOMIC JUSTICE VALUES AND PRINCIPLES TO GUIDE ACTIONS

Many problems that social workers encounter at the micro, meso, and macro levels stem from injustices that are grounded in an underlying crisis of values. Social workers need to ground their empowerment strategies and actions in values and principles that hold out hope for remedying such underlying crises of values. Psychosocial and economic explanations for problems social workers encounter need to be reinforced by an understanding of different and deeper dimensions and by understanding the interrelation of the personal and socioeconomic and value structures and processes. Possible actions aimed at promoting social and economic justice are many and as the empowerment model illustrates, all are important.

Values

Social workers are faced with complex decisions about which actions to take given each particular situation, and values provide a road map. In the NASW Code of Ethics (NASW, 1996a), the second of the six core values of social work is social justice. In order to guide their thinking, the following eight values are identified as being central to social workers' decision-making process as they determine how to promote social justice. They are intended to be illustrative rather than exhaustive.[10]

1. Life. Value for life is essential for all social and economic justice and human rights work. The worth of life, human and nonhuman existence, is the fountainhead for all other ideas and values that follow. Social workers are called to actively support positive and life-affirming aspects of all situations. Life is intrinsically connected and interdependent in all its parts and forms. Disruption of any aspect affects the social fabric or threatens life, thereby injuring humankind. Thus, value of life implies that suffering and death are not just individual phenomena but that they touch others. Physical health is an important aspect of the value and quality of life. Environmental deterioration, the water crisis including pollution, and the nonexistence and curtailment of health programs are some of the major life-threatening factors.

2. Freedom and Liberty. All human beings are born free and have the right to liberty. This presupposes that each human being has the freedom of choice in the conduct of his or her life. The enjoyment of this freedom is, however, frequently curtailed by material and other constraints. Freedom is likewise restricted by the principle of not infringing on the freedom of others. Yet, freedom, next to life itself, is viewed as the most precious human value, closely linked to human dignity and to the worth of human life. The quest for freedom and liberty has inspired many people to seek release from territorial or geographical domination. The quest for spiritual and intellectual freedom has inspired heroic acts of resistance. Social workers are often in the forefront of the struggle for freedom. In parts of the world where freedom does not exist, social workers pay a heavy price in oppression for pursuing their principles.

3. Equality and Nondiscrimination.   The fundamental principle of equality of all human beings is imperfectly applied in everyday life, not least in the manifold aspects of interpersonal relations. For social workers it is a crucial concept related to personal and professional attitudes. It is also the cornerstone for the all-important principle of justice, requiring serious consideration of just and unjust equality and inequality based on biological factors; on psychic, social, cultural, and spiritual needs; and on individual contributions to the welfare of others. Once the principle of equality is accepted, it becomes impossible to discriminate against any person or group of persons.

4. Justice.   Various aspects of justice have to be taken into consideration, including the legal, judicial, social, economic, and other aspects that constitute the basis by which a society upholds the dignity of its members and ensures the security and integrity of persons. Social workers have long promoted such principles and are conscious of the fact that human rights are best upheld by a law-abiding state. Impartiality in the administration of justice is an important tool to safeguard the rights of the vulnerable members of society who make up the majority of social work clients. The pursuit of justice, however, has wider implications that are less easily codified. Social justice encompasses satisfaction of basic human needs and the equitable sharing of material resources. It aims at universal access to fundamental services in health, education, equal opportunities at the start, protection for disadvantaged persons or groups, and a degree of moderation in the areas of retribution, consumption, and profit.

5. Solidarity.   This is a fundamental intrinsic value that implies not only understanding and empathy toward humankind's pain and suffering but also identifying and taking a stand with the sufferers and their cause. Social workers are expected not only to stand by people who are struggling but also to express their solidarity in words and in deeds in the face of any form of denial of people's political, civil, social, economic, cultural, and spiritual rights. The social work profession must identify itself with victims of violence, torture, expulsion, and curtailment of freedom anywhere in the world.

6. Social Responsibility.   This is action undertaken on behalf of sufferers and victims: standing for them, championing their cause, and helping them. Social responsibility is the implementation corollary of solidarity. The principle of social responsibility is crucial for a profession such as social work because service and commitment to the poor and the needy are its *raison d'être*.

7. Evolution, Peace, and Nonviolence.   The values mentioned so far are determining factors for the quality of interpersonal relations. Peace, as a distinct value, and not simply as the absence of organized conflict, is one additional value. It is to be nurtured and striven for, with the ultimate goal of achieving harmony with the self, with others, and with the environment. Although conflicts in human relations are unavoidable, ways to solve them can be either peaceful or violent, constructive or destructive. The revolutionary "raze all and build anew" approach has held fascination for people over the centuries, producing untold human suffering. An evolutionary approach is slower, often less immediately rewarding, but in the end longer-lasting and therefore more effective. It is an approach often chosen by social workers in relation to conflicts. Confrontation and resistance in the quest for freedom are not eschewed. Neither are justice and social justice. Violence is. Although the world is not ready to abandon the use of arms, and just causes for revolutions clearly exist, it should be recognized that arbitration and conciliation are effective tools to overcome seemingly irreconcilable differences provided they are practiced consistently and with respect, understanding, and knowledge.

8. Relations between Human Beings and Nature. Respect for other species and a quest for harmony with nature are more often permeating human consciousness in the 21st century. Environmental degradation cannot be ignored. The world economic order, faulty development models, inequality with regard to all resources, consumption patterns, and nuclear, industrial, and other pollution in industrialized as well as developing countries are recognized as causes of the earth's serious plight. Excessive consumerism and extreme poverty endanger nature as well as vulnerable groups of people through greed, lack of information, and need for survival. Comprehensive policies to halt and, where possible, repair damage to the environment need to be complemented by comprehensive environmental education programs and advocacy campaigns. Social workers have an important role to play in this process by linking with other groups.

Principles

Empowerment strategies and actions, grounded in the eight values set out previously, can be guided by the following five principles (NASW, 1996b, pp. 6–8).

Development. Community development is based on tapping into and building the integrity and leadership of the members of the community. Breaking the cycle of violence and injustice and promoting social and economic justice are development processes that local people must direct and ultimately sustain. No imported scheme can substitute for bottom-up ingenuity.

Participation. Participatory community development is needed to counter the powerlessness, isolation, and exclusion that is the result of oppression and injustice and that is often expressed through violence. Sustainable development must have the participation of community members. Successful participation calls for engaging people, unleashing their creativity, building their capacities, and giving them a sense of ownership.

Reciprocity. Successful development calls for an equitable relationship between "the givers of help" and "the recipients of help" and a blurring of who receives from whom. Assisting a community requires one to become involved with it, to learn from it, to be influenced and changed by it—in a sense, to join it. Homegrown strategies to address injustice must be retrieved and exchanged, and new methods must be devised to share learning about what works and why.

Innovation.   As budget cuts and managed care change the face of social service delivery, U.S. social workers must become innovative. As in resource-poor developing countries, accomplishing more with less and pooling resources to achieve otherwise impossible goals are becoming increasingly important. The infusion of more communitywide approaches to treating societal issues must become part of the day-to-day jobs of social workers. Innovation demands that social workers review the root causes of problems so that they can begin to institute positive change for more people at less cost.

Global Learning.   The gap between home and abroad, between "us and them," is rapidly shrinking. Not only do so-called Third World conditions exist in neighborhoods across America, but the globalization of the economy, immigrant flows, environmental degradation, and a host of other factors all combine to make interdependency a fact of life. Armed with a more sophisticated knowledge base by which to analyze and understand current situations and policies, social workers can enhance their effectiveness. The search for solutions to societal problems should not be limited to U.S. communities and policies.

CONCLUSION: IDENTIFYING, ANALYZING, AND RESPONDING TO SOCIAL INJUSTICES

Social workers work with clients on a variety of levels—micro, meso, and macro—nationally and internationally. Concerns about human rights, social inequities, oppression, and other forms of injustice need to be identified on all levels. Social workers can be guided by the values and principles suggested in the previous section. They also can be assisted by tools for analyzing situations and making decisions about strategies and actions.

The case example in Tools for Student Learning 3.3 illustrates how two individuals in two different countries are connected by the bonds of exploitation, oppression, and poverty. In both situations, industrial initiatives that are motivated solely by the desire for profits and that confer value on individuals only to the extent that they produce profits exploit the very people who should benefit from the economic development in their communities. A framework for analyzing and responding to the social justice issues inherent in their life circumstances is provided as a tool for thinking about their situation and other client situations.

TOOLS FOR STUDENT LEARNING 3.3

Case Study: Randy Conway and Angelica Hernandez

Randy Conway is 44 years old and lives with his wife and three children in the small town of Mount Vernon, Missouri. He worked 20 years in a Zenith factory making televisions. Zenith had moved from the northern United States to Missouri in 1976, in search of workers who were willing to toil for lower wages and without the benefit of trade unions. By 1992, Randy was making $11 per hour, but then Zenith moved 20,000 of its U.S. jobs to Mexico, including most of the jobs in Missouri. Randy is now out of work. Zenith spokesperson John Taylor admitted that "the wage structure in Mexico is a primary reason for our relocation there."

Angelica Hernandez has worked in Zenith's Reynosa, Mexico, factory since 1988. She works in a noisy plant with hazardous chemicals all around and takes home $35 for a 48-hour week. Angelica, her husband, and their seven children live in a shack with a dirt floor that measures 12 feet by 18 feet and has no electricity or running water (*GATT and NAFTA*, n.d.).

An Analytical Framework[11]

In order to fully understand the social justice and human rights issues and determine possible responses in the case example as well as other client situations, an analysis of the causes, symptoms, shortfalls, and the potential of the population (or clients) for action and solutions needs to be undertaken. The overriding justice theme inherent in Randy's and Angelica's situations is poverty. The following framework can be used to guide your thinking about the role of social workers in advocating for social and economic justice. The framework can be used in relation to other overriding justice themes (e.g., racism, gender discrimination, environment and development, religion, etc.) and vulnerable populations (e.g., children, women, people of color, refugees, people with disabilities, etc.).

I. *Aspects of the Situation*

A. Quality of life
B. Food
C. Employment
D. Housing
E. Health
F. Education
G. Environment/pollution
H. Access to property (land, housing)
I. Other aspects:

II. *Analysis*

A. *Causes* (e.g., inequality in global resource distribution, industrial exploitation, nonunionization)
B. *Symptoms* (e.g., powerlessness, unemployment, hunger, health)
C. *Shortfalls* (e.g., lack of social security provisions and legislation protecting workers, lack of trade unions)
D. *Potential of the population for solutions* (e.g., self-help groups, bulk purchases of products, political mobilization, union organizing efforts)

III. *Social Work Intervention*

A. Social work intervention has a long tradition and has spearheaded innovative action through cooperation with poor people themselves, nongovernmental organizations, and other partners that reinforce advocacy and a concerted thrust to combat poverty situations such as these.

B. Consider here the following question: What is the scope and what are the limits of social work interventions at different levels (micro, meso, macro)?

IV. *International Human Rights Instruments*

A. Consider the main international instruments addressing the theme of poverty and how they might be used to advocate for change (e.g., the Universal Declaration of Human Rights—1948, the International Covenants on Economic, Social, and Cultural Rights and on Civil and Political Rights—1966, and the Declaration on the Right to Development—1986).

Questions for Social Workers and Social Work Students

1. What particular human rights issues (e.g., rights to life, to work, to an adequate standard of living) that are linked to the issues of poverty are illustrated in the case example?

2. What attitudes of social discrimination, marginalization, stigmatization, and injustice need to be combated?

3. In what way can clients—individuals, families, communities—become empowered to bring about change in their own situation and in the attitudes of others toward them?

4. In what ways can social workers become empowered to alleviate or eliminate poverty and facilitate empowerment of people in the face of industrial and global exploitation? What are the barriers to their own empowerment, and how can they overcome those barriers?

NOTES

1. These statistics were taken from V. Quadrini and J.-V. Rios-Rull, (1997, Spring), Understanding the U.S. distribution of wealth, *Federal Reserve Bank of Minneapolis Quarterly Review, 21*(2), 22–36.
2. World Declaration on the Survival, Protection and Development of Children, World Summit for Children, United Nations, September 30, 1990.
3. *U.N. Focus, Refugee Women: In the Spirit of Survival,* March 1991, p. 1.
4. Preamble of the World Declaration on Education for All, 1990, World Conference on Education for All, Jomtien, Thailand, 1990.
5. *From Crisis to Consensus: The United Nations and the Challenge to Development,* p. 1. Keynote speech delivered by Mme Therese Sevigny, United Nations Undersecretary-General for Public Information, at the 1990/1991 inaugural conference, University of Ottawa, Institute for International Development, November 14, 1990.
6. The World Bank, *World Development Report 1991,* Oxford University Press, p. 25; United Nations Department of Public Information, *Development Forum, 19*(6)/*20*(1), November 1991–February 1992.

7. These instruments are described in more detail in United Nations (1992), *Teaching and Learning about Human Rights: A Manual for Schools of Social Work and the Social Work Profession*, New York: The United Nations.
8. This section is adapted with permission from M. S. White and D. Van Soest (1984), *Empowerment of People for Peace*, Minneapolis, MN: Women Against Military Madness.
9. From A. Cook and G. Kirk (1983), *Greenham Women Everywhere* (Boston), as quoted in M. S. White and D. Van Soest (1984), *Empowerment of People for Peace*, Minneapolis, MN: Women Against Military Madness, p. 18.
10. The values are drawn from United Nations (1992), *Teaching and Learning about Human Rights: A Manual for Schools of Social Work and the Social Work Profession*, New York: The United Nations, pp. 14–19.
11. Adapted from United Nations (1992), *Teaching and Learning about Human Rights: A Manual for Schools of Social Work and the Social Work Profession*, New York: The United Nations, pp. 52–53.

PART TWO

A Cultural Competence Framework

Part Two introduces the reader to a cultural competence framework that is built on two levels, generalist and advanced, and four areas of cultural competence: cultural awareness, knowledge acquisition, skill development, and inductive learning. Although the terms remind one of social work education curriculum models, our intent is to offer a broad and open structural outline and to articulate a series of competency statements that characterize social workers who interact with ethnic and cultural clients. We believe the starting point is the development of cultural self-awareness or an understanding and appreciation of one's own culture as well as a genuine interest in cultural other-awareness or a seeking out of cultural nuances from the client. Next, we believe it important to cover a body of cultural and ethnic knowledge theory and related information in order to develop a sense of competence as well as skill development, which translates knowledge into "how to help" steps. Finally, we introduce the need to constantly refresh our existing state of cultural competence by learning about new cultural and ethnic groups entering our community and nation. We call this ongoing quest *inductive learning*.

CHAPTER FOUR

A Framework for Cultural Competence

DOMAN LUM

We have introduced the concept of cultural competence with two pretests and have presented the social context of diversity as the person-centered context and racism, sexism, homophobia, discrimination, and oppression as the environment-centered context. The first three chapters provided a preparatory background for understanding a practice framework for cultural competence. We hope that as you read this chapter, you will be involved in developing cultural awareness, knowledge acquisition, skill development, and inductive learning as a social worker. The particular framework in this chapter is based on a series of cultural competence statements, each of which is explained in detail. Each cultural competency is embedded in the pretests of the research instruments you took in Chapter 1. Moreover, you will notice that there are two levels of cultural competence in the framework: generalist and advanced. In social work education, the professional foundation during the undergraduate social work major and the first year of the graduate master social work level is called generalist social work. The second year of the master's of social work degree program in the United States is called the advanced curriculum. The framework of generalist and advanced levels is designed to address the needs of both undergraduate and graduate social work students.

A framework for cultural competence serves as a point of reference and a guideline for social workers who are developing competencies in working with ethnic groups in practice settings and service delivery structures. This framework is designed to orient social workers toward cultural self-awareness, knowledge acquisition, skill development, and inductive learning. It identifies specific concerns in each of these four areas. It also provides the social worker with a degree of flexibility to explore related themes unique to the cultivation of cultural competence.

DEFINITION AND CHARACTERISTICS OF A FRAMEWORK

A framework is a structure that serves to hold the parts of a system together. For example, in the construction of a house, the framework establishes the room layout and the roofline and holds together the various components of the house. Likewise, the frame of an automobile is the basic structure that determines the essence of the car. A good course outline is also a framework, holding together a set of ideas and/or facts. An effective instructor generally teaches from a theoretical framework, and a good textbook is usually built around a framework.

The term *framework* is derived from three Latin root words that illuminate its meaning: (1) *framen*, which means a structure, frame, or problem; (2) *frami*, which connotes profit or benefit; and (3) *frama*, which denotes "to further." These root words describe a structure that provides a benefit or furthers some aim. A framework gives shape, establishes an operational perimeter, identifies procedural principles, and provides flexible application.

A framework for cultural competence has these basic characteristics:

- The framework has a systems theory foundation that links and integrates categories. Accreditation Standard 1 of the Council on Social Work Education's *Handbook of Accreditation Standards and Procedures* (CSWE, 1992) identifies mission and goal inputs, program and curriculum throughputs, and program and curriculum outputs in a systems interaction. A major component of curriculum outputs is outcome measurements.
- The framework is a helpful point of reference in social work cultural competence discussions.
- The framework sets an operational perimeter, identifies characteristics of cultural competence, and offers procedural principles for social workers to follow.
- The framework teaches assumptions, principles, and skills, and provides a road map for social work practice.
- The framework supports the development of social work outcome measures relating to cultural competence.
- The framework brings together a number of themes (e.g., cultural awareness, culture, ethnicity) and components of social work practice (such as process stages, generalist and advanced levels). There is an opportunity to create new terminology from basic concepts.
- The framework advances the state of the art of culturally competent practice by evaluating the existing multicultural counseling competencies model and proposing a social work cultural competencies orientation.

SOCIAL WORK CULTURAL COMPETENCIES: GENERALIST AND ADVANCED

Cultural competencies are a set of culturally congruent beliefs, attitudes, and policies that make cross-cultural social work possible. Cultural competence exist as points along a continuum, ranging from cultural destructiveness, cultural incapacity, cultural blindness, and precompetence to cultural competence and, finally, cultural proficiency (Cross et al., 1989). Cultural competence includes acceptance of and respect for cultural differences, analysis of one's own cultural identity and biases, awareness of the dynamics of difference in ethnic clients, and recognition of the need for additional knowledge, research, and resources to work with clients (Lu, Lim, & Mezzich, 1995). The Association for Multicultural Counseling and Development (AMCD) is the first professional group to adopt and operationalize multicultural counseling competence standards (Arredondo et al., 1996). The categories suggested pertained to awareness, knowledge, and skills that are still advocated. Smith and others (2004, p.11) cite these concepts:

Awareness refers to therapists' personal self-awareness: awareness of their worldview, values, assumptions, expectations, privileges, biases, theoretical orientation, and so on. *Knowledge* refers to therapists' understanding and knowledge of human diversity in all its forms: racial, cultural, religious, gender, sexual orientation, and so on. *Skills* refers to therapists' ability to use their personal awareness and knowledge of client culture and diversity in a therapeutic manner during the treatment process.

Sue (2001) has a multidimensional model of cultural competence in counseling that looks at a three-dimensional perspective:

- Dimension I: Group-Specific Worldviews, which includes human differences associated with race, gender, sexual orientation, physical ability, age, and other reference groups
- Dimension II: Components of Cultural Competence, which focuses on awareness, knowledge, and skills, particularly one's own biases and assumptions of human behavior, knowledge of particular groups, and culturally appropriate intervention strategies
- Dimension III: Foci of Therapeutic Interventions, which critically evaluates biases at the individual, professional, organizational, and societal levels

Culturally competent practice model building is an ongoing task for practitioners in the field. However, we sought to delineate a similar model that contains these components but that also is concerned about heuristic learning and two levels of understanding. In the following sections, we explain our model concepts.

From a social work perspective, the term *cultural competence* denotes the ability to understand the dimensions of culture and cultural practice and apply them to the client and the cultural/social environment. This ability is developed in the classroom and in the field experience of the social worker in culturally diverse practice. To facilitate this learning, it would be helpful to have an agreement among multicultural social work educators and practitioners regarding a set of practice-oriented criteria for social work cultural competencies.

At present, the volume of literature devoted to culturally diverse or multicultural social work practice is growing at a steady rate (Congress, 1997; Devore & Schlesinger, 1999; Green, 1999; Lum, 2000). The Council on Social Work Education's (CSWE's) *Educational Policy and Accreditation Standards* (2002) mandates curriculum content on diversity, populations-at-risk, and social and economic justice, although its requirement of field experience in working with people of color needs to be strengthened.

The social work cultural competencies framework I propose here addresses generalist and advanced levels in each cultural competency area. The generalist level describes the professional foundation of social work practice. According to the CSWE's 1992 *Curriculum Policy Statement*, there are five generalist practice characteristics:

1. An emphasis on professional relationships characterized by mutuality, collaboration, and respect for the client system
2. A focus on practice assessment that examines client strengths and problems in the interactions among individuals and between people and their environments
3. Knowledge, values, and skills to enhance the well-being of people and to help ameliorate the environmental conditions that affect people adversely
4. The skills of defining issues, collecting and assessing data, planning and contracting, identifying alternative interventions, selecting and implementing appropriate

courses of action, using appropriate research-based knowledge and technological advances, and termination

5. Approaches and skills for practice with clients from different social, cultural, racial, religious, spiritual, and class backgrounds and with systems of all sizes

The generalist level of cultural competence should be taught in foundation multicultural social work courses. Likewise, there is an advanced level of cultural competence that coincides with the standards of the advanced level of social work practice. This level consists of the following: (1) advanced practice skills and knowledge, in accord with a conceptual framework that shapes the breadth and depth of knowledge and practice skills to be acquired; and (2) content areas that are designed to prepare students for advanced practice. Both the generalist and advanced levels are familiar to those in social work education and distinguish this cultural competence model for social work.

The social work cultural competence model involves four areas, as mentioned in Chapter 1: (1) personal and professional awareness of ethnic persons and events that have been part of the upbringing and education of the worker; (2) knowledge acquisition related to culturally diverse practice; (3) skill development related to working with the culturally diverse client; and (4) inductive learning, which forms a continuum of heuristic information on culturally diverse persons, events, and places. Table 4.1 provides an overview of the social work cultural competencies framework.

TABLE 4.1 *Social Work Cultural Competencies, Generalist and Advanced*

Cultural Awareness	Knowledge Acquisition
Generalist level:	*Generalist level:*
• Awareness of own life experiences related to culture	• Understanding of terms related to cultural diversity
• Contact with other cultures and ethnicities	• Knowledge of demographics of culturally diverse populations
• Awareness of positive and negative experiences with other cultures and ethnicities	• Development of a critical thinking perspective on cultural diversity
• Awareness of own racism prejudice and discrimination	• Understanding of the history of oppression and of social groups
	• Knowledge of the strengths of people of color
Advanced level:	• Knowledge of culturally diverse values
• Assessment of involvement with people of color throughout various life stages	*Advanced level:*
• Completion of course work, fieldwork, and research focused on cultural diversity	• Application of systems and psychosocial theory to practice with clients of color
• Participation in employment experiences with culturally diverse clients and programs	• Knowledge of theories on ethnicity, culture, minority identity, and social class
• Academic and employment evaluation on the progress toward attaining focused cultural awareness of academic material and professional career experiences with cultural diversity	• Mastery of social science theory

TABLE 4.1 *(continued)*

Skill Development	Inductive Learning

Skill Development

Generalist level:

- Understanding of how to overcome client resistance
- Knowledge of how to obtain client background
- Understanding of the concept of ethnic community
- Use of self-disclosure
- Use of a positive and open communication style
- Problem identification
- View of the problem in terms of wants or needs
- View of the problem in terms of levels
- Explanation of problem themes
- Excavation of problem details
- Assessment of stressors and strengths
- Assessment of all client dimensions
- Establishment of culturally acceptable goals
- Formulation of multilevel intervention strategies
- Termination

Advanced level:

- Design of social service programs in ethnic communities
- Understanding that services must be accessible
- Understanding that services must be pragmatic and positive
- Belief in the importance of recruiting bilingual/bicultural workers
- Participation in community outreach programs
- Establishment of linkages with other social agencies
- Fostering a conducive agency setting
- Involvement with cultural skill development research

Inductive Learning

Generalist level:

- Participation in continuing discussions of multicultural social work practice
- Gathering new information on cultural competence and culturally diverse practice

Advanced level:

- Participation in inductive research on cultural competence and culturally diverse practice
- Participation in writing articles and texts on cultural competence and culturally diverse practice

Cultural Awareness

The first cultural competence area is cultural awareness. For culturally diverse social work, it is crucial to develop an awareness of ethnicity and racism and its impact on professional attitude, perception, and behavior.

Generalist Level. The following paragraphs describe competencies related to cultural awareness at the generalist level.

The social worker is aware of life experiences as a person related to a culture (e.g., family heritage, household and community events, beliefs, and practices). Everyone has a set of unique life experiences related to family, community, beliefs, and practices that are embedded in culture. However, many persons in the United States have blended ethnic backgrounds as a result of intermarriage over many generations and are unable to point to a predominant ethnic and cultural heritage. They see themselves simply as Americans. But, on closer examination, the experiences of these people may reflect regional and sectional culture (southern culture, New England culture, Midwestern culture, California culture) or residual traces of recognizable Irish, German, or English cultural behavior patterns. It is important for the social worker to talk about recognizable cultural life experiences. It is the beginning of cultural awareness for the social worker and prepares the worker for future discussion of cultural recognition with clients.

The social worker has contact with individuals, families, and groups of other cultures and ethnicities. As a person of culture, everyone knows another person, family, or group who is either like or unlike him or her. As the social worker widens the range of contact, patterns emerge regarding cultural groups and communities. In some cities and rural areas, ethnic communities are still intact as functioning groups. Newly arrived cultural and ethnic groups have thriving neighborhoods. Some small ethnic communities are homogeneous and have minimal contact with individuals or families of different cultural and ethnic backgrounds. It is important to talk about the degree of contact a person has with other persons of distinct and blended cultures and ethnicities. Contact is established through school, work, sports activities, clubs, church, festivals, and other events. Contact could be sporadic or constant, superficial or intimate, short-lived or for a lifetime.

The social worker is aware of positive and negative experiences with persons and events of other cultures and ethnicities. Contact causes a set of positive and/or negative experiences to occur in the life and mind of a person. A positive or negative experience either dispels or confirms a stereotype. A positive experience with an individual of another culture or ethnicity may dispel a previous negative stereotype about this group. A negative experience may confirm an already held negative stereotype. Based on a series of such experiences, our stereotypes about other groups are deeply rooted in our psyches. Positive and negative experiences with persons and events of other cultures and ethnicities should be discussed, shared, and examined. A cultural awareness session is an opportunity to investigate stereotypes and beliefs based on our unique experiences and biases.

The social worker evaluates the cognitive, affective, and behavioral components of his or her racism, prejudice, and discrimination. Racism, prejudice, and discrimination are related to the cognitive, affective, and behavioral dimensions of an individual. Racism is the cognitive belief in the superiority of one group over another. Prejudice is negative feelings toward a group or its individual members. Discrimination is an unfavorable behavioral response or reaction to members of an ethnic or racial group. Racism, prejudice, and discrimination are universal; we are the oppressed recipients and the oppressive agents. The social worker must become aware of his or her own racism, prejudice, and discrimination. Uncovering and dealing with these inherent tendencies helps the worker be effective with a culturally diverse client.

Advanced Level. The following paragraphs describe competencies related to cultural awareness at the advanced level.

The social worker assesses his or her involvement with culturally diverse clients in childhood, adolescence, young adulthood, and adulthood. It is important to take a longitudinal view of one's involvement with people of color in the various developmental stages of life. Childhood and adolescence represent the formative years of living and learning when incidents of racism, prejudice, and discrimination have a lasting effect upon the mind. Further contacts with people of color in young adulthood and adulthood may confirm or change attitudes from earlier developmental periods. Conducting a self-study of involvement uncovers an understanding of how past and present perceptions, attitudes, and beliefs about people of color affect the worker–client relationship. The social worker internalizes positive and negative experiences with people of color based on a series of developmental encounters during various life stages.

The social worker does academic course work, fieldwork, and research on culturally diverse clients and groups. Social work education requires course work on diversity that may include consideration of groups distinguished by race, ethnicity, culture, class, gender, sexual orientation, religion, physical or mental ability, age, and national origin. A social work student is expected to have taken a course on racial, ethnic, or cultural diversity. A field practicum or a research project involving people of color as clients or subjects may or may not be a part of social work education. This does not mean that a social work student must intern at an ethnic field placement or conduct research with a primary focus on an ethnic population. Though ideally a social work student has seen several culturally diverse clients in a field agency or interviewed culturally diverse human subjects in the course of conducting social work research, there is no guarantee that every social work student has been exposed to this range of experiences. To ensure cultural competence might mean that a social work program provides every student with a planned series of course work, fieldwork, and ethnic social research focusing on cultural diversity.

The social worker has professional employment experiences with culturally diverse clients and programs. A social work career takes a person through a meaningful set of program and client experiences in the social service sector. Along the way it is crucial to have employment experiences with a wide range of culturally diverse clients and to be responsible for program services that impact this population. Career employment experiences with culturally diverse clients and programs will help the social worker to grow—in his or her general competence, as an effective professional, and in his or her specific competence, as a culturally sensitive person.

The social worker evaluates academic material and professional experiences related to cultural awareness and cultural diversity. The beginning social worker relies initially on the body of academic knowledge and field experience on cultural diversity gleaned in school. Increasingly, the social worker reads new books and studies reports on racial, ethnic, and cultural factors that affect programs and services of his or her agency. Culturally diverse clients may be sources of new insights for the social worker. Interaction with ethnic colleagues and collaborative ethnic service agencies may broaden the understanding and perspective of the worker. Ideally, the social worker grows in his or her career through such contacts with cultural diversity and culturally diverse clients.

Knowledge Acquisition

Knowledge acquisition involves the acquisition of a body of information that organizes material about a topic into sets of facts that plausibly explain phenomena. Social work has been sensitive to the need for a theoretical foundation ever since the *Flexner Report* (Flexner, 1961), which criticized that social work was not a profession because it had no theory base.

Generalist Level.   The following paragraphs describe competencies related to knowledge acquisition at the generalist level.

   The social worker understands the following terms: ethnic minority, multiculturalism, diversity, and people of color. The social worker understands and can explain a number of basic terms that are essential to culturally diverse social work. *Ethnic minority* denotes a numerically smaller or politically powerless group in relation to a larger, controlling, and dominating majority and was used during the civil rights struggle for political, economic, legal, and social opportunities for African, Latino, and Asian Americans, and First Nations Peoples. *Multiculturalism* recognizes the pluralistic nature of cultures and societies and has been associated with academic and political movements. The term has been used in a positive sense to denote the collective movement of people who are committed to the realities of cultural differences, and in a negative sense by detractors who associate the term with being politically correct. *Diversity* emphasizes the similarity and dissimilarity between numerous groups in society that have distinguishing characteristics. There is diversity in this country in terms of ethnicity, culture, gender, sexual orientation, age, religion, and related areas. *People of color* is a collective term that refers to the major groups of African, Latino, and Asian Americans, and First Nations Peoples who have been distinguished from the dominant society by color.

   The social worker has a knowledge of demographic profiles of culturally diverse populations. The 2000 U.S. Census reflects a major influx of immigrants, refugees, and aliens into the United States, mainly from Asia, Central and South America, and Eastern Europe. Accordingly, it is important to study shifting area population trends to determine how new ethnic groups have changed the face of the local community. What are the emerging social problems that have resulted from this influx? Have communities changed as a result? Have there been adverse or positive reactions to the socioeconomic situation of a locale? What new social service programs are needed to respond to these changes? These questions are crucial to the discussion of changing cultural profiles.

   The social worker has developed a critical thinking perspective on cultural diversity. Kurfiss (1989) defines critical thinking:

> [T]he process of figuring out what to believe or not about a situation, phenomenon, problem or controversy for which no single definitive answer or solution exists. The term implies a diligent, open-minded search for understanding, rather than for discovery of a necessary conclusion. (p. 42)

Critical thinking is an assessment of the nature of a problem or issue and an open-ended search for understanding of the cause-and-effect relationship. It is a mind-set that is applied to a number of different situations.

Alter and Egan (1997) identify five social work critical thinking skills: (1) the ability to understand social work theories, (2) the ability to divide a theory into its components (assumptions, concepts, propositions, hypotheses), (3) the ability to assess the practice implications of a theory, (4) the ability to develop and apply criteria for evaluating a theory, and (5) the ability to identify common errors in reasoning. These skills are developed later in this book.

The social worker understands the history of oppression and of multicultural social groups. People of color share a common history of oppression, although there is variation in the histories of multicultural social groups. First Nations Peoples and African, Latino, and Asian Americans attest to a history of domination by the European–American majority society. Oppression occurs when one segment of the population systematically prevents another segment from obtaining access to resources or denies a fair and equal playing field. First Nations Peoples were victims of genocide and were forced to relinquish their lands, their children, and their freedom of movement on reservations. African Americans were victims of slavery and have fought racism, prejudice, and discrimination in employment, housing, and related forms of segregation. Latino Americans have been the victims of political, social, and economic discrimination and have been the sources of cheap labor. Asian Americans were historically used as cheap labor, have been underrepresented in their political and legal rights, and have been the objects of hostility from the dominant society.

The social worker has knowledge of the strengths of men, women, and children of color. Previously in psychiatry, psychology, and somewhat in social work, there has been an emphasis on the pathology of people of color. A focus on psychological and socioeconomic disorders conveys a sense of the deviance of members of ethnic groups. The trend in education has shifted toward a focus on the cultural survival and familial strengths of gender and age groups. Building on this trend moves social work education toward a perspective that empowers men, women, and children of color.

The social worker has knowledge about culturally diverse values. Multicultural values revolve around collective structures such as family, spirituality, and group identity. These values are the source of group solidarity, cultural networks, and hierarchical authority. People of color have internal and external values that are a part of their own being and existence as cultural and ethnic persons. Cultural consciousness, personality, attitudes, emotions, and perceptions are internal processes that are manifested in the external behavior of people of color who persist in the struggle for dignity and equality.

Advanced Level. The following paragraphs describe competencies related to knowledge acquisition at the advanced level.

The social worker applies systems theory and psychosocial theory to multicultural social work. Systems theory orients the client and the worker to a field of interrelated systems. In a cultural context, systems such as nuclear and extended family, clan/tribe/family associations, and ethnic/religious affiliations and bonding are interdependent and thus rely on each other. The social worker is able to understand interactions in terms of systems analysis and structuring and to devise new ways to formulate emerging arrangements.

Psychosocial theory views the individual, family, and/or group in the context of its interchange with the social environment of organizations, community, and region or nation. The social force field of the environment impacts the psychological persona of people in various arrangements. The social worker is able to analyze the dynamics of this exchange and explain them to the client.

The social worker has knowledge of theories on ethnicity, culture, minority identity, and social class. Theories on ethnicity deal with the racial heritage that is passed on from generation to generation. Theories of culture focus on the way of life of a particular group and encompass language, norms of behavior, values, religion, beliefs, customs, practices, food, music, and the arts. Theories on minority identity address an individual's or group's status in the dominant society and how it affects the response of and interaction with members of the whole society. Theories on social class involve social, economic, and political arrangements that affect power and social status.

The social worker draws on a range of social science theory from cross-cultural psychology, multicultural counseling and therapy, and cultural anthropology. Cross-cultural psychology has focused on East–West comparisons of group characteristics and has spread to other parts of the world. Multicultural counseling and therapy has been termed a fourth force in the field of counseling psychology (Pedersen, 1991) in view of the fact that it has its own standards, theory base, and academic visibility. (The other three forces are the psychodynamic, behavioral, and humanistic movements.) Cultural anthropology has been the forerunner of cultural studies and has sought to understand various cultures by interviewing members of a particular culture. Social work draws on applied cross-cultural social science theories and disciplines to construct relevant knowledge systems.

Skill Development

Skill development, which occurs when the worker applies what he or she knows to the helping situation, is based on cultural awareness and knowledge acquisition. Skills are developed from a set of practice principles in the course of working with a client.

Generalist Level.   The following paragraphs describe competencies related to skill development at the generalist level.

The social worker understands how to overcome the resistance and lower the communication barriers of a multicultural client. At the outset of the helping relationship, it is important to minimize resistance and to maximize motivation (the mini–maxi principle). Overcoming resistance involves the willingness of the worker to reveal background and to build structure in the relationship with the client, to be a good person who is worthy of trust, and to be a part of the client's life situation. At the same time, lowering communication barriers is initiated by polite conversation, inquiry about the cultural story of the client, and decreasing language, stereotype, and stress barriers.

The social worker obtains personal and family background information from a multicultural client and determines the extent of his or her ethnic/community sense of identity. The worker should discover the personal and family background of the client to understand the person and to build a psychosocial profile. It is important to determine whether the client relates to his or her ethnic community. Being a part of an ethnic community means that the client has a degree of support from significant others such as family and community members. Being isolated from one's ethnic community may have an adverse effect on the client.

The social worker understands the concept of ethnic community and practices relationship protocols with a multicultural client. The social worker should understand the demographics of the ethnic community served by the agency. An ethnic community has a unique history, set of problems, and needs that influence the life of a person who is part of the community. It is crucial for the worker to study these facts. Relationship protocols involve the expression of respect toward the client and/or the client's family. Parents, grandparents, and related significant others should be consulted about the problem situation. Rather than telling the client what to do, it is important to ask the client about his or her perspectives.

The social worker uses professional self-disclosure with a multicultural client. The worker takes the initiative in building a relationship with the client by disclosing an area of interest they have in common. The purpose of professional self-disclosure is to humanize and deprofessionalize the helping relationship and to model the sharing of meaningful information. This relaxes the client and encourages him or her to disclose vital personal problem material in return.

The social worker develops a positive and open communication style and uses open-ended listening responses. The communication style of the worker is important in eliciting responses from the client. Many years ago when I was a young doctoral graduate in my first community mental health center job, I encountered a professor of psychiatry who conducted teaching interview sessions before large numbers of mental health professionals. Whenever it was his turn to preside over grand rounds (a session where various patients are examined before a teaching/learning audience in a hospital setting), I could anticipate his line of questioning. Indeed, the professor of psychiatry was schooled by a famous classical psychiatrist who taught his students to conduct extensive probing. In the interview process, the poor client/patient was asked question upon question based on his or her answers. This single line of probing responses underscored to me as a young clinician the need for the worker to vary his or her responses by asking open-ended questions that offered an opportunity for the client to take the worker through a number of locked mental doors. At the same time, the worker's follow-up responses to open-ended questions should involve reflecting, summary, and directive expressions.

The social worker obtains problem information, facilitates problem area disclosure, and promotes problem understanding. Problem identification entails gathering the essential facts of the person and the social environment surrounding the problem by facilitating a positive process so that the client willingly discloses the problem area. The result is that both the client and the worker understand the problem from their different perspectives. Succeeding in uncovering the problem in a concise and careful way takes skill on the part of the worker, who has laid the groundwork since the initial contact.

The social worker views a problem as an unsatisfied want or an unfulfilled need. Reid (1978) described a problem as an unsatisfied want or an unfulfilled need. This perspective gets behind the pathology of a problem by understanding that a problem has a positive aspect. That is, a problem exists because of a lack of satisfaction (unsatisfied want) or a lack of fulfillment (unfulfilled need). If the worker can help the client to reframe the problem around this perspective, the client can be redirected in a *positive* direction, toward ways in which to achieve need satisfaction and fulfillment.

The social worker classifies problems on micro, meso, and macro levels. From the social work practice vantage point, problems are multidimensional. The micro (individual, family, and small group), meso (community and organization), and macro (complex organization, geographical population) levels of a problem persist and interact with each other. For example, problems resulting from welfare reform involve a macrolevel federal law that mandates the restructuring of welfare and employment, mesolevel state and county mandates to implement the law, and microlevel effects on single women, dependent children, and legal immigrants.

The social worker explains problem themes of racism, prejudice, and discrimination, and their expressions. Part of problem identification is uncovering the dynamics of racism, prejudice, and discrimination that may be present in the problems of the multicultural client. It is important to rule these themes in or out. Racism is a cognitive belief about superiority and inferiority, dominance and subordination learned from parents, neighborhood, and community. Prejudice is the negative attitude or emotional result of racism, whereas discrimination is the behavioral expression of racism and prejudice through a negative action taken against a person of color. Problems may be infected with racism, prejudice, and discrimination.

The social worker finds out problem details. Multicultural problems encompass a wide spectrum, ranging from psychosocial dysfunction during transitional adjustment for immigrants to persons who have indirect ways of expressing problems such as storytelling. The worker must be patient and assess the situation, often piecing together aspects of who is involved, when and where the problem occurs, and what the major issues are.

The social worker assesses socioenvironmental stressors, psychoindividual reactions, and cultural strengths. Psychosocial assessment takes into account both the socioenvironmental stressors and the psychological reaction to these stressors experienced by the client. The client generally has coping skills to process environmental stress and conflict. However, these resources may temporarily fail and the client may experience psychosomatic reactions that are symptomatic of internalized stress. The worker should also assess cultural strengths and both internal and external resources for change.

The social worker assesses the biological, psychological, social, cultural, and spiritual dimensions of a multicultural client. Social work practice normatively speaks about biopsychosocial assessment. However, from a multicultural viewpoint, assessment must address the cultural and spiritual aspects along with the physical, psychological, and social dimensions. A person is mind, body, and spirit in an environmental system. As such, a full assessment of the assets of the person considers the interaction and exchange between and among the biological/physical, psychological/mental, social/environmental, cultural/ethnic, and spiritual/religious aspects of the person.

The social worker establishes joint goals and agreements with the client that are culturally acceptable. Contracting with the client around mutually agreeable and culturally sensitive goals is the initial intervention step. In a cultural context, the agreement may be verbal rather than written because in many cultures verbal agreements are binding. Goals provide an opportunity to structure the course of the change strategy.

The social worker formulates micro, meso, and macro intervention strategies that address the cultural and special needs of the client. Multicultural clients operate in interdependent spheres involving the individual as part of the family; the family and extended family as part of an association, clan, or tribe; and the group as part of a neighborhood, community, or organization. As a result, micro, meso, and macro intervention strategies should be devised to address these multiple levels. Individual and group empowerment, family and network casework, and use of church and community social services are examples of these three levels of intervention.

The social worker initiates termination in a way that links the client to an ethnic community resource, reviews significant progress and growth, evaluates goal outcomes, and establishes a follow-up strategy. Termination is the end of a beginning. New linkages to a sense of identity and helping persons in the ethnic community, recital of past progress, evaluation of goals that have been achieved, and follow-up on emerging problems are part of a continuing pattern.

Advanced Level. The following paragraphs describe competencies related to skill development at the advanced level.

The social worker designs a service delivery and agency linkage and culturally effective social service programs in ethnic communities. Service delivery design involves identifying workable program principles for agencies that wish to adopt and implement culturally sound programs for multicultural clients. Organizing a service program structure provides a vehicle for an agency to deliver a unit of service to a client in an effective manner.

The social worker understands that services must be accessible to the ethnic community. Location is basic to service delivery. An agency program must be located near the target population. It should be within walking distance or near main transportation routes, in community storefronts, recreation centers, and churches. Locating programs should be a joint decision between the agency and community leaders.

The social worker understands the importance of pragmatic and positive services that meet the tangible needs of the ethnic community. Pragmatic and positive services mean useful and stigma-free services arising from a survey of community needs. A mental illness connotation should be avoided. Family education, child-care, and parenting themes should be promoted. The community can be asked for a list of its needs.

The social worker believes that it is important to recruit bilingual/bicultural workers who reflect the ethnic composition of the clientele. The staffing pattern of an agency program should reflect the ethnic, gender, and age composition of its constituencies. Staff should be able to speak another language in rudimentary and fluent levels and should know another culture. In this sense, the entire staff has some bilingual and bicultural skills and knowledge.

The social worker should advocate for community outreach education and prevention with visible services, culturally sensitive programs, and credible staff. The ethnic community should be exposed to the staff of an agency through extensive community outreach programs that reach the home, the church, the school, and related community institutions. Community outreach builds the visibility, credibility, and integrity of the program and staff, and is an effective way to build referrals to the agency.

The social worker establishes linkages with related social agencies, which ensures rapid referral and program collaboration. It is important to build working relationships with colleagues in other social agencies who can refer cases. When there is an emergency same-day referral, collaborative colleagues can help each other.

The social worker fosters a conducive agency setting with a friendly and helpful atmosphere. The agency setting establishes a tone for the worker–client interaction. The most important person in the office is the receptionist because that person is the first program contact for the client. A friendly, helpful, and bilingual person is a necessary ingredient. The decor of the office, staff tempo, and morale should convey a sense of nurture and caring.

The social worker is involved in cultural skill development research to gain new insights on new principles. The importance of relationship protocols and skills such as professional self-disclosure was recognized more than 15 years ago when I began to write a social work practice text on people of color (Lum, 1986). New skills are needed to keep up with ways of working with people from diverse cultures. Culturally diverse social work practice needs to foster an empirical basis for confirming skills that are appropriate and effective for culturally sensitive practice with clients of color.

Inductive Learning

Inductive learning is concerned with teaching social work students and social workers creative ways to continue developing new skills and insights relating to multicultural social work so that new contributions are made to this field. Graduation from a social work program commences the acquisition of one's own knowledge and skill based on professional work experience, study, and reflection. Van Den Bergh and Crisp (2004) affirm the need for this culturally competent component:

> The addition of an ongoing learning perspective is consonant with an empowerment approach to practice, which includes the idea of praxis. The latter term refers to the continual evaluation of one's practice by processes of action, reflection, evaluation, potential modification of practice approaches, and a reemergence into action. Inductive learning is the heuristic outreach and investigation of new cultural groups that emerge on the scene, such as recent migrant and refugee groups coming to America. (p. 224)

Generalist Level. The following paragraphs describe competencies related to inductive learning at the generalist level.

The social worker has dialogues with culturally diverse social work educators, practitioners, students, and clients on cultural competence issues, emerging cultural trends, and future directions for multicultural social work. Initiating a multicultural professional study and discussion group offers a way of fostering new knowledge and insight into the growing field of multicultural social work. Sharing client helping experiences, readings from texts, agency workshops and university courses, and program research findings are important resources for piecing together new data.

The social worker finds new information about cultural competence and culturally diverse practice. Education is a constant quest for learning from books, courses, clients, colleagues, and current events. Formal education should merge into informal individual education. The social worker should be constantly reading on his or her own, reflecting and recording the thoughts and observations of clients, and thoughtfully interpreting these ideas on paper.

Advanced Level. The following paragraphs describe competencies related to inductive learning at the advanced level.

The social worker conducts inductive research on cultural competence and culturally diverse practice, using survey, oral history, and/or participatory observation method of research. Even the social worker with a case overload in a busy and demanding agency should make time for research. The relevance and effectiveness of a social service agency is dependent on new inductive research about clients, communities, and social problems, which should direct the winds of change in an organization. Good inductive research makes no assumptions. Rather, it asks open-ended questions about a subject area and records the findings without bias. Survey, oral history, and participatory observation research are examples of inductive research areas and methodologies that are inquiring, open-ended, and expansive.

The social worker participates in the writing of articles and texts on cultural competence and culturally diverse practice. The final act of social work cultural competency is to make a written contribution to this field of culturally diverse practice. Many social workers have written articles based on graduate school and social service agency research studies on cultural competence and culturally diverse practice. Several have contributed chapters to social work multicultural practice books. There is a need for many more published articles and books to deepen the knowledge of the field.

SUMMARY

This chapter has presented a framework that addresses cultural competence and competencies from the perspective of culturally diverse social work practice. The cultural competence social work model addresses cultural awareness, knowledge acquisition, skill development, and inductive learning as essential components with generalist and advanced levels. I hope that social workers will understand and use cultural competence and competencies in their practice perspective. In the succeeding chapters of this book, the four areas of social work cultural competence are explained in detail with useful teaching and learning exercises.

CHAPTER FIVE

Cultural Awareness

DOMAN LUM

The road to cultural competence begins with an understanding of your own personal and professional cultural awareness. From the personal perspective, a search for cultural self-awareness involves cultural group experiences and contacts with people of various diverse backgrounds. In turn, personal cultural awareness has a direct effect on how you as a social work professional will interact with a variety of diverse clients. Social workers bring a set of cognitive, attitudinal, and behavioral responses to the helping situation and must be aware of how these dynamics affect the relationship.

The purpose of this chapter is to lay out the first cultural competence area, cultural awareness, from both personal and professional perspectives. First, we define *cultural awareness* in a contextual setting. Next, we explore the fragmentary nature of cultural identity and the need for a cultural search, rediscovery, and formulation on our part. Then we explain the philosophical assumptions that underlie a cultural awareness perspective. We also focus on the individual, family, group, and community dimensions of personal cultural awareness. These entities shape who we are and how we see ourselves. As a result, we learn cognitive, affective, and behavioral responses. Finally, the chapter identifies principles of professional cultural awareness that should be practiced in the worker–client helping relationship.

Reynolds (1995) points out that "cultural self-awareness is a vital first step toward cultural sensitivity" (p. 320). In turn, beliefs and values are best explored through introspection and reflective self-evaluation in an environment of trust and openness. The classroom is an effective laboratory in which to explore these thoughts and feelings in a nonthreatening manner.

DEFINITION OF CULTURAL AWARENESS

The term *cultural awareness* has several levels of meaning for our discussion. Awareness deals with conscious attention and knowledge through the mind and the senses. In other words, a person's awareness has both cognitive and sensory dimensions. Culture involves the transmission of beliefs, values, traditions, customs, and practices from one generation to the next. Cultural awareness involves the self in a cultural context. Hardy and

COMPETENCY STUDY 5.1

Cultural Awareness in an Interview

The available research, however indefinite, suggests that workers can conduct a productive interview despite ethnic, racial, age, and sexual orientation differences between interviewer and interviewee if interviewers observe some cardinal principles of good interviewing.

Interviewers must:

- Be conscious of cultural factors that may intrude on the interview
- Acknowledge any stereotypical ideas they hold regarding the group the client represents
- Apply such stereotypes flexibly with a conscious effort to modify or discard the generalization if it appears inappropriate for the particular interview
- Take the responsibility to learn about the culture of the interviewee so as to better understand any culturally derived behaviors the interviewee might manifest
- Respond to interviewees with respect, empathy, and acceptance, whatever their differences. Effective cross-cultural interviewing combines an acknowledgment of cultural differences with the general principles of good interviewing applicable to all groups of interviewees (pp. 343, 344)

Laszloffy (1995) describe cultural awareness as the learning of cultural background, issues, and relationships in a contextual sense. The emphasis on cultural context is important to our understanding of cultural awareness.

In Competency Study 5.1, Kadushin and Kadushin (1997) remind us that good cross-cultural interviewing involves cultural awareness on the part of the worker.

Sanday (1976) categorizes individuals as relating to cultural contexts in one of four different ways that affect cultural awareness and involvement:

- *Mainstream* individuals have assimilated the values of the dominant society and attempt to emulate these values in their behavior. In the United States, the Americanization of people involves individualism, freedom of expression, casual and fashionable dress, youthful appearance, patriotism, and mergence into the predominant thinking and behavior.
- *Bicultural* individuals move in two distinct cultural worlds: the mainstream, dominant culture of work and society; and their culture of origin, which may have traces of old world traditions, beliefs, and practices. They have a dual commitment to survive and maintain themselves in both spheres, which have meaning and purpose for them.
- The *culturally different* have been exposed to the mainstream culture but have chosen to affiliate and focus their activities in a culturally different and distinct structure. They have made a conscious choice to remain in their cultural and ethnic enclave. They become self-contained residents of Chinatown, Little Italy, Little Havana, or Little Saigon, where they are able to function in an autonomous ethnic setting where language, customs, food, and business exchanges occur.
- The *culturally marginal* have detached themselves from an identified cultural and ethnic identity and live their lives apart from distinct groups. They may be people who were raised away from their ethnic group and now feel neither a part

of that group nor a member of their adopted group. American Indian children who were removed and placed in White foster care may now feel a part of neither the tribe nor the White culture. Due to limited acceptance and lack of a sense of belonging to either party, they are marginal people caught outside their ethnicity and the dominant society. The same may be true of the person who rejects his or her own ethnic group, marries and seeks to identify with another racial group, alters physical appearance for assimilation purposes, and realizes there is limited acceptance in both the original and the alternative ethnic group.

These categories underscore the importance of cultural context when considering the degree of cultural awareness of an individual. What is your own sense of cultural awareness as a person strongly, moderately, or slightly related to a cultural context? How has your individual, family, neighborhood, and community context affected your cultural self-awareness and your awareness of other people's cultures? How would you classify yourself according to Sanday: mainstream, bicultural, culturally different, or culturally marginal? How would Sanday's categories help you to understand a multicultural client?

Cultural context or knowledge of the cultural environment is a critical determinant of how one evolves as a cultural being. Personal relationships with family, neighbors, primary peers, and local community groups, events, and experiences occur in a cultural context. In turn, these relationships have a profound impact on a person's memories, beliefs, attitudes, and actions.

THE DILEMMA OF AMERICANIZATION

The dilemma of Americanization is everyone's dilemma of finding out about their ethnic background and culture of origin. The term *Americanization* involves being American in character, manners, methods, and ideas and the assimilation of U.S. customs, speech, and other characteristics. Americanization should not be confused with *Americanism*. The latter term refers to the devotion or loyalty to the United States or to its traditions, customs, and institutions. The dilemma involves the loss of one's culture of origin to the point of being unable to connect it to one's present American culture.

Some people are first-generation American born and have parents who come from other countries and still speak their native language. Their culture of origin is fairly well intact because of language, customs, and traditions still practiced in the family. Others come from an ethnic community in either rural or urban America where generations have preserved language and customs from the Scandinavian countries, or from Southern or Eastern Europe. Little Italy sections, Norwegian communities, and Finnish enclaves exist and have maintained strong cultural and ethnic ties.

Many Americans are many generations removed from great-grandparents who immigrated to the United States and are the products of multiple ethnic European groups blending with other non-White ethnic groups. These people have a difficult time reconstructing their ethnic and cultural origins. All of us contact our cultural and ethnic roots in varying ways. I was born in a small town in southwestern Ohio. We were the only Chinese American family in the city. As a teenager, I moved to Honolulu, Hawaii, and became immersed in a multicultural society. However, it took me years to discover and sort out my cultural and ethnic heritage as a Chinese American. Fortunately, I married a

CULTURAL COMPETENCY IN ACTION

The Hernandez Family: A Case Study

Mr. Platt is the social worker who has been assigned to the Hernandez family. The family includes a father and mother who were born in Mexico and have immigrated to California, and three children, one of whom has a school learning and behavior problem. Mr. Platt has sought to become culturally aware of his own ethnic background and those of ethnic clients. In his social work education, Mr. Platt received undergraduate and graduate degrees in social work and took several ethnic studies and multicultural practice courses. In one class, he wrote a paper explaining his ethnic background and cultural beliefs and practices.

His first-year MSW field placement was in an East Los Angeles social service center that served Spanish-speaking clients. He did a research paper on the family structure of Latinos.

On a personal level, Mr. Platt has endeavored to integrate the cultural dynamics of the dominant social and his own ethnic culture with his knowledge of Latinos. He still is learning about the similarities and differences among these three cultural orientations as he strives to integrate culture into his life.

TASK RECOMMENDATIONS

The following questions form the basis for a discussion of cultural awareness from the social worker's perspective:

- How can Mr. Platt increase his personal sense of cultural awareness so that he can be effective with the Hernandez family?
- How can Mr. Platt become aware of the Hernandez family's culture?
- How can a person who is from the mainstream society become culturally self-aware and aware of the cultural beliefs and practices of others?

Chinese American woman whose mother was from China and who spoke the language and knew certain customs and traditions.

Giordano and McGoldrick (1996) start their discussion of European Americans with the comment of a colleague who said, "Come on, White ethnics today don't have ethnic issues; they're totally American" (p. 427). Giordano and McGoldrick point out the following interesting facts about European Americans:

- They are the majority population. European Americans form 80 percent of the U.S. population and involve 53 categories. The largest groups are German Americans (58 million), English Americans (41 million), and Irish Americans (39 million). This is because U.S. immigration policy favored Western and Central Europeans until the 1965 McCarran Immigration Act, which opened immigration from countries in Asia and Central and South America.
- They are multigenerational in the history of the United States. Most families from European American groups have been in the United States for three or more generations. This would mean that an American descendant of the Jamestown colony of 1608 would be 20 generations removed from Europe. In the nearly 400 years since the first colony, most traces of European culture and ethnicity have been reduced to residual fragments. Cultural awareness of European roots has simply faded over time.

- Anglo Protestant culture, religion, and values have been dominant due to the presence of Western European settlers in the United States. We know from the history of social welfare that the founding fathers of this country represented the White English American privileged class of the time. The first Irish Catholic president of the United States was John F. Kennedy, who was elected in 1960. Until that point, there had been strong resistance to a non-Protestant in the White House. The English (Anglo-Saxon) brought with them their racism, prejudice, and discrimination. In England, the Irish were termed "savages" by the British. This label was transferred to the American Indians in the New World. The Protestant work ethic influenced the dominant negative social attitude toward welfare recipients. The moral virtue of the society affected social attitudes toward gays and lesbians.
- European Americans display ambivalence about particular ethnic identity and achievement of success in the dominant society. Giordano and McGoldrick (1996) observe:

Ethnicity persists in the consciousness of European Americans, in their perceptions, preferences, and behavior, even while mass production and mass communication homogenize their outward appearances. Psychologically, European Americans are often ambivalent about their identities, and are constantly trying to balance the pull of their family histories and experiences with their individual desires to be accepted and successful in the larger society. (p. 439)

It is difficult to build cultural awareness in European Americans who have become so blended into the American culture. Many simply respond with "I am an American" when asked to trace their ethnic and cultural background and distinctive traditions, values, and practices. However, this may be a dilemma of Americanization for the majority of us. Green (1995) observes:

White Americans often view the matter differently for . . . many of them have difficulty in thinking of themselves as "ethnic." Typically they resort to national labels when asked to describe themselves culturally, and their idiom of ethnic affiliation is more geographical. As the dominant group, whites hear the claims of shared substance . . . made by Latinos, Asian Americans, and others whose ethnicity they can easily see, but they do not find anything like that in themselves. That is because for them ethnicity is perceived only in the surface features. . . . From the point of view of whites, that is a convenient perspective to have, especially in a political sense. It locates ethnicity exclusively in others and excuses them from having to consider their own participation in the management and enforcement of separateness. (p. 21)

Going beyond the dilemma of ethnic disengagement and lack of identification, we must consider the need to incorporate a sense of cultural awareness in our social work practice with clients. Learning to discover one's own cultural awareness, to raise it to a conscious level, and to incorporate it into one's life and professional helping are worthwhile goals. Green (1995) offers a number of practical ways to increase our cultural awareness:

- Adopting a systematic learning style and developing a supportive agency environment that recognizes culturally distinctive modes of behavior with appropriate responses.
- Acknowledging the cultural characteristics of client communities, the realities of power and systematic inequality, and the need for staff and administration

commitment to follow through on training initiatives in order for cultural awareness to penetrate the social work profession.

- Participating in discovery of the beliefs and thinking of the client, comparing these to the life and experiences of the worker, and trying to understand the meaning of differences between the two.

In sum, willingness to learn about self and others and to bridge the gap between worker and client is key to reducing the dilemma of Americanization.

PHILOSOPHICAL ASSUMPTIONS ABOUT CULTURAL AWARENESS

Philosophical assumptions about cultural awareness are important to discuss if one believes that the training emphasis in social work cultural competence education depends on cultural orientation. Everyone has a culture; the culturally competent social worker must become aware of his or her own and the cultures of others. Kadushin and Kadushin (1997) discuss cultural competence in terms of cultural self-awareness and cultural awareness of others. In Competency Study 5.2, they explain the importance of this dual awareness (cultural self and cultural other).

CULTURAL COMPETENCY IN ACTION

The Hernandez Family: A Case Study

Gaining cultural competence means developing a sense of cultural self-awareness. The White American dilemma is a reality facing many social workers who are from families of European American origin. It may be difficult to articulate an ethnic or cultural identity. It is natural to respond with a national origin ("I am an American") or a geographic label ("I am a Midwesterner"). Can we transcend this dilemma, discover our cultural awareness, and incorporate it into our lives?

Mr. Platt seems to have made efforts along these lines. In his social work education, he looked for ways to learn about his culture and other ethnic groups and sought out agency experiences with multicultural clients. He has been willing to take a diverse caseload and to reflect on various cultural behavior traits, including his own and his clients' traits.

TASK RECOMMENDATIONS

- Think about the White American dilemma regarding yourself and discuss this theme in class. Do you agree with the comment: "Come on, White ethnics today don't have ethnic issues; they're totally American"?
- Are we socially segregated from people who do not look, act, or think like us?
- Have we sealed ourselves off in selected homogeneous social groupings from other people who are ethnically different from us?
- Are we part of a diverse community where we have a variety of friends and acquaintances who represent a cross-section of ethnic groups?
- Is there an Americanization dilemma, or is this a false dichotomy that is an unnecessary concern?

Cultural Self-Awareness and Other-Awareness

COMPETENCY STUDY 5.2

Competence in multicultural interviewing is different from interviewing competence in general. General interviewing competence is a necessary but insufficient basis for effective multicultural interviewing.

The best interviewer, then, has cultural sensitivity and general competence in interviewing.

What does the culturally sensitive interviewer need to know and do to maximize the possibility of conducting a successful cross-cultural interview? What characteristics identify the culturally sensitive interviewer?

White interviewers need to recognize that they too have a culture—have been taught that certain ways of doing things are right and proper, to think in a certain way, perceive the world in a certain way, for example, as a White, Christian middle-income female. Just as everyone else has an accent and we don't, we fail to recognize that we are products of our culture. We are like fishes who, never having experienced anything but water, are unaware of the water. White people generally tend not to clearly identify themselves as being racially White. They do not see themselves as a people of color, having a sense of racial identity and a distinct culture. Culturally sensitive interviewers are consciously aware of their culture and are explicitly knowledgeable of the stereotypes associated with it.

Culturally sensitive interviewers are aware of the stereotypes they hold in regard to others and test them flexibly against the reality of the individual client with a readiness and willingness to modify or discard the stereotype in the attempt to understand the individual. (p. 345)

Competency Study 5.2 raises some philosophical issues concerning how one regards oneself as a cultural being and how one views the client as the other cultural being in the helping relationship. Carter and Qureshi (1995) have developed a typology of multicultural philosophical assumptions that offers five perspectives about cultural knowledge and self-awareness: universal, ubiquitous, traditional, race-based, and pan-national. These alternative orientations illuminate our discussion of worker cultural awareness. Although there are philosophical similarities and differences between and among all five, our task is to explain each viewpoint and to apply them to our discussion of training social workers in cultural awareness.

The universal approach. The universal or etic (culture-common) approach to culture believes that all people are the same, as human beings with greater intragroup (within group) differences than intergroup (between group) differences. There is a humanistic vision of all people living in harmony with minimal group differences. Primarily, all people are seen as human beings, and secondarily, their experience and identity are derived from ethnicity, race, and gender. People have many common characteristics and yet are unique as individuals. The individualized or emic (culture-specific) perspective focuses on the person from the group who may or may not match the total characteristics expected from being a representative of that group. Ridley (2005) discusses the nomothetic perspective, which focuses on the prominent characteristics of the group to which an individual belongs (etic) and the idiographic approach which understands the personal meaning of the client as a particular person, not just a representative of certain groups (emic) (p. 86).

From a training standpoint, special populations are understood from a unifying perspective that uses the analogy of a salad bowl: separate groups tossed together in a unified whole. Cultural differences are minimized and said to result from socialization of a particular group. From a social work perspective, common cultural traits exist that transcend particular ethnic groups and are true of all cultures, such as family and values of freedom and acceptance. Universal cultural competencies apply to clients in general and to multicultural clients in particular. The principles of relationship protocol (communication of respect to the client, particularly the head of a household) and professional self-disclosure (the worker's sharing a common experience as a bridge and point of reference) can be applied to all clients, regardless of ethnicity and culture.

The ubiquitous approach. The term *ubiquitous* means omnipresent or being present everywhere at the same time. The particular emphasis of the ubiquitous approach is cultural difference. Being different is common across special populations according to ethnic, gender, or disabled status. Ethnic groups are placed in different status levels by superordinate cultural patterns as other races are subordinated to one's own racial group. Cultural differences must be acknowledged. This results in a focus on multiple group differences.

From a training perspective, students must be aware of their own culture and others' as well as the stereotypes and prejudice associated with differences. Social work students and practitioners must be aware of cultural and ethnic differences between European, African, Latino, Asian Americans, and First Nations Peoples. Students must learn culture-specific elements (such as unique ethnic group characteristics).

The traditional approach. The traditional approach holds that culture is the context in which differences find their unique expressions. Carter and Qureshi (1995) explain:

> Culture provides and limits the range of possible experiences. An individual's cultural (identity) development is, for the most part, a function of how the individual interprets his or her world according to the possibilities and limitations set forth by his or her culture. Thus, one interacts with external factors in a strictly adaptive manner. (p. 248)

Shared background is the basis of culture. That is, one's identity is related to worldview, which influences upbringing and life experiences. A person's cultural membership responds to the surrounding environment of different races, ethnic groups, and social arrangements.

In terms of training, the student must be exposed to another culture and increase cultural knowledge through a series of learning contacts. One must develop rapport with the culturally different. Ethnic and cultural prejudice are seen as erroneous individual beliefs. Discussion of sociopolitical power dynamics is minimized, and the consequences of racism and intergroup sociopolitical power dynamics are deemphasized.

The race-based approach. Carter and Qureshi (1995) use the term *race*, although this concept has little scientific credibility. Ethnic mixing has led to no pure race existing. *Ethnicity* is the preferred term rather than *race*. However, they have chosen to use this concept in the section of their discussion on typology.

Race is the locus of culture in the United States. People are classified according to race and grouped by skin color, language, and physical features. The race-based approach highlights the issues of American races and racist practices and looks at interactive culture from sociopolitical history and intergroup power perspectives. Membership in a racial group is seen as the primary experience and the ultimate measure of social exclusion and inclusion. Race is considered to be a visible issue between Whites and other racial groups that determines individual psychosocial development.

Racial boundaries have occurred and are still in place across the United States. One's place in society, where one lives, what one is allowed to learn and later earn, and one's access to social services are part of the social and psychological boundaries established by history, tradition, and law. Early White America's interactions with American Indians and Africans formed the basis for educational, social, political, moral, religious, and economic systems organized along color lines. Racism and racial boundaries are invisibly and visibly understood and are in place in the United States. Racial identity, attitudes, and status must be seen in parallel attitudes, thoughts, feelings, and behaviors between ethnic minority racial groups and the dominant White racial group.

CULTURAL COMPETENCY IN ACTION

The Hernandez Family: A Case Study

Which philosophy of cultural awareness orients you in your work with multicultural clients? Mr. Platt, the social worker, could relate to the Hernandez family in a number of ways based on different philosophies about cultural awareness with varying emphases. As you recall, Mr. and Mrs. Hernandez are a legal immigrant couple who understand Spanish and speak some English. Mr. Hernandez is a gardener who works long hours while Mrs. Hernandez stays home and cares for the three elementary school-age children. She works part-time when the children are in school or when her husband returns from his work.

Discuss an emphasis based on the Carter-Qureshi typology that would be appropriate for Mr. Platt as he relates to the Hernandez family.

- The universal approach emphasizes the primary humanity and commonality of people and the secondary experience and identity of ethnicity, race, and gender.
- The ubiquitous approach recognizes both cultural differences between worker and client in a multiple society and culture-specific factors (such as unique group characteristics) that must be kept in mind.

- The traditional approach appreciates that culture is the context where the expression of cultural uniqueness and differences takes place.
- The race-based approach recognizes the reality of racism and racial barriers between people as something that must be recognized and worked through in the relationship between the social worker and the client.
- The pan-national approach embraces an indigenous non-Eurocentric view of ethnic history, culture, and behavior and may reject traditional social work problem analysis and intervention strategies.

TASK RECOMMENDATIONS

- Which approach or combinations would be effective with the Hernandez family in order to establish cultural competency?
- If, in your opinion, none of the five approaches fits this family, what perspective on cultural knowledge and awareness would you offer as an alternative?

From a training perspective, students must scrutinize their own racial identity development, racism, and the psychological intercultural effect of their own race and that of the client. The racial identity level of the worker and the client affects the helping relationship. One must face racism, power differentials, White ethnocentrism, and feelings of superiority. These racial dynamics are often painful to explore and much easier to ignore. Carter and Qureshi (1995) aptly state: "[A]ll people who are White identified seem to have no interest in working toward developing consciousness of the inequities inherent in the status quo, or in taking any action to effect any kind of social or psychological change" (p. 254). These authors suggest a number of areas that should be investigated during training: the trainee's racial identity; social, cultural, and institutional racism; and the linkage of sociopolitical and historical dynamics to current events. At the same time, the race-based approach requires a painful, discomforting, and soul-searching journey of self-exploration and understanding. Facing one's own racism and oppression leads to a greater awareness of the racial and ethnic dynamics between worker and client.

The pan-national approach.   The pan-national approach holds that racial group membership determines culture in a geographic global sense. Developed by non-Europeans as an alternative to European and American culture, pan-Afrocentrism is an example of this model. It emphasizes Afrocentric psychology in terms of African self-consciousness, spirituality, and social theory. It views colonialism and slavery as a distortion of African self-consciousness and supports the Black struggle for survival and liberation. Because of the violence of colonialism and slavery, non-European people of color have been alienated from themselves and their cultures, while Whites have developed a culture based on violence. Oppressed people are alienated from a worldwide sociopolitical context.

From a training standpoint, a pan-national approach rejects Eurocentric social work and advocates knowledge of ethnic history and shared racial and cultural characteristics and experiences. Ethnic self-consciousness, personality and culture, and the psychology of liberation are areas for cultural learning.

The universal, ubiquitous, traditional, race-based, and pan-national approaches emphasize different facets of training in the development of cultural awareness. The universal approach suggests that universal characteristics are common cultural links between worker and client as people, whereas the ubiquitous approach points out that cultural differences must be understood and mastered if the worker is to be effective with multicultural clients. The traditional approach asserts that the worker must acquire traditional cultural knowledge about ethnic groups and draw on this body of knowledge in working with people of color. The race-based approach forces the worker to confront his or her own racism and racial identity in order to understand the racial dynamics of the helping relationship. Finally, the pan-national approach underscores the need to uncover indigenous ethnic beliefs and practices and to incorporate them into the worker's helping repertoire.

EXPERIENCES OF FAMILY CULTURAL SELF-AWARENESS

Cultural self-awareness is the starting point in the helping process. The worker must be aware of his/her own culture. There are positive and negative dimensions to cultural self-awareness. Potocky-Tripodi (2002) focuses on background:

[A] first step in developing culturally competent practice is to be aware of one's own racial, cultural, and ethnic backgrounds, and how these have influenced one's life experiences and outlooks. By doing so one also becomes aware that the decisions one makes may be ethnocentric. (p. 131)

Later, she discusses developing self-knowledge and recommends:

Social workers' awareness of their own ethnicity may be limited to what they have personally experienced in their lives. Self-knowledge requires workers to actively learn about their ethnic backgrounds. This learning can include such methods as reading about their ethnic groups, interviewing family or other ethnic group members, and participating in traditional activities. (p. 142)

Perez, Fukuyama, and Coleman (2005) pinpoint biases and state: "Culturally competent counseling and therapy begins with therapists' examination and awareness of their own cultural contexts and the existence and sources of personal biases that may hinder effective and culturally competent therapy with clients" (p. 162).

Recently, Yan and Wong (2005) have been critical of cultural self-awareness as too mechanistic and worker oriented and centered. They state:

There are at least three problematic assumptions in the conception of self-awareness in the cultural competence model, namely, the notion of human being as cultural artifact, the use of self as a technique for transcending cultural bias, and subject–object dichotomy as an organizing structure of the worker–client relationship. On the one hand, existing discussion of the cultural competence model suggests that both social workers and clients are culturally determined. On the other hand, through the professional use of self, workers can control the influence of their culture on themselves during the intervention process. (p. 184)

Yan and Wong argue for egalitarian cultural self-and-other awareness. They state: "The unidirectional social work process leaves no space for the possibility of equal involvement between two equal human beings. The exclusion of that possibility is one of the major deficiencies of the present cultural competence model" (p. 185). Later, they observe: "[T]he social work process is an engagement of two human subjects who bring their own cultural values into the interpretation process" (p. 185). Yan and Wong want to emphasize reflexive awareness and intersubjective reflection into cultural self-and-other awareness: "[S]elf exists only in relation to others, those conversation partners who were essential to self-definition and crucial to one's self-understanding", and "[T]he self is an ongoing, fluid construction linked to social context and in dialogue with other people's perceptions of who the self is" (p. 186). Cultural self-and-other awareness pertains to the worker and the client. Yan and Wong further speak about a dialogic space: "[A] dialogic process in which both worker and client interactively negotiate, understand, and reflect on their cultures with reference to their understanding of the problem presented by the client" and "creating a dialogic space in which workers allow the inclusion of the client's world into theirs" (p. 186). Mutual learning and changing through mutual understanding occur with both the worker and the client:

On the one hand, the worker learns from the client's experiences in ways that may make him or her a different person. On the other hand, the client may also find himself or herself changing when she or he experiences full understanding and acceptance from someone. (p. 187)

Weighing both these perspectives and working through and resolving those areas of concern are important in the quest for positive self-awareness.

Others, such as Van Den Bergh and Crisp (2004), have sensitized us toward developing self-awareness in working with sexual minority clients and offer a number of suggestions:

- Self-reflect on one's own sexual orientation in terms of its development, influences, and experiences.
- Reflect on one's previous contact with GLBT (gay, lesbian, bisexual, transgender) individuals, both personally and professionally.
- Evaluate one's reaction to GLBT individuals, in terms of both positive and negative experiences.
- Self-evaluate the cognitive, affective, and behavioral components of one's responses to GLBT individuals in order to develop awareness of potential heterosexism or homophobia.
- Participate in personal and professional activities that foster a greater understanding of GLBT individuals and culture.

We are reminded to check our cultural self-awareness on many different levels.

Green (1995) points out that each individual exists in a cultural matrix and not as a unique entity, stating that "both clients and professional helpers swim in their own cultural pond, and neither has much experience outside of it" (p. 164). If the worker and the client each are a part of a different cultural pond, there will be experiential differences between them. Thus, a primary task of building cultural competence is to assist the worker in exploring his or her cultural pond and becoming aware of the client's cultural pond.

Individual and family experiences are central to an understanding of one's cultural pond. The discovery of family of origin uncovers family heritage or cultural history. Past family events influence present family attitudes and cultural life experiences. Beliefs and practices from parents and grandparents have a major effect on an individual. The family is the individual's primary group, representing the familiar, the intimate, the positive, the similar, the in-group. In their section on culture and families, Gushue, Greenan, and Brazaitis (2005) discuss between-group cultural differences and within-group cultural differences. In Chapter 2, we touched on the concept of diversity within diversity. Now we are focusing on intergroup (between-group) and intragroup (within-group) diversity. The between-group cultural differences describe differing cultural and ethnic patterns of family functioning, whereas the within-group cultural differences draw attention to significant differences among families of the same culture. The worker must recognize that these two dynamics often exist simultaneously. Family life experiences and practices shape the worker's beliefs, attitudes, behavior, and view of life and the surrounding world.

McGoldrick and Giordano (1996) point out that each ethnic culture has its own unique set of experiences. In Competency Study 5.3, they draw distinctions among different cultures in terms of how verbal communication is used.

Family and culture fulfill our needs. They are the source of our self-perception and worldview. From our family, we view, interpret, and respond to the outside world. The family provides protection, comfort, and care throughout our lives, particularly during times of transition and major change. We derive strength for coping and survival from our family, who become our natural support system. In brief, family and culture help the individual become a fully functioning person.

How Different Cultures Use Words

- In Jewish culture, articulating one's experience may be as important as the experience itself for important historical reasons. Jews have long valued cognitive clarity. Clarifying and sharing ideas and perceptions helps them find meaning in life. Given the anti-Semitic societies in which Jews have lived for so long with their rights and experiences so often obliterated, one can understand that they have come to place so much importance on analyzing, understanding, and acknowledging what has happened.
- In Anglo culture, words are used primarily to accomplish one's goals. They are valued mainly for their utilitarian value. As the son says about his brother's death in the movie *Ordinary People:* "What's the point of talking about it? It doesn't change anything."
- In Chinese culture, families may communicate many important issues through food rather than through words. They generally do not accept the dominant American idea of "laying your cards on the table."
- Italians often use words primarily for drama, to convey the emotional intensity of an experience.
- The Irish, perhaps the world's greatest poets, used words to buffer experience—using poetry or humor to somehow make reality more tolerable, not to tell the truth, but perhaps to cover it up to embellish it. The Irish have raised poetry, mystification, double meanings, humorous indirection, and ambiguity to an art form in part, perhaps, because their history of oppression led them to realize that telling the truth could be dangerous.
- In Sioux Indian culture, talking is actually proscribed in certain family relationships. A woman who has never exchanged a single word with her father-in-law may experience deep intimacy with him, a relationship that is almost inconceivable in our pragmatic world. The reduced emphasis on verbal expression seems to free Native American families for other kinds of experience of each other, of nature, and of the spiritual realm. (p. 11)

McGoldrick and Giordano (1996) stress that it is crucial for the worker to understand his or her own ethnic identity. Cultural awareness lessens negative reactions to ethnic characteristics of clients and judgmental attitudes about group values. As McGoldrick and Giordano observe,

When people are secure in their identity, they act with greater flexibility and openness to those of other cultural backgrounds. . . . [I]f people receive negative or distorted images of their ethnic group, they often develop a sense of inferiority, even self-hate, that can lead to aggressive behavior and discrimination toward outsiders. (p. 9)

Exploring and affirming the cultural identity of the social work student and practitioner enables culturally sensitive relationships with clients.

CULTURAL OTHER-AWARENESS

It is important to explore personal contacts with individuals and groups of other cultures and ethnicities in order to determine the breadth and depth of one's experience with people of diverse cultures. Perez and colleagues (2005) observe:

[I]t is important that therapists gain cultural awareness and understanding of their clients' experiences and the way presenting concerns or difficulties may be influenced by racial and ethnic variables as well as the intersection of those variables with issues of racism or other forms of societal oppression. (p. 163)

Human service workers cannot mask their feelings toward multicultural clients. Green (1995) observes:

As most social workers know, countertransference is projection onto the client of the therapist's feelings and experiences from previous relationships. These feelings may have resulted from prior frustrations or from a lifelong pattern of dislike of certain people. In the service encounter, they become part of the dynamics of the event and may be difficult to mask or control. (p. 169)

Thus, it is mandatory to revisit the range of previous contact experiences—both positive and negative—in order to become aware of feelings toward culturally different others. Cultural awareness provides a perspective on the worker's contacts outside his or her own cultural and ethnic group, an evaluation of relationships and experiences, and an understanding of individual reactions and biases.

Cultural other-awareness challenges us to look beyond a White–Black dichotomy society. Delgado, Jones, and Rohani (2005) make the point that immigration and its accompanying changing ethnic demographics move us beyond a mind-set of a dominant White majority and an oppressed Black minority. They observe:

Many people would argue that this nation's view of the world was greatly shaped and influenced by the centrality of slavery in the nation's social fabric. As a result, race relations have historically been viewed from a Black–White perspective. However, the shift in demographic composition has largely been fueled by immigration. The number of newcomers from Latino countries in the Western Hemisphere . . . has been so pronounced that this trend, combined with high fertility and low death rates, have converged to make Latinos the largest "minority" in the United States. (p. 233)

A similar case could be made for Asians, which are the fastest-growing ethnic group in this country. All this reminds us to think of cultural other-awareness in terms of multiple cultural individuals and groups.

Increasingly, with the population explosion of immigrants and refugees, we need to find out about this dimension of cultural other-awareness. Potocky-Tripodi (2002) explains:

The population of immigrants and refugees in the United States is growing rapidly. Within the next four to five decades, immigrants and refugees will account for 65 percent of the country's population growth, and first- and second-generation immigrants and refugees will make up more than 25 percent of the population. Thus, all social workers are likely to encounter refugee and immigrant clients in their practice. (p. 479)

Segal (2002) has a helpful framework for immigration that is useful for uncovering the important aspects of the journey from one's home country to the receiving country, which is a crucial part of cultural other-awareness. Her model includes eight aspects:

Conditions in Home Country
- Economic, political/legal, social, cultural/religious

Status in Home Country
- Economic, social, political

Experience in Home Country

- Education, vocation, class/caste

Reasons for Leaving Home Country

- Push: Lack of opportunity, persecution (political/legal/religious), natural disasters, adventure
- Pull: Increased opportunity, freedom/safety, family reunification, adventure

Transition to Country of Immigration

- Emigration: planned/unplanned, voluntary/forced, legal/illegal, safe/dangerous, easy/difficult
- Immigration: easy/difficulty, pleasant/traumatic, direct/indirect, legal/undocumented

Response to the Immigration Process

- Immigrant's resources for immigration: psychological strengths, language competence, social supports, professional/vocational skills, economic resources, color of skin
- Readiness of receiving country for acceptance of immigrant: immigration policies, opportunities, obstacles, programs and services, language facility, skin color

Adjustment to the Receiving Country Lifestyle and Culture

- Acculturation and assimilation, segmented assimilation, integration, accommodation, separation, marginalization, rejection

Implications for the Human Services

- Public policy and law, health and mental health, social welfare, housing and urban issues, education, vocational training, social and economic development, social/cultural/emotional adjustment, private and public services (pp. 4–37)

(For more details, see Segal's [2002] *A Framework for Immigration: Asians in the United States*, Chapter 1 Introduction: A Framework for the Immigration Experience.)

A number of approaches exist for the subject of previous contacts with diverse people. One can recall one's life-span development and focus on specific incidents where there was significant contact with a diverse person. Childhood incidents are often formative building blocks that shape later beliefs and attitudes about and behavioral responses to diverse people. Did you have meaningful contact with European, African, Latino, Asian American, and First Nations Peoples individuals and families in your childhood years? Did you live in a homogeneous White neighborhood or a heterogeneous, diverse neighborhood? Who were your neighborhood and school friends? Did you attend an integrated school system? Do you recall positive and/or negative incidents involving you and a diverse person of color that made a lasting impression on your life? These are significant questions to ask from a life-development perspective.

Based on past and present contact with diverse people, it is crucial to ask about the degree of tolerance and/or acceptance of cultural differences that you have felt. Tolerance is the degree of acceptance of views, beliefs, and practices that differ from one's own. It also denotes the degree of freedom one has from internalized bigotry or prejudice. Finally, it includes the willingness to allow, permit, and respect the divergent beliefs and practices of others. In sum, tolerance is the willingness to accept another person and to allow him or her to be what he or she wants to be, as long as the individual does not harm someone else.

Tools for Student Learning 5.1 provides an opportunity to explore in a discussion format your own cultural life experiences and contacts outside your own cultural and ethnic group. You should answer the questions before attending class and then spend at least 30 minutes in a small-group laboratory discussing your answers and those of others. These self-help and self-discovery groups are vehicles by which you can help each other with these areas of living.

TOOLS FOR STUDENT LEARNING 5.1

Family Cultural Life Experiences and Contacts Outside One's Own Cultural/Ethnic Group

This is a self-assessment of your family cultural life experiences and your significant contacts with members of other cultural and ethnic groups in your neighborhood and community. You are asked to provide the following information and to bring it to class for group discussion.

1. My ethnic family background is: (circle those that apply)

    a. European origin

1. Amish	6. Greek	11. Scandinavian
2. English	7. Hungarian	12. other (please explain)
3. Dutch	8. Irish	13. combination of the
4. French Canadian	9. Italian	following:
5. German	10. Portuguese	

    b. Slavic

1. Polish	4. Czech
2. Slovak	5. other (please explain)
3. Russian	6. combination of the following:

    c. Jewish

1. American	4. European
2. Soviet	5. other (please explain)
3. Israeli	6. combination of the following:

    d. First Nations Peoples

1. tribe	3. combination of the following:
2. other (please explain)	

    e. African origin

1. African American	3. Haitian
2. Jamaican	4. African American Muslim

      5. Nigerian   7. combination of the following:

      6. other (please explain)

  f. Latino

      1. Cuban   5. Central American

      2. Mexican   6. other (please explain)

      3. Puerto Rican   7. combination of the following:

      4. Brazilian

  g. Asian American

      1. Chinese   6. Indonesian

      2. Japanese   7. Filipino

      3. Korean   8. other (please explain)

      4. Vietnamese   9. combination of the following:

      5. Cambodian

  h. Asian Indian

      1. Hindu   4. other (please explain)

      2. Christian   5. combination of the following:

      3. Muslim

  i. Middle Eastern

      1. Arab   5. Armenian

      2. Iraqi   6. other (please explain)

      3. Iranian   7. combination of the following:

      4. Lebanese

2. My level of acculturation is: (circle one)

  a. very Americanized   d. traditional culture of origin

  b. somewhat Americanized   e. other (please explain)

  c. bicultural

3. My regional culture (circle one) does/does not influence me. If it does, my regional culture is: (circle one)

  a. Southern   f. New England

  b. Midwestern   g. New York

  c. Eastern   h. California

  d. Northern   i. Texas

  e. Western   j. other (please explain)

4. The keeper of culture in my family is: (circle one)

  a. my mother   d. my sister

  b. my father   e. my brother

  c. my mother and father   f. my grandmother

    g. my grandfather   i. other (please explain)

    h. my grandmother and grandfather   j. no one (please explain)

5. My family observes the following cultural practices: (check relevant ones)

    a. ethnic holidays   f. ethnic birthday traditions

    b. ethnic religious worship   g. ethnic funeral traditions

    c. ethnic and cultural food   h. other (please explain)

    d. ethnic conversational language   i. none (please explain)

    e. ethnic marriage traditions   j. all of the above

6. My best friends in my neighborhood were: (check one)

    a. the same race

    b. different races (please specify)

    c. other (please explain)

7. My best friends in school were: (check one)

    a. the same race

    b. different races (please specify)

    c. other (please explain)

8. My closest friends are: (check one)

    a. the same race

    b. different races (please specify)

    c. other (please explain)

9. I have a partner or will probably have a partner who is: (check one)

    a. a person of my specific ethnic subgroup   d. uncertain

    b. a person of my general ethnic background   e. other (please explain)
      (e.g., European-European, Latino-Latino)

    c. a person of another race

10. My levels of contact with individuals, families, and groups outside my own cultural and ethnic group in the following settings are: (check relevant ones)

Level of Contact	Setting			
	Neighborhood	School	Social Activities	Work
minimal				
moderate				
frequent				

11. My experiences with people of other cultures and ethnicities have been: (circle relevant ones)

positive   negative   mixed

    a. Describe a positive experience: c. Describe a mixed experience:

    b. Describe a negative experience:

12. I have a number of stereotypes about the following groups: (circle relevant ones)
    a. European Americans
    b. African Americans
    c. Latino Americans
    d. Asian Americans
    e. First Nations Peoples

    Give an example of a group stereotype that you have:

13. People have a stereotype about me due to: (circle relevant ones)
    a. my ethnic background
    b. my gender
    c. my appearance
    d. my student status
    e. my career choice
    f. my income
    g. my place of residence
    h. the make of my car
    i. other (explain)

14. I (circle one) would/would not like to increase my cultural awareness. If so, I am interested in the following areas: (circle relevant ones)
    a. studying my ethnic/cultural family roots
    b. visiting my country of origin
    c. learning my ethnic language
    d. learning about other ethnic and cultural history, beliefs, and interaction patterns
    e. working with multicultural clients in social service agencies
    f. learning a multicultural language
    g. working in my country of origin
    h. working in a Third World country
    i. other (please explain)

RACISM, PREJUDICE, AND DISCRIMINATION

In Chapter 2 we discussed racism, sexism, homophobia, and ageism as important factors in an environment-centered context. We recognize that each of these factors triggers prejudice and discrimination but we want to make the case for the centrality of racism as the underlying dynamic that has caused the major division in this country since the beginning of our nation. From the genocide of First Nations Peoples, the slavery of African Americans, the cheap labor of Latino and Asian Americans, the moral cause of the Civil War, and the Civil Rights Acts of 1870, 1875, 1964, and 1965, racism has been the primary social problem that periodically reemerges in the life of our society.

Racism, prejudice, and discrimination are universal characteristics of all people. Europeans, Africans, Latinos, Asian Americans, and First Nations Peoples experience racism, prejudice, and discrimination as victims and also victimize others as agents of racial oppression. As a person of color and a university professor, I have often observed students and faculty of color in controversy. They exclaim in frustration and anguish, "I am a victim of racism!" when related factors of ability and performance are clearly in question. This is not to discount that racism and racial bias are still alive today.

CULTURAL COMPETENCY IN ACTION

The Hernandez Family: A Case Study

Cultural awareness includes appreciation of family cultural life experiences. How can Mr. Platt, the social worker, learn about this area of the Hernandez family? Green (1995) mentions that every individual exists in a cultural matrix (a place of origin) and swims in his or her own cultural pond. Individual and family experiences—past, present, and future—influence our attitudes and life perspectives. Family and culture fulfill our needs. Positive or negative ethnic and cultural identity experiences have an effect on how we feel about ourselves and how we treat others.

TASK RECOMMENDATIONS

- Describe the cultural matrix and cultural ponds of the following people: Mr. and Mrs. Hernandez, the Hernandez children (Ricardo, Isabella, and Eduardo), and Mr. Platt, the social worker.
- How would you bring these cultural ponds together? Would you attempt to swim in any of these ponds? Would you combine these ponds so that everyone could "jump in" and have a good time swimming together?
- How would you describe your cultural matrix and cultural pond?

A newspaper article entitled "School District Shuffles Bosses: Board Changes Job of 25 Administrators" (1997) reported the reaction of a Latino middle-range administrator whose school district job was changed: "I believe I have been targeted for demotion because of my race and my support of the previous board." Later in the news story, the school district superintendent reported that overall, the reassignments or demotions would affect 18 minority educators and 14 Whites, and that 52 percent of the district's management posts and 60 percent of the principals were ethnic minority members. Like most school organizations, the school district was top-heavy with administrators and required major overhauling and trimming of personnel, but some charged that racism and racial discrimination were the reasons for the bureaucratic downsizing.

Overt and covert expressions of racism, prejudice, and discrimination exist. Racism is an ideological belief that it is right for one social or ethnic group to dominate another. Generally, White European Americans have assumed the racist role, whereas people of color have been subjugated in the history of American racism. People of color accuse Whites, who are the majority population, of racism. In turn, Whites subtly or openly may make people of color feel unwelcome and uncomfortable. This is an example of intergroup racism. There is also intragroup racism based on social class, language fluency, skin color, and educational attainment. Examples of elites who assume a superior role in their ethnic groups include light-skinned African Americans from wealthy, established families, who are alumni of prestigious Black private colleges; Mandarin-speaking Taiwanese-born Chinese American professionals from upper-class families; and Cuban-born, light-skinned, wealthy families living in the Miami area. They and other similar groups make social class distinctions that border on racism, prejudice, and discrimination within their ethnic groups.

The issue of racism raises some interesting questions:

- Are White European Americans, who form the majority of the population of the United States, racists in light of the history of ethnic oppression in America? Is racism a White American problem?
- Are there racists, and is there racism in all cultures and societal groups? Is racism a universal reality?
- Has the charge of racism been used as a diversion or an excuse to deflect the pressing issues confronting a person or society? Some would argue that this was the case in O. J. Simpson's trial, Clarence Thomas's confirmation hearings before the Senate Judiciary Committee, and former California Governor Pete Wilson's campaign for Proposition 189 on illegal immigrants, which focused attention away from the state of the California economy during Wilson's first term in office.

You may wish to discuss these controversial issues as you confront racism in American society.

Prejudice is an attitudinal response that expresses racist beliefs in an unfavorable feeling—such as hatred, anger, or hostility—toward an excluded group or individual members. Discrimination is an unfavorable behavioral response directed at members of an excluded ethnic or racial group. It is a visible or a subtle action that denies equal opportunity in society.

How does a person confront racism, prejudice, and discrimination and seek to change these realities in individuals, groups, and society? Pope (1993) offers the multicultural change intervention matrix (MCIM), a helpful step-by-step procedural model that copes with these issues. The MCIM addresses systemic planned change, multicultural organization development, and multicultural interventions and activities. The matrix has two dimensions: target of change (individual, group, institution) and type of change (first-order change, second-order change). At the individual target level of changing racism, the first-order change involves awareness, knowledge, and information about one's own racism. The second-order change at the individual level is education to restructure thinking about racism. This involves the examination of racist belief and thought systems, interactive or experiential new learning, and consciousness raising about where racism came from and how we need to transcend racism.

At the group level, the first-order change is a change in the composition of the group so that members of unrepresented groups are added. Change in the group composition forces the issue of how people relate to each other and dispels stereotypes about people of color. It also reverses the majority–minority numbers. More diversity in group composition results in more diverse thoughts, feelings, and behaviors that move away from racism, prejudice, and discrimination. The second-order change at the group level involves restructuring a program based on an examination of existing group composition, values, philosophy, purposes, and goals, and the infusion of a program with a new mission, goals, and members. For example, the introduction of multicultural staff recruitment, cultural knowledge about dealing with multicultural clients, and lending personnel for community service in underserved areas might be new directions for a business organization committed to making a contribution to diversity.

At the institutional level, the first-order change involves a program intervention that addresses the problem of racism and offers a change effort that undergirds the institutional values and structure. Examples are an ombudsman or advocate for multicultural staff and clients, a staff position devoted to multicultural activities and affairs, or a university chair in social ethnic or multicultural social work studies. The second-order change examines institutional values, goals, and evaluation, and links them to multicultural values and efforts. Multicultural content and effort pervade the entire institutional system, which is transformed toward a multicultural emphasis and moves away from a racist viewpoint. Major initiatives and institutional decision making proceed from this commitment.

The MCIM is a useful paradigm for addressing racism at the individual, group, and institutional levels. It suggests six first-order and second-order steps toward change that are fluid and dynamic. It begins with individual awareness of racism and moves toward institutional system change. Along the way, it plots a course of action to cope innovatively with racism.

Tools for Student Learning 5.2 offers some discussion questions about racism, prejudice, and discrimination. It considers the past and present status of a person who has been influenced by racism and how to move such a person beyond this stage of belief, attitude, and behavior. Coping with and facing racism, prejudice, and discrimination in our own lives and the life of our nation is an essential part of developing cultural awareness.

TOOLS FOR STUDENT LEARNING 5.2

Discussion Questions on Racism, Prejudice, and Discrimination

1. Describe racism, prejudice, and discrimination based on your experiences in your own words.

2. Who teaches a person to be a racist, to show prejudice, and to discriminate against another person?

3. Do you know a racist? Is everyone in the world a racist?

4. Is there anyone in your family who is a racist? Are you a racist?

5. How can you cope with racism? Can a racist person change?

6. Can racism be eliminated in the United States? What positive steps can be taken toward transcending racism?

7. What are your present thoughts about racism, prejudice, and discrimination?

MULTICULTURAL INVOLVEMENT OVER THE LIFE SPAN

All of us have a unique story about our multicultural involvement at different stages of our life. Throughout our lives, the extent of our contact with people of color may vary. Most Americans are a part of the predominant European American culture that forms the majority society. Many Americans are of English, Irish, French, and German ancestry. Most Americans have singular contacts with various people of color. Neighborhoods are still segregated communities, whereas multicultural contact is prevalent at school and in the workplace. But even in these settings, people are selective in their choice of school friends and work colleagues.

My life story begins with World War II, the year before England and France declared war on Nazi Germany over the invasion of Poland. I was born on September 23, 1938, in Hamilton, Ohio (population 60,000). Situated on the Miami River in southwestern Ohio between Cincinnati and Dayton, the city was a small industrial center for two quality paper manufacturing companies, Champion Paper and Beckett Paper, and an internationally known manufacturer of safes, Mosler Safes. My parents were both from Honolulu, Hawaii. My father was a 1923 graduate in chemistry from the University of Chicago and the only one of seven children to graduate from college. He settled with my mother in Hamilton in the late 1920s to learn the paper-making business. He was the chief chemist of the Beckett Paper Company. His dream was to return to China to help the new Republic of China under Dr. Sun Yat-Sen, its first president, with a paper factory. Unfortunately, the Sino-Japanese War in the early 1930s ended his vision.

During the 1940s and 1950s, Hamilton, Ohio, was a Republican, conservative, and segregated town. The Miami River divided the city into the west and east sides. The west side was all White; in fact, we were the sole minority family on that side of town. The east side consisted of the downtown; residences of low-income White families; and an isolated, segregated section by the river for African Americans, who in those days were called Negroes, colored people, or "the colors." This area contained a public housing project called Bamboo Harris.

My elementary and junior high schoolmates were all White. I was the only minority child in my schools. I grew up during World War II and the postwar era. I remember going to the Saturday afternoon movies (two cowboy Western features, cartoons, and a thriller serial for a dime) and being threatened by older children during intermission. They were going to beat me up because they thought that I was "a Jap." I remember telling them: "I am Chinese—one of your allies."

My mother attended the local United Presbyterian church and took her children to Sunday school. It was an all-White church but the members readily accepted us. Her social life centered on a few church-women friends. Many years later, my father remarked that he was never invited to his friends' homes because he was Chinese.

During my childhood and early adolescence, I experienced racial slurs and stares. As a child, I was invited to neighborhood birthday parties, but as I attended junior high, invitations to private parties and dates with White girls ceased. About that time, my older sister, a beautiful teenager, was seriously involved with a White boyfriend, and my parents decided that it was time to move back to Honolulu, Hawaii.

It was a difficult transition. My father did not have a job and was in his middle 50s. He struggled financially for several years until he finally got a position as a safety engineer with the State of Hawaii. Moving from a small, all-White culture to a large, island, multicultural environment took years of adjustment for me. I was a "banana": yellow on the outside but White on the inside. Island teenage boys were mean to this Oriental "haole" (White foreigner). Most of my junior high and high school classmates were Japanese, Chinese, and Filipino, with some White, Hawaiian, and Portuguese. There were no Blacks in my high school in Hawaii. Most of my teachers during high school and university were White. We lived in a predominantly Asian neighborhood, and I attended a Chinese Protestant church where I became accepted and active in the youth group.

I never lost my mainland English accent, but I adopted the island culture and lifestyle. My dates were mainly Asians, although there were no serious romantic relationships in my adolescence. I never learned to speak Chinese, although this was my ethnic background. I knew little Chinese cultural history and few of the beliefs and practices. I was an American Chinese rather than a Chinese American.

I left to attend graduate school in southern California at two institutions in Pasadena and Claremont. My classmates and professors were predominantly White, with a few Asian and some Black students. I attended several Chinese churches to maintain my ethnic contact and lived in dorms on campus. Several Chinese students who got together on occasion for dinner and conversation served as a support system.

My first romantic relationship was with a Chinese girl in her late teens, but her father did not like me and ended the relationship. However, several years later I met a Chinese woman at church who had come to Los Angeles to teach elementary school. She became my wife after a year and a half of courtship. Years earlier, my mother had taken me aside and said, "I want you to marry a nice Chinese girl." Those words had become a part of my subconscious. Although I dated many ethnic women, I remembered my mother's words and obeyed her wishes. I was able to pass on my ethnic heritage and culture and my family name to the next generation. We have two sons and two daughters.

As a young married couple, we spent five years in Honolulu. We attended a Japanese church, built close relationships with three Asian couples, and maintained contact with them over the years. We lived in a small apartment complex surrounded by young adult Asian singles and married couples.

I returned to graduate school in Cleveland, Ohio. My doctoral graduate class consisted of eight Whites, two Jews, one African American, and me. I was able to complete classes in a calendar year and wrote my doctoral dissertation during my second year. We lived in a suburban community (Euclid, Ohio) in a large apartment complex that was predominantly White. My wife attended a large state university in Cleveland. Her education classes were composed of White and Black students who sat in their separate groups. As an Asian, she was baffled about where to sit and sat next to a young Black woman who became her friend. After the first year, my wife worked in several elementary schools in a school district outside Cleveland, where she was the only minority teacher. During a beginning-of-the-year open house, several parents criticized my wife about being Asian and not being able to speak English correctly. They were forbidden to trespass on the school campus during the year by the principal, who stood up for her, as did several teacher friends. This is the only racial incident I can remember from our two years in the greater Cleveland area. I was treated well by my university professors and classmates. Our oldest daughter was born in Taiwan and adopted by us during our last year in Cleveland.

Our 32 years in Sacramento have been filled with my teaching and writing at California State University, Sacramento. There have been racial tensions on our faculty and at the university and community levels. However, one-third of the social work faculty are people of color. I have had an opportunity to grow and to develop multicultural theory and practice in social work. We live in south Sacramento in an area called Greenhaven, which has been a wonderful place to raise four children. We live in a predominantly White and Asian community on a double cul-de-sac and have friendly neighbors. Our children's friends are multiracial and predominantly Asian. Our two oldest are away in Los Angeles and Fresno, and the two youngest are living at home and going to community college. My wife works at an elementary school as a first-grade teacher.

I share these experiences knowing that my life journey as a Chinese American has been limited by living situations, life choices, and educational and career experiences. Each of us sharing our life background will help us understand where we are coming from and where we have to go in our journey with people on this earth.

It is important to share aspects of your life journey with others who will appreciate and understand you. Tools for Student Learning 5.3 will help you explore your childhood adolescence, young adulthood, and adult years in relationship to contact with people of color. Please fill out this exercise and bring it to class for sharing.

TOOLS FOR STUDENT LEARNING 5.3

Multicultural Involvement over the Life Span

This questionnaire surveys your involvement with people of color in childhood, adolescence, young adulthood, and adulthood. You are asked to provide the following information and to share it in class discussion.

1. I was born in: (name of city, population)

2. My ethnic group is: (circle one)
   a. European American
   b. African American
   c. Latino American
   d. Asian American
   e. First Nations Peoples
   f. other (please explain)

3. My childhood years were spent in: (name of city or cities)

4. When I was a child, my neighborhood was predominantly: (circle one)
   a. European American
   b. African American
   c. Latino American
   d. Asian American
   e. First Nations Peoples
   f. multiracial (list ethnic groups)

5. When I was a child, my contact with people of different ethnic groups was as indicated. (circle one in each category)
   a. African Americans: rare / somewhat frequent/ frequent
   b. Mexican Americans: rare / somewhat frequent/ frequent
   c. Puerto Rican Americans: rare / somewhat frequent/ frequent
   d. Cuban Americans: rare / somewhat frequent/ frequent
   e. Chinese Americans: rare / somewhat frequent/ frequent
   f. Japanese Americans: rare / somewhat frequent/ frequent
   g. Korean Americans: rare / somewhat frequent/ frequent
   h. Vietnamese Americans: rare / somewhat frequent/ frequent
   i. First Nations Peoples: rare / somewhat frequent/ frequent

6. When I was a child, my impressions about people of different ethnic groups were as indicated. (circle one in each category)

    a. African Americans: favorable / somewhat favorable / unfavorable

    b. Latino Americans: favorable / somewhat favorable / unfavorable

    c. Asian Americans: favorable / somewhat favorable / unfavorable

    d. First Nations Peoples: favorable / somewhat favorable / unfavorable

7. As a child, I formulated my impression about people of color from: (circle relevant ones)

    a. my parents' attitudes   d. my peer group

    b. my experiences with ethnic individuals   e. other (please explain)

    c. neighbors' attitudes

8. My adolescent years were spent in: (name of city or cities)

9. When I was a teenager, my neighborhood was predominantly: (circle one)

    a. European American   d. Asian American

    b. African American   e. First Nations Peoples

    c. Latino American   f. multiracial (list ethnic groups)

10. When I was a teenager, my close friends were predominantly: (circle one)

    a. Whites   d. Asian American

    b. African Americans   e. First Nations Peoples

    c. Latino Americans   f. multiracial (list ethnic groups)

11. As a teenager, I dated predominantly: (circle one)

    a. Whites   d. Asian American

    b. African Americans   e. American Indians

    c. Latino Americans   f. multiracial (list ethnic groups)

12. When I was a teenager, my impressions from childhood about people of different ethnic groups changed (or not) as indicated. (circle one in each category)

    a. African Americans:

       remained the same / changed more favorably / changed less favorably

    b. Latino Americans:
       remained the same / changed more favorably / changed less favorably

    c. Asian Americans:

       remained the same / changed more favorably / changed less favorably

    d. First Nations Peoples:

       remained the same / changed more favorably / changed less favorably

Explain the reasons for your change in impressions about specific ethnic groups.

13. As a young adult, I lived in: (name of city or cities)

14. I went to the following colleges and universities:

15. My undergraduate college major was:

16. My college degrees are: (circle relevant ones)
    baccalaureate   master   doctorate

17. When I was a young adult, my close friends were predominantly: (circle one)
    a. Whites
    b. African Americans
    c. Latino Americans
    d. Asian Americans
    e. First Nations Peoples
    f. multiracial (list ethnic groups)

18. When I was a young adult, my serious romantic relationships were predominantly with: (circle one)
    a. Whites
    b. African Americans
    c. Latino Americans
    d. Asian Americans
    e. First Nations Peoples
    f. multiracial (list ethnic groups)

19. When I was a young adult, my first full-time job after graduation from college was with an organization whose employees were predominantly: (circle one)
    a. Whites
    b. African Americans
    c. Latino Americans
    d. Asian Americans
    e. First Nations Peoples
    f. multiracial (list ethnic groups)

20. As an adult, I have lived in: (name of city or cities)
    I now am living in: (name of city)

21. As an adult, I married or am living with a partner whose ethnic background is: (circle one)
    a. the same as mine
    b. different from mine (please explain)

22. As an adult, I live in a neighborhood that is predominantly: (circle one)
    a. White
    b. African American
    c. Latino American
    d. Asian American
    e. First Nations Peoples
    f. multiracial (list ethnic groups)

23. My present employer is: (name of the company)

24. My fellow employees are predominantly: (circle one)
    a. White
    b. African American
    c. Latino American
    d. Asian American
    e. First Nations Peoples
    f. multiracial (list ethnic groups)

25. Throughout my life, the degree of contact and involvement with people of color that I have had has been: (circle one)
    a. minimal   b. somewhat frequent   c. frequent   d. other (please explain)

INTERGENERATIONAL ACCULTURATION

We have just covered multicultural involvement over the life span. As a result of life-span cultural interaction between the individual and related groups, there is the need to consider how one acculturates over various life stages. When individuals, families, and ethnic and cultural groups and communities experience acculturation over many generations, intergenerational acculturation is at work. *Acculturation* is the process of adapting to a new or different culture and involves making a transition from one's culture of origin to the dominant and majority new culture. *Intergenerational acculturation* relates to how the acculturation process affects each succeeding generation, from grandparents to parents to children and their offspring. Over the generations, one witnesses degrees of transformation toward the new culture as well as preservation of traditional cultural practices, beliefs, customs, and values. An intricate pattern of weaving together a *bicultural integration* of American and country of origin perspectives makes sense and becomes functional for each individual who is in this process. Lum (2004) discusses the *paracultural perspective*, which depicts and explains four related intergenerational stages (recent immigrants who are confronted with two distinct cultures; first generation, American-born who undergo acculturation; second generation, American-born who experience Americanization; and third generation, American-born who are often drawn toward the rediscovery of culture-of-origin elements).

In order to understand the dynamics of intergenerational acculturation and how they impact, for example, a second-generation family as the social worker engages various family subsystems, an intergenerational acculturation model would be a useful tool in the helping process. Portes and Rumbaut (2001) have created intergenerational models of acculturation to understand parent–child dynamics in immigrant families. These dynamics interact with such contextual factors as racial discrimination, urban subcultures, and labor market opportunities. In turn, these elements can affect the child's social, academic, and economic outcomes.

Three ideal type relationships exist between parents and child and form the basis for consonant acculturation, dissonant acculturation, and selective acculturation:

- *Consonant acculturation* describes the situation where both the parent and the child abandon their native culture and assimilate to the dominant American culture. A variation of this is the situation where parents and child resist acculturation and remain rooted within their ethnic community. These families are most likely to return to their home countries.
- *Dissonant acculturation* occurs when the child abandons his/her native culture of origin in favor of integration into the American mainstream while parents lag behind. This situation may lead to intergenerational conflict. Moreover, if the parents do not have ties to the ethnic community as a support system, role reversal may occur where the parents rely on their child to interact with institutions and others in society because the child has learned the language and is able to communicate and broker services for the parents.
- *Selective acculturation* occurs when both parents and child maintain ties to their native culture while also learning the English language and American customs. This seems to be the most desirable form of acculturation because there have been strong associations among continued contact with ethnic communities and academic achievement (Bankston & Zhou, 1995; Portes & Hao, 2002), and little

intergenerational conflict between parents and child and fluent bilingualism for the child when there is a mutual acculturation transition made by both parents and child (Portes & Rumbaut, 2001).

Portes and Rumbaut (2001) tested this model using data from the Children of Immigrants Longitudinal Study (CILS), a national sample of Asian and Latin American second-generation youth. They measured *dissonant acculturation* by limited bilingualism (fluency in one language and poor command of another) and parent–child cultural conflict, which measured the difference in viewpoints and frequency of arguments between parents and child. They found a strong negative influence of dissonant acculturation on middle school grade-point averages that continued through high school. *Selective acculturation* was operationalized by fluent bilingualism and the presence of co-ethnic friendships (friends of the child from both the culture of origin and the dominant culture), which had a strong positive effect on middle school grades but was not significant for high school grades. Nevertheless, strong empirical research evidence bolstered these models of intergenerational acculturation.

In light of this research, social workers should work with immigrant and refugee families to ensure that selective acculturation is achieved. This means selectively identifying useful elements from the culture of origin and simultaneously providing resources that will help both parents and child learn the English language (English as a second language for school children and adults) and American customs as a family unit. This family interaction pattern based on language ability, socioeconomic resources, and sociocultural supports contributes to educational, social, and cultural achievement of immigrant and refugee groups and serves as a basis for understanding other ethnic groups.

CULTURALLY DIVERSE SOCIAL WORK PRACTICE

In the preceding sections of this chapter, we have made the case for cultural awareness in terms of self, others, and societal responses. Social workers need such cultural background as tools for learning to work with a variety of individuals, families, and groups. Culturally diverse social work practice involves working with clients from a perspective of cultural awareness. Green (1999) has set forth a help-seeking behavior model that enhances cultural awareness from the client's perspective. Green is a cultural anthropologist who has applied ethnographic interviewing principles to social work practice. The Green model consists of four major components:

1. The individual's definition and understanding of an experience as a problem. Green discusses this principle in terms of perspective taking; that is, the willingness and ability of the practitioner to elicit the client's understanding of his or her needs. The procedure is primarily to gather information about the client's willingness to communicate and to give feedback that the client's position has been heard by the worker.
2. The client's semantic evaluation of a problem. Language is the medium of cultural knowledge about an individual and an ethnic group. It is crucial to know and understand the meaning of cultural and ethnic words, what Green describes as "cover terms" or special categories of ideas, objects, concepts, or relationships that are familiar and part of the client's cultural experience. These cover terms have cultural significance and psychological reality to the client. Green also uses "ethnographic descriptors" to explain the meaning of cover terms and suggests the importance of a

cultural guide who serves as a teaching resource to explain the subtleties and complexities of a particular community and to interpret cover terms to the worker.

3. Indigenous strategies of problem intervention. Here Green is seeking appropriate sources of help that are a part of the client's culture. Rather than imposing external social work intervention modalities, Green is concerned about ethnic community resources, family and extended family support, indigenous advice giving from respected community authority figures, religious resources, and use of meditation and exercise.

4. Culturally based criteria of problem resolution. Green suggests a focus on how people generally solve their problems in their own communities and what reasonable outcomes to those efforts are from their perspectives. The worker should be knowledgeable about the recent history and daily experiences of the client's ethnic community. The worker should also be aware of the cultural variations that may exist in a particular community and how different clients may respond to specific therapeutic techniques.

An essential part of the cultural awareness practice model centers on ethnographic interviewing. Thornton and Garrett (1995) believe that ethnography is a crucial bridge to multicultural practice. In Competency Study 5.4, they explain how to incorporate ethnography into practice.

COMPETENCY STUDY 5.4

Cultural Awareness and Ethnographic Practice

Social workers who work cross-culturally must know not only how to conduct an ethnographic study but also how to apply this knowledge in practice. Becoming familiar with a culture is not enough, just as listening alone is not enough to help clients solve the problems. Social workers should learn about clients both as individuals and as members of their culture or ethnic community, they should investigate the relevance of culture to the clients' lives, and then they should build on this knowledge and incorporate it into the helping process. Although social workers need to "start where the client is," they also need to help clients move beyond that starting point. Goal development must be based on clients' perceptions of needs (Goldstein, 1983). As obvious as this sounds, the meaning of clients' problems may depend upon the culture in which they are based. Cultural practices that appear problematic or dysfunctional to outsiders may be acceptable or normal when viewed within the context of the culture (Bourguignon, 1979). Therefore, the problems, goals, and outcomes determined by clients may differ from those chosen by workers.

Preconceived solutions are inappropriate in cross-cultural social work. Services tend to be ineffective when they are incongruent with clients' expectations and cultural backgrounds (Leigh & Green, 1989). Social workers who use ethnographic interviewing have established themselves as learners in their client's culture. Clients are viewed as experts on their lives and cultures, workers as experts on the problem-solving process. The two become collaborators, working together to find *ways* to meet client needs in an effective and culturally acceptable way. (pp. 70–71)

The Abdullah family is featured in this chapter on cultural awareness as well as in the next two chapters on knowledge acquisition and skill development. Competency Study 5.5 focuses on applying cultural awareness to the following case study:

The Abdullah Family and Cultural Awareness

Abdullah Abdullah, age 35, his wife, Risah Abdullah, age 30, and their two children, Mohammed, age 10, and Osama, age 5, have recently come to Sacramento, California, from Afghanistan. They have been sponsored by a local mosque and have been referred to the Sacramento New Comers Center where you are a social work intern. You have been asked to find out about their culture, identify important information, and devise a plan for intervention, thereby increasing cultural competence with this family.

Using Green's help-seeking behavior model of cultural awareness, how would you devise an ethnographic approach that would focus on the family's definition and understanding of their experiences in Afghanistan and California and their semantic evaluation of a problem perspective?

Because Muslim men are socialized to be providers and family heads, they are "the face of the family" according to The Cultural Orientation Project ("Muslim refugees in the United States," n.d.). They are closely involved in family life and the care and raising of their children, accompany their wives and children to medical appointments and other family excursions, and are concerned about their children's academic progress. There is a strong traditional value of caring and taking responsibility for one's family. They are the gatekeepers of many family-oriented decisions and activities. For Muslim men, the refugee experience in the United States may be daunting, particularly if they lack English language skills or have professional credentials and work experience that are not recognized by U.S. institutions. They may not be able to find work in their professional field or find work at all and may be completely dislocated. As a result, some Muslim men may exhibit self-destructive behavior as coping mechanisms or may turn to strict observance of Islamic traditions as a way of holding on to something familiar to them. They may require that their wives wear hijab (fully covered from head to foot) and may become more controlling of where, when, and with whom their wives and children may go outside the house. They may become verbally or physically abusive when their wives are more successful than they are at finding work or adapting to the new environment.

Social workers should be aware of these tensions and potential repercussions and should cultivate a respectful relationship with husbands and fathers, deferring to them for their viewpoints and opinions. Building mutual trust will facilitate a willingness to accept assistance and recommendations from the worker. Many Muslim men will not feel comfortable discussing or acknowledging problems with a stranger, particularly a woman. Working with social services provided by a local mosque or other Islamic organizations may be more effective with Muslim refugee men.

Rather than focusing on the problems of the family, discuss how you would work with Mr. Abdullah in the following cultural awareness areas:

1. How would you communicate your sense of cultural awareness to this family?
2. How would you find out about this family's culture in order to build cultural other-awareness?

Green's model underscores the importance of cultivating and applying cultural awareness to the helping relationship. He explains the nature of the ethnographic approach. Rather than superimposing a foreign social work practice intervention, the worker starts with the client's cultural understanding of the problem, moves toward examining the meaning of semantic concepts surrounding the culture and the problem, and then seeks indigenous intervention strategies and problem resolution from the ethnic community perspective. This cultural awareness procedure arises from the recognition that the client's culture is primary and holds the key to solving the problem itself.

The Hernandez Family: A Case Study

Cultural awareness is an integral part of cultural competence. Mr. Platt, the social worker, found that Mr. Hernandez has two jobs and has been away from the family due to long working hours. He usually helps his son, Ricardo, with his homework but has not been able to do so because of work. As a result, Ricardo's schoolwork has suffered and he has become disruptive in the classroom.

TASK RECOMMENDATIONS

The Green help-seeking behavior model is applicable to the Hernandez family. Describe how you would apply the following principles to the Hernandez case:

- The individual's definition and understanding of an experience as a problem. The worker elicits the client's understanding of needs. Would you ask Mr. Hernandez, Mrs. Hernandez, or their son Ricardo to define the problem?
- The client's semantic evaluation of a problem. Particular cultural and ethnic language describes

the problem in specific detail. A cultural guide is suggested to interpret the client description of the problem to the worker. Would you enlist a resource person from Mr. Hernandez's community who is fluent in Spanish and English to come and explain the problem in both languages?

- Indigenous strategies of problem intervention. Cultural sources of help include ethnic community resources, family and extended family support, indigenous advice giving, religious resources, and meditation and exercise. Which strategies would you use for intervention?
- Cultural problem resolution. This focus is on how people in their own communities solve their problems. Problems confronting the Hernandez family are the absence of Mr. Hernandez due to his working at two jobs, Ricardo's school problems, and the immigration of relatives from Mexico. Is it advantageous for the social worker to ask Mr. and Mrs. Hernandez how people in their ethnic community would solve similar problems?

SUMMARY

This chapter has defined cultural awareness from both personal and professional perspectives. It has encouraged you to assess your own cultural background and identity as well as your contacts with groups and individuals of other cultures and ethnicities. It has urged you to confront your own racism, prejudice, and discrimination, challenging you to explore and resolve this aspect of your beliefs, attitudes, and behavioral responses. It has emphasized the importance of cultivating essential knowledge and skills in social work education and employment experiences. Ideally, you will not be hindered by past negative events and people and can work competently with multicultural clients in the present. As a result, clients will feel affirmed and can work on the pressing problems facing them.

CHAPTER SIX

Knowledge Acquisition

Doman Lum

Cultural competence rests on a foundation of *knowledge*—information, facts, theories, and principles that facilitate culturally diverse social work. The social work student needs to master a body of knowledge and become familiar with certain basic issues and theories. *Theory* may consist of single propositions or of a series of general principles that provide a systemic explanation.

This chapter surveys the range of knowledge related to culturally diverse social work that is essential to cultural competence. Weaver (2004) points out: "A culturally competent helper must have knowledge about a client's culture, have certain values and attitudes that include respect for diversity and emphasize helper self-awareness, and have the ability to integrate this knowledge and values/attitudes with helping skills" (p. 21). This chapter on knowledge acquisition begins with demographic trends that contribute to general and ethnic group profiles. Next, it focuses on critical thinking as a means of analyzing knowledge. It explores the effect of the history of group oppression on how knowledge about cultural diversity is formulated. It addresses gender issues, particularly multicultural feminist themes, and examines values that influence how the client and the social worker formulate and interpret social problems, make choices, and implement behavioral change. Gelman (2004) concurs with a similar list of knowledge concerns:

> As this sampling of the social work literature attending to cultural competence with the Latino population illustrates, the importance of possessing knowledge of Latino demographics, diversity, history, immigration patterns, and the problems facing this population is emphasized. Furthermore, an understanding and respect for cultural values identified as characteristic of many within the Latino population is considered necessary. (p. 86)

On an advanced level, cultural competence is enhanced by knowledge of systems and psychosocial theory, as well as theories about ethnicity, culture, minority status, and social class. Finally, the chapter presents social science theory and its application to social work practice with culturally diverse clients.

THE DEMOGRAPHICS OF AMERICANS

In survey research, *demographics* is understood to mean the distribution of a sample population. The word *demography* comes from *demos* (the people) and *graphia* (writing), which describes the process of writing about the people under study. In a social work context, the demography of the client population is the basis for program planning and evaluation.

According to the 2000 U.S. Census, out of a total population of 281,421,906, there were slightly more females (143,368,343 or 50.9 percent) than males (138,053,563 or 49.1 percent). The median age of the average American was 35.3 years. There were 105,480,101 total households in the United States. Family households numbered 71,787,347 (68.1 percent) with married couple families (54,493,232 or 51.7 percent) and female households with no husband present (12,900,103 or 12.2 percent). Nonfamily households numbered 33,692,754 (31.9 percent). Households with individuals under 18 years were 38,022,115 (36 percent), and households with individuals 65 years and over numbered 24,672,708 (23.4 percent). The average household size was 2.59, and the average family size was 3.14 (American FactFinder, 2000, pp. 1–3).

Some interesting profiles exist from the 2000 U.S. Census. Nearly 4 million homes in the United States have three or more generations of families living under the same roof. Households with multiple generations are likely to be recent immigrants or families where there are housing shortages or high costs. The three groups of households are grandparents living with children and grandchildren; parents living with their children and their own parents; and homes with four or more generations. Five states are among the leaders with multiple-generation households: California (8.2 percent), Hawaii (5.6 percent), and Mississippi, Louisiana, and Texas (5 percent each) (MSNBC, 2001d, pp. 1–2).

The gender gap is narrowing, with females about 5 million more than males, who are catching up according to the 2000 U.S. Census. Women numbered 143.4 million (a 13 percent increase from 1990), whereas men numbered 138.1 million (a 14 percent increase from 1990). There were 96.3 men for every 100 women in 2000. The slight increase in men is due to declining death rates for men and the increase in the number of men immigrating to the United States (MSNBC, 2001a, pp. 1–2).

Regarding employment and women, fewer mothers with infant children are working, particularly mothers over 30 years old, White, married, and with some college. In 1998, a record high 59 percent of women with infants worked in the labor force. In 2000, 22 million women with infants were in the labor force. The rates have not dropped for younger mothers, African American and Latino American women, and women with less education (MSNBC, 2001b, pp. 1–2).

Finally, more Americans are living to age 100. There were 50,454 Americans age 100 and older in 2000, an increase of 13,000 (35 percent) from 1990. By 2050, there may be 1 million centenarians. Americans aged 80–84 increased to 4.9 million (26 percent increase from 1990), whereas people aged 90–94 numbered 1.l million (45 percent increase from 1990). A number of factors contributed to increased longevity: healthy and active lifestyles, medical advances, and genetics. California had the largest number of centenarians (5,341 or .016 of its population). In the 65 years and over group, the ratio of men to women increased from 67 men per 100 women in 1990 to 70 men per 100 women in 2000. Of all the older groups, the largest increase was in people who are in the 50–54 years category, with an increase of 55 percent from 1990 (17.6 million in 2000) (MSNBC, 2001c, pp. 1–3)

The Demographics of Cultural Diversity

The demographic profile of ethnically diverse people in the United States is constantly changing due to significant growth in this population in the last 30 years. The 2000 U.S. Census uncovered the following demographic trends (Westphal, 2001):

- Race alone or in combination (multiracial totals) reflects the following ethnic profiles: White (216,930,975), Black or African American (36,419,434), Hispanic or Latino (of any race) (35,305,818), some other race (18,521,486), Asian (11,898,828), American Indian and Alaska Native (4,119,301), and Native Hawaiian and other Pacific Islander (874,414).
- Racial and ethnic minorities accounted for up to 80 percent of the nation's population growth in the 1990s.
- The number of minorities, led by a huge increase in the Hispanic population and fast growth among Asians, was nearly 87 million in 2000, up 43 percent from 1990.
- Hispanic and racial minorities comprise nearly one-third of the 281 million population of the United States.
- Nearly 7 million or 2.4 percent marked two racial categories with a multiracial option yielding up to 63 racial combinations, which increases the complexity of diversity.
- The Hispanic population has reached a population parity with African Americans, which has political and cultural implications.
- The growth of the Hispanic population was fed by immigration and high birth rates, and the Asian population grew due to an intense period of immigration.
- More Americans are identifying themselves as American Indian and Alaska Native.
- An estimated 3.3 million population undercount exists that especially affects minorities.

California, the largest state in the union, reflects the diversity makeup of population trends that may eventually affect the rest of the country. The total population of California was 33,871,648 according to the 2000 U.S. Census. The ethnic population of California consisted of Whites (15,816,790 or 46.7 percent), Latinos (10,966,556 or 32.4 percent), Asians (3,648,860 or 10.8 percent), African Americans (2,181,926 or 6.4 percent), people of mixed race (1,607,646 or 4.7 percent), American Indians (178,984 or 0.5 percent), Pacific Islanders (103,736 or 0.3 percent), and people of some other race (71,681 or 0.2 percent) (Korber, 2001). The Latino and Asian populations of California were larger than the African American group, and a growing presence of people checked two ethnic groups or more as mixed race. The combined non-White ethnic groups outnumbered the White by 53.3 percent, which has political and social implications.

These demographic trends have implications for health care, housing, education, employment, social services, and related human service areas. Such data are the raw material for social welfare planning, programs, and administration of services. Moreover, demographic knowledge is a strong pointer to new and significant findings. It increases our understanding of new immigrant adjustment patterns, customs, family structure, and related data, which furthers our cultural competence.

CRITICAL THINKING ABOUT CULTURAL DIVERSITY

Critical thinking is a learning process that can help anyone:

- Formulate, analyze, and assess a problem, question, or issue
- Segment an argument or assertion into its components (points of view, major concepts and ideas, theories and underlying assumptions, reasoning, interpretations, and implications and consequences) (Paul, 1992, p. 11)
- Differentiate theories about culturally diverse social work practice issues
- Build theories of cultural diversity as sources of new knowledge

Critical thinking is relevant to culturally diverse social work practice. Mumm and Kerstling (1997) have presented a list of five interrelated skills that promote critical thinking for social workers: (1) the ability to understand social work theories; (2) the ability to divide a theory into its components (assumptions, concepts, propositions, hypotheses); (3) the ability to assess the practice implications of a theory; (4) the ability to develop and apply criteria for evaluating a theory; and (5) the ability to identify common errors in reasoning. These authors propose a number of critical thinking ways to evaluate theories:

- Historical perspective, or a discussion of how and why a theory developed in a historical context
- Assumptions, or a discussion about the explicit and implicit premises of a theory concerning the client, human nature, the role of the social worker and the client, and the change process
- Logical flaws, or a discussion about the logic, contradictions among theories, fit with the mission of social work, and errors in reasoning
- Usefulness in practice, or a discussion about the application of a theory to one's own practice
- Strengths and weaknesses of a theory and a comparison of theories and their potential benefit to specific problems, clients, or settings
- Practice dilemmas, or a discussion of how theories apply to specific problems, clients, or settings

New theories regarding ethnic-sensitive social work practice (Devore & Schlesinger, 1999), cultural awareness in the human services (Green, 1999), and social work practice with people of color (Lum, 2004) emerged in the 1980s and are still in development, as described in Competency Study 6.1. We can apply critical thinking skills to these theories.

UNDERSTANDING THE HISTORY OF OPPRESSION AND OF OPPRESSED GROUPS

History, which chronicles past achievements, mistakes, and failures, provides valuable lessons for the present and the future. It is a chronological narrative of a series of events that reflect cause and effect or circular repetition. We should not be sentenced to repeat the mistakes of the past but should strive to overcome present and future challenges with a historical perspective by asking critical questions about people, events, and happenings in order to gain an accurate picture of the circumstances. In short, history is a record of the past that has implications for the present and future.

Applying Critical Thinking to Three Theories of Culturally Diverse Social Work Practice

COMPETENCY STUDY 6.1

Devore and Schlesinger (1999), in their theory of ethnic-sensitive social work practice, use a number of theoretical building blocks: the case method in teaching and learning; ethnic stratification, ethnic conflict theory, and social class, which are subsumed under the concept of ethnic reality; and a seven-layer model of understanding involving values, knowledge and skills, self-awareness, the client, and the social worker. The concepts of ethnicity, social class, and layers of understanding are the major theoretical underpinnings that could be discussed in a critical thinking context.

Among the critical thinking questions that could be posed about Devore and Schlesinger's assumptions are the following:

- What are the major components and emphases of the ethnic reality involving ethnicity and social class issues?
- Are ethnicity and social class important elements in understanding the background and behavioral dynamics of clients?
- How can the seven layers of understanding be explained and interrelated as the foundation for ethnic-sensitive practice?
- Do the seven layers of understanding illumine the client's situation from the perspective of a generalist practice, direct practice, macro practice, and applications to refugees and new immigrants, families, public sector, and health care settings?

Green (1999) builds his multiethnic cultural awareness practice approach by integrating cultural anthropology with social work practice. Ethnicity is a primary theme, expressed as ethnic group relationships, ethnic community, and ethnic competence. The help-seeking behavior model is based on an inductive ethnographic interviewing approach. The major components are the client's definition and understanding of an experience as a problem, the client's semantic evaluation of a problem, indigenous strategies of problem intervention, and culturally based criteria for problem resolution. Cross-cultural social work consists of cross-cultural learning and ethnic competence, which involve entering an unfamiliar community, key respondents as cultural guides, and participant observation. Language, working with a translator, and ethnographic interviewing are involved in the process.

Green's approach evokes a number of critical thinking questions:

- Is the cultural anthropology concept of ethnography compatible with multiethnic cross-cultural social work?
- Green's help-seeking behavior model is based on ethnographic interviewing principles that focus on the client's definition and understanding of the problem, semantic evaluation of the problem, indigenous strategies, and culturally based problem resolution. Does this approach offer a specific way to focus culturally diverse social work practice, or is it too narrow a perspective?

Lum's (2004) theory of social work practice with people of color advocates culturally diverse social work. The underpinnings of this approach center on the meaning of culture. Lum has devised five perspectives on culture: transcultural, cross-cultural, paracultural, metacultural, and pancultural. Culture is the basis for understanding clients from various ethnic groups.

The culturally diverse approach deals with emic (culture-specific) and etic (culture-common) dimensions of culture. Close analysis of Lum's text reveals that themes such as family, religion, and identity are common to various ethnic groups, and at the same time, culture-specific distinctions are made about each separate group. These culture-common and culture-specific themes are consistent throughout his system.

This theory tries to infuse culturally diverse meaning into clinical and community terms such as *resistance, communication barriers, service delivery*, and *micro-meso-macro intervention*. It also introduces new concepts that have multicultural meaning such as relationship protocols, professional self-disclosure, communication style, socioenvironmental impacts, psychoindividual reactions, and cultural and spiritual assessment. These themes are applied in a process-stage approach where the social worker and the client engage in contact, problem identification, assessment, intervention, and termination. There are three major paradigms: a framework for culturally diverse social work practice, a multicultural problem typology, and an intervention levels and strategies model.

Among the critical thinking questions that could be raised concerning Lum (2004) are:

- Is the cultural diversity orientation a reflection of current culture and diversity emphases?
- Are etic (culture-common) and emic (culture-specific) distinctions necessary when discussing people of color as an etic entity and as separate and distinct emic groups such as African, Latino, Asian Americans or First Nations Peoples?
- Is the infusion-of-new-meaning approach to classic practice terminology helpful or is it a distortion of the intent of these concepts?
- Is the introduction of new and distinctive multicultural concepts a validation that culturally diverse social work is able to stand as a specialized field of practice?

You are encouraged to apply critical thinking questions to increase your cultural competency. Ethnic-sensitive social work practice, cultural awareness in the human services, and culturally diverse social work practice are still in the process of development. You should apply critical thinking to these approaches.

The history of African, Latino, and Asian Americans and First Nations Peoples reaches into the oldest existing civilizations in the world. The history of these groups in the United States represents only a fraction (about 400 years) of their cultural past.

The theme of oppression features prominently in the American experience with ethnic minority groups. Oppression occurs when one segment of the population keeps another segment from obtaining social, economic, political, and related human rights through institutional practices and social stratification. The dynamics of oppression involve the oppressor, with presumed power and control, and the oppressed, who is powerless. The victimization of the oppressed by the oppressor or oppressive forces occurs in a social and political context.

Oppression began in the United States with the concept of Republicanism (Takaki, 1990) that advocated the virtuous self-control of the American population during colonial times. Morality, education, and virtue were the hallmarks of the White American male. Women were the bearers of children, the property of their husbands, and the teachers of their male offspring. African American slaves were inferior, and American Indians were savage (a term used by the English to describe the Irish in their country before the settlement of the Americas).

The history in America of African, Latino, and Asian Americans and First Nations Peoples reveals a number of common themes:

- African, Latino, and Asian Americans and First Nations Peoples were exploited for their land and cheap labor and became subservient to White Americans from social, economic, and political perspectives.

CULTURAL COMPETENCY IN ACTION

The Hernandez Family: A Case Study

Critical thinking is a major tool to uncover our practice approach to the Hernandez family. It is appropriate to critically analyze the rationale behind how the social worker deals with clients. Critical thinking helps us to question and justify what we do as social work practitioners. With critical thinking as a form of reflection, we have an opportunity to think about what we are doing before we engage the client in the social work helping process.

Among the critical thinking aspects of theory related to this case are the following:

- A historical perspective on social work theory. From a historical perspective, one could assert that the theory of historical oppression applies to the economic and social struggle of the Hernandez family. They represent the legal immigrant minority poor of this country.
- Client, worker, and change process assumptions of social work theory. From a client, worker, and change process perspective, critical thinking advocates the use of indigenous cultural change practices that arise from the Latino community

rather than traditional middle-class social work interventions.
- Theory application to specific problems, clients, or settings. From a theory application perspective, it is important to develop a culturally diverse social work practice approach that uses cultural beliefs, behavior, and mutual assistance. The Hernandez family believes in helping members of the extended family who in turn aid them. The Latino community operates under mutual obligation through religious, employment, and educational resources.

TASK RECOMMENDATIONS

- Discuss the meaning of critical thinking and its applications to the issues of the Hernandez family in a cultural competence context.
- Are the critical thinking issues (such as historical oppression, indigenous cultural practice, and mutual obligation and assistance) relevant to the Hernandez family?

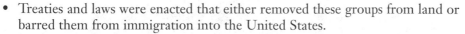

- Treaties and laws were enacted that either removed these groups from land or barred them from immigration into the United States.
- African, Latino, and Asian Americans and First Nations Peoples lived in segregated, isolated communities—such as reservations, Harlem, or Chinatown—and were barred from equal education, employment, and housing opportunities.
- Ethnic minority groups used the legal court system in their struggle for civil rights and equal justice under the law.
- Poverty, family fragmentation, and social dysfunction are major symptoms of class stratification affecting the Black underclass, reservation Indians, Mexican farm workers, and recent waves of Southeast Asian refugees.

A case could be made for women of color. Lum (2004) has traced the historical relationship between White feminism and African American women beginning with the abolition of slavery movement and the suffrage movement where there was racism in women's suffrage and a historical parting of the ways between White and African American women due to the Fifteenth Amendment to the Constitution. Not only has White male-dominated society oppressed women but also White women have discriminated against women of color.

Lum (2004) has also documented the history of oppression of gays and lesbian people in terms of the struggle for open and affirming church acceptance and marriage, the civil rights of gays and lesbians, and the exclusion of gay and lesbian people of color from the White gay and lesbian community and their own cultural and ethnic communities. There is major concern about sexual minorities who have experienced oppression in the dominant heterosexual culture and society. Van Den Bergh and Crisp (2004) address oppression in "a nonsupportive sociocultural environment that engenders a variety of forms of prejudice" (p. 230). They list such incidents as social repercussions for showing affection to a partner in public, intolerant reactions of family, friends, and coworkers when GLBT (gay, lesbian, bisexual, transgender) clients disclose their sexual orientation, pressure to censor details about their experiences as a GLBT person, and hate crimes where at least 14 percent are based on the victim's sexual orientation.

Single histories of oppression could be written about multiethnic/multiracial people, the elderly of color, poor people, the homeless, and other groups. However, a person has multiple identities that transcend solely one category. For example, we could be focusing on an African American–Irish American multiethnic lesbian woman of color who is 65 years old, living alone in substandard housing, and solely dependent on Social Security. No longer are single ethnic, gender, sexual orientation, or social class groups and populations-at-risk important, but the person who is a composite of these identities emerges as a real individual who has experienced oppression and needs liberation.

A major task in the area of gaining knowledge for cultural competence is an investigative study and analysis of oppression on a group-by-group basis. The historical remnants of oppression are still a part of contemporary social history.

CULTURAL COMPETENCY IN ACTION

The Hernandez Family: A Case Study

History is a source of knowledge as we strive to learn from the past. Ethnic minorities have historically been oppressed. Mr. and Mrs. Hernandez are a part of this history affecting poor Latinos.

Mr. and Mrs. Hernandez are legal immigrants from Mexico who live in the barrio. They speak little English and have relatives who recently migrated from Mexico like themselves. Mr. Hernandez is a hard-working gardener, and Mrs. Hernandez works part-time in a laundry. Thus, both are service workers. Historically, Latinos have been sources of cheap labor who were exploited in low-paying jobs. These dynamics of oppression are still seen in the Hernandez family.

TASK RECOMMENDATIONS

- Are historical remnants of oppression operating in the Hernandez family background?
- Can the Hernandez family be liberated from socioeconomic oppression?
- Can the Hernandez children have a better life than their parents?

KNOWLEDGE OF GENDER AND CULTURAL DIVERSITY

Multicultural feminist theory is concerned with women of color (African, Latino, and Asian Americans, and First Nations Peoples) in the United States. Major contributions to studies on women of color have been made in texts by Mirkin (1994) and Comas-Diaz and Greene (1994). Along with the development of texts on women of color, an alternative knowledge base (social constructionism) has emerged that relies on personal narratives of experiences of individual women of color and lays the basis for establishing some common themes (Holland, Gallant, & Colosetti, 1994; McNamee & Gergen, 1992; Radtke & Stam, 1994). Moreover, White feminist therapy has recognized that racial, ethnic, social class, and related issues need to be addressed along with gender opposition (Greene, 1994; Kliman, 1994; Kopacsi & Faulkner, 1988).

During the 1970s and 1980s, limited research existed on ethnically related gender differences and feminist issues in culturally diverse populations due to the domination of feminist therapy by White women writers. Gender oppression and therapeutic solutions dominated the scene at the expense of recognizing the problem of ethnic/racial oppression and its resulting consequences in the lives of women of color. During the 1990s, there was a gradual dawning of awareness that racial, ethnic, and cultural factors are just as important as gender oppression for women. Moreover, women of color practitioners (Aguilar & Williams, 1993; Collins, 1990; Comas-Diaz & Greene, 1994; Greene, 1994; Kliman, 1994) began to reflect and write on the unique problems and issues facing multiethnic and culturally diverse female clients. These contributions represent crucial components of the women of color mosaic that delineates particular helping approaches. For example, Congress and Kung (2005) point out the conflict between traditional and American gender roles and role reversals that produce conflict and domestic violence. They state:

> Traditional gendered roles within the family also exert significant impact on the family, especially when circumstances change after migration. For example, in some cultures women are expected to take care of internal familial affairs, including household chores and child care, while men are expected to work outside and be income earners. However, changes in socioeconomic status of the family after migration may necessitate both spouses to work outside of home. If the role of domestic caretaker continues to be rigidly assigned only to women, they may become overburdened. In situations in which the woman is able to find a job while the man is unemployed, if the family lacks flexibility in their role adaptation, conflict, blame, and burden within the family may become so enormous that it may threaten the survival of the family unit. (p. 14)

Working with both spouses to ensure the socioeconomic transitions of marriage, family, and economic survival is a major task.

Regarding the etiology of a multicultural feminist perspective, Brown (1990) analyzed the limitations of existing feminist therapy and the need for multicultural theory building. On the one hand, feminist therapy and feminist therapy theory were developed by White women who excluded diversity issues that were the concerns of women of color, poor or working-class women, and non–North American women. Past feminist therapy theory was based on a sociological description of the external reality and social context (that is, gender and societal oppression) and a phenomenological recollection of the lived and inner reality of women's life experiences. Both approaches describe the interactive relationships of internal and external realities of predominantly White working-class and middle-class women.

Brown (1990), on the other hand, advocated the development of an alternative culturally diverse gender knowledge. There are four goals of multicultural feminist therapy theory:

1. The creation of a multicultural, non-White, and non-Western feminist database reflecting the varieties of female experiences, connected with research questions and data gathering that are guided by a feminist consciousness
2. The de-emphasis of gender oppression as the primary central issue for women of color, poor women, and women from non-Western cultures, and the inclusion of multicultural female socialization experiences, which may vary according to ethnic and cultural factors
3. The search for how internal reality is shaped by diverse external experiences utilizing phenomenology (observable reported experiences) and introspection (personal sharing of an ethnic-cultural perspective in relationship to one's culture of origin and participation in the dominant society) as tools for theory development
4. The acknowledgment of cultural factors outside the control of particular group members that shape the internal experiences of individual women related to a particular ethnic group and become symbolic representations of how women accept culturally defined roles and yet transcend them to become liberated people in their cultural society

Yet Brown (1990) warns educators and practitioners concerned with cultural diversity:

> If we do not soon undertake the process of making feminist theory a multicultural theory, we may lose our chance and become yet another white, exclusionary system. Some therapists who are women of color and feminist in their theoretical perspectives have refused to take on an identification with feminist therapy in part because of its overly white bias, and in part because feminist political theory has seemed to deny to women of color the importance of their racial and cultural identities. (p. 17)

We must move beyond refusal and criticism of past feminist theory and forge ahead with the development of systematic multicultural knowledge that addresses understanding and helping women of color in their personal growth and life development. Most feminist groups in the 1990s recognized the need for a multicultural emphasis that addresses racism, social class inequality, and homophobia along with sexism. Renzetti and Curran (1995) state:

> If the movement is to remain strong and make up ground lost as a result of the conservative backlash of the 1980s, then the needs and experiences of diverse groups of women must not just be taken into account by the powers that be within feminism, they must reshape the focus and course of the movement itself. (p. 566)

As mainstream feminists incorporate multicultural concerns, there must be adequate principles on working with women of color.

In Competency Study 6.2, GlenMaye (1998) offers some practical ways that social workers can empower women.

Nonsexist resocialization involves enacting liberating changes in family, education, religion, economy, and politics while preserving the best of traditional social values. To this end, we hope that gender barriers will be removed and that the potentials of women and men as respected and genuine people will be realized in significant ways.

Empowering Women

1. Practitioners must acknowledge and understand the role of oppression in the lives of women. This understanding will grow as practitioners themselves undergo the process of personal and political consciousness raising.
2. The empowerment of women requires an environment of safety, trust, and support in which women are encouraged to believe in themselves and their own reality and to find their voice to speak their truth. The presence of other women is integral to the creation of this environment.
3. Women must be given concrete opportunities to experience their own capability, strength, and worth. For instance, women who have experienced physical assault should be encouraged to find ways to experience bodily and emotional strength, and women who have experienced social indignities and assaults, such as homelessness, poverty, or racism, should be presented with opportunities to regain dignity and worth.
4. Though empowerment for women is fundamentally related to autonomy and self-determination, women must also work together to change themselves and society. Rather than work merely for individual solutions to individual problems, practitioners must find ways to bring women together and to work with women clients toward social change.
5. The many roles of the practitioner in empowerment practice include educator, supporter, advocate, activist, option clarifier, facilitator of concrete experiences of power, and model of lived empowerment. (pp. 49–50)

KNOWLEDGE OF CULTURALLY DIVERSE VALUES

Values are beliefs about preferred choices that govern conduct, life decisions, and related normative action by individuals, families, groups, and society. Social institutional values are broad in nature and protect and promote social well-being and the public good. Individual values are personal idiosyncratic choices based on the orientation of the person and influential significant others such as peers, parents, and family members. Cultural values are rooted in ethnic, religious, and generational beliefs, traditions, and practices that influence individual and social values. In strong traditional communities, cultural and religious values are the basis for how community members interact with each other.

Knowledge of culturally diverse values is part of cultural competence. Although there is a range of culturally diverse values, five values are central to our discussion: family, respect, harmony, spirituality, and cooperation.

The multicultural *family* revolves around interdependent collective and/or hierarchical structures. The family is the basic transmitter of cultural values and traditions. It is the source of ethnic identity from biological, psychological, and social perspectives. In many ethnic families, the individual's sense of freedom and choice are subsumed under the good of the family as a whole. The individual family member is interdependent, not independent of or dependent on the family. The family may operate on a collective, extended basis with nuclear/extended family systems or similar social networks. The collective nature of the multicultural family fosters mutual support and may center on a hierarchical authority figure such as a parent, grandparent, or godfather.

Closely related to the value of family is the concept and practice of *respect*. The word *respect* comes from the root word *respicere*, which has a past tense meaning (to look back on) and a present tense understanding (to look at). The implied meaning is that one shows honor and regard for those who are held in high esteem in the past and the present. Many cultures express respect for ancestors. Latinos often name children in honor of past and present relatives, and Asians reverently remember their parents and grandparents in ancestor worship. First Nations Peoples have undergone spiritual quests to communicate with the spirits of their ancestors, and African Americans have communed with their deceased loved ones in quiet and prayerful conversations.

Respect is shown toward father and mother, older relatives and adults, and people in general. Polite manners, formal address, and deference of children to the wishes of parents are manifestations of respect in African and Latino American cultures. Respect for the personhood of people communicates a sense of reverence for life, which is an important value for Asian and First Nations Peoples traditional cultures.

Harmony is a sense of congruity and agreement in feelings, actions, ideas, and interests within and between people. *Harmony* comes from the Greek word *harmos*, which means a fitting or joining. For First Nations Peoples, harmony is essential to maintain balance in the universe. Illness is the absence of harmony or an imbalance in the body or in relations to self, others, and the world. For Asian Americans, it is important to maintain harmony or peace rather than conflict or disharmony in ethnic group relationships. Harmony is a part of individual and group continuity rather than alienation. As a result, many Asian Americans avoid confrontation and defer argumentation to maintain a higher order: interpersonal harmony.

Spirituality refers to a personal sense of meaning and purpose based on belief in a transcendent cosmic Being or Ultimate Truth. Spirituality may encompass a sense of morality or a personal code of ethical behavior. African, Latino, and Asian Americans traditionally have practiced their spirituality in an institutional religious setting through ethnic churches. First Nations Peoples have combined cultural and spiritual rituals of cleansing and healing through ceremonies presided over by a medicine man.

Cooperation is a value that brings ethnic families and groups together in a common sense of purpose. For African Americans, cooperation or pooling of resources is essential for survival in terms of housing, child care, and related necessities of life. For Latino Americans, cooperation involves helping extended-family members who are immigrant newcomers or working together on church and community projects. Japanese Americans have worked together to support legal, political, and social causes in the Asian community through local churches and legal rights organizations such as the Japanese American Citizenship League. Among First Nations Peoples, there is a sense of purpose when Native people celebrate their cultures in powwows and sweat lodge ceremonies and run Indian gaming casinos for the good of the tribe.

Many more values beyond these five are important to each ethnic group. For example, Manning, Cornelius, and Okundaye (2004) identify an Afrocentric value orientation that underlies a number of clinical principles: assessing the relationship between racism and oppression and mental health and health problems; using empowerment to assess the ego functioning and group consciousness strengths of African American clients; assessing the level of spirituality and religious involvement such as value orientation and participation in church activities; considering the value orientation of African Americans in developing

CULTURAL COMPETENCY IN ACTION

The Hernandez Family: A Case Study

Cultural values are held beliefs that assist clients of color to function in their communities as they interact with family, friends, and neighbors. We identify the important values of family, respect, harmony, spirituality, and cooperation. As a social worker, Mr. Platt has uncovered these values in the Hernandez family:

- Strong sense of family: hard-working father, caring mother, family as the center of life.
- Mutual respect: father's concern for the social and educational well-being of his son, division of labor in parental-sibling roles.
- Harmonious relationship: minimal conflict, ability to get along with each other, parental response to the concerns of Ricardo's teacher.

- Spiritual practice; mother goes to church, family goes to Catholic Social Service for follow-up referral.
- Cooperation: father and mother work with the social worker to resolve family problems.

TASK RECOMMENDATIONS

- Discuss the importance of values such as family, respect, harmony, spirituality, and cooperation and provide further examples in the Hernandez family.
- Describe practical ways in which the social worker can mirror these values in his relationship with this family.

Afrocentric, empowerment, and ego psychology intervention strategies; integrating ego functioning and group consciousness from Afrocentric perspective, empowerment, and ego psychology to enhance cultural competence; and advocating for African Americans experiencing stress from racism and oppression. Values reflect a range of cultural beliefs, practices, and behaviors that come from ethnic traditions. Culturally competent social workers must understand and respect these cultural values, which are essential to the well-being of people of color.

EMERGING THEORIES

Cultural competence as a practice orientation requires a theory base. Theory is an organized set of principles about a subject area. Although space does not allow for a survey of all existing cultural and ethnic theories applicable to social work practice and cultural competence, several recent theories have intriguing possibilities. We offer them here for your understanding and to give you an opportunity to reflect on the possibilities.

The emerging theory known as social constructionism has an inductive approach that asks open-ended questions about a person's life experiences. Pieper (1994) has moved research-oriented social work practice toward a naturalistic and qualitative compatibility with social constructionism. Identity development theory is a process-stage approach to understanding how individuals, groups, and communities react to and cope with racism, sexism, social classism, and homophobia and move toward resolution. Cultural competence practice theory summarizes recent conceptual building by social work educators who focus on skills, interventions, and evaluations.

Social Constructionism: Definition and Characteristics

Social constructionism is an emerging theory that emphasizes the situational interchanges between people, particularly the historical and cultural influences on how a person's world is constructed. The ways that a person describes his or her experiences and activities are important ingredients in constructing an understanding of an individual. The term *social constructionism* alludes to these aspects of social interaction among and between people.

Norton (1993) introduces the social construction of meaning and ecology as an epistemology of social cognition. People use the ecology of their environment to construct meaning for themselves based on their experiences. Relationship stages are part of a person's life development. Norton describes how children construct meaning as a part of their families:

> Children who are immersed in the environment of their families and neighborhoods begin to build on their perceptions about their world and gradually construct what is reality to them. The content of that construction is determined by their personalities in interaction with their social, physical, linguistic, historical, and cultural experiences determined primarily by their families. The children extract information from these experiences at all levels and organize it into schemas that are consistent with their personalities. These schemas help them make sense out of the environment. The process is both interdependent and circular, with the environment and the individual influencing each other. This construction of meaning largely determines the children's behavior. (p. 84)

The individual constructs a worldview from life experiences throughout the life span.

Social construction theory has been applied to people (Gergen & Davis, 1985) in the helping relationship. Therapy is seen as a process of social construction. Anderson and Goolishian (1992) outline the following principles that are important in this process:

- Social construction encourages a therapeutic conversation or dialogue where the therapist and client undergo a mutual search for understanding and exploring problems. It involves a "talking with" rather than a "talking to" one another. There are new narratives, open spaces for conversation, and "not-yet-said" stories.
- In social construction, the therapist adopts a "not-knowing" position or takes on an open, inquiring stance of wanting to know about what has been said, being informed by the client, and joining a mutual exploration of the client's understanding and experience.
- The personal narrative or the story about one's life describes individual problems that provide an opportunity to enter this person's world. Important in the narrative is the client's language and problem metaphors.

Anderson and Goolishian further explain:

> Telling one's story is a re-presentation of experience; it is constructing history in the present. The re-presentation reflects the teller's re-description and re-explanation of the experience in response to what is not known by the therapist. Each evolves together and influences the other, as well as the experience, and thus, the re-presentation of the experience. (p. 37)

Epston, White, and Murray (1992) state:

> The "story" or "narrative" provides the dominant frame for live experience and for the organization and patterning of lived experience. Following this proposal, a story is a unit of meaning that provides a frame for lived experience. It is through these stories that lived experience is interpreted. We enter into stories; we are entered into stories by others; and we live our lives through these stories. (p. 97)

This discourse with others is a co-construction of two people and a framework for lived experience.

- The focus of helping is an interpersonal construction process and a context for problem solving, evolution, and change. The emphasis is on the interpersonal and social dynamics and processes in the experience between the therapist and the client (Froggeri, 1992).
- Social construction has drawn on cultural assumptions and frameworks to express stories relevant to the individual (Sivan, 1986). The individual may use cultural themes and attributes from relatives and community leaders or interpret events and experiences based on cultural patterns. These cultural influences are housed in the mind of the individual who carries and uses them (Geertz, 1973; Parker & Shotter, 1990).
- The practitioner offers a client alternative themes to make sense of experiences and encourages self-observation, reflections, and developments. The client may reflect on patterns, explore alternatives, and understand experiences in a self-help approach that is a different response to the past. Both parties help to make sense out of daily experiences with others in relationship. This is the re-storying of life stories (Holland, Gallant, & Colosetti, 1994).
- Social work practice has emphasized the need to focus on client strengths and capacities and to develop meaning and direction to deal with the issues of daily living. This leads to empowerment or mastery of challenges. The client's own strengths, energy, and insights become resources for learning. Holland, Gallant, and Colosetti (1994) observe: "The constructivist approach to teaching social work practice emphasizes the student's strengths, rather than deficits, emphasizes exceptions or times when problems were not overwhelming, and builds upon those times when something the student tried did work effectively" (pp. 49–50).

In Competency Study 6.3, Holmes (1992) discusses empowerment research and focuses on the story narrative and strengths perspective, which are related themes of social constructionism.

Social construction theory facilitates several avenues to working with culturally and ethnically diverse people. It highlights the importance of the cultural perspective of clients in terms of their worldview and interactions with other people. Cultural beliefs, customs, and traditions learned from parents, family, and extended family are crucial connections to understanding how multicultural clients react and respond to normal problems of living and to crisis situations. Cognitive beliefs, affective feelings, and behavioral actions can be traced back to cultural learning from the family as it interacts with a friendly or hostile environment.

COMPETENCY STUDY 6.3

Life-Story Narratives

Empowerment research in social work attempts to identify sources and varieties of, and the means to extend, participatory competence. Romanyshyn (1982) argued that human psychological life is characterized not by fact but by story. Stories are autobiographical "I" narratives of personal meaning (Goldstein, 1986, p. 355). As Sacks (1987) expressed it, "We have, each of us, a life-story, an inner narrative—whose continuity, whose sense, *is* our lives" (p. 110). Life stories are vital to social work's understanding of how the individual perceives his or her life condition in relation to having or not having power to act. Ideally, the social work encounter and social work research help client groups understand their own strengths and potentials to alter or embellish definitions of life as lived. And as life is lived, we can assist client groups to redefine their experience of the world, to act within it from a position of greater human potential and power. (p. 164)

Social construction emphasizes the value of narratives or life experience stories, where the practitioner and the client talk with each other. In many cultures, information about the client and the problem situation is communicated indirectly through story. Indeed, the life of a client is a story of the past, present, and future that is unfolding. The story of a diverse person contains ups and downs, joys and concerns, heartbreak and happiness.

As the story unfolds, the practitioner and client endeavor to bring meaning to what has happened in the client's life. It is particularly important to highlight the strengths rather than the pathology of the person. Building on the strengths enables a multicultural client to move forward and to make necessary changes based on affirmation of self and self-empowerment of culture and person. In these ways, social construction theory includes many emerging themes associated with culturally diverse social work practice.

Identity Development Theory

Identity development theory focuses on an understanding of how a culturally diverse person begins to shape a growing sense of what it means to be an ethnic person. Morton and Atkinson (1983) and Helms (1990) have discussed racial and ethnic identity development in terms of various stages of growth. Although it is important to recognize that an individual may not necessarily go through all the stages of development, identity development theory does provide an understanding of the range of growth that is possible and may pinpoint a certain critical stage for the worker and the client.

The first stage of identity development may involve the internalization of the culture's negative imagery. Often in this stage there is a self-hatred of one's own ethnicity and a strong desire to be accepted by members of the dominant social group. One may intuit the racism, sexism, homophobia, and oppression of society, depending on one's identity, and suffer internalized stress.

The second stage may result in the expression of anger as the result of social prejudice and discrimination. The anger is directed outwardly toward the dominant society. The person may become hostile and act upon these emotions. Injustice may be seen through these lenses.

The third state is immersion, where the person turns to his or her own culture as a source of strength and support. Rather than reacting to the dominant culture, members of the dominant group become less important and relevant. The person begins to participate in the activities of his or her own ethnic and social group. There is a reevaluation of one's identity and a lessening of anger.

The fourth and final stage is integration of life as parts and as a whole. An opposition to prejudice and discrimination may continue, but one is able to distinguish between supportive and unsupportive group members of the dominant society. There are satisfying relations with them and resolution.

Rosenblum and Travis (2000) discuss identity development in terms of stigmatized and nonstigmatized statuses and have various stages for both situations.

Tanemura Morelli and Spencer (2000) conducted research on community attitudes toward multicultural and antiracist education in five school districts in Idaho, Montana, Oregon, Washington, and Wyoming. In terms of identity development from the community perspective, they found among 44 school administrators, teachers, and professional services staff the following school and community trends:

- Continuing racist and bigoted attitudes in the form of violent acts, threats, and harassment against minority groups
- Toleration and perpetuation of racism and bigoted behavior in school and community environments
- Reluctance to discuss racism and homosexuality in the classroom due to retribution from the community

In short, a student of color or a gay or lesbian student would be in jeopardy in such an environment in terms of being stuck in the first and second stages of identity development. At the same time, the majority population is a part of community identity development that requires proactive education and supportive policies to end discrimination in the public schools. Tanemura Morelli and Spencer (2000) sum up the mood of their study: "More than 30 years since the zenith of the civil rights movement, the effects of racism and bigotry remain an enduring part of the human landscape in this country. Institutional and tacit racism continue to elude systemic change" (p. 174). Identity development theory leads us to venture forth into immersion and integration that will bring some resolution.

Cultural Competence Practice Theory

Fong and Furuto (2001a) reflect an emerging body of cultural competence practice theory related to social work. In an important work, *Culturally Competent Practice: Skills, Interventions, and Evaluations* (Fong and Furuto, 2001a), a number of social work educators have advanced cultural competence in social work along several theory development themes. There has been a major *paradigm shift* to biculturalization and multiculturalization. Fong (2001a) calls for the recognition of the interracial interblending of cultures in a single ethnic group and the need for assessments and interventions to deal with multiethnic identities and the differing environments of clients. This is a timely shift away from a static description of various people of color ethnic groups, particularly as we recognize the multiple identities of people and the intersectionality of their backgrounds. That is, a growing number of people are multiracial in ethnic identity and understand themselves along ethnic, gender, social class, and sexual orientation lines. The question should be: What is the particular set of individual, family, and group multicultural variables that must be identified in order to understand the client? Fong goes on to state that values and belief systems comprising traditions and cultural norms are central to understanding the ethnic client's functioning.

The starting point is the indigenous culture itself, particularly the ethnic social environment of the client and the parallel use of Euro-American norms as a complement to the client's ethnic reality. One might call this a multicultural social construction approach. That is, in order to fully understand and work with a client, the worker must start with the client's cultural context (the culture of the client and his or her surrounding environment) and find useful cultural helping approaches. Next the worker should identify useful and complementary social work interventions that support the cultural ones. It is not an either/or approach; rather, it is a both/and, side-by-side integration of the helping process from both perspectives.

The particular paradigm model of the preceding shift is Fong, Boyd, and Browne's (1999) *biculturation of intervention approach*. It brings together the client's culture and worldview and the adaptation of Western interventions. This model incorporates appropriate ethnic group norms and practices, and supplements them by using Euro-American practices as well. It is analogous to the Asian approach of integrating and blending Eastern and Western medicine where there is a common belief and practice of using Eastern herbal medicine and Western medication and surgery.

Fong, Boyd, and Browne's model (1999) identifies the important values in the ethnic culture that can be used to reinforce therapeutic interventions; chooses a Western intervention whose theoretical framework and values are compatible with the ethnic cultural values of the family client system; analyzes an indigenous intervention familiar to the ethnic client system in order to discern which techniques can be reinforced and integrated with a Western intervention; develops a framework and approach that integrates the values and techniques of the ethnic culture with the Western intervention; and applies the Western intervention, at the same time explaining to a client family how the techniques reinforce cultural values and support indigenous interventions (p. 105).

Fong (2001) identifies some crucial *connecting points* starting with moving from worker self-awareness to client other-awareness, from cultural values to client strengths, and making connections between assessment and intervention. Regarding the assessment and intervention connection, Fong explains:

> The assessed strengths of the client's cultural values should determine the design and planning of interventions. If the cultural strength of extended family is assessed, then recommending and implementing individual therapy may be contraindicated. If spirituality is central to the belief system of a culture, to omit or neglect it is no longer acceptable for culturally competent practice. (p. 6)

Making culturally sensitive and competent connections in an intervention plan for the client is good social work practice.

There is also a *positive power orientation*. A detailed study of Fong and Furuto (2001a) reveals an overwhelming consensus among these social work educators writing about culturally competent practice regarding the strengths perspective and empowerment intervention. The two go hand in hand and interconnect with each other. The strengths assessment and the empowerment intervention approaches are discussed side by side (Acevedo & Morales, 2001; Brown & Gundersen, 2001; Browne & Mills, 2001; Daly, 2001; Davis, 2001; Furuto, Nicolas, Kim, & Fiaui, 2001; Gilbert & Franklin, 2001; Grant, 2001; Kanuha, 2001; Lewis, 2001; Puig, 2001; Weaver, 2001; Westbrooks & Starks, 2001).

Westbrooks and Starks (2001) combine the strengths and empowerment themes in a joint model called SPICE (Strengths-Perspective-Inherent-in-Cultural-Empowerment). Among the lead questions of this assessment model using an ecocultural approach are the following:

- *Strengths.* What is the focal system? Who are the identified clients? What is the status of the challenge? What are the current strengths? What is the client's perspective of what is working?
- *Perspective.* What are the goals of the client? How does the client envision the future? Internally and externally? Subjectively and objectively? Look at positive projections.
- *Inherent in.* How does the client system define itself? What are its roles? Discuss gender, racial identity, education level, job/career, and family structure.
- *Cultural.* What are the cultural antecedents? What are the client's racial and intergenerational experiences? How does the client present the problems?
- *Empowerment.* What are the physical, emotional, economic, spiritual, familial, formal, and informal resources? What is the degree of energy going out of versus coming into the system? (p. 110)

Cultural competence has focused on the strengths assessment and empowerment intervention combination because it moves away from a pathology diagnostic assessment and deals with the problem of powerlessness among people of color, women of color, and gay and lesbian people of color. Both strengths and empowerment underscore the positive power orientation that characterizes discovering the strength assets of people and building on this foundation for empowering people to change their problem situations.

A number of social work knowledge and skill competencies exist. Leung and Cheung (2001) have created social worker self-evaluation competency questions that are relevant to the client's cultural expectations. There are five competency areas related to information, intellect, interpersonal, intrapersonal, and intervention:

1. *Informational competencies*
   - Ethnic differences related to diversity among clients and their families in languages, customs, values/religions, communication patterns, food preferences, and other cultural components
   - Family history pertaining to American-born, legal or illegal immigrants, or permanent residents; visa holders; generations residing in the United States, special family history, and immigrant background
   - Minority identity development regarding personal identity (families of origin, ethnic history, immigration, peers, schools, jobs, friends, neighbors, people of the same or different ethnic backgrounds)
   - Specific information on special needs and ethnic interests; legal, ethical, and political rights; social policies affecting clients and their families due to ethnic backgrounds; client's purpose for seeking help, access to receiving social services

2. *Intellectual competencies*
   - Information gathering on the means to assess the needs of individuals and families; the use of psychosocial assessments, genograms, or other tools to assess family history impact and family functioning
   - Assessment on analyzing the past (immigration, war trauma) and current situations (migration, cultural adjustment) to make future decisions; analyze resources and strengths; offer suggestions without imposing values; interpret data according to the client's cultural expectations
   - Goal setting to prioritize mental health concerns related to cultural needs; mutual goals balancing client demand and social work mission; evaluation of cultural constraints in achieving goals; alternatives in formal and informal systems; client options selection

3. *Interpersonal competencies*
   - Relationship building addressing ethnic comfort level between worker and client; showing genuineness in the midst of cultural differences between worker and client; demonstrating positive regard when the client sees the worker as an authority figure; rapport building; a trusting relationship
   - Communication skills making a client feel safe and at ease; using nonverbal communications; inviting family members to attend sessions; communicating with family to ensure trust and safety; negotiating among family members to resolve disagreements; exercising assertiveness without intimidation; encouraging family members to speak when there is a family spokesperson

4. *Intrapersonal competencies*
   - Values and attitudes differing between worker and client; helping client and family voice concerns; adapting to the client's situations and circumstances when making an assessment; assessing client needs related to cultural beliefs and values
   - Personal qualities and characters such as creativity in planning client services; awareness of worker biases; openness to lifestyle variation; acceptance of client when there is disagreement; respect for kinship solidarity system and family balance and harmony; valuation of family practice; address of men and elders in initial contacts; respect for traditional role of women

5. *Intervention competencies*
   - Intervention according to the needs, constraints, and cultural expectations of families; cultural expectations influencing the service plan; formal and informal client support systems; various rates of family acculturation; wish to seek or not to seek family advice; balancing of interpersonal relationships rather than confrontation over conflict avoidance behavior
   - Termination involving preparing the client; another starting point; cultural rituals related to termination

These competency knowledge and skill areas offer detailed performance task concerns that further our understanding of training and outcome measurements.

In terms of *cultural competence model building*, Fong and Furuto (2001b) offer a micro-, meso-, and macro-level model that starts with large systems. In order to build cultural

CULTURAL COMPETENCY IN ACTION

The Hernandez Family: A Case Study

Social constructionism as a theory teaches that people construct meaningful experiences and relationships from the environment. Among the principles relevant to the Hernandez case are:

- Therapeutic conversation: a mutual search for understanding and exploring problems, which is part of contact and problem identification; the emergence of new and yet-to-be told stories
- Open, inquiring stance: no presuppositions or assumptions on the part of the worker; the client as the information giver
- Personal narrative and storytelling of life experiences: many cultures communicate thoughts, feelings, and actions through telling one's story; the content, expression, and personal style of storytelling are as important as the story itself
- Re-storying of life stories: the piecing together of various story segments into a coherent whole; the worker and the client cooperate in this process of

constructing the story into realistic connecting chapters
- Client strengths and capacities: the ability to develop meaning, direction, and purpose; the will to persevere in the problems of daily living; the affirmation and empowerment of cultural self and family

TASK RECOMMENDATIONS

- Describe how Mr. Platt could use the social construction approach with Mr. and Mrs. Hernandez and their children.
- Imagine the new stories, storytelling, and personal narratives that might emerge from each member of the Hernandez family.
- Describe how Mr. Platt might help the family put their stories together in a coherent form so that the family understands past, present, and future segments.

competence between cultures, they suggest that we start with the macro level of seeking out and identifying key societal cultural group values. From there, on a meso level one moves toward within-group or intragroup variations of value choices with an emphasis on particular cultural values as strengths in assessment and intervention. Finally, on the micro level the creation and integration of biculturation intervention combines indigenous and Western matches with congruent underpinnings and adopts cultural contextual evaluations of interventions rather than culturally inappropriate outcome measures. The starting emphasis on cultural group values and their variations (diversity within group diversity) is an attempt to be true to the values of a culture. It might be described as maintaining the cultural value authenticity that is the basis for biculturation integration or attempting to integrate a native intervention approach based on cultural values and a Western intervention treatment. The test is whether or not the cultural context has been affected by the marriage of these two bicultural interventions without sacrificing the integrity of the native cultural values, which is the foundation of the whole enterprise.

Cultural competence practice theory builds on an inductive understanding of biculturalization or multiculturalization that is indigenous to the client's ethnic values and experiences.

It makes connections between worker self-awareness and client other-awareness and between cultural values and client strengths. It carefully constructs the relationship between a strengths assessment and an empowerment intervention approach, creating a sense of positive power for the worker and the client. The five related competency areas and the model building address detailed areas of culture and the relationship between the client, family, community, and the social worker.

THEORIES ON ETHNICITY, CULTURE, MINORITY STATUS, AND SOCIAL CLASS

Ethnicity, culture, minority status, and social class have been the focus of theories essential to culturally diverse practice. Devore and Schlesinger (1999) have emphasized ethnicity (ethnic reality) and social class (working, middle, and under classes) and have borrowed Gordon's (1978) term *ethclass* to describe the fusion between ethnicity and social class. Green (1999) has explained ethnicity in terms of its categorical and transactional features. The former relate to ethnicity as a combination of traits such as color, musical styles, foods, and sometimes poverty; the latter include relations across ethnic boundaries, ethnic distinctions, and individual management of ethnic identity. Iglehart and Becerra (1995) underscore the historical struggle of ethnic minorities who suffered discrimination, racial violence, and social/legal injustice as well as exclusion from the social work system. These themes are examined from social work practice and policy perspectives.

Ethnicity involves ancestry and racial origin, present membership in an ethnic family and community group, and future participation in generations of ethnic offspring. Ethnicity is a powerful unifying force that gives an individual a heritage and a sense of identity and belonging. From ethnicity flows a history of forebearers and country of origin; racial and language identity; family membership and participation; and social, economic, and religious ties to an ethnic community.

Culture is closely allied to ethnicity. However, it deals with prescribed ways of conduct, beliefs, values, traditions and customs, and related life patterns of a people or community group. Culture has a flexible range of applications. Cultural pluralism involves the coexistence and interrelations of various cultural communities with particular styles, customs, languages, and values. Bicultural conflict involves the tension and incongruities between the dominant culture and one's culture of origin in terms of values and behaviors. Traditional culture-of-origin parents and acculturated children who identify with the dominant culture are major players. Cultural duality contrasts the nurturing culture that is part of the indigenous culture and provides psychological and social gratification and identity, and the sustaining culture that provides the necessary goods and services for survival and is associated with the dominant culture.

Acculturation involves the adjustment and adaptation of the individual from the culture of origin to the dominant culture. Paniagua (2005) examines four models of acculturation: (1) the assimilation model where a highly acculturated client strongly identifies only with the dominant or host culture; (2) the separation model where the client values only the behaviors and beliefs of his/her own culture; (3) the integration model where the client displays behaviors and beliefs of both the traditional and host or dominant cultures; and (4) the marginalization model where the client rejects the behaviors and beliefs of the traditional and host (dominant) culture (pp. 13–14). Depending on the particular acculturation of the person, acculturation may or may not involve rejection of the culture of origin. Bicultural integration occurs where an individual evaluates aspects of both cultures and connects them in a functional way. Cultural barriers are societal and exist along a continuum from segregation (geographic, social, educational, and marital separation of races and socioeconomic classes) to assimilation (acceptance and adaptation into the dominant society, particularly in terms of social and marital inclusion).

Minority status relates to the inferior and unequal rank in power and access to resources of a subordinate and disadvantaged group in relation to the superiority in power and resources of the dominant majority. Racial myths and stereotypes, prejudice, and discrimination are invented and practiced by the majority group. Legislation as well as civilian and military force are used to maintain the status quo. On the other hand, throughout the history of the United States, the courts and the legal system have been used to overturn unjust laws and practices on behalf of people of color, women, and gays and lesbians.

Shifts in population, political representation, and social policies and programs are occurring that have implications for minorities. People of color, specifically Latino Americans, are projected to be the numerical majority of the population in the 21st century. Political power, social policies, legislation, and programs have yet to shift in favor of the needs of ethnic minorities. With the White majority in control of political and economic power, it is doubtful that there can be major changes away from the status quo.

Social class is closely related to minority status because it addresses social stratification or the social hierarchical arrangement of people based on economic, power, and status differences. People of color tend to be class bound due to racial discrimination and socioeconomic constraints. Social class affects our perspective on life. Devore and Schlesinger (1999) observe:

> Social class is about inequality. It refers to the fact that some people have more income, find themselves in more highly valued and rewarded occupations, and have more prestige than others. This in turn affects well-being in such respects as health and illness, the ability to exert power and influence to achieve desired ends, the sense of self-respect, and the degree of dignity conferred by others. Differences related to wealth, occupation, and education are generally referred to as social class differences. (p. 44)

Social class distinctions reflect degrees of social inequality based on economic (wealth, income, consumption, occupation), social (influence, community power, group identification), and family status. These social boundaries reinforce the belief that ethnic groups are class bound.

Minority status and social class reinforce negative determinism for people of color, who constantly struggle to transcend minority and class barriers and to move toward social equality and social justice. At the same time, ethnicity and culture are motivators and sources of strength for those who draw on their ethnic identity and cultural beliefs. Ethnicity, culture, minority status, and social class interact and are closely linked. The culturally competent worker must be aware of the dynamics of these four themes.

In Competency Study 6.4, we return to the Abdullah Family case study.

COMPETENCY STUDY 6.4

The Abdullah Family and Knowledge Acquisition

As you recall from Chapter 4, the focus was on cultural awareness and working with Mr. Abdullah as the main point of contact of the family. In this chapter on knowledge acquisition, our attention shifts to *Mrs. Risah Abdullah*, age 30, who is the wife of Mr. Abdullah Abdullah and the mother of Mohammed, age 10, and Osama, age 5. Mrs. Abdullah lived under the eight-year reign of the Taliban regime in Afghanistan and was oppressed as a woman.

Unlike the treatment that Mrs. Abdullah endured under the Taliban, Islam emphasizes the equality of all people, particularly that men and women are equal in the eyes of God. Islam gives women the right to decide on marriage, divorce, and inheritance. They may maintain their own personal property and wealth in marriage and play important family and community roles in socializing children, transmitting religious beliefs, and participating in community charity activities and family and religious traditions.

However, there may be discrepancies in Islamic community practices. Some Islamic countries have laws that restrict the role of women in the public sector. Most Muslim families are patriarchal, with males in the household holding positions of authority. Some Muslims interpret their religion as requiring the submission of women to males in their household. Muslim men are socialized as heads of households and breadwinners, whereas women take responsibility for child care, elder care, and household work. A few Islamic cultures confine women to their homes.

Muslim immigrant women face major transitions in the United States. Many are employed in entry-level or blue-collar jobs, whereas some Muslim men are unemployed, intermittently employed, or underemployed. In addition to work, Muslim women face multiple burdens as homemakers, responsible for the children's behavior and their religious and cultural knowledge. These multiple responsibilities may be daunting and exhausting for Muslim women. They may lack traditional supports from their family of origin, in-laws, or friends and neighbors. They may be unwilling to seek non-Muslim social services. Muslim women's organizations such as the North American Council for Muslim Women or Muslim Women in the Arts may be available to meet the needs of Muslim women. Many local mosques have programs for tutoring children, English language acquisition, job searching, housing assistance, domestic violence response programs, and youth supports ("Muslim refugees in the United States," n.d.).

Based on the range of knowledge acquisition themes and knowledge theories in Chapter 5, select and discuss three important knowledge areas, detailing some sample questions that you would ask Mrs. Abdullah after you received permission from Mr. Abdullah to discuss these matters with his wife:

___family background	___values	___ethnic background
___culture	___demographics of the country	
___minority status	___spirituality	___social class
___oppression under the Taliban	___gender roles	___related knowledge areas

Select and explain a knowledge theory and apply it to Mrs. Abdullah's situation:

___social constructionism	___identity development theory
___cultural competence practice theory	

SOCIAL SCIENCE THEORY AND CULTURALLY DIVERSE SOCIAL WORK

Social work practice draws on a wide range of social theories because it serves a diverse target population with many needs. The culturally competent social worker is well read and broadly educated in the social sciences. The liberal arts approach to social work education prescribes background courses in psychology, sociology, anthropology, government, history, ethnic and women's studies, economics, and related areas. The continuous development of social science theory means translating it and applying it to the field of social work.

Social science theory is transmitted to and transformed by social work and filters through the social work education process to particular curriculum areas. Diversity and populations-at-risk are two content areas on which culturally diverse social work focuses. Culturally competent faculty, program resources, and administrative leadership and commitment are necessary to translate social science theory into program realities for students of culturally diverse social work.

Cultural competence develops when faculty and program resources are committed to a multicultural approach. The accrediting body for counseling psychology programs is the American Psychological Association (APA), whereas the accrediting counterpart for counseling education programs is the Council for Accreditation of Counseling and Related Educational Programs. Ponterotto (1997) reports on a 22-item multicultural competency checklist survey of 66 program training directors regarding multicultural competence aspects of their programs (49 APA-accredited doctoral programs in counseling psychology and 17 non–APA-accredited programs). The survey was divided into six sections: (1) faculty, student, and staff minority representation; (2) multicultural curriculum content, teaching, and methods issues; (3) counseling field and supervision; (4) faculty and student research considerations; (5) student and faculty competency evaluation; and (6) physical environment of the program.

Of the 22 items, 10 items received affirmative responses from more than 60 percent of respondents. Under curriculum, 94 percent of the programs indicated that written and oral assessment methods were used to evaluate student performance and learning; 89 percent had a required multicultural counseling course; 89 percent used a diversity of teaching strategies and procedures; and 62 percent required or recommended one additional multicultural course besides the required multicultural counseling course. Regarding research, 88 percent reported the use of quantitative and qualitative research methods in faculty and student research; 86 percent had at least a faculty member whose primary research interest was multicultural issues; 83 percent had clear faculty research productivity (journal publications and conference presentations) in multicultural issues; and 80 percent indicated faculty–student mentoring and coauthored work on multicultural issues, research, and dissertation topics. On student and faculty competency evaluation, 74 percent reported that multicultural issues were a part of student comprehensive examinations. Finally, on counseling practice and supervision, 73 percent indicated that multicultural issues were considered an important component of clinical supervision.

Seven items received affirmative responses from fewer than 35 percent of respondents. Concerning minority representation, 33 percent stated that at least 30 percent of students were from racial/ethnic minorities; 29 percent of the programs had at least 30 percent of faculty members from racial/ethnic minorities; and 29 percent had 30 percent of support staff from racial/ethnic minorities. Regarding counseling practice and supervision, 20 percent had a faculty–student multicultural program leadership and support steering committee called a multicultural affairs committee. On student and faculty competency evaluation, 18 percent reported faculty teaching evaluations with items measuring the instructor's ability to integrate multicultural issues into the course and assessing faculty ability to make all students feel equally comfortable in class. Similarly, on physical environment, only 17 percent had a multicultural resource center where students could convene and use multicultural resources in a cultural diversity setting.

In a discussion of these findings, Ponterotto (1997) recommended strengthening multicultural research competency, infusing cultural issues throughout the curriculum, exposing students to minority clients during the practicum, including multicultural issues on faculty and student evaluations, and recruiting more minority faculty members and students from an enlarged pool. Along the same lines, Ridley, Espelage, and Rubinstein (1997) have suggested a number of multicultural course topic areas: prejudice, racism, and power; psychological assessment and diagnosis; therapy process variables and outcome goals; intervention strategies; multicultural counseling research; racial identity development; ethical issues in multicultural counseling; and normative group information on the major racial/ethnic minority groups.

Multicultural counseling is in the process of setting up standards and program content for counseling psychology. Similar efforts in social work education have been structured since the late 1960s. A modification of Ponterotto's multicultural competency checklist survey for social work education may reveal a similar pattern. Coverage of a body of knowledge about cultural diversity is an essential component of any social work program committed to cultural diversity in program structure, curriculum, and faculty–student representation.

Tools for Student Learning 6.1 measures your comprehension and retention of the essential emphases of this chapter. You should complete the test outside class and come to class prepared to review and discuss the items covered.

TOOLS FOR STUDENT LEARNING 6.1

Test of Knowledge Basic to Cultural Competence

This test covers the essential information included in Chapter Six. It is designed to measure the extent to which you have comprehended the various aspects of knowledge basic to cultural competency.

1. Define the following terms:

   a. *Knowledge* is

   b. *Theory* is

2. List the two fastest-growing ethnic groups of the 2000 U.S. Census:

3. Racial and ethnic groups account for what percentage of population growth in the 2000 U.S. Census? (check one)
   ___ 60%   ___ 70%   ___ 75%   ___ 80%

4. *Critical thinking* is

5. List five interrelated skills that promote critical thinking for social workers, according to Mumm and Kerstling.

6. Name the three ethnic and cultural social work practice texts used to illustrate theory assumptions and pose critical thinking questions in this chapter:

7. *Emic* means _____ whereas *etic* means _____.

8. Name three common themes of group history of oppression:

9. List five multicultural feminist issues facing women of color:

10. A *value* is

11. List five multicultural values:

12. *Social constructionism* is

13. *Identity development* is

14. *Cultural competence practice theory* involves

15. Culture, ethnicity, minority status, and social class are interrelated in the following ways:

16. On his multicultural competency checklist survey, Ponterotto found more than 60 percent agreement in the following areas: (check appropriate ones)
    ___ faculty, student, and staff minority representation
    ___ multicultural curriculum content, teaching, and methods issues
    ___ counseling field and supervision
    ___ faculty and student research considerations
    ___ student and faculty competency evaluation
    ___ physical environment of the program

17. On the same survey, Ponterotto found less than 35 percent agreement in the following areas: (check appropriate ones)
    ___ faculty, student, and staff minority representation
    ___ multicultural curriculum content, teaching, and methods issues

___ counseling field and supervision
___ faculty and student research considerations
___ student and faculty competency evaluation
___ physical environment of the program

Scoring: There are 45 items in this test, and each item is worth 2 points.

90–80 = excellent
79–70 = good
69–60 = fair
59–50 = needs review
49 and below = needs comprehension

SUMMARY

Knowledge about cultural diversity is a foundational component of cultural competence. This chapter has surveyed a wide range of cultural diversity knowledge for social work students and practitioners. Starting with demographic trends, it focused on critical thinking; history of oppression; gender knowledge; values; the emerging theories of social constructionism, identity development, and culturally competent practice; the themes of ethnicity, culture, minority status, and social class; and social science theory. These areas of knowledge are crucial to master in the development of cultural competence.

CHAPTER SEVEN

Skill Development

DOMAN LUM AND YUHWA EVA LU

Skill development is the creation of a repertoire of behaviors for the social worker to use in the helping situation. Skills represent the practical application of cultural awareness and knowledge acquisition. The word *skill* comes from the root word *skel*, which means the ability to separate or discern. In the helping sense, skills are practical tools for working with the client that have been discerned from knowledge of working with people generally and particularly with culturally and ethnically diverse clients. Helms and Richardson (1997) define skills as "the capacity to use awareness and knowledge to interact effectively with clients and colleagues regardless of their racial classification or cultural origins" (p. 75). Skills are applied at the interface between the social worker and the client and are the heart of social work and culturally competent practice.

Ridley, Espelage, and Rubinstein (1997, p. 140) speak about "culturally responsive skills" that reflect cultural sensitivity. A wide range of skills is identified: the ability to work with multiple roles and identities and multiple layers of environmental oppression (Comas-Diaz, 1994; Reynolds & Pope, 1991); advocacy and assertiveness training for women; identification of community resources for lesbian, gay, and bisexual clients (Fassinger & Richie, 1997); multicultural assessment, particularly process and outcome assessment (Dana, 1993); varied communication and intervention skills; and development of a therapeutic style (Fassinger & Richie, 1997).

Competency Study 7.1 identifies eight essential skills for working with people in general and multicultural clients in particular (Giordano & Giordano, 1995, pp. 23–24). You may wish to talk about these skill principles in class. This list of dos and don'ts provides useful guideposts for working with culturally and ethnically diverse clients. However, we want to build on this foundation of skill development and organize some skill areas for you.

In the following sections of this chapter, we cover types of skills, process-stage skill clusters, service delivery and agency linkage, design and implementation, and examples of skill development research. We will focus on certain skill principles in order to help you build a repertoire of tools you can use as you work with a client. The Hernandez family case study is a complementary series of exercises to help you apply practice principles and enhance your skill development. We encourage you to read the principles in the text and then connect them to the Hernandez case study as you work through this chapter.

COMPETENCY STUDY 7.1

Skills for Cultural Diversity

- *Assess the importance of ethnicity to clients and families.* To what extent does the client identify with an ethnic group and/or religion? Is his or her behavior pathological or a cultural norm? Is the client manifesting "resistance," or is his or her value system different from that of the therapist?
- *Validate and strengthen ethnic identity.* Under great stress, an individual's identity can easily become diffused. It is important that the therapist foster the client's connection to his or her cultural heritage.
- *Be aware of and use the client's support systems.* Often support systems—extended family and friends; fraternal, social, and religious groups—are strained or unavailable. Learn to strengthen the client's connections to family and community resources.
- *Serve as a "culture broker."* Help the family identify and resolve value conflicts. For example, a person may feel pride about some aspects of his or her ethnic background and shame about others, or there may be an immobilizing "tug of war" between personal aspirations and family loyalty.
- *Be aware of "cultural camouflage."* Clients sometimes use ethnic, racial, or religious identity (and stereotypes about it) as a defense against change or pain, or as a justification for half-hearted involvement in therapy. A person who says, "I'm late for our session because I'm on Puerto Rican time" may be trying to avoid a difficult issue.
- *Know that there are advantages and disadvantages to being of the same ethnic group as your client.* There may be a "natural" rapport from belonging to the same "tribe" as your client. Yet, you may also unconsciously overidentify with the client and "collude" with his or her other resistance. Unresolved issues about your own ethnicity may be "mirrored" by client families, exacerbating your own value conflicts.
- *Don't feel you have to "know everything" about other ethnic groups.* Ethnically sensitive practice begins with an awareness of how cultural beliefs influence all our interactions. Knowing your own limitations and ignorance and being openheartedly curious will help set up a context within which you will have mutual learning with your clients.
- *To avoid polarization, always try to think in categories that allow for at least three possibilities.* Consider, if you are exploring Black and White differences, how a Latina might view them. Consider, if you are thinking of how African Americans deal with male–female relationships, how a black lesbian might view it. Consider, when exploring Italian and Irish differences, how an African American might think about them.

TYPES OF SKILLS

Skill development is generally process-oriented in social work practice. Social work is seen as a process with a beginning, middle, and end, during which the worker exercises skills having to do with engagement, psychosocial assessment, intervention strategy, and termination/ending. These skills, applied to individuals, families, groups, organizations, and communities, serve as stepping stones to move the worker and the client through the helping process to a successful conclusion. You may wish to envision how you can use these skills as you work with various population sizes.

Interviewing from a culturally competent perspective is a basic skill arena for social work. It is the first contact skill of beginning with the client. Interviewing skills are strongly emphasized because social workers generally conduct the initial intake sessions for mental health and child and family services.

In Competency Study 7.2, Kadushin and Kadushin (1997) list a number of interviewing skills for the culturally sensitive interviewer. As you read these interviewing skills, take a mental inventory of your skill background and abilities and note the need to develop certain areas.

Culturally Competent Interviewing Skills

COMPETENCY STUDY 7.2

1. The culturally sensitive interviewer approaches all interviewees of whatever cultural background with respect, warmth, acceptance, concern, interest, empathy, and due regard for individuality and confidentiality.
2. The culturally sensitive interviewer exerts maximum effort in the early part of the interview when the interviewee's mistrust and suspicion are highest, when the interviewer is apt to be perceived as a stereotype rather than an individual, and in terms of the interviewer's status as a representative of the mainstream culture rather than as a person.
3. Culturally sensitive interviewers strive to develop an explicit awareness that they have a culture as a member of a particular racial or ethnic, gender, age, and occupational group and as such have been socialized to beliefs, attitudes, behaviors, stereotypes, biases, and prejudices that affect their behavior in the interview.
4. Having achieved such awareness, culturally sensitive interviewers are comfortably undefensive in their identity as a member of a cultural group.
5. Culturally sensitive interviewers are aware of the cultural factors in the interviewee's background that they need to recognize and accept as potential determinants of the interviewee's decision to come for help, the presentation and nature of the problem the client brings, and the choice of intervention.
6. The culturally sensitive interviewer is ready to acknowledge and undefensively and unapologetically raise for discussion cross-cultural factors affecting the interview.
7. Culturally sensitive interviewers recognize that the great variety of culturally distinct groups makes it impossible to have knowledge of all of them but accepts the obligation to study the cultural background of interviewees most frequently served by their agency.
8. Culturally sensitive interviewers are ready to acknowledge the limitations of their knowledge of an interviewee's cultural background and are ready to undefensively solicit help from the interviewee in learning what they need to know.
9. The culturally sensitive interviewer communicates an attitude that cultural differences are not better or worse but rather legitimately diverse and respects such differences.
10. Culturally sensitive interviewers are aware of indigenous cultures' strengths, culturally based community resources that might be a source of help, and that some kinds of help may be culturally inappropriate.
11. Culturally sensitive interviewers are aware of the problems of disenfranchisement, discrimination, and stigmatization frequently associated with minority group status.
12. Although sensitive to cultural factors that might be related to clients' problems, the culturally sensitive interviewer is aware that such factors may be peripheral to the situation of a particular client, that personality factors may be of more significance than racial or ethnic cultural factors, and that culture does not adequately define the interviewee, who is unique. (pp. 347–348)

As you review the 12 skill areas of interviewing in Competency Study 7.2, ask yourself which ones you already have in your helping repertoire and which ones you need to incorporate into your culturally competent practice with people.

A helpful way to organize skill development principles is to cluster them into useful sets. Bernard (1979) distinguishes three types of skills in the helping relationship: *process skills*, *conceptualization skills*, and *personalization skills*. These three themes are useful ways of grouping skills and are reminders of essential ways of working with clients and checking yourself in the process. The three types of skills are defined as follows:

- *Process skills* refer to the following therapeutic techniques and strategies: opening the interview smoothly; using reflection, probing, restatement, summary, or interpretation; helping the client say what is on his or her mind; using nonverbal communication to enhance verbal communication; implementing intervention strategies; and achieving closure.
- *Conceptualization skills* include deliberate thinking and case analysis abilities: understanding what the client is saying; identifying themes of the client's messages; recognizing appropriate and inappropriate goals; choosing strategies that are appropriate to the client's expressed goals; and recognizing subtle client improvement.
- *Personalization skills* have to do with learning observable and subtle behaviors, and with the personal growth of the worker: communicating authority in the helping relationship and taking responsibility for specialized knowledge and skills; hearing client challenges and feedback without becoming overly defensive; being comfortable with the client's feelings and attitudes; and respecting the client.

Process, conceptualization, and personalization skills are important skills to develop. Generally, process skills are the primary focus of skill building because they provide the worker with tools to move the client through the helping process.

Conceptualization and personalization skills are generally developed in the student field practicum with agency supervision. An audiotape or a videotape assists the worker and the supervisor with cultivating such conceptualization skills as the analysis of verbal and nonverbal communication, processing of problem themes, goal setting, and selection of the intervention strategy. Careful supervision helps the beginning student worker with the development of conceptualization skills.

Likewise, personalization skills focus on the worker's response to the helping situation. It is important to process how the client affects the worker. "What were you feeling when the client said that she was ready to scream at her mother?" "What was happening to you when the client became angry and said that you were a lousy social worker?" Investigating the worker's feelings of insecurity, threat, fear, and uncertainty are examples of developing personalization skills. The focus is to help the worker realize that the client may be projecting feelings intended for someone else. At the same time, the worker must own up to the feelings of the client who may need to confront the worker. Keeping composure and asking, "What is going on in this exchange?" helps the worker to maintain an objective perspective in the situation.

The development of process, conceptualization, and personalization skills is essential for cultural competence and requires hours of supervision. In the next section, we turn to five process stages: contact, problem identification, assessment, intervention, and termination. Each stage encompasses a cluster of process, conceptualization, and personalization skills.

PROCESS, CONCEPTUALIZATION, AND PERSONALIZATION SKILL CLUSTERS

Lum's (2000) framework for social work practice with people of color is built around a systematic process-stage approach, following the classic formula of beginning, middle, and end. The beginning process stages are contact and problem identification; the middle stages include assessment and intervention; and the ending stage is termination. We invite you to read *Social Work Practice and People of Color* (Lum, 2000), which details these process-stage areas and their accompanying skills. In this section, we select several key skill area principles and identify those process skills necessary to move clients in general and the multicultural client in particular through these five stages, along with essential conceptualization and personalization skills.

Contact

Contact Process Skills. The establishment of the relationship between the social worker and the multicultural client is basic to the contact stage. Relationship building is the primary requisite for retaining the client. Culturally diverse contact has a skill cluster consisting of understanding the ethnic community, following a relationship protocol, engaging in professional self-disclosure, and developing an effective communication style.

Understanding the ethnic community means that the social worker has a working knowledge of the client community's demographic profile. Studying the 2000 U.S. Census local demographics on a particular area, as well as recent city and state study reports, may give you a handle on ethnic, social, economic, and related trends and indicators such as unemployment rates, income levels, housing, and related information. A social worker should be well versed in the history, problems, and profiles of an ethnic community. A local community newspaper, recent books and articles about a community, and interviews with grassroots community leaders will uncover a wealth of information you can piece together in order to understand the community and the people who are your client groups.

The worker can consult community study reports, but it is important to walk through a community and observe where people congregate and exchange information. This participant observation and thoughtful interaction with the people who live in a community are most helpful. Be sure to patronize businesses and talk with storeowners and customers about the news of the community. Show up at social, cultural, and educational community events and observe how people spend their leisure time. Talking with people living in the community provides valuable knowledge about current issues facing residents. Shadow a staff member of a social service helping agency in the community and get a sense of how one relates effectively with residents. It is important to listen and gain information while also establishing credibility as a reliable and believable person of integrity.

The ways in which individuals in a particular cultural community express their gratitude are important to observe and understand as the community interacts with each other. Vasquez (2005) talks about giving and receiving gifts and cites a client's healthy expression of care, which may be a genuine expression of thanks. She observes:

> On the other hand, when a Latina client who works near a restaurant brings me tacos because I squeezed her in during my lunch hour when she was in crisis, we don't need to spend half an hour processing the meaning of the tacos. We know that she felt appreciative, that it was a relatively easy, warm gesture, and that food is a common gift among Latinas. Sometimes a taco is just a taco! (p. 105)

Looking and listening, understanding local ways of relating and conducting business, and placing the needs of people first before getting results are some community-understanding guidelines.

Relationship protocols are cultural ways of relating to a person. A protocol is a code of ceremonial formality and courtesies. Every locale has a particular way of beginning a relationship or a contact with another person. It is important to find out the specific ways in which people relate to each other in initial conversation. In many cultures, a relationship protocol is a prelude to conducting business. It may involve a formal greeting, inquiry about the health and well-being of family, and other friendly topics of conversation. This communicates a message of genuine concern about the well-being of another person and a common exchange of daily activities that are considered important topics of conversation. It may be considered rude to proceed directly to the main order of business or to the presenting problem without proper protocol conversation. Friendly, warm, and thoughtful feelings are important to communicate at the beginning.

Following a relationship protocol involves the communication of respect and recognition to the head of household, grandparents, and other adults. It is important to practice a relationship protocol regarding the father and mother in a family situation, which means supporting their authority and roles rather than undermining their family influence. This may involve relating to and respecting traditional male, female, and age role relationships of a particular cultural and ethnic group. A professional protocol is to assure a client that a level of confidentiality will be maintained in the helping relationship as far as information sharing is concerned. Clients furthermore appreciate structure in the helping relationship to the extent that the worker sets forth flexible and clear guidelines and directions in the sessions.

The following are examples of relationship protocol responses:

- Worker to the Hernandez family: Good evening, Mr. and Mrs. Hernandez. My name is John Platt. I am pleased that you and your family are here. Could you introduce your children to me? (Later) Let me get everyone some refreshments, and then I would like to get to know you better.
- Worker to the Hernandez family: Good evening, Mr. and Mrs. Hernandez. I am John Platt, a social worker here at the Family Service Agency. Mr. Hernandez, I am happy that your whole family is here tonight. Let me open this window and cool the room. How has the weather been affecting you lately?

Professional self-disclosure is an extension of the professional use of self, an important social work principle. Often a client comes to the helping session with distrust, anxiety, and fear of the unknown. Professional self-disclosure is an effort on the part of the worker to reveal a commonality between the worker and the client. Rather than hiding behind the professionalism of social work, the worker takes the initiative by disclosing an area of interest shared by the client. The intent is to become a real person and to humanize the relationship.

Finding out about the background of the client may open appropriate topics of self-disclosure, such as travel, children, cars, clothes, shopping, and other areas of common interest. Professional self-disclosure begins to create a sense of community and bonding between the worker and the client. Among the practical suggestions for professional self-disclosure are introducing yourself; sharing pertinent background about your work and role, family, and helping philosophy; and finding a common area of interest with the client that you might reveal in order to build a bridge between the two of you.

The worker should be judicious in the sharing of a professional self-disclosure. Current problems of the worker that are parallel to the client's problems may not be appropriate. Neutral common areas of interests may be more effective to bridge the gap of the unknown between the worker and the client. Professional self-disclosure should put the client at ease, generate rapport, and increase spontaneity and openness.

Lum (2000) suggests three levels of professional self-disclosure:

1. Level One: self-disclosure about common areas of interest to humanize the relationship and to establish a sense of openness with the client, usually at the first session as a point of contact
2. Level Two: self-disclosure of empathy and related warmth from the worker (e.g., how the worker felt as the client was able to express genuine feelings about a problem situation)
3. Level Three: self-disclosure at the problem identification stage when the client is sharing a significant problem and needs support from the worker who may have experienced a similar situation

Self-disclosure should be used discreetly and appropriately as the helping relationship progresses with the worker and the client. Examples of professional self-disclosure at the three different levels are as follows:

- Level One/Worker to Mr. Hernandez: Mr. Hernandez, what is your hometown in Mexico? I took a recent trip to Mexico City to see a high school friend, Alex Garcia, who is working for Volkswagen.
- Level Two/Worker to Mrs. Hernandez: Mrs. Hernandez, thank you for sharing your feelings about your son, Ricardo. As you were talking about your love for him, I could sense your deep feelings about helping him with his schoolwork. It reminded me about how my mother cared for me when I was Ricardo's age.
- Level Three/Worker to Ricardo: Ricardo, you really miss the support and help of your father with your schoolwork. I know that he would like to spend more time with you but has needed to work in the evenings. I remember my father, who was away on many business trips. I missed him, too, and wished he were at home to help me. I think that I know what you are going through.

An effective *communication style* gives a positive message to the multicultural client. The agency environment sets the tone for the initial contact between the worker and the client. A friendly bilingual receptionist, an accessible location, an attractive facility, a private room, comfortable furniture, light refreshments, and a casual approach create a positive atmosphere. Agency setting communicates a tone of cultural and ethnic sensitivity to people who come to a center for help.

Body language, bilingual staff, use of an on-call trained translator or interpreter, and familiarity with cultural mannerisms and gestures make for effective communication. Body language should convey an open and approachable stance. Sitting with the client without a barrier such as a desk, leaning toward the client with arms and open palms of the hand, and legs uncrossed are nonverbal signs of open communication. There should be allowance for personal space between the client and the worker.

Generally, physical contact such as shaking hands is appropriate at the beginning of a session. Further contact such as hugging at the end of a session should be explored with the client in terms of appropriate cultural expressions of support and related behavior patterns. Likewise, the worker should note eye contact of the client. In some cultures, indirect and minimal direct eye contact may denote a respect for the worker as an authority figure. Looking away and the lack of direct eye contact may not connote avoidance or resistance. Talking about sensitive topics in the session may be accompanied by the lack of eye contact because of the serious nature of the conversation. The client may feel uneasy and embarrassed by the topic and may look away or down at the ground as a result. Staffing patterns should mirror the demographic population of the clients served. Allow the behavior of the client to lead and to tell you what an appropriate response is. If a worker has questions about these areas, it would be helpful to get clarification from the client. Likewise, a professional colleague of the same ethnic group as the client may be a good sounding board to give advice and to orient the worker before the beginning session with a particular client from an unfamiliar cultural and ethnic group.

Bilingual and bicultural staff matching the language and cultural needs of clients conveys a sense of familiarity and expressiveness to clients who are comfortable speaking their culture-of-origin language. Translators should be trained by the staff of the agency to understand and interpret correctly medical and clinical terms and concepts. The worker should address and maintain contact with the client rather than the translator and should continuously ask the client for feedback to determine the level of understanding between the two.

Active listening responses that vary according to the content of the message and the feelings of the messenger should be used. Strive to offer *open-ended questions* that will open avenues of information and feelings rather than close-ended questions that trigger brief and dead-end answers. Supportive, understanding, probing, interpretive, and evaluative (SUPIE) responses are examples of varying listening skills. *Supportive responses* restate the essential thoughts and feelings of the client without using the same words. A paraphrase by the worker reassures the client that he or she has been heard. *Understanding responses* focus on the client's meaning and the perception of the problem. They verify that significant thoughts have been understood and comprehended. *Probing responses* seek further information on problem issues that are to be explored or those that are in progress. Open-ended probing may be used to elicit more information, and close-ended probing may help pinpoint a particular detail yet to be uncovered. *Interpretive responses* seek to bring meaning and organization to the various facts, events, and experiences shared by the client. Such responses order the series of events, provide meaning about what has been going on, and bring a sense of rationality. Finally, *evaluative responses* offer various alternative directions that the client may take based on his or her readiness to move on the problem situation. They summarize the themes and provide a range of available solutions. Examples of SUPIE are as follows:

- *Supportive response:* Mr. Hernandez, I hear you saying that it has been difficult coming here and discussing your problems. You have always been a person who has been able to figure things out.
- *Understanding response:* Mrs. Hernandez, I sense that you want to help Ricardo with his homework but are frustrated because you cannot speak English.
- *Probing response:* Ricardo, could you tell me when your problems at school started?
- *Interpretive response:* It seems that when you started working at two jobs and were unable to work with Ricardo on his homework, Ricardo started having problems at school. Have you made a connection between these two events?
- *Evaluative response:* Based on what you have been saying, we have a number of ways that we can solve some of the problems you have all talked about tonight. Ricardo, what do you think about a tutor for you to help you with your schoolwork? Mr. Hernandez, do you think that it would be possible to reduce the hours on your night job? Mrs. Hernandez, what about the possibility of attending an English as a Second Language class? Let's talk about these areas.

In Competency Study 7.3, Hepworth, Rooney, and Larsen (2002, p. 107) offer some thoughts on the importance and limitations of empathic communication.

Contact Conceptualization Skills. Ethnographic skills are important to conceptualization in the contact stage. *Ethnography* is derived from *ethnos* (people) and *graphics* (writings, drawing) and literally involves the recording (writing and drawing) of the behavioral culture of a person or a group of people. Ethnography is concerned with the words, thoughts, and feelings of the client from a participant observation stance. In the contact stage, we must constantly ask ourselves as workers what clients are saying about themselves, their families, and their primary groups. We must have an ethnographic discipline to record words, thoughts, and feelings and then to translate them as teachable moments for us to learn and uncover new and different ways of understanding and relating to people.

Empathic Communication Contact Skills

COMPETENCY STUDY 7.3

The importance of knowledge of cultural factors was documented almost 40 years ago by the research findings of Mayer and Timms (1969), who studied clashes of perspectives between clients and social workers. Based on their findings they concluded: "It seems that social workers start where the client is psychodynamically but they are insufficiently empathic in regard to cultural components" (p. 38).

Although empathic communication is important in bridging cultural gaps, it can be used to excess with many Asian Americans and American Indians. Many members of these groups tend to be lower in emotional expressiveness than other client groups and may react with discomfort and confusion if a practitioner relies heavily on empathic communication. Still, it is important to "read between the lines" and to sensitively respond to troubling emotions that these clients do not usually express directly. Like other clients, they are likely to appreciate sensitive awareness by a practitioner to painful emotions associated with their difficulties.

In this text and in our social work courses, we learn how to discover concepts from the contact phase. Ethnographic skills have a number of parallels in the following areas:

- Qualitative inductive survey research begins by framing a research question and interviewing a sample population without a priori assumptions. Likewise, ethnographic skills in the contact stage encourage open-ended questions about the client's family, work, children, and related background areas.
- Social constructionism focuses on life story or narrative and is interested in how a person has constructed his or her life from various pieces of experience. Again, ethnographic skills include the telling of life stories by the person, which is a familiar and nonthreatening way for a multicultural client to open segments of his or her life.
- Emic and etic understanding views the multicultural client from two perspectives. Emic understanding seeks to comprehend the unique particulars of the client in order to understand what sets the person apart from others in his or her culture. Etic understanding is concerned about the link between the client and his or her cultural group. Sobeck, Chapleski and Fisher (2003) describe the emic perspective in research:

The purpose of emic research is to seek categories of meanings based on how the group being studied defines things. Its research strategy includes conducting interviews in the native language, seeking to discover meaning and relying on the research participant's explanation for their own behavior. (p. 74)

A number of applications have been made to feminist research and to American Indian communities. Ethnographic contact skills cover these areas and remind us of the importance of open-ended interviewing, finding out about the life story narratives of clients, and determining what is culture-common and culture-specific about individuals, families, and groups.

Green (1995) offers some practical suggestions about ethnographic interviewing:

- The social work interview must have a mutually accepted purpose and must focus on how the client uses language and what language suggests about the client's state of being and thinking.
- Our concern must be on the salient cultural data bearing on the presenting issue or the cultural context of the problem.
- It is important to understand the perspective of the client and how the client explains the veracity (truthfulness) of cultural expressions and communication.
- The client is our teacher who best explains cultural differences.

Green (1995) explains:

The intent of ethnographic interviewing is . . . to recognize ideas, beliefs, and patterns of behavior in the contexts where they are meaningful—all as an aid to informed understanding of people's problems and appreciation of what one will have to do to effectively help resolve them. (p. 146)

Contact conceptualization skills enable the worker to learn about the client in an inductive manner and assist us with conceptualizing some preliminary notions about the person at the beginning of the helping process.

Contact Personalization Skills. What happens to the worker in the contact stage? The range of subjective feelings on the part of the worker may include normal anxiety and curiosity about the reasons for the client coming for help, positive interest in and empathy for the client, or uneasy feelings about the client due to manipulation, personal attack, racism, and other issues. The worker should constantly check his or her feelings and ask: "What am I feeling and sensing as I listen to and interact with this client?" "What is the client's message?" "Am I able to help with the client's problems?" The worker needs to process these feelings and reactions both internally and with a supervisor or colleague.

Subjective reflection about the first impressions of the client is a part of the personalization skills at the contact stage. Likewise, the client is sizing up the worker and decoding verbal and nonverbal messages and related behavioral responses. Paniagua (2005) discusses attrition, where the client fails to return, and estimates that 50 percent of clients terminate after one contact with a mental health professional (p. 110). The preceding principles on contact are designed to keep the client coming for help. The personalization process involves listening to one's self and becoming curious about how one reacts to the client, the problem situation, and significant others involved. Identifying and checking out these reactions helps with self-learning and provides an opportunity to receive feedback from a third-party source who objectively analyzes the situation. Fieldwork supervisors in social work field education play a vital role as teachers who are able to heighten the personalization skills of social work students in helping situations.

In Competency Study 7.4, we again focus on the Abdullah family case study, particularly on the two children.

The Abdullah Family and Skill Development

COMPETENCY STUDY 7.4

Mohammed, age 10, and Osama, age 5, as well as the entire Abdullah family, have lived under the Taliban rule, which has shaped the education and upbringing of the two children. Muslim refugee children have three cultural needs: identity, language, and religion ("Muslim Refugees in the United States," n.d.). Along the way the Muslim child must negotiate at least four sets of values in the transition from a country of origin Muslim culture to a dominant host society: (1) his or her family's culture, (2) U.S. cultural norms as learned within the context of the education system, (3) the culture communicated by peers and the mass media, and (4) the teaching of Islam.

As Mohammed and Osama settle into life in the United States, they are negotiating these values in terms of their cultural, social, and religious identity. Mr. and Mrs. Abdullah may not be aware of the subtle conflicts and sorting-out process that their children are undergoing because as parents they are coping with their own survival, losses, and adjustments. Observant Muslim parents ensure that their children are raised with an understanding of Islam and live their faith. They depend on the local mosque to provide religious instruction to their children and socialization with other Muslim children of the same age.

Muslim adults may invoke the authority of religion when they are concerned about maintaining tradition and control over their children. Mr. and Mrs. Abdullah must sort out the differences between cultural traditions from Afghanistan and Islamic practice as taught in the mosque of a city in the United States. There are major transitions, gaps, and leaps that the entire family must take as individuals and as a family unit. Adjustment may be more difficult for the parents but equally as challenging for the children.

Many Muslim refugee children accept cultural traditions and integrate themselves into American society. Others negotiate parental demands and expectations or hide their activities from their parents, or even participate in risky behaviors. They may turn to their Muslim peers for answers or to school counselors or youth leaders in the local mosque. Enlightened Muslim community leaders and social caseworkers are important resources to guide children in mitigating social risks.

Mohammed and Osama may experience prejudice and hostility at school because they are foreign born, have a different appearance, and have a different primary language. American-born peers may have stereotypes about them because they came from a country that was invaded by Western coalition powers and because they have names that are associated with the tragic events of September 11, 2001. They may be subject to cruel humor, shunning, hazing, or physical abuse even though President Bush issued a public warning about discrimination against the Muslim community after 9/11 and school districts have set a zero-tolerance policy toward negative incidents focusing on Muslim children in schools.

Mohammed and Osama need time to sort out their culture, experiences in Afghanistan and California, and their journey from a war-torn, divided country to a strange and different country of resettlement. In this chapter, we have covered 12 interviewing skills and practice principles related to contact process, conceptualization, and personalization skills. In small groups, answer the following questions about your involvement with these two children:

1. If you were working with Mohammed and Osama, how would you develop a relationship with them that may lead to utilizing practice skills in exploring where they are in their lives?
2. What kind of interviewing skill principles that were previously covered would you employ in working with the boys?
3. What would be some contact process, conceptualization and personalization skills guiding your time with Mohammed and Osama?

CULTURAL COMPETENCY IN ACTION

The Hernandez Family: A Case Study

Contact involves the process skills of establishing the relationship between the worker, Mr. Platt, and the Hernandez family as well as employing ethnographic conceptualization skills and reflecting on feelings and reactions as personalization skills. Contact process skills are the foundation of the relationship. The social worker should do the homework of understanding the ethnic community of the client.

In this situation, Mr. Platt should be familiar with the local Latino community. Relationship protocols are important to establish, such as formal greeting, friendly conversation, and respect for each family member. Professional self-disclosure reveals a common point of reference for both parties and is initiated by the social worker.

TASK RECOMMENDATIONS

- State the essential information that Mr. Platt should know about the local Latino community before he meets the Hernandez family.
- Give examples of the use of relationship protocols and professional self-disclosure between Mr. Platt and the Hernandez family.
- Suggest a number of open-ended ethnographic questions about the Hernandez family that Mr. Platt can pose on work, children, and other familiar and nonthreatening topics, as beginning subjects for discussion.
- Anticipate the feelings and reactions of the worker after the first session with the family and process them in class.

Problem Identification

Problem-Identification Process Skills.   It is crucial to spend as much time as possible cultivating contact in order to retain the client. However, the presenting problem eventually emerges, and the worker must employ problem-identification process skills. Among them are problem-area disclosure, problem orientation, and identification of racial/ethnic themes.

Problem-area disclosure is a skill based on the understanding that a multicultural client may have a difficult time expressing a problem directly to the worker. The client may feel shame and hesitation and may have a guarded attitude toward disclosing family secrets to a stranger. Hepworth, Rooney, and Larsen (2002) give some suggestions about establishing rapport in Competency Study 7.5.

The worker should be patient and allow the client to set the pace in revealing the problem. It is important not to rush the client prematurely. The client may ask indirect questions ("I have this friend who has a problem. How would you help her?"), make oblique or circular comments that approach a problem in a slanted or peripheral way ("I don't know why I am here, but something is bothering me"), or make similar efforts toward problem disclosure. Part of the reason for this communication style may be that *the client, particularly the person of color, has learned to communicate with cultural understatement.* Rather than spelling out all the negative details and unburdening one's self in humiliation, one learns to infer and allude to problem issues. In turn, the worker must read between the lines and piece together the inferences. As a result, it may more be culturally appropriate for the worker to figure out the problem, spell out the details, and ask for comments from the client, who is excused from disgracing himself or herself. A culturally competent social worker is able to pick up on this approach and decipher these indirect messages from the client.

A natural way to begin problem-area disclosure is to take a history of the family. This is a nonthreatening way of helping a person talk about himself or herself. Questions such as "Could you tell me about your family?" "What are they like?" "Where are they living?" help to break the barrier and to begin conversation about the family unit and the client's membership in the family.

Establishing Rapport

COMPETENCY STUDY 7.5

Revealing problems to others may be perceived as a reflection of personal inadequacy and as a stigma upon an entire family. The resultant fear of shame may thus impede the development of rapport with clients from this ethnic group (Kumabe, Nishida, & Hepworth, 1985; Lum, 1996; Tsui & Schultz, 1985). African Americans, First Nations Peoples, and Latinos may also experience difficulty in developing rapport because of distrust that derives from a history of being exploited or discriminated against by other ethnic groups (Longres, 1991; Proctor & Davis, 1994).

Clients' difficulties in communicating openly tend to be even more severe when their problems involve allegations of socially unacceptable behavior, such as child abuse, moral infractions, or criminal behavior. In groups, the pain is further compounded by having to expose one's difficulties to other group members, especially in early sessions when the reactions of other members represent the threat of the unknown. (p. 47)

Problem orientation is the core of problem identification. Problems are normally viewed as negative intrusions in our lives. However, problems are opportunities for growth and learning. In our orientation, the problem is viewed as an unsatisfied want or an unfulfilled need (Reid, 1978), which is a way of interpreting the problem in a positive light. That is, behind every problem are wants that have not been satisfied and needs that have not been fulfilled. Our task is to restructure the problem so that we can reorient the client toward positive growth. This is called *reframing the problem.* The worker and the client reframe the problem and change the point of reference from negative pathology to positive want satisfaction or need fulfillment. Greene, Lee, and Hoffpauir (2005) explain reframing:

> The reframing process involves offering clients a plausible, alternative positive interpretation for something they have defined as negative and undesirable or unchangeable. Once clients accept the plausibility of the new and more positive reality represented by the new category, they cannot go back to using only their former, more narrow worldview. (p. 272)

This changes the orientation toward the underlying need and perspective away from the negative aspects of the problem in the cognitive mind-set of the client. *A problem becomes an opportunity for satisfaction and fulfillment.* This redirection reinterprets the problem as an opportunity for positive change and gets behind and beyond the problem as a motivating force for change. The culturally competent worker repositions the client and the problem by reframing the problem. As part of the reframing process, one begins *to mobilize client strengths and resources to fulfill the want and satisfy the need.*

As an exercise, state a problem that is confronting a person and then reframe the problem so that one understands the unsatisfied want or the unfulfilled need that underlies the supposed problem. Ask how this reinterpretation of the problem could be a motivator for change and growth.

Racial/ethnic themes may be a part of problem identification. Multiple problem levels may occur simultaneously and require analysis and unraveling. Fong (2004) describes the layer-upon-layer problems of immigrants and refugees coming to the United States. She describes them:

> At the macro-level, poverty, discrimination, racism, language, immigration laws, and legal and illegal status characterize many of their experiences. At the meso-level, families often struggle with role reversal, husband–wife tensions, grandparent relations, and questions of abandonment and loyalty. At the micro-level, a father may encounter problems with his traditional role as the head of house and loss of authority, because he lacks command of the host-culture's language. At the micro-level, for the mother, accepting employment may introduce tension about her role as wife and mother. At the micro-level, for the child, tensions may be related to school and language deficiency. Children may also have conflicts due to illiteracy, the necessity to interpret for parents, and pressure to achieve and hurry through childhood. (pp. 12–13)

The culturally competent worker explores possible problem themes of racism, sexism, and homophobia (ideological beliefs), prejudice (attitude), discrimination (behavior), and expressions manifested in oppression, powerlessness, exploitation, acculturation, and stereotyping. Racism, sexism, and homophobia are related concepts that have similar dynamics: in-group/out-group, superiority/inferiority, domination/submission, power/powerlessness, and systemic-institutional/individual. They are cognitive beliefs learned from parents, neighborhood, community, and society. Prejudice is a negative attitudinal and affective response based on prior cognitive belief, whereas discrimination is the behavioral response expressed as denial, refusal, and rejection. (See the section in Chapter 2 on environment-centered context for a more detailed discussion of these concepts.)

Racism, prejudice, and discrimination result in oppression, powerlessness, exploitation, acculturation, and stereotyping. *Oppression* occurs when a group with power and control systematically prevents another group from attaining access to scarce and valued resources and creates a hierarchy where oppressed groups are placed at the bottom. *Powerlessness* is the inability to control self and others, to alter problem situations, or to reduce environmental distress. There is a feeling of impotence so overwhelming that a person is at a loss of knowing what to do in a situation. *Exploitation* occurs when a person is manipulated or used unfairly in an economic, political, or social situation for the benefit of members of the dominant society. This may be due to ethnicity, gender, social class, age, or other related factors. *Acculturation* involves the adoption of the dominant culture to the exclusion of maintaining the culture of origin. To a certain extent, there is normal adjustment and adaptation of the dominant society's behavior patterns and modification of cultural beliefs, traditions, and customs. Forced acculturation is harmful when there is an either–or choice made between the dominant culture and the culture of origin so that the latter is rejected or given up in favor of the former. *Stereotyping* is a negative label placed on all members of a group based on a prejudicial generalization without regard to individuals of the stigmatized group. These five expressions are played out in organizational and interpersonal ways between social institutions and victimized individuals (Lum, 2000). The culturally competent worker looks for racist dynamics that may be a part of the problem set.

Problem-Identification Conceptualization Skills. Ethnographic problem-identification skills involve how the multicultural client formulates the problem. Green (1999) explains his help-seeking behavior model that relates four principles to problem identification and resolution: the individual's definition and understanding of an experience as a problem; the client's semantic evaluation of a problem from his or her language explanation; indigenous cultural strategies of problem intervention; and acceptable culturally based problem resolution. That is, rather than defining the problem for the client, it is vital to understand how the client defines and understands his or her problem situation. It may well be that because the client wears another set of cultural and ethnic lenses, his or her perception of the problem is different from the worker's. For example, when working with refugees, Chen and colleagues (2003) assert:

> They are more likely to have language difficulties, less likely to have high human capital and socioeconomic status, and they experience a forced separation from their familiar culture and life style. Since they are less likely to have marketable skills in the U.S., they are more likely to be unemployed and more likely to live on welfare, which in turn makes them more likely to be a target of discrimination. As refugees, many had traumatizing experiences even before they entered this country. (p. 24)

However, we cannot assume that this problem identification description fits all refugees. We must ask the client to share his or her own unique story, which may be similar and different from our assumptions. Moreover, language may explain the problem with a different semantic meaning, so it is important to know, understand, and use the language explanation for a problem. What appears to be clinical depression in Western countries may be considered extreme fatigue in Eastern countries. Finding out how the client and his or her family name a problem from a linguistic perspective may give us a clue to how the client understands and handles a problem situation. Furthermore, from a bicultural vantage point, one may ask an ethnic caregiver for information and advice on appropriate indigenous ways of intervening and solving a problem. Cultural practices, group support, and medicinal cures may all play a role in problem solving. It is important to determine how traditional a client is and how receptive a person might be to applying a combination of indigenous healing and clinical therapy practices to a problem situation. This is an example of the biculturation of problem-solving practices.

CULTURAL COMPETENCY IN ACTION

The Hernandez Family: A Case Study

Problem-identification process skills involve problem-areas disclosure (the particular way that the client may allude to the problem); problem orientation (the reframing of the problem as an unsatisfied want or an unfulfilled need); and the identification of racial/ethnic themes of racism, prejudice, and discrimination, which lead to oppression, powerlessness, exploitation, acculturation, and stereotyping.

Problem-identification conceptualization skills are concerned with the client's formulation of the problem from his or her cultural and linguistic perspectives. The conceptualization should be inductive and indigenous, arising from the cultural context of the client. Problem-identification personalization skills concentrate on the worker's reaction to the problem to determine whether it is appropriate and natural.

The Hernandez family's problems are twofold: (1) Mr. Hernandez's two jobs, long hours, and economic burdens precipitated by having to support two families of in-laws who recently migrated from Mexico, and (2) Ricardo's academic and social problems at school, caused by the unavailability of Mr. Hernandez to help his son with his schoolwork.

TASK RECOMMENDATIONS

- Formulate some direct and indirect ways in which Mr. Hernandez might express his problems.
- Reframe the Hernandez family's problem in terms of an unsatisfied want or an unfulfilled need.
- Determine whether racism, prejudice, and/or discrimination are involved in the problem.
- Express how the Hernandez family members may describe the problem rather than a social work problem description.
- Suggest an appropriate personalized response to the problem on the part of the social worker, Mr. Platt.

These problem identification concepts provide a cultural context for inductive and indigenous problem identification that is not superimposed from the social worker's vantage point. It is important for the culturally competent worker to obtain the client's expression and explanation of the problem. The next step might be to ask to what extent the client conceptualizes the problem along the traditional versus contemporary continuum of care.

Problem-Identification Personalization Skills. It is important for the worker to determine his or her own reaction to the problem. Does the worker grasp the cultural and ethnic implications of the problem? Has the worker misidentified the problem? Has the worker strived to reframe the problem with the client and thus brought new insights and directions? Does the problem have clinical, ethnic, cultural, gender, social class, and/or sexual orientation implications? Does the problem involve a single dimension or a multiple set of dynamics? Is there a problem or are there problems? Does the problem shock the worker in its sensationalism or taboo nature? Is the problem so overwhelming that the worker privately recognizes that problem resolution is not likely to happen? Is it better to sustain the client through supportive maintenance than to push for a rapid solution? Is the problem a part of a problem cluster that will take time to unravel, and should the worker direct the client toward a series of modest solutions? The culturally competent worker must consider these questions and others in the problem-identification stage.

Assessment

Assessment Process Skills. Assessment process skills involve a psychosocial perspective that analyzes environment and person. Some factors in the social environment are related to maintaining basic survival needs, such as food, housing, clothes, employment, health care, and education. Other related environmental stressors include ethnic identity formation, intergenerational disputes, and related cultural conflicts. These areas are termed *socioenvironmental impacts*.

The individual interacts with and responds to the environment. Normally, people use coping skills to process socioenvironmental impacts and are not overwhelmed by stressors. Ego strength, support systems, and community resources play a part in the processing of these demands. Sometimes, however, system overloads result in psychosomatic symptoms and psychosocial dysfunctioning. It is well-known that Asian Americans tend to internalize their stresses rather than deal with the external causes or people involved. They manifest physical and somatic complaints that can be treated by a family medicine physician rather than admit to mental and emotional problems that may need the services of a psychiatrist. Physically based problems are recognized, but mental illness is a social stigma. These *psychoindividual reactions* must be understood as a response to the immediate environment confronting the person.

The *psychosocial perspective* views the environment as socioenvironmental impacts and the person as psychoindividual reactions. This is especially helpful in the assessment process because the worker explains the concept of social/environmental stressors affecting the individual and causing psychological stress reactions (Lum, 2000). Interpreting this view to the client helps the worker to keep this perspective of the interaction between environment and person. However, clients in major transition may experience these stress points in terms of newcomer acculturation, psychosomatic reactions, psychological identity issues, and related survival adjustment concerns. Newcomer acculturation consists of culture shock and culture dislocation, language barriers, legal and immigration problems, employment/unemployment/welfare, and school adjustment for children. As indicated earlier, clients in transitions may have psychosomatic reactions such as anxiety and depression with accompanying insomnia, weight loss, and lack of energy; headache, back pain, and shoulder pain; hypertension; and loneliness and isolation.

Psychological identity may be impaired due to ethnic identity confusion, conflict, and ambivalence; cultural value conflict; family role conflict; dating, mate selection, and intermarriage; and youth delinquency and gang activities. Imparting this psychosocial perspective helps to process and interpret assessment in practical terms.

Emphasis is placed on the positive nature of psychosocial assessment. Cultural and spiritual strengths must be tapped as positive resources for the person in the environment. Assessment ought to uncover the resources available to the client because *assessment* is derived from the root word *asset*, which means worth, resources, and value. Saleeby (2002) lists the following lexicon of strengths: empowerment, membership, resilience, healing and wholeness, dialogue and collaboration, and suspension of disbelief. His principles of the strengths perspective have implications for a strengths-oriented assessment:

- Every individual, group, family, and community has strengths.
- Trauma and abuse, illness, and struggle may be injurious, but they also may be sources of challenge and opportunity.
- Assume that you do not know the upper limits of the capacity to grow and change, and take individual, group, and community aspirations seriously.
- We best serve clients by collaborating with them.
- Every environment is full of resources.
- Caring, caretaking, and context. (pp. 9–18)

Cultural strengths are a focus of social work assessment in line with the asset resource understanding advocated by Saleeby (2002) and Cowger (1994). This assessment emphasis discovers internal strengths of the person and external ethnic group strengths from the culture. Examples of cultural strengths are religious beliefs, historical achievements, ethnic pride, capacities for endurance and hard work in the family, and related areas. Bricker-Jenkins (1997) talks about supporting the life world and strengths of the client from a cultural perspective:

> The workers who engaged networks skillfully had two competencies that were essential: They were *"culturally competent,"* knowing how to get "inside the skin" of a culture not familiar to them; and they *used the oral histories* of clients to assess their strengths and understand their systems of meaning. Thus they were able to place clients not only in time and situation but in their ethnic and class medium as well. These workers were able to assume, with patience and sensitivity, the "standpoint" of their clients. (p. 141)

This example of cultural strengths assessment in social networks should be incorporated into our procedures for conducting culturally competent assessments.

In Competency Study 7.6, Dupree, Spencer, and Bell (1997) write about the need to promote resilient coping strategies among African American children, which has implications for all clients in general and for people of color specifically.

The cultural strengths perspective emphasizes the discovery of strengths in the person and the culture, the motivation toward perseverance and change based on inner strength and endurance, and the environment as full of resources at the family, group, and community levels.

The inclusion of cultural and spiritual assessment expands the concept of biopsychosocial assessment beyond the biological, psychological, and social categories to include cultural and spiritual dimensions. African American, Latino, Asian American, and First Nations

African American Children

Sources of stress, such as poverty and low socioeconomic status, neighborhood dangers, and daily hassles, which are often prevalent in African American communities but not limited to these communities, reveal an increasing need for innovative strategies with which to relate to these children and youth. Avoid thinking that the aforementioned factors reflect the experiences of the entire African American community. Similar cultural characteristics may be shared but they are in no way a homogeneous group. In fact, counseling with African American children and youth requires a case-by-case, situation-specific approach. One of the goals of counseling with African American children and youth is to promote resilient coping strategies under unique circumstances. Therefore, one should avoid using methods that encourage clients to accept their negative environmental circumstances and adapt to such an environment. Methods providing information that promotes the effective use of underutilized resources or resources that are unattainable within their community should be employed. Help-seeking strategies and greater social mobility will enable them to survive in their environment. (p. 258)

Peoples cultures recognize this interconnectedness. Part of culture is the spiritual and part of spirituality is the culture. In African American, Latino, and Asian American cultures, the ethnic church is the source of imparting spiritual values and celebrating cultural events. For First Nations Peoples, the cultural and spiritual aspects of life are a part of rituals and group gatherings.

Psychiatric cultural assessment (American Psychiatric Association [APA], 1994) addresses cultural identity, cultural explanations of illness, psychosocial environmental levels of functioning, and cultural elements between the worker and the client. Cultural identity is concerned about the degree of involvement that a person has with both the culture of origin and the host culture as far as language abilities, use, and preference. Cultural explanations of illness are important to determine in relation to cultural expressions of stress, cultural group norms and perceptions of symptom severity, local perspectives on cultural forms of illness, cultural explanations of dysfunction, and the blending of professional and indigenous helping. Psychosocial environmental levels of functioning involve culturally sensitive interpretations of social stressors, available social supports, and the role of religion and kinship networks. Finally, the relationship between the worker and the client is important to determine the degree of difficulties in language communication, understanding the cultural significance of symptoms, negotiating an appropriate relationship, and determining whether a behavior is normative or pathological.

Indigenous or ethnic cultures are natural support systems that include significant other people in families and extended families, as well as neighborhood, church, and ethnic community organizations. Although some ethnic clients may lack natural support systems, resources are generally available in ethnic community groups. The culturally competent worker should contact cultural network leaders and helping associations and link multicultural clients to them.

Regarding spiritual assessment, linking spirituality and social work is a growing movement in social work education and professional practice (Amato-von Hemert, 1994; Clark, 1994). Part of the movement recognizes the importance of religion and spirituality in people's life, and another part is active in churches, synagogues, and mosques. From a cultural competence standpoint, it is appropriate to understand and explore past and present spirituality and religious faith in the life of the client. Some of the following questions might be asked:

- Could you tell me about your religious faith or spiritual beliefs to help me understand your thoughts about your spirituality?
- What particular beliefs and spiritual practices have directed your life in the past and present?
- How has spiritual faith been a source of strength to you lately?

Of course, the worker should ask the client for permission to discuss these areas. Spiritual assessment may be an important strength area for a client.

Assessment Conceptualization Skills. A culturally competent social worker must not equate assessment with using the *Diagnostic and Statistical Manual of Mental Disorders.* To do so is to give up the unique perspective of social work psychosocial assessment. Selling this birthright is a capitulation to psychiatric mental health assessment. Culturally sensitive assessment reinterprets and reconceptualizes psychosocial factors as socioenvironmental impacts and psychoindividual reactions; it also acknowledges cultural strengths and includes both the cultural and the spiritual (Lum, 2000). This extension of the conceptual framework should be included in any meaningful discussion of culturally sensitive assessment.

Green (1995) has some helpful recommendations for workers attempting to hone their assessment conceptualization skills:

- A worker should think about clients in terms of group characteristics and group strengths as well as clinical pathology and agency protocols of problem resolution.
- A worker should examine group strengths as they are understood by community members themselves, and should view the client as a potential teacher to the worker as well as the recipient of services.
- A worker should openly use indigenous sources of help, which may mean granting credence to lay practitioners from ethnic communities.
- A worker should have a systematic learning style and a supportive agency environment that recognize culturally distinctive modes of behavior and respond to them appropriately. (pp. 80–81)

The biological, psychological, social, cultural, and spiritual dimensions of assessment point out the importance of understanding the dynamics and subject areas of human behavior. Life-span development, theories of personality, and theories of understanding individuals, families, groups, organizations, and communities are parallel information areas that inform and enlighten areas of assessment. For example, Schriver (2001) speaks of alternative paradigms or worldviews that make up the environments of our own world. He offers a paradigm shift that encompasses culture and society, ethnicity, and multiple meanings of race (race as biology, culture, or both; race and power; race as biology, culture, and power); social work and cultural competence that addresses diversity, cultural assessment, the dynamics of difference, and cultural knowledge; and social and economic justice and empowerment. Such a worldview has implications for shaping and understanding person and environment assessment.

Balanced Assessment

COMPETENCY
STUDY 7.7

Behaviors that could be characterized as pathological, such as viewing a social worker with great suspicion at a first meeting, may be adaptive and quite comprehensible when displayed by a person who has been denied rights or has been the victim of hate violence (Barnes & Ephross, 1995). Social stressors are often intense in minority communities, and people under stress behave in ways that have different meanings that need to be understood. Ethnic clients, in particular, need to be listened to carefully as they define from their perspective the problems they face. Social workers need to be careful, indeed, before assuming a stance that we know better than the client what the client needs.

At the same time, we are concerned that genuine and painful self-destructive pathologies not be concealed beneath a cloak of ethnic diversity. A simple theory of social causation can blind a worker to problems that can be solved and pathology that can be treated.

Effective assessment in social work practice requires balance and joint participation of client and worker to the maximum feasible point, empathic awareness of cultural differences, and the best, most trusting, communication possible. No one of these elements substitutes for another. Using the assumed or supposed characteristics of an ethnic group to solve a worker's own identity confusions or to express a worker's resentments against the majority culture can be harmful to ethnically identified clients. (pp. 35–36)

Assessment Personalization Skills. Psychosocial assessment provides an opportunity to evaluate the positive potential of the client. One must not be trapped into focusing on negative pathology. Cox and Ephross (1998) point out the need for a balanced assessment in Competency Study 7.7.

Assessment ought to mobilize positive resources that support change intervention strategies. In a pathology-oriented assessment, the worker is confronted with an extensive assessment workup filled with client liabilities. How does one move from pathology assessment to change intervention? It increasingly becomes a dilemma for the social work professional.

In Competency Study 7.8, Hines and Boyd-Franklin (1996) cite the role and dilemma of the African American father.

African American Fathers

COMPETENCY
STUDY 7.8

The identity of African American fathers, regardless of income, is linked to their ability to provide for their families. Success in being a provider, however, often is limited by discrimination. Franklin (1993) introduced the concept of the "invisibility syndrome" to explain the marginalization of African American men. This refers to the paradox that White Americans, while keenly aware of Black Americans' skin color, fear them and treat them as if they were "invisible," thus denying African Americans validation and marginalizing them. Frequently therapists assume that Black fathers are absent and uninvolved, particularly if there has been no formal marriage. It also is not uncommon for therapists to overlook males in the extended family system, including the father's kinship network and the mother's male friends, who may be involved in the children's lives. (p. 69)

A client's strengths and weaknesses are a given reality. However, a conscious effort to focus on positive client potentials and strengths helps to create intervention strategies that draw on these resources. We reframe the problem as an unsatisfied want or an unfulfilled need and the assessment as an evaluation of client potentials and strengths. As a result, intervention builds on these preceding stages in a substantive way. The worker has positive confidence based on these building blocks.

Intervention

Intervention Process Skills. The purpose of intervention is to affect a positive change between the person and the problem situation. Among the intervention process skills are goal setting and agreement; the selection of culturally diverse intervention strategies; and micro, meso, and macro levels of intervention. An intervention plan must be based on the needs of the client.

Goal setting and agreement is a cooperative effort between the client and the worker. It involves the detailed formulation of goal outcomes, expected behavioral changes, task objectives, and contracting.

Goal outcomes are terminal achievements accomplished at the end of the intervention stage. They are specific areas that give direction to the client. It is important to write down the exact words of the client as far as a goal outcome is concerned. Begin by asking the client what he or she wishes to accomplish based on resolving the problem. For example, in the Hernandez case study, Mr. Hernandez might want to work toward the following goal outcome: Father at home—Mr. Hernandez would like to work at his regular job and be home in the evenings with his family.

Expected behavioral changes are specific ways the client is willing to alter existing patterns and introduce a positive and alternative way of handling a situation. In the Hernandez case study, Mr. Hernandez is willing to leave his part-time night job as soon as his brothers-in-law are able to secure jobs to support their own families, which will free Mr. Hernandez to help Ricardo and the other children with their school homework. These elements comprise the scope of an intervention plan.

Task objectives are intermediate steps that are taken to move toward the achievement of goal outcomes. For instance, a task objective for Mr. Hernandez might be to gradually taper off his second job as the brothers-in-law secure part-time work and to arrive home at 8:00 p.m. to help the children before they go to bed. He would assist Ricardo and the other children with difficult homework assignments and encourage them to help each other with familiar schoolwork. This would be a realistic task objective that would be a first step.

Contracting involves bringing all client parties (e.g., family members) together to initially discuss the goal setting (goal outcomes, expected behavioral changes, and task objectives), sketch them on a board or on a piece of paper, then draw up a written or verbal agreement that is realistic and fair for all client parties involved.

The culturally competent worker utilizes intervention skills by selecting relevant *micro, meso, and macro strategies* based on the problem identification and assessment workup of the case. Among the multiple intervention strategies is the *empowerment intervention* approach. In a recent text, *Culturally Competent Practice: Skills, Intervention, and Evaluations* (Fong & Furuto, 2001), the major intervention strategy advocated by the authors is empowerment.

CULTURAL COMPETENCY IN ACTION

The Hernandez Family: A Case Study

Assessment process skills are concerned with an analysis of person and environment, cultural strengths, and the inclusion of cultural and spiritual dimensions in the biopsychosocial perspective. Person and environment are viewed as interacting, in that socioenvironmental impacts on the person result in psychological reactions. Cultural strengths are essential to the assessment process because the root of the word *assessment* emphasizes the assets or resources of the person. The incorporation of cultural and spiritual assessment expands the notion of biological, psychological, and social levels.

Assessment conceptualization skills focus on recognizing ethnic group characteristics and strengths, indigenous community resources, and culturally distinctive modes of behavior. Assessment personalization skills enable a social worker to evaluate the positive potential of a client. Assessment is a stepping stone toward intervention based on problem reframing and resource potentiality. The natural personal reaction of a social worker is to move in this direction.

Socioenvironmental factors impacting the Hernandez family are the uncertain economic conditions, Mr. Hernandez's need to work two jobs, and the family obligation of assisting two other immigrant families who are relatives. Psychoindividual reactions include Mr. Hernandez's fatigue and neglect of his family, and the determination of the husband and wife to work to meet the financial demands.

TASK RECOMMENDATIONS

- Contrast the socioenvironmental stress impacts and the psychoindividual reactions of Mr. Hernandez and his son, Ricardo, with the internal and external cultural strengths and the cultural and spiritual dimensions available to them and the family.
- Conceptualize the Latino values of hard work, extended family network, and support from indigenous church and ethnic grassroots agencies available to the Hernandez family.
- Evaluate the positive potential of the Hernandez family members from a personal perspective.

According to Browne and Mills (2001), empowerment is "the gaining of power by an individual, family group of persons, or a community" (p. 23). Empowerment presupposes a state of powerlessness on the part of the client group. Powerlessness is the inability to control self and others, to alter problem situations, or to reduce environmental distress (Leigh, 1984). Empowerment is a process that involves the individual micro level, the group meso level, and the institutional macro level. Empowerment is such a unique and useful intervention because of the range of change strategies (micro, meso, macro) applicable to client problems. Crafting an empowerment intervention plan that addresses all three levels is a practice skill.

On the *micro level*, empowerment is the mobilization of the uniqueness and self-determination of the client to take charge and control his or her life, to learn new ways of thinking about the problem situation, and to adopt new behaviors that give more satisfying and rewarding outcomes (Cowger, 1994). In the empowerment process, the client recognizes that social forces have negatively affected his or her life and moves toward an internal locus of control over the outcome of his or her life as well as an external locus of responsibility to improve his or her life. The client is able to mobilize personal and community resources and control and master the environment. The focus is on client strength and responsibility (Gibson, 1993). Pinderhughes (1989) emphasizes the need to help clients with a sense of positive strength:

> Empowerment requires the use of strategies that enable clients to experience themselves as competent, valuable, and worthwhile both as individuals and as members of their cultural group. They no longer feel trapped in the subordinate cultural group status that prevents them from meeting their goals. The process of empowering requires helpers to use their power appropriately to facilitate this shift. (p. 111)

The social worker is a vital resource to nurture the client and to help him or her in this self-discovery. At the same time, a person experiences empowerment as a member of a group. In order to make this empowerment transition, micro individual empowerment is interconnected to meso group empowerment.

Meso-level empowerment relies on the development of group consciousness and participation. The individual must reach for his or her internal power and at the same time be energized by the group. Group consciousness involves developing an awareness that there is collective power in a group and that political structures affecting individual and group experiences need to be changed (Gutierrez, 1990). Collective action and change take place on the meso group level. Such collaborative partnerships between clients and social workers, client groups, and constituents focus on program and service changes. Browne and Mills (2001) suggest:

> Strategies that encourage empowerment practice in social work settings include: (1) the creation of an employment setting that provides for participatory management, (2) the ability of social workers to make independent decisions about their work, (3) support and open communication patterns with administrators, and (4) opportunities for skill development. Social work administrators and practitioners alike must commit themselves to ideas and principles of democracy, equality and equity, social justice, nonviolence, and nonintimidation. (p. 27)

As social workers model empowerment in their agencies, it becomes the basis for clients to change groups that affect them.

Macro-level empowerment addresses large-scale organizational and institutional change. Group empowerment involves the ability to work with others to change social institutions. Political power and resource allocation for those who are powerless but who have mobilized a group's efforts are a part of rebalancing traditional power and control. Macro level empowerment involves connecting groups with a number of social, political, and economic advocates and agencies who are sensitive and responsive to disenfranchised and powerless individuals and groups. This networking on the macro level is a demonstration of large-scale empowerment. It involves redistributing resource allocations (distributive justice), initiating class action discrimination suits (corrective justice), and working with state and federal legislators on fair and just social programs (political justice).

Empowerment as an intervention strategy is appropriate to clients of color, in particular. In First Nations Peoples settings, empowerment is useful to empower an individual to function as an integral part of creation. Gaining or developing power is seen as "securing help from the spiritual and natural world for a higher purpose than the individual self—to benefit the *Oyate* (Lakota Nation)," according to Yellow Horse Brave Heart (2001, p. 165). Empowerment and sovereignty have been linked in that there is the protection of power to advocate for rights, beliefs, and values. Traditional American Indian forms of governance are important to maintain in light of internalized oppression and the impact of colonization. Empowerment and resiliency are two critical themes in this circumstance (Weaver, 2001).

With African Americans, the powerlessness and empowerment themes were first used by Solomon (1976) to describe the situation of Black communities. African American spiritual beliefs and churches have been the source of community empowerment. In large urban areas, African American churches provide recreational, social service, housing, and other tangible economic programs (Manning, 2001). Empowerment is grounded in African American principles of self-determination and an equitable distribution of political, economic, and social choices. Grant (2001) states:

> Three goals of empowerment evaluation in this context are to help the African American organization or community (1) gain the skills necessary to make important decisions, (2) develop skills necessary to taking socioeconomic control in accessing resources and opportunities, and (3) educate the broader society regarding African American history and its importance to the well-being and strength of the United States. (p. 363)

Manning, Cornelius, and Okundaye (2004) have identified strengths as an expression of empowerment theory:

> The client's support system, as a strength, can provide physical resources such as shelter, financial assistance, and emotional comfort. Individual strengths might be certain innate capacities like the ability to communicate, interact with others, or function under difficult circumstances. The role of the social worker is to help the client identify these strengths and then maximize their usefulness by identifying how these supports can be accessed to benefit the African American client. (p. 231)

These areas of concern are empowerment themes.

Regarding empowerment with Latino Americans, Negroni-Rodriguez and Morales (2001) remind us that Latinos have natural strengths among extended family members, traditional support and healing systems, and levels of biculturalism and bilingualism. It is important to draw on these natural structures in empowerment interventions with this group. At the same time, they caution that it is important to "assess the ability to help Latino clients move from self-blaming and powerless views to being agents of change." This involves working with Latino clients to build a relationship of collaboration and partnership in problem solving and to impart social work knowledge and skills. Client preparation is crucial to launching an empowerment intervention strategy. Latinos may have suffered socioeconomic and sociocultural oppression (racism, colonialism, economic exploitation, and cultural domination) and internal oppression (gender, sexual orientation, race, and class) (Acevedo & Morales, 2001). As a result, it may take longer to sort through these areas as part of the empowerment process.

Intervention Conceptualization Skills.   Intervention strategies should be based on the unique experience of the multicultural client (Ridley, Espelage, & Rubinstein, 1997) and tailored from a broad repertoire of intervention strategies to apply specifically to the client's problem situation. This involves recognizing the unique factors related to the client, the problem, and the social/cultural environment. Boehm and Staples (2004) identify six essential conceptual characteristics of empowerment:

1. Empowerment is both a process and an outcome. As a process it involves individuals and groups moving from relative powerlessness to increased power and as an outcome it has end products whereby a measure of power is achieved such as access to information or increased economic resources.
2. Empowerment is operative at both the personal and collective levels. Personal empowerment relates to the way people think about themselves as well as the knowledge, capacities, skills, and mastery that they possess such as increased levels of self-esteem, assertiveness, self-determination, social responsibility, critical consciousness, participatory competencies, and hope. Collective empowerment refers to individuals joining together to break their solitude and silence, to support and help one another, to learn together, and to develop skills for collective action.
3. Empowerment assumes that even when people are in situations of relative powerlessness, they have capacities, skills, qualifications, and assets that serve as resources for individual or collective change.
4. Empowerment cannot be created for another person, but professionals, such as social workers, can help facilitate the empowerment process through consumer self-determination and critical consciousness where people gain understanding of their sociocultural reality and their ability to change social conditions.
5. Empowerment underscores the need for consumers to make decisions and take initiatives as well as establish a partnership between social workers and consumers to share power, joint responsibility, and division of labor.
6. Empowerment focuses on oppressed groups in society, on better understanding of the way inequality and lack of power perpetuate personal and social problems, and a concern for stigmatization and unequal structural relations of power and the means for achieving social and economic justice. (pp. 270–271)

They also conducted research on empowerment with 145 respondents (84 consumers, 61 social workers) and reported that mastery and competencies were basic elements of empowerment: physical mastery including the use of equipment and technology; mastery of emotions and behavior; mastery of information and decision making; mastery of social systems; efficient mastery of time and the effective use of time; mastery connected to autonomy and individual freedom; and planning mastery to prevent negative situations and to actualize positive ones.

Empowerment intervention presupposes conceptualizing a plan that addresses micro individuals, meso groups, and macro communities and organizations. The worker conceptualizes a responsive plan with the client who needs to be well prepared before initiating an empowerment approach.

Another conceptual skill of empowerment intervention involves using the client's belief system and culture as sources of strength and empowerment. Conceptualization of indigenous interventions identifies natural cultural ways of helping and reconciling differences, such as the family group resolution effort in Hawaiian culture called *ho'ponopono*.

There are other ways that ethnic groups and communities introduce intervention change. Ron Lewis, a Native American social work educator, asserts that it is important for an Indian with a drinking problem to attend and participate in pow-wows in order to contact his or her First Nations Peoples culture and tribe. These elements help an Indian person cope with alcoholism (Ron Lewis, personal communication, March 1985). Conceptualizing an indigenous intervention with a particular client offers indigenous expressions of empowerment.

Greene, Lee, and Hoffpauir (2005) advocate the solution-focused approach, which is based on a strengths and competence orientation:

> The solution-focused approach operates from the assumption that change is occurring much of the time and that there are times when the problem is less frequent, intense, severe, or even not present. The language of solutions facilitates identifying the strengths, resources, and competencies clients use to make these exceptions to the problem occur. (p. 272)

They further explain (2005):

> The language of solutions never attempts to deny the existence of problems; rather, it emphasizes the fact that people have strengths, competencies, resources, potentials, and creativity which they or others are ignoring, forgetting, or underutilizing. By focusing the therapeutic dialogue on solutions and strengths, the power of language can facilitate the client and clinician in co-constructing a view of reality that contains an expanded definition of self that includes competence, skills, power, and personal agency. (pp. 272–273)

Conceptualizing interventions that accent empowerment, strengths, competencies, and solutions to problems are directions that culturally competent practice should take.

Intervention Personalization Skills. The culturally competent worker is concerned about intervention implementation. Is the client motivated to make a change? To what extent will the intervention strategy be successful? How can I be a source of encouragement and facilitate the change process? These are some questions of a worker who is going through the intervention stage with a client.

Motivation for change often comes from the pain and suffering experienced by the client as a result of the problem. A person changes when he or she is uncomfortable or has reached a threshold of pain. For example, the best time to reach an alcoholic is when the person has "hit bottom" and is suffering pain, embarrassment, and guilt. These painful moments of suffering are motivators for change. Personalizing the uncomfortable nature of the problem situation and having the client own responsibility are some practical worker skills. How does one know if a client is ready to implement empowerment? Part of the empowerment process is the exploration of painful experiences and the reconciliation of putting our lives together as much as possible. Working through self-esteem and experiences of oppression is part of the empowerment healing process.

A structured agreement based on specific goals reminds the client about change directions. The worker assigns homework with a prescriptive list of change actions. Daily and weekly task assignments between sessions are structured ways to implement empowerment tasks and change on a step-by-step basis.

CULTURAL COMPETENCY IN ACTION

The Hernandez Family: A Case Study

Intervention process skills consist of drawing up goals and an agreement, selecting an intervention strategy, and orchestrating the micro, meso, and macro levels of change. Goal setting and agreement between the worker and the client involves detailing goal outcomes and behavioral tasks in a contract. Intervention strategies entail specific plans to effect change in the psychosocial situation. Micro, meso, and macro levels of intervention, for example, assemble an array of approaches to the Hernandez family case: problem solving and family therapy, church and community support systems, and community organizing.

Intervention conceptualization skills entail the careful selection of an intervention plan that addresses the particular problem situation and fits the belief system and culture of the client.

Intervention personalization skills focus on the reaction of the worker to the client's motivation for change, the potential success of the intervention strategy, and the client's power to make choices. One must consider working with the Hernandez family on the intervention process, conceptualization, and personalization skill levels.

TASK RECOMMENDATIONS

- Suggest a set of goals and an agreement between the social worker, Mr. Platt, and the Hernandez family.
- Select a culturally diverse intervention strategy (one that will result in liberation, empowerment, parity, maintenance of culture, and unique personhood) and micro, meso, and macro levels of intervention.
- Determine whether the intervention plan addresses the particular problem(s) of the Hernandez family and fits their belief system and culture.
- Ascertain whether members of the Hernandez family are motivated toward change and whether the intervention plan has the potential for succeeding.

The worker recognizes that the client has the power to make choices. The worker cannot and should not assume this responsibility. If the worker has structured the necessary means for change, the client has choice in determining the process. Hepworth, Rooney, and Larsen (2002) discuss client involvement in intervention in Competency Study 7.9.

COMPETENCY STUDY 7.9

Client-Selected Intervention

A useful guideline to planning interventions with ethnic minority people (and other clients, for that matter) is to solicit their views as to what needs to be done to remedy their difficulties. Their suggestions will be in harmony with their beliefs and values. Moreover, their views about essential changes are often on target: they lack only the "know-how" required to accomplish the changes. Deficiencies in the latter are associated with limited knowledge about available resources and about the complexities of our service delivery systems. Determining clients' views enables the practitioner to suggest interventions that clients will perceive as relevant and to couch the rationale for selecting them in terms that make sense to clients. Including clients in the planning of interventive strategies enhances their cooperation, as we noted previously. (p. 362)

Termination

Termination Process Skills. Termination, or the ending stage of the social work process, is a critical transition time for the client. On the one hand, a meaningful relationship between the worker and the client is ending, but on the other hand, the client is making a transition, with the worker's help, to coping with the normal problems of living. Potocky-Tripodi (2002) urges the need for cultural competence to focus not only measuring worker behavior (cultural competencies measurement of skills) but ". . . measuring client outcomes such as accessing services, staying in treatment, satisfaction with treatment, resolution of problems, and achievement of goals" (p. 124). She indicates that far too often, these areas are not fully addressed in cultural competence. These are client concerns at the termination process stage, part of practice and program evaluation, and legitimate areas of termination.

Lum (2000) describes four of the process skills:

- Helping the client connect with an ongoing support network: family and friends, ethnic community resources, a referral to another agency for follow-up care
- Conducting retrospective analysis of the problem situation and the growth that has occurred during the helping relationship
- Ascertaining whether the goals and outcomes agreed upon in intervention planning have been achieved
- Establishing a sensible plan for follow-up such as periodic phone calls, visits for checking in, and rechecks that gradually taper off

Termination Conceptualization Skills. Termination is a critical stage, but it is least considered in social work practice. Hepworth, Rooney, and Larsen (1997) conceptualize the ingredients for positive termination in Competency Study 7.10.

COMPETENCY STUDY 7.10

Positive Termination

Most clients in individual, marital, family, and group therapy experience positive emotions in termination. Benefits of the gains achieved usually *far outweigh* the impact of the loss of the helping relationship. Indeed, clients often report an increased sense of mastery, and both practitioners and clients are likely to experience joy over such accomplishments. This is especially true when practitioners have employed a strength-oriented, problem-solving approach. Furthermore, the participants have experienced mutual enrichment from the deep, personal, and authentic human encounter, and, in a very real sense, the self of each person has been expanded by the contacts with the other.

Until very recent years, the literature on termination reactions has stressed that sadness, loss, ambivalence, apprehension, and other negative reactions are associated with termination on the part of both practitioner and client. Research findings (Fortune, 1987; Fortune, Pearlingi, & Rochelle, 1992), however, have refuted these widely accepted beliefs. These findings indicate that in both open-ended and time-limited treatment the common reactions are positive feelings related to success and progress, positive feelings about the therapeutic experience, increased constructive activities outside of treatment, more free time, more financial resources to spend on other activities, and feelings of pride about accomplishments and/or independence gained through treatment. Negative reactions on the part of both clients and practitioners are not common. (p. 605)

CULTURAL COMPETENCY IN ACTION

The Hernandez Family: A Case Study

Termination process skills help the client to connect with a follow-up network (e.g., family and friends, ethnic community agency), conduct a retrospective analysis of the problem and the growth achieved, and determine whether goal outcomes have been accomplished. Termination conceptualization skills are concerned with factors surrounding early and premature case dropouts as well as successful case completions. Conceptualizing about termination assists the social worker with facts and figures to improve the quality of services in an agency. This is a mark of cultural competence from a termination viewpoint.

Termination personalization skills focus on the positive and negative effects of cases on the social worker as a person and a helper. Intensive casework leading to a successful resolution of problems tends to energize a social worker, whereas chronic and complex cases with no closure tend to burn out a worker. If the burnout is compounded by a shortage of staff, heavy caseloads, and mounting paperwork, a social worker reaches a point where personal and professional needs must be nurtured. A culturally competent worker knows when and where to turn for consultation and assistance.

Appropriate intervention strategies for the Hernandez family might involve schoolwork tutoring for Ricardo from a responsible high school senior, the reduction of Mr. Hernandez's workload to allow him to spend more time with his family, and encouraging the personal growth and development of Mrs. Hernandez through her education and community activities. A whole array of intervention possibilities exists based on cultural competency that students are able to devise from this case.

TASK RECOMMENDATIONS

- Propose a termination plan for the Hernandez family that connects them in a continuing helping network, conducts a retrospective analysis of growth and progress, and ascertains the achievement of goals.
- Determine the factors surrounding the Hernandez family that made this a successful case.
- Suggest how Mr. Platt, the social worker, could be debriefed by a social work supervisor on the Hernandez case.

It is important for a worker in an agency to study the termination rates of clients. What is the agency doing to conclude successful client cases? In cases of premature or unsuccessful termination, what are the agency elements that may have contributed to unresolved cases? Follow-up on unsuccessful cases may teach the worker and the agency as much as analyzing successful cases. Exit interview surveys and follow-up on premature termination are important because of the high dropout rate of multicultural clients. Research and reflection on early termination and clients of color are helpful at this stage.

Termination Personalization Skills.   Termination triggers a range of responses on the part of the worker. The caseload number and intensity, along with the stress of unsuccessful resolution of problems, take their toll on the social worker. The daily demand on staff is apparent in many service agencies. Many agencies are using case management to broker a network of services for their clients, group treatment with crisis intervention on serious cases, brief treatment with community referral, and other strategies to deal with the volume of clients. As a result, intensive casework with single clients is the exception rather than the rule of service. Short-term treatment with reachable, concrete, and practical goals results in frequent termination and reliance on social services, the family, indigenous community agencies, and ethnic church and community.

CULTURALLY DIVERSE SERVICE DELIVERY

Developing skills to design culturally diverse service delivery program structures is a prerequisite to working effectively with clients. Service delivery deals with structuring programs, facilities, staff, funding, and administration on behalf of serving the needs of client populations in a geographic area. Service delivery design through an ethnic lens is crucial to culturally diverse services.

In Competency Study 7.11, Cox and Ephross (1998) discuss the ethnic lens from both the client and the provider perspectives.

Have you ever thought about how you would design a new service delivery program for a client group population? Let us pretend that you have been appointed by your executive director to create such a program and have been given a staff team with a $10,000 planning grant for a program proposal. How would you proceed with this project? What are some *principles of service delivery* that you would use to guide you and your team in your planning process?

Service delivery is based on the philosophy of social services reflected in the administrative unit and the board of directors of an agency. It may change as a series of events occurs or as new policies are made that alter how services are organized and delivered to clients. Iglehart and Becerra (2000) observe: "Service delivery as a system or organizational process continues to be a dynamic process that is altered by technological, ideological,

COMPETENCY STUDY 7.11

The Ethnic Lens of Service Delivery

Designing social services that are effective in reaching and serving ethnic groups is a major challenge to the profession. The ethnic lens, as it affects clients' perceptions of services and practitioners' perceptions of clients and their needs, plays a pivotal role in social work's ability to meet this challenge. Consequently, it is incumbent upon agencies to ensure that these lenses are free from distortion.

One of the first issues ethnic groups are likely to confront in their perception of the agency is whether the agency is fundamentally "ours" or "theirs," whether it is one that welcomes "people like us" or has staff "like us." Often, this question is not resolvable simply by official policy or statement, because past experiences have frequently taught many ethnic groups that such statements are not reliable. Informal comments, community gossip, rumors, and personal references from former clients can count for much more than stated policies.

Staff persons who are "like us" can make communication easier, due to the histories they share with prospective clients. The terms used to describe the discovery of an Italian-American or African-American staff member are themselves powerful. Reports of a "paisan" or a "brother" among the staff can affect the entire ethnic lens. The agency is transformed into a place that is both welcoming and accommodating to "us." (p. 116) political, and economic factors. The mode of service delivery has varied from specialization to integrated, comprehensive services" (pp. 244–245). These authors offer the following observations about social service delivery:

- Social service delivery systems are changing as the population of the United States becomes more diverse and as there is an increased challenge to provide services to ethnic minority groups.
- The client–worker relationship is important in the delivery of ethnic-sensitive services, because the client experiences the agency through the worker as the worker interprets the policies of the agency and implements its services.
- In service delivery planning and implementation there is a need to accept and respect the client's ethnicity and culture and to increase sensitivity to the cultures and values of minorities.
- In service delivery arrangements the client is a member of other systems such as groups, communities, and other service delivery systems that are bounded by ethnicity, culture, and community.
- Effective ethnic-sensitive service delivery utilizes and incorporates the client's community and community services in the service delivery process so that the ethnic minority agency is a focal organization with minority staff, services, and access to the minority group and community.
- Service delivery occurs in the context of a system that is shaped by the culture, values, and ideologies of groups and individuals who plan and implement services.
- The ethnic agency captures the interface between a social service delivery system and a client system that blends use of services with community and ethnicity.
- The history of social work reveals racism and exclusion in the charity organizations and settlement house movement, which resulted in disregard for the needs, concerns, and rights of ethnic minority groups and partially explains the current lack of minority clients in these types of agencies.

Lum (2000) has written about the essential characteristics of multicultural service delivery in terms of location and pragmatic services, staffing, community outreach programs, agency setting, and service linkage. The agency should be located in or near areas with a large ethnic population and be accessible to public transportation. It should offer needed and attractive services, such as health care, family services, and/or child care. Mental health services may have a social stigma attached in ethnic communities, and services should not be advertised as such. There should be bilingual/bicultural staff in a ratio that reflects the ethnic and gender composition of the service population. There should be strong community outreach programs to schools, churches, and family associations in order to build agency/staff credibility and integrity. The agency setting should be friendly and informal with a bilingual receptionist, clean and private offices, and an ethnic-friendly decor. There should be service linkage and a working relationship between ethnic agencies and other organizations that serve the same client population base.

Cox and Ephross (1998) reiterate these principles of service delivery when they discuss availability, accessibility, acceptability, and ethnic staff in Competency Study 7.12.

When planning a new service delivery program, you must be aware of a number of interrelated factors that create a "political climate" for the planning group, the host agency,

Ethnic Service Delivery Principles

COMPETENCY STUDY 7.12

Services, regardless of the type of agency offering them, are used when they are available, accessible, and acceptable to the intended population (Wallace, 1990). Availability refers to the location and amount of services provided and whether they are sufficient to meet the group's needs. A clinic located outside of an ethnic community, although on a bus line, may be perceived as unavailable if persons are uncomfortable leaving the boundaries of their particular neighborhood. Obviously, a limited amount of services, such as English classes, can seriously curtail service availability.

Accessibility depends upon persons' knowledge of programs and having the necessary resources, such as finances, insurance, or transportation, needed for utilization. Accessibility is also affected by the degree of coordination or fragmentation among services.

Accessibility also depends upon service providers' ability to reach those in need. Language can be a major barrier to accessibility. Making sure that the person who answers the agency telephone is fluent in the language of the residents is of prime importance, since he or she is often the first contact that the potential client has with the agency. Having workers who speak the same dialects as the residents and assuring that their accents are compatible with the group are important factors in accessibility.

Service accessibility is also dependent upon the effectiveness of the outreach activities. Outreach involves actively informing the community about the service and its goals and making them attractive to the residents. Outreach workers are active in the community describing their services and making them attractive to potential clients. Rather than waiting for persons to come to the agencies, they attend local functions, give talks at community organizations, and meet with people in the neighborhoods. The aim is to encourage service use by demonstrating the accessibility of the program. Involving local leaders such as the clergy, media personalities, and teachers can be important in the success of the outreach activity.

Finally, even the titles of agencies can affect accessibility. Within ethnic communities, mental problems are often a source of shame, and mental health counseling is not trusted. Consequently, calling a service "Center for Mental Health" is likely to deter access. Instead, a title which emphasizes growth or acceptable concerns such as "healthy living" may encourage persons to seek further information regarding services.

In order for services to be used, they must be acceptable to the ethnic group. Cultural values and traditions as they affect attitudes and behavior are major influences in acceptability. For example, services such as day care, family planning, and mental health counseling may strongly conflict with traditional values. However, as persons become assimilated into the greater society and its values, these traditional values are often modified.

Staff from the same ethnic background as the clients often have an easier time establishing rapport with community members than do those from outside the ethnic group. Persons are less likely to feel that they have to explain or justify themselves to workers from the same background who share the same history and experiences. Language barriers are also reduced, which enables practitioners to obtain a clear understanding of the problem and to more easily discuss with the client possible interventions.

Clients are often suspicious of ethnic group members returning to a neighborhood as agency staff. Because staff have left the traditional community, persons frequently find it difficult to trust them or their motives.

Staff of their own ethnicity may be perceived as less qualified and less competent. In these situations, clients who are compelled to see an ethnic worker are liable to resist the relationship. In fact, the possibilities for misperception in these situations are great. The agency is likely to believe that by providing ethnic clients with an ethnic worker, they are sensitively attempting to meet their clients' concerns. However, the clients may perceive that, by being assigned this worker, they are being stereotyped and are being denied workers of equal worth. (pp. 105–107, 111) related organizations, and the target population client groups. Iglehart and Becerra (2000) identify seven external and five internal forces of agency change to accommodate an ethnic-sensitive service delivery system. The external catalysts for change are the following:

- Changing funding policies with funding regulations that stipulate the inclusion of specific ethnic populations as service beneficiaries
- Shifting funding priorities to seek new client populations (such as ethnic minority senior citizens) as funding for services to these groups becomes available
- Out-group protests on behalf of underserved ethnic groups that cause some agency change, inclusion of ethnic populations, and increase of ethnic utilization
- New constituencies resulting from the creation of new minority voting districts that elect minority representation who support ethnic-sensitive services
- New agency leadership (e.g., new directors or staff with particular skills and political positions) shifting the agency toward the concerns of clients of color
- The worker as a change catalyst for the client and the agency
- Routinization of change where special programs for specific ethnic groups are absorbed as a part of permanent agency structure

The internal forces for change in agency service delivery include the following:

- The ideology of the agency in terms of ethnic client perception, situational causes, worker and client roles, and desired outcomes
- The technology of the agency and worker–client activities in terms of process stages, desired outcomes, and client movement
- The structure of the agency regarding the rules and ethics governing worker–client interaction, agency contact encounters, and agency hierarchy
- Client inputs about and assessment of services
- The accountability of the agency in terms of the recognition of the ethnic community as an agency constituency, procedures for ethnic community input about agency services, and agency accountability to the ethnic community

How would you cope with these trends in funding, out-group protests, new constituencies, new agency leadership, existing staff, anticipated changes, the ideology and technology of the host agency, rules and regulations, community inputs, and agency and project accountability? How would you plan a process where you would consider and allow a number of constituent groups to participate and interact with your planning group in order to receive input and exchange ideas? How would you incorporate relevant recommendations into your final proposal plan? These external and internal forces offer avenues for introducing change into existing agencies in order to make them more responsive and sensitive to ethnic populations.

AGENCY LINKAGE, DESIGN, AND IMPLEMENTATION

In order to design and implement culturally diverse service delivery, it is important to understand how agency services interrelate. This is called *agency linkage or interorganizational relations*. Service delivery cooperation and coordination are crucial as funding shrinks or shifts toward specialized needs, ethnic populations increase with new immigrant influx, and qualified ethnic practitioners become scarce resources.

Iglehart and Becerra (2000) offer 10 propositions about agency linkage:

1. Ethnic agencies are not in competition with mainstream social services for clients, but they do receive funding for specialized services to ethnic groups.
2. In an interorganizational relationship, the ethnic agency does have access to a particular ethnic population because of its presence in the ethnic community and its relationship with specific target populations.
3. Ethnic agencies are participants in alternative service delivery as services are redefined and new interorganizational relations emerge.
4. Ethnic agencies will extend more services to special populations due to privatization (purchase of service contracts, contracting).
5. Interorganizational relationships are likely to develop between public and ethnic agencies because public agencies are mandated to meet the needs of the general population, public agencies provide funding and ethnic agencies use the funds to provide services in an exchange relationship, and ethnic agencies with access to ethnic communities have power and bond with public agencies over funding.
6. Changing federal funding requirements develop partnerships between mainstream agencies and ethnic agencies.
7. The availability of funding governs the interface between mainstream agencies and the ethnic agency in terms of the development of partnerships, reduction in service duplication, and reaching special populations.
8. Ethnic agencies are particularly vulnerable to service contract cuts and grants in terms of financial austerity.
9. Ideological conflict can occur between the ethnic agency and mainstream agencies.
10. The problems of societal race relations may permeate the relations between ethnic and mainstream agencies.

These propositions on service delivery and agency linkage serve as the basis for the design and implementation of culturally diverse service delivery. *Service content* changes as various ethnic target groups emerge on the scene: the ethnic elderly, legal immigrants, and former welfare recipients. The *needs of ethnic and racial groups* are defined by public agencies that are the funding source: alcohol and drug abuse, AIDS, gang violence prevention. These trends may be determined *by* federal and state policies and legislation that cope with social problem areas and include application to ethnic populations. Programs should be derived from *the changing needs of the ethnic community*, which should influence ethnic-sensitive public social services or ethnic-responsive indigenous community agencies. With decentralization and downsizing of government services, it is politically and fiscally expedient to contract with ethnic agencies that serve ethnic populations.

Agency ideology and philosophy, technology, staffing, and structure may change in light of federal and state funding of ethnic-related programs. *Funding requirements and stipulations* can transform the service delivery of an agency.

There are five delivery design elements: programs, staffing, facilities, funding, and administration. *Programs* are based on community research data and public and private grants. Program planning incorporates social planning principles, funding proposals, and social service legislation. Bilingual, bicultural, and gender-balanced *staff* should reflect the

CULTURAL COMPETENCY IN ACTION

The Hernandez Family: A Case Study

Practice skill development must be set in the context of a service delivery structure. Our philosophy of delivering services to multicultural clients determines an agency's programs, facilities, staff, funding, and administrative oversight. In turn, these structural components impact the lives of clients with problems.

Iglehart and Becerra (1995) and Lum (2000) emphasize a number of service delivery principles:

- That the worker embodies service delivery and that the client experiences the agency through the worker
- That the ethnic agency is the focal organization that contracts services from the public government sector and is the bridge between the ethnic community and ethnic clients in need

- That bilingual/bicultural staff should reflect the population's ethnic and gender profile
- That facilities should be located near the service population in the existing ethnic neighborhood community

TASK RECOMMENDATIONS

- Design a Latino family service center that addresses the needs of the Hernandez family. Specify location, program services, staffing, community outreach, agency setting, and interagency service linkage.
- Detail a funding plan for the Latino family service center that could be supported by federal, state, and county monies, private foundations, and ethnic community support.

service area population and should meet degree and professional experience requirements. *Facilities* should be accessible to the service population and should use existing ethnic social service buildings or neighborhood churches. *Funding* is based on various local, state, and federal public monies as well as private foundation and United Way monies. Program *administration* is vested in a program director, a community-based board, and a clear chain of command with job descriptions at all levels.

Agency program implementation usually involves a three-year cycle: start-up, initial and full implementation, and periodic program evaluation. Agency implementation starts with federal and state regulatory compliance or the terms of the grant. Regional consortiums may pool resources in a cooperative effort. Cooperative projects are the preferred choice for university program training, research evaluation, and/or community-based agencies.

Iglehart and Becerra (2000) discuss agency linkage between ethnic and mainstream agencies:

A continuum of services seem to unfold in which the ethnic agency may serve as the first line of defense for filling service gaps, for responding to the needs of marginalized groups, and for helping when no other agency does. It may also substitute for public agencies in delivering uniquely packaged and specially tailored services. In the quest for ethnic-sensitive practice, it seems to be a resource that has been underutilized. Mainstream social services and agencies will continue to vary in the degree to which they adopt ethnic-sensitive practice. The variation is due to agency history, ideologies, structure, and technologies. Mainstream agencies are responding to the needs of a mainstream America, and shifts in paradigms do take years to accomplish. (p. 283)

Specifically, there are a number of helping suggestions to build a multicultural organization with a cultural competence emphasis (GLSEN, 2001):

- Form a cultural competence committee within your organization with representation from policymaking, administration, service delivery, and community levels that serves as a governing body for planning, implementing, and evaluating organizational cultural competence.
- Write a mission statement that commits the organization to cultural competence activities.
- Find out what similar organizations have done and develop partnerships, gathering the processes and information from other groups that are consistent with your organizational needs for cultural competence.
- Use free resources from federally funded technical assistance centers that catalog information on cultural competence.
- Do a comprehensive cultural competence assessment of your organization that will result in a long-term plan with measurable goals and objectives incorporating cultural competent principles, policies, structures, and practices and that will change your mission statement, policies, procedures, administration, staffing patterns, service delivery practices, outreach, telecommunications and information dissemination systems, and professional development activities.
- Find out about cultural groups in the community and the degree to which they access community services.
- Have a brown bag lunch to involve staff in discussion and activities about their attitudes, beliefs, and values concerning cultural competence.
- Ask your staff about their development needs regarding interacting with cultural groups in your area.
- Assign a part of your budget to staff development in cultural competence, particularly conferences, workshops, and seminars.
- Include cultural competency requirements in job descriptions in the hiring process and discuss the importance of cultural awareness and competency with potential employees.
- Be sure your facility's location is accessible and respect of difference, for example, how to show respect to racial and ethnic elders.
- Collect resource materials for staff use such as free online resources, printed material, and library books on culturally diverse groups.
- Build a network of natural helpers, community informants, and other experts that have valuable knowledge of cultural, linguistic, racial, and ethnic groups in the community.

These authors make a strong case for culturally diverse service delivery and agency linkage between ethnic and mainstream agencies. We encourage you to develop service delivery planning skills along with your skills of working with individuals, families, and groups.

RESEARCH ON SKILL DEVELOPMENT

Research on skill development is important because it constantly gives us a fresh perspective on how to develop new skills and confirms or modifies our skill base. Beach and colleagues (2005) conducted research evaluating interventions to improve the cultural competence of health professionals from 1980–2003 and found the following results of 34 studies:

> There is excellent evidence that cultural competence training improves the knowledge of health professionals (17 of 19 studies demonstrated a beneficial effect), and good evidence that cultural competence training improves the attitudes and skills of health professionals (21 of 25 studies evaluating attitudes demonstrated a beneficial effect and 14 of 14 studies evaluating skills demonstrated a beneficial effect). There is good evidence that cultural competence training impacts patient satisfaction (3 of 3 studies demonstrated a beneficial effect), poor evidence that cultural competence training impacts patient adherence (although the one study designed to do this demonstrated a beneficial effect), and no studies that have evaluated patient health status outcomes. There is poor evidence to determine the costs of cultural competence training (5 studies included incomplete estimates of costs). (p. 356)

Further research is needed to show how cultural competence improves patient adherence to therapy, health outcomes, and equity of services across racial and ethnic groups.

Similarly, Stanhope and colleagues (2005) call for more empirical evaluation of cultural competence. They state:

> Both the training in and evaluation of cultural competence continues to inform the development of good empirical measures for behavioral health providers and their agencies. Ultimately, the key to effective cultural competence training is the extent to which it generates positive outcomes for clients, not merely increased awareness, knowledge, and skills of trainees. (p. 232)

Client results are being asked for.

More work needs to be done on the cost effectiveness of cultural competence training on program impacts. Culturally diverse health care and social work practice skills are in constant development. This section describes a number of cultural competence skills that are now emerging, according to research.

Personal Styles and Clinical Process

Relationship-building between the worker and the client results in case effectiveness and client/problem situation change. Research has claimed that psychological characteristics (cultural attitudes, emotional well-being, values, attitudes, beliefs, expectations, clinical relationships) of the clinician and the client, and the style match between the two, affect the clinical efficacy and make significant impacts on client change. The subjective personal style differences between the clinician and the client contribute to the dynamics of the clinical process (Bergin & Garfield, 1996).

These personal styles were researched and named *achieving styles* by Lipman-Blumen, Handley-Isaksen, and Leavitt (1983). Subsequently, the Achieving Styles Inventory (ASI) was revised and standardized to assess both individual and organizational styles. Three major sets of domains (direct, instrumental, and relational) contain three related but distinctive styles. Altogether there are nine achieving styles, each of which is a preference pattern for a particular orientation or situation. The concept of personal achieving styles is discussed in business, education, and counseling. Specifically, an achieving style is an individual preference that reflects the behavior, value system, and strategic reasoning of a person. It refers to various learned ways to accomplish tasks or achieve goals, regardless of the specific nature of these goals (Lipman-Blumen, Handley-Isaksen, & Leavitt, 1983).

An individual's achieving style is shaped by his or her attitudes, norms, values, and cultural boundaries (Spence, 1985). On a practical level, it involves an individual's way of thinking, talking, and feeling, particularly as a person acts and interacts with others. These styles are profoundly influenced by the individual's personal experiences and cultural/social context. Beginning in childhood, we learn different ways or strategies to get what we want. These thinking, feeling, and behaving patterns become personal styles for accomplishing tasks or achieving goals. A person uses his or her unique set of achieving styles to project himself or herself, accomplish life goals, and relate to the world. These personal achieving styles seem adequate for accomplishing tasks until we are confronted by a difference or mismatch of interpersonal styles in cross-cultural encounters. An individual is not conscious of his or her achieving styles without a deliberate and conscious examination of himself or herself.

Social work has been concerned about worker–client effectiveness in the helping process due to *interaction relationship patterns.* Personal achieving styles research is a way to examine this concern. Clinicians often have little awareness of their own personal achieving styles that closely link and relate to their own clinical practice. Clinicians with *direct achieving styles* tend to focus their attention on the task and use direct problem-solving approaches. They tend to offer direct advice as a helping authority for clients. Clinicians with *instrumental achieving styles* frequently use their own credibility, influence, professionalism, or a support system to resolve problems. They rely on clients to assume partial or full responsibility for their actions. Clinicians with *relational-cognitive behavioral achieving styles* allow clients to select the means and the ends of their goal accomplishments. They use collaborative or contributory approaches to help clients accomplish their own goals through group efforts.

Social work interventions tend to offer a choice of approaches: direct (problem solving or task centered), instrumental (family therapy), and relational-cognitive (functionalism, existentialism). However, what is the personal and idiosyncratic nature of the worker's helping approach? Are there cultural and ethnic differences between practitioners? These are some of the questions answered by skill development research.

Just as the clinician's choice of skills and intervention strategies is shaped by his or her cultural self, the client comes with his or her culturally contained self. Consequently, an important element of effective cross-cultural clinical practice is the clinician's awareness of this value choice's impact on the clinical process. Recognizing the importance of having styles match is essential for a successful cross-cultural clinical process.

Empirical Research on Achieving Styles

Research on skill development has used the variables of therapeutic alliance, achieving styles, and practitioner ethnic background. This section reports on European, Asian, Latino, American Indian, and African American helping professions and reveals differences in achieving styles based on ethnicity.

As a part of regional studies of achieving styles related to skill development, Lu, Lum, and Chen (2001) reported on a number of research studies that examined the relationship between linguistic and cultural differences and individual achieving styles among social workers. The Achieving Style Inventory (ASI) instrument (Lipman-Blumen, Handley-Isaksen, & Leavitt, 1983) was used for the following populations.

Asian American Population. Lu, Lum, and Chen (2001) conducted achieving style research on 146 clinicians in southern California from two groups (64 bilingual/bicultural Asian American clinicians and 82 non–Asian American clinicians. Of the 146 clinicians, 18.2 percent held BA degrees, 55.5 percent had MA degrees, 13.1 percent were PhDs, and 13.1 percent were MDs. The mean and median for education were both 18 years. There were 36.6 percent males and 63.4 percent females. Age consisted of 38.2 percent (35 years and younger) and 61.8 percent (36 years and older), with 40 years as the mean and 39 years as the median. Statistical analyses were employed using t-test, correlation, and regression. Findings showed that the language/culture variable was significantly related to the differences between the two groups as far as achieving styles were concerned, controlling for gender, age, and education. Most significant was that Asian bilingual/bicultural clinicians used vicarious-relational and collaborative-relational styles more frequently than non–Asian American clinicians.

Latino Population. Lu, Organista, Manzo, Wong, and Phung (2002) studied 53 Latino American clinicians who were members of the Bilingual Association of Spanish Speaking Clinicians and Advocates in the San Francisco Bay Area and 47 non–Latino White American clinicians from county mental health agencies in the Bay Area. There were 44 males and 63 females. Thirty-six were less than 39 years old; 33 were between ages 39 and 50; and 35 were 50 years old and older. Seventy-three held MAs or MSWs, and 28 were PhDs or MDs. Using multivariate analysis of variance and multiple regression, the researchers found a significant difference between the ASI profiles of the two groups. The non–Latino White American group scored higher on the power-direct style, the self-instrumental style, and the reliant-instrumental style, and lower on the relational style, whereas Latino clinicians were more collaborative and relationship-oriented with clients.

American Indian Population. Lu, DuBray, Chen, and Ahn (2000) surveyed 18 American Indian social workers and social work faculty who were affiliated with the California American Indian Social Work Association and the American Indian Social Work Faculty Association, as well as 47 European American professionals from the San Francisco Bay area county mental health agencies. There were 21 males and 43 females, with 29 who were 45 years old or younger and 33 who were 46 years old or older. Forty had MAs or MSWs, and 22 held PhDs or MDs. Cross-tabulations and t-tests were used to determine their ASI scores. The American Indian group scored higher on relational style but lower on the direct styles than the European American group.

African American Population. Lu, Lum, and Chen (2001) conducted a parallel study of 188 African American clinicians and 181 White non-Hispanic clinicians who were members of the National Association of Social Workers, New York City chapter. There were 89 males and 279 females, with 189 who were less than 44 years old and 73 who were 44 years old and older. Master's or MSW degree holders numbered 312, and PhDs or MDs numbered 20. Based on the Wilks' Lambda statistic, significant differences existed based on race/ethnicity. African Americans scored higher on competitive-direct style, intrinsic-direct style, social-instrumental style, contributory-relational style, and vicarious-relational style but lower on power-direct style than their White counterparts.

Summary of Achieving Styles Research. Although this research is preliminary and exploratory, Lu, Lum, and Chen (2001) offer some advice:

- With Asian Americans, use vicarious- and collaborative-relational styles such as empathic listening, joint participatory problem solving and task assignments, and mutually agreed-upon empowerment strategies.
- With Latino Americans, employ nondirective and relational styles that offer self-exploration, relationship building, and nonconfrontational trust.
- Work with First Nations Peoples around relational styles that focus on the search for personal growth experiences and the forming of life stories.
- Focus with African American clients on a direct style that communicates honesty, advice, recommendations for change with an empathic relationship, and a positive contribution to the person's life.

SUMMARY

Culturally competent skill development is the core of a discussion of culturally competent practice because it affects the worker–client helping relationship. This chapter defined three types of skills—process, conceptualization, and personalization skills—and related them to the social work practice stages of contact, problem identification, assessment, intervention, and termination. Culturally diverse service delivery was discussed and related to agency linkage, design, and implementation. Finally, research on culturally competent skill development was examined.

CHAPTER EIGHT

Inductive Learning

FRANCIS K. O. YUEN, ANDREW BEIN, AND DOMAN LUM

This chapter will help you to develop competencies in the area of inductive learning. It encourages the reader to participate in continuing discussions of how to practice with culturally and ethnically diverse clients and explains how to gather information about new population groups who enter the local social service scene. The chapter describes participation in inductive learning using action participatory research tools. It connects cultural competence and inductive learning. As the NASW *Standards for Cultural Competence in Social Work Practice* (2001) explains:

> Cultural competence is never fully realized, achieved, or completed, but rather cultural competence is a lifelong process for social workers who will always encounter diverse clients and new situations in their practice. Supervisors and workers should have the expectation that cultural competence is an ongoing learning process integral and central to daily supervision. (p. 5)

We fully support this continuing learning emphasis and believe that inductive learning is a methodological tool that fulfills this task. Inductive learning begins in the social work classroom and carries over into professional worker–client relationships.

As a social work educator and practitioner, Ruth G. Dean is concerned about how a social worker evaluates his or her own practice after completing his or her formal education. Dean (1994) writes:

> As a teacher, supervisor, and clinician I see social workers evaluating and reflecting on their practice all the time. These evaluations are not systematic nor are they written. Sometimes they occur in discussions between colleagues or in supervisory sessions and sometimes they simply occur in the clinician's mind. But a form of evaluation goes on continuously. The challenge is to find the bridge between qualitative methods and the kinds of questions that social workers do ask when they evaluate their practices. If we could pay more attention to these questions and start where the practitioner is, then I think we could integrate qualitative forms of research with practitioners' needs. (pp. 279–280)

We have a similar concern about culturally diverse social work practice. That is, after graduating from a social work program, how does a social work professional evaluate multicultural practice and continue the learning process to explore new information about this field of practice? What questions, issues, and insights from the multicultural client and the cultural diversity–oriented social work practitioner arise in the helping process that might contribute new data to this area? What are the practical qualitative research and practice tools that support inductive learning?

This chapter focuses on inductive learning as a lifelong process of continuous discovery about the changing nature of multicultural individual, family, and community dynamics. The chapter begins with a definition of inductive learning and the characteristics of the inductive research approach. It next moves to the inductive learning process, which emphasizes the need for the social worker to continue learning as practitioner and researcher. It makes a case for professional research-oriented practice in the social work tradition. Qualitative research is an integral part of social work education in the practice and research curriculum; this chapter offers practical suggestions on combining research-oriented practice and culturally diverse social work practice. Discussions on learning about diversity from people and strategies for change are also included. Finally, we argue that inductive learning is more than a subject of social work research and practice; it is a framework for thinking and learning about diversity.

INDUCTIVE AND DEDUCTIVE REASONING

In learning, people gather information and gain knowledge about a certain subject matter. Learning can be accomplished with or without a preset agenda. Through the study and discovery process, an individual develops a new understanding about the topic. At the end, the person usually arrives at a conclusion that leads to a claim regarding the subject matter. This claim, which represents an individual's belief toward a particular area under discussion, is that person's argument. Moore (1998) defines an argument "as a group of statements, one of which—the conclusion—is claimed to follow the others—the premises" (p. 2). Accordingly, an argument "consists of three parts—a group of premises, a conclusion, and an implicit claim" (p. 5).

Arguments can be presented deductively or inductively. Moore (1998) explains the difference between deductive argument and inductive argument. She cites the primary example of deductive reasoning: "All men are mortal. Socrates is a man. Therefore, Socrates is mortal" (p. 5). A conclusion about a specific situation is drawn from the truth of general premises. The premises, in fact, contain more information than the conclusion, and the conclusion follows from the premises. In this situation, no matter how much more information is available on Socrates, he is still mortal and the conclusion still stands. Deductive reasoning provides a more precise and confident assertion than does inductive reasoning.

In an inductive argument, individual specific situations are used to make a generalization. "Socrates was mortal. Sappho was mortal. Cleopatra was mortal. Therefore, all people are mortal" (Moore, 1998, p. 6). The premises of three people's situations become the evidence and the basis for the conclusion that applies to all people. In this case, the conclusion bears more information than the premises, and that conclusion might be altered as new information arises and is incorporated. The inductive conclusion is more of the nature of probability, correlation, or contribution than is a causal determination made through deductive reasoning.

Inductively, people can learn about situations and make generalizations through analogy and inductive generalization. Moore (1998) explains that learning through analogy involves the use of similar situations to comprehend new or little known situations. Using information from a member of a set to make a generalization to all members of that set is inductive reasoning. Such reasoning provides many avenues for learning about diversity.

DEFINITION OF INDUCTIVE LEARNING

The learning process is a part of life and living. At birth, a person begins the process of receiving, processing, and integrating stimuli from significant others (parents, family, friends), events, and experiences. This series of learning experiences becomes the basis for intelligence, knowledge, and action.

During undergraduate and graduate education, social work educators teach students about social work practice, behavior, policy, research, diversity, populations-at-risk, values and ethics, and economic and social justice. These social work education areas are introductions to a lifelong series of learning encounters where social workers integrate classroom theory and agency practice. This requires constant refinements and applications of new knowledge and experiences in clinical, organizational, and community situations.

Learning, denoting the acquisition of knowledge or skills, has some interesting root meanings. The German word *lernen* means to learn and teach. The connotation is that as one learns, there comes the opportunity to teach what has been learned. In a real sense, the students of today are the teachers of tomorrow. The current social work students are the future social work educators. The Latin word *lira* means track or furrow. The implication is that as one learns, there is imprinted in one's mind a track or furrow or a memory of that learned experience. In an agricultural sense, a furrow is made for planting a seed that grows into a crop. A learning furrow becomes the ground for a seed or an idea to grow into a body of knowledge. As social work educators, we hope to teach culturally diverse social work practice and cultural competence so that we will implant seeds of ideas in the minds and hearts of students that will grow and flourish in ways beyond our teaching aspirations and dreams.

A researcher doing social survey is constantly asking questions about areas of concern in an inductive manner. A survey researcher uses inductive reasoning in assembling particular facts about a subject or individual cases and then drawing general conclusions based on findings. A good inductive researcher asks open-ended research questions and draws conclusions based on findings. The inductive method is the opposite of the deductive method. Deduction is a process of reasoning from a known principle that serves as a guide or benchmark to a conclusion that confirms the given. The deductive method may go from the general to the specific or from a premise to a logical conclusion.

From an inductive learning perspective, the social worker begins by ascertaining the background and problems of the multicultural client. Based on careful inquiry and investigation, the social worker learns about the unique issues confronting the client. Similarities may exist between multicultural clients. At the same time, unique characteristics may emerge and differ from those found in the existing literature. Inductive learning helps the social worker to become a careful and caring practitioner and offers new insights on emerging information that may differ from the body of knowledge on multicultural clients. This may be especially relevant with new immigrant groups from countries where unique cultural knowledge about these people may be lacking.

Inductive learning often associates with everyday real life experience. Social work practitioners in the field are rich sources for inductive learning about problems from the multicultural front lines. As they uncover new client information through an open-ended inductive process, they help develop new insight as well as practice knowledge and skills. Qualitative research in social work should assert its social work birthright and articulate inductive learning methods for culturally diverse social work practice.

THE INDUCTIVE RESEARCH APPROACH

The inductive research approach fits our concern for inductive learning. Several features of inductive research are described here.

Analytic induction is a procedure for verifying theories and propositions based on qualitative data. A hypothesis is tested, revised, and retested on a case-by-case basis across a broad range of cases until the hypothesis adequately explains in all cases the phenomenon being studied (Sherman & Reid, 1994, p. 434). This form of inductive research is useful to the development of theories about cultural diversity.

The grounded theory (Glaser & Strauss, 1967) approach is a type of qualitative inductive research. Its purpose is the discovery of relationships among concepts, processes, and patterns. Grounded theory researchers enter the field with an open inductive mind, pit the emerging empirical findings against new data, and modify findings to fit the data. In short, they practice constant comparison within and across cases. Mizrahi and Abramson (1994) explain: "The constant comparative method is a process of developing categories, concepts, and broader themes or theory inductively from the data and testing them out at each step by returning to the data to evaluate their fit and appropriateness" (p. 140). This approach combines the openness of induction with the deductive processes of hypotheses testing and cross-validation of empirical findings with the existing literature (Gilgun, 1994).

Grounded theory researchers discover understanding through their open-minded observations and analyses. They do not enter the observation with the intention of confirming or disconfirming certain preconceived working hypotheses. Instead, through inductive observations, they detect certain patterns or concepts, and thus form the working hypotheses that are to be modified by further observations. This process continues until the researchers reach the conclusion that no more insights can be gained or the existing findings will not be altered from more observations. Grounded theory approaches support those who practice with diverse populations—that is, those who work with clients in their natural environments without preconceived bias, understand the native perceptions, and engage in ongoing explorations and modifications.

Ethnography is another type of qualitative research that utilizes participant observation, family interviewing, autobiographies, and detailed descriptions of the events of all participants (Fortune, 1994). Ethnographic research often uses inductive reasoning in its approach. It moves from observation to conceptualization of meaning, with relevance for cross-cultural practice.

The ethnographic researcher may ask questions indirectly by implication rather than in a direct way in order to obtain oblique perceptions of the problem or issue at hand. For example, Lum (2000, pp. 162–165) discusses disclosure of problem areas where ethnic clients may feel a sense of shame and hesitation. Before disclosing the problem, the client might say in an indirect, oblique manner, "I have a friend with a certain problem. What would you suggest if this were the case?" The worker might also respond in an oblique way by offering a helpful and practical suggestion and building trust. Both understand the real circumstances but practice a respectful approach to dealing with the issue in a nonobtrusive manner.

Fortune (1994) distinguishes between microethnographic and macroethnographic studies. The former deal with individual clients, subgroups, organizations, and programs, and their interactions. The latter are concerned with enhancing knowledge of whole cultures in relation to their setting and perspective.

Monette, Sullivan, and De Jong (1994) suggest four categories to be observed and recorded in ethnographic participant observation research: (1) the setting, or a description of the general physical and social setting being observed by the researcher–practitioner; (2) the people, or a physical and social description of individuals who are the focus (number of people, physical appearance, age, gender, socioeconomic characteristics); (3) individual behavior, or interactions, communications, and behavioral sequences; and (4) group behavior, or the composition, interrelationship, and cliques of groups on the scene.

Ethnographic methods, according to Yegidis, Weinbach, and Morrison-Rodriguez (1999), employ both the *emic* (insider standpoint) and *etic* (outsider standpoint) perspectives to help researchers understand the social structures, norms, beliefs, values, and other cultural elements of the groups being studied. These methods allow "the outside investigator to function as an insider through participant observation and other methods that will enhance the understanding of the cultural context" (p. 135). By combining the insider's understanding of the subtle cultural nuances and the outsider's critical questioning and pursuit, ethnographic methods allow for a detailed understanding of the client's various social and cultural realities.

Rubin and Babbie (2005) point out that an ethnographic study using grounded theory approach "emphasizes an inductive process, [although] it also can incorporate deductive processes" (p. 437) through constant comparisons. They explain that using inductive observations, researchers identify certain patterns that lead to the development of specific concepts and hypotheses. Similar cases are further selected for more observations that could be compared to the earlier concepts and hypotheses. When the researchers find the observations of similar cases can no longer generate new insights, the researchers will select a new type of cases and will replicate the same process. This process will repeat until "the researcher believes that further seeking of new types of cases will not alter the findings" (p. 437).

The theory-building process of qualitative inductive research involves categories evolved from the data leading to the development of conclusions. "What does the data tell us?" is the crucial inductive and reflective question posed by the practitioner–researcher. Lang (1994) suggests that the questions "What do I know from this processing?" and "Therefore, what should I do?" are "the guiding questions of such data processing" (p. 275). Inductive data gathering and processing lead to abstracting or generalizing and later conceptualization.

This line of thinking inductively and generalizing theory from data is a part of the critical mind-set that is important for students and practitioners of culturally diverse social work. As social work students graduate and become professional practitioners, it is incumbent on them to establish a research-oriented line of inquiry. Lang (1994) explains:

> [T]he earliest experiences in class and field for the beginning student practitioner should include inquiry about "what is" and "how does it happen," so that upon entry into the profession, the social work practitioner is habituated to asking questions, thinking about practice, and exploring "what the practice tells."(p. 276)

In brief, intervention ought to be derived from practice data that come from client and community knowledge.

Stern (1994) reaffirms the need to move from data to theory building; to build knowledge inductively in order to discover new practice theory, and to connect inductive and deductive data processing.

Social constructivist research is a type of naturalistic inquiry in which the researcher focuses on the "cognitive schemes that construct the subject's experience and action and lead to new interpretive frameworks or structures" (Rodwell, 1998, p. 254). *Cognitive schema* is the cognitive map or diagram of a person. The term "can also refer to the way individuals categorize to make sense out of complexity" (p. 262). This schema is often the result of one's data analysis processes. This cognitive map informs how one perceives and understands reality. Through linguistic negotiations and other narrative exchanges that are achieved intersubjectively, researchers gain understanding of the development of the new reality and meaning. In other words, through the communication process, new common referent terms and understandings between individuals are achieved, and they shape and construct the new reality. For example, suppose a social worker is working with a newly arrived refugee who is still traumatized by the war and torture he suffered. Through extensive dialogues that include genuine support and direct challenges, the social worker can gain the trust and understanding of the client and can attempt to help him sort out and make sense of his war experience and his life in a new land. The social worker and the client together write a chapter of his history and coauthor a new chapter of his future that is sensible to the client.

Analytic induction, the grounded theory approach, ethnographic participant observation, inductive theory building, and social constructivist research are examples of qualitative research approaches in social work that have relevance for culturally diverse practice. In the next section we discuss inductive social work practice, which integrates the inductive qualitative approach, a strengths perspective, and grounded theory.

INDUCTIVE SOCIAL WORK PRACTICE

Inductive approaches are particularly appropriate for cross-cultural social work practice. Practitioners move beyond cultural stereotypes or etic (universal) categorization of psychosocial dynamics when they listen to and appreciate the client's own story. Clients tell social workers about what events, conditions, behaviors, and decisions mean to them, and social workers understand the client's narrative on the client's own terms. When clients *teach* social workers about their lives, clients experience having their voice count, being respected, and knowing they are not judged.

The nature of inductive understanding is illustrated in Competency Study 8.1.

COMPETENCY STUDY 8.1

Inductive Understanding

Suppose a Latino male adolescent is struggling with behavior problems in a school that is less than 2 percent Latino. We do not assume or even construct a hypothesis that family and individual ethnic identity issues underlie the youth's struggles. The inductive approach is not about measuring how well a client's experience conforms to an already determined theoretical construct—in this case *ethnic identity confusion;* instead, we build our understanding about this youth's reality upon the family's and the youth's narrative as well as our observations of the youth in various environments. We may learn, for example, that the youth's behavioral struggles are recent and coincide with his learning that his father is terminally ill. We may learn that the youth's mother is African American, that the youth has comfortably identified himself as African American, and that 50 percent of the school's students are African American.

Theoretical concepts like ethnic identity confusion do, however, have some utility. High school students of color may struggle with issues of ethnic identity, and these struggles may be significant forces in their lives. An understanding of the potentially destructive consequences of racism also prepares practitioners to tune into elements that may be salient in the client's life. Overall, cross-cultural theory prepares practitioners to hear information related to identity and racism themes, place it within a context, and ask intelligent questions.

However, although the hypothesis-testing, deductive practitioner starts with a theoretical framework (such as identity theory) and tests the theory's utility and relevance for a given client, the inductive practitioner–researcher grounds his or her inquiry on information gleaned from the client's narrative and from observation of the client within his or her ecological system. Theoretical concepts are utilized to sensitize workers to possibilities rather than to lock workers into narrow frameworks from which to view clients (Glaser & Strauss, 1967; Strauss & Corbin, 1990).

Reactions to the professional golfer Tiger Woods ("The Question of Race in America," 1997) provide a simplistic illustration of inductive and deductive approaches. Some people strive to categorize Tiger Woods's identity through invoking general sociological theory. They proclaim that because of how larger society acts toward him and because of the history of oppression suffered by African Americans within larger society and, in particular, the sport of golf, Tiger Woods (1) is African American, (2) has a social responsibility to declare himself as African American, and (3) is somehow deficient for not declaring himself as African American. Others look at Tiger Woods and state that because he is one-fourth Chinese, one-fourth Thai, one-fourth Black, one-eighth White and one-eighth American Indian, he should have the option of checking any appropriate boxes or a new box labeled "multicultural."

On the other hand, the inductive approach toward understanding a multicultural person such as Tiger Woods involves asking Tiger Woods to talk about his identity. How does he see himself and define himself, and what is significant for him about the various ethnic groups that he mentions? How meaningful is "multicultural"? How important are these identity issues for him? What is it like to have demands placed upon him to identify himself in a certain way? How, in his perception, does his ethnic identity relate to larger social issues involving identity? What kind of family support or stress is present in his life regarding these issues? By answering such questions, Tiger Woods teaches us about his identity. He perhaps raises issues around multicultural or ethnically blended identity for which we are not prepared because there is so little established theory (Root, 1992).

TABLE 8-1 *Strengths Perspective Principles*

1. Client knowledge and experience are valued.
2. Client gifts and talents are emphasized.
3. Learned hopefulness is promoted.
4. The practitioner recognizes that people are more successful when moving toward something than when moving away from something.
5. The practitioner avoids labels and the victimizing effects of labels, and uses concepts such as resiliency rather than at-risk.
6. Positive expectations are integral to the relationship.
7. In the client–worker relationship, the qualities of openness, clarity of expectations, genuineness, and supportiveness are emphasized.
8. Change in one area reverberates in other areas of life.

A STRENGTHS PERSPECTIVE

Students and practitioners who have integrated a strengths perspective (Delgado, 1997; Saleeby, 2002) are best prepared to work with clients in a respectful, open, and nonjudgmental manner. In the absence of a thorough grounding in the strengths perspective, students and practitioners can easily view their clients through a lens distorted either by individual or societal racism or stereotyping, or by overly general social psychological theory. The strengths perspective directs practitioners to emphasize clients' strengths, gifts, and talents beyond the situation that has overwhelmed and challenged their coping abilities. It sets the tone for a client–worker *partnership* and orients social workers toward embracing clients and looking for health rather than pathologizing clients and looking for dysfunction. Among other principles in the strengths perspective (see Table 8-1), client knowledge and experience are valued.

The culturally competent practitioner thus combines the inductive researcher's mentality—which involves learning and discovering with clients, asking questions, and observing—with a strengths perspective that orients the practitioner to embrace clients' positive behavioral styles, belief systems, and coping patterns. When the inductive and strengths traditions are linked, social workers not only approach clients with an open, inquiring mind but also they sincerely believe that clients have the capacity to do things correctly and that clients can teach them about overcoming difficult situations and solving day-to-day dilemmas (De Jong & Miller, 1995). Clients could shed light and offer new perspectives on how to behave, think, and feel in given social situations. They inform us of psychosocial dynamics that may be useful in our work with similarly situated clients, but which we, as practitioners, may never have considered.

The Search for Client Meaning

Grounded Data Collection—Client Narrative. The way a client thinks about and comes to understand his or her dilemmas, victories, self-identity, and hopes represents the client's search for meaning. The data collection process is considered *grounded* because it begins with the client's narrative rather than the practitioner–researcher's theoretical constructs or predictions about who the client is or the nature of the client's

CULTURAL COMPETENCY IN ACTION

The Hernandez Family: A Case Study

The inductive process begins with the practitioner's commitment to be a learner and to have the client assume a teacher's role. The practitioner adopts a strengths perspective and sincerely values the client's knowledge, perspectives, and coping strategies. The social worker frames the initial encounter (1) to help manage the anxiety that the individual or family may feel in assuming the teacher role; (2) to orient the client to expect solutions and, thus, help the client maintain hope that the worker's inquiry has a purpose; and (3) to convey respect to the client through asserting that the client's perspectives are valued.

Mr. Platt, the social worker, learns that the Hernandez family is concerned about the disruptive school behavior of 10-year-old Ricardo. He observes the family's reluctance and nervousness during their session and tells himself that these reactions are normal. He informs the family that they will address Ricardo's school situation. However, he would like to first learn about who they are. This approach may be in accordance with a Latino emphasis on *personalismo*, a cultural orientation that emphasizes personal warmth and connectedness. When Mr. Platt learns about Mr. Hernandez's two jobs and willingness to support his extended family, he conveys his admiration of Mr. Hernandez's work ethic and dedication to his family. He inquires about the family's decision to leave Mexico and praises Mrs. Hernandez's courage and her resolve to enhance the economic well-being of her family. Ricardo and his younger siblings are attentive to their parents' words. They are affirmed by the social worker as "respectful, caring children."

Inductive exploration addresses the issue that brought the family for service: Ricardo's school struggles. Mr. Platt works from a strengths perspective and assumes that the parents want Ricardo to experience school success. They have valuable knowledge about Ricardo, and Ricardo has valuable knowledge about himself. Mr. Platt addresses the following areas:

- What are the issues in school for Ricardo?
- What do Ricardo's parents do to prepare him to be successful in school?

- What is Ricardo's behavior at home?
- What kinds of successes do Mr. and Mrs. Hernandez have with Ricardo, and how do they manage to have these successes?
- What should Mr. and Mrs. Hernandez tell Ricardo's teachers so that the teachers have a better understanding of Ricardo?
- What is the relationship like between the teacher and the Hernandez family?

TASK RECOMMENDATIONS

Inductive inquiry and the strengths perspective are advanced as cornerstones of culturally competent practice. Discussing these questions will clarify the applications and implications of this overall approach:

- How *respectful* is Mr. Platt toward the Hernandez family compared to practitioners you have observed in agencies? What does it mean for a client to feel *respected?*
- What follow-up questions may be helpful to facilitate the collection of more specific data?
- Weick (1992) states that "when people's positive capacities are supported, they are more likely to act on their strengths" (p. 24). Mr. Platt frequently invokes the metaphors of the family's strong work ethic, courage, and resourcefulness. How can these capacities be mobilized to positively affect Ricardo's academic success?
- How would the social worker's approach be similar or different if the client or family were in counseling involuntarily?
- Suppose the family presented itself as highly distressed because Ricardo had set a fire at school.

How would you modify or not modify Mr. Platt's approach?

FIGURE 8.1 *The Inductive Process for the Practitioner–Researcher*

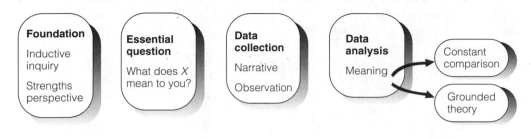

problems. The practitioner–researcher develops a strong orientation toward learning about the client's unique reality and accepts and embraces the client's perspectives vis-à-vis this reality. It should be noted that acceptance does not imply approval, because some behaviors, beliefs, or values may be the source of the client's struggles and may contribute to why the social worker is involved in the client's life. Acceptance, instead, is a vehicle for entering the client's world and understanding as completely as possible this person's beliefs, feelings, and behaviors and how these are influenced by this person's cultural and social conditions. When clients interact with practitioner–researchers who incorporate a strengths–inductive learning perspective, the clients feel empowered and much more prepared to tackle major life issues (Bein, Torres, & Kurilla, 2000).

Figure 8.1 illustrates that a strengths–inductive learning orientation serves as a foundation for practitioner–researchers to approach clients with a fundamental question: What does X mean to you? The symbol X can refer to a family or social experience, or to feelings, beliefs, or cultural meanings. Social workers address this question through eliciting the client's narrative and through observing the client's behavior in interactions with the worker and in the client's natural environment. The client's narrative deepens when the worker asks open-ended questions and invokes facilitative communication skills (Lum, 2000). Interpretations are offered sparingly to clients and in such a way that clients are free to reject, modify, or accept them. Questions such as the following facilitate the development of the client's narrative:

What does having an autistic son mean to you? How do you maintain your strength? What's it like to have a father who is in jail?
Can you tell me what it's like for you as a Hmong teenager to go to the doctor?
How do you manage to keep your family together when you don't have enough income and you've been homeless?
How is it for you as a Latina to be thinking about leaving your abusive husband?
How does being that angry toward the world affect your life?
What was it like for you to be told by Child Protective Services that you could not take care of your kids?
What was it like when the worker came to your house and put your kids in her car?

Out of context, some of these questions may seem insensitive or, perhaps, ineffective. Some clients may be looking for immediate, concrete help, and a narrative-generating question that is poorly timed could be interpreted as off-base, insensitive, or indulgent on the worker's behalf. In nearly all cases, however, there is a time and a place for questions of this nature. Clients wish to feel understood, accepted, and respected, and relish opportunities to tell their story to a worker who is eager to learn from them. Most important, this kind of data gathering is likely to yield fruitful results in cross-cultural interactions.

The practitioner–researcher adopts the same spirit of open-ended inquiry with regard to understanding the client's experience of the social work service. The social worker engages the client in *directive narrative consultation*, where the client becomes the expert on the utility of the social worker's involvement. In this role, the client talks with the social worker about what is and is not working, which elements of the social worker's style are appreciated and which elements are not, and what the social worker needs to do in order to facilitate gains. One client may state that he or she needs direct advice; the social worker is not clear enough and needs to play an expert role. Another client may state that the social worker is pushing too hard in a particular direction; the client wants to feel more supported regardless of his or her decisions and wants the social worker to be more active in setting up employment opportunities.

The social worker should learn about the client's past involvement with helping professionals and nonprofessionals and develop a sense of the client's expectations for the present helping encounter. This area of inquiry frames the present helping encounter as fluid and open to client input.

Grounded Data Collection—Client Observation. In addition to client narrative, grounded data collection also involves observation. A child, for example, may not discuss his or her peer relationships in much detail; however, a worker might observe the child in various interactions and notice that the child appears withdrawn. Through child, family, or teacher interviews, the worker would learn about the meaning of this withdrawn behavior. In other words, rather than forming a quick hypothesis regarding the etiology of the withdrawn behavior (the child does not feel accepted because of his or her ADD, because he or she is in foster care, because of inadequate social skills), the social worker learns "from the ground up" the meaning of the child's behavior. The worker would want to see whether there were instances where the child is not withdrawn and identify the differences. He or she would want to understand how the child experiences being removed from others and what staying alone represents.

Grounded Data Analysis and Theory Building. When the practitioner–researcher works with individual clients, families, or systems, he or she relies on narrative or observational data to develop an understanding of the client's reality. The worker does not seek higher-level theoretical constructs when working with the individual client; instead, the worker attempts to weave gathered data into useful, data-driven themes. The social worker discusses these themes with the client so that the client can confirm them, build upon them, or reject them.

The constant comparison process ensures that the grounded theorist does not attempt to explicate theory based upon a few cases; in fact, the grounded theorist makes an extensive search to uncover exceptions to the developing categories. Ultimately, the grounded theorist realizes that no matter how elegant the theory and how all-inclusive it appears to be, it is actually fluid and subject to revision (Gilgun, 1994).

CULTURAL COMPETENCY IN ACTION

The Hernandez Family: A Case Study

The inductive practitioner seeks to understand the meaning of life events and circumstances for the client. The worker's involvement is not based on how Ricardo's teacher constructs the case (Ricardo needs help with his homework and Ricardo's father is working too much); nor is it based on overly general constructions about how Latinos are supposed to respond in counseling.

Mr. Platt seeks to understand how the parents view their own role in Ricardo's schooling and education. How much is the teacher viewed as the guardian of Ricardo's education and what role do the parents see for themselves? Can the parents imagine a facilitative role that they can play in assisting Ricardo in school? What lessons about life and about their history can the parents impart? What does Ricardo say about his acting-out behavior? How much would he link his behavior to his academic difficulties versus problems with his teacher or peers? What kinds of school successes has he experienced? What strategies does he have for becoming more successful in school?

TASK RECOMMENDATIONS

Cross-cultural theory sensitizes Mr. Platt to the possibility that parent involvement may have unique meaning to the Hernandez family that is salient to this case. Before establishing a contract regarding Ricardo's completion of homework (perhaps the teacher's desire), the social worker seeks to understand the parents' beliefs about what they can contribute. Mr. Platt is also aware that many people of color, and Mexican immigrants in particular, internalize racist ideology and believe that their life stories and life lessons have little relevance for the education of their children. The parents' narrative regarding these themes deepens Mr. Platt's understanding of what Ricardo's school struggles *mean* to Mr. and Mrs. Hernandez. The exploration is validating for the parents and it provides a fertile environment for a new family paradigm that the worker and Mr. and Mrs. Hernandez jointly construct. For example, Mr. and Mrs. Hernandez have valuable wisdom about Ricardo. They can contribute to his academic success. Their life lessons are powerful educational tools.

Assessment and intervention issues regarding a narrative-generating approach are addressed through the following questions:

- How easy or difficult would it be for you to resist the pressure to impose upon the family an immediate solution or condition (such as a homework contract)? Is this dynamic different if the parents are behaving destructively? Please explain.
- How would you assess the additional resources to be utilized on behalf of the family or Ricardo?
- What questions would you ask the Hernandez family to ascertain their level of satisfaction with your helping effort and the likelihood that they would continue in counseling?
- What intervention with Ricardo's teacher can you suggest that would enhance the probability of positive outcomes?
- What meso level interventions could assist the school to become more effective with the Hernandez family and with others similarly situated?
- What kinds of observations fortify your data collection process?

Cross-cultural social work theory at its core has always taken exception to the universal categorization of complex phenomena (such as a healthy process of dying) and has argued for an emic or more client- and culture-specific understanding of issues (Devore & Schlesinger, 1999; Green, 1999; Lum, 2000). A grounded approach to data collection makes sense even where established theory exists, but especially where theory is undeveloped (e.g., regarding identity issues for mixed-ethnicity individuals, recovery from posttraumatic stress disorders for refugees, successful coping patterns for families affected by welfare reform).

Inductive social work practice is part of the inductive learning experience, which needs to be taught in the repertoire of social work interventions. In the next section, we propose an inductive learning process that can be used in the practice and research classroom and later translated to the social work agency.

THE INDUCTIVE LEARNING PROCESS

We have made a case for inductive learning and qualitative inductive practice and research. We have surveyed various types of qualitative research and qualitative inductive practice and have argued for the need to prepare social work students and practitioners in culturally diverse research-oriented practice. In this section, we explain Lang's three-stage model of integrating practice and research.

Lang (1994) pushes for the needed integration between the data processing of qualitative research and social work practice in order to advance the practitioner as knowledge builder. She maintains an emphasis on the practitioner as primary and qualitative research in social work practice as secondary, while at the same time comparing and contrasting the varying research and practice methodologies. Her emphasis, like ours, is on the research-oriented practitioner; that is, culturally diverse social work should educate practitioners to work with multicultural clients and also to do clinical and community ethnic research.

Lang's threefold model encompasses data gathering, data processing and data transformation, and integration of qualitative research and social work practice. These three stages should be taught in social work practice and research classes. They become the structure for professional social work practice in social service agencies.

Data Gathering

Data-gathering strategies consist of firsthand observation and writing down those observations in process descriptions that record important client–worker verbal and nonverbal interactions. The social work practitioner is concerned about the following questions: What is discovered? How does it happen? What needs to be done? How can I contribute? The practitioner must uncover information from observation and must also determine a course of action. Observation is used to develop practice directives. Practitioner observations occur at critical junctures in the helping process: at the beginning of a new client relationship, at various stages of the relationship, and when a client terminates.

The written description of observations captures significant details and constitutes the data for practice analysis and directives. The emphasis is on self-supervision through scrutinizing practice records. Lang (1994) believes that it is important to record practice sessions as material for qualitative research: "The promotion of and provision for large-scale process recording by numerous practitioners as a professional requirement would enable the profession to enter an era in which qualitative research methods could become widely used for theory-building purposes" (p. 268). Lang's suggestion underlines the need to bring together social work education programs and social work agencies on a local level. The creation of a multicultural study and discussion group consisting of multicultural

CULTURAL COMPETENCY IN ACTION

The Hernandez Family: A Case Study

The inductive practitioner–researcher relies on collection of the client's narrative and his or her own observations to build an understanding of the client's reality. Data-driven themes are discussed with the client so that the client can confirm, reject, or further construct them. The culturally competent social worker maintains a researcher's mentality when working with the individual client or family; eventually the practitioner–researcher assigns conceptual names to what is happening in the client's environment.

School officials and teachers frequently admonish parents to play a larger role in their child's education. This admonishment is well intentioned and is based on the well-established correlation between parent involvement and child academic success. However, the Hernandez family has been accustomed to having the teacher and the school be responsible for their child's education. They do not perceive a role for themselves. If anything, the parents feel ashamed about their lack of formal education and their Spanish monolingualism.

TASK RECOMMENDATIONS

Working within the grounded theory tradition, Mr. Platt compares the Hernandez case with other cases regarding parent involvement issues. After conducting qualitative interviews with Latino parents of other underachieving children, he realizes that (1) parents do not see themselves as the primary "authors" of their child's education and their child's future; (2) parents believe that their lack of English and math skills severely limits their ability to help; (3) parents do not know what "doing well" means for their early-age school child; (4) parents have limited time to help their child (Garcia & Dryer, 1996).

Mr. Platt uses these findings to theoretically sensitize himself in his work with other families. He does not mechanically apply these newfound concepts to each family with whom he works. Rather, he maintains an inductive, strengths-based posture, and then compares the new family's narrative with the already existing categories. New data contribute either to the enriched description of existing categories or to the emergence of new categories. He uses emergent knowledge to plan interventions and conducts case studies to document the effectiveness of various efforts.

Mr. Platt prepares the Hernandez family to meet with Ricardo's teacher. He talks with them about the value of their information and prepares the teacher to listen to the parents and validate them. Mr. Platt talks to Mr. and Mrs. Hernandez about a successful social worker whom he knows whose Latino parents were monolingual farm workers. Mr. Platt's story describes how these parents monitored their child's homework and gained the support of other potentially helpful adults in order to contribute to his childhood academic success. The social worker talks to Mr. and Mrs. Hernandez about an available homework group that exists on the school grounds.

- Researcher bias is a potential pitfall in grounded theory building. The practitioner–researcher may superimpose initial impressions and analysis on subsequent cases. How do you guard against this tendency?
- What is the difference between approaching a case with "theoretical sensitivity" and approaching a case with a formulated hypothesis to be tested about the client's problems and intervention strategies?
- How much do Mr. Platt's approaches flow from the inductive assessment of the case's dynamics?
- How can processes involving inductive knowledge building or systematic research become incorporated into a social service site?
- What dynamic or topic can you imagine systematically investigating with an inductive approach?

social work educators, students, and practitioners is an opportunity to discuss multicultural cases that have implications for learning and to implement social work practice and qualitative research methodologies.

The Lang model suggests a focus group that would meet to discuss systematic ways to conduct uniform data gathering of multicultural case material. Hardcastle, Wenocur, and Powers (1997) explain that a focus group is "a small number of individuals meet[ing] together with a trained facilitator to discuss a narrow topic in a detailed, guided way" (p. 172). Its purpose is to air ideas, to react to each other, and to refine opinions.

A focus group has the atmosphere of a study group. It provides valuable information and insights into issues, describing ways in which people react to areas of concern. It also tests the waters and may provide themes and key concepts for formulating an area of concern. Finally, a focus group provides specialized assessment of some subject matter, tasks to be pursued, and the population under study. Members of a focus group could gather various theoretical and clinical/community case study data in completing Lang's first stage.

Data Processing and Data Transformation

The first level of data processing consists of abstracting and generalizing. Abstracting primary features and characteristics from the data has a twofold effect: reducing the data by selection, and transforming the data into an abstracted, generalized form. Generalizing involves linking similar features and making connections in the data. Categorizing and sorting comparable items and naming them as a class is the next step after abstracting and generalizing. It begins to focus and elaborate the inquiry to a higher level of abstraction. It creates the beginning of a classification scheme or typology. Next, there is conceptualizing into a profile, model, or paradigm. Finally, there is contextualizing, where the new theory is placed in the context of relevant existing theories.

Two emerging patterns of data processing are the action-focused and knowledge-focused patterns. The action-focused pattern derives appropriate interventions for immediate practice implementation. It is motivated by the demand for action in the immediate helping situation. Lang (1994) explains:

> Thus the practitioner in the action-focused pattern may run on a short cycle of inductive data processing limited to the first level of abstraction and generalization, followed by a deductive process involving interpretation of data in the light of theory, derivation of action, and a return to the concrete. (p. 270)

The knowledge-focused pattern involves the matching of previous and current data with knowledge building and developing. The practitioner evolves classifications and conceptualizations and turns quickly to theory for an immediate explanation. The issue is to know what to do and which action to take.

A focus group consisting of social work educators, students, and practitioners can become a force committed to processing and transforming data. This involves, for example, working on a major area of multicultural study and abstracting concepts and findings that are selected and related to each other. This task is best done by a group of people who are familiar with the existing body of knowledge and skill relating to a major aspect of culturally diverse practice. Cultural competencies in the classroom are enlarged and strengthened through participation in the focus group.

Generalizing, conceptualizing, and contextualizing involve creative effort by academicians who are able to develop theory and by clinicians who understand the relationship between theory development and skill application. On a local or regional level, such a focus group would have to be highly committed to a major undertaking that involves many hours, weeks, and months of steady work and creative data refinement.

Integration of Qualitative Research and Social Work Practice

Lang (1994) calls for social work educators and professionals to commit themselves to qualitative research methodologies in social work practice. This involves the development of a social work curriculum requirement to teach qualitative research methodology. At the same time, the role of the social work practice professional is to participate in the inductive pattern of data processing and abstracting and generalizing from qualitative research data.

The social work practitioner is involved in process recording so that knowledge is retained and practice theory is generated from data. Lang (1994) points out:

> We have not thought of the practitioner as knowledge builder, yet no social worker is in practice very long before accumulating expert knowledge from practice experience. We recover only a fraction of this knowledge because it may not be articulated or formulated into a transmittable, shareable state and because our emphasis in practice is on doing. (p. 277)

In the end, Lang believes that we must integrate the practice and research methodologies of data processing. The integration begins with the education of social work students in research-oriented practice.

Tools for Student Learning 8.1 outlines five phases of integrating practice and research based on Lang's model. They are: (1) getting started; (2) gathering the data; (3) processing the data; (4) categorizing, classifying, and contextualizing the data; and (5) integrating qualitative research and social work practice. This exercise uses the focus group as the discussion and investigatory vehicle.

TOOLS FOR STUDENT LEARNING 8.1

Structuring the Inductive Learning Process

The purpose of this group exercise is to implement Lang's three-stage model of integrating practice and research in social work classes. This exercise clarifies how a group might process qualitative research data and apply it to social work practice in order to build knowledge about cultural diversity. It further supports the interchange between research-oriented practice and practice-oriented research. It outlines the entire inductive learning process and can be spread over a series of sessions that might actually occur over weeks and months.

Phase 1: Getting Started

1. The creation of a focus group is crucial to bringing together various key members who have theoretical, didactic, clinical, and research interests and experiences in culturally diverse social work practice issues. Describe the composition of such a focus group with members' specific qualifications.

2. Data gathering begins with sharing firsthand observations from experiences of culturally diverse practice. List various clinical and community experiences with culturally diverse clients.

3. Lang suggests that in order to concentrate on specific topics and issues, the focus group should answer certain general questions. Lum adds a multicultural perspective to these questions:

- What have I discovered about working with clients of color?
- Have these observations and experiences about this client group been a part of my practice?
- What needs to be done to uncover and develop further knowledge about a specific theme that emerges from my discovery?
- How can I make a contribution to refine a multicultural topic that interests me?

4. After an initial discussion, list the range of topics on the board and based on group consensus, select a single area of interest.

- Why did the group focus on this particular theme?
- Why did the group agree that this area was worthy of further investigation and development?
- What particular aspect of the social work practice process involving people of color does this theme relate to—contact, problem identification, assessment of client/environmental strengths, intervention, or termination?

Phase 2: Gathering the Data

1. What basic observations does the focus group have about its selected area of interest based on case experiences, readings, review of the literature, professional insights, classroom discussion, and other avenues of knowledge?

2. Are there any case process recordings from the practitioner group members, articles or chapters of books from the academic group members, or research material uncovered by the student group members on this topic? Are there any local experts who could speak to the group about the topic under investigation?

Phase 3: Processing the Data

1. Which people in the group are able to select material that could be assessed in a thoughtful way, arranged into subcategories, and interpreted to the whole group?

2. Based on Lang's guidelines, answering the following questions is crucial to processing the data:

- What features and characteristics can be abstracted from the data?
- What linkages (similarities, connections) can be made among features and characteristics to arrive at generalizations about the data?
- What action-focused areas of the data lend themselves to immediate application with clients?
- What knowledge-focused areas of the data make a contribution to theory building and understanding?

Phase 4: Categorizing, Classifying, and Contextualizing the Data

1. The group is moving into data transformation, where systematic arrangement of the data takes place. Can the group build a framework, model, or paradigm around the categories of material? Various group members might take leadership roles in the creation of a conceptual scheme that brings together components of the topic in a logical and meaningful way.
2. The initial framework may need refinement based on individual scrutiny and group review. Initial drafts of the model should be given to group members for critical analysis, further discussion, and revision.
3. After building consensus, the new model should be assessed in light of how it fits into the current literature on social work practice and people of color.

Phase 5: Integrating Qualitative Research and Social Work Practice

1. As a follow-up to the focus group, an effort should be made to ensure that qualitative research methodologies are taught in social work programs. Content should include practice-oriented research and research-oriented practice. The focus group is an excellent resource to interact with social work research classes and to share their deliberations and results. The interaction would provide an illuminating example of how academicians, professionals, and students can work together on a joint project committed to qualitative research.

INDUCTIVE LEARNING AREAS

Learning about Diversity from People

Diversity among people and cultures calls for social workers to learn and formulate differential and culturally appropriate interventions in working with clients of different backgrounds. These interventions involve finding approaches that are suitable to the client's culture and background. Learning about diversity starts from knowing oneself and how one relates to others. This process involves a series of key questions: Who are we, and who is this person? What and how do we know? How are we different, and how are we similar? How do we relate to each other? Yuen (1999) discusses acculturation and the four sources of knowledge—tradition, experience, common sense, and scientific knowledge:

> Tradition is customs and beliefs that have been handed down from generation to generation. It is not necessarily logical or rational, but it makes sense to the people who practice it. Experience is the person's firsthand observation. . . . Experience is unique and sometimes can only be understood by the individuals involved. . . . Common sense is the combination of tradition and experience. Obviously, what is common sense for one person may not be for another person, particularly if the two people have different traditions and experiences. Scientific knowledge is developed mainly through logical and rational validations. It is not the source of absolute knowledge, but it provides the objective means of knowing in addition to the other more subjective ways of knowing. (pp. 106–107)

Tradition and culture have a reciprocal relationship in that they affect each other. Experience is a personal account that is more subjective than objective. Inductive reasoning involves attempts to learn from the person in question and view the world from that person's perspectives. In effect, inductive learning tries to describe reality from the person's traditional background and personal experiences of the given situation. In turn, the researcher may develop a certain extent of capacity to comprehend the common sense of the people being studied. Coupled with logical and systematic ways to collect, organize, and analyze field notes and other data, the inductive learning process provides a qualitative and scientific practice-research approach for social workers. This approach also equips the social worker and other professionals with reverent ways of "looking into" the lives of people of diverse cultures instead of the more intrusive and not necessarily respectful ways of "looking at" such populations (Gould, 1995; Leigh, 1983).

Equally, each social worker learns through his or her own personal and professional tradition, experience, common sense, and scientific/professional education. The interplays of these variables in learning between the social workers and their clients form almost endless possibilities and dynamics of learning and growth. The following scenario provides additional insight.

A young Asian male social worker who was raised in a middle-class suburban neighborhood of Los Angeles can use some time to learn more about his new client, Mrs. Johnson, who is 78 years old. Mrs. Johnson is an African American who was born and raised in a rural town in Alabama. She has a large family and had lived in the same town for many generations until her recent move to New York City to be with her oldest daughter. Last month, she was transferred from a local hospital to a skilled nursing home after surgery for an accidental fall that broke her hip. Her daughter, who is single, runs a rather successful small business and is not able to provide around-the-clock care. Nursing home staff have complained that Mrs. Johnson shows no trust to any staff in the facility. Most importantly, she is unwilling to take her prescribed medications. She uses some type of folk medicine that is not approved by the nursing home physician, and she hides it under her bed. In order to be able to work with Mrs. Johnson, this new social worker needs to learn, at least minimally, about Mrs. Johnson's tradition in family and health care; her personal experience with the established authorities; and her sound and prudent but often unsophisticated ways in dealing with daily struggles and, in fact, life in general. The social worker's scientific and often textbook training will help him give a proper DSM diagnosis but will not help him understand Mrs. Johnson's issues from her perspectives, which are influenced by her upbringing and life experience as well as her age, values, and culture.

The states of diversity and the learning of diversity are fluid in that they evolve continuously. They can range from basic awareness to sophisticated competency. Yuen (2003) discusses the different extents of learning and commitment to diversity by distinguishing several major terms including cultural awareness, cultural sensitivity, cultural diversity, cultural pluralism, and multiculturalism:

The awareness of cultural diversity or human diversity suggests the acknowledgment of the existence of people of different cultures. People who accept cultural diversity do not remain culturally apathetic and are well aware of different cultures. . . . Starting at the level of cultural awareness, individuals of different backgrounds who are culturally aware interact in a manner that is sensitive to one another's culture. . . . Often, these cultural sensitivity skills can be well performed behaviorally; they are, however, no guarantee of attitude changes. . . . Cultural pluralism implies the recognition, the intention, and the practice of working with people of different backgrounds. It involves the advancement from cultural awareness to cultural sensitivity and the development of the ability to effectively interact cross-culturally. Cultural pluralism treats all cultures as equal and valid and asserts that all should be respected. . . . Multiculturalism not only recognizes differences and similarities among diverse cultures but also requires a framework of thinking that is inclusive and transcultural. This framework demands the ability to develop beyond cultural sensitivity to the level of cultural competency in interacting with people of various backgrounds. It requires one to think and act not only from the ethnic or cultural specific perspective but also from a multiple and collective perspective that allows one to conceive of common good and understanding among all people. (pp. 22–23)

Many prepackaged cross-cultural workshops or outdated publications on various cultural groups provide information that increases awareness and certain intercultural communication skills. Some of them, however, may in fact inadvertently reinforce the stereotypical images of the very groups they intend to de-stereotype. For example, there is the idea that all Asian American families take care of their elderly and do well in school. Subsequently, this "model minority" myth may steer social workers away from genuinely learning about the family conflicts, elder abuse, and school failures that affect many Asian American families. Effective social work practice with diverse populations calls for more than cultural awareness, sensitivity, or even cross-cultural communication. It requires social workers to respect the inherent values and contributions of different cultures in this culturally pluralistic society. In time they should also develop the needed knowledge, attitudes, and skills for a higher level of multicultural and transcultural practice. Nevertheless, social workers' awareness of issues faced by cultural groups certainly is the beginning step toward further advancement to competency.

Learning about Overcoming Discrimination

As a profession, social work values diversity and is committed to social justice. Part of becoming a professional social worker is learning to overcome discrimination and to promote social justice. This can be achieved through the proper use of inductive learning.

Discrimination can result from distorted inductive learning and its subsequent overgeneralization and oversimplification. For example,

> I know a new hire in my office who is African American. As far as I know, he is not any better than the other applicants who happen to be White. I guess we hired him because of Affirmative Action. He was lucky. Someday when I become the director, I will not hire any more of them. It is not fair.

Inductive learning, however, is also an effective means of taming discrimination. For example,

> When I was growing up, I was told many negative things about the Hispanic Americans and how we should deal with them. For the last year, I have been placed on an important project and have to work very closely with several Latino team members. At first, I did not

like the idea of working with them. Later, I decided to be open-minded and give it a try. Through my contacts with each one of them, I have come to recognize many of those negative stereotypes are, in fact, unfounded and untrue. I was kind of ashamed of my own ignorance.

Stereotype, prejudice, discrimination, and *oppression* are terms often used in social work literature. Yuen (2003) asserts the following:

The term *stereotype* is the oversimplification and overgeneralization of a particular group of individuals based on few characteristics. It is an ill-informed knowledge that may include both positive and negative attributes of the group. For example, a stereotype exists that Asian American students do well in school, excel at math, but do not have the capacity to be good managers. *Prejudice* is a negative attitude that is based on the stereotypical knowledge. This attitude is one's belief that may or may not turn into discriminatory actions. However, when one acts out the prejudice and violates the civil rights or human rights of any individuals, then that is *discrimination.* An employer who has a prejudice against Asian Americans as managers, hurtful as it may seem, simply has a personally held negative attitude. When the employer refuses to hire or to promote any qualified Asian Americans as managers, then discrimination has taken place. When the discriminatory behaviors are being act out in an organized manner at the systemwide or societal level, a situation of *oppression* has occurred. The happenings of discrimination and oppression have forced the situation beyond personal virtue and then become legal, social, and civic concerns. (p. 27)

Discrimination involves behaviors that are acquired or learned. Efforts aimed at challenging stereotypes and questioning one's prejudices are the initial step in overcoming discrimination. At the micro and meso levels, there are many effective inductive learning processes. Facilitating opportunities for individual discourse among people of different backgrounds, promoting open-mindedness in interactions, individualizing each person within the cultural context of the person, and discovering each individual's personhood through improved exchanges and experience among diverse people are just some of the examples of such efforts.

A social worker who works with youth gangs plans to organize a treatment group in a youth detention center. It is very likely that the group will include members from rival ethnic gangs. The social worker's obvious first step would be to control or minimize the risk of having violent conflicts in group. However, the worker would be most interested in attaining the likely benefits of mutual sharing, and hopefully improving the understanding and acceptance of each member as a worthy individual. One of the group objectives would be to provide planned opportunities for group members to have genuine dialogues, to challenge old prejudices, to identify common grounds, and to develop new understanding of oneself and others.

At the macro level, social policies that aim to prohibit discrimination and promote mutual respect and understanding in society need to be continuously updated and improved. Human service providers need to ensure the provision of programs and services that promote and implement such policies. In some situations, compromising strategies may not work, and confrontational social actions such as petition, protest, or demonstration may be needed. These more aggressive actions call the seriousness of the problem to the attention of the public, the authorities, and the discriminators, as well as the discriminated.

Part of the difficulty in overcoming discrimination is the denial and ignorance from both sides of the issue. The interactions, if any, of both sides are often defensive, emotionally charged, and political. In this situation, productive exchanges are nearly impossible, and the interactions are more confrontational and argumentative. As suggested earlier, education and provision of opportunities to have productive exchanges on individual, small-group, and macro levels can help facilitate genuine dialogue. These incremental gains in promoting mutual understanding and overcoming discrimination are small but important. These steps allow inductively developed individual discourse and build shared tradition and experience. Only by learning the individuation of the counterpart and understanding how culture and other backgrounds affect the person and his or her significant others can true appreciation of diversity be achieved.

Similarly, collective group and family issues also need to be understood within appropriate cultural frameworks. During the 1990 Los Angeles riot, African Americans and Korean Americans were caught at odds with each other. Their conflicts were made vivid by the news reporting of looting and armed defense of businesses and properties. Some African Americans made the accusation that new Korean immigrants had taken over their neighborhoods and businesses but returned no jobs, opportunities, or community improvements. Korean Americans had their own complaints, including some that involved cultural stereotypes and personal virtues. Some leaders from both ethnic communities, including many social workers in human service agencies and community organizations, saw the dangers of such senseless accusations and decided to seriously address this issue. Through many individual and group dialogues, exchanges of personal and family stories of struggle and survival, and knowing of each other (at least those who participated) as a person rather than a member of another ethnic group, the residents were able to develop the common understanding to construct agreements on future cooperation and partnership.

The following sample questions are designed to help one to start exploring the experience of discrimination:

- Can you tell me what it is like for you to be the only minority person in the room?
- Does being a minority person increase your sense of need for personal security?
- Does being a minority person make you a person of an oppressed group?
- What is it like being a person from an oppressed group?
- What kind of behaviors would you consider as discriminatory actions toward you?
- What does having the experience of being discriminated against mean to you?
- In facing discrimination, how and where do you get and maintain your strength?
- Looking back, have you been the person who discriminates?

Learning about Change Strategies

The social work profession is a value-laden one. Although there is a lack of common agreement among social workers about the complete list of these values, respect for human dignity, mutual responsibility among people, and belief in the possibility of change in people and systems are usually cited as the most basic social work values. Change can take place at three different levels: knowledge, attitude, and behavior.

Knowledge is about what one knows, attitude is about what one believes, and behavior is about one's actions. Although it is common to assume that knowledge change will bring about attitude and behavioral change, in reality this may not be the case. To a certain extent, they exist independently. Take smoking tobacco as an example. It is common knowledge that tobacco use causes many health problems. It is, however, surprising to discover how many health care providers stand around the back doors of hospitals and medical clinics taking their break and smoking cigarettes. When asked about the dangers of tobacco use, many of them have expert knowledge about the damages of tobacco use and the related health problems. They also have a rather negative attitude toward such use. They are, however, behaviorally having trouble quitting smoking, although they have tried various smoking cessation methods over a long period of time.

Discrimination is as evil and damaging to society as tobacco use is to one's health. Educational programs, workshops, and group discussions may help people develop better cultural awareness and sensitivity through improved knowledge about the different cultural groups and their experiences. However, this is only the first step toward positive change. The change needs to be more than just a change in knowledge, attitude, or behavior; rather, it must be in all three areas: improved understanding of the lives and realities (knowledge) of other individuals and cultural groups; educated opinions, feelings, and mind-sets (attitudes) toward those individuals and groups; and proper manners and interactions (behavior) with people of different backgrounds. Behavioral change without attitude and knowledge change is just a performance of "political correctness." Knowledge and attitude changes without behavioral change, or knowledge and behavioral changes without attitude change, represent both the incongruence and the inertia of change within the person. Social work students are expected to take classes to learn more about human diversity, challenge their own systems of belief and values to expand their perspectives, and acquire proper skills in working with clients and colleagues of various backgrounds.

Isaac Newton's laws of motion in physics, although they appear to be unrelated to social work and to the issue of discrimination, are indeed quite appropriate. Newton's first law of motion states that an object at rest will remain at rest and an object in motion will continue in motion at the same speed in the absence of any interaction with something else. This property of matter, in which an object is disinclined to change its state of rest or its uniform motion, is known as inertia. Basically, objects will do what they have been doing unless they are acted upon by an outside force. Newton's third law says that when an object exerts a force on another object, the second object exerts on the first a force of the same magnitude but in the opposite direction. Applying these concepts to the strategies for change, we need to have forces that produce friction and that push and pull to transform inertia and create motions of change (first law). Meanwhile, the application of such forces should be carefully calculated so they do not become counterproductive (third law).

Although Newton made breakthroughs for science with his new understanding of the physical world, he might not have intended to apply his framework to understanding human beings and minds. The independence, autonomy, interaction and networking, interdependence, emotion, and particularly intelligence and the ability to reflect and to develop insight may be the forces that generate motion in human lives. The belief in human capacity to make change is the very basic view that gives reason and hope for the practice of social work interventions.

Another major consideration for change is that currently many diversity promotions treat "multiculturalism as merely a 'practice' extension of the minority perspective" (Gould, 1995). In fact, we should consider changing this to a "framework that can help all groups in society orient their thinking at a transcultural level" (p. 202). For social workers, this is more than a practice issue; this is a framework of thinking and an issue of change that demands a paradigm shift.

Change strategies via inductive learning take place simultaneously and independently in multiple areas (knowledge, attitude, and behavior) and at multiple levels (micro, meso, and macro). Individuals, families, cultural groups, communities, and society as a whole all need to be involved in the transformation. There is no designed starting point or scope for the initiation and implementation of change. We have witnessed individual struggles, such as those of Cesar Chavez and Martin Luther King, Jr., transform the nation. As well, we have seen the efforts of endless numbers of families, communities, and organizations in promoting understanding and appreciation of diversity through participation and policy change. We also have observed the implementation of some government legislation and social policies designed to bring about social justice and fairness. All these changes demand the participation, learning, and understanding of people who are willing to share and to shape their tradition, experience, and common sense with the input of valid research data to gain improvements in what we know and how we view, and interact with one another.

TOOLS FOR STUDENT LEARNING 8.2

An Exercise on Diversity, Discrimination, and Social Change: A Self-Assessment

The purpose of this exercise is to provide an opportunity for students to perform a self-assessment of knowledge, attitudes, and behaviors toward different oppressed populations in our society (Rothman, 1999, pp. 38–40). This assessment gives the student an opportunity to further understand how he or she relates to other groups, both minority and the dominant. It also helps students to understand discrimination and helps to set a stage for making plans for change. To do this exercise, students are to fill out each one of the cells within the grid. Most importantly, students need to complete the My Next Steps column. Students should complete this grid on their own. If it is appropriate and under instructor supervision, students may form a group meeting to review and reflect on their responses on this grid. Additionally, students should explore individual and collective ways to promote positive social change.

The following is an example of the use of this grid.

My name is Ali. I am a 23-year-old ethnic Palestinian and an American. My parents came to the United States from Jordan in 1971. My father brought his family to Alabama, and he worked as an engineer for a steel mill. I was born in the United States and consider myself as both an American and a Palestinian. I was raised in a middle-class suburban neighborhood. Most of my friends from school have been White. I also know a few other Palestinians through our small Islamic mosque. I was a fair student in high school and was the starting quarterback for the school football team. I have had several girlfriends, and all of them were White.

In filling out the Self-Assessment Grid, I identify the following as part of the oppressed groups: (Race) African Americans and Middle Easterners, (Ethnicity or national origin) Palestinian Americans, and (Social class) people from the lower social class. Although I am part of the oppressed groups, I have been socialized more with people from the dominant group. I have had several African American friends and teammates; however, I know very little about them and their culture. In fact,

I have not been exactly open and receptive toward the African American people and culture. I consider myself bicultural. Yet, often I feel I don't belong and am not welcomed by either the Palestinian or the American culture. Many of my friends are White, but I have also experienced the strongest rejections from them. My middle-class family background shields me from understanding the effects of social class and poverty. I want to critically evaluate my attitudes toward diversity, and plan to actively learn more about African American and my own cultures.

Diversity Self-Assessment Grid

Categories	I am a . . .	Who is (are) the oppressed group(s)?	Who is (are) the dominant group(s)?	What is my knowledge about the oppressed and dominant groups?	What are my attitudes toward the oppressed and the dominant groups?	What have been my behaviors toward the oppressed and dominant groups?	My next steps . . .

A Partial View of Ali's Diversity Self-Assessment Grid

Categories	I am a . . .	Who is (are) the oppressed group(s)?	Who is (are) the dominant group(s)?	What is my knowledge about the oppressed and dominant groups?	What are my attitudes toward the oppressed and the dominant groups?	What have been my behaviors toward the oppressed and dominant groups?	My next steps . . .
Race	Middle Easterner	Middle Easterners and Blacks	Whites and Blacks	I know a lot about Whites, but little about Blacks	Middle Easterners are misunderstood. Blacks have been oppressed. Whites are okay.	I have friends of all races. Most of them are White, and a few of them are Blacks. So far, I have only dated White girls.	Learn more about the Blacks and my own race.
Ethnicity or national origin	Jordanian-Palestinian American	Foreign-borns and their children	American-born Blacks and Whites	I know a lot about Whites and the new immigrant families. I don't think I know enough about Blacks.	I think the foreign-borns are being misunderstood and being discriminated against by the local-born Blacks and whites.	I was not quite sure about my self-identity as a Palestinian. The Blacks and Whites have been fair to me. I also treat them with respect.	Better understand the multicultural reality of the United States. Become more active in my mosque.
Social class	Middle	Lower	Middle	Hard work determines one's future.	Lower-class people do not work hard enough. If they do, many of them will become middle class.	I offer help to lower-class people who have worked and tried hard themselves. I firmly believe that the middle class is the backbone of America.	Find ways to promote work ethics and to work with the strengths of the lower and the middle classes.

QUALITATIVE RESEARCH AND SOCIAL WORK EDUCATION

There is a strong case for qualitative research as an integral part of social work education. Cultural competence hinges on research-oriented practice and practice-oriented research in multicultural settings from the inductive learning perspective. In this chapter, we have discussed how qualitative approaches enhance our multicultural practice and knowledge base. Examples have illustrated how inductive qualitative approaches help social workers to construct an emic (culture-specific) understanding of client reality and lead students, educators, and practitioners to learn from clients and help them feel accepted, respected, and heard in the learning and helping process.

The inductive qualitative approach to research is especially consonant with social work's emphasis on "starting where the client is" (Gilgun, 1994). Not only is this a practice dictum, but it is also an inductive learning principle for research. Rather than initiating client or research interviewee contact with a preformed hypothesis about client or interviewee dynamics, the inductive practitioner–researcher establishes rapport, tunes into client or interviewee strengths, and utilizes communication skills in guiding the process and letting the client's or the interviewee's story unfold. The storytelling process becomes an empowering event: an interviewee in a research project becomes a *teacher* rather than a *subject* and experiences a sense of contribution and connectedness (Bein, 1994). Ultimately, the inductive practitioner–researcher seeks to minimize "the extent to which constraints are placed on output(s)" (Patton, 1990, p. 41). Rather than asking a client or interviewee to respond "never," "sometimes," or "always" to a given question framed by the practitioner–researcher's theoretical orientation, the practitioner–researcher engages the client or interviewee in a joint process of discovery where an infinite number of data possibilities are present.

The empowerment and social justice traditions embedded in social work demand that practitioner–researchers provide opportunities for clients to "give voice" to their experiences. Hartman (1994) exhorts the social work profession to enhance the opportunities for knowledge—to listen to the stories that arise out of practice with clients, and to learn about their wisdom, lived experience, and vision of the world.

SUMMARY

This chapter provided a framework for learning based on a foundation of inductive research and respect for cultural strengths. This framework was then applied to social work practice, and a process of inductive practice was advanced. The chapter further discussed the utilities and strategies of using inductive learning to understand diversity and to create change. This chapter discussed the practitioner–researcher's tasks within this process and provided case examples. Finally, it was argued that qualitative research makes an important contribution to the social work knowledge base and is consonant with social work perspectives emphasizing client uniqueness and empowerment. The culturally competent practitioner–researcher may want to consult the literature cited in this chapter to gain a deeper understanding of various qualitative research traditions.

PART THREE

Culturally and Ethnically Diverse Groups

Cultural and ethnic diverse groups comprise what is called populations-at-risk in the Council on Social Work Education's *Educational Policy and Accreditation Standards* (EPAS). The focus of this section of the text is on cultural and ethnic groups: primarily First Nations Peoples, African Americans, Latino Americans, and Asian Americans. Chapters also discuss gender and sexual orientation, specifically women of color and gay and lesbian persons of color. These two groups, which have received minimal coverage in the social work and related helping professional literature, are included here to foster further reading, reflection, and research on them.

The discussion of these six groups brings together a variety of knowledge, expertise, and insight from a talented group of social work educators/scholars across the United States who have made recognized contributions to the understanding of these populations. There is a uniformity of common themes in these chapters that bind them together; each chapter addresses cultural competence, diversity, historical and current oppression, cultural awareness, knowledge acquisition, skill development, inductive learning, and social and economic justice.

At the same time, there is deep regret that space has made it impossible to cover other diverse populations such as the elderly, people with disabilities, immigrants and refugees, gays and lesbians in general, and the religious or spiritual person. The reader is encouraged to pursue information about these groups in current texts such as the following: Appleby, G. A., Colon, E., and Hamilton, J. (Eds.), *Diversity, Oppression, and Social Functioning: Person-in-Environment Assessment and Intervention* (Boston: Allyn & Bacon, 2001); Balgopal, P. R. (Ed.), *Social Work Practice with Immigrants and Refugees* (New York: Columbia University Press, 2000); and Van Hook, M., Hugen, M., and Aguilar, M. (Eds.), *Spirituality within Religious Traditions in Social Work Practice* (Pacific Grove, CA: Brooks/Cole Thomson Learning, 2001).

The populations-at-risk standards of the 2002 Council on Social Work Education, *Educational Policy and Accreditation Standards*, have been our markers for this second section.

- Contributing factors that constitute groups being at risk
- Group membership influencing access to resources
- The dynamics of risk factors and responsive and productive strategies to redress them

We hope you will find that these chapters address the concerns of CSWE's diverse populations.

253

CHAPTER NINE

Cultural Competence with First Nations Peoples

HILARY N. WEAVER

Many First Nations Peoples have an image of a social worker as someone from a government bureaucracy who takes children away, not only from parents but also from the indigenous community. The child is then raised by a White family with no knowledge of culture, traditions, or an indigenous identity. In this sense, social workers threaten more than a particular family. If we forget our cultures, we will no longer exist as distinct people. Thus, social workers are perceived as a threat to the very existence of First Nations Peoples. Although it is common for clients from many cultural groups to hold negative perceptions of social workers, the social worker who serves Native American clients is likely to face distinct challenges.

This chapter presents information that social workers need to know in order to provide culturally competent services to First Nations Peoples. The chapter begins with a discussion of defining cultural competence with First Nations Peoples, including an understanding of the vast diversity present in this population and an overview of key historical and contemporary issues. The chapter presents information on the social service needs of Native people including the knowledge and skills important for serving this population. This information will help readers not only to provide culturally competent clinical services but also to use social work skills to advocate for social and economic justice.

Before moving further into a discussion of cultural competence with First Nations Peoples, it is important to clarify the terminology used in this chapter. There are many different terms for the indigenous people of North America including *American Indian*, *Native American*, and *First Nations Peoples*. There is no consensus about which term is best, yet some Native people have strong preferences for one term over the others. These terms all include many different groups of distinct people. Use of such broad terms tends to obscure diversity. Generally, when speaking of a particular Native person or nation (such as Comanche or Oneida), it is best to use the specific label used by those people rather than a more general term such as *Native American*. In the context of this chapter, which covers a variety of Native groups, the terms *Native American*, *Native*, *indigenous*, and *First Nations Peoples* are used interchangeably.

DEFINING CULTURAL COMPETENCE WITH FIRST NATIONS PEOPLES

The need for cultural competence has been identified as an ethical imperative by the National Association of Social Workers in its Code of Ethics (NASW, 1999). In fact, some scholars have determined that competent practice and culturally competent practice are so intertwined that it is impossible to be competent without being culturally competent (Coleman, 1998). The Council on Social Work Education (CSWE) has also recognized the importance of cultural competence and requires that content on diverse populations be included in all accredited social work programs (CSWE, 2000). Clearly, a belief exists within the social work profession that cultural competence is important, yet operationalizing this concept can be challenging.

In current social work literature, knowledge, skills, and values/attitudes are consistently identified as important components of cultural competence. Until recently, these components had not been clearly operationalized or empirically tested. At this time the profession is taking an important step in moving beyond practice wisdom as researchers begin to identify specific knowledge, skills, and values/attitudes associated with cultural competence with particular populations. Additionally, significant diversity exists among First Nations Peoples, and working with different Native groups may require different elements of cultural competence.

Cultural competence with First Nations Peoples involves blending knowledge about specific First Nations cultures, history, and contemporary realities with social work skills and knowledge. Additionally, social workers must be self-reflective, nonjudgmental, and willing to learn from clients. This will enable social workers to assess clients within their cultural context and to choose culturally appropriate interventions.

Cultural competence, a necessity in direct practice with First Nations Peoples, is also critical in other levels of practice. Administrators and policy makers must apply the principles of cultural competence in order to ensure social justice throughout all aspects of social services. Cultural competence includes an understanding of how organizational or institutional forces can enhance or impede services to diverse populations (Sue et al., 1998). For example, cost containment strategies such as managed care may undermine the work of culturally competent helping professionals by limiting the type and amount of service provided (Abe-Kim & Takeuchi, 1996).

Green (1999) asserts the following: "The service provider who is culturally competent can deliver professional services in a way that is congruent with behavior and expectations normative for a given community and that are adapted to suit the specific needs of individuals and families from that community" (p. 87). In order to strive for cultural competence with First Nations clients, social workers must develop a basic understanding of these culturally based behaviors and expectations. Cultural competence also involves a recognition of macrolevel problems and ongoing social injustice. Activism and advocacy are key skills that culturally competent social workers can use to confront problems such as violation of treaty rights, threats to sovereignty, contamination of the environment, and lack of adequate housing. Social workers also have a role to play in educating the large government bureaucracies that serve First Nations Peoples and in educating social work agencies in order to make their programs more culturally appropriate and effective with this population.

This chapter frequently cites the findings of a study of Native Americans in the field of social work (educators, social workers, and students) and their beliefs about culturally competent practice. This study sought to identify what specific knowledge, skills, and values/attitudes are needed for culturally competent social work practice with First Nations Peoples. (See Weaver, 1999b, for a detailed description of this study.) As both Native people and social work professionals, the respondents were in a unique position to begin to identify the specific components of culturally competent practice with First Nations Peoples. The respondents emphasized that social workers need to be knowledgeable in four broad areas: (1) diversity; (2) history; (3) culture; and (4) contemporary realities of Native people. Likewise, they identified the importance of having strong skills in general and of having, in particular, containment skills such as having patience and allowing silence. Culturally competent social workers also need to bring certain values and attitudes to their work with indigenous people. These values and attitudes include (1) helper wellness and self-awareness; (2) humility and willingness to learn; (3) respect, open-mindedness, and a nonjudgmental attitude; and (4) social justice.

UNDERSTANDING DIVERSITY AMONG FIRST NATIONS PEOPLES FOR ASSESSMENT, PLANNING, PRACTICE, AND RESEARCH

Social workers need to understand the vast diversity that exists among First Nations Peoples. The 2000 U.S. Census identified 4.1 million Native Americans in the United States (1.5 percent of the population). This includes 1.6 million individuals who identified themselves as both Native American and another ethnic group (Ogunwole, 2002). Over 500 distinct Native American nations exist within the boundaries of the United States. These nations differ in terms of language, religion, social structure, political structure, and many other aspects of their cultures. Some of these nations are quite small and have fewer than 100 members, whereas 5 nations (the Cherokee, Navajo/Dine, Choctaw, Lakota/Dakota/Nakota, and Chippewa/Ojibway) have populations of over 100,000. Additionally, many immigrants from Latin America identify primarily as First Nations People. The census identified more than 100,000 Latin American indigenous people living in the United States in 2000. These six different groups accounted for 42 percent of all Native Americans in the United States (Ogunwole, 2002).

Substantial variation among Native Americans exists in other areas such as land holdings. Some nations like the Navajo/Dine of the southwestern United States have a large reservation, and inhabitants may live in very isolated areas. Other Native nations like the Cayuga of New York state have no reservation land base at all. Indeed, the perception that most Native people live on reservations has not been true for some time. Less than one fourth of First Nations Peoples live on reservations.

Native Americans vary substantially in their income. Some Native people, most notably Native people in the northeastern United States and Southeastern Canada, like the Mohawks, have entered in substantial numbers the well-paid profession of iron working and are largely responsible for building many major structures such as the bridges around New York City (Mitchell, 1991). Some Native people also receive per capita payments from casino revenues. On the whole, though, Native Americans are some of the poorest populations in the United States. In 2004, 21.9 percent of Native Americans lived below the poverty level. This was even higher for those who identified soley as Native American (25.1 percent) than those having heritage from another ethnic group as well. Although there has been some improvement over time, the poverty rate has fluctuated instead of following a steady trend. For example, the poverty rate for Native Americans in 1987 was 28.8 percent, dipped to 23.9 percent in 1989, rose to 31.3 percent in 1991, dipped to 23.6 percent in 1993, and rose to 31.0 percent in 1995 (U.S. Bureau of the Census, 2005).

Extensive diversity also exists among people within Native nations in terms of their cultural identity. Some people are very knowledgeable about and grounded in their indigenous culture, whereas others are not. Sometimes this is based on choices an individual has made; however, it is more often the result of decades of damaging U.S. policies designed to assimilate Native people. These policies were deliberate in their attempts to eradicate indigenous cultures. Many people lost their ability to speak their language and lost touch with their cultural traditions when they were forcibly taken away from their community and sent to government or church-run boarding schools. This sort of cultural loss impaired their ability to pass on cultural traditions to their children and left many Native people with limited knowledge of their indigenous heritage.

Individuals also may be more or less grounded in their indigenous culture at different stages of their lives. Waters (1990) found that it is common for people to report their ethnicity differently at different points in their life. This may be particularly true for people of mixed heritage. Many indigenous people who have grown up with limited knowledge of their culture take steps to learn more and claim their heritage as they get older.

Given the vast diversity that exists among Native people, it is important that social workers examine cultural affiliation as part of a basic assessment. Only an individual client knows what his or her cultural identity means to him or her, and the social worker must take steps to seek out this information. An important first step is to identify whether a client is a First Nations person and, if so, his or her nation. It is not always possible to identify a Native person by physical appearance or name. There are many Native people who appear phenotypically White, Latino, African American, or Asian. Social workers often may not even be aware they are working with a Native client unless they ask or the client volunteers this information. Likewise, the social worker who expects all Native people to have colorful names like in the movies is likely to overlook the fact that some clients are Native American. Indeed, many Native people have names like Smith and Johnson, and the names White and Hill are particularly common in some First Nations communities.

Damaging Hollywood images have objectified indigenous people and have promoted stereotypes. Thus, social workers may have developed certain ideas about what indigenous people look like or what their values are. Rather than being guided by stereotypes, social workers must be open to understanding how their clients identify as Native people and what is meaningful to them. Additionally, social workers should be prepared to actively challenge damaging stereotypical images like that of the "drunken Indian" that are used to label Native people and deny their basic humanity and strengths.

A number of assessment tools have been applied with Native clients, but social workers should be cautious in using such tools. Some of these standardized instruments were initially developed for use with other populations. For many reasons, people may or may not speak a language associated with their cultural group. It is important to challenge the assumption that people have given up speaking their language as part of a free choice to assimilate. Indigenous people have been subjected to large-scale federal policies designed to eradicate language and culture. Although there is certainly a link between language and culture, it is a complex one. It would be inappropriate to assume that a Native person who does not speak an indigenous language does not value or have a strong connection to his or her culture. Indeed, social workers should be sensitive to the fact that many indigenous people feel awkward when they cannot speak their indigenous languages, and this may have an impact on their sense of self.

Another concern with standardized cultural assessment tools is that many still place culture on a continuum; for example, if you are more grounded in one culture, you must be less so in another. Scholars who focus on cultural identity have begun to move beyond linear models to orthogonal models. Although *orthogonal* is a term used commonly in geometry to identify a right angle, social scientists increasingly use it to identify factors that exist independently. In other words, a strong connection to one culture does not limit an individual's ability to be strongly grounded in other cultures. Studies of First Nations youth have found that it is common for them to identify with more than one culture, thus supporting theories of orthogonal cultural identification (Oetting & Beauvais, 1991; Weaver, 1996).

Given the limitations of the standardized tools available for assessing culture in First Nations clients, social workers may wish to avoid using these instruments or at least to use them with caution. Culture can be assessed in a less structured manner. The following are some possible areas of inquiry for exploring culture. Information about culture may be obtained, in part, by inquiring about family history. For example, it may be revealing to know about family members that were placed in boarding schools (a common policy through the 1970s) and what this has meant for the client's ability to continue cultural traditions. Additionally, it can be helpful to know whether the client follows traditional spiritual practices, pan-Indian practices such as the Native American church, or is affiliated with a Christian denomination. Choices about how children are raised and the client's relationships with extended family and other members of the Native American community also can reveal information about how a client experiences his or her culture. As the social worker continues to work with the client, issues of values, behavior, and priorities that emerge during sessions also will reflect aspects of the client's culture.

It is important to incorporate diversity in planning both for individual clients and for programs. All planning must be done based on the assessment in order for it to be relevant. Well-meaning service providers are likely to miss the mark if they attempt to incorporate diversity without considering the particular needs of the client or client population. For example, one midwestern social service agency with many clients from the First Nations of the Great Plains region decided to incorporate traditional practices in their interventions. The staff were astonished when in spite of their efforts, the vast majority of clients left the agency before completing the program. In hindsight, the staff realized that although the interventions contained material that was culturally appropriate for the people of that region, the clients in this particular program were all alienated from their cultural heritage and, in fact, felt even more inadequate when presented with the culturally infused interventions (Gurnee, Vigil, Krill-Smith, & Crowley, 1990). In planning for interventions and programs, it is critical to assess the level of cultural connection of clients and to find an intervention that is a good match.

Although extensive diversity exists among First Nations clients, some theoretical models may be more appropriate than others for guiding interventions. Models that tend to focus heavily on the individual may not be a good fit given the importance placed on extended family and community connections in many Native cultures. Interventions that are based on systems theories that emphasize the importance of the social environment are likely to be most effective.

It is helpful not only to acknowledge the importance of family and community members but also to incorporate them in the work. Connecting youth with elders can reinforce both their cultural identity and positive behaviors that serve as protective factors against substance abuse and other social problems. Elders are typically perceived to be strong and vibrant members of their communities who are able to pass on the core elements of culture to others. Angell, Kurz and Gottfried (1997) give a poignent example of how a social worker assisted a troubled adolescent who had attempted suicide by connecting him with a respected elder who helped him become more grounded in his culture. Additionally, helping elders to reestablish or strengthen meaningful roles in their communities can be therapeutic. One urban First Nations social agency had elders make beaded red ribbons that were later sold to promote awareness and raise funds for HIV prevention. This task gave the elders a way to make a difference in their community while using traditional skills.

Social workers must give thoughtful consideration to the best ways to reach culturally diverse clients. Techniques that have proved effective with some Native people will not necessarily work with others. Schafer and McIlwaine (1992) found techniques that worked well for interviewing Seminole children who may have experienced sexual abuse were inappropriate and ineffective when applied to sexually abused Navajo children. Interviewers successfully engaged Seminole children and encouraged them to talk about what happened to them by stating that elders had already been notified of the allegations and urged the children to cooperate fully in the investigation. This approach backfired with Navajo children who were shocked that investigators would have talked with elders and refused to cooperate for fear that information would quickly spread throughout their community and damage their reputations. When interviewing Navajo and Hopi youth, it is helpful to respect personal space by sitting slightly off to the side and avoiding eye contact. It is also helpful to know the timing of ceremonies to decide when best to conduct an interview and to use these as markers to identify when an event happened.

Because Native Americans are a relatively small population, researchers rarely have adequate samples to examine intertribal differences. Overlooking diversity among Native Americans results in distorted data regarding strengths and challenges faced by indigenous people. One example of this can be found in the research on First Nations Peoples and the use of alcohol. Substantial variation exists in the drinking patterns of people from different Native nations. Men and women also tend to have very different drinking patterns. Likewise, drinking tends to be prominent in some age groups and not in others. Unfortunately, when researchers report only findings about drinking and Native Americans as a general category, it obscures the fact that alcohol abuse is more of a problem in some nations than others and that it tends to be most problematic for young men. Although clearly methodological challenges exist in getting an adequate sample of Native people to examine these differences, if researchers continue to treat indigenous people as a monolithic group, they will contribute to stereotypical images—in this case, the perception that alcohol presents a widespread problem for all Native people. This stereotype of the drunken Indian perpetuates the belief that indigenous people are biologically predetermined to alcoholism and that they are helpless, hopeless, passive victims.

Social workers and researchers must move beyond stereotypes to see the unique aspects of First Nations cultures and peoples. For clinicians, this means keeping an open mind and examining all the various factors that contribute to a client's use of alcohol rather than assuming that all Native people are prone to alcoholism. Likewise, the researcher should frame research questions and choose methodologies that are not based on the assumption that alcohol is a problem in all First Nations communities.

The diversity among Native American groups and among people within these groups cannot be overemphasized. Significant differences continue to exist among the people that fall into the general category "Native American." Just as it would be inappropriate to assume that all Europeans are the same, it is often inappropriate to generalize from one Native group to another. A Miccosuki person is likely to be quite different from a Klamath person, just as a Greek person is different than a Belgian. These differences must be considered in all aspects of social work practice, from clinical work to policy development to research.

TOOLS FOR STUDENT LEARNING 9.1

The Case of Melissa Two Bulls

You work at an agency that specializes in counseling family issues, and you have just received a referral of a new client, Melissa Two Bulls. The referral information indicates that one of her three children is currently in foster care because of charges of negligence related to her drinking. The family is to be reunified shortly. The focus of your work will be to help the family through this transition and to help Melissa develop parenting skills.

1. How will you assess the root cause of the family's difficulties?

2. How will you determine how to integrate culture in your interventions?

3. What empirical support is available to support your choice of an intervention plan?

4. Historically, many Native children have been removed from their families and the families have been charged with neglect because of cultural misunderstand-ings. How will you know if there was institutional bias in the removal of Melissa's children?

5. If you determine that institutional bias played a role in the removal of Melissa's children, what steps can you take to change the system so this does not happen again?

6. Develop a plan for a single-subject research design to evaluate the effectiveness of your work.

RECOLLECTING FIRST NATIONS PEOPLES' HISTORICAL AND CURRENT OPPRESSION EXPERIENCES

In order to effectively work with First Nations Peoples, it is important to have an under-standing of the historical events that have led to the circumstances of today. Within many Native American cultures, there is a sense of existing within a time continuum. The people of today maintain strong connections to ancestors, and contemporary actions are under-taken with future generations in mind. The concept of Seven Generations is present in many First Nations cultures, although it is defined somewhat differently by different people. For some, the ancestors seven generations ago were planning for the people of today, and these plans are the reason there is still land, language, and culture left for indigenous people. The people of today have the responsibility to ensure that the needs of future generations will be met in the same way. Some Native people interpret the Seven Generations concept as looking back to the ancestors three generations ago, looking forward to the children of the next three generations, with the current generation in the middle. Either way, indigenous people have a sense of being related to other generations through a time continuum. This sense of responsibility for future generations is a frequent message in prevention programs such as those that encourage abstinence from alcohol during pregnancy.

The ancestral connection felt by many First Nations Peoples is important to be aware of in understanding the importance of history. Some scholars have suggested that Native Americans have never been able to adequately mourn the events that happened to ancestors, and this unresolved grief is the root of many contemporary social problems (Brave Heart-Jordan & DeBruyn, 1995). Historical events that may be relevant to a particular client's case situation will vary by individual and by tribal affiliation; however, the following key events are likely to be relevant to many First Nations clients.

After Europeans came to the Americas, disease epidemics devastated many Native nations. Many of these epidemics were not the result of unfortunate circumstances but were the result of deliberate acts of germ warfare perpetrated on indigenous people. The fact that such devastating diseases were deliberately spread by both the British and Americans has been clearly documented (Stiffarm & Lane, 1992). The decimation of Native populations, by some estimations the loss of 95 percent to 99 percent of all indigenous people in what is now the United States (Stiffarm & Lane, 1992), occurred largely because of diseases such as smallpox, measles, and cholera (Claymore & Taylor, 1989; Native American Leadership Commission on Health and AIDS, 1994). The intergenerational memory of the effect of disease on Native people helps support a climate of suspicion around contemporary issues such as HIV/AIDS. Some First Nations Peoples fear that HIV/AIDS will have an even more devastating effect on their communities than previous epidemics. Additionally, some Native people feel that HIV/AIDS has been deliberately spread or that promising treatments have been purposefully withheld in First Nations communities.

Much has been written about the use of alcohol as a tool of oppression and a way to cheat indigenous people of their land and other natural resources. Although not all Native communities have been equally affected, alcohol has had a devastating effect on some Native communities and is often linked to other social problems like violence, suicide, and sexual abuse (Bachman, 1992).

One of the most devastating parts of the history of colonization and oppression of indigenous people in the United States and Canada has only recently begun to receive significant attention. Beginning in the late 19th century and extending into the late 20th century, it was federal policy to separate Native children from their families and to educate them in boarding schools that were often hundreds or thousands of miles from their home communities. The slogan of these schools, "Kill the Indian: Save the man," reflected the belief of the times that all cultural, linguistic, and spiritual practices of First Nations Peoples must be eradicated in order for them to be civilized and have a place within White society. The mission of the schools was essentially cultural genocide. Often, children were taken to these schools for years at a time, where they were beaten for speaking their languages or for following their spiritual practices. During this time, they had limited contact with their home communities. When they eventually left school, they no longer were able to speak to their relatives or fit into their home communities. Growing up in institutions with no models of parenting other than the severe discipline of the military or religious personnel who ran the schools led to generations of Native people with no parenting skills (Morrisette, 1994). The physical and sexual abuse that was pervasive in some boarding schools is now replicated with succeeding generations in many First Nations communities. Likewise, the devastating effects of the schools have left many Native people with a severe mistrust of education and other dominant-society institutions.

National policies of relocation and termination have also had negative effects on indigenous communities. Ever since first contact with Europeans, Native people have been forced by warfare and federal policies to leave their traditional lands. The most famous removal was that of the indigenous people of the Southeast and their forced march on the "Trail of Tears" in the 1830s to what is now Oklahoma. Likewise, the people of the Southwest were subject to removal on a forced march called the Longest Walk. Since the inception of the reservation system, the federal government has forced First Nations Peoples onto land a fraction of the size of their traditional territories, only to have some reservations reduced in size or eliminated all together at a later date.

Beginning in the 1950s, the United States entered what is known as the "termination era," a time when the federal government took steps to legally end the existence of many Native nations like the Klamath and the Menominee. Through legal maneuvers, the United States revoked its promises made in treaties and took land previously set aside as reservations. Thus, members of terminated nations lost all access to social and health benefits that had been previously guaranteed to First Nations Peoples under treaties and other laws.

It is important to remember that Native nations are recognized as sovereign by the U.S. government, as acknowledged in all treaty agreements. According to the U.S. Constitution, treaties are the supreme law of the land and are not subject to modification by subsequent legislation. Sovereignty means that indigenous people retain their own governments with the ability to make laws and policies to govern themselves. Although existing within the physical boundaries of the United States, Native nations often have their own courts, schools, and social welfare systems. Thus, Native Americans are not simply an ethnic group. In addition to cultural distinctiveness, they have legal distinction from other groups in the United States. Although some federal laws infringe upon and limit sovereignty, in most cases, Native nations retain as many or more rights to self-governance as states and localities retain.

Oppression and violation of the rights of First Nations Peoples is not a thing of the past. In the 1970s, the Alaska Native Claims Settlement Act (ANCSA) combined some of the most devastating parts of earlier federal policies and applied them to Native Alaskans. The status and sovereignty of these First Nations Peoples was severely eroded by legally deeming nations to be corporations with stockholders. Native people born after 1971 were not even entitled to be stockholders, thus effectively ending the future (legally speaking) of indigenous people in Alaska (Churchill & Morris, 1992). By establishing a cutoff date for new stockholders, the federal government was able to limit future claims for land and other resources. As a result of ANCSA, First Nations Peoples in Alaska have less legal recourse than other Native Americans. Some questions have even been raised about whether major pieces of federal legislation like the Indian Child Welfare Act (ICWA) apply to Native people covered by ANCSA, because legally they are no longer defined as Native nations. Fortunately, most social policies continue to treat Native people in Alaska as having the same rights as First Nations Peoples in the rest of the country; however, ANCSA opened the door to the possibility of legally sanctioned loss of access for Native Alaskans to all Native-specific social programs.

The challenges to indigenous people continue as conservative, reactionary Americans try to deny indigenous people their inherent rights to traditional means of subsistence such as fishing, whaling, and gathering medicines. In some regions of the United States like Washington state, Michigan, and Wisconsin where the battles over traditional subsistence have been heated, it is common to see signs and bumper stickers advocating violence such as "Spear an Indian, save a fish." First Nations Peoples also face challenges when they try to make a living in more modern ways but within a context of sovereignty. In the late 1990s, the state of New York attempted to tax the First Nations within its borders for the sale of cigarettes and gasoline (Weaver, 2000). Such a tax, if collected, would have a devastating effect on the economies of these First Nations. Although many indigenous people and their advocates viewed imposition of the tax as a violation of treaties and a devastation of their sovereignty, the Supreme Court of the United States found otherwise. The state of New York took steps to collect the tax, which included imposing on reservations an embargo that prevented the delivery of any fuel including home heating oil. State troopers were frequently shown on the news beating indigenous people as part of the standoff.

Another example of the continued oppression of First Nations Peoples is the ongoing paternalism and mismanagement of resources overseen by the federal government. Native Americans are still often seen as not fully competent to manage their own lives; thus, the federal government continues to consider them its wards. In this capacity, the federal government holds 11 million acres in trust and collects from timber sales, oil and mineral exploitation, and agricultural leases, money that it is legally obligated to distribute to the Native people. This is called Individual Indian Monies (IIM). Although some money is distributed to Native people (about $450 million annually), there has been a growing scandal that the federal government has not been allocating all the money collected. Some Native people are not receiving payment for use of their lands at all, whereas others do not receive payments regularly. There have been accusations that billions of dollars owed to First Nations Peoples are unaccounted for. A pending class action lawsuit alleges the federal government has grossly mismanaged IIM accounts (Unclaimed Assets.com, 2005). A federal investigation has been ordered into historical accounting practices (U.S. Department of the Interior, 2005).

Just as Native Americans are not a thing of the past, neither are oppression and social injustice. Social workers can play an important role in fighting continued oppression by publicly opposing social policies and laws that seek to further undermine indigenous sovereignty. Policies such as ICWA that encourage First Nations control over Native children being placed in foster care or adoptive homes should be supported. Other important ways of combating oppression include fighting to remove stereotypical images of First Nations Peoples used as mascots for sports teams, and challenging environmental racism that has led to a variety of health problems and birth defects in First Nations communities.

TOOLS FOR STUDENT LEARNING 9.2

The Case of Dean Marshall

You have been meeting with Ho Chunk client Dean Marshall for three months. The Ho Chunk (formerly known as the Winnebago) is a nation of people who traditionally farmed in Wisconsin near Green Bay before being relocated several times. Some remain in Wisconsin and have repurchased 2,000 acres of their traditional homelands. You have been trying to assist Dean in his goals of completing his GED and obtaining employment that would enable him to support his family of five. During your time working with him, he has disclosed how his grandparents were forced to go to boarding school where they were punished for speaking their language and were not allowed to practice their religion. His mother spent most of her childhood in various non-Native foster homes and was eventually adopted by a non-Native family where she suffered sexual abuse. There are few jobs in the area where Dean lives, and he struggles with having to leave the area and his extended family in order to find employment. He has expressed hopelessness in his ability to remain in his community and support his children at the same time. He feels overwhelmed and powerless.

1. Describe how you could empower Dean to look at his family's endurance and survival using tools such as a genogram to identify resilience across generations.

2. Describe how you could empower Dean to find employment opportunities and perhaps facilitate economic development that would bring opportunities to his community. It may be helpful to begin with an assessment of Dean's skills and interests as well as reviewing what the economic base of the Ho Chunk people has been in the past.

3. Describe how societal oppression and institutionalized racism have impacted Dean's life.

4. What clinical skills will be most useful in exploring Dean's feelings about himself and his environment?

5. Identify how social work skills might be used to work toward societal change and social justice to reduce oppression and racism. Are there oppressive factors in the contemporary social environment of First Nations Peoples that may be relevant to Dean's situation?

6. How can community organizing and advocacy skills be used to enhance employment?

7. How can you, as a social worker, address your own feelings of being overwhelmed by the situations of clients like Dean who face many difficult obstacles?

IDENTIFYING CULTURAL AWARENESS AND SOCIAL SERVICE NEEDS OF FIRST NATIONS PEOPLES

Many stereotypes exist about Native Americans, so it is important for social workers to make sure they are choosing interventions and designing programs that accurately target needs rather than fulfill assumptions that are not based in reality. The social service needs of each Native community are likely to vary, so it is important to do an accurate assessment. As with assessing an individual, the needs of Native communities must be assessed in a thoughtful, culturally competent manner.

Weaver (1999a) presents a model of how one urban First Nations community conducted a needs assessment to determine the effectiveness of its current social service programs and to identify gaps in agency-based services. Focus groups were used as a culturally congruent method of gathering information on social service needs. Although outside observers might expect such a needs assessment to identify the need for services in areas such as substance abuse, in fact, this particular community identified its most critical challenge as integrating culture in all facets of service delivery from direct work with clients to agency administration. In addition to incorporating cultural factors in the helping process, the needs assessment revealed a need to change the physical layout of the agency so that members of the First Nations community would feel comfortable dropping in and spending time in the setting, something not supported by a typical agency setup with a receptionist and waiting room. Culture also needed to be integrated in service delivery through methods such as honoring foster parents at traditional dancing events known as socials and by making use of traditional knowledge and the teachings of the elders as well as the professional knowledge of social workers (Weaver, 1999a).

The social service needs of urban Native American elders are extensive and often go unmet. Native people residing in urban areas often do not have access to health and social services offered under tribal auspices. A study of urban elders found that they suffer from many health problems. They often do not seek help from agencies and helping professionals because of significant mistrust of dominant-society organizations (Kramer, 1992a, 1992b). Helping professionals need to do culturally appropriate outreach in order to successfully engage this population.

In choosing an intervention or designing a program, social workers should keep in mind the following principles:

1. The intervention should fit with the particular culture of the clients being served. In other words, a program based on Hopi culture is not likely to be a good fit for an Abenaki client.
2. The intervention should be based on the needs and level of cultural connection of the specific client. For example, offering an intervention grounded in Choctaw culture to a Choctaw client who knows nothing about his or her traditions is not likely to be productive. The exception to this would be an intervention designed specifically to reconnect a client to his or her culture.
3. The best information on whether an intervention or program is a good cultural fit will come from clients. Social workers should acknowledge that clients are experts on their own lives and needs. This acknowledgment can be very empowering for clients.

4. Some culturally based interventions, particularly those of a spiritual nature, are likely to be outside the purview of social work. Social workers should support clients who choose to seek help from traditional healers in addition to or instead of social work services.

Social work interventions that are most likely to be helpful for First Nations clients are ones that acknowledge, validate, and respect indigenous cultures. Empirical validation has been found for a variety of culturally grounded prevention programs that use a cognitive behavioral approach. Programs that target substance abuse prevention for First Nations youth have been effective at reducing the use of alcohol and drugs in many instances (Parker, Jamous, Marek, & Camacho, 1991; Schinke, Tepavac, & Cole, 2000). Although research has yet to test the effectiveness of most types of interventions with First Nations Peoples, those that incorporate culture clearly have face validity and the support of many experienced clinicians (Thomason, 2000).

EXPLORING KNOWLEDGE ACQUISITION AREAS ABOUT FIRST NATIONS PEOPLES

In order to be culturally competent, social workers must understand the extraordinary diversity that exists among Native people, be knowledgeable about the culture of specific clients or groups they are working with, and be knowledgeable about the history as well as contemporary realities of First Nations clients (Weaver, 1999b). Clearly, the diversity theme underlies the other three areas of knowledge because culture, history, and contemporary realities will vary depending on the particular Native client or nation.

In becoming knowledgeable about indigenous cultures, social workers can seek information from reservation and urban social service agencies, from indigenous journals such as *American Indian/Alaska Native Mental Health Research* and *American Indian Quarterly*, and from individual Native people who give public speeches or workshops and may be willing to serve as key informants or cultural guides in First Nations communities. In particular, social workers need to learn about indigenous values such as the emphasis placed on family and community. Extended family networks and strong community ties are common in First Nations cultures. These connections are likely to exist among urban Native people as well as those living on reservations (Red Horse, 1978; Weaver & White, 1997). Respect, responsibility, and generosity are also key values commonly found among First Nations Peoples. Respect determines how people interact with each other and the environment. Native people are often reluctant to impose on each other or to interfere with each other. A classic article on noninterference by Native social worker Jimm Good Tracks outlines how these values may conflict with social work interventions (Good Tracks, 1973). Responsibility and generosity also influence interactions between people. The sense of responsibility to other members of the community often results in support and mutual aid in caring for the elderly or teaching children. The generosity that permeates Native value systems is clearly illustrated by contemporary "giveaways," particularly common among First Nations Peoples from the Northwest, in which someone who is celebrating an event such as a graduation, birth, or anniversary gives away possessions.

Elders are particularly valued members of Native American societies. Not only do they have important roles to fill but also there is a strong belief that they are entitled to be cared for in their later years. Native elders are often cared for by their children or younger relatives who view this as a natural part of their responsibilities. In fact, about half of Native elders age 75 or older live with their families. It is important to note, however, that these families are more than three times as likely as White families to be living in poverty and thus, could benefit from increased use of social programs (Kramer, 1992a).

Understanding the history of First Nations Peoples can help in comprehending contemporary realities. As discussed earlier in this chapter, some First Nations social workers attribute contemporary social problems, such as the substance abuse and violence that trouble some Native communities, to historical unresolved trauma and grief (Brave Heart-Jordan & DeBruyn, 1995). Thus, it is important to identify the root cause and to validate historical trauma when addressing contemporary problems.

First Nations Peoples as a whole appear to suffer disproportionately from substance abuse due to a variety of factors such as cultural loss, prejudice, and poverty. In part, these problems have persisted because of helping professionals' lack of cultural competence when working with indigenous peoples (Mitka, 2002). It is important to recognize, however, that substantial variation exists in the extent of substance abuse problems among the various First Nations. This variation typically has not been recognized by researchers and practitioners, and inappropriate generalizations have been made that substance abuse is a significant problem across First Nations groups. Reliable data on trends or patterns of alcohol and drug use are scarce due to significant problems in the research (Weaver, 2001). Although social workers may well recognize substance abuse as being a significant issue for some of their Native clients, the extent and nature of this problem for First Nations Peoples has not been adequately documented.

In order to understand the current realities of First Nations Peoples, social workers need to understand the urban Native community as well as the reservation experience (Weaver, 1999b). Urban First Nations Peoples deal with issues that are both similar to and different from their reservation-based peers. Social workers need to develop culturally appropriate programs tailored to meet the needs of urban youth (Moran, 1999) and elders (Kramer, 1992a, 1992b). Social workers should recognize that urban Native people may be strongly grounded in their cultures. Walters (1999) found that urban First Nations Peoples "have survived by taking the best of both worlds, integrating them, maintaining and transforming native cultures, and, ultimately buffering against negative colonizing processes through the internalization of positive identity attitudes and the externalization of negative dominant group attitudes" (pp. 163–164). Some urban Native people experience homelessness; however, this phenomenon differs significantly from homelessness experienced by White urban dwellers. Even though First Nations homeless people experience higher poverty, less consistent employment, higher misuse of alcohol, and lower use of mental health services than their White peers, they receive a higher level of support from family and friends (Westerfelt & Yellow Bird, 1999). This illustrates the strong value that First Nations Peoples place on interpersonal connections, even under dire circumstances.

Many Native communities are taking positive steps to prevent further erosion of culture and language and are indeed working to reclaim these vital aspects of their heritage. As an example of this, one Native American social agency has recently been awarded a federal grant to assess the state of the six languages indigenous to New York State. This program, called Haudenosaunee Empowerment through Language Preservation (HELP), will begin by determining how prevalent these languages still are and will identify steps that can be taken to preserve them and keep them as vital parts of Haudenosaunee culture. It is particularly noteworthy that this effort is being made by an urban social agency, given that most Native people live in urban areas, but the majority of Native people who speak their language fluently are likely to remain on reservations.

Cultural competence with First Nations Peoples requires a basic understanding of sovereignty issues and policies that apply to indigenous people, such as the Indian Child Welfare Act and the Indian Health Service (Weaver, 1999b). When Europeans first came to what is now the United States, they dealt with First Nations Peoples on a government-to-government basis as an acknowledgment that the people who were already here existed as members of sovereign nations, just like other countries with complete rights to self-governance. Sovereignty is not something that one nation can give to another. It is an inherent characteristic. Over the centuries, the U.S. government has passed laws that have infringed upon the sovereignty of First Nations Peoples. Because the United States has grown stronger and has become able to enforce its will upon the First Nations, it has been able to put limits on indigenous sovereignty, yet it still recognizes Native people as members of domestic dependent nations, with many rights of self-governance still in place. An edited collection, *The State of Native America: Genocide, Colonization, and Resistance* (Jaimes, 1992), provides important background information that can help readers develop a basic understanding of historical and contemporary issues of indigenous sovereignty. With an understanding of the sovereignty of indigenous people, it becomes clear why many laws and policies exist that apply exclusively to First Nations Peoples.

Because Native nations still retain vestiges of sovereignty, they are able to operate casinos, even when this is prohibited by state law. Beginning in the mid-1980s, some First Nations began to look to casino revenue as a form of economic development. For some nations, this has proved to be quite lucrative. Tribal gaming has grown from earning revenues of $5.4 billion in 1995 to $19.4 billion in 2004 (National Indian Gaming Commission, 2005). Some casinos with a prime location to bring in large numbers of tourists have been particularly successful. For example, in 2003, 43 tribal gaming enterprises (out of a total of 330) brought in over $100 million each. However, the largest number, 73 (out of 330), brought in under $3 million. Some casinos are not financially viable, particularly for tribes in remote locations. The 330 tribal gaming enterprises operating at the end of 2003 is a decline from the 348 operating at the end of 2002 (National Indian Gaming Commission, 2005).

Those casinos that have become profitable have been able to invest profits in tribal infrastructure (i.e., supporting governance and social service programs) as well as supporting their members (i.e., scholarships and per capita payments). This may even be seen as a way to reclaim independence and reduce dependence on the federal government (Napoli, 2002). Gaming revenue has also been used for disaster aid to meet the needs of those effected by Hurricanes Katrina and Rita that devastated Gulf Coast regions in September 2005 (National Indian Gaming Association, 2005). On the other hand, gaming is still highly controversial in many Native communities as well as the larger communities that surround them. Some people (Native and non-Native) view gaming as bringing additional problems rather than being a solution. In particular, the compact that must be signed with states in order to operate casinos may be viewed as irreparably damaging tribal sovereignty and largely benefiting states and non-Native communities.

Social workers working with First Nations Peoples must be familiar with the Indian Child Welfare Act of 1978 (ICWA), one of the most significant policies affecting First

Nations Peoples. Although the act has existed for almost a quarter of a century and is a federal law that social workers must follow regardless of where they practice, many social workers are ignorant of the law's requirements or may not have heard of the law at all. The law was passed in response to the large numbers of First Nations children who were removed from their families and communities and were raised outside of an indigenous context, either through foster care or adoption. Under ICWA, a social worker who works for an entity other than a Native nation may not have jurisdiction to work with a Native child who is being taken into foster care or placed for adoption. Although the "best interest of the child" is a concept common throughout many child welfare policies, it is rarely defined. Under ICWA, the best interest of the child is clearly defined as cultural continuity. Indigenous children who must be removed from their parents should be placed with the extended family when possible, or with someone from their own tribe/nation, with a First Nations family, or with any family, in that order of preference. (For more information on ICWA, see Barsh, 1996; MacEachron, Gustavsson, Cross, & Lewis, 1996; Mannes, 1995; Wares, Wedel, Rosenthal, & Dobrec, 1994; Weaver & White, 1999.)

In addition to being knowledgeable in the areas mentioned, social workers need to develop certain attitudes or values to bring to their work with First Nations Peoples. In a survey of First Nations social workers, four general categories of values or attitudes were identified as important to cultural competence with Native people: (1) helper wellness and self-awareness; (2) humility and willingness to learn; (3) respect, open-mindedness, and a nonjudgmental attitude; and (4) social justice (Weaver, 1999b).

The importance of self-awareness is mentioned repeatedly in the social work literature. It is critical that social workers be able to reflect on their own feelings and biases and how these may influence their work with clients (Mason, Benjamin, & Lewis, 1996; Ronnau, 1994; Sowers-Hoag & Sandau-Beckler, 1996). Supervision can be an important venue for developing self-awareness and examining biases. It is important that a social worker feel safe enough to openly discuss these feelings in a confidential setting with a trusted senior colleague. One tool that can be helpful in this task is the process recording. Process recordings are an important learning tool in which social workers are encouraged to write down their feelings and reactions next to a description of the content of an interview with a client. The process recording is used as a learning tool that encourages self-reflection and is not something that becomes part of a client record; thus, it is a safe place for a social worker to begin to disclose feelings honestly.

Closely related to self-awareness is the value of helper wellness. Social workers must be able to take care of their own well-being and make sure they are not trying to inappropriately meet their own needs through interaction with clients. In recent years, Native values and spirituality have often been exploited through the New Age movement. This cultural and spiritual misappropriation has a devastating impact on First Nations Peoples. People with a spiritual hunger and need for balance in their lives have sought these out through attempting to replicate (often in inappropriate ways and with gross distortions) indigenous practices. Social workers need to make sure they are not trying to meet their own needs through asking Native clients questions about their culture, values, and traditions. Social workers need to find other ways to maintain their own well-being in this often stressful profession, and to not do it at the expense of their clients.

Humility and willingness to learn are important values for social workers to have, regardless of the type of clients they serve, but these attitudes/values are particularly important in doing cross-cultural work. Social workers must realize that there are many different ways of helping and that they do not know everything; they should always display a willingness to learn. Sometimes learning comes through formal channels such as workshops, but some of the most important learning comes through less formal channels like listening to and learning from clients. This is particularly important when working with Native American clients. Social workers must be willing to learn from clients the role that culture plays in their lives. Through active listening, the social worker will learn whether clients have strong cultural connections and the nature of those connections. Some clients who do not have a strong cultural connection may feel a sense of pain and loss that can be traced back to federal policies that promoted assimilation and cultural loss, such as the boarding schools. It is important to learn how clients experience such losses. Are they filled with self-blame because they do not know their traditions? Are they angry at the dominant society (and those they perceive to be its representatives, such as social workers) over what has been taken from them? Only by careful listening and learning from clients will social workers be able to choose and implement appropriate interventions.

An appropriate intervention is one that is culturally congruent for the client. Social workers who serve First Nations clients must learn to take time to form a relationship during the engaging phase prior to probing for sensitive information. The pace of the interaction is likely to be fairly slow, allowing time for trust to build. Respecting silence is important in the interview.

Respect, open-mindedness, and a nonjudgmental attitude are also important values for working with First Nations Peoples. In doing cross-cultural work, social workers are faced with clients whose values and lifestyles may be quite different from those of the social worker. It can be challenging to be open-minded enough to respect differing practices when they seem to be diametrically opposed to the social worker's own values. Voss, Douville, Little Soldier, and Twiss (1999) emphasize that social workers must be knowledgeable about and respectful of the traditional, non-Christian value systems held by many indigenous people. A social worker who comes from a strong Judeo-Christian orientation may have difficulty working with a client who follows traditional indigenous spiritual practices. For many years, ceremonies like the Sun Dance were outlawed and perceived as barbaric because they differed from spiritual practices more commonly found in the dominant society. Indigenous spirituality was often seen as pagan and un-Christian rather than simply as a different and equally valid spirituality. Although it may be challenging for social workers to respect practices that differ significantly from their own, displaying a nonjudgmental attitude is an important part of cultural competence with First Nations Peoples.

Striving for social justice is inherent in culturally competent practice. Social workers can begin the struggle for social justice by examining the policies and procedures in their own agencies. This level of self-reflection must go hand in hand with a growing awareness of individual biases that influence practice. For example, a social worker in a foster care setting might reflect on the agency's policies and examine whether criteria for foster parents may contain a bias against Native families who may have limited income, space limitations, and several children already in the household. Likewise, social workers need to reflect on national policies and bureaucracies. For instance, a culturally competent social worker can reflect on legislation such as the Adoption and Safe Families Act and question how its implementation may interact with and possibly undermine legislation such as the Indian Child Welfare Act. Social workers can use advocacy skills to work to implement culturally appropriate policies and to confront policies that have a differential or negative impact on First Nations Peoples. It is impossible to do culturally competent practice in an environment filled with social injustice; therefore, social workers must focus efforts on the macro level as well as the micro level.

FOSTERING PRACTICE SKILL DEVELOPMENT ABOUT FIRST NATIONS PEOPLES

Many of the skills needed for work with First Nations clients are the same as those used with clients from other backgrounds. Good communication skills and problem solving skills are important with this population (Weaver, 1999b). Social workers must be able to communicate clearly with their indigenous clients. Cross-cultural social work can often be hampered when clients and social workers do not share a mutual understanding of the work to be done. The problem-solving approach with clear and practical steps for addressing concerns has been identified by First Nations social workers as being culturally congruent for most Native American clients (Weaver, 1999b). It is also important for social workers to approach their work with indigenous clients from a strengths perspective, given the deficit perspective that permeates the stereotypes of Native Americans. Although it is true that as a whole, Native Americans are among the poorest groups in the country, have many health problems, and have a comparatively short life span, they also have many strengths as a population that has survived more than 500 years of colonization and policies designed for assimilation and both physical and cultural destruction. Some of the strengths that have enabled indigenous people to survive include a strong sense of community, values placed on tradition and cultural continuity, and respect for all people and parts of creation. These strengths must not be overlooked.

In addition to possessing strong general social work skills, it is particularly important that social workers who work with First Nations Peoples have good containment skills (Weaver, 1999b). Containment skills are those that require less activity on the part of the social worker (Shulman, 1999). In particular, social workers need to display a lot of patience in working with clients. It is important to spend a lot of time listening rather than talking. Although many social workers, particularly those new to the profession, may be uncomfortable with silence in the social work interview, it is important that silence be allowed to happen. Many Native Americans have a different pace to their communication than do people from the dominant society. Silence is common in communication and often reflects the Native person's thoughtfully considering things previously said or taking time to choose just the right words. A social worker who rushes to fill silence prematurely is likely to cut off the client and discourage further communication.

Once a social worker recognizes the importance of containment skills when working with First Nations clients, the social worker can begin to reflect on this aspect of his or her work. The social worker can review past interviews to pinpoint times when the use of containment skills might have been important. When beginning new interviews, the social worker can consciously monitor the pace of the interview and allow the client additional time to respond to questions or statements. Showing patience in this way is likely to result in additional material being disclosed or a client discussing current material more fully.

TOOLS FOR STUDENT LEARNING 9.3

The Case of Mrs. Grey

Mrs. Grey is a 79-year-old Houma woman who recently fell and broke her hip. The Houma are a southeastern nation with French cultural influences who are recognized by Louisiana but not by the federal government. Many Houma people experienced significant devastation as a result of Hurricane Katrina in 2005. As the hospital social worker, your job is to make arrangements for Mrs. Grey's discharge. She will not be able to return to her own apartment unless someone can stay with her during her recovery. You have presented her with all the facts of her medical needs, but you have not been successful at getting her to discuss her preferences or options.

1. Are there particular ways that you can go about engaging Mrs. Grey because you know she is Houma?

2. How can you employ containment skills such as patience and the use of silence when there is a pressing need to make discharge decisions?

3. You are vaguely aware that sometimes tribes offer social services to their members. How can you find out if there are specialized resources available to Mrs. Grey as a First Nations person?

4. How might the devastation caused by Hurricane Katrina influence this case?

GENERATING NEW INDUCTIVE LEARNING ABOUT SOCIAL WORK WITH FIRST NATIONS PEOPLES

Although readings, classes, and workshops on social work with Native Americans can be helpful, it is also important to participate in experiential learning activities. Sometimes internships are available at urban or reservation-based Native American agencies. These can give valuable opportunities for social work students to have supervised practice experience with First Nations Peoples. Briefer experiential learning activities can supplement such internships or provide important contact with Native communities when internships are not a practical option.

Spending time in First Nations communities, even for short periods, can present valuable learning experiences. Some schools of social work have developed immersion projects that send students to reservation communities for several days or weeks to learn about indigenous cultures. For example, students at Arizona State University School of Social Work can participate in a five-day cultural immersion exercise on the Navajo reservation in a class entitled "The Ecological Context of Social Work Practice." This class gives students an opportunity to learn through participation, not simply observation (DeGraw, 1989). This type of project can be a valuable source of learning, but students must be prepared to enter indigenous communities with respect and an open mind, and to not treat community residents as subjects to be studied.

Attending Native American activities can be a good source of learning. One social work student who attended a powwow in the western United States was startled to hear so many people speaking indigenous languages rather than English. Even though the reservation was just a few miles from his home, he had no idea that indigenous language and culture were still a vital part of the lives of many First Nations Peoples. Other social work students have become exposed to First Nations cultures through attending indigenous festivals that are open to the public. This is a good way of learning about cultures, values, and traditions. Sometimes cultural activities are sponsored by social service agencies. For example, a human service agency may sponsor an honoring event that includes social dancing to honor foster parents or graduates of a drug rehabilitation program. Such events give insight not only into indigenous cultures themselves but also into how cultural elements can be integrated into social services.

It is difficult to enter experiential learning activities with a truly open mind. One way to begin to consciously be aware of assumptions and preconceived notions is to write them down before entering the experience. The cross-cultural learner can ask him- or herself: What is it that I think I know about the people I plan to interact with? How do I think they will act? What do I think they will look like? How do I think they will react to me? By reflecting on questions like these, the learner becomes more aware of assumptions and thus more able to put them aside and enter the experience prepared to learn and to have assumptions challenged.

UNDERSTANDING AND ADVOCATING SOCIAL AND ECONOMIC JUSTICE FOR FIRST NATIONS PEOPLES

Social justice is a crucial element of cultural competence with First Nations Peoples (Weaver, 1999b). Social workers must be prepared to use their advocacy skills to confront the social and economic injustices that continue to be perpetrated upon First Nations Peoples. Native children are still removed from their families and communities in numbers large enough to threaten the future of indigenous nations. Knowledgeable social workers can play an important role in educating other social workers, people in the legal system, and the general public about the Indian Child Welfare Act (ICWA). This act has always been under attack by people who misunderstand or feel threatened by it. Thus far it has withstood all legal challenges, and it has not been affected by later legislation such as the Multiethnic Placement Act and the Adoption and Safe Families Act. It is likely that attacks on ICWA will continue. Social workers can assume an important role in helping others to understand the importance of this law and in making sure that the law is not overturned or watered down.

Economic development is an issue that presents challenges as well as hope in First Nations communities. First Nations Peoples, particularly those living on reservations, experience some of the highest unemployment rates in the country. Many reservations offer few job opportunities other than working directly for the tribe. Casinos and other gaming enterprises have offered some First Nations reservation communities a major source of employment and revenue. Although some Native people view these as positive developments, others see them as violations of cultural traditions, as addictive influences, and as something that opens the door to organized crime. Additionally, some gaming enterprises have been very profitable, whereas others have not been self-sustaining and have gone bankrupt.

Some First Nations communities have been approached by the federal government to act as storage sites for nuclear waste and other toxic materials. This presents a dilemma, particularly for impoverished communities. Federal contracts of this type are likely to bring in a substantial amount of money to struggling reservation economies, but what will be the cost in the long run? The value placed on planning for seven generations echoes in the minds of indigenous people confronted with such options. Although accepting toxic waste would give First Nations communities the money needed to feed hungry children and elders, fund social programs, and invest in college educations for young adults, the environmental destruction and health consequences are likely to compromise the future of generations to come.

First Nations communities will continue to be faced with the challenge of seeking economic development opportunities that help the nations and their members to be self-sustaining without compromising their own well-being. The relatively small, sometimes isolated nature of most reservations, and the lack of technologically skilled labor make it difficult to attract many employers. Indigenous people are confronted with difficult decisions about developing sustainable and culturally appropriate types of jobs in their communities.

Currently, Native nations still retain some sovereignty that includes the right to govern themselves, set laws, and develop social policies. Reservations often have their own tribal social service offices, health clinics, and legal systems. Through the years, sovereignty has been infringed upon by the passage of various federal laws and by Supreme Court decisions (Robbins, 1992). Given the current political climate in the United States, challenges to sovereignty are likely to continue, and long-established treaty rights may be lost. The current configuration of the Supreme Court has consistently ruled against the rights of First Nations Peoples, and President George W. Bush has made public statements that there is no such thing as sovereignty for Native American nations. Social workers can play an important role in advocating for just and fair social and economic policies.

Social workers can play a number of activist roles on behalf of First Nations Peoples while still respecting a context of indigenous sovereignty. A much-needed role for social work activists is that of putting political pressure on federal and state entities that make policies and laws affecting First Nations Peoples. Social justice in a First Nations context means challenging the colonial structures and mind-set that undermine sovereignty and self-governance. This can be done through traditional advocacy efforts such as letter writing, voting, and community organization, as well as through more radical methods that challenge U.S. and state governmental structures (Weaver, 1999a).

Rarely acknowledged or critically examined, ethical dimensions are embedded in many aspects of social work practice with First Nations people. It is important for social workers to reflect on their practice and examine any ways in which they might be replicating the colonizing practices implemented by the federal government and its representatives. This includes conscious reflection and acknowledgement of the power dynamics inherent in social work practice. These reflections must be expanded to include all aspects of social work practice. Areas to consider include (1) What are the ethical implications of not being culturally competent in service provision? (2) What are the ethical implications of not advocating for social justice? (3) What are the ethical implications of agency policies and administrative practices as they relate to First Nations Peoples? (4) What are the ethical impications of social policies as they apply to First Nations peoples? and (5) What are the ethical issues to consider in conducting research with First Nations Peoples?

TOOLS FOR STUDENT LEARNING 9.4

The Indian Child Welfare Act Case Exercise

The Indian Child Welfare Act (ICWA) has the goal of keeping First Nations children within an indigenous context when they need to be placed in foster care or placed for adoption. It sets forth specific procedures for protecting cultural continuity, which is deemed as being in the best interest of the child. Unfortunately, some social workers do not understand or support this law. Proposals that would water down the ICWA are frequently introduced in Congress. Your supervisor has stated, "I don't know why Indians get special treatment anyway."

1. What are your own feelings about a law that applies only to First Nations children?

2. What can you say in response to your supervisor's comment?

3. What can you do about congressional attempts to limit or eliminate the ICWA?

SUMMARY

Social workers must continue to strive for cultural competence. This involves the ability to interact with clients in a way that is knowledgeable and respectful of the clients' cultural context. Although it is not possible to know everything about every indigenous group, culturally competent social workers will take steps to be knowledgeable about the culture, history, and contemporary realities of the indigenous people they work with, keeping in mind the extraordinary diversity that exists among Native people. Culturally competent social workers will possess strong skills in general and will make sure they use containment skills that emphasize patience and listening and that allow for silence. Social workers must show respect, have an open mind, and be nonjudgmental with First Nations clients. Self-awareness and helper wellness are critical attributes, as are humility and a willingness to learn. Cultural competence is not just relevant to direct practice but also must permeate the way programs and policies are developed and administered. Without social and economic justice, cultural competence on a micro level is severely limited.

Social workers who work with First Nations Peoples face the challenge of overcoming stereotypes to be effective in their work. In addition to gaining realistic, strengths-based perspectives of their Native clients, social workers must help clients see social workers in a new way. Many First Nations clients see social workers as culturally incompetent representatives of government bureaucracies that pose a threat to Native families, communities, and nations. Through culturally competent work, social workers can demonstrate respect for indigenous values and traditions. Once both clients and social workers are able to get past the stereotypes they hold of each other, it will be possible for them to work together in healthy, productive ways within a climate that respects indigenous cultures.

CHAPTER TEN

Cultural Competence with African Americans

RUTH G. McROY

DEFINING CULTURAL COMPETENCE WITH AFRICAN AMERICANS

Cultural competence is "the ability to understand the dimensions of culture and cultural practice and apply them to the client and the cultural/social environment" (Lum, 1999, p. 29). In social work practice, cultural competence is achieved through development of personal and professional cultural awareness, knowledge acquisition, skills, and inductive learning about a specific population. This chapter examines these dimensions in relation to African Americans.

In 1989, Cross, Bazron, Dennis, and Isaacs proposed a continuum of competence that ranges from *cultural destructiveness* to *cultural incapacity, cultural blindness, cultural precompetence, cultural competence*, and finally, *cultural proficiency*. According to their continuum, *cultural destructiveness* refers to situations in which individuals exhibit attitudes and behaviors designed to crush or destroy a culture. In practice, this includes harmful acts such as denying people who are often disempowered access to resources. Historical practices that have denied African Americans employment or educational opportunities due to race are examples of cultural destructiveness (*Oppression*, 1998). Practitioners who are *culturally incapacitated* are not actively culturally destructive, yet they may adhere to values and beliefs that perpetuate racist stereotypes of African Americans. For example, those who fall in this domain of the cultural competence continuum might believe that African American families are pathological or that all African American children perform poorly in school and might expect that they will be overrepresented in special education classes. They are likely to "blame the victim" (Ryan, 1976). Consideration of systemic factors as potential causes is unlikely among these individuals.

Cultural blindness refers to situations in which practitioners deny any differences between groups and assume that practices used with the majority population, generally Whites, may work equally as well with African Americans. For example, an adoption worker who finds that the majority of families who attend an adoption information meeting are White might assume that Whites are the only families who want to adopt, without considering factors that may be serving as barriers to African American families coming forward to adopt. Moreover, culturally blind practitioners may assume that no special efforts or changes in services are needed to recruit and retain African American prospective adoptive families.

Individuals who have *cultural precompetence* recognize their strengths as well as weaknesses in providing services to African Americans and seek to become more culturally sensitive and aware. Social workers at the precompetence level might suggest the need for staff diversity training, might enroll in prejudice awareness training, or might express the need for greater diversity among the staff or board. They are less likely to "blame the victim," and sometimes they begin to recognize their own personal biases. These practitioners are often comfortable attending diversity trainings that increase awareness of difference but are not yet comfortable acknowledging the existence of oppression or "White privilege" (McIntosh, 1992).

Culturally competent practitioners openly express a commitment to diversity and obviously value diversity. For example, they recognize the impact of societal institutions and systemic factors that may lead to an increase in African American single-parent families rather than blaming the families or culture. These practitioners tend to understand the need to consider the social context and diversity among African Americans. They may seek guidance from experts in diversity and may commit to training for their staff. Culturally competent practitioners often recognize the need to hire more than one African American staff member and insist that African Americans are included in the pool of all potential staff hires or board members.

Finally, those practitioners who are *culturally proficient* hold African American culture and diversity in high esteem. They recognize the need to go beyond tokenism in hiring and are likely to include on a regular basis mandatory diversity or anti-racism training for all staff, may hire a director of diversity, and may include and continually assess the effectiveness of diversity and/or social justice mission statements and goals in their policies and procedures. They believe in holding the agency accountable for diversity and may evaluate collaborators in terms of their willingness to require diversity training and to demonstrate their valuing of diversity. To these practitioners, diversity training means more than awareness; it means a commitment to hire African American staff and to train all staff in prejudice reduction or undoing racism, as well as a commitment to social and economic justice. It also means a commitment to gaining knowledge about effective strategies for serving African American clients including Afrocentric practice approaches based on African principles and values.

The following sections are designed to highlight the multidimensionality of cultural competency with African Americans. They focus on knowledge, skills, and inductive learning.

UNDERSTANDING DIVERSITY AMONG AFRICAN AMERICANS FOR ASSESSMENT, PLANNING, PRACTICE, AND RESEARCH

There is much diversity among the African American population in terms of origin, appearance, experiences with oppression, identity, demographic characteristics, residential patterns, social class, interpersonal styles, and patterns of functioning and lifestyles. It is essential to understand each of these aspects of diversity in order to effectively assess, intervene, and become involved in research and practice.

Physical Characteristics, Ethnic Labels and Identification, and Respectful Language

African Americans range from those having much African genetic ancestry to those with primarily European ancestry. Phenotypic characteristics vary in terms of body size, skin color, and physical characteristics (Diller, 1999). Skin tones may range from very fair (almost white) to very dark. These variations reflect the racial mixing that has occurred over many generations. Just as there is diversity in skin tones, there is diversity in other physical attributes. For example, nose shapes may vary from very narrow and keen to very broad and flat. Lips may be pencil thin to large and full (McRoy & Grape, 1999). Hair texture may vary from very straight to very curly or kinky. Although some believe the stereotype that "all Blacks look alike," the tremendous variation in physical attributes as well as colors demonstrates that there is great diversity within this population.

Just as there is diversity in appearance among African Americans, there is much diversity of opinion about how they refer to their ethnic background. It is important for practitioners to know what racial category to use in referring to the population in general as well as how to refer to the racial identity of an individual client. *African Americans*, and *Blacks* are the terms generally used in the 21st century to refer to this racial group. Some writers differentiate between *African American* and *Black* by using *African American* to refer to Blacks who are descendents of African slaves brought to the United States and *Black* to refer to all people and cultures of African descent, including but not limited to Black people from the West Indies, Africa, and the Americas (Grace, 1992). Some believe that the term *African American* is the most appropriate of all as it gives respect to the African heritage. Historically, however, African Americans have been referred to as *colored*, *Negroes*, and later *Blacks* and *Afro Americans* (Diller, 1999).

Some individuals, however, may resent being called *African American* and may express a preference for being called *Black*. Others use the terms interchangeably, as will be done in this chapter primarily for readability purposes. As practitioners develop rapport with clients or in the community, it is best to listen closely to see how individuals refer to one another, or to ask specifically what they prefer to be called. There are some persons of mixed racial descent who do not want to be referred to by one racial label at all and define themselves as *bicultural*, *mixed*, or *biracial*.

Similarly, in interactions with African American youth, practitioners must feel comfortable asking them to explain terminology with which the practitioner may not be familiar. Terms and phrases such as "It's crunk" or "That's tight" (fun, a happening place, good) are often used by African American youth today. It is better to ask questions about these cultural idioms and thus empower the client, rather than make assumptions about their meaning or fail to clarify and therefore reduce the chances of developing rapport and forming an effective, therapeutic relationship (Lum, 2000).

Use of titles such as *Mr., Mrs., Ms.,* or *Dr.* followed by their last names represents a sign of respect for African Americans. This is necessary until the client gives the practitioner permission to use first names. This not only empowers the client, but it also demonstrates a rejection of historically dehumanizing precedents when Whites called African American adults by their first names (e.g., Susie) while expecting African Americans to refer to White adults and often children by title and name (e.g., Mr. Bob or Miss Jones; *African Americans*, 1998; Robinson, 1989).

"Black" Immigrant Populations

In recent years, increasing numbers of "Black" immigrants from the Caribbean and from sub-Saharan Africa have come to the United States. In fact, the U.S. Census reported 881,300 Africans, representing almost 3 percent of the total "foreign born" population. More than half of these African immigrants entered in the 1990s. Thirty-six percent are from West African including such countries as Ghana, Nigeria and Sierra Leone (Wilson, 2003). They are accustomed to referring to themselves based upon their country of origin and may be called Africans, Nigerians, or Somalis, and so on. Although often referred to in the United States as "Black," and viewed as "Black" based upon their phenotypical characteristics, they have a completely different history and cultural background. Many recent immigrants resent being "grouped." For example, there are approximately 420,000 Haitians in the United States, and the majority live in Miami and New York. However, growing numbers are locating in Massachusetts and New Jersey. Many were refugees from the political crisis in Haiti. Some were diplomats, professionals in Haiti seeking asylum in the United States. They continue to fight for their identity and recognition in the United States, and they advocate for their homeland (Newland & Grieco, 2004; Stepick, 1998). Understanding their past experiences and history as well as their present goals is essential in becoming culturally competent in working with immigrant populations.

Residential Patterns

Recent population statistics indicate that 55.3 percent of the 36.2 million African Americans in this country reside in the South. This is compared to 18.1 percent in the Northeast, 18.1 percent in the Midwest, and 8.6 percent in the West (McKinnon, 2003). Most (52 percent) African American families live in central cities of metropolitan areas. In contrast, only 21 percent of Whites[1] live in central cities. Those who live in inner cities have greater susceptibility to the negative consequences of downturns in the economy, leaving more families vulnerable (Burbridge, 1995).

Marital Status

Many believe that African American families have always been predominantly female-headed. However, up until 1925, just before the Great Depression, the following was true:

> [With] the modernization of southern agriculture afterward—the typical African American family was lower class in status and headed by two parents. This was so in the urban and rural south from 1880 to 1900 and in New York City from 1905 to 1925. Such families were just as common among farm laborers, sharecroppers, tenants, and northern and southern urban unskilled laborers and service workers. This family style accompanied the southern Blacks in the great migration to the North that has so reshaped the United States in the twentieth century. (Harrison, 2000, p. 189)

In fact, from the mid-1700s to the mid-1920s, less than one-fourth of Black families were female-headed. In 1960, still only 22 percent of Black families were female-headed (Billingsley, 1992, p. 36). However, this number began to significantly increase, and by

---

1. In this chapter, White or Whites refer to persons of non-Hispanic origin.

1970, 33 percent were female-headed. In 2002, 48 percent of African American families were headed by married couples, 43 percent of African American families were headed by women with no spouse present, and 9 percent were headed by men with no spouse present. This is in comparison to 82 percent of non-Hispanic White married-couple families, 13 percent of White families headed by women, and 5 percent of White families headed by men with no spouse present. (McKinnon, 2003).

In looking at the profile of African American children, only 33.3 percent of African American children live in married-couple families compared to 75.2 percent of non-Hispanic White children. Forty-six percent of African American children live in single parent families, 12 percent live with neither parent, and 13.1 percent live in grandparent-headed households (Annie E Casey Foundation, 2003). Many of these grandparent-headed households have limited income resources.

Age, Education, Social Class, Employment, and Gender

To better understand and assess African American families, it is important to understand the diversity in terms of age, education, social class, employment, and gender. African Americans are generally younger than Whites, with 33 percent under the age of 18 compared with 23 percent of Whites. Similarly, African Americans are less likely to be over 65. In 2003, only 8 percent of African Americans were 65 or older compared to 14 percent of Whites. Although the population over 65 is small in comparison to Whites, the poverty rate for African Americans 65 or older is 23.9 percent, which is more than twice the rate for the elderly in general. African American women over 65 are especially vulnerable as almost 28 percent live below the poverty line. A primary reason for the high poverty rate among older African Americans is that most (80 percent) rely on Social Security as their primary and often only source of income. Only 5.3 percent of older African Americans receive income from dividends, and only about 24 percent receive income from interest (Beedon & Wu, 2004). The limited income of African American elderly has a direct bearing on their lifestyles and options available to them. In African American families, many elderly parents who are no longer able to live on their own live with an adult child, rather than in a nursing home. Historically, these shared housing arrangements have allowed the elderly family member to remain active in the community and often in the church, as adult children often provide transportation and ongoing connections to extended family and friends (Chatters et al., 1989).

African American families historically and still today tend to view education as the vehicle most likely to ensure economic security (Logan, 1990). In 2002, 79 percent of all Blacks 25 years of age and over had at least a high school degree. Black women were more likely to have a college degree than Black men. In 2002, 18 percent of Black females and 16 percent of Black males aged 25 and above had completed at least a bachelor's degree.

A look at leading economic indicators suggests that although Blacks represent only about 13 percent of the population, they continue to be disproportionately poor. Although the poverty rate for African Americans is the lowest ever measured by the Census Bureau, it is still much higher than for non-Hispanic Whites. In 2001, 23 percent (8.1 million) of African Americans were poor, compared to 8 percent (15.3 million) of Whites. Thirty percent of Black children under the age of 18 are poor, and 22 percent of Blacks 65 and over are poor. Black women are more likely to be poor than Black men.

In 2001, 20 percent of Black men and 25 percent of Black women were poor. These percentages are two and a half to nearly three times higher than the rate for Whites in the same age and gender categories; 7 percent of White men and 9 percent of White women were poor. The highest poverty rates occur among families headed by women. Thirty-five percent of Black families and 19 percent of White families maintained by women with no spouse present are in poverty (McKinnon, 2003).

The median annual income for African Americans in 2001 was $29,470, compared to $53,635 for Asian and Pacific Islanders, $46,305 for Whites, and $33,565 for Hispanics (U.S. Census Bureau, 2002). Although 8 percent of African American married couples and 3 percent of White married couple families are poor, married couples in general are likely to have more income; 52 percent of African American couples, 13.7 percent of African American female heads of households, and 25.5 percent of African American male heads of household earn $50,000 or above. About 19 percent of African American married couples, 58.1 percent of Black female householders with no spouse present, and 37.6 percent of Black male householders with no spouse present make less than $25,000 a year.

For over 50 years, the African American male unemployment rate has been over twice that of White males (Jaynes & Williams, 1989, p. 308). Currently, 12 percent of Black men and 10 percent of Black women are unemployed, compared to 6 percent of White men and 4 percent of White women. Among workers between ages 20 to 24, however, 16.8 percent of Blacks are unemployed, whereas only 6.5 percent of Whites are unemployed. For Black males between the ages of 16 and 19, 60 percent are not in the labor force, compared with 43 percent of Whites in that age range who are unemployed (Cose, 1999). It is clear that some African Americans are doing better than in prior times, but in comparison to Whites, significant differences remain.

Much diversity exists within African American communities, and culturally competent practitioners recognize that poverty is not synonymous with African American culture. Nineteen percent of Black men and 27 percent of Black women are employed in service occupations, and 28 percent of Black men and 9 percent of Black women are likely to be employed as operators, fabricators, and laborers (McKinnon, 2003). Twenty-six percent of Black women are in managerial and professional specialty positions, and 18 percent of Black men are in such jobs. Many of these African Americans are classified as being in the middle or upper classes.

The upper-middle class, sometimes referred to as the Black bourgeoisie (Diller, 1999) after the Great Depression, historically meant a privileged class of persons who aspired to send their children to elite schools. Currently, many members of the African American upper-middle class live in predominantly White communities; hold professional positions such as doctors, lawyers, professors, engineers, and computer scientists; and often define themselves as bicultural or acculturated. Some participate in traditionally upper-middle class Black organizations such as The Links, Inc., Jack and Jill of America, Inc., and the Sigma Pi Phi Boule. However, it is important to note that indicators of social class used by Blacks (e.g., income, education, and occupation) are sometimes different from those used in the White community (Billingsley, 1968; Hill, 1978). For example, Logan (1990) notes, "[U]pper class Blacks comprise families of judges, businessmen, and physicians who would be middle class on the basis of criteria used by Whites" (p. 26). In 1987, Hill described African American households with incomes of $50,000 or more as upper class, and those with incomes between $20,000 and $49,999 were designated as middle class. Upper-class status, by White standards, is often based on much greater wealth (e.g., millions) that is either inherited or acquired through a successful independent business, and less often from a salaried position.

Finally, there is a very rich group, in a class by themselves (multimillionaires), among African Americans who often serve as prominent role models for children. This group, mostly composed of wealthy athletes and entertainers such as Oprah Winfrey, Michael Jordan, and Janet Jackson, is considered among the Black elite.

Sexual Orientation

Another very important issue that must be considered in developing cultural competence in working with African American families is understanding the unique challenges faced by African Americans who are gay, lesbian, bisexual or transgender. The challenges of being a member of a racial and ethnic group are compounded when also a member of a sexual minority. The limited research on African American gays and lesbians suggests that many men and women are reluctant to disclose their sexual orientation due to fear of rejection by family members and the church (Mays et al., 1998). These institutions have historically provided support to African Americans, yet often have very negative attitudes toward homosexuality. Such attitudes have led some African American gay men and lesbians to engage in self-denial and sometimes bisexuality "out of cultural guilt or to salvage a bruised sense of masculinity" (Icard & Nurius, 1996, p. 39). In any considerations of identity formation, family and community relationships, help seeking behaviors, practitioners must be aware of the impact of sexual orientation and identity as well as racial identity and socialization experiences.

Interpersonal Styles

Bell and Evans (1981) suggested that African Americans demonstrate four interpersonal styles that are associated with one's degree of acculturation. Those persons who have assimilated into the White mainstream culture and whose actions suggest that they wish to deny or reject their Blackness in favor of White mainstream culture are often identified as having an *acculturated interpersonal style*. Many are more comfortable relating to Whites and limit their social and business contacts with other Blacks.

Those who choose to adopt a Black frame of reference and reject White mainstream culture, norms, and values are defined as *culturally immersed*. Their orientation is very Africentric, and they are less likely to have many White close friends. They may view many Whites with suspicion and distrust.

There are others who are considered to be *bicultural* as they are comfortable with both Black and White society. They may have both Black and White friends, and they usually work in settings in which they have to exhibit "double consciousness" (Du Bois, 1903), in which they function well in both the African American and Anglo-American culture. They typically adjust their behavior to the identity of the persons with whom they interact and demonstrate bicultural competence (*African Americans*, 1998; LaFromboise, Coleman, & Gerton, 1993).

Finally, those who adopt a *traditional* interpersonal style tend to value their Blackness and typically have limited contact with persons outside the Black community. Many are elderly or from impoverished backgrounds and adhere to traditional Black family norms. Some may show deference to Whites as was expected many years ago. They may be reluctant to call themselves Black and instead still feel comfortable with the term *Negro*.

Some theorists exploring the development of interpersonal styles, such as Sanders-Thompson (1994), suggest the need to go beyond racial identification as the key component of interpersonal styles for African Americans. Sanders-Thompson proposes a multidimensional model that includes four parameters: the physical parameter involves an acceptance of African American physical features, and the cultural parameter indicates an awareness of African American culture and values. Attitudes toward economic and social issues are included in the sociopolitical parameter, and one's sense of belonging to the group is included in the psychological parameter.

Other theorists have begun to examine factors that may influence differences in cultural orientation among African Americans. Noting that racial identity (one's beliefs or feelings about the racial group to which one belongs) is possibly independent of level of acculturation, Landrine and Klonoff (1994) suggest:

> [H]ighly acculturated African Americans (e.g., who have adopted some aspects of White culture in order to succeed in some specific predominantly White context) may accept and take pride in their race or may reject and deny their racial group membership. (p. 125)

These authors have recently developed a new acculturation scale to further empirically examine ethnic difference in acculturation (Klonoff & Landrine, 2000).

Whichever approach is taken, it is essential for practitioners to be cognizant of the within-group diversity among African Americans. As mentioned earlier, some persons of African American descent do not value a particular racial identity at all and may suggest that they are multiracial due to mixed racial genetic origins. In fact, according to anthropologist Munro Edmonson, the average American Black person has 25 percent traceable White genes ("What Makes You Black?" 1993).

In exploring an individual's racial and cultural identity to determine appropriate treatment approaches, as well as to assess whether the client is experiencing any conflict regarding his or her identity or racial background, a number of factors can be considered, including: (1) racial self-identification, (2) physical appearance, (3) race of mother and father, (4) economic status and occupation or profession, (5) education, (6) church membership and other social affiliations, (7) relationship with extended family, (8) language (i.e., use of Ebonics), (9) lifestyle factors (i.e., living environment—predominantly White, African American, or racially mixed), and (10) experiences with racism. Data collection on all of these factors can provide useful information in better understanding the client's interpersonal style and the significance of race and culture in the client's life (McRoy, 1990).

It is essential to understand the diversity among African Americans in order to provide effective services as well as to conduct research with this population and interpret findings appropriately. Questions must always be asked of researchers studying African American populations: Who was in the study? What was their socioeconomic class? What was the attrition? How was the sample selected? What attempts were made to get greater participation? What was the race of the interviewer? Who was involved in conducting the evaluation? What types of instruments were used? Have the instruments or measures been normed on African American populations? A lack of knowledge about the myriad of systemic factors that affect this population and the extreme diversity of economic conditions, lifestyles, and interpersonal styles can lead researchers to make false generalizations or erroneous assumptions about the population or program (Grace, 1992). Culturally proficient researchers recognize this and use a variety of data-gathering methods, including case studies and ethnographic techniques, to examine cultural uniqueness.

To better understand the cultural uniqueness of African Americans, the following section examines the impact of their African origins on the history of race relations in the United States.

RECOLLECTING THE AFRICAN AMERICAN HISTORICAL AND CURRENT OPPRESSION EXPERIENCES

African Americans have a unique historical background characterized by involuntary migration, slavery and segregation, and continued oppression (Billingsley, 1968, 1992). From the 16th to the mid–19th century, coastal West Africans were forcibly removed from their homes and transported to America. They came from various ethnically distinct tribes (e.g., Mandingos, Yorubas, Ibos, Fantins, Ashantis, and Hausas) who spoke different languages and came from different cultural traditions. They were taken from their homelands in which the family, children, and elders were highly valued. Their rich culture was characterized by "communal aid, religious rituals and celebrations, music and art" (McRoy, 1990, p. 4). Historians have noted that Africans were a very proud people who did not consider themselves inferior to Europeans (Bennett, 1982, p. 33).

Despite this rich history, European slave traders who supplied the labor to the huge American plantations, enslaved Africans to provide cheap labor to work in tobacco, sugar, and cotton fields to support the southern agricultural economy. Originally, unsuccessful attempts were made to use European immigrants as indentured servants, and then to enslave Native Americans, but many died from diseases or were able to escape because they knew the land. Africans were more visible and could not blend in, did not know the land, and seemed to be in great supply. They were captured in large numbers, separated from their families, shackled, and forced to march hundreds of miles to the African coast, where they were examined like cattle and packed tightly like parcels into the hull of ships for the dreaded Middle Passage to the Americas. Many were tortured and murdered at sea, others were thrown overboard due to sickness, and some committed suicide. Ten to 15 percent of slaves who left Africa died along the Middle Passage (Alter, 1997). It is estimated that over two and a half centuries, more than 100 million Africans in all were involved in the African Diaspora, the forcible dispersion of peoples from Africa. Many who survived the journey were taken to Brazil, Cuba, Jamaica, and Haiti, and some were later sold to America from there.

Most African slaves in America arrived on slave ships landing in the southern ports of Virginia and the Carolinas (Winkleman, 1999). They were auctioned and sold to the highest bidder. Considered bondsmen, or slaves for life, these Blacks were treated as "objects" or "things" that were owned by the master and could be bought and sold like any property. In many cases families were separated to increase profitability. Children of slave mothers also became slaves. Slaves had no civil status and could not enter into legal contracts, so they could not legally marry, own property, sue, or be sued. They were not allowed to be educated, and they were forbidden from assembling, voting, and holding political office (McRoy, 1990, pp. 4–5).

The majority of slaves lived on southern plantations located in seven states, but an estimated 500,000 Blacks worked in cities as domestics, factory workers, or skilled artisans (Bennett, 1982). Women worked either in the fields or as house servants. Typically viewed as sexual objects or property, they were often exploited sexually by plantation owners. To further dehumanize slaves for the purpose of determining the number of congressional representatives, the 1767 U.S. Constitution stipulated that each slave would be counted as three-fifths of a person (Alter, 1997).

Some Blacks were free because they were born in a non-slave state, had been set free by a master, had run away, or had bought their freedom. However, they were only free from physical bondage, not free from oppression. In the late 1780s, there were about 59,000 free Blacks and about 697,000 Black slaves. By 1860, the number of free Blacks had increased to about 500,000, and most lived in the Southeast. The rights of free Blacks varied from state to state. However, most had low-status and low-paying jobs. Most sought education as a means of self-improvement and advancement, and many were engaged in antislavery organizations and developed natural helping networks to combat poverty and provide services to Blacks (McRoy, 1990, p. 8).

The church played a major role in protecting slave families. According to McRoy (1990), church gatherings gave slaves a brief respite from the toils of their day, gave them a place to release their pent-up feelings of despair and to express their desires for freedom, and gave them an opportunity to develop group solidarity and promote mutual aid.

Drawing upon the helping tradition characteristic of African society, slave families helped one another, whether biologically related or not. Individual slaves looked out for one another and felt a sense of obligation to support family and non-family. Fictive kin (non-kin adults close to the family) were often referred to as *Aunt* or *Uncle*.

Slave rebellions, the abolitionist movements, the secession of the southern states from the Union, and the Civil War were among the factors that eventually led to the end of slavery. In 1863, the Emancipation Proclamation was signed, which freed slaves living in the rebel states of the South during the Civil War. At that time, an estimated 5 to 20 million Africans were enslaved in the United States (Bennett, 1986). In 1865, slavery was officially abolished for all slaves with the signing of the Thirteenth Amendment.

However, the abolition of slavery did little to alter the historically oppressive relationship between Blacks and Whites in the United States. The dehumanization and "thingification" of Blacks, justified by theories of inferiority and subhuman status, laid the groundwork for the economic, political, and social discrimination and oppression that characterized the post-slavery era. During this period, Black codes of conduct restricted the movement of freedmen, and "Jim Crow" laws legalized segregated facilities for Blacks. The systematic separation of Blacks and Whites in such places as schools, restaurants, theaters, buses, cemeteries, funeral homes, water fountains, and restrooms had legal sanction for over 58 years. These segregated facilities for Blacks were not only separate but also inadequate or inferior to comparable White facilities. In 1954, the Supreme Court began to dismantle the policy of "separate but equal" in the *Brown v. Board of Education, Topeka, Kansas* decision, making school segregation unconstitutional.

Beginning in the 1950s and 1960s, the civil rights movement, led by African American religious leaders such as the Reverend Doctor Martin Luther King, Jr., eventually led to the passage of the Civil Rights Act of 1964 and the Voting Rights Act of 1965. Over the years, the struggle has continued for African Americans to be given equal access to housing, jobs, and educational opportunities. In recent years, efforts to redress past wrongs, such as affirmative action policies in higher education, have come under siege.

Another form of oppression that stemmed from slavery is "skin color" oppression. During slavery, the offspring of interracial unions, "mulattoes," were often given more favored status on the plantation (e.g., as house servants) and may have been sold for higher prices at slave auctions (Comer & Poussaint, 1975; Drake & Cayton, 1962; McRoy, 1999; Myrdal, 1962; Neal & Wilson, 1989). Higher social status was often accorded to those Africans who had more "White characteristics." However, according to laws in the upper south and in the north, any person with "one drop" of Black blood had the legal status of a pure African (Russell, Wilson, & Hall, 1992, p. 14).

Some African Americans have internalized this racist belief that characteristics associated with Whites (straight hair, thin lips, small pointed nose, and light eyes) are considered to be "good" or preferable, as they are more "Whitelike" and thus may be more acceptable to Whites. Those physical characteristics associated with Blacks (kinky hair, large lips, wide, flat nose, and dark eyes) are considered by some to be less desirable because they are less like the appearance of Whites (McRoy & Grape, 1999). Historically, persons with lighter skin tones were more likely to obtain higher status positions and earn more money than those with darker skin tones (Keith & Herring, 1991). As a result of the Black pride movements of the late 1960s and 1970s and changing perspectives on beauty over the years, many began to reject White standards of beauty. Despite this change in attitude, however, "the consequences of having a particular skin shade have not disappeared" (Keith & Herring, 1991, p. 777).

Still today, those with more "Whitelike" characteristics are defined by many Blacks and Whites as more acceptable to Whites and, therefore, may be given more opportunities. Bond and Cash (1992) found that although the majority of African American college women in their study were satisfied with their skin tone, those who desired a different skin color preferred a lighter tone. Keith and Herring (1991), using data from the National Survey of Black Americans (1979–1980), reported that skin tone is a more consequential predictor of occupation and income than parental socioeconomic status. They found that darker-skinned respondents were twice as likely to report being victims of discrimination within the last month than lighter-skinned respondents (p. 775). They concluded that despite progress in race relations, skin tone variations, both historically and now, have an influence on stratification outcomes.

Similarly, Blacks were not only systematically oppressed during slavery, but they continue to suffer discrimination. Equal rights for Blacks in the United States have always had to be fought for, and despite greater access and opportunities, Blacks still experience a great deal of discriminatory and oppressive attitudes and behaviors from the dominant White society. Legislative gains have been made, but it is not possible to legislate White attitudes (Billingsley, 1968).

Even the term *minority*, often used to refer to African Americans and other groups of color, is based on underlying racist assumptions. As Logan (1990) states, the term *minority* actually refers to "power and privilege, not to numbers" (p. 19). The emphasis on power differentials can become an obstacle to helping, as it exacerbates the already unequal power relationship between client and clinician.

IDENTIFYING CULTURAL AWARENESS AND SOCIAL SERVICE NEEDS OF AFRICAN AMERICANS

Historically, many African Americans have been reluctant to seek help from social service agencies for a variety of reasons stemming from a distrust of society due to the history of institutional racism and discrimination. Institutional racism refers to the recurring ways in which injustice is perpetuated on Blacks in the United States. According to the National Council of Churches: "Both consciously and unconsciously, racism is enforced and maintained by the legal, cultural, religious, educational, economic, political, environmental and military institutions of societies. Racism is more than just a personal attitude; it is the institutionalized form of that attitude" (as cited in Feagan & Sikes, 1994, p. 3). Institutional racism is a form of oppression maintained through a reliance on White norms, stereotyping, assimilation, and tokenism in which people with power mismanage cultural differences (*Oppression*, 1998; Pinderhughes, 1989). One of the most blatant forms of oppression was the enslavement of African Americans in the United States, which was followed by legalized segregation. These racist practices have negatively impacted the economic and social lives of African Americans and therefore must be acknowledged in considering the social service needs of this population.

Neighbors and Taylor (1985) reported that the majority of Blacks still did not use social services. Those who did (14.4 percent) tended to be poor and sought services from public assistance programs (McRoy, 1990, p. 13). After slavery, however, as segregation and discrimination limited social services to African Americans, self-help efforts including day care centers, orphanages, private services, and other forms of mutual aid developed within Black communities for families in need. Although never referred to as "volunteerism," Blacks have always cared for each other in their homes, in their neighborhoods, and throughout their communities (Harper, 1990, p. 240). The Black church in particular has always been very much involved in serving Black families and is one of the few institutions that is Black-owned and controlled. It remains a source of material, emotional, and spiritual assistance (McRoy, 1990). Agencies must find ways to collaborate with families and communities to build on these natural helping tendencies and to enhance service provision.

Understanding spiritual belief systems also offers some guidance in the provision of services to African Americans. Spirituality for African Americans may include church attendance but actually includes more of a belief in a superior power who can provide solutions for problems. Some view problems as punishments from God, and others see the church as one's personal salvation. Because of these beliefs, many African Americans are very involved in missionary societies, Bible study groups, and prayer meetings and have a great deal of faith in preachers (Dana, 1993). For this reason, social service agencies need to recognize the influence of the church and use this as a resource to build relationships within the African American community. Some Blacks maintain a belief in voodoo, witchcraft, and folk medicine. These are beliefs that remain from African belief systems; they also must be explored (Dana, 1993).

According to data from the National Survey of Black Americans (Neighbors & Jackson, 1984), gender, age, and type of problem may influence help-seeking among Black families. African American women are more likely than men to seek help as well as to use informal networks. Men are less likely than women to talk with informal helpers about their concerns and problems. This study also found that older Blacks are less likely than younger Blacks to use professional and informal networks. Crawley and Freeman (1992) reported similar findings. Logan (1996) noted other factors that may influence African American help-seeking behaviors, including "lack of diversity among service staff, location of service delivery system, negative perception of the service system, manner in which Black families conceptualize problems and needs and the manner in which Blacks conceptualize strategies for resolving problems" (p. 196).

Assumptions that race is nothing more than a physical attribute can lead to misunderstandings in client–worker relationships. Robinson (1989) notes that "by choosing not to acknowledge the clients' perspective regarding race, the therapist risks disrupting the formation of an alliance that the client experiences as sympathetic" (p. 323). This can lead to early withdrawal from therapy by the African American client. Practitioners must understand racial dynamics as well as racism and oppression and be willing to address these issues in treatment.

As agencies strive to become culturally competent and proficient, their staff must first become acutely aware of how personal stereotypical assumptions about African Americans can affect interactions. It is important for social workers to become self-aware of their own biases and recognize how these can act as an impediment not only to the use of services but also to the accurate assessment of problems (Gary, 1985). Moreover, practitioners must acknowledge that racist behavior can occur within social service agencies. A commitment to "undoing" racism, through trainings, ongoing self-assessments of practitioners, and agency policies and procedures, is needed to better meet the needs of African American clients.

Therefore, it is critical for social workers to adopt a multicultural perspective that "recognizes the multifaceted configurations of ethnicity and race in social work practice" (Dungee-Anderson & Beckett, 1995, p. 459) and accounts for the impact of environmental stresses such as racism and discrimination (*African Americans*, 1998). It is also important to utilize the ecological perspective in developing social service programs for African Americans, in order to focus on the dynamic interaction between the person and environment over the course of the life span.

Dana (1993) suggests that African American clients may go through some of the following stages as they consider becoming involved in the helping process. In the first stage, "appraisal," the African American client may appear very guarded, reserved, or aloof. In the second stage, "investigative," the client may begin to try to equalize the power differential between client and practitioner by challenging the practitioner and raising questions about the practitioner's background and approach. For example, an African American client may ask a clinical supervisor why he or she was assigned an African American worker instead of a White worker. This "challenging" or "investigative" approach begins to alter the status disparity. In the third stage, "partial identification with the practitioner," the African American client attempts to establish a more personal relationship. The final stage, "loyalty and personal regard for practitioner," occurs when the African American client begins to feel comfortable with the practitioner and becomes less defensive. These stages are considered fluid, and clients may alternate between these responses at various times in the therapeutic relationship (Dana, 1993).

To further establish trust, the culturally sensitive practitioner must acknowledge any racial concerns of the client. If the client and practitioner differ in their ethnic background, African American clients often may assume that the practitioner has less familiarity with their situation and may not be likely to recognize or acknowledge the impact of racism and oppression on the presenting problem. Some may exhibit "healthy cultural paranoia" (Grier & Cobbs, 1968) in their interactions with the practitioner by demonstrating uneasiness and lack of trust in the initial encounters. This may manifest in more "hostile" reactions or reluctance to confide in non–African American practitioners. Instead of assuming this is resistance, practitioners should recognize that it is adaptive coping.

Because of the hesitancy of many African Americans to utilize a social service agency, the practitioner needs to demonstrate sensitivity by acknowledging that the client may have experienced lengthy waits for service in the past, or may not have received adequate services in the past. Devore and Schlesinger (1996) suggest adjusting agency hours and service delivery patterns to facilitate the involvement of African American men in the helping process.

In assessing African American clients, workers should use a "strengths perspective" rather than defining all behaviors and problems as pathological. Finding positive coping strategies and looking for family strengths are essential in working with African American families. The pathological deficit approach is a sure way of losing a potential opportunity to help an African American client.

Some practitioners overlook the concrete needs of a family and want to immediately begin to address psychosocial problems. However, many families cannot begin to address issues like parenting behaviors until the immediate stressors are eliminated through the provision of concrete services. Lum (2000) noted that many problems may be triggered by environmental deficits, and coping is often enhanced when these deficits are reduced.

Because African Americans are more likely to use informal helping networks, Logan (1996) suggests ways to empower African American communities by developing community directories of resources and making them available to families, creating community support groups for single parents or others with special needs, and creating linkages with churches and fraternal groups to aid in planning and implementing programs.

Finally, in working with African American clients, it is essential to consider the practitioner's level of acculturation and experiences with racism. It should not be assumed that African American workers are automatically able to accept and communicate with African American clients. Many African American social workers are products of traditional educational experiences and may not have had much experience with the realities of African Americans in other social classes. Similarly, White workers who believe that race is not an important factor to an African American client or who believe traditional stereotypes of African American clients will have difficulty in establishing positive working relationships with African Americans. Those who overemphasize the significance of race, blame racism and discrimination for everything, and fail to help the client see his or her part in an issue also are not going to be effective practitioners with African Americans (McRoy, 1990).

TOOLS FOR STUDENT LEARNING 10.1

Social Service Needs of Blacks

1. List questions or comments you have heard social workers, educators, or other service providers raise or state about reaching the African American community.

2. Identify five factors that may influence help seeking among African Americans and African immigrant populations.

3. Discuss pitfalls or problems agencies may encounter in appropriately serving African American clients.

4. List ways to address these problems or pitfalls.

EXPLORING KNOWLEDGE ACQUISITION AREAS ABOUT AFRICAN AMERICANS

In order to prepare to meet the needs of African American clients, social work practitioners need to have knowledge of the unique history experienced by African Americans in the United States and to understand the impact of contemporary racism and oppression. These factors must be integrated into assessment, intervention, and evaluation of service delivery to this population. Moreover, the impact of social and economic issues that have affected African Americans in the United States is essential knowledge in preparing to serve this population.

In developing cultural competence with African Americans, social workers need to have general knowledge in the following areas:

- The diverse demographic profiles of African Americans
- African American history, culture, values, and traditions
- The impact of racism, discrimination, oppression, and poverty on behavior, attitudes, and values
- Relationships between African Americans and immigrant populations
- Challenges faced by African American gays and lesbians
- Help-seeking behaviors of African Americans
- Language, speech patterns, and communication styles
- The impact of social service policies and practices on African Americans
- Resources (informal helping networks)
- Power relationships with Whites and other ethnic groups and their impact on African Americans
- Levels of acculturation and their impact on the helping relationship
- Possibility of conflict between professional values and values and needs of clients (Saldana, 2001)
- Theoretical approaches that work well with diverse African American populations, including a range of social classes and levels of education and acculturation (Pinderhughes, 1989)

- Ways to apply ecological theory and psychosocial theory to African American families
- Theories of ethnicity, culture, African American identity, and social class
- Africentric helping approaches
- Stereotypes African American clients may hold toward service providers
- The impact of gender, class, age, sexual orientation, and race on African Americans
- Strengths of African American men, women, and children, as well as of the community
- Critical analysis of contemporary issues and problems faced by African Americans
- Ways to operationalize the strengths perspective
- African American family functioning and family forms
- Disproportionate representation of African American children in special education and in foster care
- The differential impact of social policies on African American families

Social workers also need to have specific knowledge about these areas for each client or client system. For example, the worker needs knowledge about the following:

- Specific issue or problem facing the client
- Client's culture (history, traditions, values, family systems, etc.)
- Prior experiences of client or client's population with service providers
- Client's strengths, family resources, informal helping, network, and help-seeking behaviors
- Client's family functioning and family forms
- Potential stereotypes toward service providers
- History of help-seeking
- Impact of gender, class, and ethnicity on client
- Experiences with racism, discrimination, and oppression
- Power and privilege and their impact on the family
- Client's interpersonal style and perceptions of racial identity and relationships

Diller (1999) suggests:

To the extent that White providers can acknowledge the centrality of race to a non-White client and at the same time grasp the nature of their own attitude toward racial differences, the cultural distance between them can dramatically be reduced. (p. 23)

To accomplish this, social workers working with African American populations should possess self-knowledge about the following:

- Level of cultural competence in relation to African Americans
- Ways in which racism, oppression, and discrimination have affected the worker both personally and professionally
- Worker's own racial and cultural heritage as well as how the worker's interpersonal style can affect his or her personal and professional relationships with African American clients (Diller, 1999)
- Ways in which power and privilege have differentially affected African Americans and Whites in the United States.

TOOLS FOR STUDENT LEARNING 10.2

Experience and Knowledge Self-Assessment

Please complete the following self-assessment of your experiences with and knowledge about African Americans. Answer true or false, unless otherwise specified.

1. When I was growing up, my parents had many friends who were African American. ____ True ____ False
2. When I was growing up, African Americans were among my closest friends. ____ True ____ False
3. I have taken a course on African American families or social work practice with African Americans. ____ True ____ False
4. I feel that I have a very open communication style. ____ True ____ False
5. I believe I can learn a great deal from African Americans. ____ True ____ False
6. I see myself as being a. acculturated b. bicultural c. culturally immersed (within own culture) d. other (please explain)
7. When I hear others make pejorative comments about African Americans, I challenge them. ____ True ____ False
8. I am uncomfortable when I hear others make pejorative comments about African Americans. ____ True ____ False
9. I believe knowledge about African Americans will assist me in my practice. ____ True ____ False
10. I have had mostly positive experiences with African Americans. ____ True ____ False
11. I grew up believing the following stereotypes about African Americans:
12. I have the following questions about providing services to African Americans:

FOSTERING PRACTICE SKILL DEVELOPMENT ABOUT AFRICAN AMERICANS

According to Saldana (2001), there is much potential for failure in cross-cultural therapeutic work. In each phase of the process, from engagement through case closure, it is important to recognize and acknowledge the potential for miscommunication. For example, African American clients who are seeking help, exhibiting the healthy cultural paranoia discussed earlier, may begin the encounter as follows: (1) assuming the therapist will not understand the situation due to the racial or cultural difference; (2) perceiving social distance between the therapist and client; (3) expressing fear of being judged by the professional; and (4) exhibiting anxiety due to these concerns. Therapists who are unaware of these potential client perceptions may sense the social distance, feel anxious, fall back on stereotypes to explain the client's behavior, and fail to recognize, acknowledge, and address their own or the client's anxiety.

As the therapeutic relationship continues, a client may maintain feelings of being misunderstood, fail to develop rapport, have greater feelings of distrust, and become less communicative in the encounter. The therapist may respond to the lack of disclosure by assuming the client is resistant and may view the client as unmotivated. A client may then cancel appointments or drop out of treatment without any further interaction with the therapist. In such a case, the therapist may exhibit frustration and could potentially misdiagnose, attributing failure to the client rather than to the worker for failing to appropriately develop rapport and overcome the initial social distance with the client.

Freeman (1990) and Saldana (2001) identified specific professional skills needed to work with culturally diverse populations. Many of these skills can be considered "good practices" with all populations. However, the following is an adaptation of these skills for specific use with African American families:

- Ability to communicate accurate information: being comfortable in assuming a "one-down" position and asking sensitive, nonjudgmental questions to obtain information from the client's perspective
- Ability to openly discuss racial and ethnic differences: acknowledging obvious differences between worker and client and exploring how they may affect the interaction
- Ability to assess the meaning that ethnicity has for individual clients: identifying and understanding the worldview of African American families as being distinct from that of larger society
- Ability to discern between the symptoms of intrapsychic stress and stress arising from the social structure
- Interviewing techniques that enable the client to feel comfortable sharing personal information
- Ability to apply strengths perspective in evaluating strengths within the client, family, and community: assuming the existence of strengths such as strong kinship bonds; spiritual orientation; work orientation; adaptability or fluidity of family roles; high tolerance for environmental stress, ambiguity, and ambivalence; and high achievement orientations (Hill, 1972; Jones, 1983)
- Ability to utilize the concepts of empowerment on behalf of African American clients and communities: assessing strengths within the family and community, including the role and impact of significant others on the client
- Ability to recognize self-help structures in the community: recognizing the traditional family self-help approaches such as the fluidity of family roles, taking in kin, and the role of community agencies and churches in the family's life
- Ability to use resources on behalf of African American clients and their communities: giving appropriate referrals for concrete services if needed before more psychosocial services are provided
- Ability to recognize and combat racism, stereotypes, and myths about African American families: challenging self and others in an attempt to begin to undo the impact of racism and stereotypes in society
- Ability to evaluate the validity of using new therapeutic approaches, research findings, and knowledge with African American populations (Saldana, 2001, pp. 4–5)
- Ability to overcome client resistance and reduce communication barriers
- Ability to use open communication style
- Ability to self-disclose lack of experience or information and to ask questions in a respectful manner
- Ability to modify services to make them accessible and culturally sensitive
- Ability to recognize the need for having African American professional staff as part of the agency

Afrocentric Practice Approaches

It is important to understand the diversity as well as the commonalities within African American communities. As someone once said, Black families are like all other families, some other families, and no other families. Nevertheless, an understanding of the ethos of African Americans allows one to understand the special characteristics that identify them as a group and that set the group apart from other groups. Ethos refers to the common beliefs and emotional responses that stem from a common historical heritage and worldview based upon contemporary experiences that include discrimination, oppression, biased media portrayals, and struggles for equality (Crawley, 1996).

Many believe that the prevailing Western/Eurocentric perspectives are not suited for remedying the conditions faced by many African Americans. Instead, an Afrocentric paradigm has been proposed. The term *Afrocentricity* (sometimes used interchangeably with *Africentricity*) has been used to describe "the cultural values of people of African descent" (Schiele, 1996, p. 284; Akbar, 1984; Daly et al., 1995; Everett et al., 1991). According to Oyebade (1990), "Afrocentricity is a search for those values that will make man relate to man in a humanistic way and not in an imperialistic or exploitative way" (p. 237). Most current social service programs are not designed using African-centered principles for service delivery. Such principles, based on the Nguzo Saba value system, are as follows (Oliver, 1989, pp. 27–32):

- *Umoja* (unity)—to strive for and maintain unity in the family, community, nation, and race
- *Kujichagulia* (self-determination)—to define ourselves, name ourselves, create for ourselves, and speak for ourselves instead of being defined, named, created for, and spoken for by others
- *Ujima* (collective work and responsibility)—to build and maintain our community together, to make our sisters' and brothers' problems our problems, and to solve our problems together
- *Ujamma* (cooperative economics)—to build and maintain our own stores, shops, and other businesses and to profit from them together
- *Nia* (purpose)—to make our collective vocation the building and developing of our community in order to restore our people to their traditional greatness
- *Kuumba* (creativity)—to do always as much as we can, in the way we can, in order to leave our community more beautiful and beneficial than when we inherited it
- *Imani* (faith)—to believe with all our hearts in our people, our parents, our teachers, our leaders, and the righteousness and victory of our struggle (Crawley, 1996, p. 119)

By using such a collective approach, workers may be able to design practice strategies emphasizing group and family strengths that may work more positively with African American populations.

A collective Afrocentric practice approach recognizes that African American families reflect African traditions, Christian beliefs, and adjustments made to slavery ("The American Black Family," 1987, p. 26). According to Schiele (1996), this approach calls for the personalization of the professional relationship by downplaying "aloofness between social worker and client" (p. 291). Similarly, this perspective calls for reciprocity in the helping relationship as social workers recognize the potential for learning from the knowledge and experiences of the client. Social workers who acquire the aforementioned practice skills are likely to be very successful in providing culturally competent services to a variety of African American clients.

GENERATING NEW INDUCTIVE LEARNING ABOUT SOCIAL WORK WITH AFRICAN AMERICANS

According to Lum (1999), inductive learning "is a lifelong process of continuous discovery about the changing nature of multicultural individual, family, and community dynamics" (p. 146). It is based upon the premise that we must move beyond cultural stereotypes through listening to the meanings clients give to their lives and experiences and through observing clients within their ecological systems. Workers' assessments are based upon learning and discovering with clients, asking questions, using a strengths perspective, and embracing clients' behavioral styles, belief systems, and coping patterns (Lum, 1999, p. 152). Moreover, this approach draws upon qualitative research strategies that include inductive data gathering to seek an understanding of clients' perspectives on their problems. This approach empowers clients, as they assume the role of teacher, and the social worker is in the role of learner.

The inductive process leads the practitioner to approach the client with questions such as "What does X (an experience, belief, person, family, etc.) mean to you?" As the client describes the meaning, the practitioner engages in a data-gathering process through the client's narrative as well as the practitioner's observations. Using such narrative-generating questions and observations, the worker is able to develop an understanding of the client's reality. This data is then used to look for common themes that can be discussed with the client, who can then "confirm them, build upon them, or reject them" (Lum, 1999, p. 158). This approach leads to a more client- and culture-specific understanding of issues.

In practice with African American clients, the inductive approach suggests moving away from generalized, often stereotypically negative beliefs about African Americans to more of a practitioner–researcher approach. It means that the worker will utilize a strengths perspective by looking for positives rather than pathologizing clients. This is particularly important with African American clients, as so much has been written on this population from a pathological perspective. Using a strengths approach, the worker is able to form a client–worker partnership, and jointly the client and worker examine the client's knowledge and experience. This allows the worker to understand and embrace the client's behavioral styles, belief systems, and coping patterns (Lum, 1999). In this perspective, the worker clearly values the client's knowledge, beliefs, strengths, talents, and coping strategies. This approach is empowering to the client and serves to move the client from a position of learned helplessness to one of learned hopefulness. Instead of workers being in the role of informants to clients, the clients inform the workers and offer their own perspectives on how they think, feel and behave in specific situations. This tends to broaden the knowledge of practitioners and to increase the likelihood of a successful intervention based on client reality rather than only the worker's evaluative perspective, which is often more narrow.

TOOLS FOR STUDENT LEARNING 10.3

The Case of Mariah

Review the following case and respond to the questions listed after it.

Mariah is an 18-year-old African American girl who is currently single and pregnant with her first child. She dropped out of high school during her senior year but hopes to get her GED and eventually to become a special education teacher. Currently, she is living in a transitional living program for pregnant and parenting teens because she has just aged out of foster care and has no permanent home. Her baby is due in three months. Her current boyfriend is not the father of her baby. She met the African American boyfriend at a shelter for drug dependent youth that is located not far from the transitional living program. Her boyfriend hopes to "get clean" and get a job and support Mariah and her child. Mariah is having difficulty getting employment right now because she is six months pregnant, so she is very hopeful that her boyfriend will be able to support her. She has no contact with the Anglo father of her child but believes he is in jail for burglary. Her White foster parents moved to another town right after Mariah turned 18. She planned to be on her own but discovered she was pregnant, and she had no job or place to live. Mariah was physically abused in the home of her birth parents by her stepfather and was removed at the age of 4. She has been living in foster homes since her removal. She has two older brothers who were also removed; she has had no further contact with either of them. The social worker, Ms. Martin, first met Mariah when she was assigned her case at the transitional living program.

1. Using an inductive approach, what questions would Ms. Martin want to ask to better understand the meaning of this situation for Mariah?

2. What other forms of data collection should Ms. Martin use to better understand Mariah's situation?

3. How would Ms. Martin utilize a strengths perspective in working on this case?

4. How would Ms. Martin develop a positive client–worker partnership with Mariah?

UNDERSTANDING AND ADVOCATING SOCIAL AND ECONOMIC JUSTICE FOR AFRICAN AMERICANS

Gaining knowledge and understanding of the historical as well as contemporary inequities that many African Americans have experienced leads social workers to become more involved in advocating for social and economic justice. Social justice "refers to the manner in which society provides resources for its members" (Miley, O'Melia, & DuBois, 1995, p. 17). Historically and currently in the United States, the dominant White society has differentially held power, privilege, and resources and has treated persons of color inequitably. To maintain this sense of power, some members of dominant groups try to obscure or rationalize the unequal distribution of resources through the process of moral exclusion by assuming that some groups do not merit fair treatment (Staub, 1987). This allows those who have power and privilege to justify maintaining this system. For example, the lower educational attainment of African Americans, as compared to Whites, is often attributed to their lack of ability rather than to the fact that they have had limited access to well-funded public schools and, therefore, have not had access to equal educational opportunities.

Slavery, segregation, and "Jim Crow" laws are all examples of oppressive uses of power (Billingsley, 1992; *Oppression*, 1998). Society's unwillingness to challenge everyday practices of discrimination that result in oppression is defined as structural–cultural violence (Van Soest & Bryant, 1995). A related aspect of oppression is the internalization of oppression in which disempowered people carry out stereotypes and sometimes behave in ways that conform to the negative images society has of them. This internalization process further limits the opportunities for members of oppressed groups. Moreover, some disempowered people find that not only are they isolated from dominant society but also they are made to feel that the problems they experience are self-imposed rather than being imposed by society. For example, in 1965, the Moynihan report characterized African American families as primarily "female-headed," deviant, and pathological. However, in reality, a number of social and political factors were responsible for the undermining of the Black family, including social welfare policies beginning in the 1950s (e.g., AFDC, which required male absence from the house for a woman to receive assistance). Such policies began to force men out of the family while "systematically entitling women, and not their husbands, to benefits" (Jewell, 1988, p. 25).

Culturally competent and proficient practitioners can acknowledge and explore the effects of power and privilege, look beyond cultural stereotypes and explanations, and recognize the impact of social policies on families. They seek to become effective advocates for African Americans and to develop strategies for shifting power to and sharing power with African American clients (*Oppression*, 1998). The use of the inductive method of data gathering (discussed earlier) is an example of one of these empowering strategies. Moreover, social workers must commit to the development of strategies for moral inclusion, operate from a strengths perspective, build coalitions with oppressed groups, call attention to inequities, and commit to advocating for social and economic justice in their professional lives.

SUMMARY

This chapter has focused on the unique attributes of African Americans in the United States. Beginning with their forced transplantation from Africa that started four centuries ago and continuing with the ongoing racial oppression and discrimination that African Americans experience in U.S. society today, African Americans are the most racially stigmatized and stereotyped ethnic group in the United States. Due to the history of exclusion, segregation, and separation, much distrust, paranoia, and hostility still exists between Whites and Blacks. Although Blacks have made substantial economic gains in the recent past, major economic disparities still exist in terms of employment opportunities and earnings. African Americans continue to be underserved in many service areas, including the health care delivery system, and to be overrepresented in the population of persons who are poor, in prison, and in out-of-home care.

Vast diversity exists among African Americans, including physical characteristics, socioeconomic status, perceptions of racial identity, and interpersonal styles. Most African Americans have experienced racism, oppression, and discrimination, and those experiences influence their interactions and worldviews.

Many social service agencies continue to find it difficult to reach this population, and social workers are challenged to become more culturally competent to facilitate communication, interaction, and intervention. The utilization of a strengths-based, inductive, practitioner–researcher approach tends to increase the likelihood of effective interventions with African Americans. Afrocentric approaches also need to be implemented and evaluated to determine whether they may be more effective than traditional Eurocentric approaches with some African American clients. Finally, social workers must become cognizant of and be willing to challenge the effects of ongoing inequities and oppression and to advocate for social and economic justice for African Americans.

CHAPTER ELEVEN

Cultural Competence with Latino Americans

BETTY GARCIA AND MARIA E. ZUNIGA

The Latino population in the United States is increasing faster than it did in the 1990s and represents the fastest-growing sector of the population. Latinos account for half of the growth in U.S. population since 2000 and represent 14 percent of the U.S. population, not counting Puerto Rico. Whereas 41.3 million out of a national population of 293.7 million Hispanics represented 40 percent of the population increase in the 1990s, the Latino population represented 49 percent of the total population increase between 2000 and 2004 (Cohn, 2005; U.S. Department of Education, 2003). Currently, one-half of adult Latinos are immigrants (Cohn, 2005). In contrast to the "graying" of America where half of non-Hispanic Whites are over 40, half of Latinos are under the age of 27. Undocumented immigrants outnumber incoming immigrants with visas (Passel, 2005), and births have outpaced immigration increases with one in five children in the United States under the age of 18 being Hispanic. With 11 percent of Hispanics under the age of 4, Latinos have a higher number of preschoolers than any other group (U.S. Department of Education, 2003). Moreover, projections suggest that by 2020, one in four children will be Hispanic, up from one in five (Freking, 2005), and by 2050, Latinos will represent 24 percent of the population, reflecting a 188 percent growth (Bergman, 2004). Mexicans continue to represent the largest group within this heterogeneous population and constitute 64 percent of all Latinos. Latinos of other national origins, such as Cubans and Central and South Americans, each represent 3 percent of Latinos (U.S. Department of Education, 2003).

A review of the socioeconomic profile of Latinos shows that in 2004, almost 22 percent lived in poverty, which is unchanged from the 2003 poverty rates (Wollman, n.d.). Fifty-eight percent of Hispanics aged 25 and older have a high school education, and 13 percent have a bachelor's degree, compared to 31 percent of Euro-Americans who have bachelor's degrees (U.S. Department of Education, 2003). Latinos represent 5 percent of the total population aged 65 and over, whereas Euro-Americans represent 15 percent (Bernstein, 2005).

Practice with Latinos assumes that social work professionals will become knowledgeable about the heterogeneity of the Latino population. Social workers are challenged to consider multiple variables in individualizing their clients; they are also challenged to consider the complex problems this population encounters in U.S. society. For example, some Latino subgroups have the highest high school dropout rates (Roderick, 2000) and the lowest rates of high school completion in the country. The realities experienced by

Latinos who have been in the United States for four generations are similar in some ways to those experienced by Latinos who are immigrants to the United States, yet there are some major differences. The experiences of immigrants from Central American countries torn by civil war, particularly those immigrants without documentation, are similar and yet quite different from the experience of undocumented immigrants from Mexico. The experiences of Cuban Americans are similar in terms of the Spanish language to those of Puerto Ricans or Latinos of Mexican heritage, yet each group has a unique political history from which the people derive special insights and meanings from their "construction of reality" (O'Brien & Kollock, 2001).

Latinos are a heterogeneous group comprised of a multitude of national origins from all parts of Latin America and the Caribbean. Although Mexicans represent the largest number of Latinos in the United States, it is becoming increasingly common, depending on what region one lives in, to encounter Latinos with diverse national origins. A perspective that views all Latinos as a monolithic group that has more sameness than difference denies the unique historical, social, cultural, and political characteristics of this rich, multifaceted population. Ethical and culturally competent practice requires both process and content skills that demonstrate an ability to engage as well as to gather and use information about a culture. Content skills require having sufficient information about the history and context of a particular population and serve as a foundation for developing hypotheses with which to learn about the actual reality and social identity of Latino client(s). However, process skills used in engagement and rapport building require transparency by the professional and are motivated by curiosity and respect for diversity. Process skills and skillful engagement allow discovery of the uniqueness and worldview of the client. Everything else is conjecture and risks operating on the basis of stereotypes.

A practice approach that appreciates one's limitations in knowing other cultures, values learning about diversity, develops hypotheses about one's clients, and suspends making conclusions until one is informed by the clients has been referred to as "informed, not knowing" (Anderson & Goolishian, 1992; Laird, 1998). Maintaining a compassionate posture with the client as expert attends to the feelings that get triggered in transactions with diverse clients, requires managing what can be quite uncomfortable, and deals with ambiguity. Holding onto impressions or feelings without drawing conclusions can be uncomfortable and yet is essential in one's practice with unfamiliar cultures, settings, or individuals.

Culturally competent practice with Latinos must be premised on knowledge of the diverse sociopolitical complexity of Latinos, based on national origin, immigrant status, social identity, experience of oppression, level of acculturation, and other factors such as religion and socioeconomic class that influence the psychosocial characteristics of individuals and families. The following section will first address factors related to national origin and will follow with discussion of current research and writing before discussing cultural competence.

NATIONALITY AND LATINO AMERICAN COMPLEXITY

Historically and demographically, Latin America is complex in that virtually every world ethnic, racial, and religious population has immigrated to various parts of Latin America. Although Spain has been the major colonizer of a majority of Latin America, and thus most Latinos have the Spanish language as their heritage, Dutch, Portuguese and British colonizers have also had a presence in South America and have left legacies of cultural influence. Some generalizations about shared cultural values can be made about Latinos; however, these must always be made in the context of socioeconomic class, national origin, and class and/or color privilege. Also, as the following suggests, it is essential to understand potentially significant factors in the individual's and family's life course experiences. More will be said on this in the discussion on assessment.

The history of oppression in U.S. society and contemporary negative stereotyping of Latinos contribute to the ongoing experience of discrimination and racism toward Latinos. Practice with Latinos requires that social workers be knowledgeable about the consequences of low social power and institutional racism within the United States.

The following narratives on a few of the many Latino countries are provided to provoke further exploration on the vast diversity in the national origins of Latino Americans. This chapter does not permit full treatment of essential information on the richness of these nations.

Mexican Heritage

The Treaty of Guadalupe Hidalgo resulted in the sale of what is now California and New Mexico to the United States for $15 million in 1848. This negotiation was an outcome of the U.S.-Mexican War and led to long-standing tensions between the native Mexican residents and the new U.S. settlers. Aggression against Mexicans during this period resulted in Mexicans being hunted and killed (Acuna, 1972) and was accompanied by the growth of negative stereotyping about Mexicans as inferior. Activism by Reies López Tijerina, who was imprisoned for his militancy regarding the land appropriation in New Mexico, has brought attention to support of the United States in unethical and illegal maneuvers of Euro-American private interests to divest residents of their land grants. Because many of these residents' families received land grants from Spain, they were the first to identify as Hispanic due to the identification with Spain (Acuna, 1972).

The history of Mexican Americans in California has several contentious points. Wartime stress is attributed with having a role in the Los Angeles Zoot Suit Riot of 1943, a week-long clash between White, off-duty U.S. sailors and Mexican American youths who dressed in what were called "zoot suits." Naval personnel reportedly battered and taunted Mexican immigrants and residents with little to no interference by local police. The Lemon Grove Incident in San Diego in 1931 (Alvarez, 1986) represents one of the earliest successful desegregation cases. In this instance, the Mexican American community rallied when their children were ordered to attend a segregated school. The Mexican American community succeeded in assuring that their children would attend desegregated schools. This occurred during a period when anti-immigrant sentiment in southern California led to hundreds of thousands of Mexican nationals and U.S. citizens being deported to Mexico.

Legislation known as Proposition 187, voted on in California in 1994, is viewed as one of the most controversial initiatives in history. Under Proposition 187, immigrants residing in the United States without legal documentation, mainly Mexican immigrants, were restricted from receiving public health services, social services, and education and welfare benefits (Cowan, Martinez, & Mendiola, 1997). Proponents of the bill argued that the legislation would ensure economic savings for California, and opponents pointed to the measure as a form of racial discrimination and a direct assault on the California Latino community (Cowan et al., 1997). Although the legality of this proposition was immediately challenged in court, the Coalition for Humane Immigrant Rights of Los Angeles (CHIRLA) noted that hate crimes toward Latino immigrants increased after the proposition's passage (CHIRLA, 1995). More recently, the increasing number of border deaths between Arizona and Texas since 2000 has attracted growing attention. U.S. Customs and Border Protection declared in September 2005 that 415 deaths had occurred in the last 11 months alone, surpassing the high of 383 deaths in 2000. The oppression of Mexican-heritage persons continues and is buttressed by the abuse of academic scholarship, such as Harvard political scientist Samuel Huntington's warning that Mexican immigration to the United States "looms as a unique and disturbing challenge to our cultural integrity. . . ." (Lindsay & Michaelidis, 2001, p. B7).

Puerto Rican Experiences

Oppression of Puerto Ricans stems from the political situation of Puerto Rico as a colony of the United States, as well as from racial discrimination (Negroni-Rodriguez & Morales, 2001). The United States appropriated Puerto Rico in 1900 (Foraker Act) as an unincorporated territory after the Spanish-American War ended 400 years of Spanish rule, and in 1917, the Jones Act imposed U.S. citizenship on the residents of Puerto Rico (Montijo, 1985). As American citizens, Puerto Ricans serve in the American military and are subject to most American federal laws. English was enforced as the language of instruction until 1930; however, a change to the policy of instruction in the Spanish language was not passed until 1948. The question over commonwealth versus statehood status remains a flashpoint for heated debate among Puerto Ricans on the island and in New York City, where there are large settlements. Extensive testing of birth control methods in remote parts of Puerto Rico in the 1950s by international interests left a significant portion of women in that generation infertile. Also, in the 1990s the presence of the United States military and ongoing practice bombing maneuvers on the island of Vieques captured public attention in the United States and informed the American public of opposition to the U.S. presence on the island (*Orlando Sentinel*, 2001).

Cuban Experiences

Cuba's history with the corrupt regime of the Cuban dictator Fulgencio Batista began with a coup in 1933. The regime benefited from collusion with U.S. corporations and endured until 1959 with the Marxist revolution led by Fidel Castro. The effects of the political regime were buttressed by an economy based on gambling, and international commerce contributed to the revolution when the disenfranchised and low-income Cuban population pushed for a government that was more responsive to the needs of the Cuban community. The revolution initially resulted in thousands of Cubans, primarily from privileged classes, fleeing their homeland to the United States.

The subsequent *Cubanization* of such cities as Miami resulted in anti-immigrant attitudes that manifested as anti-Cuban. The waves of immigration that occurred over time elicited from U.S. citizens varied reactions, such as efforts to maintain English as the official language in Florida. In 1980, the refugees from Mariel, who are also called the

Marielitos, represented one wave of immigrants. This group did not meet the open arms that greeted Cuban refugees prior to 1980, primarily because this boatlift was allegedly overrepresented by criminals, prostitutes, and people who had been jailed in Cuba. However, research confirmed that only about 10 percent of this population had, in fact, been jailed in Cuba (Clark, Lasaga, & Reque, 1981, as quoted by Puig, 2001). Moreover, one of the reasons often cited for the difference in reception was that 35 percent of the Mariel refugees were Black males of limited education and employment skills (Clark et al., 1981).

The various waves of immigration from Cuba to the United States most often represented privileged classes of European phenotype. One consequence of this phenomenon is that the demographic profile of Cuba is increasingly African Latino with Cubans of European phenotype becoming the minority. Also, in the United States, the Cuban response to the immigration and refugee experience, the increase of Cuban professionals as refugees, and the growth of the number of Cuban business owners has resulted in anti-Castro, conservative attitudes. Cubans have a high profile in the media industry, and Latinos who secure federal appointments or achieve political office, particularly in the East and Southeast, are often Cuban. The intersection between socioeconomic class privilege and European phenotype and conservative political leanings suggests that it is essential to understand the meaning of these distinctions for the Cuban individuals, families, and communities.

Central American Experiences

It is important to understand the political, economic, and social demographics of diverse Central American immigrants in the United States. Their diversity challenges generalizations about them. Differences abound in relation to the socioeconomic class, colonizers' language (i.e., English, Spanish, Portuguese), and demographics of the country of national origin in relation to indigenous, mestizo (combination of European and indigenous), or European phenotype.

The population of Belize, former British Honduras, speaks both English and Spanish. The influx of immigrants from Jamaica and other Caribbean islands for the building of the canal in Panama in the early 1900s has also resulted in English and Spanish language proficiency. Panama's political situation into the late 20th century was problematic due to a dictatorship by President Noriega.

In the 1970s and 1980s, when the civil wars in Nicaragua, El Salvador, and Guatemala were front-page news, the United States experienced a major flow of immigration from those countries. It is estimated that more than a million Salvadoran and 200,000 Guatemalan refugees live in the United States (Melville & Lykes, 1992). Central American immigration was heavily composed of children and youths (Benjamin & Morgan, 1989). These young immigrants sometimes witnessed people being beheaded or gunned down before their eyes, the kind of premigration trauma that leads to serious psychological distress if not addressed. The political tensions in Nicaragua and El Salvador, marked by civil wars that split families along political lines, led to the deaths of thousands, left others seeking refuge in the United States, oftentimes with fear of death should they return to their homeland. Nicaraguans experienced political oppression first with the Somoza government, which ended in 1979, and later with the subsequent Sandinista regime.

Denied refugee status by the United States, these immigrants often entered the country as undocumented immigrants. The unevenness in deciding who could be classified as a refugee and who could be viewed as an illegal immigrant was determined by the former INS (Immigration and Naturalization Service), which often presented an oppressive challenge that could overwhelm immigrants who had already suffered so much in their former country (Potocky-Tripodi, 1999).

The civil war that ravaged El Salvador in the 1980s ended in 1989; however, the vestiges of that war have been felt internationally. For example, the growth of gang activity by the "Mara Salvatrucha" began with the deportation of a small group of Salvadoran youths from Los Angeles back to El Salvador in the early 1980s. The combination of gang activity in Southern California and civil war experiences resulted in violence between gangs in 33 states in the United States and in El Salvador, Honduras, and Guatemala. It is estimated between 40,000 and 100,000 gang members exist in Central America alone (Salinas, 2005).

South American Experiences

The South American continent is characterized by vastly diverse countries with differences in demographics with indigenous populations such as those in Ecuador, Bolivia, and Peru. Others have a mix of mestizo and European phenotype, as in Chile and Venezuela, or a mixture of mestizo, European, and African phenotypes as found in Columbia. Argentina's demographics, on the other hand, have strong European phenotypes based on huge waves of immigration from Italy, Spain, England, and Germany; most of the indigenous population was nomadic and was either pushed to the north or disappeared. The political situations are likewise extremely varied with a few having gained more international attention than others, such as Chile's struggle to deal with the Pinochet coup of Salvador Allende's government in 1973 by bringing Pinochet to trial in the 21st century.

For many Latinos, issues of language, cultural, historical, and socioeconomic differences highlight their immigrant backgrounds and make them vulnerable to discrimination and racism from U.S. residents. Latinos who are dark skinned or have indigenous or African phenotypes face racism, occasionally even in their own families. For low-income families, daily management of ongoing hassles, societal stereotypes, and negative expectations can often feel overwhelming.

Elderly Latinos

A growing body of literature focuses on the needs of Latino elderly and their caregivers. Ayalon and Huyck (2002) found that Latino caregivers with relatives with Alzheimer's disease are most often females caring for parents or parents-in–law, and that they underutilize social services. Research on the toll of aging and caregiving has examined how health problems associated with aging have depleted finances (Kim & Lee, 2005). Latina Alzheimer's caregivers report lower levels of stress, greater perceived benefits of caregiving, and greater use of religious coping compared to Euro-American caregivers (Coon et al., 2004). Latino caregivers' appraisal of satisfaction has been found to effect depression and a sense of personal gain (Morano, 2003).

Research on hospices and Latinos has found that Latinos use hospice services at lower rates than Euro-Americans do (Colon & Lyke, 2003). Limited knowledge of hospice programs, fear of discrimination, possible costs, low-income status, lack of health insurance, low levels of education, and language concerns may inhibit the use of hospice services by Mexicans (Gelfand, Balcazar, Parzuchowski, & Lenox, 2004; Randall & Csikai, 2003).

Zunker, Rutt, and Meza (2005) found that Mexican elders valued knowledge from life experience and raising a family and viewed quality of health as being related to socioeconomic status, family support, chronic disease, and earlier life circumstances. Mexican elders also reported having poor health and believing that it is difficult to access quality health care. Bertera (2003) found that elderly Latinos over 60 years of age were more likely to be unaware of having a high glucose level and to have low levels of social support and affiliation compared to other groups.

Cuellar, Bastida, and Braccio (2004) found that acculturation, age, and gender account for more depression among Mexican immigrants aged 45 and over, compared to Mexican Americans. Puerto Rican elders who report low incomes, recent migration to the northeast United States, perceptions of poor health, limited interaction with relatives on a monthly basis, and a need for emotional support were more likely to be depressed than other Puerto Rican elders (Robison et al., 2003).

Grandchildren's problem behavior contributes to Latino grandparents' negative affect, and parents' presence in the home during Latino grandparenting contributes to grandparents having a greater sense of well-being (Goodman & Silverstein, 2005). Hill, Angel, Ellison, and Angel (2005) found that attending church once a week reduces risk of mortality among Mexican Americans.

Ethnocultural factors appear to influence the stress of caregiving for Puerto Ricans (Ramos, 2004). Likewise, acculturation factors in utilizing support services for aging Latino parents (Radina & Barber, 2004). Gallagher-Thompson and colleagues (2003) found that providing skill building to Latino female caregivers of elderly relatives with dementia is more effective than managing caregiving distress through support alone. Weitzman, Chang, and Reynoso (2004) examined how middle-aged Latino women prefer female doctors, compared to older Latino women who preferred male doctors, and although both groups valued trustworthiness in physicians and preferred Spanish-speaking physicians, they did not want physicians of their own ethnicity.

Latino Gay and Lesbian Research

A small body of research on gay and lesbian issues has identified, among Latino gay males, histories of verbal and physical abuse, mistreatment, discrimination due to sexual orientation, as well as poverty and increased psychological distress (Diaz, Ayala & Bein, 2004). Williams and colleagues (2004) found histories of sexual abuse among HIV seropositive Latino males. Rosario, Schrimshaw, and Hunter (2004) suggest that Latino youths disclose less about sexual orientation compared to Euro-American youths, and that cultural factors possibly delay integration of identity. Colon's (2001) ethnographic study of gay and bisexual Latino males examined immigration, acculturation, cultural values, health, and mental health beliefs in relation to social functioning. Adams, Cahill, and Ackerlind (2005) found six themes in their understanding of the intersection of Latinos and sexual orientation. Three of the themes are awareness of being different, prejudice from one's ethnic group, and issues related to identity management in the workplace. Parks, Hughes, and Matthews (2004) discovered that lesbian women reported having to confront norms and expectations of both majority and ethnic cultures.

Latinos and Ethics

Very little research and writing has focused on Latinos and ethics. The NASW Code of Ethics (1996) provides a guide for a perspective on professional responsibilities and the necessity of commitment to social change. A small body of work has addressed how the vulnerability of migrant farm workers based on low socioeconomic status makes it particularly important that researchers who study this population be rigorous in utilizing methods that inhibit the potential harm by research (Cooper et al., 2004), provide clarity on informed consent without assuming participants would indicate if they did not understand (Adams, 2004), realize ethical and policy issues associated with the dilemma of rationing care to undocumented children (Young, Flores, & Berman, 2004), and recognize the importance of community-based participatory designs with this population (Martin & Latnos, 2005). Research regarding adolescents from an ecological-ethical viewpoint has shown that specific stressors related to immigration, such as poverty and discrimination, can lead to greater parental involvement that can compete with tasks related to education and peer engagement and can also result in adolescents feeling a greater sense of personal and interpersonal competence (Jurkovic et al., 2004). Also, Lazzari, Ford, and Haughey (1996) identified many complex realities in the lives of Mexican American women that heighten the need for ethically bound interventions.

Ethical practice with Latinos must demonstrate knowledge, values, and skills premised on the NASW Standards for Cultural Competence (2001), developed by the National Committee on Racial and Ethnic Diversity (NCORED). In addition to identifying standards related to ethics and values, these standards also identify criteria related to self-awareness, cross-cultural knowledge, cross-cultural skills, service delivery, empowerment and advocacy, diverse workforce, professional education, language diversity, and cross-cultural leadership. These standards identify a wide range of domains based on ethical professional behavior that include development of self-awareness and extend to macro-level professional advocacy. Self-awareness professional responsibilities evoke learning about one's own personal heritage in relation to the family's national origins, the internalization of societal biases, and the recognition of how fear and ignorance feed into racism and ethnocentrism.

WHAT IS CULTURALLY COMPETENT PRACTICE WITH LATINO AMERICANS?

Cultural competence is defined as a set of congruent behaviors, attitudes, and policies that become integrated in a system, agency, or among professionals and, in turn, enable that system, agency, or those professionals to work effectively in cross-cultural situations (Cross et al., 1989). Cross and colleagues (1989) indicate five elements essential to ensuring that a system, institution, agency, or professional is able to become more culturally competent: (1) valuing diversity; (2) having the capacity for cultural self-assessment; (3) being conscious of the dynamics inherent when cultures interact; (4) having institutionalized cultural knowledge; and (5) having developed adaptations to diversity, basing practice on accurate perceptions of behavior, constructing impartial policies, and demonstrating unbiased attitudes (p. v).

Appreciation of diversity applies not only to the ethnic, racial, and cultural forms of diversity but also to socioeconomic class diversity. A challenge for a social worker from a middle-class background when assessing problem-solving methods of a low-income person is not to evaluate, devalue, or compare his or her judgments to middle-class expectations. For example, for the middle-class worker who is accustomed to using a budget and anticipating long-term goals, a Latino client's decisions on how to spend a lump sum of money from an overdue disability check may evoke conflicts in the way the client uses the money. Issues of value preferences, style, and survival experiences may be very different between the two class cultures. Can the worker refrain from devaluing what the client does with the money but think how to enable the client to learn to problem solve in expanded and future-oriented ways? Teaching a client another way to view the problem is a tool; devaluing the way a client uses his or her money is unethical. The negative criticism does not teach but only diminishes the client's self-esteem.

Latino social workers who come from a subgroup that is different in socioeconomic class or have different cultural expectations, meaning-making, or value preferences of clients, face challenges to suspend their assumptions about these clients. Rather, they must check their perceptions by undertaking thorough assessments. The issues of nativity, phenotype, acculturation, generation level, and native-born and foreign-born differences, to name a few factors, can make a difference both in how the worker will relate to a client and in the kinds of interventions that will be more or less effective with a Latino client or family system. Regardless of ethnic, racial, or class background, Latino social workers must learn how to develop the appropriate knowledge and skill repertoire for this vast population in order to ensure that their practice is culturally competent.

The question workers must ask themselves is, "Can I work with clients and not demean, devalue, or project attitudes that clients feel devalue them and their behaviors?" This is where Cross and colleagues' (1989) requirements for conscious use of self and analysis of the intersection between cultures are critical and must undergird our interventions with clients who are diverse from us. That is, we must be aware of how we employ ourselves in a helping situation and how our cultural understanding relates to another person's culture. For middle-class Latino professionals, this self-awareness is particularly necessary because they may assume they have the cultural competencies to serve Latinos without recognizing the differences that exist.

Cultural competency faces challenges regarding workers' attitudes relating to a Latino client's undocumented status. Utilization of the term *illegal aliens* construes a value stance and bias about their status. Some people in society consider undocumented immigrants as criminals who have broken the law. These immigrants are viewed in such a negative fashion that they are dehumanized and are seen as less moral, which then allows society to feel less compassion for their plight.

Immigrants are acting on a right to improve their life and often make life-threatening journeys to cross the U.S.–Mexican border in order to work and finance their family's well-being. Once in the United States, they are at major risk for poor living conditions, economic exploitation, and racist treatment (Perez Foster, 2001). It is important for social workers to view them or treat them not as criminals but as people who have a right to resources. According to the NASW Code of Ethics, social workers are obligated to facilitate access to resources for those clients who come to them in need. They must respond to the client's plight in an unbiased fashion; holding negative sentiments toward those who are not in the United States legally is unethical (Zuniga, 2001).

Undocumented status is one factor that contributes to Latino groups' diversity. The following text discusses other areas of difference for social workers to consider in their assessment, planning, practice, and research.

DIVERSITY: ASSESSMENT, PLANNING, RESEARCH, AND PRACTICE

Assessment: Language, Immigration, and Acculturation

Assessment demands that workers examine the complexity of clients to formulate interventions with them. The following discussion reflects some of these themes.

Language. Language differences must be considered. Many Latinos in the process of acculturation lose their Spanish language skills, especially by the third generation. Although this is an important marker of acculturation and integration of the American culture, the worker must not be confused and make erroneous assumptions. Values of reliance on family and the family-centeredness that often characterize this population may still be operating in acculturated individuals and families and must be woven into the planning and intervention processes.

In addition, each Latino national origin group speaks Spanish with a cultural style that highlights group differences. Each group has idioms and metaphors that belong exclusively to that group. Workers who are bilingual in Spanish and English must look for differences in expressions and idioms; they should not be fearful of asking clients to clarify the terms they use. Workers also can ask clients whether they comprehend the workers' idioms. Although language is discussed more fully in the practice section later in this chapter, an important aspect of the assessment process is to determine the client's language preference. Some bilinguals prefer to be served in English or Spanish if the agency offers that resource. Others can be served effectively only in Spanish, in which case the agency needs to ensure this resource is available—at a minimum, through the services of a translator.

Immigration. The Immigration and Naturalization Service (INS), formerly the sole agency to oversee immigrants' applications for a visa and/or citizenship, split into two agencies with the 2002 establishment of the Department of Homeland Security. Depending on their immigration circumstances, immigrants potentially can have contact with both the Bureau of Border Security that oversees patrolling of the borders and/or the Bureau of Citizenship and Immigration Services that oversees applications for visas, asylum, naturalization, and refugee status (U.S. Department of Homeland Security, n.d.).

Immigration history represents a realm of life experience that demands close examination due to the range of factors that can influence its meaning in the lives of individuals, families, and communities. Attachment theory suggests that age at the time of immigration is a significant psychosocial factor (Rodriguez, 2004). Developmentally, distinct considerations exist according to whether the person was in childhood, adolescence, transitional youth stage, mid-life, or older adulthood at the time of immigration. In addition, migration must be considered in the context of three stages: (1) Predominant feelings of sorrow, fear of the unfamiliar, loneliness, and isolation. Prior feelings of unresolved loss can get activated through this process. An ability to move into a role (i.e., work, career) and create connections in the new location that are similar to those in the homeland can assist the transition. Other variables that can exacerbate or assist the transition are the extent to which the new culture is different from that of the national origin, the quality of responsiveness of the host culture, the success or failure in the new environment, and the acquisition of legal status. The language adjustments are critical because of the role of language in identity; (2) Feelings and thoughts that the immigrant had denied in order to manage the potentially overwhelming task of moving and adjusting can begin to surface and/or break through their awareness; and (3) the immigrant has worked through feelings of loss and mourning for what was left behind and is well underway integrating into life the elements of the new host environment and culture. He or she feels like a member of the new society and maintains a positive relation to his or her national origin, language, and culture. It is possible that for some, the process of mourning remains a lifelong process (Rodriguez, 2004).

Sluzki and Ransom (1976) and, more recently, Drachman (1992), have outlined stage-of-migration frameworks for use in clinical assessment. Perez Foster (2001) studied work by Desjarlais and colleagues (1995) that elucidates four migration stages during which there exists the potential for traumatogenic experiences that can lead to serious psychological distress. These stages include the following: (1) premigration trauma experienced just prior to migration or caused by the move itself; (2) traumatic events the immigrant undergoes during the journey; (3) continued traumatic experiences while in the process of asylum-seeking and resettlement; and (4) below-standard living conditions due to unemployment, isolation, and discrimination once in the country.

Workers should examine the literature on immigrant populations and select a framework that readily fits the immigrant population they are working with. Workers must be sensitive to the needs of traumatized immigrants to avoid discussing the trauma as a defense and must work diligently not to collude with clients in avoiding the details of trauma they experienced before or during their migration (Perez Foster, 1998, 2001).

A variety of difficulties arise as a result of many immigration-related issues, such as why the immigration took place (e.g., forced to leave as refugees, economic motivation), who was left behind and for what reason (e.g., siblings, parents), how the immigration was arranged and managed (e.g., agents, such as a "coyote" who, for a large fee, takes undocumented immigrants into the new host country or arranges passage through other persons), and experiences during their journey (e.g., robbery, rape). There is some evidence that women traveling alone from Central America or Mexico are at risk for months-long sexual assaults and forced labor as payments to coyotes or illegal travel brokers (Perez Foster, 2001). The process for many Mexicans crossing the U.S. border without documents can lead to experiences that are the basis for post-traumatic stress disorder (PTSD) and clinical levels of anxiety and depression (Desjarlais et al., 1995).

Workers must learn how to assess immigration history in a fashion that does not further exacerbate the negative emotions, such as fearfulness and anxiety, associated with the immigration process. Because the immigrant may be at a point where he or she has not begun to process the experiences and may be dissociating from the painful aspects of the experience (Perez Foster, 2001; Rodriguez, 2004), workers need to learn how to probe these experiences with sensitivity by beginning with asking "safe" questions about the experience and slowly, once rapport is established, moving into more sensitive areas. This supports the person in bearing the pain that is triggered as he or she talks about the guilt and anguish associated with adaptation to the new culture. It can feel like carrying a full load of emotional baggage as one is attempting to navigate through a new world. The stories of the immigrants are extremely sensitive narratives that oftentimes cannot be shared easily or quickly but are of the utmost importance in evaluating the extent to which this kind of trauma affects their ability to adapt.

Workers need to clarify unique aspects of the client's experience such as whether the client has documented or undocumented status (Perez Foster, 2001). Workers must decipher as a crucial assessment pathway what country clients are from and whether war or civil strife was part of their experience. All immigrants have to suffer the difficulties of adapting to a new country, new culture, and new language in addition to possibly managing difficulties related to documentation or histories of war in their countries.

New Geographic Settlements. Oppressive circumstances began to arise more often in the latter part of the 20th century as Latino immigrants settled in such states as Iowa, North Carolina, and South Carolina. Although the draw of employment (e.g., in poultry-packing industries) offers important financial resources, the lack of experience of the areas' institutions in working with this population contributes to discrimination and rejection for these immigrants (Ewell, 2000). Latino immigrants settling in these new frontiers do not have the enclaves found in cities in such states as Texas, Illinois, and California, where Spanish-speaking immigrants have traditionally found comfortable networks and cultural supports quite readily, which helps to temper the discrimination experiences. These immigrants have to learn how to adjust to their new locations without the cultural ties, resources, and supports that De Anda (1984) identified as facilitating the adaptation of new immigrants.

An important assessment feature the worker must undertake is to determine what natural support networks are available for clients in the cities or regions in which they live. Are there resources offered by churches or community organizations that will support the immigrants' adaptation? Such cultural traditions as parades, festivals, and church groups were seen as contributing to the development of organizations and community activists for the Puerto Rican community in Hartford, Connecticut (Cruz, 1998, as noted by Acevedo & Morales, 2001).

Acculturation themes. A major area that makes a difference in meaning making or value choices and interaction preferences is level of acculturation. Acculturation is the process wherein the ethnic values, behaviors, and rituals clients hold from their traditional culture change over time and integrate with the values, behaviors, and rituals of the majority or host culture (Levine & Padilla, 1980). The term *assimilation* refers to the end product of those who have completely removed all aspects of their traditional culture and replaced them with those of the host culture. An ultimate gesture may be to even change their name, for example, from Martinez to Marten, in order to be viewed as fully American.

Latinos fall along a continuum of change where some maintain their traditional culture while integrating some aspects of U.S. culture so that they can hold a job or participate fully in educational experiences. Others are unconsciously impacted by their education and social influences so that their adherence to cultural values and behaviors is closer to that of people in the U.S. mainstream. Others are bicultural and can function effectively in both their traditional culture and the majority culture.

It is important to assess where persons fall along this cultural continuum in order to determine what intervention formats would respect their value and behavior preferences. Value preferences are especially sensitive around the issue of sex roles, where change inevitably occurs (Comas-Diaz & Greene, 1994). Working with a traditional family requires acknowledgment of the role of the father as the patriarch as a baseline for interventions. For example, if a member of the family must undergo surgery, the father must be consulted so that he comprehends what is needed and supports the procedure. Families encounter stressors when women can obtain employment more easily than the male heads of households; this may result in an unbalanced family system, often leading to violence and substance abuse (Comas-Diaz & Greene, 1994).

The theme of respecting traditional family roles can become particularly sensitive when it relates to the medical needs of the wife. Especially in areas such as contraception choices, workers must be concerned with planning ways to ensure that they do not inadvertently "set up" the wife for marital conflict by advocating for her right to free choice, when this advocacy is contraindicated by a traditional marital scenario. If the worker is a feminist, Cross and colleagues' (1989) edict about being unbiased becomes especially challenging. The worker is caught in a bind of not wanting to further contribute to a woman's oppression, yet acculturation and family themes must be examined in terms of what the request for service is and how that request can be met in a culturally competent manner. How do social workers support a woman who wants to change traditional family roles? It is critical that they help her anticipate the consequences of this power change so her choices are informed and are truly choices, and not those of the worker. By helping women examine closely the costs of their choices or gender-style preferences, workers can help them to determine if they are willing to pay the costs. A conception of change may be so costly the client will not be willing to act on it immediately; however, this conception could become part of a long-term goal toward which the client might plan to work, and the worker can help the client to formulate and implement that goal.

Acculturation can become problematic when it is related to intergenerational dynamics. Szapocznik and colleagues (1997) detail how acculturation of children and youths often sets up major intergenerational conflicts between children and their traditional parents who are threatened by the new culture's values and behaviors that are the new cultural norms for the youths. Parents often react to the threat of what they perceive as sexualized music, dress, and values by becoming more rigid and inflexible with their teenagers. The teens then react, sometimes with drugs, poor school performance, or other acting-out behaviors as they attempt to break from what they consider "old ways." Ascertaining what cultural conflicts exist between traditional, especially immigrant, parents and their teenagers helps to lay the foundation for competent planning and intervention formats.

Acculturation scales and assessment instruments have been used to ascertain clients' levels of traditional versus modern cultural values (Levine & Padilla, 1980; Szapocznik et al., 1997). These scales enable social workers to assess acculturation levels as a format for tailoring their interventions. Workers may prefer a brief instrument, so their time for counseling is not spent in asking questions, or they may want a longer scale that will provide them with more depth regarding their clients' preferences in such areas as their recreational activities. Various subgroup experts have provided insights into these themes (Castro, 1977; Negroni-Rodriguez & Morales, 2001; Szapocznik et al., 1997). In illustration, the instrument of Szapocznik and colleagues (1997) helps to identify generational differences that provide workers with insight when working with a family. Acculturation assessment is a powerful and necessary method for ensuring the individualization of intervention with Latino clients and family systems.

Social workers must consider the situation or context in which Latinos find themselves. How do different-sized systems affect this population? How does a social worker plan strategies with a client to achieve interventions that must address the impact of systems on the Latino family or individual?

Planning: An Ecological Perspective and Case Example

When clients come for help from a social service agency, they often focus on one complaint, need, or problem area, or are in crisis. The worker can utilize a process-stage approach to ensure culturally competent services. This includes contact, problem identification, assessment, intervention, and termination (Lum, 2000). Thorough and sensitive assessment will allow the worker to examine the context in which the person lives and ways that context may be a resource or feed into or exacerbate the problem about which the individual or family is concerned. Planning the process and the steps that must support a problem-solving format demands thoughtful attention to the particular circumstances presented. An ecological perspective examines if and how the various systems that affect family systems function to enable them to adapt (Germain, 1991). What is the fit between people and the environments in which they find themselves? Social workers must examine the interface between client systems and their relevant environment. Using this perspective, the worker also examines the quality of that interaction.

An ecological view determines whether the client or family system is developing an ability to function so as to (1) be competent in fulfilling their roles; (2) be autonomous; (3) establish social ties or support, or what Germain (1991) calls "relatedness"; and (4) have a positive sense of themselves (esteem) (i.e., CARE for competence, autonomy, relatedness, and esteem). The assessment should examine what systems may be obfuscating the person or family's ability to successfully address these adaptations. Considering this information enables the worker to establish a planning format that includes these assessment elements.

TOOLS FOR STUDENT LEARNING 11.1

The Case of the Lopez Family

The Lopez family came to the social service agency very concerned about their oldest son, Mando, who was in a gang, had been involved in various gang activities, and had been in the emergency room twice in the past year for a stabbing and a gunshot wound that was the result of a rival gang attack. The family had not been to a social service agency before, although they had asked for help from the school Mando attended. The worker, Andrea, was a young Euro-American woman who did not speak Spanish. The worker spent a few minutes greeting them, talking to them about the resources the agency provided, and explaining why she as the worker would need to ask various questions (Tsui & Schultz, 1985).

These relational aspects of the *contact phase* are crucial for setting a tone Latino clients can relax in. They allow clients to experience an interchange that is formal but underpinned by a caring and concerned worker. Helping them comprehend why seemingly intrusive questions are necessary enables them to feel more secure as they provide the worker with information. It is also important to highlight the normative aspects of seeking help and to reinforce the integrity and strength displayed by a family in seeking help when it is such a new and difficult process for them. Acknowledging and reflecting to the family such a strengths view helps them to feel respected (Saleeby, 1997). This "orientation" process is an important format for enabling the family to assess the humanity of the worker and for establishing trust during the contact part of a process-stage approach (Lum, 2000).

Although Mando, 18, wanted out of gang life, he was fearful he would be gravely hurt if he left his gang. He expressed to his mother that he felt his life was worthless and that he knew he would be dead within a year. He was fearful about accompanying his family in asking the agency for help. He was afraid gang members would discover this and retaliate.

Mrs. Lopez and her two oldest daughters—Irene, age 27, and Maribel, age 20—came to the agency to seek help. They did not know what to do. They were fearful for Mando's welfare. They also felt embarrassed about this problem and were afraid the worker would look down on them because Mando was in a gang. The worker underscored the family's strength in seeking help and indicated the appropriateness of their actions.

The daughters were also fearful for their mother's health because she suffered chronic insomnia that was triggered by her fear for her son's welfare. In later sessions, they hesitantly disclosed another family secret: All members of the family had papers except for Mrs. Lopez. Because of this immigration problem, the daughters feared for the safety of their mother in seeking health care. Mrs. Lopez had not been examined by a doctor in years, and the daughters were afraid she might have more medical problems than she was willing to disclose to them.

This family was still reeling from the recent separation of the parents; the father had returned to Tijuana, Baja California, Mexico. They were barely able to sustain themselves economically, so they were struggling to be autonomous. The mother and daughters felt helpless and incompetent in their ability to ensure the safety of their son/brother; they also had apprehension about issues related to Mrs. Lopez's undocumented status. The neighborhood and school systems that would normally provide resources for a teenager were viewed as alienating aspects of this family's environment. The school system had claimed that its hands were tied and that it did not have resources to offer the family when they asked for help with getting Mando out of his gang. Mando's fellow gang members were enrolled in this same high school, yet gang intervention efforts were not available. One of the reasons Mando dropped out of school was to remove himself from gang influences while at school.

Moreover, Mando's neighborhood, which offered housing that was affordable for this family, was on the border of rival gang turf. Weekly gang struggles occurred in that area to such an extent that children were not allowed to play outside their homes. The neighborhood, which normally provides social, recreational, and support networks, was instead a system that was dangerous and resulted in families being cut off from each other, fearful of gang activity and disempowered. The interaction of important systems such as school and neighborhood with this family was of dubious quality and was only challenging this family negatively, rather than serving as a resource.

Various planning sessions with the family, attempting to identify options that would enable Mando to exit his gang without reprisal, resulted in a creative plan the 20-year-old daughter presented: Why couldn't they move to San Diego where they had relatives and where they could also be in proximity to their father? Would it be possible to move the family to San Diego as a way to remove Mando from his gang turf, freeing him in a legitimate way from gang membership? This would offer a new beginning for this teenager and his family members, albeit at some costs. Perhaps establishing a new environment in a literal sense would change the quality of interactions.

Mrs. Lopez worked cleaning hotel rooms, but she felt that the move would not be a problem related to work; a niece in the area would be able to obtain similar employment for her despite her undocumented status. The worker's sensitive inquiries about where support systems existed for this family suggested they would have more support by leaving their city and moving to San Diego. Assessment of the father's relation to the family indicated that the mother felt having Mando's father in close proximity would provide the male input she could not provide for her son's socialization.

The worker and family listed all the positive reasons for moving and then identified all the difficulties and resources that would be needed for this change. A critical area that was assessed was whether the move and resettlement in a new city might be more risky for the mother's undocumented status. Although the worker felt uncomfortable in asking this sensitive question, the discussion helped the family assess this important area and consider this theme as a critical element in their planning. The family examined the issues over several sessions and formulated their plan and commitment to move.

Between sessions, the worker found social service agencies in San Diego that would support Mando's need to be in a school with a gang prevention resource and located a free clinic that could attend to his mother's health needs without concern for her legal status. Although Mando had dropped out of school, he was motivated to start again if they moved to San Diego.

Planning with this family took several sessions wherein they examined budget issues, how they were to obtain rent deposit resources, how they would actually move, and how Mrs. Lopez would obtain employment before the move to ensure some source of income. One of the daughters, Maribel, had also initiated a job search for herself. Because the family would be moving to San Diego, they would not have to pass through an Immigration and Naturalization Service (INS) station; thus, the physical move would not place the mother at risk for detection. Even though the oldest daughter was married and had her own family, she participated in all the planning activities because her mother did not speak English well. This daughter also helped to make telephone calls regarding employment, social service contacts, and housing contacts before the move actually transpired.

Evaluation by the worker after the move indicated that Mando and his younger brother were enrolled in new schools. Due to a specific contact made by the social worker in the new city, Mando was enrolled in an alternative high school that would allow him to take extra credits to make up for the time he had lost. This school had a collaborative gang prevention program that (1) provided Mando with pre-employment training, (2) offered counseling and support services, and (3) helped to tutor him so that he would be eligible for graduation within the year. Mando graduated from high school, obtained a job through the gang prevention program, and began contributing to his family's welfare because they still struggled economically. He developed his ability to speak to teenagers on the dangers of gangs, using his experiences to illustrate the dangers both he and his family survived.

Although this family also needed to address their grief related to the parents' separation, the worker focused first on the survival issues they faced. The life-or-death issue related to gang membership is a major threat to teens who live in inner cities (Morales, 1995). Workers must be flexible and offer creative problem solving in aiding families that have scarce resources to find realistic options. A major underpinning in this family's solution strategy was to consider where extended family and supports would be most available. Coupling the family's natural networks with the worker's delineation of formal networks provided a solution, though difficult, that was acceptable to this family. Together, the worker and the family figured out a way to provide the family with a different environment. An important piece of the worker's job was to identify resources that would not jeopardize the mother's undocumented situation.

In the assessment process, in the planning endeavors, and in operationalizing strategies, the worker always asked for the family's evaluation of the worthiness of the plan. The fact that the 20-year-old daughter identified the option that became real illustrates the importance of working with as many family members as possible.

1. How would you feel about Mando if you met him, knowing his history of gang assaults?

2. Mando did not come to see the worker because he feared retaliation from his gang members. Do you think this was a legitimate reason for his not attending the meetings with his family or just an excuse for not facing his responsibilities?

3. The 27-year-old daughter attended each session, even though she had her own family. Do you think this could have been a boundary violation, and if so, why?

4. What was your comfort level when you read about the discussion of Mrs. Lopez's undocumented status, and why did you feel that way?

5. How would you identify resources in another city for a family if you were not familiar with that city and its resources?

Research Needs

The Lopez family's situation highlights the great need for research that examines the unique situations of many Latinos like them. The research being done must be enlarged to provide more insights that practitioners can utilize. How does a family manage their anxiety and stress when all but one of the family members have documentation? Gangs are an ongoing concern for the Latino community and immigrant families. Social workers need to know what kinds of programs have been effective for working with these high-risk youth.

A research area of crucial importance is the strengths that immigrant Latinos and their families rely on that can provide workers with new perspectives on how to work with these client systems. Later, this chapter identifies some of the limited research examining the issues of PTSD with immigrant Latinos, and especially with children and youths. Research on the trauma these immigrants experience must be expanded. Finally, although we talk about the importance of religion to this group, more research is needed to examine broader issues of the reliance on spirituality and its meaning for this population (Hutchinson, 1999). This assortment of research would help to drive more specific and culturally appropriate practice.

Practice Themes

Although the Lopez case focused on problem solving that was based on survival themes, the family was also referred to counseling services in their new location. The worker elaborated on their need to discuss their grief and anger around the parental separation and identified a Spanish-speaking counseling center in the neighborhood to which they moved. Cities and regions have different ranges of services; some cities have more culturally sensitive services than others, which facilitates a worker's ability to make culturally appropriate referrals. In the case example, an ecological perspective enabled the worker and the Lopez family to find an environment with the needed formal resources—services offered in Spanish, services that would not jeopardize the mother, and a location where they could access natural support systems, which is crucial for the adaptation of Latino families (Valle & Vega, 1980).

The Lopez case points to the basic kinds of services many Latino client situations demand. Although the worker helped the family to feel more competent in protecting its children, more autonomous in its ability to choose options, and more connected to social supports to enhance related themes, issues of identity were not given similar attention. However, the worker made the referral to counseling services, hoping that issues related to the more emotional aspects this family was contending with would be addressed. She hoped that identity themes would be elaborated on in this format. For Latinos, the fluidity of the acculturation process exacerbates identity issues for children as well as for parents.

A variety of practice intervention approaches are particularly suited for Latinos. Crisis intervention, when the case demands this kind of approach, is a method that enables families or individuals to experience firsthand the results of a helping relationship. Workers can build on this once the crisis has been resolved to engage the Latino client system in counseling or family work because a trusting relationship has been established. "Platicas," or educative forums of group work with parents, is another format that is preventive but offers Latinos experiences with professionals that enable them to recognize the value of professional input. Support groups to address stressful issues and organizing groups to promote advocacy efforts play into the cultural ethos of the collective that is valued among Latinos. The group context enables parents or youth in groups to feel less threatened or embarrassed about participating. Adding a social element to group work, such as asking parents to bring refreshments for break time, plays into the Latino cultural format that values this social time. Both individual and group formats must be based on a humanistic stance that connotes to Latino clients that their culture is being respected and that racist elements are not present.

IDENTIFYING CULTURAL AWARENESS AND SOCIAL SERVICE NEEDS OF LATINO AMERICANS

Learning how to be culturally competent without contributing to negative stereotypes about Latino clients involves workers being willing to examine their own cultural backgrounds. They must examine their socioeconomic status and discern the degree and extent of their own cultural programming. If workers come from recent immigrant backgrounds, what is their level of acculturation, and what insights do they have about the complexities of this process? Are countertransference issues present that might evolve from having similar backgrounds to clients? If immigration experiences are not part of workers' backgrounds, they must read about the experiences of immigrants, even utilizing contemporary novels or films like *El Norte* as initial entrées into discovery of this experience. As Lum (2000) has noted, learning about diversity is a lifelong process. Exposing oneself to the culture and community of the population(s) one serves helps the worker to become more comfortable and familiar with differences that exist.

Each Latino client system also teaches us about how Latinos utilize their culture—that is, in what ways they are unique and in what ways they share similar Latino values, attitudes, and behaviors. The one commonality we can agree on, however, is that all Latino clients *are* unique; therefore, we cannot make cultural assumptions about them. There is more heterogeneity within the Latino group than between Latinos and other groups; there is more similarity across different groups. We must always ask how a cultural theme pertains to them, if at all. Nevertheless, there are certain factors that workers should pay close attention to in performing assessments.

Religion

Diversity in religion among Latinos can be a challenging experience for social workers. For example, we no longer can assume that all Latinos are Catholic. Maldonado (2000) elucidates why this impression has been so vivid. The Spanish colonization of the New World had as one of its goals the conversion of native peoples. Consequently, the Catholic Church and its missionaries took drastic measures to destroy indigenous native religious traditions. The result has been a diversity of Latin American cultures with what Maldonado (2000) describes as "the common thread of Catholicism at the core of national and cultural identities" (p. 99). Moreover, he notes that Latino cultural, religious, and personal identities were formed in societies embedded with Catholicism.

Yet, over the years, religious diversity has increased among Latinos and includes Protestant denominations such as Methodists, Baptists, Presbyterians, and Lutherans, as well as such groups as Mormons, Seventh-Day Adventists, and Jehovah's Witnesses. The fastest-growing Latino religious groups are the Pentecostal and evangelical denominations (Diaz-Stevens & Stevens-Arroyo, 1998). Maldonado points out that Pentecostalism's rise in Latin America has been a major religious phenomenon that is changing the religious picture in Latin America and now indirectly in the United States.

Why is knowing about the religion of a Latino client important? The increase in both the Latino population and its religious diversity has prompted an increase by Catholic and Protestant denominations in establishing outreach structures to the Latino community. Catholic, Lutheran, and Episcopalian churches also have earmarked social service resources for this population via Spanish-speaking workers and programs structured to address their unique needs, such as special immigration and advocacy services. In illustration, Puig (2001) describes the partnership the Cuban community developed with the Archdiocese of Miami to address the need to teach English to the "balseros" or Cuban refugees who left Cuba in 1994.

In different regions and cities, many denominations provide special support to Latinos in need. Social workers need to know if a Latino client belongs to a certain denomination to ascertain if that religious institution offers services in Spanish and programs that address needs as immigration matters. This is crucial information about referral resources for workers dealing with undocumented immigrants who may be eligible for certain services only from the private rather than the public sector. Workers must know what services undocumented immigrants are eligible for because certain services can jeopardize any opportunity for future legal immigration (Zuniga, 2001). During the Clinton administration, clarification was provided on service eligibility for federal programs to enable clients as well as professionals to comprehend the ramifications of appropriate resource use (Bellisle, 1999).

Another reason why determining the religious preference of Latino clients or families is crucial is that clients' or families' specific religion may be a profound asset in their ability to find meaning in their struggles and to find emotional resources (Hutchinson, 1999). In working with an elderly, acculturated Mexican American woman, for example, asking about her belief system may allow the worker to incorporate her daily prayer ritual as a clinical prescription for enabling her to address a situational crisis she is experiencing (Zuniga, 1991). Moreover, in enabling families like recent immigrants to develop social ties and a sense of relatedness, referral to a place of worship may be an important adjunctive intervention for enabling them to initiate their cultural networking. Also, if one is helping a family learn to become more cohesive, asking them to attend church service as a family may provide a family systems intervention that will help them function in a more collaborative and connected manner (Minuchin, 1974).

Family

The value of family is a core dimension in the Latino culture. Despite acculturation, even third-generation Latinos in a California study still held onto values that are family centered (Hurtado et al., 1992). Roland (1988) points out the importance of a family orientation in most traditional cultures, a value stance that supports a collective sense of oneself in relation to the world. In a society like the United States that has such an ingrained sense of individual rights and the value of independence, it is difficult for a worker who is unaware of his or her own individualistic stance to be objective or unbiased about the more collective approach that Latinos utilize both in their problem solving and in their sense of interpersonal responsibility.

Latinos can be easily misassessed as being enmeshed with their family when they choose to live at home and/or not move out as other young adults in the majority culture often do. For example, one social work student felt that two teenagers she was working with, a 14- and 16-year-old sister and brother, were enmeshed with their grandmother. When asked to identify the behaviors on which she based her assessment, the student noted that each time the teens left their house, especially for recreational activities, they went to their grandmother, knelt before her, and asked for her blessing. The student was viewing a ritual as a weakness when, in fact, it was a family strength. It honored the role of the grandmother as the wise "protector" of the family and also depicted a strong intergenerational tie that is a strength for a Latino family, especially when acculturation processes often work to place young and old at odds with one another (Szapocznik et al., 1997).

The "connections" and sense of responsibility that Latino family members experience must be evaluated to assure that enmeshment is not occurring. However, workers must be cautious not to misconstrue interactions that are unfamiliar, like the example of the grandmother's blessing, as dysfunctional. They must seek consultation to learn what the rituals can mean and reevaluate whether they are viable in their own right or in fact may be contributing to enmeshed or dysfunctional behaviors.

The vignette about the Lopez family demonstrated how work with as many members of the family as possible is an important method for utilizing their resources. In that case, the creative solution to the Lopez family's problem was offered by a 20-year-old. Using a family systems approach (Minuchin, 1974) is a more natural way to work on problems that affect family members.

The Challenge of Including Fathers

Engaging fathers to participate in family sessions can be difficult, often due to work responsibilities and constraints. Frequently, the idea of seeking help may be a challenging experience when faced with personnel and agencies that are foreign to an immigrant father. In particular, the idea of being evaluated by someone who may misconstrue his traditional role as head of the family and to whom he feels no connection puts off many fathers' motivation to seek "counseling," something that was typically not undertaken in an immigrant's country of origin. Finally, the literature points out how Western perspectives on psychological function and dysfunction, particularly the use of "Western European criteria to distinguish idiosyncratic pathology from culture-specific behavior in new immigrants" (Perez Foster, 2001), can contribute to misassessment of the immigrant Latino client.

Given Latinos' lack of experience with counseling or therapy, how can the social worker engage a family in a practice to which the family is not accustomed? The response to this is complex. However, if workers can "demonstrate" their "personableness" and allow the family, especially the parents, to see that their motivation is for the welfare of the family, this can initiate the "cultural connection" that needs to be developed. Often workers can reframe the problem so that they indicate to the parents, especially the father, that family problems, such as those with a child, need the father's expertise. The worker or clinician is then asking for the parent's help in being able to know how to work effectively with the presenting complaint. This role assignment is not manipulation by the clinician but an earnest attempt to collaborate with the father and use his wisdom and knowledge of his family system. Also, by indicating in a genuine fashion that the worker needs the help of fathers as cultural consultants, the worker creates another reframe for underscoring the recognition for cultural differences that can be misconstrued by the professional.

Making home calls to provide service when possible helps to lessen the threat of the situation for the family and offers the parents and family more control. This is also a viable manner by which to ensure that the worker's assessment truly incorporates an ecological perspective because the worker sees firsthand what kinds of streets, stores, bus transportation, and resources surround the family's home. A worker who encounters gang graffiti close to where a family lives, for example, can ask the family about their experiences with gang phenomena. This may provide insights that otherwise might not be provided and uncover important areas to examine, such as the safety of children.

In short, many Latinos need social services that are offered in Spanish and with the cultural frameworks that respect and utilize a family and its cultural strengths. Information and referral services to enable the client and family to address survival issues should always be given priority. The need for knowledge of culturally relevant community services and agencies demands that the worker become familiar with the Latino community and its resources (Zuniga, 2003).

The Value of the Collective: Group Services

The family-centeredness that characterizes Latino culture is interwoven with a concern for and emphasis on the collective. This emphasis can be used by workers to provide educational, informational, and problem-focused services by using group formats. In particular, the use of parent groups to inform parents about school policy or to address special topics, if driven by a culturally sensitive format, can be especially effective. Because so many Latino families immigrate to this country to ensure good educational resources for their children, developing services in collaboration with schools to strengthen the relationship between parents and the school systems is a critical need area.

Cultures like those of Latinos are viewed as "high-context" cultures wherein communication not only involves the words offered to convey a message but also relies heavily on personal delivery that resonates the affective as well as the factual (Harry, 1992). The meaning includes personal perceptions and is dependent on personal interaction. In contrast, low-context cultures use written communication such as letters or memos to parents, a device often used in U.S. public school systems. Utilizing a group process in which parents feel the support of other parents as they interact with representatives, professionals, and social workers from the sending institution or agency is a method that lessens the threat of dealing with a foreign institution, allows parents to provide support to one another, and incorporates the ideas and recommendations of these parents to ensure more culturally appropriate outcomes. It offers the parents the opportunity to assess the affective dimensions presented by the professional; if this affective component is genuine and shows the worker has "un corazon buena," or a good heart, that helps to support culturally sensitive communication avenues. Although this speaks more to the style and format that social workers must incorporate if they are to provide culturally competent services to Latinos, there are also arenas of knowledge acquisition that must be recognized.

EXPLORING KNOWLEDGE ACQUISITION AREAS ABOUT LATINO AMERICANS

A critical new area of cultural competence required in working with Latinos is knowledge of how best to serve the nation's new immigrants. Perez Foster (2001) highlights several questions that the mental health worker should consider: "Does the trauma of war and disaster permanently impair the human psyche? Do people ever recover from psychological and physical torture? How do clinicians intervene so that people ultimately adjust to new host environments, and move on with productive lives?" (pp. 153–154).

This chapter cannot provide the substantive discussion that these questions warrant. However, it will point the readers to the arenas of knowledge that they need to develop through both examining the literature and seeking training and consultation from clinicians who have the experiences and expertise in working with Latino immigrants who have suffered trauma.

Perez Foster (2001) identifies a variety of literature on immigrants, including research that focused on new immigrants' mental health and socioenvironmental needs. These included insights into the various losses immigrants experience—such as loss of family, community, and physical environment and loss of familiar networks—and issues of isolation. In general, these themes address the multiple demands of life in a foreign environment (Boylan, 1991; Desjarlais, Eisenberg, Good, & Kleinman, 1995).

In addition to losses and isolation, immigrants often experience a downturn in their economic circumstances. For example, some who are well educated must take on low-status jobs because of their lack of English fluency and lack of licensing (Perez Foster, 1996). Immigrants who relocate as a family adapt better than those who make the journey alone (Kinzie et al., 1986). The re-sorting of gender roles and power has major implications for immigrants (Comas-Diaz & Greene, 1994). Women often help the family by willingly taking on menial and low-paying jobs, while males may remain unemployed. The reshuffling of marital and familial roles can result in despondent men who have difficulty sustaining such power shifts. In short, the migration is linked to major adjustment stressors with resulting challenges to the mental health of this population.

Pertinent Isolation Themes

Due to language, cultural, and economic issues, immigrants often find themselves without the moral support and networks that enabled them to function. In particular, families who have left relatives in their country of origin have weakened support networks. In his investigation of the social integration of Salvadoran refugees in Canada, Jacob (1994) found that social relationships were critical to satisfying the refugee's need for communication and to mitigate isolation. Such places as the workplace provided the most significant nonfamily support networks.

Because social support plays such a dramatic role in anyone's adaptation, but especially that of an immigrant, workers must develop knowledge of the varied kinds of social support that can be developed in immigrant communities. Examination of the social support literature for Latinos may provide exemplars that can be replicated for other communities (Cohen, 1985; Valle & Bensussen, 1980; Vega & Kolody, 1980).

Another area of knowledge development involves how immigration and trauma experiences affect children. Because Latinos tend to have more children than the majority population, insights into the impact of immigration on children should be developed. As cited by Zea, Diehl, and Porterfield (1997), Espino and colleagues (1987) examined Latino immigrants dwelling in Washington DC in relation to the intersection of education and risk issues. This study of the academic and cognitive functions of children noted that 35 percent were functioning two or more years below expected grade level. Although some might interpret the delay as related to lack of English proficiency, even Spanish school achievement tests showed that 72 percent demonstrated this kind of delay. Espino and colleagues (1987) were concerned that once a child or teen reaches this grave level of academic delay, achievement motivation weakens intensely. The children are then at risk for severe self-esteem and shame issues related to their school skills. Their self-identity suffers, and they view themselves as incompetent. These perceived deficiencies can contribute to delinquent maladaptations, such as gang behaviors. In addition, their poor identity and sense of incompetence can challenge their ability to be autonomous in their school setting, which also can deter normal social relations and friendships, the areas of an ecological perspective that focus on adaptation (Germain, 1991). Other risk themes that prevail include drug abuse and early teen pregnancy.

Research on children and youth from war-torn countries like El Salvador and Nicaragua (Arroyo & Eth, 1985) elucidated how exposure to violence resulted in suicidal behaviors, serious antisocial acts, insomnia, separation anxiety, defiance, somatic complaints, and school problems. Work by Mancilla (1987), as quoted by Zea and colleagues (1997), identified the emotional kinds of losses these children endure. Similarly, Melville and Lykes's (1992) study of Guatemalan children identified the hunger issues that impacted the children, among other critical themes. Studies like these provide ideas of areas to assess that workers might not otherwise consider. This kind of knowledge also demands practice skill development to fit these need areas.

FOSTERING PRACTICE SKILL DEVELOPMENT ABOUT LATINO AMERICANS

The Lopez vignette in this chapter illustrates how workers can use a process-stage approach in working with Latinos (i.e., contact, problem identification, assessment, intervention, and termination) (Lum, 2000). We will highlight some of the worker–system practice issues, noting the workers' tasks as they proceed through this stage approach.

Contact

Workers who find Latino children, youth, and families in their caseloads must examine whether these clients are immigrants, have legal entry issues, come from war-torn countries, and whether they suffered trauma during their immigration sojourns. Workers must learn to present their questions within a framework that will educate the family: they need to convey that they can be trusted, that they are not mandated to inform the immigration service, and that they are developing their knowledge about resources undocumented clients can utilize.

Relationship Protocols

Effective practice skills require that workers be personable and respectful so as to match the cultural mode of Latinos (Tsui & Schultz, 1985; Zuniga, 1992). They must develop trust when serving those who fear deportation. *Self-disclosure* must be used to adhere to boundary considerations and demonstrate one's humanness. Workers who are parents and are working with parents, for example, can disclose shared experience of the responsibilities and concerns of parents; however, they must always be clear about how the disclosure will assist the client. Workers might display concern about the special stressors immigrants face, and demonstrate optimism by noting how, with a little help, many Latino families or individuals have been able to adapt quite well.

Style of communication must be personable, patient, and formal, yet with special kindness and consideration shown. When interviewing a family, a worker who asks the parents whether he or she can give the children a snack or candy shows the hospitality that is valued in Latino culture. If Spanish is not the worker's first language, but he or she speaks it well enough to work with the family, the worker can ask them to forgive his or her limited competence in the language, which displays humility and a respect for the client's culture. One who is bilingual Latino also can apologize for his or her level of Spanish, to demonstrate humility, as a way to even the playing field. A worker also can use a *dicho*, or a folk saying, to create a cultural ambience clients will be comforted with; using a dicho that is comical may allow the family to relax (Zuniga, 1991).

Workers who are delving into sensitive areas with clients, especially if a mental status exam is being undertaken, must recognize the importance of clients responding to questions in their first language to ensure a more accurate assessment. In mental health scenarios, the assessment of Spanish-speaking clients using their second language resulted in more inaccurate reflections of their mental health status (Marcos, 1994).

If a Latino worker acts impatient, impersonable, or "better" than the client, only distrust and dislike of the worker will result. If the Latino worker discloses a bit of history about his or her family, for instance, where or when they immigrated, this indicates that the worker is familiar with the experience. Making just a brief comment of how difficult it was for one's parents initially but how with time things worked out, will signify both the worker's insight on the clients' issues and a sense of optimism.

Problem Identification

When clients present, noting a problem or a need, underlying issues and needs may exist that they may not immediately want to disclose out of fear, shame, or distrust. Underlining the theme of strength, the worker can applaud them for seeking help, recognizing the difficulty of this process. Under problem identification, the worker might be able to slip in questions about legal documentation, clarifying that the reason for asking is not to report the clients but to seek services that will not endanger them. When the worker highlights client concerns about deportation, this offers a respite from their anxiety about this theme.

By acknowledging legal documentation, the worker can more easily evaluate what level of problem exists. In the Lopez vignette, although the mother's legal status was not part of the core problem, it could be related to the types of resolutions that were needed to help her son, Mando, and had to be acknowledged and addressed (in that vignette, as a referral to private health care).

Interventions

Although intervention will depend on the presenting problem, social workers should always consider the following questions about practice:

- Does the intervention help solve the problem without putting the client in harm's way regarding detection by immigration authorities?
- Does the intervention respond to the cultural orientation and preferences of this client rather than imposing societal or worker's cultural values and priorities?
- Does the intervention include natural support networks that would make the intervention more culturally relevant?
- Does the intervention acknowledge the stressors that immigration presents by offering resources or solutions that mitigate adaptation risks?
- Does the intervention give priority to survival issues before imposing talk therapy?
- Is the intervention offered in such a manner that facilitates adaptation, especially in such areas as development of competence, autonomy, relatedness and esteem?
- Does the intervention utilize such resources as the client's religion, spirituality, or belief system?
- Does the intervention incorporate known culturally viable techniques like narrative therapy (Falicov, 1998), use of metaphor or dichos (Zuniga, 1991), or family systems work (Szapocznik et al., 1997)?
- Does the intervention address different-sized system elements that may demand advocacy types of work?

GENERATING NEW INDUCTIVE LEARNING ABOUT SOCIAL WORK WITH LATINO AMERICANS

Workers can enhance their knowledge and skill base in working with the Latino population by seeking consultation from culturally competent Latino workers with extensive experience serving this population. Inquiring about certain behaviors and beliefs that clients present will help workers to expand their awareness and knowledge. Volunteering one's case for formal case review provides another avenue for exploring the variety of perspectives that can be applied to understanding and enabling the worker to develop his or her own perspective. In addition, comparing how a Latino worker with cultural competence assesses the case as compared to workers without this competence will elucidate the cultural perspectives that are crucial for effective service delivery.

Workers can also enhance their knowledge and skills by seeking out recent literature on practice developed by practitioner–researchers who are culturally competent with the Latino population. This will allow workers to add the new elements and practices that are identified in the research. Attending conferences, like the ones offered in such areas as Texas or California by Latino social workers, will ensure that workers are exposed to the variety of expertise that is growing and developing nationally. All of these experiences enable workers to extend their competencies with this group.

UNDERSTANDING AND ADVOCATING SOCIAL AND ECONOMIC JUSTICE FOR LATINOS

In U.S. society, each person has a right to benefit from societal resources, especially the right to a fair wage and decent working conditions as mandated by legislation. Moreover, society's resources such as health care, education, and housing should be accessible to all segments of the population. Demographic data on the labor force participation rate of Latinos, at least in California, indicate this group has the highest labor force participation when compared to African Americans and Euro-Americans (Hurtado et al., 1992). Latinos who live in the United States or who come to the country as immigrants have a strong work ethic underpinned by their value for providing for their families' sustenance. Yet, the experience of Latinos continues to be one of exploitation related to employment. Often they are underpaid or not given benefits such as health insurance. Access to education remains remote and has not been provided in an equitable fashion. Moreover, institutional and individual discrimination have denied Latinos equal access to societal resources like health and mental health services. When one examines these themes in relation to Latinos who are immigrants lacking access to resources, it is obvious that exploitation and discrimination are exacerbated.

The literature on immigrants identifies exploitation as a common theme in such areas as employment and housing (Perez Foster, 2001). Knowledge of a family's undocumented status can give way to a landlord charging excessive prices or not responding to requests for correcting problems such as an insect infestation or plumbing problems. Landlords realize these families typically do not make formal complaints out of fear of apprehension. Workers must identify what organizations support advocacy efforts, such as agencies that are community-run or sponsored by religious organizations, and work with such entities when undertaking advocacy efforts.

Working with organizations that support advocacy efforts can provide the expertise and momentum that will make system entities more responsive. For example, in one instance parents worked with a community agency in seeking the removal of a local school principal who was insensitive to their children's needs (Zuniga, 2003). Parents who form groups become empowered and feel less threatened by their undocumented status because they know they will be supported in their efforts to ask for system change (Street, 1992).

Although advocacy efforts may take workers who are clinicians out of their normal role performance, culturally competent work with Latinos demands that social workers take on multiple roles and work with different-sized systems to ensure justice-oriented outcomes. Workers must learn to be flexible in their roles so that they can facilitate empowering experiences for clients (Zuniga, 2003). This demands a role repertoire that includes not only the role of clinician but also that of educator, organizer, collaborator, counselor, broker, and advocate.

Social workers need to model their work from experiences of professionals like those at The Family Centre in New Zealand. This model elucidates the critical nature of therapeutic work that not only addresses the marginality issues presented by indigenous clients but also critically examines justice issues that are viewed as being as urgent and central to therapy as traditional "talk therapies" (Van Soest, 1994; White & Tapping, 1990). In the New Zealand experience, workers expanded their boundaries so they were not just office-limited but learned to enter the clients' communities and establish collaborative efforts to develop resources that did not exist or were not accessible. By participating in community work, therapists become schooled in the clients' culture and their contextual or ecological realities. Such an experience offers therapists the opportunity to see the problems from the client's perspective; it gives them a real sense of the "stressors" their clients experience when they leave the therapist's office.

SUMMARY

The diversity of the Latino population requires that social workers develop a large knowledge base if they are to ensure culturally competent services. Substantive political and historical differences exist among Latino groups. With the dramatic growth of immigration in some Latino subgroups, workers are challenged to entertain all the elements that should be considered both for assessment and intervention formats.

This chapter highlighted the special ecological contexts that immigrants experience. Within this group, the unique stressors of those who reside in the United States without documentation indicate that the worker must be prudent, sensitive, and yet pragmatic in serving this particular subset of clients. Knowing what services can be utilized without jeopardizing their situation is paramount when working with these kinds of clients. Also, digging further in a sensitive manner to ascertain if clients were traumatized in their countries of origin or became traumatized in their sojourn to the United States demands therapeutic work that addresses post-traumatic stress disorder issues. Recognition of such experiences in children and youth who immigrate is critical to ensuring that misassessment does not occur with them.

Whether a worker is Euro-American, African American, or Latino, working with a Latino population demands that the worker seek out literature, research, and consultation that will continually upgrade the worker's competencies with this population. An ongoing and critical aspect of this competence demands that workers continuously monitor themselves in terms of their values, attitudes, and reactions to each Latino client or family system.

TOOLS FOR STUDENT LEARNING 11.2

Goal: This exercise enables you to reflect on the anxiety and needed watchfulness that immigrants often experience when they live in the United States without documents.

Go to a shopping mall and undertake normal shopping experiences such as buying groceries for your family, buying stamps at the post office, and visiting the drug store. Pretend you are here as an immigrant without documents, although you can speak some English. First, think about how lack of documents might preside over each transaction you undertake. What things, people, or circumstances might make an immigrant concerned and anxious? On returning home, think about the emotional costs an immigrant parent, in particular, pays in undertaking even the normal tasks of a few hours of shopping.

- What incidents could have been especially sensitive?

- What transactions might have made an immigrant particularly concerned (e.g., showing an identification to pick up a prescription)?

- What officials, such as security guards walking around stores, did you encounter that might make an immigrant feel self-conscious?

- How tired did you feel at the end of this exercise?

Implications: Workers need to be sensitive and have insights into the kinds of experiences that, although others consider them normal, add to the pressures and anxieties of an undocumented person. Such insights allow workers to consider how to ask clients about their experiences and enable workers to debrief clients and alleviate their anxieties. It also teaches workers how to prepare immigrants for referrals and help them to address normal tasks with less emotional expenditure.

CHAPTER TWELVE

Cultural Competence with Asian Americans

Rowena Fong

Diversity in multiple races and ethnic identities challenges social workers in the 21st century to reexamine culturally competent practices in serving ethnic minority populations. The 2000 U.S. Census (U.S. Bureau of the Census, 2001) now reports seven possible categories of race and origin rather than the "one-drop" rule (Daniel, 1992). Thus, individuals can now self-identify with various race mixings. Spickard, Fong, and Ewalt (1995) forewarned that no one ethnic grouping would be sufficient and that the "multiplication of racial categories suggests a deconstruction of the very notion of race" (p. 581).

Because of the growing diversity among and within ethnic groups, social workers are to be evermore aware of subtle differences. In delivering culturally competent social work services, cultural awareness, knowledge acquisition, and skill development need to be reexamined for each ethnic grouping. Asian Americans and Pacific Islanders are no exception. Within the last two decades, the Vietnamese, a Southeast Asian group, had a growth rate of 134.8 percent (Hing, 1993). With growth come challenges and problems. Fong and Mokuau (1994), in their literature review on Asians and Pacific Islanders (API), reported that researchers, educators, and practitioners would need to distinguish between Asians (South Asians, and Southeast Asians) and Pacific Islanders, separate Asian Americans into different ethnic groups, and discern the differences between immigrants and refugees.

Social problems within the API groups have expanded. Substance abuse and family violence are growing concerns with Native Hawaiians and other API populations (Mokuau, 1999, 2001; Straussner, 2001); stress, coping, and depression among the Korean and Chinese elderly (Mui, 1996, 2001); cultural conflict and pressure for scholastic achievement among Hmong and other Southeast Asian children (Caplan, Choy, & Whitmore, 1991; Chan, 1994; Trueba, Jacobs, & Kirton, 1990); and somatic and social suffering among survivors of the Cambodian killing fields (Morelli, 2001; Uehara, Morelli, & Abe-Kim, 2001). Bigotry, discrimination, unfair employment, hate crimes, and insufficient funding for immigrants services were expected to be problematic for Asian Americans in the 1990s and 2000s (U.S. Commission on Civil Rights, 1992).

Thus, theories, practices, and social services should be modified and delivered in a manner that addresses the diverse, complex, and multifaceted needs of these clients.

Social workers ought to examine new paradigm shifts and integrate the intersection of ethnicity, gender, age, social class, physical and mental abilities, and religion into present and future culturally competent practices. Rather than using the traditional paradigm of approaching APIs with ethnicity as the primary variable, social workers need to create new paradigms that also embrace sexual orientation and religion and physical and mental abilities as equally important factors in the clients' lives.

This chapter will begin with a definition of cultural competence as it applies to Asian and Pacific Islander Americans (APIA). An explanation and discussion of diversity within the APIA population will follow in order to give a context to the historical and current oppressions faced by this ethnic population. Cultural awareness, knowledge acquisition, skill development, and inductive learning will be elaborated upon with an attempt to intersect ethnicity with gender, age, sexual orientation, religion, social class, and physical and mental abilities. Social and economic justice issues will be analyzed before closing with a summary and suggestions for future direction.

DEFINITION OF CULTURAL COMPETENCE

The definition of culture is often presented as the starting point (Lum, 1999, p. 2) to the discussion on cultural competence. Gordon (as cited in Lum, 1999) defines culture as "the way of life of multiple groups in a society and consists of prescribed ways of behaving or norms of conduct, beliefs, values, and skills" (p. 2). However, in social work practice, the term *cultural competence* has evolved in the last couple of decades with a range of conceptualizations including culturally competent system of care (Cross, Bazron, Dennis, & Issacs, 1989), ethnic sensitive practice and ethnic realities (Devore & Schlesinger, 1999), social work practice and people of color (Lum, 2000), culturally competent social work practice (Lum 1999), and biculturalization of interventions (Fong, Boyd, & Browne, 1999).

Lum (1999) defines cultural competence as "the set of knowledge and skills that a social worker must develop in order to be effective with multicultural clients" (p. 3). He advocates for cultural awareness, knowledge acquisition, skill development, and inductive learning. Operating from a strengths-based, solution-focused, culture-valued framework, this was modified by Fong (2001), and the terms were redefined as follows:

- *Cultural awareness:* The social workers' understanding and identification of the critical cultural values important to the client system and to themselves.
- *Knowledge acquisition:* The social workers' understanding of how these cultural values function as strengths in the client's functioning and treatment planning.
- *Skill development:* The social workers' ability to match services that support the identified cultural values and then to incorporate them in the appropriate interventions.
- *Inductive learning:* The social workers' continued quest to seek solutions, which includes finding other indigenous interventions and matching cultural values to choose appropriate western interventions. (p. 6)

Fong's framework presupposes that social workers are fully familiar with the cultural values important to the client system. The traditional values of ethnic groups represent strengths in the assessment process of social work and provide resources in treatment planning and implementation. For example, in traditional Asian cultures values of patriarchy, family loyalty, cohesion, and harmony are highly revered. Thus, it is important to include these variables in the planning of how to treat these clients. Galan (2001) states that the "culturally competent relationship is helping each family member achieve internal consistency among values, beliefs, behaviors, and identity within a social context" (p. 264). He describes the "processing of cultural beliefs" and defines it to be "helping the client [to] know how to weigh cultural information and how to prioritize with respect to choosing appropriate behavior in order to maintain integrity in one's belief and behavior nexus" (p. 263).

The definition of cultural competence as it applies to APIA groups includes knowledge of cultural values, indigenous interventions, and Western interventions to support and not contradict or detract from the traditional cultural values. With many ethnic groups, macro-level societal values dominate the meso and micro levels of functioning of family and individual. Fong (1997) warns that in working with immigrants from the People's Republic of China and assessing problems and issues, social workers must study the macro-level societal values, which shape the behaviors and performance of family members and individuals. This approach serves to address cultural competence at the macro, meso, and micro levels of practice. However, to build upon Cross and colleagues' work (1989), cultural competence also needs to be addressed at the macro level in working with communities that support the ethnic families. In most Asian groups, the community family associations may play a big role in offering support and services to people within their own ethnic group.

This framework of starting with macro-level societal values supports and builds upon the previous literature of cultural competence. Devore and Schlesinger's (1999) ethnic sensitive practice framework examines the layers of understanding in ethnic-sensitive social work practice. These seven layers cover social work values, knowledge of human behavior, knowledge and skill in agency policy and services, self-awareness into ethnicity, impact of the ethnic reality, and the relationship between social worker and the delivery of social services. Cross and colleagues (1989) examine cultural competence from a macro system of care framework that includes attitudes, behaviors, and policies as they apply to individuals, agencies, and organizations. For Hawaiian, Samoan, and Chamorro communities, cultural competence is "having staff, with a deep understanding of the people and place, an understanding reflected in program content, policies, procedures, and the living character of the program" (Furuto, San Nicolas, Kim, & Fiaui, 2001, p. 329). Each ethnic community program is a representation of a distinct part of the culture reflected in different languages and customs. The "living character of the program" is reflected when bilingual and bicultural social workers are hired to bring cultural meaning in words and behaviors into the agency and services for clients.

In defining cultural competence, this chapter will emphasize several points: (1) It is a way of life that consists of values and beliefs; (2) it involves cultural awareness, knowledge, skills, and inductive learning (Lum 1999); (3) it includes cultural values as strengths, which should be included in assessments and biculturalization of interventions (Fong, 2001); (4) it is the "processing of cultural beliefs" (Galan, 2001); and (5) it starts at the macrosocietal level and interacts with meso and micro levels (Fong, 1997).

UNDERSTANDING DIVERSITY

Diversity is a term that has evolved in the social work profession to encompass race, ethnicity, culture, class gender, sexual orientation, religion, age, national origin, and disability. According to the Council on Social Work Education's *Educational Policy and Accreditation Standards* (1994), diversity is the differences and similarities in experiences, needs, and beliefs of people. Diversity exists between the Asians, Southeast Asians, and Pacific Islanders; and within one single Asian or Pacific Islander ethnic group, there are many differences because of people's national origin, gender, sexual orientation, religion, age, and social class.

Diversification among the ethnic groups has been evident with the growing census population numbers. The 2000 U.S. Census reflects how Asian and Pacific Islander Americans and other ethnic groups have evolved. Historically, Asian Americans were clumped together to include all groups of Asians, and Pacific Islanders were included in that group. However, during the 10-year period between 1980 and 1990, the total Asian American population increased 107 percent (Sandhu, 1997, cited in Ross-Sheriff & Husain, 2001). But the 2000 U.S. Census subdivides the peoples of Asian countries into the major groupings of Asian, Southeast Asian, Asian Indian, and other Asian. These groups include people who are Chinese, Filipino, Japanese, Korean, Vietnamese, Cambodian, Hmong, Laotian, Indian, Pakistani, Thai, and other Asians; whereas the peoples of the 25 islands in the Pacific are categorized as Native Hawaiian, Guamanian or Chamorro, Samoan, or other Pacific Islander. Leung and Cheung (2001) report that prior to the 2000 U.S. Census, "[even though] Asians and Pacific Islanders represent at least twenty-three ethnic groups with thirty-two linguistic groups and more than one hundred dialects, these culturally diverse populations have been conveniently grouped for statistical purposes" (p. 426). Historically, Pacific Islanders were grossly omitted from considerations of reporting mechanisms. But with growing Pacific Islander populations throughout the United States, particularly on the West Coast, it is very important not only to acknowledge them but also to understand and respect their distinct cultural values and history.

Diversity has made its impact on racial categorizing. Lott (1998) criticizes the racial groupings of Asian Americans and claims that "Asian Americans in the United States were first defined not as a racial category or ethnic group but as a legal status. For almost a century they were defined as aliens ineligible for citizenship" (p. 87). Thus, it was only in the 1970s that the Asian American category was expanded to include Pacific Americans. Only 30 years later, however, the 2000 U.S. Census was recategorized to include six race-alone categories (White, Black or African American, American Indian and Alaska Native, Asian, Native Hawaiian and other Pacific Islander, and some other race such as one of Hispanic origin including Spanish, Hispanic, or Latino) and one category for two or more races (U.S. Bureau of the Census, 2001).

According to the 2000 U.S. Census, Asian, Native Hawaiian, and other Pacific Islander are each considered to be separate race categories. The total U.S. population in 2000 was 281,421,906 with 3.6 percent (2,475,956) reported to be Asian and 0.1 percent (398,835) to be Native Hawaiian and other Pacific Islander. The population of two or more races was 6,626,228. Of the API population, the subgroupings according to the 2000 U.S. Census are as follows:

Asian Americans	Chinese, Japanese, Filipino, Korean
Southeast Asians	Cambodian, Hmong, Vietnamese, Laotian, Thai, Malaysian, Singaporean
Asian Indian	Bengalese, Bharat, Dravidian, East Indian, Goanese
Other Asian	Bangladeshi, Burmese, Indonesian, Pakistani, Sri Lankan

Among the Pacific Islanders, the largest groups are Hawaiians, Samoans, and Guamanians (Chamorros). Other groups are Tongan, Fijian, Palauan, Tahitian, North Mariana Islanders, and other Pacific Islanders.

In a 2000 U.S. Census special report entitled "We the People: Asians in the United States," current demographics report Asians to be 11.9 million or 4.2 percent of the total population (Reeves & Bennett, 2004). Within the 11.9 million, 10.2 million are Asian only (3.6 percent) and 1.7 million or 0.6 percent are Asian and at least one other race. This report offers a breakdown of the 10.2 million Asian-only population: Chinese 2,422,970; Filipino 1,864,120; Asian Indian 1,645,510; Vietnamese 1,110,207; Korean 1,072,682; Japanese 795,051; Cambodian 178,043; Hmong 170,049; Laotian 167,792; Pakistani 155,909; Thai 110,851; and Other Asian 478,636.

Within each ethnic group, distinctions may exist among individuals based on immigrant, refugee, and transnational status (Lott, 1998, p. 99). Immigrant status would distinguish between those people who are native and those who are foreign. Transnational status would distinguish those people who, like the Chinese, emigrate from one country to two or more countries, such as Hong Kong to Canada and then to the United States. Within the transnational identity, some immigrants have left living environments with political policies affecting family size, structure, and functioning.

Diversity concepts are to be explained in the context of race and ethnicity, cultural values, religions, languages, and refugee and immigrant status. The immigrant and refugee status should not be ignored. The issues for immigrants overlap concerns for American-born Asians, but a host of complex issues plagues immigrants. They have problems with undocumented-alien status and discriminatory Immigration and Naturalization Service (INS) experiences. Lee, Lei, and Sue (2001) report anxiety stressors associated with the process of leaving family members behind and encountering poor living conditions upon arrival in America.

Besides differences in political status, language, foods, beliefs and traditions, the Asian and Pacific Islander populations can be further distinguished by religions, marriage patterns, and occupations. Although no one ethnic group is the same and there are many within-group differences, historically and even in current practices, Buddhism, Hinduism, and Catholicism have been major religions for several Asian groups. Interracial marriage tended to be more dominant in some Asian groups than others, and depending on the time cohort of the immigrant and refugee arrivals, occupational choices also tended to differ by Asian ethnic group. For example, Ross-Sheriff and Husain (2004) write:

> As a group, South Asians who came after 1980, as a result of the family reunification laws and green card lottery, are different from their previous counterparts. There is a much greater chance that neither parent of these immigrant families speak English or have a college degree. Unlike their predecessors who arrived after 1965, these immigrants have not settled in suburbs but rather in neighborhoods with low-cost or public housing. (p. 166)

Some of the Asian immigrant groups have settled into communities such as Chinatowns, Japantowns, or Koreatowns. These communities historically have been located in large cities such as San Francisco, Los Angeles, New York City, and Seattle. However, Asian communities have grown in Monterey, California (Chinatown); Portland, Oregon, and San Jose, California (Japantowns); and Atlanta, Georgia (Koreatown). In April 2005, *The Korea Times* newspaper printed an article entitled "Grocery Giants Battle in Atlanta Koreatown," reporting competition among five big grocery stores for the Asian and Latino customers (Chang, 2005). The Asian immigrant population continues to grow, sometimes with overlapping and tension-filled issues related to their own ethnic community or other minority groups.

Besides the immigrants, two other growing populations within the APIA population who are encountering stressors and are in need of attention are biracial and mixed-race children, adults, and families. This category encompasses the children born from inter-marriages who will become biracial or multiracial adults. Dhooper and Moore (2001) report the major needs and problems of biracial/mixed-race American groups to be related to mixed-race status, mixed-race families, biracial homosexuals, and biracial children and adolescents. Identity formation, divided loyalties, and conflicted choices between cultural heritages are some of the common dilemmas for this population.

Another growing population within the Asian group that will need attention in the future is the rising number of Chinese female (mostly) babies from the People's Republic of China who are being adopted by families. This trend eventually will cause social workers to examine their practice and deal with diversity issues. Fong and Wang (2001) write about the differing political and social environments between the United States and the People's Republic of China and the potential identity conflicts these infants may face as young adults with the absence of birth family knowledge. Chinese infants in both Chinese and non-Chinese families will struggle with the same issues of identity that American-born Asian children and adolescents face, but they also will have to struggle with national identity because the values and traditions of the People's Republic of China differ greatly from those of Hong Kong and other non-Communist environments. National identity issues may arise when the Chinese girls ask their adoptive parents about their birthplace, and parents might have to grapple with their personal and political thoughts about the People's Republic of China's stance on human rights. As Ross-Sheriff and Husain (2001) remind social workers, "[O]verall the common concern regarding work with Asian Americans is that the practitioner must recognize and plan to address the complex and multifaceted nature of their diversity" (p. 87). Certainly, the Chinese infants, many of them with physical disabilities, born in a Communist country but raised in a democratic political environment, some with parents of a different race, might someday need very skilled social workers who can explain when these teenagers ask why their Chinese parents abandoned them. Culturally competent skills are needed in working with all these facets of diversity.

Assessment and Planning

Assessment and planning is the process of determining the problem and its roots from the biopsychosocial cultural perspectives of the client. It usually mandates an investigation of the impact of the social environment upon the client system. In working with people of color, when assessing and planning for problem identification, it is important to clarify and understand the role that cultural values play in the psychological, social, and biological functioning of the client. Cultural values acknowledge and reflect the diversity of social environments. Thus, in performing biopsychosocial cultural assessments with ethnic minority groups, a social worker would start with understanding of the culture of the client and determine how cultural values impact biological, psychological, and social functioning. For example, in Asian and Pacific Islander families, the unit of analysis or functioning is the family. Thus, the family unit has an impact on the individual's biological, psychological, and social functioning in API populations.

Usually in working with Asian and Pacific Islander populations, a biopsychosocial cultural assessment would have different emphases because of life-span development. When working with API youth, there may be a developmental life-span emphasis on the social rather than the psychological. However, in working with the aged population, the literature has documented that in working with the API elderly, assessment needs to be done in understanding the cultural component because psychosomatic symptoms frequently are indicators of mental health dysfunction as well as biological impairments (Browne & Broderick, 1994; Mui, 2001; Takamura, 1991). This is reflective of the traditional API cultural value of keeping problems in the family or denying that a psychological problem exists. It is a more common occurrence among the elderly who keep to traditional practices of not acknowledging mental health that they would acknowledge a biological rather than psychological problem.

Chinese American family therapist Marshall Jung (1998) describes his elderly mother's somatization of her psychological discomforts:

> As my mother grew older, she appeared to be plagued with an increasing number of physical ailments: headaches, backaches and stomach pains, and an inability to move joints. One day, my brothers Chester, Douglas, and I watched her coming out of the kitchen in the back area of our grocery store. She was dragging one leg and had her right hand on her forehead as she complained of having a severe headache. It looked [so] contrived that it seemed comical, instead of eliciting feelings of sympathy. We looked at each other thinking that she was a hypochondriac. Later, I learned that to the Chinese, somatization is a valid way of expressing inner conflicts and that physical, rather than psychological, complaints are an acceptable way to obtain attention. (p. 46–47)

Although some elderly do somatize feelings, others struggle with mental health issues. Studies have been done on Asian American elders and stress, coping, and depression (Mui, 1996; Mui, 2001; Mui & Burnette, 1996). But researchers and practitioners have found that "despite substantial prevalent rates, symptoms of depression can go unrecognized, undiagnosed, and untreated due to patient- and health-care-related barriers and problems in the organization and financing of mental health services for older adults, especially minority elders" (Mui, 2001, p. 283).

Whether the client is elderly or youthful, in Asian and Pacific Island cultures, there are many cultural values, with the most dominant ones to be love for and loyalty to family, respect of elders and authority, love of land and education, harmony and unity, and avoidance of loss of face and shame. These cultural values may be used as strengths in assessments in that they will explain much of the meaning behind behavior and thinking. In the area of Asian mental health, this is particularly important because the psychological and physical functioning of the individual are intricately related. The cultural components affect the psychological thinking, which may indeed affect the biological functioning.

Many cultural values dominate throughout the various Asian, Southeast Asian, and Pacific Islander cultures. A strong appreciation for family and extended family members is probably the most common. For some API groups, the cultural value of spirituality in various manifestations is very important. In working with Southeast Asians, Morelli (2001) writes about Cambodian meaning systems and the cultural value of spirituality and how it is intertwined with animism, sorcery, and magic. Asians hold strong Buddhist and Taoist beliefs as well as traditional Protestant and Catholic beliefs. Pacific Islanders honor their gods and strongly connect spirituality to their love of the land.

Although cultural values are related to religion and ethnicity, another diversity variable of sexual orientation adds complexities when these foci intersect. Kanuha (2001) warns that for gays and lesbians, another layer of complexity exists:

> . . . due to the importance of family loyalty, "saving face," and other cultural values that are integral parts of many Asian and Pacific Island communities, social workers who work with individual or family levels with Asian/Pacific Island American (A/PIA) gay men and lesbians must be sensitive to the myriad ways this population balances cultural aspects of A/PIA family life while also learning to know themselves as gay and lesbian persons. (p. 315)

She suggests that social workers "assume that every A/PIA client who is dealing with his or her sexuality, whether or not they are gay, may also be conflicted in part by their racial/ethnic beliefs and traditions" (p. 320).

TOOLS FOR STUDENT LEARNING 12.1

Determining Cultural Values—Case Study: The Hawaiian Way

The presenting problem is a Hawaiian Chinese family with a 15-year-old son, who was suspended from school because of marijuana use. The Chinese mother phoned the family service agency wanting help, despite her hesitation to reveal family problems. The Hawaiian father did not want his son to be permanently hooked on drugs or kicked out of school, so he agreed to have the social workers come to his home.

The family had three children ages 15, 12, and 9 but were part of a larger extended family system that generally could deal with all the problems presented by family members. Both parents admitted regular use of marijuana when younger. However, they were worried that their son was using "too much." They were worried that he might become incarcerated like the other cousins who used "too much."

The social workers established goals for the family. The first was to have the family work together on the problem. The mother wanted the father more involved and active in the parenting because she was tired of dealing with the son's problems on her own. The father wanted the mother to be less angry and demanding and more attentive to his (the husband's) needs. The other two kids wanted the parents to stop fighting all the time.

The social workers had to discern what values were important to the family that would help them direct the problem-solving process and select the appropriate culturally competent interventions for this family.

The following questions help to determine what values are important to the family as a system:

1. What cultural values are important to Chinese families?

2. What cultural values are important to Hawaiian families?

3. What cultural values are important to this Chinese-Hawaiian family?

4. How can social workers use these cultural values as strengths in treatment planning?

Practice

Because of the diversity within an ethnic group and the growing numbers of mixed groupings, culturally competent practice needs to continually be examined in several ways to accommodate changes. Questions to ask include the following: (1) Does the diversity within the single ethnic group warrant practice modifications? (2) Do practice methods account for the interactions of ethnicity, gender, sexual orientation, age, religion, social class, and physical or mental ability? (3) Do practices include indigenous strategies? (4) Are new practice models being developed to reflect cultural values? When social workers discuss practice methods and diversity, there should be a recognition that indigenous strategies, which are usually grounded in cultural values, ought to be an integral part of practice methods.

Examples would be *o'hana* conferencing or deep cultural therapy in the Hawaiian culture in which cultural values of family and land are reflected in the interventions. Fong, Boyd, and Browne (1999) look at combining Western interventions and indigenous interventions in the process of biculturalization of interventions. Lee (1997, p. 15) recommends structural family therapy because of the hierarchal and structural orientation to most Asian families, the generalist practice problem-solving approach, and the Bowenian approach to explore family dynamics. Structural family therapy reinforces the emphasis of many Asian cultures on family structure, roles, and authority domination. Jung (1998) advocates working with Chinese families from a Chinese American family therapy (CAFT) perspective, which also examines Chinese traditional values and Western-oriented therapies for families.

Because Asians and Pacific Islanders are mostly family oriented, various family theoretical models have been used in social work practice. Family group conferencing (FGC) is another model being used in Asian and Pacific Islander family work. Having originated with the Pacific Islander Maori group in Australia, FGC has been used in child welfare and mental health fields. Pennell and Buford (2000) report how family group conferencing and decision making tap into the strengths of the families and communities and brings families together who may be struggling with domestic violence and child welfare issues. With the rising incidence of family violence and substance abuse among Native Hawaiian families, Mokuau (2001) proposes "culturally-based solutions" such as *ho'oponopono*, a Native Hawaiian family-focused approach to problem prevention and resolution.

TOOLS FOR STUDENT LEARNING 12.2

Family Group Conferencing—Case Study: The Hawaiian Way (continued)

The Hawaiian Chinese parents agreed to work with the social workers but were uncomfortable with the proposed intervention plan of having their son attend a group for substance users while they sought a marriage counselor to discuss their communication difficulties. Instead, family group conferencing (FGC) was proposed where this family and their extended members could gather to discuss how to go about treating the substance use and the parents' difficulties. The four phases of FGC (Merkel-Holguin & Ribich, 2001) were explained by the social workers as follows:

Phase One: Referral phase
Phase Two: Preparation and planning
Phase Three: The family group conference
Phase Four: Follow-up

The social workers worked with the parents in phases two and three, in preparing, planning, and actually holding the conference.

In the preparing and planning phases, the social workers had the parents define what they meant by family in order to determine which "family" members were necessary to invite. Relationship building among the extended family networks is important in order to protect emotional and physical safety during and after the family conference. Unresolved family issues are addressed as much as possible before the family conference begins. During the actual family group conference for this Hawaiian Chinese family, the coordinator made introductions of everyone present (family and relatives, professionals, school officials, community members). Professionals delineated the facts of the case during the time of information sharing. People present identified the strengths of the family and discussed available resources. Private family time was given after the concerns, strengths, and pertinent information on the case were laid out. All the professionals left it to the family, friends, and relatives to come up with a treatment plan to help the 15-year-old boy and his parents with his substance abuse problem.

Once a decision was made and a plan was developed, the professionals were invited into the room again to discuss the plan and make sure it was reasonable and could be implemented. When everyone present agreed upon the plan, it was signed and a copy was offered to all participants. The follow-up phase was very important because resourcing and monitoring needed to be carefully implemented.

The following questions are important to consider in conducting a family group conference:

1. How is "family" defined in the clients' culture, and who are the important participants to invite?

2. Are all the strengths of the family system identified and used as resources?

3. Did every participant "buy into" the plan?

4. What assurance is there for the resourcing and monitoring of the plan?

Despite the proposed changes in practices, social workers need to be culturally sensitive as to why ethnic clients may refuse social work practice services. Leung and Cheung (2001) report that Asians and Pacific Islanders may refuse to seek help for mental health problems either to avoid shame or because they assume natural healing will occur. Clients may not seek help for the following reasons:

1. They do not recognize or acknowledge there is a mental health problem.
2. They are afraid of being stigmatized if they seek help.
3. They do not want to address negative comments about their traditional healing practices.
4. They do not have access to bilingual, bicultural services.
5. They assume the social service provider will not be culturally competent.

Thus, the worker is not thought to understand the client's culture even if the provider is the same ethnicity as the client (Leung and Cheung, 2001, pp. 428–429). Social workers need to try to work with the refusals and hesitations of clients by creating culturally competent practices. This would include helping the clients feel safe in knowing that a psychosomatic problem can be treated without shame-based activities or negative stigmas. Bilingual and bicultural workers who are of the same level of acculturation and who speak the same dialect can assure API clients that they will receive help in a manner that is sensitive to and respectful of their culture. Using indigenous treatments in place of or in addition to Western interventions assures API clients through familiar experiences that they are receiving help in a culturally competent manner.

Morelli (2001) asserts that "in cross-cultural practice we fail to fully assess, advocate for, and facilitate culturally appropriate interventions and services that have a greater potential for meeting the clients' needs" (p. 427). Ross-Sheriff and Husain (2001) warn:

[P]ractitioners must realize that, regardless of their efforts to customize current assessment and interventions techniques to suit Asian-Americans, there will remain biases from the dominant Euro-American worldview and its values. Guided by their zeal to assist the client, the practitioners may involuntarily impart notions of what is healthy and normal based on Euro-American standards. (p. 87)

Practitioners need to examine their worldviews and be sure to have enough knowledge about their clients' ethnic culture in order to plan and implement treatment based upon values, beliefs, and ethnic practices of the clients. This will work to counteract culturally biased definitions of normal and abnormal attitudes and behaviors.

Research

Research is an integral part of practice in that it evaluates the effectiveness of interventions, services, and programs. Historically, the traditional research paradigm had positivistic, scientific, objective, and quantitative characteristics (Schriver, 2001). However, an alternative paradigm for understanding human behavior and doing research is one with characteristics of interpretive, intuitive, subjective, and qualitative dimensions (Schriver, 2001). In doing research with Asians and Pacific Islanders, several alternative paradigms have been used. Some of these alternative methods are participatory action research, oral histories and traditions, and ethnographies.

Matsuoka (2001) describes the need to do participatory action research (PAR) whose purpose is "documenting particular social realities in order to enable constituencies/communities to advocate for communities and the resources needed to sustain them" (p. 444). Matsuoka asserts that the traditional role of the researcher where participants play a passive role and are not actively engaged "in the technical and interpretative stages of research is antithetic to the goal of documenting indigenous realities" (p. 444). As described by Matsuoka,

> [PAR] is a process that involves establishing networks between representatives of a locale or community, research consultants, and bureaucrats. The goal of this process is to discover and document aspects of a community in order to preserve or ameliorate such aspects in an effort to sustain or improve the quality of life. (p. 444)

People's lives and indigenous realities are reflected in people's stories. In working with Asians and Pacific Islanders, using oral histories is important. Mokuau, Lukela, Obra, and Voeller (1997), in their work about Native Hawaiian spirituality, capture oral histories and traditions from their focus group research. Oral histories and traditions are recorded through interviews using key informants in qualitative research methods. The histories and traditions are rich with descriptions of key events and their cultural meanings as well as human behavior affiliated with these activities. It is important for social workers to work on cultural competence skills in communication. Leigh (1998) advocates that social workers "must strive for the degree of understanding that can derive only from information provided by a member of the contrasting cultural group. Failure to achieve this means the social worker cannot enter the senses of the other. The social worker must comprehend the cultural context and meaning of these sensibilities. Only then will the social worker comprehend what is it that the person knows and how it is used in everyday life" (p. 15).

Ethnographies and ethnographic interviewing are other methods used in research. Ethnographic methods are "suggested for the culturally competent social worker because [they foster] a fellowship with the minority person of color" (Leigh, 1998, p. 12). Morton's (1996) ethnography on Pacific Islander children describes her research method as an ethnopsychological approach where she examined the "interaction of socialization, language socialization research, and accounts of tradition and cultural identity" (p. 10). She explains, "[T]he emphasis on interaction, agency, and context as a feature of recent psychological and sociological approaches to socialization is a feature of the ethnopsychological approach in anthropology" (p. 10). Interdisciplinary work often enhances the explanation of the contexts of the culture and the environments.

Leigh's (1998) work on communicating for cultural competence stresses the importance of ethnographic interviewing. He writes:

> Ethnographic interviewing holds much promise for social workers who wish to attain cultural competence. Ethnographic interviewing can be very helpful when working with ethnic minority persons of color. Essentially, ethnographic interviewing is highly cognitive and word-oriented. It assumes that language and words, in particular, are windows to the world of the ethnic minority person. By ethnographic methods of inquiry, the social worker elicits the story. The story of a person can be seen as narrative through which the storyteller's perspective is revealed. Narrative is the universal metacode from which cultural messages and the

nature of a shared reality are transmitted. For effective helping, it is essential that the social worker hear the content of the narratives, as the content provides valuable information about how other people experience others as well as themselves in interaction with others. (p. 13)

Although quantitative and positivistic research does occur with APIAs, Leung and Cheung (2001) write about the involvement of Asians and Pacific Islanders in satisfaction surveys. They warn that in the Asian context,

. . . such an approach can be misinterpreted as either a dissatisfaction assessment or a means for pleasing others. Some API may think they should only report something that is undesirable and disregard the survey even if satisfaction is found. Others may solely focus on positives even if dissatisfaction is evident. (pp. 427–428)

Because many APIs tend not to express negative information or not to express their true thoughts and feelings, discernment is needed to discover what the clients truly feel and think about situations.

Furthermore, Leung and Cheung (2001) state: "No literature has addressed these phenomena because cultural factors [of APIs not expressing real feelings and emotions] are mixed with situational factors [of complying and responding to authority-associated activities] in Asian clients' responses to surveys" (p. 428). As social workers grapple with the complex issues that come with the diversity of the APIA population, it is hoped that innovative research endeavors will be created to meet new challenges encountered in evaluating traditional cultural responses in order to discern the real answers to ethnic clients' problems.

HISTORICAL AND CURRENT OPPRESSION EXPERIENCES

The history of the oppression of Asians and Pacific Islanders is best told by recounting the discriminatory experiences of Asian immigrants, the racist attitudes and behaviors toward American-born Asians, and the colonialist practices toward Pacific Islanders, particularly Native Hawaiians. Although it is acknowledged that probably all Asian, Southeast Asian, South Asian, and Pacific Islander groups have endured unfair discriminatory, racist, and colonialist attitudes and behaviors, space limitations allow for only a brief discussion of some Asian and Pacific Islander groups' experiences.

Discriminatory Experiences of Asian Immigrants

Discriminatory experiences for Asian immigrants have been many and are ongoing. The first Asian immigrant group to enter the United States was the Chinese in the 1840s. Mostly single men, these sojourners were looking for their "mountain of gold" (Sung, 1967) in order to make good money, buy a business or land, and return to China as prosperous successes. This was their dream. Their reality in California in the 1800s and 1900s was hostile confrontations, exclusions, and even fatalities because of riots against them. In 1882, legislation was passed (the Chinese Exclusion law) that halted immigration and exacerbated the already discriminatory practice of not allowing Chinese immigrants to become citizens. Although in 1943 the Exclusion Act was finally repealed, much pressure, such as being driven out of their work and communities, was put upon the Chinese laborers to return to China. Some succumbed, but despite the racist and discriminatory practices against them because they worked for wages lower than their Euro-American counterparts, many remained in the United States and formed Chinatown communities (Fong, 1992; Takaki, 1993).

The next Asian groups of Japanese, Korean, and Filipino immigrants fared no better than the Chinese in adjusting to the United States except that they could learn from experiences of the Chinese. Japanese immigrants, mostly laborers and indigent students who started coming to America in the 1890s, were carefully screened before being allowed to leave Japan. They were "predominantly males who worked at difficult low paying jobs; they faced racism and were relegated to the bottom of society" (Kitano & Nakaoka, 2001, p. 9). Although in 1907 the Gentleman's Agreement passed between the United States and Japanese governments restricted the emigration of male laborer immigrants, it did not apply to female immigrants. Between 1910 and 1920, the Japanese government allowed farmers and laborers to summon their wives in order to avoid the bachelor society the Chinese men had had to endure (Fong, 1992; Ichioka, 1988). Japanese women were able to join their husbands and form a "family society" in the United States, but many women also came as "picture brides" or prostitutes (Ichioka, 1988). Whether male or female, single or married, the Japanese immigrants, like the Chinese, experienced hostility and discrimination. The anti-Japanese movement was as virulent in the 1900s as was the anti-Chinese movement in the 1800s.

When the next immigrant groups of Koreans, Asian Indians, and Filipinos entered the United States in the 1900s, they too experienced exclusion, harassment, and violence. Filipinos confronted difficulties and hardships created by the United States government despite their U.S. national status. Anti-Filipino sentiment was rampant on the West Coast because of competition for jobs with white laborers. Asian Indians and Koreans also experienced prejudice, discrimination, and racism in jobs, workplace, housing, and educational opportunities.

In 1900, Asian immigrants consisting mostly of Chinese and Japanese occupied 1.5 percent of the total foreign-born U.S. population (Kitano & Nakaoka, 2001, p. 12). But Hing (1993) reports that demographic predictions are that by the year 2020, Asian Pacific Americans will be 54 percent of the foreign-born population (p. 127). Foreign-born Asians will dominate social work services, and culturally competent services will need to be changed to reflect that change in status.

Racist Attitudes and Behaviors toward American-Born Asians

First- and second-generation Asians, Southeast Asians, and Asian Indians born in the United States experience many discriminatory practices, as did their forefathers from overseas. Employment discrimination with unfair labor laws and below-normal wages continue to be practiced. In the 1940s, the Japanese interned during World War II experienced what the American Civil Liberties Union described as the "greatest deprivation of civil liberties by government in this country since slavery." Evacuation, incarceration, and resettlement were imposed on Japanese American citizens who felt that "their government did not trust them and that the Constitution did not protect them from forced removal and incarceration without charges or trial" (Nishi, 1995, p. 103).

Almost 30 years later in the 1970s, at the end of the Vietnam War, the Amerasian children, offspring of American GIs and Southeast Asian women, were also treated with racial bias and hostile attitudes, despite negotiations between the South Vietnamese and

American governments. These refugees, although given U.S. citizenship by birth, were not well received in America. Nor were their other Southeast Asian counterparts. Poverty and poor housing and living conditions are some of the many problems these Southeast Asians have faced living in America.

Colonialist Practices toward Pacific Islanders

The history of Pacific Islanders and the story of their oppressive encounters with people who forcibly try to dominate the land and the peoples document the colonization practices. In the history of the *kanaka maoli* or indigenous Hawaiians, it is written that James Cooke arrived in Hawaii in 1778 and "unleashed five devastating interrelated forces of depopulation; foreign exploitation; cultural conflict; adoption of harmful foreign ways; and neglect, insensitivity, and malice from the ruling establishment" (Blaisdell & Mokuau, 1991, p. 132). Native Hawaiians and other Pacific Islanders have experienced colonization, which diminishes their attempts and ability to self-govern (Trask, 1984–1985). Foreigners have come to the islands and exploited native lands for private ownership. They have supplanted ruling chiefs by indebtedness to avarice merchants and suspended native language, dances, and healing methods for Westernized religious practices (Mokuau, 1991). The sovereignty nation movement of Hawaiians in the 1990s was an attempt to empower the entire nation (Ewalt and Mokuau, 1995), but opposition remains to Native Hawaiian self-determination from internal (factions among the Hawaiian people) and external (practices of colonialization) sources. Ethical questions arise when the practices of colonialization go unquestioned, and social and economic injustices continue to plague the Native Hawaiian population.

Current Oppression Experiences

Native Hawaiians have struggled to own their land and receive the federal rights and entitlements bestowed upon Native peoples. Federal legislation was proposed to give Native Hawaiians the same federal recognition as Native Americans by Senator Daniel Akaka, who has been spearheading this effort since 1999. In January 2005, he introduced S147, the Native Hawaiian Government Reorganization Act of 2005, which would (1) establish the Office of Native Hawaiian Relations in the Department of Interior to focus on Native Hawaiian affairs; (2) establish the Native Hawaiian Interagency Coordinating Group; and (3) provide a process of reorganizing the Native Hawaiian governing entity. Akaka's bill was proposed and passed through the House in 2000 but was not immediately approved by the Senate. The delay perpetuates the denial of Native Hawaiians' rights and entitlements.

The United States Commission on Civil Rights (1992) reported that in the 1990s Asian Americans faced discrimination and barriers to equal opportunities because of the "model minority" stereotype that wrongly labels some Asian groups with high average family incomes, educational achievement, and occupational status as representing all or most Asian American family situations (p. 19). The poverty of recent immigrants and "glass ceilings" in employment and academic admissions in higher learning institutions for second-, third-, or fourth-generation individual members are ignored. Negative perceptions of being "foreigners," of lacking communication skills, of having limited English proficiency, and of adhering to non-Western religious beliefs and practices tend to still plague many American-born Asians (pp. 20–21).

CULTURAL AWARENESS AND SOCIAL SERVICE NEEDS

Cultural awareness is defined as "the learning of the cultural background, issues, and relationships in a contextual sense" (Hardy & Laszloffy, 1995, as cited in Lum, 1999). Understanding the cultural background and the contextual sense is important because the context will dictate the services needed. Sanders (as cited in Mokuau, 1991) predicted a decade ago that the services for Asians and Pacific Islanders would include the following considerations:

1. More changes and intergenerational problems impacting parents, children, and the elderly
2. A need for a more holistic perspective in services addressing "life, relationships, and services" and less of a "dichotomy between the body and mind, psyche and soma"
3. An emphasis on change that comes from a "preventive and developmental perspective" committed to "maximizing the strengths and capacities of individuals, families, and communities"
4. A cross-cultural, pluralistic perspective in working with clients and services
5. Greater emphasis on "total family and family support systems" (pp. 236–239)

Sanders identifies some needs, but developing the services to meet those needs is challenging. Even if the services are developed, they need to be made culturally competent and appropriate if APIA needs are truly to be met.

The social needs for services are great for Asian and Pacific Islanders. Among Japanese Americans, the impact of internment on families may still require services dealing with PTSD issues. Asian and Pacific Islander elderly suffer from depression and Alzheimer's disease, and caregivers' stress due to filial piety and obligation cultural values is also problematic (Mui, 2001). Chinese immigrants deal with language discrimination, employment, and naturalization problems. Intergenerational conflicts arise in parent–child relationships, and acculturation difficulties exist because of value conflicts, communication misunderstandings, and psychological isolation (Lee, 1997).

Filipinos struggle with employment discrimination and often end up in service-oriented jobs because of their immigrant status. Asian and Southeast Asian immigrants need bilingual services. Vietnamese and other Southeast Asians struggle with mental health problems because of acculturation stress and drastic changes in environmental disruptions (Ngo, Tran, Gibbons, & Oliver, 2001). Families have been separated, and Amerasian children have been forced to relocate to an American environment that initially did not welcome or support them. In Vietnamese and Korean immigrant family systems, there are role reversals and abuse of the women (Scheinfeld, Wallach, & Langendorf, 1997; Tran & Des Jardins, 2000; Zhou & Bankston, 1998).

Morelli (2001) writes that, in working with Cambodian refugees, social workers need to pay attention to five areas in assessment:

1. The need for trained competent language translators who have a sound understanding of differences in cultural beliefs and values regarding family, social customs, and health care between the host and immigrating cultures
2. The need for understanding of sociocultural traditions and health care
3. The need to be in consultation with community leaders and family elders regarding health care issues

4. The need for social workers to understand the disorders from both a Western and a culturally specific perspective
5. The role that policies and geopolitical histories have played and the consequent importance of macro perspectives when assessing needs for service provision (p. 208)

Among the Pacific Islander populations, abuse of Hawaiians continues because cultural traditions have been stolen and the land is largely owned by trusts and oligopolies, forcing Native Hawaiian families to live in poverty. Native Hawaiian families experience disproportionate levels of substance abuse and family violence, and their children may consequently experience or witness domestic violence more than others will (Mokuau, 1999). Samoan children suffer high rates of child abuse, and their parents have financial difficulties, environmental and mental health concerns, and domestic violence problems. Chamorros suffer from high suicide rates among youth, drug abuse, alcoholism, family violence, and high crime rates.

Among the Asian and Pacific Islander GLBT (gay, lesbian, bisexual, and transgender) population, Kanuha (2001) makes the point that the gay or lesbian person from an ethnic group has sexual orientation needs in addition to ethnicity. Poon (2000) reports interracial same-sex abuse between Asian and Caucasian gay men and concludes that same-sex violence in Asian communities produces a need for 24-hour hotlines, shelters and safe houses, public awareness, and advocacy in the criminal justice system. Poon offers six risk factors contributing to intimate violence in Asian-Caucasian relationships:

1. Homophobia in Asian cultures
2. Issues of professional assistance and support
3. The dominant idea of beauty and Asian images in western countries
4. Age differences
5. Income disparity and its implications in relationships
6. Cultural values of family (p. 40)

Although the cultural value of family is usually a positive attribute, the shame and "loss of face" as well as privately keeping affairs within the family may discourage or prohibit help-seeking efforts.

In addressing these many needs for services within the API population, social workers need to be ready to provide social services that are based on cultural values and include indigenous strategies and interventions. They must also grapple with the interactions of ethnicity, sexual orientation, gender, and national origins that may result in cultural tensions.

EXPLORING AREAS OF KNOWLEDGE ACQUISITION

For social work practitioners, knowledge acquisition is the process of acquiring information that will enhance their understanding and effectiveness in providing culturally competent services to Asian and Pacific Islander clients. The question to be asked is this: What kind of knowledge is needed to enhance culturally competent practice with Asians and Pacific Islanders? One proposal would be to explore how knowledge acquisition relates to the interaction of theory development, cultural values, and practice methods to affect Asian and Pacific Islander clients.

Although the theoretical framework of person-in-environment, the ecological model, and the oppression or colonization theories are germane to APIA knowledge development, theory development still needs to be compatible with the cultural values of the ethnic group. In the culture of First Nations Peoples, colonization theory guides the understanding of oppression (Yellow Bird, 2001; Brave Heart, 2001). Traditional Native culture also advocates historical trauma theory (Yellow Bird, 2001) to help explain the Lakota tribe's response to "massive cumulative group trauma across generations and within the current lifespan" (Brave Heart, 2001). This is an example of how cultural values guide theory development in Native people's culture.

In the Chinese culture, Chung (1992) offers the Confucian model of social transformation. It is a model for social change used in Asian countries that has been adapted for use in the universal generalist social work practice (p. 131). This theory is based on the values of Confucianism. There are seven steps in the model to change individuals and society:

1. The investigation of things or variables
2. The completion of knowledge
3. The sincerity of thought
4. The rectifying of the heart
5. The cultivation of the person
6. The regulation of the family
7. The governance of the state (p. 131)

This model demonstrates taking cultural values from Confucianism and creating a theory that supports those cultural values.

Another example is Morelli's (2001) statement:

[C]ritical to deeper understanding of Cambodian constructions of trauma and healing is the knowledge that the Khmer concept of pain and its expression in suffering is significantly different from western beliefs and forms. In the Khmer culture, the concept of pain extends beyond pain as an indication of illness. It is part of a larger process of suffering, which continually contributes to their kinship and familial solidarity and reciprocity, and ethnic identity maintenance. (pp. 202–203)

Morelli's point is that the Cambodian cultural value of suffering shapes the building of family and extended family relationships and connects them to the cultural value of suffering.

Thus, in working with Asians, Southeast Asians, Asian Indians, or Pacific Islanders, social workers must have a planned way to explore areas of knowledge acquisition that will allow them to better know the ethnic culture of their API clients and to use the cultural values to develop theories to explain their ways of thinking and behaving. This is closely tied into skill development and generating new inductive learning. Social workers need to know that if a Khmer client is expressing suffering and pain (a biological and psychological adjustment), the client may be using the strength of the Khmer cultural norm as a reciprocal endeavor to solidify kinship and ethnic identity. In other words, the suffering and pain should be taken as a strength for family solidarity rather than family dysfunction.

New theory development and practices need to be formulated for API families affected by policies and societal change. For example, Lee (1997) describes five types of constructs by which to understand Asian American families: traditional, "cultural conflict," bicultural, "Americanized," and interracial (pp. 11–13). Lee's five constructs assume that the Asian American families are intact families and that the differences stem from generational gaps (traditional) in differing environments with labels such as "cultural conflict" or "Americanized." Missing from Lee's constructs are Asian American families that are not intact, where the husband and wife are divorced; families where the partners are of the same sex or not married; and families with adopted children from other countries. Chinese infants from the People's Republic of China are now creating Asian American families that are more complex, with multifaceted factors. In working with Asian families, particularly Chinese families who have come from the People's Republic of China since the passing of the 1979 single-child policy, it would be erroneous for a social worker to assess the family's problem without understanding the cultural value of having only one child, particularly a male child to continue the traditionalist custom of name and family preservation.

Another area for knowledge acquisition is the interaction of the various diversity variables. Cultural values need to inform theory development and be interwoven with ethnicity, sexual orientation, gender, age, social class, religion, and physical or mental ability. This leads to some questions: How do social workers develop a framework that integrates these variables rather than treating them as separate entities? How does a social worker, for example, use knowledge about a lesbian Japanese woman to discern whether she is most concerned about her gender, sexual orientation, or ethnic cultural values? Probably all of these are important to her. To compound matters, how does a social worker take culture-specific problems and sift them though the lenses of a multicultural client? How do we help clients with the "processing of cultural beliefs" (Galan, 2001) in the midst of dealing with severe problems such as chronic depression, sexual abuse, or domestic violence? These are the questions and areas that social workers need to continue to explore in knowledge acquisition to improve their abilities as culturally competent social workers.

FOSTERING PRACTICE SKILL DEVELOPMENT

Skill development, according to Lum (1999), is "the creation of a repertoire of behaviors for the social worker to use in the helping situation. Skills represent the practical application of cultural awareness and knowledge" (p. 112). In working with Asian Americans, it is important for social workers to learn how to foster the development of relevant and culturally sensitive and competent skills.

Lee (1997) discusses skills needed in the assessment and data collection stages in working with APIAs:

1. Family's ethnocultural heritage, migration stress, postmigration experience and cultural shock, impact of migration on individual and family life cycle, acculturation level of each family member
2. Work and financial stresses
3. Family's place of residence and community influence
4. Family stresses caused by role reversal
5. Stress caused by legal problems and sponsor relationships
6. Family's experiences with racism, prejudice, and discrimination

7. General skills plus specialized skills in substance abuse and family violence (pp. 16–24)

Leung and Cheung (2001) recommend that social workers use three principles in working with Asian and Pacific Islander clients and families in clinical practice:

1. To positively convey the concept of mental health and to address the purpose of counseling services according to cultural expectations
2. To evaluate the client's decision to seek, or not seek, family support
3. To recognize clients' strengths as well as evaluate their limitations that may block the optimal use of their potential in the environment (p. 426)

However, the two new areas that need to be fostered in skill development with APIs are (1) viewing cultural values as strengths in selecting appropriate or compatible Western interventions, and (2) dealing with multicomplex situations such as international adoptions.

Social workers need to develop skills in assessment from alternative paradigm perspectives. Rather than following the traditional paradigm of using Western treatment models, social workers need to start skill development of treatment planning with Asian and Pacific Islander traditional ways of healing and then match them with Western interventions. They need to evaluate whether the Western interventions foster the cultural values and ask whether programs that they are designing are accessible, available, and accountable to the ethnic community. For example, Chow (2001) advocates that a "multiservice, one-stop neighborhood center is considered a culturally appropriate approach for Chinese immigrant communities in the United States" (p. 217).

Another area in which to foster skill development is selecting the assessment and intervention skills that meet the complexities of problem situations involving the intersection of multiple variables such as physical disability, national origin, ethnicity, and multiple race. For example, in the area of international adoptions, Fong and Wang (2001) researched how parents prepared for and shaped the identity development of their adopted daughters from the People's Republic of China. Findings included the following: (1) creating a birth heritage, (2) instilling pride in the child's Chinese identity, (3) integrating the adoptive parents' background, (4) explaining the abandonment, and (5) coping with physical and medical special needs. The authors concluded:

> [T]he adoptees in the study have a composite identity of having special needs, being orphans, and becoming Chinese Americans born in Communist China but who are raised by non-Chinese parents in democratic America. The findings in the study strongly suggest the monitoring of the development of the ethnic identity of the adoptees. . . . Because the Chinese adoptees are born in the People's Republic of China and because Chinese culture is different from America, Hong Kong, or Taiwan, this heralds a new Chinese-American experience completely different from the "Chinatown" or "model minority" Chinese Americanness. . . . Multiple identities will intersect, such as adoptee, orphan, daughter, female, Chinese, American, and Chinese-American. The added intricacies of adoption, abandonment, foreign birthplace, and a second set of invisible parents [unidentifiable birth parents] call for new research endeavors. (p. 29)

New practice skills will also have to be developed to handle the complexities of these adoptive situations. Although the Korean, Romanian, and Russian international adoptive situations offer some comparative experiences and insights, the fact that accessibility to Chinese birth parents does not exist will create the need for social work skills to be developed to accommodate complex situations with adoptive parents, teachers, doctors, social workers, and therapists. Social workers working in international adoptions may have to develop closer ties with the medical community to understand the Chinese medical system and normative childhood medical conditions in China and compare them to American childhood diseases.

Newly developed practice skills would include understanding international social work; crossing disciplines between child welfare and health; and understanding Chinese language efficiency, health, mental health, and education. Research skills would be developed in alternative paradigms, and policy advocacy skills would be important to have in promoting human rights and social justice for the female special needs infants.

GENERATING NEW INDUCTIVE LEARNING

Inductive learning involves several steps and processes: (1) discerning the backgrounds and problems of the client; (2) improving the practitioner's skills; (3) collecting new information on problem formation; and (4) continuing to do informal and formal research to contribute to the enhancement of multicultural knowledge and skills. To generate new inductive learning, social workers will have to assess what they currently know about their minority client populations, discern what new information has been accrued recently, update their knowledge base and practices, and decipher where the gaps are and how to fill them.

Inductive learning about Asians and Pacific Islanders will have to focus on the following areas: (1) new diverse groupings and identities; (2) clashes of cultural values when clients transition between differing social environments; (3) indigenous strategies; (4) commonalities between the APIA groups; (5) differences between the groups; and (6) differences within the same group. Another area where new inductive learning needs to occur is to develop a means to automatically intersect race and ethnicity with age, gender, sexual orientation, social class, religion, and disability with each ethnic grouping within the Asian American population. For example, Asian Americans and Pacific Islanders need to be adressed by life-span development from infancy to older adulthood with attention to male and female as well as gay and lesbian issues and needs. Disabilities need to be addressed during each developmental period, the differences between males and females need to be addressed; and attention must be paid to homo-, bi-, and heterosexuals and the impact social class and religion has on them. The perpetual argument given is that the populations of the various Asian subgroups are too small to warrant a separate discussion. This reasoning is no longer justifiable, given the increasing diversity among the Asian and Pacific Islander American minority groups as well as many other ethnic populations.

UNDERSTANDING AND ADVOCATING FOR SOCIAL AND ECONOMIC JUSTICE

Social and economic justice is promoted by the Council on Social Work Education and the National Association of Social Workers (NASW). As early as the 1980s, the NASW standards for practice in social justice and economic justice were viable tenets for practice. Social workers were expected to understand the dynamics and consequences of social and economic injustice.

For Asians and Pacific Islanders, social and economic issues revolve around land rights and welfare reform for immigrants. For Pacific Islanders, specifically Native Hawaiians, land rights are crucial. Fong and Furuto (2001) reiterate that "indigenous communities need to organize themselves around issues of sovereignty as a means by which to develop themselves and their communities" (p. 457). Furuto, San Nicholas, Kim, and Fiaui (2001) advocate that for Chamorros and Hawaiians, social justice would be the return of their land or the payment of fair compensation for it. For the Japanese internment people, social justice was achieved when they were compensated for their imprisonment.

For Asians, welfare reforms continue to economically oppress and intimidate immigrants. In writing about Public Law 104-193, the Personal Responsibility and Work Opportunity Reconciliation Act (known as the welfare reform law), Swingle (2000) states, "[T]he passage of the welfare reform rendered immigrants an 'undeserving group' and an 'economic drain'" (p. 605). He maintains that immigrants "are living in fear that if they utilize any public health services they will be considered a public charge resulting in possible deportation" (p. 605). This increasing fear is

> . . . resulting in immigrant women not getting appropriate pre-natal care, and parents not getting their kids immunized or participating in nutrition programs. Health professionals are concerned that this problem will result in serious public health consequences affecting not only immigrants but also the larger population. (pp. 606–607)

Proposed is a public charge rule where legal immigrants are subject to public charge consideration if they receive "cash assistance for income maintenance." The protection offered under the proposed public charge rule is another form of labeling and does not really address the immigrants' economic dilemma. The fear of being rejected is not diminished by substituting one label for another. Social workers can assist immigrants to better cope with economic, social, and political pressures by understanding their situations and having as much background information as possible about their cultures in order to be competent cultural translators. Misunderstandings cause a lot of trauma for immigrants, who are often victims of racist and discriminatory practices.

Sanchez-Hucles (1998) asserts that racism is a form of emotional abuse and creates psychological trauma for ethnic minorities. She exhorts the mental health field to better understand racism to mitigate emotional abusiveness and trauma. She asserts that racism persists because of "inaction, passivity, tolerance, and denial" (p. 71). These discriminatory and racist practices will stop when Asians and Pacific Islanders, and other ethnic minority groups, are treated equally, fairly, and justly. Despite the increasing census numbers, attitudes still need to be changed.

SUMMARY

Culturally competent practice with Asian and Pacific Islander Americans is diversifying so that social workers in the 21st century have the task of clarifying that the Asian American category as a single category is obsolete. The 2000 U.S. Census offered 17 categories for Asians, Pacific Islanders, and mixed groups of interracial identities in which Asians and Pacific Islanders are included. Thus, the single ethnic categories need to be broken down into the multiple racial combinations and variations within single ethnic groups. Culturally competent practice also involves the challenge of including the intersection of ethnicity and race with gender, sexual orientation, religion, social class, and physical and mental abilities.

In defining cultural competence, many aspects must be considered, but the main focus is on cultural awareness and social service needs, the exploration of knowledge acquisition, the fostering of skill development, and the inductive learning process. The definition primarily follows a strengths perspective, and cultural values are identified as key components to understanding diversity in assessment and planning, practice, and research. Cultural values are reflective of the culture, norms, and behaviors preserved by each ethnic group. Galan (2001) discusses the "processing of cultural beliefs whereby the client weighs cultural information, prioritizes to choose appropriate behavior, and maintains integrity in belief and behavior" (p. 456).

Social and economic justice needs to be achieved for the Asian and Pacific Islander groups because so many discriminatory, racist, and oppressive experiences have been imposed upon these people and other ethnic minorities in the United States. Macrolevel shifts in attitudes and policies need to be made in order to achieve culturally competent practice with Asian and Pacific Islander clients.

CHAPTER THIRTEEN

Cultural Competence with Women of Color

GWAT-YONG LIE AND CHRISTINE T. LOWERY

HUMAN RIGHTS AS A LENS AND A PEDAGOGY

As world economies shift and cultural practices are homogenized, culturally competent practice with women of color must be considered within a global context of human rights. A human rights lens on global conflict and violence, socioeconomic policies and poverty, racism and oppression, and culture, language, and religion provides the social worker a framework for understanding the history of gender oppression and inequality worldwide, including the United States. Women worldwide share issues of rights and lack of access to formal economic power, education, and security. And, often women carry the power to address these very issues.

When goals for strong and healthy people are broad and encompass social justice, we can better see what Jean Bertrand Aristide (2000) calls "the third way." The third way offers direction outside limiting dichotomies: healthy or unhealthy, good or bad, rich or poor, Black or White. The third way offers a fresh and startling perspective on habitual thinking and action. The third way essentially surpasses those in power using indigenous knowledge to actualize social conscience and social justice. Paulo Friere (1994) understood the third way from this perspective, "When decisions are made for the people without the people they are often made against the people" (p. 37). Aristide (2000) promoted the idea of people governing or *demos cratei*, "Women, children and the poor must be the subjects, not the objects of history. They must sit at the decision-making tables and fill the halls of power" (p. 41). Mind and spirit are a powerful combination in what Paulo Friere called true dialogue. When we tap into this resource, we help unleash the power of the people to help heal themselves.

Meintjes (1997) describes a human rights ethos that emphasizes self-determination, shared power or a horizontal relationship with others, a focus on relationships, critical reflection and action. These elements are descriptive of a systemic understanding of social work. Critical to a dynamic understanding of human rights education is the acknowledgement that the empowerment–disempowerment relationship is relative. For example, men who brutalize their families cannot be marginalized or ignored in human rights education. They, too, are victims. They and their families must be included in a human rights process to empower to address political and social problems (Meintjes, 1997).

Women's Rights as Human Rights

Globally, the United Nations Decade for Women (1975–1985) placed women on the international, intergovernmental agenda and supported women's cooperation globally (Friedman, 1995). Since then, World Conferences for Women have taken place in Mexico (1975), Copenhagen (1980), Nairobi (1985), Beijing (1995), and New York (2000). In the 1993 Vienna conference, women around the world forced acknowledgment of women's vulnerability and violations of women's rights onto the human rights agenda. These violations are significant: from war crimes and rape to political and domestic violence against women in patriarchal countries, including the United States. Consider the sexual enslavement of Korean women by the Japanese army in the 1930s and the cultural genocide by rape of women in Bosnia by the Serbian army in the 1990s. On the current media scope, at long last, are the isolation and brutality against Afghani women by the Taliban. Economic violence against poor women and their children throughout the world is perhaps the most widespread violation.

> When we speak of the "poorest of the poor," we are almost always speaking about women. Poor men in the developing world have even poorer wives and children. And there is no doubt that recession, the debt crisis, and structural adjustment policies have placed the heaviest burden on poor women, who earn less, own less and control less. (Vickers, 1991, p. 15)

Women and the Potential for Economic Power

On the other hand, women entrepreneurs and their small-scale trade form the backbone of the informal market in many countries: Haiti, 91 percent; Ghana, 88 percent; Thailand, 54 percent; and Brazil, 28 percent (Vickers, 1991). In some countries, the women-dominated informal sector can be three times the formal economic sector. In the United States, 9.1 million women-owned businesses employ 27.5 million people and contribute $3.6 trillion to the economy (United States Small Business Administration, n.d.). Still, divorce, separation, widowhood, and migration contribute to the worldwide increase in female-headed households, which can be among the poorest in the world (Vickers, 1991).

Women worldwide have constraints on their mobility and time, including the time required for domestic duties, productive activities, and management of community resources. Because of socialization and inequity of access worldwide, girls from low-income households are at higher risk for dropping out of school (Bamberger et al., 2001). And yet, an educated mother raises healthier children, has fewer children, and encourages these children to become educated. An educated woman is more productive at home and in the workplace and makes more independent decisions (United Nations, 1995).

When health, welfare, and child-care services are cut, women must bear the burden of finding other resources for their families. When food prices rise and fall, women's work as food providers for their families is sometimes reduced to survival (Vickers, 1991). Economic disruptions (unemployment, layoffs, recessions) contribute to family conflicts and domestic violence. Still a private matter in many countries, domestic violence puts a whole family at risk through physical, cultural, and social isolation but may result in death or injury of the woman in the family. Legal status and the rights of women are often ambiguous in some countries or are culturally or religiously defined or denied (Bamberger et al., 2001). The poor, especially women, are often denied voice. They are excluded from the social and economic processes that may cause and shape their poverty. The lack of decision-making power in institutions, in civil society, or even households from childhood is pronounced, even when women organize to influence policy changes on behalf of their children (Bamberger et al., 2001).

Yet, women's role as sustainers of culture is significant. The United Nations High Commissioner for Refugees (UNHCR) estimates that 23 million refugees and 26 million internally displaced people have left their homes in the face of human rights abuses and the consequences of conflict, including famine and lawlessness (United Nations, 1995). More than three-fourths of these refugees are women and dependent children, up to 90 percent where males have been conscripted, killed, or taken prisoner. With war comes sexual violence and torture, and women are targeted.

> While refugee women play an economic and social role, they also play a role in sustaining the culture. They have the power to nurture future generations, re-establishing the family and culture in exile and recreating it again on return to their homeland. . . . [Yet], UNHCR activities have not always been planned with full regard to the needs, abilities, and aspirations of refugee women. (p. 12)

Women's issues have shaped an imperfect but worldwide sisterhood. Although felt unevenly and debated vigorously in many sectors of the world, this emergent sense of connectedness is foundational for social justice on an international scale. What should touch us deeply as social workers is the injustice of poor children and poor women in our nation, in our hemisphere, and in other countries. When we recognize our obligations as citizens of the world, we can move beyond our privileged positions as tourists, beyond the curious, beyond the ability to visit and leave. Instead, we can work with compassion within our ability to own another woman's plight, and together recognize the strengths and oppressions of cultures and nations and address inequities locally and globally.

DEFINING "WOMEN OF COLOR"

For the purposes of this chapter, the term *women of color* refers to women who are of Hispanic/Latina, African American, Native American (commonly labeled in census data as "American Indian and Native Alaskan"), Asian American, and Hawaiian and other Pacific Island heritage. The term also includes women of mixed-race/ethnic heritage and acknowledges the diversity that exists within each subgrouping. The diversity may be based on the following:

- Different national origins (e.g., Guatemala, Mexico, or Venezuela), even though individuals share a common language (Spanish), as in the case of Latinas
- Different dialects (e.g., Navajo, Choctaw, or Kickapoo), even when sharing a common racial designation (i.e., American Indian)
- Different religious affiliations (e.g., Baptist, Catholics, or Muslims) while sharing a common racial identity (e.g., African American)
- Different languages (e.g., Korean, Mandarin, and Japanese), different national origins (Korea, China, and Japan), and different religious affiliations (e.g., Buddhism, Taoism, and Shintoism) among those with the common racial label of Asian American

- Different experiences in life development, spiritual growth, family history, education, employment and economic conditions, health and illness, geographical place, race, class, and sexual orientation

DEFINING CULTURALLY COMPETENT PRACTICE WITH WOMEN OF COLOR

Collins (1994) argues that although the term *women of color* implies unity, the term may flatten the diversity of the lived experiences of these women. There exists no "universal truth" about women and gender buried beneath diversities shaped by racial classification, ethnicity, social class, and sexual orientation (p. xv). Closer to reality are the intersections of other inequalities and the gendered experience (Zinn & Dill, 1994, p. 3). Race, class, and gender create a matrix of domination that women of color experience (and resist) on three levels: "the level of personal biography, the group level of the cultural context created by race, class and gender, and the systemic level of social institutions" (Collins, 1986, pp. 514–515). For these reasons, Crenshaw (1995) draws attention to our responsibility "to account for multiple grounds of identity" (p. 358).

In other words, culturally competent practice with women of color demands that service providers and practitioners, at minimum, educate themselves about the multiple identities and the resulting diverse and unique circumstances that define women of color. In addition, service providers must be willing to intervene at multiple levels, that is, micro (individuals, groups, and families), meso (neighborhoods and communities), and macro (society and institutions) systems levels, even though contact with the person may have been initiated at the micro level (e.g., seeking therapy or counseling services).

WOMEN'S VOICES . . . 1

What does it mean to be culturally different and to speak, at the level of culture, in a different voice? The question is generally answered by those with the power to mark others (or the "other") as different, rather than by those whose difference is in question in relation to the majority, or main members of a given group. To be culturally different is not the same as being individually different or different by virtue of one's age or sex. If I am in a group among other women with roughly the same kind of education and occupational interests as myself and if we are roughly of the same age, what will mark me as culturally different is that I am, in today's terms, a Latina—a name that, while pointing to some aspects of my background, also erases some important aspects of my individuality and the actual specifics of my cultural genealogy, which includes Caribbean, Latin American, and Western European background. (Ofelia Schutte, 2000, p. 52)

UNDERSTANDING DIVERSITY AMONG WOMEN OF COLOR

The multiple identifying characteristics imbued in women of color begins with the sociodemographic descriptions offered by the U.S. Bureau of the Census (2000b, p. 631). The intent is not only to illuminate the similarities as well as disparities among women of color but also to instigate thoughtful and reasoned discussion over the implications of these findings for practice. As Liu (2000) notes, "[R]ecognizing the differences among women should lead us to ask how our different lives and experiences are connected." The connectedness

TABLE 13.1 *Population of the United States in 1990, 2000, and 2004*

Race/Ethnicity	Census 1990[1]		Census 2000[2]		Projections 2004[3]	
	Numerical	Percent	Numerical	Percent	Numerical	Percent
Total	**248,709,873**	**100.0**	**281,421,906**	**100.0**	**293,655,404**	**100.0**
European American	188,128,296	75.6	194,552,774	69.1	197,840,821	67.4
African American	29,216,293	11.7	33,947,837	12.1	35,963,702	12.2
Hispanic/Latino/a	22,354,059	8.9	35,305,818	12.5	41,322,070	14.1
Native American/Alaska Native	1,793,773	0.7	2,068,883	0.7	2,206,748	0.7
Asian American	6,968,359	2.8	10,123,169	3.6	12,068,424	4.1
Native Hawaiian/Other Pacific Islanders	–		353,509	0.1	398,161	0.1
Other	249,093	0.1	467,770	0.2	–	
Two or more races	–		4,602,146	1.6	3,855,478	1.3

1. Source: U.S. Census Bureau, American FactFinder; Tables P001Persons (STF 1), P008 Persons of Hispanic Origin (STF 1), P010 Hispanic Origin by Race (STF 1). http://factfinder.census.gov/servlet/DTTable?
2. Source: U.S. Census Bureau, Modified Race Data Summary File, Technical Documentation for the Census 2000 Modified Race Data Summary File; Issued September 2002. http://www.census.gov/popest/archives/files/MRSF-01-USl.html; retrieved 8/12/05.
3. Source: U.S. Census Bureau, Population Estimates Program; State Population Estimates—Characteristics; Annual Estimates of the Population by Race Alone and Hispanic or Latino Origin for the United States and States: July 1, 2004. http://www.census.gov/popest/ states/asrh/tables/SC-EST2004-04.xls; retrieved 8/12/05.

of experiences and the social justice consequences do not imply the formulation of common action and common solutions but could energize and inform deliberate customized strategies to alleviate individualized predicaments.

Sociodemographic Profile

The total population of the United States as of July 1, 2004 was estimated to be close to 294 million, which represents about 4.3 percent more than the estimates for 1999 and about 18.0 percent more than the estimates for 1989; see Table 13.1.

Not all segments of the population grew at the same rate between 1990 and 1999. Asian American and Pacific Islanders (AAPI) (about 10.5 million in 1999) were a fast-growing group, increasing by roughly 3.4 million in the 10 years between 1989 and 1999. In the 1990 U.S. Census, Asians and Pacific Islanders were grouped together, but for the 2000 U.S. Census, "Asians" were an independent category, and a new (to census reports) classification, "Native Hawaiian/Other Pacific Islanders," emerged. The AAPI composite group accounted for 2.8 percent of the total population in 1989. In the four years between 1999 and 2004, the AAPI group added another 1.9 million to their ranks and accounted for 3.7 percent of the total population, registering a 0.9 percent increase in ranks.

Hispanic[1] residents, the fastest-growing group, increased by about 13 million, from 22.3 million in 1989 (8.9 percent of the total population) to an estimated 35.3 million in 1999

---

1. The term *Hispanic* refers to people who trace their origin or descent to Mexico, Puerto Rico, Cuba, Central and South America, and other Spanish cultures. Hispanics may be of any race, and data in Table 13.1 represent a deliberate attempt to ensure that the estimates shown for the other races have been clearly delineated as "not of Hispanic origin" (Office of Management & Budget, 2000).

(12.5 percent of the total population). By 2004, projections were for the Hispanic/Latino/a group to add another 6 million people, for an estimated total of 41.3 million. Migration from abroad was a major contributor in the growth in both the AAPI and Hispanic population segments. According to the U.S. Census Bureau *News* (February 22, 2005), foreign-born population in the United States numbered 34.2 million in 2004, which is 12 percent of the total population. Of those who were foreign-born, 53 percent were born in Latin America, 25 percent in Asia, 14 percent in Europe, and the remaining 8 percent in Africa and Oceania, that is, Australia, New Zealand, and all the Pacific Island nations.

From 1989 to 1999, the African American population sector, which accounted for about 11.7 percent of the total population in 1989, grew by an additional 4 million—from 29.2 million to 33.9 million (12.1 percent of the total population). From 1999 to 2004, the estimates show a steady growth trajectory from 33.9 million in 2000 to over 35.9 million in 2004 (12.2 percent of the total population). Native American/Alaskan Natives also gained in numbers from 1989 to 2004 and have maintained a steady 0.1 percent share of the total U.S. population since 1989.

In 1999, females outnumbered males by 5.3 million: 143.4 million to 138.1 million. By 2004, the projected estimates showed females losing some ground to males in terms of population numbers: 149.1 million to 144.5 million, or a difference of about 4.6 million. Women outnumbered men in all ethnic/racial categories in 2000 and 2004, except in Hispanic/Latino/a where males accounted for over 51 percent of the members of the group and in the Native Hawaiian/Other Pacific Islander group where the sex distribution was about equal. See Table 13.2.

The ethnic/racial composition of the approximately 143.4 million women in 1999 was 99.8 million European American women and 43.5 million women of color. In 2004, the estimates indicated that the total population of women in the United States had increased by about 5.7 million to 149.1 million. European American women accounted for 100.8 million, and women of color, 48.3 million (see Table 13.3a). Together, women of color accounted for 30.3 percent of the total female population in the United States in 1999 and almost a third (32.4 percent) of the total female population in the United States in 2004.

TABLE 13.2 *Sex and Racial/Ethnic Characteristics in* 2000 *and* 2004

	Census 2000[1]				Projected Estimates 2004[2]			
	Female		Male		Female		Male	
Race/Ethnicity	Numerical	Percent	Numerical	Percent	Numerical	Percent	Numerical	Percent
Total	**143,368,343**	**50.9**	**138,053,563**	**49.1**	**149,117,996**	**50.8**	**144,537,408**	**49.2**
European American	99,879,733	51.1	95,695,752	48.9	100,801,786	50.9	97,039,035	49.1
African American	18,019,958	52.5	16,293,049	47.5	18,845,139	52.4	17,118,563	47.6
Hispanic/Latino/a	17,144,023	48.5	18,161,795	51.5	19,974,997	48.3	21,347,073	51.7
Native American/Alaska Native	1,061,200	50.6	1,036,240	49.4	1,117,539	50.6	1,089,209	49.4
Asian American	5,343,833	51.6	5,012,971	48.4	6,221,682	51.4	5,846,742	48.6
Native Hawaiian/Other Pacific Islanders	181,485	49.4	185,619	50.6	197,132	49.5	201,029	50.5
Other	—		—		—		—	
Two or more races	1,738,111	51.0	1,668,137	49.0	1,959,721	50.8	1,895,757	49.2

TABLE 13.3a Women in the United States in 2000 and 2004

Race/Ethnicity	Census 2000[1]		Projected Estimates 2004[2]	
	Numerical	**Percent**	**Numerical**	**Percent**
Total	**143,368,343**	**100.0**	**149,117,996**	**100.0**
European American	99,879,733	69.7	100,801,786	67.6
African American	18,019,958	12.6	18,845,139	12.6
Hispanic/Latino/a	17,144,023	11.9	19,974,997	13.4
Native American/Alaska Native	1,061,200	0.7	1,117,539	0.7
Asian American	5,343,833	3.7	6,221,682	4.2
Native Hawaiian/Other Pacific Islanders	181,485	0.1	197,132	0.1
Other	–		–	
Two or more races	1,738,111	1.2	1,959,721	1.3

1. Source: U.S. Census Bureau, National Population Estimates—Characteristics, Annual Estimates of the Population by Sex, Race and Hispanic or Latino Origin for the United States: April 1, 2000 to July 1, 2004 (NC-EST2004-03). http://www.census.gov/popest/national/asrh/NC-EST2004/NC-EST2004-03.xls; retrieved 09/15/05.
2. Source: U.S. Census Bureau, Population Estimates Program; State Population Estimates—Characteristics; Annual Estimates of the Population by Race Alone and Hispanic or Latino Origin for the United States and States: July 1, 2004. http://www.census.gov/popest/states/asrh/tables/SC-EST2004-03.xls; retrieved 9/12/05.

Of the 43.5 million women of color (100 percent) in 1999, there were 18 million (41.4 percent) African American women, 17 million (39.4 percent) Hispanic/Latina women, 5.3 million (12.3 percent) Asian American women, 1 million (2.4 percent) Native American/Alaskan Native women, 181,000 (0.4 percent) women of Native Hawaiian/Other Pacific Islander heritage, and 1.7 million (4.0 percent) women of mixed heritage (see Table 13.3b). Hispanic/Latina as a proportion of all women of color increased from 39.4 percent in 1999 to 41.3 percent in 2004. Similarly, Asian American women increased proportionally from 12.3 percent in 1999 to 12.9 percent in 2004. In contrast, African American women accounted for 41.4 percent of all women of color in 1999, but the number shrank in proportion by about 2.4 percent to 39.0 percent in 2004, even though in numbers the group had increased from 18.0 million in 1999 to 18.8 million in 2004. All other ethnic/racial groups of women increased in numbers but remained proportionally constant relative to the total number of women of color.

African American Women

The median age of African American and Asian American women in April 2000 was 28.3 years, and in May 2004, 28.8 years.[2] The marital status of women 15 years and older (14.2 million) in March 2000[3] was as follows:

2. http://www.census.gov/popest/national/asrh/NC-EST2004/NC-EST2004-04.xls (accessed 08/12/05)
3. U.S. Bureau of the Census (2000b)

TABLE 13.3b *Women of Color in the United States in 2000 and 2004*

Race/Ethnicity	Census 2000[1]		Projected Estimates 2004[2]	
	Numerical	Percent	Numerical	Percent
Total	**43,488,610**	**100.0**	**48,316,210**	**100.0**
African American	18,019,958	41.4	18,845,139	39.0
Hispanic/Latino/a	17,144,023	39.4	19,974,997	41.3
Native American/Alaska Native	1,061,200	2.4	1,117,539	2.3
Asian American	5,343,833	12.3	6,221,682	12.9
Native Hawaiian/Other Pacific Islanders	181,485	0.4	197,132	0.4
Other	–		–	
Two or more races	1,738,111	4.0	1,959,721	4.0

1. Source: U.S. Census Bureau, National Population Estimates—Characteristics, Annual Estimates of the Population by Sex, Race and Hispanic or Latino Origin for the United States: April 1, 2000 to July 1, 2004 (NC-EST2004-03). http://www.census.gov/popest/national/asrh/NC-EST2004/NC-EST2004-03.xls; retrieved 09/15/05.
2. Source: U.S. Census Bureau, Population Estimates Program; State Population Estimates—Characteristics; Annual Estimates of the Population by Race Alone and Hispanic or Latino Origin for the United States and States: July 1, 2004. http://www.census.gov/popest/states/asrh/tables/SC-EST2004-03.xls; retrieved 9/12/05.

- Never married: 42.4 percent
- Married, spouse present: 28.9 percent
- Divorced: 11.8 percent

The other categories (married, spouse absent, widowed, and separated) each accounted for less than 10 percent of all African American women aged 15 and older. In terms of educational attainment, the 2000 U.S. Census data showed that 78.3 percent (8.7 million) of African American women aged 25 years and older had, at minimum, attained a high school diploma. About 16.7 percent had a bachelor's degree or more.

In 1999, the percentage of Black women who were foreign-born was 15.5 percent (1.1 million). More than half (57.4 percent) of Black foreign-born women were not citizens; the other half (42.6 percent) were naturalized. Turning to information on labor force participation, the 1999 U.S. Census data showed that about 46.6 percent of all African American women were in the civilian workforce, and of these almost all (92.6 percent) were employed. In contrast, whereas less than half (48.6 percent) of White/Caucasian women were in the civilian labor force, almost all (96.7 percent) in the labor force were employed.

In 1999, the major occupational category in which the largest proportion (38 percent) of African American women were employed was the technical, sales, and administrative support category. Almost equal proportions of African American women (25.2 percent) were in managerial/professional occupations and service occupations (25.8 percent). Similarly, about 38 percent of White/Caucasian women were in the technical, sales, and administrative support line. Almost equal proportions were in managerial/professional (22.2 percent) and service occupations (25.6 percent).

TABLE 13.4 *Median Earnings in the Past 12 Months (in 2004 Inflation-Adjusted Dollars) of Workers by Sex*

Race/Ethnicity	Median Earnings		Women's Earnings as a Percentage of Men's Earnings
	Female	Male	
European American	$32,034	$42,707	75.0
African American	$28,581	$32,686	87.4
Hispanic/Latino/a	$24,030	$26,749	89.8
Native American/Alaskan Native	$25,752	$32,113	80.2
Asian American	$36,137	$46,888	77.1
Native Hawaiian and Other Pacific Islanders	$27,989	$32,403	86.4
Other	$23,565	$26,679	88.3
Two or more races	$30,729	$37,025	83.0

Source: U.S. Census Bureau's American Factfinder. http://factfinder.census.gov/servlet/STTable?; retrieved 09/15/05.

Examination of the earnings (full-time, year-round earnings for people aged 15 years and over) showed that the median earnings for African American women in 1999 were located in the $20,000 to $24,999 earnings range. In comparison, the median income for White women was located in the next earnings range of $25,000–$34,999; the median income for White men was located in a still higher range, $35,999–$49,999. In 2004, estimates from the American Community Survey showed the median earnings for African American women to be about $28,581, which is 87.4 percent of the median earnings of African American males, which, at $32,686, is comparable to the median earnings of $32,034 for White females[4] (see Table 13.4). African American households had the lowest median income in 2004 ($30,134) among race groups.[5]

When tying in income and educational attainment, the census data for women in general (not broken down by race/ethnicity) showed that the 1999 median income for women aged 25 and older who worked year-round and full-time and held a bachelor's degree was $36,000. However, the median income for those who held a high school diploma was only $16,300 (U.S. Bureau of the Census, 2000b).

The poverty rate for *all* families (not just African American families) in 1999 was at 9.3 percent, a 20-year low.[6] By 2004, the official poverty rate was estimated at 12.7 percent.[7] Female householder families in general (not specific to African Americans) with no husband present had their poverty rate drop to a record low of 27.8 percent in 1999 and 28.4 percent in 2004.[8] Even so, female householder families had a significantly higher poverty rate than married couple families (4.8 percent in 1999). The total number of poor African Americans of both sexes in 1999 was estimated at 8.4 million, and up to

---

4. http://factfinder.census.gov/servlet/STTable? (accessed 09/13/05)
5. http://www.census.gov/Press-Release/www/releases/archives/income_wealth/005647.html (accessed 09/13/05)
6. U.S. Bureau of the Census (2000c)
7. http://www.census.gov/hhes/www/poverty/poverty04/pov04hi.html (accessed 09/13/05)
8. http://www.census.gov/hhes/www/poverty/poverty04/table3.pdf (accessed 9/13/05)

9 million by 2004.[9] The poverty rate for African Americans in general in 1999 was 23.6 percent, the lowest ever measured, and 24.7 percent in 2004.[10] Among African American women, 26.6 percent fell below the poverty level, which in 1999 was $8,501 for a single individual or $17,029 for a family of four (U.S. Bureau of the Census, 2000c). The poverty level in 2004 was $9,645 for a single individual or $19,157 for a family of four.[11]

Hispanic American Women/Latinas

In April 2000, the median age of Latinas was 25.4 years; in May 2004, it was 26.7 years.[12] The marital status of Latinas aged 15 years and more (total of 11.5 million)[13] was as follows:

- Married, spouse present: 49.5 percent
- Never married: 28.9 percent
- Other categories (widowed; divorced; separated; married, spouse absent): each accounted for less than 10 percent of Latinas

The proportion of foreign-born people of both sexes from Latin America was 51 percent in 1999 (up from 19 percent in 1970). Two-thirds of Latino/as were from Central America and Mexico. The estimated number of Latinas who were foreign-born was 6.2 million (38 percent), of whom 73 percent were not citizens and 27 percent were naturalized (U.S. Bureau of the Census, 2000a). The foreign-born were less likely than the U.S.-born Latino/as to have a high school diploma. The share of high school graduates among the Latino/a population was 48 percent. Educational attainment statistics showed that 57.5 percent (about 5 million) of Latinas aged 25 years (not distinguished by date of birth) had attained at least a high school diploma. The proportion with a bachelor's degree or more was 10.6 percent.

Turning to labor force participation rates, the 2000 U.S. Census data showed that over half (56.6 percent or 6.3 million) of Latinas were in the civilian (as opposed to military) labor force. The employment rate among these women was 92.3 percent. Of all Latinas aged 16 years and older who worked (about 5.8 million), 38 percent were employed in the technical, sales, and administrative support sectors. Another quarter (25.6 percent) worked in service occupations, whereas 17.8 percent held jobs in the managerial/professional sector, and 13.1 percent worked as operators, fabricators, and laborers. According to the 2000 U.S. Census, median income for Latinas (15 years and older; full-time, year-round workers) was located in the $15,000–$19,999 earnings range (for White women, it was $24,000–$34,999; for White men, it was $35,000–$49,999). The median earnings range for Hispanic women/Latinas was $24,030 as compared to median earnings of $26,749 for Hispanic men/Latinos[14] (see Table 13.4).

9. U.S. Bureau of the Census (2000c)

10. http://www.census.gov/Press-Release/www/releases/archives/income_wealth/005647.html (accessed 09/13/05)

11. http://www.census.gov/hhes/www/poverty/threshld/thresh04.html (accessed 09/13/05)

12. http:// www.census.gov/popest/national/asrh/NC-EST2004/NC-EST2004-04.xls (accessed 09/15/05)

13. U.S. Bureau of the Census (2000a)

14. http://factfinder.census.gov/servlet/STTable? (accessed 09/13/05)

Median income for Hispanic households was $34,241 in 2004.[15] The number of poor and the poverty rate for Hispanic families dropped in 1999 to 1.5 million and 20.2 percent, a 20-year low, from 1.6 million and 22.7 percent in 1998. The 2000 U.S. Census showed that among Latinas, the proportion living above the poverty line was about 75 percent, or three out of every four women. In 2004, the poverty rate was 21.9 percent, and 9.1 million Hispanic/Latino/a people were below the poverty line.

Asian American and Pacific Islander (AAPI) Women

April 2000 estimates showed the median age for AAPI women to be 31.5 years, whereas the May 2004 estimates showed the median age for Asian women (excluding Pacific Islanders) to be 33.2 years.[16] Among women 15 years and older (4.4 million), the marital status demographics in 1999 were as follows:

- Married, spouse present: 54.7 percent
- Never married: 28.8 percent
- All other categories (widowed; divorced; separated; married, spouse absent): each accounted for less than 7 percent of AAPI women

Between 1970 and 1999, the share of foreign-born U.S. residents (both sexes) from Asia tripled, from 9 percent to 27 percent. A significant number were refugees from Southeast Asia. Between April 1975 and September 1988, nearly 900,000 Southeast Asian refugees entered the United States, and about 45 percent (close to 396,700) were women (Office of Refugee Resettlement, 1988). The number of foreign-born AAPI women in 1999 was 3.5 million, and this subgroup accounted for nearly half (46.8 percent) of all AAPI women. Of those who were foreign-born, 53.9 percent were not U.S. citizens; 46.1 percent were naturalized.

Educational attainment statistics in 1999 for AAPI women showed that 83.4 percent had at least a high school diploma, and 40.7 percent had a bachelor's degree or more. Civilian labor force participation rates were estimated based on the employment rates of people 16 years and older. Asian American/Pacific Islander females aged 16 years and older accounted for 43.7 percent (2.4 million) of all AAPI females in the United States in 1999.

Of those in the labor force, 96.4 percent were employed, with 38.7 percent in managerial/professional positions; 32.4 percent in the technical, sales, and administrative support sector; and 17.7 percent in service occupations. The median income for AAPI women was between $25,000 and $34,999. Median earnings for Asian women in 2004 were $36,137; for Asian men median earnings were $46,888 (see Table 13.4). Asian households had the highest median income ($57,518) in 2004.[17]

Overall, the number of AAPI in poverty was 1.2 million in 1999, down from 1.4 million the year before. The poverty rate for the group was 10.7 percent (compared to 12.5 percent in 1998). The number of AAPI females living above the poverty level in 1999 was about 5 million, or 89 percent. By 2004, the poverty rate for Asians was 9.8 percent.[18]

---

15. http://www.census.gov/Press-Release/www/releases/archives/income_wealth/005647.html (accessed 09/13/05)

16. http://www.census.gov/hhes/www/poverty/poverty04/table3.pdf (accessed 09/15/05)

17. http://factfinder.census.gov/servlet/STTable? (accessed 9/13/05)

18. U.S. Bureau of the Census (2000c)

Native Women

The median age for Native American/Alaskan Native women was 26.9 years according to the April 2000 estimates and 28.5 years according to the May 2004 estimates.[19] In the case of women of Native Hawaiian and other Pacific Islander heritage, the April 2000 estimates showed the median age to be 26.3 years, and the May 2004 estimates listed 28.5 years as the median age. Unlike the other population segments, comparable socioeconomic and other demographic statistics broken down by sex are not available for Native women. Instead, the available census data are aggregated for the group as a whole and are based on 1990 data. According to Paisano (1995), nearly two-thirds of Native American families were married-couple families in 1990. Consistent with the national trend, the proportion of Native American families maintained by a female householder with no spouse present increased during the 1980–1990 decade to 27 percent in 1990.

In 1990, 66 percent of the 1.1 million Native Americans aged 25 years and older were high school graduates. About 9 percent had completed a bachelor's degree or higher. Median family income was $21,750 (compared to $35,225 for *all* families). However, the median income for a family headed by a Native American/Alaskan Native woman was $10,742 (compared to $17,414 for all families maintained by women with no husband present). Median earnings for Native American/Alaskan Native women in 2004 were $25,752 and for Hawaiian and other Pacific Islander women, median earnings were $27,989[20] (see Table 13.4).

Twenty-seven percent of Native American families were poor in 1989 (compared to 10 percent for all families in the United States in 1989). In 1989, 50 percent of Native American families headed by a female with no spouse present were poor (compared to 31 percent of all female-headed families in the United States). For the period 1997–1999, the poverty rate for Native Americans was 25.9 percent with 0.7 million poor (U.S. Bureau of the Census, 2000c). Using three-year averages (2002–2004), the number of Native American and Alaskan Native people was about 24,300, and the poverty rate was estimated at 2.5 percent, whereas the number for Native Hawaiians and Other Pacific Islanders was 13,200, with a poverty rate of 3.6 percent.[21]

WOMEN'S VOICES . . . 2

I learned about racism firsthand when I started school. We were punished if we spoke the Laguna language once we crossed onto the school grounds. Every fall, all of us were lined up and herded like cattle into the girls' and boys' bathrooms, where our heads were drenched with smelly insecticide regardless of whether we had lice or not. We were vaccinated in both arms without regard to our individual immunization records. (Leslie Marmon Silko 1996, p. 104)

Women, Health, and Diversity

Health is a social justice and human rights issue. The World Health Organization recognizes the integration of physical, mental, and social well-being as an optimum standard for health. This intersection overshadows the limited definition of an absence of disease.

---

19. http://www.census.gov/popest/national/asrh/NC-EST2004/NC-EST2004-04.xls (accessed 9/13/05)
20. http://factfinder.census.gov/servlet/STTable? (accessed 9/13/05)
21. Source: http://www.census.gov/hhes/www/poverty/poverty04/table4.pdf (accessed 9/13/05)

Such a standard supports an environmental and systemic perspective on health and frees us to examine the individual and family within the economic, political, spiritual, professional, and culture life of communities.

The Office on Women's Health, U.S. Department of Health and Human Services (2003) notes that women of color experience many of the same health problems as European American or White women but that as a group, women of color are in poorer health, use fewer health services, and "continue to suffer disproportionately from premature death, disease and disabilities. Many also face tremendous social, economic, cultural and other barriers to achieving optimal health" (p. 1). Within the group, diversity among women of color is marked when considering issues of health. Differing cultural perspectives on the body, the spirit, and illness; language barriers and language-isolated populations; and socioeconomic status and racism are factors one must consider in working with women of color. And specific populations require specific health interventions. For example, Helstrom, Coffey, and Jorgannathan (1998) report that Hepatitis B, which is transmitted from mother to child and can lead to cancer of the liver, is five times more prevalent in Asian Americans than in the general population. The genetic condition thalassemia, which can lead to stillbirth, is carried by 10 percent of Chinese and 40 percent of Southeast Asians. Because these conditions are not prevalent in the general population, routine screening in mainstream American clinics will miss these conditions. Diseases linked to lower socioeconomic status (SES) are diabetes, cerebrovascular disease, lung disease, and cirrhosis of the liver (McNair & Roberts, 1998). When comparing African American and European American women, mortality rates for African American women are higher in every major disease category: heart disease, lung cancer, breast cancer, diabetes, and HIV/AIDS (p. 821). In some cases, health outcomes are independent of SES. For example, African American women are more likely than European American to have poor reproductive health outcomes regardless of SES. Infant mortality rates in 1992 were 2.4 times higher for Black women than for White women; preterm births and low–birth-weight infants were disproportionately higher as well, even among higher-income, well-educated African American women.

Ruggiero (1998) describes a bleak outlook for women of color who have Type II diabetes or non–insulin-dependent diabetes mellitus, which is greater in women who are over 65 and obese. Generally, ethnic minority populations, particularly American Indians, African Americans, Latinos or Hispanics, and Pacific Islanders are more likely to develop diabetes and more likely to develop diabetes-related complications (American Diabetes Association, 2005). Black females have the highest prevalence rates, including the highest rates for mortality for diabetes-related deaths: "For example, in 1990 age adjusted prevalence of known diabetes was almost twice as high in African Americans as in non-Hispanic white individuals, and more than twice as high in Mexican-Americans and Puerto-Ricans" (Ruggiero, 1998, p. 615). In spite of these statistics, Ruggeiro reports a "paucity of literature" regarding women of color and cultural diversity factors.

To prevent long-term complications of diabetes, intensive management has proven most effective for Type I or insulin-dependent diabetes but may be generalized to Type II diabetes mellitus. This includes "multiple daily insulin injections, frequent blood glucose self-testing," and adherence to a special dietary and exercise plan for weight control over the life span (Ruggeiro, 1998, p. 616).

Although only 1 percent of the population, Native peoples account for almost 50 percent of the diversity in languages and tribes, and health and disease patterns among specific groups can also be diverse. Baines (1998) cautions that although different rates of disease may be prevalent in different geographic areas, the leading cause of death for American Indian women (between 47 percent and 70 percent) is cardiovascular disease, related to increased obesity among tribes and high rates of smoking. Malignant neoplasms, accidents, diabetes, stroke, chronic liver disease and cirrhosis, pneumonia and influenza, and kidney disease follow. Accidents, liver disease, and cirrhosis are related to alcohol abuse. Baines asserts that causes of mortality and morbidity among American Indian women can be addressed through prevention programs and behavior changes.

A rapidly growing health problem, especially among women of color, is HIV/AIDS. African Americans and Hispanic women/Latinas accounted for 77 percent of all AIDS cases as of 1999, even though they represented less than one-fourth of the U.S. population (Office on Women's Health, 2001). One of the 10 leading causes of death among African American women of all ages is AIDS. In 1997, these women had the highest mortality rates from AIDS of all American women: 29.3 per 100,000 people. African American women are 12 times more likely to die from AIDS than are White/Caucasian women (2.4 deaths per 100,000) (Office on Women's Health, 2001).

Hispanic women/Latinas had the second-highest mortality rate from AIDS in 1997 (6.7 per 100,000). HIV/AIDS is the third leading cause of death for Hispanic women aged 25–44 (Office on Women's Health, 2001). The mortality rate from AIDS for American Indian women was 2.0 per 100,000 in 1997; the rate was negligible for AAPI women (i.e., less than 20 reported deaths in 1997) (McNair & Roberts, 1998).

The National Women's Health Information Center (May 2003a) reported that the health problems facing a large number of African American women include the following:

- Being overweight and obese: 50 percent of African American women are overweight.
- Diabetes: Overall, African Americans are twice as likely as European Americans/Whites to have diabetes.
- Heart disease: This is the main cause of death for African American women.
- High blood pressure: One out of three African Americans suffers from high blood pressure, rendering him or her at risk for heart attacks, strokes, or kidney failure.
- Kidney disease: High blood pressure and diabetes are the two main causes of kidney disease.
- HIV/AIDS: This presents the leading cause of death for African American women between the ages of 25 and 44.
- Lupus: It is more common in African American women and other women of color than in European American women.
- Breast cancer: With the exception of African American women between the ages of 20 and 24, African American women are more likely than European American or White women to get breast cancer before the age of 40.
- Other cancers (such as colorectal, lung and bronchus, uterine corpus, and pancreatic cancer): Overall, African American women are more likely to die from cancer than are people of any other racial/ethnic groups.

- Tuberculosis (TB): African American women have the highest number of TB cases compared to all women.

According to the National Women's Health Information (2003b), health problems that affect a large number of Latinas include the following:

- Being overweight and obese: Obesity in Mexican American women is 1.5 times more common (approaching 52 percent) than in the general female population.
- Diabetes: Mexican Americans are twice as likely as European Americans/Whites to have diabetes, and diabetes is more prevalent among Latinas than among Latinos.
- High cholesterol: Among Mexican American women ages 20–74, almost half (41.6 percent) have borderline high-risk total cholesterol levels.
- Heart disease: Heart disease and death rates are higher among Mexican Americans partly because of the higher rates of obesity and diabetes.
- Stroke: Among Hispanic Americans/Latinos, the risk of stroke is 1.3 times higher at ages 35–64 than for non-Hispanics.
- HIV/AIDS: Latinas account for 19 percent of HIV/AIDS cases in the Hispanic American/Latino population but account for 23 percent of all cases reported in 2000. The rate of HIV infection is 7 times higher among Latinas than among European American/White women. Heterosexual contact is the cause of the disease for 47 percent of adult and adolescent Latinas with AIDS, and injection drug use accounts for another 40 percent of AIDS cases among Latinas.
- Depression: Major depression and dysthymia may be diagnosed slightly more frequently among Latinas than among European American/White women.
- Cancers: Hispanic Americans/Latino/as have a lower rate of new cancer cases and lower death rates for all cancers combined but a higher proportion of cases of cancer of the stomach, liver, and cervix than European Americans/Whites. Breast cancer is the most commonly diagnosed cancer and the leading cause of death among Latinas. The number of new cases of invasive cervical cancer among Latinas is about twice that for non-Hispanic women. Overall, the death rate from cervical cancer is about 40 percent higher among Latinas than for non-Hispanic women. Lung cancer is the second most common cause of cancer deaths (behind breast cancer) among Latinas.
- Alcoholism and illicit drug use: Overall, compared to the total U.S. population, Mexican Americans and Puerto Rican Americans have high rates of illicit drug use, heavy alcohol use, alcohol dependence, and need for drug abuse treatment.

Health problems for many Asian American/Pacific Islander women and native Hawaiian women as reported by the National Women's Health Information Center (May 2003c) include the following:

- Being overweight and obese: Many Native Hawaiians and Samoans are obese and at risk for various health complications, including heart disease, diabetes, and cancer.
- Diabetes: Native Hawaiians are 2.5 times more likely to have diagnosed diabetes than European American/White residents of Hawaii of the same age. Guam's death rate from diabetes is 5 times higher than that of mainland United States, and it is one of the leading causes of death in American Samoa.

- Heart disease: Overall, AAPI and Native Hawaiian women have much lower rates of heart disease than other women of color, but it is still the leading cause of death within their own group.
- Stroke: Among AAPI, the risk of stroke is higher at ages 35–64 than for European Americans/Whites.
- High cholesterol: Among AAPI women, high cholesterol rates are highest among Japanese American women. AAPI women in general have low cholesterol screening rates.
- High blood pressure: Among AAPI women, high blood pressure is more of a problem for Filipino women. AAPI women have much lower blood pressure screening rates than other women of color.
- Hepatitis B: This disease is 25–75 times more common among Samoans and immigrants from Cambodia, Laos, Vietnam, and China than any other immigrant group in the United States.
- Tuberculosis (TB): Among all women with TB, 81 percent of TB cases affect women of color. Of these cases, 26 percent are among AAPI women (second only to African American women, who make up 30 percent of TB cases among women of color).
- Cancer: New cases of cervical cancer among Vietnamese American women are nearly 5 times those of European American/White women. On average, AAPI women have lower rates of Pap test screening than do other groups. Breast cancer is on the rise among AAPI women. The rate is lower than those for European American/White and African American women, but it is higher than those for Latinas or Native American/Alaskan Native women. AAPI and Native Hawaiian women are the least likely to have ever had a mammogram. Chinese- and Japanese American women have higher rates of breast cancer than women of the same age in China and Japan. AAPI in general have the lowest death rate from cancer. Yet, Native Hawaiians have the highest death rate from breast cancer than any other racial/ethnic group in the United States. Also, breast cancer is the leading cause of death among Filipino women.
- Suicide: Asian American women have the highest suicide rate among women 65 years and older. Suicide rates are higher than the national average for Native Hawaiians. Nearly 1 out of 2 AAPI will have problems accessing mental health treatment because they cannot speak English or cannot find services that meet their language needs.
- Osteoporosis: Asian women are at higher risk because of their lower bone mass and density and smaller body frames. They also have a lower intake of calcium compared to other groups of women. As many as 90 percent of Asian Americans are lactose intolerant and cannot easily digest dairy products.

The National Women's Health Information Center (2003d) reported the following leading health concerns for Native American/Alaskan Native women:

- Being overweight and obese: In one tribal group in Arizona, 80 percent of its members were overweight.
- Diabetes: Diabetes is a serious and common problem among Native Americans and Alaskan Natives. The number of new cases of Type 2 diabetes among Native

Americans/Alaskan Natives has reached epidemic proportions. Diabetes contributes to several of the leading causes of death in Native American/Alaskan Native peoples, including heart disease, stroke, pneumonia, and influenza. Certain tribes, such as the Pima Indians in Arizona, have much higher rates; 50 percent of their members between the ages of 30 and 64 have Type 2 diabetes. Pregnant Native American/Alaskan Native women with Type 2 diabetes are at increased risk of having babies with birth defects. Serious incidences of complications from the condition are increasing. Of most concern are kidney failure, heart disease, amputations, and blindness. Infections, including tuberculosis (TB), are of particular concern.

- Smoking and lung cancer: Lung cancer is the leading cause of cancer death among Native American/Alaskan Natives. Native Americans/Alaskan Natives have the highest smoking rates and use of smokeless tobacco (chewing tobacco or snuff) of any group in the United States.
- Alcoholism: Native Americans/Alaskan Natives are five times more likely to die of alcohol-related causes than are European Americans/Whites, and they experience high rates of chronic liver disease and cirrhosis. In addition, this group has a high rate of driving under the influence and alcohol-related fatal crashes compared to the general population.
- Suicide: Of all women, Native American/Alaskan Native women ages 25–44 had the highest suicide rate in 2000.
- Sudden Infant Death Syndrome (SIDS): More Native American babies die from SIDS than do infants born to other women in the United States.
- Other infant deaths: Native American/Alaskan Natives have the second-highest number of infant deaths (from, for example, SIDS, birth defects, preterm/low birth weight, accidents, and respiratory distress syndrome) in the United States.
- Gallstones: The high levels of cholesterol in their bile place Native American women at risk for gallstones. One study found 70 percent of Pima Indian women with gallstones by age 30.
- Cardiovascular disease: Cardiovascular disease, including heart disease and stroke, is the leading cause of death for Native Americans/Alaskan Natives.

Mental Health

Differences in the prevalence, course, and outcomes for schizophrenia were noted in two international comparisons of people with psychoses in developed and undeveloped countries conducted by the World Health Organization (WHO) in 1973 and 1979. Although the reasons for the outcomes are not clear, it was significant that the course and impairment attributed to schizophrenia were "more benign in less developed societies, regardless of the nature of onset or type of presenting problems" (Castillo, 1998, p. 245). A subsequent analysis of this data by Susser and Wanderling (1994, as cited in Castillo, 1998) indicated:

> [T]he incidence of nonaffective psychoses with acute onset *and full recovery* was about twice as high in women across various research centers, and about ten times higher in the less developed societies versus the developed societies. Moreover, prevalence rates for schizophrenia were much higher in economically developed societies compared to agrarian or hunter-gatherer societies. (p. 245)

Castillo (1998) concludes that the differences in outcomes "appear to be related to social relations and the distinctions between sociocentric and egocentric societies, and premodern versus modern cultural meaning systems" (p. 246).

Cultural meaning systems are relevant in the diagnosis and treatment of mental illness in the cultural environments of both the client and the clinician. Castillo (1998) outlines a framework for how mental illness is given cultural meaning (symptoms, perceptions, relationships, explanations), which then shapes the way the one suffers and copes with mental illness. First, meaning is given through symptoms (sensations, thoughts, emotions, behavior) interpreted as an indication of illness. Second, meaning is given through cultural significance or societal constructions of what mental illness is and how society views the person and the mental disorder. Third, mental illness has cultural meaning through personal and social relationships, including relationships in the family and workplace. And fourth, the explanatory model or how mental illness is explained (onset, effects, course, treatment) "can affect the diagnoses of clinicians as well as the subjective experiences of mental patients" (p. xiii).

Clinical reality is the construction of the clinician in a clinical setting, and culture intersects this reality at many levels. Castillo (1998) summarizes Kleinman's (1980) explanatory list of culture-based elements: subjective experiences, idioms of distress, diagnoses, and treatments. The *subjective experience* of depression from a person with a Western perspective may be seen as biological or biomedical "even though no specific brain disease causing a major depressive episode has been identified" (APA, 1994, p. 323). From a Western perspective, importance is placed on depressive symptoms (*idioms of distress*) rather than on somatic or bodily symptoms, and a psychiatrist's or psychologist's help is sought. A psychiatrist or psychologist diagnoses and treats a mental illness based on his or her own cultural background—whether this is American, Brazilian, or Chinese—and professional training (*culturally based diagnosis*). A psychiatrist or psychologist trained in the United States will most likely treat the client with antidepressant medication or electroconvulsive therapy, perhaps in conjunction with psychotherapy or talking therapy (*culturally based treatment*). Now into the Western model just outlined, we inject this summary of depression from O'Nell's (1993) ethnographic report of depression and drinking in the context of the Flathead Reservation in Montana:

> Depression, therefore, can be a positive expression of belonging in this milieu. To be sad is to be aware of human interdependence and the gravity of historical, tribal familial and personal loss. To be depressed, and that includes tearfulness and sleep and appetite disturbances, is to demonstrate maturity and connectedness to the Indian world. A carefree attitude is often thought of as indicative of immaturity. (p. 461)

We recognize how Western culture has influenced the social construction of mental illness and the culturally based outcomes that will result. Cultural artifacts of the profession influence how interventions are carried out: facility, location, scheduling, medication reviews, length of therapy sessions, funding, and policies.

Lidz (1994, cited in Castillo, 1998) concludes a short paper on the evolution and future of psychiatry with a comment on the complexity of the neurochemistry and neuropathways of the brain: "It is, indeed, no wonder that psychiatrists seek to simplify their tasks by hoping to explain matters as due to abnormalities in the brain or in its functioning that can be corrected pharmaceutically" (p. 6). From another worldview, an Indian Health Service (Jewish) psychiatrist recounted that a Hopi medicine man once summarized the complexity of the brain with the word *mysterious* and left it at that.

According to *Mental Health: A Report of the Surgeon General* (U.S. Department of Health and Human Services, 2000), 22–23 percent of the U.S. adult population (44 million) have diagnosable mental disorders in a year. However, only 15 percent of the adult population receives treatment during that time. Women of color are thought to be at higher risk of developing mental illness, "due to the stress and problems linked to higher rates of exposure to violence, poverty, incarceration, and homelessness" (National Women's Information Center, 2003e, p. 1). Loss of social support, stress from cultural differences, and language barriers exacerbate the experience of isolation among immigrant women and may impede help-seeking behavior. The plight of refugee women, many of whom have been subjected to traumas such as gender-based violence (e.g., rape), torture, and genocide render them at high risk for posttraumatic stress disorder (National Women's Information Center, 2003e).

Among women of color, Hispanic women/Latinas have the highest lifetime prevalence of depression (24 percent) among women in the United States (Office on Women's Health, 2001). African American women are less likely to have this disorder (16 percent) than are White/Caucasian women (22 percent). Although African American women are less likely to suffer from major depression than are European American/White women, they are more likely to suffer from phobias (National Women's Information Center, 2003e).

Native American/Alaskan Native women and AAPI women have higher rates of depression than do European American/White women (National Women's Information Center, 2003e). Among Native American/Alaskan Native adolescent females, 14 percent were characterized as sad and hopeless, and 6 percent showed signs of emotional stress (Office on Women's Health, 2001). A significant proportion of Asian American women, especially among the Southeast Asian refugee population (e.g., Cambodian, Laotian, and Vietnamese), suffer from psychiatric disorders (Office on Women's Health, 2001, p. 15). A survey of mental health centers conducted in 1987 in Washington State (State of Washington Division of Mental Health, 1987) found that 60 percent of Southeast Asian American refugees treated in the system received a diagnosis of depression. More importantly, substantive empirical evidence links depression and/or posttraumatic stress disorder (PTSD) to the variables of victimization and poverty (Tien, 1994, citing the work of McGrath, Keita, Strickland, & Russo, 1990).

The source of the following data on suicide is the Office on Women's Health (2001). In 1997, Native American/Alaskan Native women of all ages had the highest suicide mortality rate (4.4 per 100,000). Between 1995 and 1997, the average annual suicide death rate for Native American/Alaskan Native women between the ages of 15 and 24 was 7.2 per 100,000. Asian American and Pacific Islander women of all ages had the second-highest mortality rate from suicide (3.4 per 100,000). Older AAPI women above 65 years of age were especially vulnerable, with a mortality rate of 8.8 per 100,00 between 1995 and 1997. The mortality rate from suicide for African American women was 1.9 per 100,000. Hispanic women/Latinas had the lowest rate: 1.7 per 100,000 in 1997.

Behavioral Health

Intimate Partner Violence. This section borrows heavily from Crenshaw's (1994) work and introduces the concept of *structural intersectionality*. The experience of intimate partner violence differs qualitatively across women according to race, gender, sexual orientation, and the structural inequities that exist in society. Any analysis of the dynamics of intimate partner violence and its impact on women of color is inadequate without close scrutiny and attention to the issue of *structural intersectionality* (p. 358). Crenshaw points out:

> Many women of color, for example, are burdened by poverty, child care responsibilities, and the lack of job skills. These burdens, largely the consequence of gender and class oppression, are then compounded by the racially discriminatory employment and housing practices often faced by women of color, as well as by the disproportionately high unemployment among people of color that makes battered women of color less able to depend on the support of friends and relatives for temporary shelter. (p. 358)

Therefore, in addressing the plight of battered women, the focus should not simply be on the battering and its impact on the survivor and her children. Instead, service providers must appreciate and respond to the structural factors that complicate and often severely restrict alternatives to the abusive situation.

WOMEN'S VOICES . . . 3

She thinks of all the nights she lies awake in her bed hearing the woman's voice, her mother's voice, hearing his voice. She wonders if it is then that he is telling her the messages he refers to now. Yelling, screaming, hitting, they stare at the red blood that trickles through the crying mouth. They cannot believe that this pleading, crying woman, this woman who does not fight back, is the same person they know. The person they know is strong, gets things done, is a woman of ways and means, a woman of action. They do not know her still, paralyzed, waiting for the next blow, pleading. They do not know her afraid. Even if she does not hit back they want her to run, to run and to not stop running. (bell hooks, 1994, p. 206)

Structural intersectionality. For undocumented workers, fear of the police and distrust of service providers including hospitals, social service agencies, and even attorneys only serve to keep the woman entrapped in the abusive relationship. Rasche (2000) notes that several factors may work together to keep the woman isolated and fearful. The fear of deportation prevents many from reaching out for any assistance. Almost all have few or no family or social supports in the area. Many are not aware that they can seek protection from the law for battery even as an illegal alien if the battering occurs in the United States.

The sense of entrapment is shared by women who enter the United States legally. Immigration and naturalization laws, written to protect immigrant women from battering or cruel treatment by a spouse who is a U.S. citizen or permanent resident, may in fact have the opposite effect of restraining the woman from leaving an abusive relationship. Crenshaw (1994) explains that the fear of deportation forces the woman to choose to remain in the relationship, preferring the protection from deportation to protection from her abuser. Even the passage of a waiver for hardship caused by intimate partner violence in 1990 by Congress did not ameliorate the predicament of immigrant women in abusive relationships. To qualify for a waiver, women need reports and affidavits from police, medical personnel, psychologists, school officials, and/or social service agents. Distrust and fear, limited access to these resources, and cultural barriers (e.g., the embarrassment and shame of being a battered spouse or partner) may work singularly or in concert to keep the woman in the abusive relationship. As Crenshaw notes, however, the waiver is not uniformly inaccessible to *all* immigrant women; women who are "socially, culturally, or economically privileged are more likely to be able to marshall the resources needed to satisfy the waiver requirements" (p. 360). She also notes, though, that the immigrant women who are least likely to take advantage of the waiver, "women who are socially or economically the most marginal," are most likely to be women of color.

Then there is the case of immigrant women who may be intimately related to an undocumented worker working in the United States. They may choose to suffer in silence rather than place their family in jeopardy, which is a likely outcome should they draw attention to the abuse. Crenshaw (1994) also directs attention to the many women who are partnered with or married to immigrant men; often these women are ignorant about their legal status and dependent on their partners or spouses for information. Another structural factor that limits alternatives to the abusive relationship is language. Language barriers may, for example, prevent the consumption of and follow-up on critical information about the availability of shelters, the protection that shelters provide, how to access shelter services, and eligibility criteria.

Kanuha (1994) notes that women of color may be reluctant to report being victimized by their partners as a protective measure against the historical and institutional racism to which their communities have been subjected. The fear of contributing to the stigmatization and stereotyping of people of color as pathological is yet another barrier to reaching out and seeking intervention. Gendered role expectations, traditional values such as loyalty to the family, and historical legacies (e.g., the effects of colonization on Native American communities) also have worked to silence women of color.

Political intersectionality. The experiences by women of color of racism (as compared to the experiences of men of color) and sexism (as contrasted with the experiences of White women) demand strategies that take into account the uniqueness of these experiences:

> The failure of feminism to interrogate race means that feminism's resistance strategies will often replicate and reinforce the subordination of people of color; likewise, the failure of antiracism to interrogate patriarchy means that antiracism will frequently reproduce the subordination of women. (Crenshaw, 1994, p. 360)

Here Crenshaw refers to the reluctance in releasing statistics reflecting the extent of intimate partner violence in communities of color. Apparently the articulated reason for not wanting to publicize the data was that these numbers might be used to frame intimate partner violence in the community as a "minority problem." Once perceived and labeled as an issue concerning only the "minority" community, the problem becomes undeserving of attention and resources. Crenshaw uses this example to illustrate how an antiracist strategy worked to compound rather than alleviate the problem for women of color.

Arguments that data would simply reinforce and confirm stereotypes of communities of color as "unusually violent" have in fact thwarted efforts to confront the problem in communities of color. Further, contentions that intimate partner violence "*equally* affects all races and classes" (Crenshaw, 1994, p. 363) unjustly equate the impact of battering across women without due regard to race, gender, or class. In the end, the ultimate reality that must be confronted is as follows: "Suppression of some of these issues in the name of antiracism imposes real costs: where information about violence in minority communities is not available, domestic violence is unlikely to be addressed as a serious issue" (p. 362).

Policies guiding the practice and delivery of services are often formulated by staff who are culturally different from consumers of services. Crenshaw raises the concern that the intersectional differences of women of color may not be factored into prescriptions of eligibility and admissibility. She offers an example of a woman denied admission to a shelter because she was not English proficient, the rationale being that the woman would feel isolated, would not be able to follow house rules that were written in English, and would not be able to participate in support groups conducted in English. Given the increasing diversity of communities across the United States and the increasing need for service providers to respond to the diverse needs presented by diverse peoples, there is no excuse for the presence of such policies, nor is there room for inflexible interpretations of the same.

In cases of rape, sexism and racism continue to be instrumental in the "devaluation of black women and the marginalization of their sexual victimization" (Crenshaw, 1994, p. 368). The still-pervasive stereotypic images of a Black perpetrator with a White victim and the sexualized images of the Black woman contrasted against images of the "legitimate" rape victim have contributed to the discrediting of Black women's allegations of rape. Social science research—in not examining the intersection of race, gender, and class—has likewise contributed to the continued marginalization of the experiences of women of color. According to Crenshaw, this mind-set will continue unless antirape activists commit to consistently investigating and challenging "the background cultural narratives that undermine the credibility of black women"—in other words, "the consequences of racism in the context of rape" (p. 369). Single-issue analysis of social problems faced by women of color cripples initiatives designed to develop solutions that are not only antiracist but also gender responsive and class sensitive. Instead, Crenshaw asserts, "Through an awareness of intersectionality, we can better acknowledge and ground the differences among us and negotiate the means by which these differences will find expression in constructing group politics" (p. 377).

Substance Use.   According to data collected by the Office on Women's Health (2001), in 1998, there was a reported total of 113 million drinkers, of whom 10.5 million were between the ages of 12 and 20. Of this group, 5.1 million were *binge* drinkers (five or more drinks on a single occasion during the past 30 days), including 2.3 million *heavy* drinkers (five or more drinks on one occasion on 5 or more days during the past 30 days). In 1998, 2 to 3 percent of Native American women and White/Caucasian women were classified as *heavy* drinkers. Native American women had the highest mortality rates related to alcoholism of all American women. Among 25- to 34-year-old women, 21 per 100,000 deaths were alcohol-related; for the 45–54 age group, the mortality rate from alcohol-related causes was 65 per 100,000.

The National Survey on Drug Use and Health (NSDUH) Report (Substance Abuse and Mental Health Administration, 2005) noted that in 2003, 70.1 million (63.4 percent) women aged 18 or older used alcohol during the past year, and an estimated 12.5 million (11.3 percent) used an illicit drug during the past year. About 6.5 million (5.9 percent) women aged 18 or older met the criteria for abuse of or dependence on alcohol or an illicit drug. Of these, it is estimated that 5.2 million (4.7 percent) abused or were dependent on alcohol, and 2 million (1.8 percent) abused or were dependent on an illicit drug.

Among African American women, 2 to 3 percent were considered *heavy* drinkers in 1998. The mortality rate from alcohol-related causes was 6 per 100,000. *Heavy* drinkers accounted for 1 percent of Hispanic women/Latinas in 1998. Almost half (49 percent) abstained from the use of alcohol. The proportion of AAPI women abstaining from the use of alcohol was 61 percent. While the overall rate among AAPI women for *heavy* drinking was less than 1 percent, among Japanese American women, 12 percent were considered *heavy* drinkers (Office on Women's Health, 2001). In 2003, rates of abuse of or dependence on alcohol or illicit drugs among women 18 years or older were highest among Native American/Alaskan Native women (19.9 percent), followed by European American women (6.3 percent), African American women (4.5 percent), Latinas (4.4 percent), and Asian women (3.4 percent) (NSDUH Report, Aug 2005).

In 1995, 23.2 percent of African American and 19 percent of Hispanic women reported having used illicit drugs at some point during their lifetime. Illicit drugs popular with women include marijuana, inhalants, hallucinogens, tranquilizers, sedatives, and analgesics. About 4.6 percent of Hispanic women/Latinas reported having tried cocaine. African American women were reportedly more likely to be recent and frequent users of cocaine, especially crack cocaine. The proportion of African American women who used cocaine/crack cocaine in 1998 was 4.2 percent.

The proportions of deaths from drug-induced causes for women of color in 1999[22] were as follows:

- African American women: 26.4 percent (57 percent aged 26–44)
- Hispanic women/Latinas: 7.2 percent (53 percent aged 26–44; 11 percent aged 18–25)
- AAPI women: 1.1 percent of drug-related deaths among women in 1999
- Native women: 0.6 percent of all drug-induced deaths in 1999

At the Intersection of Aging, Illness, and Addictions

According to *The Older Americans 2004: Key Indicators of Well-Being* (Federal Interagency Forum on Aging Related Statistics, 2005), nearly 36 million people 65 and over lived in the United States in 2003. Those 85 and over numbered 100,000 in 1900 and numbered 4.2 million by 2000. As the baby boomers age, the population 65 and over will grow to 20 percent of the U.S. population, or 71.5 million, between 2010 and 2030. By 2050, those 85 and older could reach 21 million. Florida, Pennsylvania, and West Virginia have proportions of older populations over 15 percent, whereas McIntosh County, North Dakota, boasts the highest proportion (35 percent) in the country of those 65 and older.

Women made up 58 percent of those 65 and older; women made up 69 percent of those 85 and older in 2003. By 2050, elderly Hispanics (of any race) will increase by 12 percent, from 2 million to 15 million and will outnumber elderly Blacks. In 2003, elderly Asians numbered a million, and by 2050, that population will increase to almost 7 million.

In 2003, the older population (65 and older) in the United States made up 12 percent of the total population, compared to 19 percent in Italy and Japan. Older women continue to outnumber older men in the United States, and women of color will be a prominent component in aging demographics until 2050 (Federal Interagency Forum on Aging-Related Statistics, 2005).

---

22. http://www.4woman.gov/owh/pub/minority/status.htm (accessed 4/26/06)

Minority aging research.   The role of positive emotional attitudes and survival is significant in working with people who are over 65. The Nun Study, a longitudinal study of Catholic sisters ($N = 180$), shows a strong relationship between positive emotional content in early handwritten biographies and the reduced risk of death of nuns in their 80s and 90s. Cognitive skills may help maintain independence as one ages, and social, cultural, and behavioral factors are influential in maintaining cognitive functioning. Physical activity and exercise are also being studied to understand their links to cognitive function (National Institute on Aging, 2001).

Since 1994, the National Institute on Aging (NIA) has worked to develop resource centers on minority aging research in an effort to reduce health disparities. One research question is, "How are the diagnostic tests for Alzheimer's disease (AD) affected by racial, ethnic, cultural or educational factors?" The Study of Women's Health across the Nation (SWAN) includes one multiracial and ethnic sample of women in midlife in a study of the natural course of menopause. Another study, Healthy Aging in National Diverse Longitudinal Samples (HANDLS), focuses on the role of socioeconomic status in age-related disease (cardiovascular, cerebrovascular) and disability (NIA, 2001).

At the intersection of a growing population of women of color and aging are two noteworthy issues. As people age, there is an increase in disability and illness. Hospital care begins to increase for people in their mid-50s. By the time people are in their late 70s, hospitalization rates increase 5 times and by their late 80s, to 12 times the lifetime rate (Foot & Stoffman, 1996). A study of primary and secondary alcohol-related diagnoses from Medicare claims data indicate the rate of alcohol-related hospitalizations (31/100,000) was higher than the rate of myocardial infarctions (20/100,000) (Brounstein, 2001). Heart-related illnesses have received more medical and research attention, although alcohol use is pervasive in the United States. Alcohol-related consequences and hospitalizations are prevalent, although 60–70 percent of older adults never drink. Concomitant with increased illness and hospitalization is the increased use of prescription and over-the-counter medications (Brounstein, 2001).

Older Americans take an average of 5.3 prescription drugs and 5.7 over-the-counter drugs daily. If these drugs are coupled with alcohol use, especially alcohol abuse, then one is dealing with potentially lethal consequences. Data show that 34 percent of older adults regularly consume alcohol, and 6.6 percent are consuming at a problematic rate. However, in 1999, nearly 39,000 inpatient admissions to veterans' hospitals were patients over 50 years old with substance abuse diagnoses. They represented more than 10 percent of all inpatient admissions to the Department of Veterans Affairs health system (Brounstein, 2001, p. 3).

Working with women of color requires that social workers understand the impact of alcohol and drugs and the intersection with mental and social health in communities of color. Social justice issues of economic development, racism, and access to health and educational resources form the context.

As couples age, women in caregiving roles often bear in silence the brunt of alcohol abuse in the family, depending on the cultural and social proscriptions or prescriptions around alcohol use. Grandmothers raising grandchildren are witness to the impact alcohol and drugs have on their adult children and their grandchildren. Elders may be at risk of financial abuse by those family members addicted to alcohol and drugs.

At the individual level, the role of alcohol or drug use in pain control, both physical and emotional (loneliness, isolation, loss), must be considered. How are hip fractures from falls in the home related to medication use? And how do our own notions about older women and addictions erect barriers for women over 65 to regular screening for prescription drug addiction or alcohol addiction?

Prostitution

Frameworks used to address issues related to prostitution include defining prostitution as exploitative of women and children, a public health concern, a "necessary evil," and a form of violence against women and children (Stout & McPhail, 1998). Public policy responses include moves to decriminalize prostitution and to recognize it as a service occupation in an attempt to address the issue of exploitation; to license and control prostitution to curb sexually transmitted diseases (STDs), including HIV/AIDS; to keep prostitution illegal and out of sight, consistent with the "necessary evil" logic; and to stop and eliminate prostitution as a form of violence waged against women and children.

According to materials distributed by Women Hurt in Systems of Prostitution Engaged in Revolt (WHISPER) in October 1990 in Austin, Texas, at the Texas Council on Family Violence Annual Conference, 85 percent of women used in prostitution are substance abusers and addicts. Stout and McPhail (1998) cite studies that attest to the correlation between prostitution and substance abuse. Depending on the parameters and foci of studies, prevalence rates of substance use among prostitutes range from 0 percent to 84 percent, with substance addiction among street prostitutes found to be relatively common (Prostitution Education Network, 2001). Violence remains a major health hazard for prostitutes.

The Prostitution Education Network (2001), using data compiled through the 1980s, noted the difficulty in estimating the number of people who currently work or have ever worked as prostitutes. It is difficult to estimate numbers involved for many reasons, including that various definitions of prostitution exist. The National Task Force on Prostitution estimates that over 1 million people in the United States have worked as prostitutes; this translates to about 1 percent of all American women (Alexander, 1987). Average prostitution arrests involve about 70 percent female and 20 percent male prostitutes, and 10 percent customers. What makes prostitution a salient women-of-color issue is the finding that a disproportionate number of prostitutes arrested are women of color, and, although only a minority of prostitutes are women of color, a large majority of those sentenced to jail are women of color (Alexander, 1987). Consequently, the public image of the street prostitute is that of an addicted and probably diseased woman of color.

Reproductive Freedom versus Population Control

Although most women's health advocacy groups see the fight for abortion rights in the context of defending the rights of all women to make their own decisions about reproduction, not all advocates of abortion rights share this perspective. Some view legal abortion as contraception or a tool of population control. Information from an Internet source (http://www.feminist.com/resources/ourbodies/test_old.html, posted July 9, 2001) offers the following point of information: Women with few economic resources, especially women of color in the United States and throughout the world, have been the targets of population control policies.

- Example 1: HIV-positive women in the United States (who are overwhelmingly women of color) are often pressured to have abortions, though only 20–25 percent of their children will be HIV-positive and new treatments during pregnancy have reduced the likelihood even further.
- Example 2: Although abortion has become increasingly less accessible in the United States, sterilization remains all too available for women of color. The federal government stopped funding abortions in 1977, but it continues to pay for sterilizations.

It is also critical to bear in mind that many families of color, because of fundamental religious or simply conservative ethnic values, may strenuously oppose abortion no matter the circumstances leading to conception. They may also prohibit the use of prophylactics to prevent conception. Several communities of color see a woman's role as essentially one of procreation, and as such, decisions about conception rest not with the woman but with the male spouse, family, and sometimes the clan or community.

Immigrant Women of Color

Almost half of all AAPI women (46.8 percent), over one-third (38 percent) of Hispanic women/Latinas (38 percent), and about 15 percent of women of African heritage are foreign-born. It therefore becomes important to consider the migration experience and the process of acculturation and adjustment within the social, economic, and political milieu in which immigrant women find themselves. Espin (1997) notes that migration may open doors of new possibilities and opportunities. Newly encountered sex-role patterns, greater access to paid employment, new lifestyles, and new opportunities for education are but some of the many possibilities that an immigrant woman might encounter. Espin also notes that, even in situations where migration was a sought-out choice, it still has the capacity to impact the individual in substantive ways:

> [T]ransitions created by immigration often result in many different feelings: the loneliness that results from the absence of people with shared experiences; strain and fatigue from the effort to adapt to and cope with cognitive overload; feelings of rejection from the new society that affect self-esteem and may lead to alienation; confusion in terms of role expectations, values and identity; "culture shock" resulting from differences between the old country and the new; and a sense of impotence resulting from an inability to function competently in the new culture. (p. 192)

One transition task that many immigrant women have to negotiate and overcome is to reorganize and sometimes redefine and reintegrate self within the new context (Espin, 1997). For children, adolescents, and young adults, because the sense of self is still formative, the adjustment process is relatively easier than it is for an older adult ensconced in the "old ways." Women who stay at home are comparatively less exposed to the forces of acculturation than women who are involved in educational (including gaining fluency in the English language) and/or employment activities. Undocumented immigrant women have reported abusive experiences at the hands of employers and even human service representatives, including law enforcement and medical personnel.

WOMEN'S VOICES . . . 4

Hello, my name is Fu Lee. I am forty-one years old, married, and I have a nine-year-old daughter. I have been living in Oakland Chinatown since I left Hong Kong twelve years ago. . . . I worked as a seamstress at Lucky Sewing Co. for two years. Before that, I worked as a seamstress at other similar sweatshops. All of the workers worked long hours, ten to twelve hours a day and six to seven days a week. We were paid by the piece, which sometimes was below minimum wage. Overtime pay was unheard of. You may think sewing is an easy job, but it requires a lot of skill. For fancy dresses, with laces, tiny buttons, and tricky fabric patterns, you really have to concentrate so you don't make any mistakes. My wage was never enough money for our family to live on. We were always worried about our daughter getting sick because we had no health insurance. (Lowe, 1997, p. 269)

Similar challenges confront refugee women who have added burdens of issues emanating from the horrors of war, forced migration, and relocation. The journey en route to the host country may have been fraught with trauma—immeasurable losses (including those inflicted by rape), dislocation, flight laced with fear, and uncertainty. Language difficulties and stark sociocultural differences are only some of the many obstacles refugee women have to overcome.

Immigrants and refugees, especially those of color, have not always been welcomed. History is replete with acts of outright prejudice and discrimination, and the experiences of many immigrant and refugee women attest to the continuing oppressive climate imposed by racism and sexism. Yet, as Espin (1997) notes, women of color have also had to deal with the oppressive burdens placed on them by their own communities. Even though the racism that is experienced may be subtle, nevertheless the immigrant (and refugee) woman finds herself wedged between the racism of the dominant society and the sexist expectations of her own community. This *gendered racism* (a term Espin attributes to Essed, 1991, 1994) underscores the need to "increase our knowledge and understanding of how the contradictions and interplays of sexuality/gender and racism in both the home and host cultures are experienced and 'made sense of' by women immigrants" (Espin, 1997, p. 198).

Refugee Women of Color

In its Fact Sheet released on January 26, 2004, the Bureau of Population, Refugees and Migration reported that majority of refugees and displaced people in the world today are women and children. The following excerpt describes the plight of refugee women and children:

From Afghanistan to the Democratic Republic of the Congo (D.R.C.), from Burma to Liberia, women have fled and continue to flee war and repression, often leaving behind fathers, husbands, sons, and brothers who are fighting; who are in jails; or who have perished. Refugee women are often single-handedly responsible for the survival of their children even when their own survival is at stake. Every day provides challenges: finding cooking fuel, carrying water—often for miles—obtaining sufficient food at distribution sites, and obtaining access to primary health care for themselves and their families. Refugee women are also exposed to violence at every stage in their flight. Sexual violence and exploitation are two of the most terrible dangers confronting refugee women and girls today.

According to the Interim Report of the Refugee Admissions Program for 2004 and 2005 (Refugee Council U.S.A., 2004), refugee groups previously recommended for resettlement and being processed in 2004 and 2005 include Liberians in Côte D'Ivoire, Meskhetian Turks in Krasnodar Krai, Somali Bantu, Lao Hmong in Wat Tham Krabok in Thailand, and Burmese urban refugees in Thailand. The report also refers to particularly vulnerable groups of refugees who "require special attention and response, including protection, specialized services, and expedited consideration and pursuit of durable solutions, including resettlement" (p. 8). It lists women and separated minors as two subgroups deserving of special outreach and leadership in the pursuit of "durable solutions" by the U.S. government. In another report, the Refugee Council U.S.A. (2005) lists refugee arrivals in the United States in September 2005 as 20,749 from Africa; 12,071 from East Asia; 11,316 from Europe; 6,700 from Latin America and the Caribbean; and 2,977 from Near East and South Asia.

Lesbians of Color

Greene (1994) describes the *zeitgeist* of lesbians of color as follows:

> Lesbian of color exist within a tangle of multiply devalued identities, surrounded by the oppression and discrimination that accompany institutionalized racism, sexism, and heterosexism. Unlike their White counterparts, lesbians of color bear the additional task involved in integrating major features of their identity when they are conspicuously devalued. Unlike their ethnic identities, their sexual orientation and sometimes their gender may be devalued by those closest to them in their families. (p. 412)

In this climate, lesbians of color are more likely to remain closeted; there is often more to lose by coming out than by remaining invisible, even to their own ethnic/racial communities (Greene, 1994).

Greene (1994) further notes that many people of color believe homosexuality to be a lifestyle choice. For these people, it follows then that the person can "un-choose" her lifestyle and return to her innate heterosexual orientation. If she refuses, this decision may be interpreted as a repudiation of her ethnicity. On the other hand, lesbians of color have reported discriminatory treatment in mainstream lesbian bars, clubs, and social and political gatherings. They frequently express feelings of marginality, of never completely belonging to any group, "leaving them at greater risk for isolation, feelings of estrangement, and increased psychological vulnerability" (p. 414).

Lesbians of color, more than their White counterparts, are likely to find themselves in interethnic or interracial relationships. When the partner is a White woman, encounters and experiences with racism add stress and strain to the relationship for both. However, Greene (1994) warns that racism may be a convenient scapegoat for a relationship that is stressed for other reasons.

When an immigrant woman of color is also lesbian, then, as Espin (1997) noted, "The crossing of borders through migration may provide, for both heterosexual and lesbian women, the space and 'permission' to cross boundaries and transform their sexuality and roles" (p. 192). Coming out may have occurred in the home country, or it may have taken place in the United States as part of the acculturation process. Or, as Espin points out, the need to come out in a safer space may have motivated the move. After the move, however, the immigrant lesbian of color may find the climate sufficiently oppressive to still remain closeted; "the host society also imposes its own burdens and desires through prejudices and racism" (p. 197). There again, many women point to a greater cultural openness regarding lesbianism in the United States than in their own home countries, resulting in a conflict of loyalties between their home and host countries.

IMPLICATIONS FOR CULTURALLY COMPETENT PRACTICE

Becoming Aware of and Knowledgeable about the Intersecting Realities of Women of Color

The poverty rate and the number of poor dropped in 1999 to 11.8 percent and 32.3 million (from 12.7 percent and 34.5 million in 1998). Every racial and ethnic group experienced a drop in both the number of poor and the poverty rate. Despite this decline, female-headed families had a starkly higher poverty rate than did married-couple families. As a result, female-householder families composed the majority of poor families (53 percent) in 1999 (U.S. Bureau of the Census, 2000c). More poor women than nonpoor women reported fair or poor health in 1996. For example, among poor women of color, 27.8 percent of African American women and 21.8 percent of Hispanic women/Latinas reported only fair or poor health (Office on Women's Health, 2001). However, in 2004, the official poverty rate increased, to 12.7 percent and 37.0 million.[23]

Inadequate income carries over into other aspects of daily life that impinge on health and mental health. Inadequate housing, malnutrition, the stress of constantly struggling to make ends meet, and limited or no access to health and dental care can have long-term effects, lasting over several generations. For example, the high African American mortality rate has been related to "the intergenerational effects of socioeconomic conditions on the growth and development of a mother from her prebirth to childhood, which may in turn influence the intrauterine growth of her child" (National Women's Health Information Center, 2001).

The stresses of constantly struggling to make ends meet may translate directly into the finding that African Americans living below the poverty level, many of whom work, have the highest rate of depression for any racial/ethnic group. Structural racism prevents access to adequate health care. Low income is strongly associated with decreased use of health services and poor health outcomes (Office on Women's Health, 2001). In other words, structural barriers, such as poverty and the lack of opportunities to improve one's socioeconomic situation, contribute to and exacerbate psychosocial and physical dispositions. In addition, structural barriers limit access to and restrict utilization of community-based resources to mitigate individual-, family-, and group-based predicaments. Thus, unless a concerted effort is made to address the plight of women of color, not just at the micro level but also at the meso (neighborhood and community) and the macro (society and institutions at large) levels, their well-being and that of their families will remain difficult to mitigate or even promote. Diverse languages, cultures, degrees of acculturation (or lack of), and histories should not excuse service providers from agitating and advocating for structural changes.

---

23. http://www.census.gov/hhes/www/poverty/poverty04/pov04hi.html (accessed 09/15/05)

Women's strength has been in their ability to organize and promote self-help. Since 1984, the National Black Women's Health Project has been organizing Black women to actively maintain their physical and mental health using local chapters and self-help groups. Projects have included "Walking for Wellness," college substance abuse programs, "Mothers and Daughters Talking Together" about sexuality, motherhood and birth control programs, and *Body & Soul: The Black Women's Guide to Physical Health and Emotional Well-being.* More information about this organization is available at the Project's website: www.nbwhp.org.

Likewise, the National Latina Health Organization (www.clnet.ucr.edu/women/nlho) raises Latina consciousness about health problems, including emotional health, and promotes health through self-empowerment. Latina diversity is recognized in regional differences in expressions used in everyday Spanish language, socioeconomic and educational backgrounds, and ethnic groupings based on geographical locations, for example, Central and South Americas and the Caribbean.

Broad social justice issues are the target of the National Asian Women's Health Organization, which advocates to improve the health status of Asian American women and families. Research, education, leadership, and public policy programs are promoted through the organization's website: www.nawho.org.

The National Women's Health Network provides up-to-date information on selected women's health issues for its members and the public. The Network seeks to protect the health of women by keeping them informed of the risks of certain medications; bringing to their attention the latest research on topics such as cancer and birth control methods; and launching campaigns against harmful drugs and devices. The Network sponsored the first national conference on Black women's health, which led to the creation of the National Black Women's Health Project. The Network maintains an extensive resource library and responds to health inquiries from individuals and health professionals. The National Women's Health Network publishes materials about women's health, for example, a pamphlet called "Taking Hormones: Choices, Risks and Benefits" and fact sheets on breast cancer for women of different ethnic groups. The Network also publishes for its members a bimonthly newsletter that contains articles on women's health concerns. For more information, call 1-202-347-1140, or visit the Network's website: www.womenshealthnetwork.org.

The Office of Minority Health Resource Center (OMHRC, 1-800-444-6472) offers customized database searches, publications, mailing lists, and referrals for women of color. Information distribution on health topics—substance abuse, cancer, heart disease, violence, diabetes, HIV/AIDS, and infant mortality—is the organization's goal.

Medical education must incorporate into its core curriculum information about the dynamics of gender, race, and class and their impact on access to and use of health care resources. The Office on Women's Health (2001) noted the need for health care providers (including social workers) to foster an environment in which patients of diverse backgrounds will be understood, appropriately diagnosed, and appropriately treated. It is also important for health care providers to learn about and incorporate indigenous practices (e.g., use of herbal remedies, and religious rites of cleansing) with respect to health care and healing. More emphasis must be given to community-based training and primary care, which is needed by women of color in underserved communities (Office on Women's Health, 2001).

The juggling of both health care costs and profit margins has had a broad impact on the humaneness of health care. Financial barriers encountered by many women of color have been tied either to income or to the availability and adequacy of health insurance. Strategies common in the private-sector marketplace have pushed their way into health care in hospitals and local clinics across the United States, with variable results. Managed care and its complexities raise questions about access and the quality of health care for vulnerable populations, including women, the poor and homeless, and the uninsured working poor.

Good health habits and health care on a regular basis are companions in prevention and early intervention and, simultaneously, influence the high costs of emergency care and extended hospital stays. Attitudes about health care and use of health care resources vary from community to community, depending on multiple elements. The history of the people—including history of oppression, displacement, immigration, and disparities in health care—and the history of disease in a community (AIDS, tuberculosis, sickle cell), as well as the characteristics of the population across the life span (infant to elder), must be considered. The influence of levels of acculturation and the maintenance of cultural ways of healing are important for a social worker to understand. Other factors that must be considered in assessing health needs include social and environmental conditions that influence availability of health care resources and access, including geographic boundaries and transportation, and locally, family systems of helping and the availability of paraprofessional and professional health workers. Policy changes, funding, improved medical technology, and even climate (severe weather, cataclysmic storms) are significant.

Managed care settings contained mixed populations. Planning and policies for health care must address the needs of women of color with different needs and histories. Mays, Cochran, and Sullivan (2000) list differing factors, such as "labor force participation, family formation, immigration status, and state eligibility requirements for publicly funded coverage," and propose "equitable outcomes" as potential criteria for reforming or financing health care (pp. 118–119). For example, in one study, Hispanics were the least likely to have insurance, but within-group differences were marked. Whereas Puerto Ricans were the most likely to be insured, women of Mexican origin were the least likely to be insured (Torres et al., 1996, as cited in Mays, Cochran, & Sullivan, 2000). When it comes to immigration factors, one's sociopolitical status and residence are often critical in health care. Puerto Rico is a territory of the United States, so Puerto Ricans have U.S. citizenship, and many reside in the northeastern part of the United States, where benefits and eligibility for Medicaid are more favorable (Valdez et al., 1993, as cited in Mays, Cochran, & Sullivan, 2000). Women of Mexican origin are more likely to be immigrants, are faced with immigration laws and racism, and tend to live in the Southwest, where states have fewer benefits and eligibility for Medicaid is more restrictive (Valdez et al., 1993, as cited in Mays, Cochran, & Sullivan, 2000).

What elements contribute to physical and mental health and the likelihood of premature death for women? Mays, Cochran, and Sullivan (2000) cite research that repeatedly demonstrates the influence of "an individual's social status of origin, an individual's achievement, as well as gender, marital status, ethnic group, and even the neighborhood in which one resides" as correlates (p. 99). These elements must be evaluated for assessment and intervention with all groups.

Because clients often are involved with several service systems at the same time, it is important to implement case coordination and management measures across service providers to ensure the following:

- The client is not overwhelmed with demands from the service system.
- Services are not duplicated.
- Certain needs do not "fall between the cracks."
- Appropriate and reasonable timing elapses between service events.
- Services rendered are indeed gender-responsive and culturally appropriate and meaningful.
- Client input and feedback are available at every stage and level of the service utilization process to allow for corrective action.
- Needs are serviced in an ethical and timely fashion.

Skill Development

Sue and Sue (1999) contend that "the worldview of the culturally different is ultimately linked to the historical and current experiences of racism and oppression in the United States" (p. 5). The culturally different client is likely to approach the help-seeking process and the utilization of services with a great deal of suspicion and distrust. One approach, designed to overcome the effects of oppression, is to take a strengths-based approach to assessment and to use cultural empowerment strategies and techniques to facilitate the assessment process. Westbrooks and Starks (2001) offer the "strengths perspective inherent in cultural empowerment" (SPICE) model that, although designed specifically for use with African American clients, has tremendous potential for use across ethnic/racial and gender groups.

Important considerations in the *rapport development/engagement phase* include the following:

- *Greetings and salutations:* Err on the side of being traditional and conservative in greetings and salutations. Social work practitioners should never presume to be on a first-name basis with individuals, especially with clients who are older than the worker. Ask the client how she would like to be addressed.
- *Deciding on the language of communication:* Espin (1997) quotes Torres (1991, p. 279), who asserts that "[t]he problem of identity emerges in discussions of language and how to give voice to a multiple heritage." Espin is joined by Lee (1997), Negroni-Rodriguez and Morales (2001), and Sue and Sue (1999) in directing attention to the importance of the client's choice of language. If the language of choice is not a language that the social worker or service provider is fluent in or is comfortable using, then the services of a professional interpreter skilled in the field should be engaged. Over the long term, the agency/organization should look into the prospect of encouraging staff to develop second- and even third-language skills or recruiting and employing native language speakers educated and trained to deliver the needed services.

  Brave Heart (2001) stresses the importance of attending to indirect styles of communication and the values of noninterference and nonintrusiveness, polite reserve, and reticence. She cautions against interpreting an individual's silence and humility during the session as ignorance and/or passivity, and she also points to the differences in sense of personal space and cross-gender interactions and the need to respond sensitively and appropriately to these differences.

- *Time:* Brave Heart directs attention to the different meanings that time may have for different ethnic groups.
- *Forming a social and cultural connection:* Many women find it difficult to talk about themselves. To "break the ice," the social worker/service provider should consider getting a woman to talk about her children, if she has any, or asking a woman if she would like a cup of coffee or tea or a glass of water and then encouraging her to talk about expressions of hospitality in her family.
- *Checking to see if the client is comfortable with a social worker/service provider of a different race or sex:* Sue and Sue (1999) suggest asking, "Sometimes clients feel uncomfortable working with a client of a different race or sex; would this be a problem for you?"
- *Identifying the event or circumstances that triggered the help-seeking behavior:* During this process, it is important for the social worker/service provider to validate feelings and to ascertain the meaning ascribed to the event or circumstances by the individual and significant others.
- *Judicious use of rapid assessment instruments, even when these have been translated to a specific language for use with a client:* Women of color may find the use of pen-and-paper measures or formal face-to-face interviews impersonal and mechanistic. In fact, practitioners should err on the side of using such measures only after developing rapport and trust with the client, and this may take time (several sessions).

In the *assessment process*, the worker should ask about the following issues:

- The primacy of the family of origin and the family of procreation in the individual's life. In addition, it will be helpful to understand the structure and the roles of family members. Be sure to defer to the client regarding the definition of "family."
- The family's ethnocultural heritage. This may include asking about the person's and family's premigration, migration, and postmigration experiences where applicable and determining levels of acculturation in client and key family members. Lee (1997) advises workers to look at the losses associated with the migration experience: material losses (e.g., property and career); physical losses (e.g., disfigurement and physical injuries); spiritual losses (e.g., freedom to practice religion and support from religious community); loss of community support and cultural milieu; and loss of family members and friends.

For the lesbian of color, losses suffered as a result of coming out or of not coming out should be explored. Appreciating what it is like to be a lesbian of color requires an awareness and understanding of the dynamics and interaction of ethnic and gender identity with sexual orientation. Specifically, Greene (1994) recommends that salient factors to be explored with a lesbian of color include the following:

- Experiences with heterosexism and homophobia, and the toll they have exacted on self and significant others
- Culturally specific gender role expectations

- Sexuality and the forms and range of accepted sexual behaviors
- The role and primacy of family and community
- The role of religion/spirituality in the lives of the person and significant others
- The experience of racism, the presence (or absence) of internalized homophobia, and the prevalence of sexism within the client's own ethnic/racial community

Intervention Strategies and Techniques

If the woman of color is seeking mental health intervention, it is crucial to understand how mental disorders are conceptualized. For example, the Chinese language has no equivalent for "depression." Instead, the experience of the condition is expressed in physical terms, leading many mental health providers to conclude that Asian American clients are more apt than other people of color to somaticize psychological distress. It is equally important to ascertain, if working with an immigrant woman, what kind of treatment she would have received in her home country (Lee, 1997). Service providers should also determine prior experiences (in the home country) with Western medicine and the quality of those experiences. Following are some of the areas that should be explored:

- Work and financial stresses: Women of color who work outside the home may find themselves holding several jobs to make ends meet or putting in long hours at work and coming home to still more responsibilities.
- Role changes: Look at the gendered role expectations subscribed to by the woman and significant others. Women may find it easier to get employment because often they are more willing than men to settle for job situations in which they may be overqualified. They may head households and make critical decisions for the family when, in their family of origin and extended family, these responsibilities are still considered a male privilege.
- Experiences with racism, sexism, classism, and heterosexism/homophobia: The aftermath of these experiences on the person and the family should be explored.
- Coping strategies: Examine personal, family-based, and cultural strengths; family and community support networks; and sociocultural practices, including the use of indigenous healers and folk remedies.
- Religious/spiritual beliefs, values, and practices: Sexuality and considerations regarding appropriate or unsanctioned sexual behavior also should be discussed.
- Reframing: Lee (1997) notes that reframing helps to validate good intentions. For example, a mother's overprotective and stifling behavior may be described as "loving well," or a mother's long hours at work can be reframed from "neglecting her children" to "sacrificing for the economic well-being of the family."
- Assuming multiple helping roles: In addition to being a counselor/therapist, the practitioner/service provider can also be a teacher, advocate, cultural broker or mediator, and resource broker (Lee, 1997).
- Mobilizing personal and cultural strengths: Strengths may include support from the extended family, a strong sense of family obligation and family loyalty, filial piety, and a strong work ethic (Lee, 1997). Noting how the person has managed to survive despite her obstacles and barriers, and noting the coping strategies she used (which may lend themselves to strengthening and modification), may help strengthen a diminished sense of self-efficacy.

New Inductive Learning

Generally, women of color have not been the focus of research, and this needs to change. In the health field, epidemiological research to determine the prevalence and incidence of different physical and psychological conditions is needed. Large-scale research that reports aggregated data plays an important role in helping society formulate policies and make funding allocations to allow for programmatic and service delivery responses. However, this should not be done at the expense of individual experiences.

Women's individual and collective voices about their unique encounters with violence, racism, sexism, poverty, and heterosexism/homophobia must be heard. These voices remind society that there is diversity in diversity—that one size does not fit all. Customizing programs and service delivery to meet cultural and gender-specific needs may be expensive in the short term. However, if over the long haul such customized approaches stop the "revolving-door" phenomenon, incalculable savings will have been made.

The search for "best practice" for women of color should fuel efforts to refine existing knowledge and generate new knowledge about what works, with whom, under what circumstances, and with what methods/strategies. Such knowledge is available through conscientious research of gender- and culture-specific behaviors and evaluation of programs and services designed to support, assuage, or eliminate those behaviors. Women of color should not only be subjects of investigation but also participate in the design of the research and the questions contained therein. In addition, they should be involved in the interpretations of findings; after all, is not the intent to describe accurately their reality?

Many instruments and measures may be culture-bound and not normed on women, let alone women of color. Every effort should be made by researchers to design and develop measures and instruments that more accurately and appropriately represent the lived realities of women of color. At the very least, existing instruments should be adapted and modified to more correctly portray the conditions and circumstances that women of color experience.

TOOLS FOR STUDENT LEARNING 13.1

The Case of Wanda

Wanda is from an American Indian tribe in Arizona and has lived, attended school, and worked intermittently on the reservation all her life. Her face is scarred from many physical fights, both in and out of bars. She usually wears a red bandana around her cropped hair, and her muscular arms are often bare in a sweatshirt cut like a tank top. She has small, self-designed tattoos on her fingers and hands, including the names Mike and Wanda tattooed across the fingers. Wanda (37) and her husband, Mike (33), have had an alcohol abuse problem since they were teenagers. Their seven-year marriage produced one son, Andy (6), who has been living with his paternal aunt, Mike's younger sister Maria (30), for a year.

Maria is married and works for the tribal government. She wants to keep Andy and raise him. Because of the time that has passed and because she has no children, she is hoping that Mike will give this child to her. Andy started school this fall. Andy knows and is attached to his mother and father, with whom he lived from birth until he moved in with Maria.

The background information received by the child welfare worker follows. A year ago, during one of their violent, alcohol-induced fights, Wanda stabbed Mike six times with a small kitchen knife. The couple was at home, and Andy witnessed the stabbing. The wounds were not life-threatening; however, Mike spent a week in the hospital. Mike agreed to have Maria take temporary custody of Andy during this emergency and has visited him about six times since Andy's placement. No plan has been made by the child welfare agency to date.

Wanda was charged with assault with a deadly weapon and was sentenced to six months in the tribal jail. She is now out of jail, has been through alcohol treatment as part of her sentence, and has asked the child welfare agency if she can see her son. She has attempted to work and has a temporary job with the tribal casino as a janitor. She admits she has been too ashamed to visit the child in Maria's home. Maria sees Wanda not as physical threat but as a threat to her own foster custody of Andy.

In the context of their reservation, Wanda and Mike have a drinking life. They are also laborers and often work temporary jobs with the tribe to make their living and are considered good workers. Andy has been seen at the local bars with Wanda and Mike, but he has never been removed from the home. Wanda recognizes that her relationship with Mike is over, and this does not seem to bother her. She is afraid she will lose contact with her son, and this is a potential source of conflict for both parents. She is also afraid Mike's sister will claim the child and that she will be cut off from a relationship with Andy because of her actions and jail history. Both she and Mike have served time in jail in the past 15 years, mostly on drunk and disorderly charges. In this community, this behavior has meant a night or two in jail, unless there was any property damage.

After this last episode, Mike quit drinking. He decided that he no longer wants to have a marital relationship with Wanda. During Wanda's incarceration, Mike established a relationship with a long-time friend, and they have moved in together. He wants to have his son returned to him and to raise him with his new partner. The new partner, Doris (35), quit drinking three years ago after a serious problem with diabetes, a hospitalization, and a conversion to Christianity. She has never been married and has worked in a clerical position for the tribe for the last 10 years.

Both Wanda and Mike come from extended families, members of which have varied histories with substance abuse and the criminal justice system, and both lost their parents before they reached the age of 30. Wanda has a particularly violent history, including assaults as a young adult. There is no specific information about Wanda's siblings.

1. What are Wanda's strengths? Name three.

2. What are Mike's strengths? Name three.

3. Should Andy remain in Maria's custody? Why or why not?

4. What should be the long-term plans for Andy? Explain your views.

ADVOCATING FOR SOCIAL AND ECONOMIC JUSTICE

Many women of color are living testimonies of the fortitude, resilience, and perseverance it takes to transcend the complexities of living imposed by gender, race, and class. Although many have triumphed and flourished, many still live at the margins. This chapter has documented the social and economic disparities that exist among women of color in particular, between the women and others in the community, and between women of color and others in society in general.

For social workers, the imperative for activism and advocacy is undeniable. Section 6.04 on social and political action in the Code of Ethics for social workers compiled by the National Association of Social Workers (NASW, 1996) discusses the professional and ethical responsibility that social workers have to address such inequities. With those mandates in mind, some examples of strategic action that could be undertaken include the following.

Get involved in social and political action to ensure that all women of color have equal access to critical resources (e.g., health insurance coverage), employment, services (e.g., culturally competent and language-appropriate services), and opportunities (e.g., for personal and professional growth and development through education and training) that they require in order to meet their basic human needs and to develop fully.

Be aware of the impact of the political arena on practice. For example, when U.S. District Court Judge Susan Webber Wright dismissed Paula Corbin Jones's sexual harassment suit against Bill Clinton in 1998, "public interest in the complexities of applying sexual harassment law" grew (Gould, 2000, p. 242). Gould (2000) urged social work participation in the emerging debate on sexual harassment for several reasons. First, citing Maypole's (1987) review of research on sexual harassment at work, Gould noted that women constitute 90 percent of all plaintiffs and the vast majority of victims; and, among unskilled women laborers in the automobile industry, women of color reported greater harassment. Second, "the complicated nature of power relationships and women's economic dependence, which at times, forces them to tolerate unwelcome advances" (Gould, 2000, p. 244) is often misunderstood even by the judiciary. Finally, given the rate of 15,500 cases filed each year and 60 new cases every working day (citing Cloud, 1998), it was clear to Gould that "the substantive area of sexual harassment is particularly relevant to social work's professional mission to oppose oppression and foster social justice" (p. 243). She called for social workers to engage in activism and advocacy by participating in efforts to reformulate the laws to overcome the combined barriers of ambiguity of wording and level of evidence required to prove a case. In other words, laws needed to be redefined so that the legal route to justice would be better understood and less onerous, and legal outcomes would be more equitable.

Advocate for changes in policy and legislation to improve social conditions so that basic human needs will be met. Finn, Castellanos, McOmber, and Kahan (2000) chronicled the history of a Montana-based grassroots advocacy and educational organization, Working for Equality and Economic Liberation (WEEL), which emerged in 1996 in response to welfare reform. With an advisory group of low-income women, WEEL crafted a mission statement that sought to change "the belief and policy systems that keep people oppressed." They hoped to accomplish "a future of equality and economic liberation for all" through "action and education" (p. 298). The WEEL organization networked with other local organizations, as well as those located in other states, in developing its knowledge and capacity. In addition to publicizing the message of welfare rights and recruiting new members, WEEL was involved in the campaign to establish a plan that provided children of uninsured working-poor parents with access to health care. It also was successful at mounting an effort "to challenge the inequity of punitive welfare sanctions in Montana." Members drafted a bill "calling for the creation of an independent oversight board composed of social workers who would review all sanctioned cases before punitive action was taken to close them." Finn and colleagues (2000) note the outcome: "The bill was tabled in House debates and referred to an interim legislative committee for further review" (p. 306).

The organizing efforts of WEEL and the organization's activism have resulted in chapters in Missoula and Helena and a student chapter at the University of Montana at Missoula. It has an active core membership of 40 people and more than 1,000 members and supporters across the state. Its goals are as follows:

- Expand choice and opportunity
- Promote conditions that encourage respect for the diversity of cultures and social diversity
- Implement policies and practices that demonstrate respect for difference
- Expand cultural knowledge and resources
- Support programs and institutions that demonstrate cultural competence
- Employ policies that safeguard rights and confirm equity and social justice

SUMMARY

The biggest challenge in the writing of this chapter has been to accurately portray the complexities and nuances of the challenges facing women of color. We used intersectionality as a conceptual framework to impress upon the reader the importance of understanding that location at the intersections of race, ethnicity, age, marital status, education, and employment is unique to a particular woman. This unique presentation elicits a multiplicity of personal, social, and political responses, all of which interact to determine the individual's access to resources. The logical choice then for perspective-taking when it comes to the writing of this chapter would have been to adopt a strengths-based, case study approach to the writing of this chapter.

Instead, we rationalized that for readers in the helping professions to be aware of the social, economic, political, medical, and behavioral health implications of being a woman of color, we needed to present nomothetic as opposed to ideographic data and information. Invariably, this perspective focuses on the challenges that women of color in general encounter as opposed to examining personal successes in overcoming life barriers and impediments. In taking this generalized approach, our hope is that we have provided you, the reader, with a checklist of conditions and predispositions for which to be alert but not to presume. It is also our hope that this checklist will inspire creativity of thinking and doing that we believe is essential to customizing and personalizing programmatic and service responses. In the end, it is our fervent hope that our call to attend to the needs of each woman of color is heard and acted upon through the rendition of individualized helping responses as a manifestation of culturally competent practice.

CHAPTER FOURTEEN

Cultural Competence with Gay and Lesbian Persons of Color

KARINA L. WALTERS, JOHN F. LONGRES, CHONG-SUK HAN, AND LARRY D. ICARD

> Differences between ourselves as Black women are also being misnamed and used to separate us from one another. As a Black lesbian feminist comfortable with the many different ingredients of my identity, and as a woman committed to racial and sexual freedom from oppression, I find I am constantly being encouraged to pluck out some one aspect of myself and present this as a meaningful whole, eclipsing or denying the other parts of self. But this is a destructive and fragmenting way to live. My fullest concentration of energy is available to me only when I integrate all the parts of who I am. . . .
>
> Audre Lorde (1984, pp. 120–121)

Sexual orientation refers to the object of a person's predominant sexual, erotic, and affectional desires (Bell & Weinberg, 1978; Kinsey, Pomeroy, & Martin, 1948). One may desire a person of the opposite sex or of the same sex, or one may desire people of both sexes. The idea of sexual orientation, that is, classifying people according to the object of primary sexual desire, is a rather new, Western construct. Although same-sex affection and sexual behaviors are manifest across cultures, the meaning attributed to same-sex desires and one's social location in relation to those desires varies widely by culture and historical era. Similarly, the terms *gay* and *lesbian* are sociopolitical constructs rooted in 20th-century advanced industrial societies. They are constructs that are still relatively novel across parts of the Western world and, to a greater degree, the non-Western world.

The term *homosexual*, another social construct, was coined in Germany in 1869 and entered the English language in 1892 (Downing, 1989). Today, *gay, lesbian, bisexual,* and *queer* are replacing *homosexual* throughout Western societies. Where the term *homosexual* emphasized sexual interests and behaviors, the newer terms refer to a broader psychosocial constellation including identity, community, lifestyle, and worldview. Among urban, educated, middle-class Whites, gays and lesbians are developing a clear set of norms around which they organize their lives. Although these norms are debated and not universally accepted, their ascendancy in lesbian and gay communities is readily apparent. These norms include (1) the idea that sexual orientation is a master status (i.e., an essential feature of one's personal and social identity in much the same way as gender, race, or class background); (2) the belief in the normality and morality of consensual same-sex

389

relationships between adults who share the same sexual orientation; (3) the construction of pride in self through the development of community life, replete with social, religious, political, and economic resources; and (4) the formation of stable "families of choice," which include supportive gay and heterosexual friendships, long-term partnerships, and children variously conceived. These norms are particularly important to social workers because they increasingly form the foundation from which social services to lesbian and gays are provided.

Yet, lesbians and gays in Western industrial societies have developed these norms somewhat at the expense of the working classes and people of color. After the Stonewall Riots, middle-class gays and lesbians, working through such White and middle-class dominated organizations as the Daughters of Bilitis and the Mattachine Society, emerged as the leaders of the movement. As they took over the movement, they promoted the constructs of sexual orientation, sexual identity, gay and lesbian identity and community, and the lifestyle that goes along with them. Although it is generally seen as liberating, many gays and lesbians of color, as well as White working-class gays and lesbians, feel alienated from its emerging middle-class norms. Although many people of color in the United States accept the labels of lesbian or gay and participate in the community, a significant number reject these labels in favor of terms more consonant with the way sex attraction is understood in their respective communities (see discussions to follow). Today, the lesbian and gay movement still tends to be led by middle-class Whites, but people of color are increasingly being incorporated. Lesbians and gays of color participate as staff or volunteers in the Human Rights Campaign and the National Gay and Lesbian Task Force—the two largest national organizations—as well as in local mainstream organizations like the Pride Foundation in Seattle. For instance, the Gay and Lesbian Alliance Against Defamation (GLAAD), a national organization that monitors the treatment of gays and lesbians in the media, maintains a People of Color program that monitors how people of African descent, Asian and Pacific Islanders, Muslims, and Latino lesbians and gays are portrayed (GLAAD, 2005). They also work with two-spirited Native Americans and their allies to ensure fair, accurate, and inclusive media coverage.

The construct of a transgendered person is an even more recent development in advanced industrial societies. Rather than sexual orientation, transgender is rooted in the distinction between sexual identity and gender identity. Sexual identity—one's biological sex—is distinguished from gender identity—one's perceptions and feelings about being male or female. Gays and lesbians are comfortable with their biological sex and are attracted to members of their same biological sex. Transgendered people, on the other hand, reject their biological sex in favor of their perceived gender. Although transgendered people may or may not be sexually attracted to members of their same transgendered self, they are defined by their gender identity, not their sexual orientation. The concept of transgendered is broadly defined to include both those who may have their biological sex wholly or partially surgically altered as well as those who think of themselves as gender nonconforming (Mallon, 1999). This chapter focuses on gays and lesbian of color (GALOCs). There are, undoubtedly, people of color who fit the notion of transgendered. Furthermore, as we will show, some historical ways of perceiving same-sex attraction in communities of color might easily fit into contemporary notions of transgendered. Although we will not do it here, this topic deserves increased attention among researchers and practitioners alike.

Social Work Practice

Practice with respect to sexual orientation has become more progressive as the gay and lesbian movement has moved forward. Where homosexuality was seen as a disorder in need of change, most helping professionals now accept the normalcy of gay and lesbian identities and aim to affirm them. Yet, in working within the norms of an evolving, largely White, middle-class gay and lesbian community, social workers may fail to accurately empathize with clients of color and their families who may perceive issues differently. Most of the research on gays and lesbians has used White and middle-class respondents (Garnets & Kimmel, 1991; Greene, 1997). Similarly, research and conceptual articles on racial and ethic group processes rarely address sexual orientation as a salient factor in the lives of people of color (Greene, 1997). Finally, in couples-based practice literature, rarely will one find a discussion on lesbian or gay couplings, and simultaneously, rarely are racial identity processes a component of understanding inter- or intraracial couplings (Greene, 1997). Although this chapter aims to fill the gap, a clear need exists for more research and practice models.

The successful development of healthy sexual and racial identities among gays and lesbians of color involves the ability to negotiate and reconcile competing demands from the dominant society at large, from the gay and lesbian community, and from one's own ethnic/racial community. Despite the recognition that a gay/lesbian identity and a positive racial identity are both important to healthy bio-psycho-social-spiritual functioning, little research has investigated how multiple oppressed statuses and the interactions of those statuses affect bio-psycho-social-spiritual functioning among gays and lesbians of color (GALOCs). Walters (1999) notes:

> For GALOCS, the integration of a consolidated racial and gay or lesbian identity is even more complex, involving negotiations of conflicting allegiances to the gay and lesbian community and the community of color. Despite the importance of understanding the complex interactions among racism, sexism, and heterosexism that GALOCS must negotiate, the social work practice literature remains inadequate in providing any practice guidelines that incorporate these issues. (p. 48)

In this chapter, we will focus on the interconnection between racial identity and sexual identity, how these identities buffer the life stressors associated with a double or triple oppressed group status (e.g., discrimination), and the corresponding conflicting allegiances that arise as a result of life stressors. We will start by contextualizing the history of same-sex sexual expression and desires among four groups of peoples: First Nations Peoples, African Americans, Asian Americans, and Latino/a Americans. Second, we will elucidate universal conflicting allegiances and identity processes among GALOCs and discuss how these processes are experienced and manifested in culturally specific ways among the four groups, with a specific emphasis on integrating these factors into culturally competent service delivery across systems levels and articulating a model for providing culturally competent services for GALOCs. Finally, we will highlight social justice implications of these processes and discuss macro level interventions for GALOC populations.

The use of the term *GALOC* in this chapter is not purported to represent a monolithic cultural group, and it is not intended to render invisible the vast within-group heterogeneity that exists between and among GALOCs from diverse racial and class backgrounds.

Rather, the term *GALOC* is used here to refer to individuals who self-identify primarily with one racial group (e.g., Asian American or Korean American), with one sexual orientation (e.g., gay man, lesbian, or some other term that reflects primarily monosexual and/or affectional object choice), and with one sexual identity (e.g., male or female). Although there are likely to be parallel process issues for bisexuals of color and for multiracial gays and lesbians, delving into these specific issues is beyond the scope of this chapter. For an excellent preliminary discussion of these issues, however, see Allman (1996), Greene (1993), Kich (1996), and Root (1996). Although the thrust of this chapter will be on uncovering common identity struggles that cut across racial group affiliations, culturally competent practitioners should use this perspective only as a set of generalizations to be accepted or discarded as the culturally specific experiences of individual clients are taken into account (Walters, 1999).

SAME-SEX SEXUAL DESIRES AND EXPRESSIONS: A TRAVEL THROUGH HISTORY BY GROUP

For a long time, anthropologists believed that homosexual conduct was not present across all societies. Using the Standard Sample of the Human Relations Area File, some concluded that although present in some societies, homosexual conduct was absent in others. In reviewing this data, David Greenberg (1988, pp. 77–78) notes that many ethnographers either did not explore the subject or accepted statements of "not allowing it" as "not having it." He also notes that some ethnographers actually observed homosexual conduct but did not report it. Broude and Greene (1976) also note that some anthropologists did not report homosexual conduct because it was not customary and because they feared not being allowed to return for further research. Read (1980), recalling his study of the Gahuku-Gama, a New Guinea people, acknowledges that he did not ask about homosexuality in spite of witnessing same-sex contact. He assumed it was not a significant part of the culture!

Contemporary anthropologists assume that homosexual conduct is a universal phenomenon (Herdt, 1990; Murray, 2000). The anthropological question is not whether same-sex conduct exists but how it is organized and structured across time and communities. The fact that homosexual behavior exists in all societies does not mean that it is universally understood in the same way. Sexual behavior is enormously flexible, a "set of potentialities" that has been shaped and reshaped across time, place, and culture. We should note, however, that although there is an abundance of research on same-sex sexual behaviors among men, there is very little research on women of color.

At the turn of the 20th century, same-sex sexual conduct and affection was medicalized as a disease throughout much of the Western world, which led to increased stigmatization of what was referred to as "homosexual" conduct. Many communities of color followed suit, distancing themselves from "homosexuality," stigmatizing any perceived homosexuals among them, and denying outright that such behaviors had ever existed in their communities. They came to believe that "homosexuality" and, subsequently, "lesbian and gay" were not only diseases but also corrupt Western imports, an example of the bad effects of acculturation and colonization. Even those with a clear communal history of same-sex behaviors came to stigmatize same-sex oriented people in their communities (Murray & Roscoe, 1998; Arguelles & Rich, 1989). The distancing came about not only because they accepted Western ideas of homosexuality as disease but also because the terms *homosexual*, *lesbian*, and *gay* were indeed unknown and foreign and so worth making a disease of. These notions of conduct and identity did not correspond with their own understanding of same-sex sexual expression and desires. Although Western-style homosexuality was stigmatized, same-sex affection within the context of their traditional norms was not necessarily stigmatized.

Gays and lesbians of color, feeling stigmatized by their communities, tended to accept the liberation promised by the lesbian and gay movement. Many became comfortable within the lesbian and gay movement, and some have emerged as its leaders. Others live on the edge, feeling a pull to the gay and lesbian community but also feeling a pull back into their ethnic and racial communities. Still others feel alienated from the lesbian and gay movement because of racism and a sense of exclusion and have worked to develop a sexual identity in keeping with their racial and ethic identity. Thus, ambivalence and resistance to notions of homosexual, or gay and lesbian, identities should be interpreted as resistance to Western-imposed constructions of sexual and affectional behaviors.

In the following text, we highlight histories and culturally specific practice issues for each ethnic group (First Nations, African Americans, Asian Americans, and Latino Americans). Each author has focused on particular themes he or she felt are particularly salient for each population; however, these themes are by no means exhaustive. Discussion of more in-depth cultural specificity (e.g., spirituality) is beyond the scope of this chapter. Further reading is encouraged to examine in greater detail culturally specific issues for each of these groupings.

First Nations Peoples (American Indians and Alaska Natives)

Finding the appropriate terminology to capture contemporary First Nations gay, lesbian, bisexual, transgendered, and/or two-spirit (FN GLBT-TS) experience is complex due to the entanglement of historical and contemporary traditional Native worldviews of gender roles, spiritual roles, and sexual behaviors with contemporary Western understandings of "sexual orientation" and "homosexuality." Disentangling these worldviews is necessary to better understand contemporary experience and practice-related issues for FN GLBT-TS.

First, it is important to note that FN Peoples generally do not classify the world in dichotomous or binary categories (e.g., gay/straight). The fluidity of self, spirituality, community, time, and space is a cultural norm that permeates worldviews and linguistic understandings of self in relation to community, ancestors, and future generations. This fluid, nonlinear worldview is critical to contextualizing FN concepts of gender and sexuality, which historically, and to some degree contemporarily, do not fit into Western concepts of gay/straight or male/female (Tafoya, 1992).

Previous anthropological literature adopted the term *berdache* to describe FN Peoples "who partially or completely take on the culturally defined role of the other [biological] sex and who are classified neither as men nor as women, but as genders of their own in their respective cultures" (Lang, 1998). It is also important to note that the term *berdache* is not used among FN Peoples due to its colonizing origins. *Berdache* is a non-FN word of Arabic origin (*berdaj*) that was used to describe male slaves who served as (anally receptive) prostitutes (Thomas, 1997). Later, the term was misapplied by anthropologists to describe biologically male Natives who functioned in gender roles outside of European gender role expectations and constructions. Because of the Western lenses through which many anthropologists initially observed same-sex sexual behaviors and gender role variances, these early observations were fraught with inaccuracies and ethnocentric biases that more often than not confounded gender roles with sexual orientation. More recently, these observations have been misused to further political needs of non-FN gay, lesbian, bisexual, and transgendered movements. Nevertheless, some important findings emerged from this early literature (for an exhaustive review of this subject, see Jacobs, Thomas, & Lang, 1997; Lang, 1998) that suggest that male-bodied berdaches (and to some degree, although not as documented, female-bodied berdaches) were held in fairly high esteem, were thought to be endowed with spiritual or medicinal powers, or, among some tribes, were seen as more secular (Lang, 1998). At the very least, Lang notes that these "women–men" or male-bodied berdaches seem to have been at least "accepted" in all FN cultures in which they were reported to exist (over 125 cultures plus tribes or bands have been studied). It is important to note that *women–men* is simply a lingua franca term to denote this other-gendered status (sometimes referred to as a third- or fourth-gendered status) that is reflected in culturally specific terminology. For example, women–men have been documented among the Cheyenne (*heemaneh'*), Hidatsa (*miati*), Oglala Lakota (*winkte*), Ojibway (*agokwe*), Mohave (*alyha* or *hwame*), and Crow (*bote'*), to name a few. Likewise, "men–women" (i.e., female-bodied women) have been documented among the Klamath (*Tw!inna'ek*), Maidu (*suku*), Mohave (*hwame* or *hwami*), Coeur d'Alene (*brumaiwi*), and Tewa (*kwido'* or *kweedo'*), among many other tribes (Lang, 1998).

Women–men generally had sexual liaisons and partnerships with biological males as well as females and among some tribes had "marriages" to biological males (e.g., among Aleut or Hidatsa, as reported in Lang, 1998). However, these partnerships were seen to be between a biological male and a third gender; thus, they were not a "same-sex" union. In fact, women–men did not have sexual relationships with one another; this would have been considered incestuous because they referred to each other as "sisters." Thus, same-sex relationships between persons of the same *gender* status were typically not formally sanctioned (Lang, 1998). Lang also notes that most women–men entered into partnerships with men (and sometimes women), ranging from brief sexual encounters to formalized ceremonial marriages that may have been polygamous, monogamous, or serial marriages. For example, among the Aleuts, marriages between men and *shupans* (i.e., women–men) were commonplace (although more frequently as a second "wife" to a biological woman) and were associated with high levels of prestige. On the other hand, among the Lakota, not all *winkte* married men. Many would remain single and live in their own tipis, where they would be visited by men while the men's wives were menstruating or during other times when sexual intercourse was forbidden (Lang, 1998). Similarly, among female-bodied women who were men–women, marriages and other forms of relational statuses have been documented as well. For example, marriages have been documented between Nevada Shoshoni *tangowaipü* and Nevada Shoshoni women, whereas among the Paiute, a *moroni noho* tended to remain single (Lang, 1998).

With a few exceptions, little data exists to support a general classification of these women–men or men–women as "homosexual" in a Western sense. In fact, as Lang (1998) notes, a more accurate way to characterize women–men's and men–women's relationships with either men or women is to characterize them as "hetero-gendered" rather than "homosexual."

From Women–Men and Men–Women to Two-Spirited. Progressing from historical understandings of same-biological-sex sexual behaviors to contemporary "traditional" understandings of such relationships is extremely complex. Colonial processes (e.g., adoption of Christianity) have undermined the continuance of these traditions within many tribal Nations. As a result, the fluidity between gender and sexuality has slowly become eroded and replaced to varying degrees with more of a demarcation between sexuality and gender expression as well as the adoption of Western understandings of sexual orientation and homosexuality. However, in the last 20 years, on the heels of the Red Power movement and retraditionalization in Indian country, communities have begun to reclaim traditional understandings of various roles within their communities. As a result, the chasm between gender and sexuality that had been developing has now been bridged with the term *two-spirit[ed]*. This fairly new pan-Indian term was created by indigenous GLBT-TS activists to capture sexual, tribal, and spiritual identity processes as well as historical statuses and traditions from which contemporary experience is reinformed, re-created, and retraditionalized. It is important to note that the term is not tribally specific. It is a term that allows contemporary FN GLBT-TS to align with ancestral roles and traditions while simultaneously enacting political resistance to White hegemony (Roscoe, 1998).

The term *two-spirit[ed]* has many meanings within different contemporary Native tribal contexts. In 1988, the term *two-spirit* was adopted to refer to a "Native American who is of two spirits, both male and female." It was also created as a way of naming oneself outside of colonizing terms imposed previously (e.g., *berdache*). Deschamps (1998) states:

> Aboriginal culture is recognized for its emphasis on balance and harmony in all of creation. No one element, force, or impulse dominates others. The term "two-spirited" originates from the First Nations recognition of the traditions and sacredness of people who maintain a balance by housing both the male and female spirit. (p. 10)

Contemporarily, two-spirited has come to signify a fluidity of gender roles (beyond the Western male/female) and sexuality (beyond the Western gay/straight) because it refers to an identity determined not solely by genital contact but also by culturally prescribed spiritual and social powers and roles (e.g., cutting down the tree for the Sun Dance ceremony among the Crow or serving in specific roles during funerals). In fact, many contemporary two-spirit activists identify the valued positions held by ancestral two-spirited peoples, such as dreamer, name-giver, and mediator, as important spiritual and traditional roles that are essential to contemporary two-spirit experience.

It is important to note that this term is not necessarily translatable into Native languages, nor is its meaning culturally equivalent across or between tribes and urban indigenous communities. Thus, the term is not without controversy regarding its "true" meaning or its appropriateness as a pan-tribal term. Moreover, the meaning of the terms varies between and within different Nations, communities, and FN individuals. For example, among the Navajo, having two spirits would be the equivalent of being possessed, and, therefore the term would not necessarily be appropriate to use in working with Navajo clients. Among some FN persons, the term represents a tribally specific spiritual, social, and cultural role that is not at all defined by sexual orientation (i.e., similar to the women–men term) or gender roles but is defined solely by one's spiritual role in relation to tribal-specific traditions. For others, the term does not represent sexual orientation per se (e.g., one can be a transgendered heterosexual who identifies as two-spirited but not as gay) but represents the fluidity of sexuality and gender roles combined with tribally specific cultural and spiritual responsibilities (inclusive of all sexualities and genders). Still others use the term in highly contextualized ways, depending on the audience. For example, one Navajo Native activist refers to himself as "*n'dleeh*-like" when interacting with Navajos, as "two-spirited" among non-Navajo FN peoples, and as "gay" among gay non-FN peoples or while in "Western society." Finally, it is also important to note that some FN individuals self-label as gay, lesbian, bisexual, or transgendered and *purposefully* do not self-label as "two-spirited" because they do not feel that they are sanctioned by their tribal communities as fulfilling social, spiritual, or ceremonial obligations warranting this generic title that might be misconstrued by others as representing a tribal-specific status, such as *winkte*. Thus, for some, the spiritual obligations associated with the term *two-spirited* precludes their use of this term and may be a main reason they will use only *gay, lesbian, bisexual, transgendered,* or *queer* as their self-label. To be inclusive, we use the term *GLBT-TS* to include both two-spirited peoples as well as those who self-label as gay, lesbian, bisexual, or transgendered.

To avoid a simplistic reductionism that equates two-spirit with being only queer or gay, Tafoya (1992) suggests that we think of *gay* as a noun and *two-spirit* as a verb. Because many Native traditions emphasize transformation and fluidity, the idea of a monolithic category that is only constructed on sexual orientation, irrespective of gender roles and spiritual/cultural roles, is simply not culturally relevant. Two-spirit essentially combines sexual orientation with gender-psycho-sexual identity with one's spiritual/cultural/tribal identity.

The ceremonial and social roles of two-spirited persons and women–men/men–women have deteriorated over the centuries with the intrusion of non-FN traditions, belief systems, and Christianity. The erosion of traditional roles associated with two-spirit people among FN Peoples have left many urban two-spirits today with a limited understanding of their traditional place and many heterosexual FN Peoples with little information regarding their two-spirit relatives. Nevertheless, many FN GLBT-TS have begun to reclaim, rename, and reorganize around a two-spirit identity as a way to heal from the cumulative trauma (i.e., the soul wound) associated with colonization.

First Nations: Culturally Specific Practice Themes. *FN GLBT-TS discrimination and sexual orientation bias.* Limited anecdotal and empirical evidence suggests FN GLBT-TS people are at higher risk for trauma and violence than their heterosexual FN counterparts and their non-FN gay or lesbian counterparts. Prejudice toward FN GLBT-TS assumes many forms, ranging from avoidance and disregard to outright murder. For example, in the early 1990s, attacks on FN GLBT-TS on a reservation in South Dakota resulted in at least one death (Roscoe, 1998). In a recent study among 14 FN GLBT-TS, the percentages reporting various bias-related experiences were equal to or greater than those reported in studies of non-FN GLBT-TS populations (36 percent physically assaulted; 36 percent assaulted with a weapon; and 29 percent sexually assaulted for being perceived as GLBT-TS) (Walters, Simoni, & Horwath, 2001).

FN GLBT-TS must contend with racism within non-FN gay and lesbian communities (Walters, 1997) as well as pervasive homophobia within FN communities (Meyers, Calzavara, Cockerill, Marshall, & Bullock, 1993). Racism in non-FN gay and lesbian communities has been manifested in the objectification or eroticization of Native images or outright denial of entrance into gay or lesbian bars.

Negative attitudes in home communities have forced many FN GLBT-TS to migrate to urban centers. For example, some have been asked to leave their reservation or a ceremony when they publicly disclosed their sexual orientation (Roscoe, 1998; Walters, Simoni, & Horwath, 2001). In some cases, FN GLBT-TS leave reservations at very young ages and with little education, eventually trading sex to survive in cities (Deschamps, 1998). Prejudice in FN communities manifests itself in the denial of the existence of FN GLBT-TS, avoidance in discussing the subject, and cultural beliefs that nonheterosexual behavior is sinful, immoral, or against traditions.

Historical traumas may also affect FN GLBT-TS experience of self in relation to community. For example, as Tafoya and Wirth (1996) note: "[B]oarding and missionary schools were a major source of physical and sexual abuse for Native boys and girls . . . some individual Native people may have difficulty reconciling their sexual orientation with their sexual abuse" (p. 58). Additionally, these authors note that the effects of boarding school experience on parenting skills and cultural knowledge have led to a "negative impact on maintaining the integrity of traditional concepts of gender and sexuality . . . as a result, many Native people have had as little informed instruction about Native sexuality and gender as most other Americans" (p. 59).

Prejudicial attitudes and discriminatory behaviors on the part of practitioners (including both FN and non-FN gay and lesbian providers) may be particularly devastating to FN GLBT-TS. Practitioner heterosexist practices range from outing or harassing clients and colleagues to more subtle forms such as not challenging negative perceptions of GLBT-TS in FN communities or not examining one's own heterosexual privilege and corresponding identity attitudes (Simoni, Meyers, & Walters, 2001). Moreover, the practitioner's lack of awareness and unconditional acceptance of institutionalized heterosexist, racist, or colonial practices may lead to "secondary victimization" of FN GLBT-TS clients (Garnets, Herek, & Levy, 1990).

Preliminary evidence among FN GLBT-TS suggests that traumas associated with one's status as GLBT-TS (Simoni, Meyers, & Walters, 2001) create particular strains, stressors, and health/mental health vulnerability among FN GLBT-TS. For example, in one study of FN men who have sex with men (MSMs) and FN non-MSMs, rates of nonpartner sexual assault (45 percent vs. 2 percent), nonpartner physical assault (45 percent vs. 6 percent), partner sexual assault (10 percent vs. 0 percent), and partner physical assault (10 percent vs. 2 percent) were much higher for FN MSMs than FN non-MSMs (Simoni, Meyers, & Walters, 2001). In this same study, regression analyses indicated that trauma and sexual orientation were equally powerful predictors of lifetime high-risk sexual behaviors.

FN GLBT-TS sexual health issues. In a national study of sexual orientation between reservation-based American Indian and Anglo-American adolescents, findings indicated a significantly higher self-reported prevalence of homosexual, bisexual, and unsure responses among FN adolescents compared to their Anglo-American adolescent counterparts (Saewyc, Skay, Bearinger, Blum, & Resnick, 1998). Additionally, gay/bisexual FN males were more likely to report early heterosexual intercourse, more consistent contraception, and a higher prevalence of abuse and running away compared to other males. Likewise, FN self-identified lesbian/bisexual females were more likely to report early onset of heterosexual intercourse, more frequent intercourse, and running away compared to their FN heterosexual counterparts (Saewyc, Skay, Bearinger, Blum, & Resnick, 1998). These findings are consistent with research on interracial same-sex couples where a higher rate of self-reported heterosexual experience or "functional bisexuality" was reported among FN persons compared with other ethnic groups (Tafoya & Rowell, 1988). Tafoya and Wirth (1996) hypothesize that this fluidity of sexual relationships may reflect cultural values associated with fluid gender and sexual roles associated with traditional two-spirited peoples.

The interactions among trauma, sexual risk taking, and alcohol–drug use pose serious potential health risks to FN GLBT-TS and should be contextualized within historical and contemporary traumas. Injection drug use (IDU) has been established as an important risk factor for HIV infection among FN populations (Loecker et al., 1992). According to the Centers for Disease Control (CDC, 1999), among FN males, the most common exposure category is MSM (57 percent), followed by MSMs who inject drugs (17 percent). Among FN MSMs, the combined MSM-IDU exposure rate is highest for FN Peoples compared to any other ethnic group. The mixing and phasing of injection drug use and risky sex among FN MSMs places them in a very vulnerable position for health-related problems. On a positive note, Calzavara and colleagues (1999) note that circular migration is associated with safer sexual behaviors (e.g., higher rates of condom use) among FN MSMs.

Despite negotiating the deleterious effects of colonial processes, including discrimination, historical trauma, and elevated risk of HIV infection, FN GLBT-TS remain committed to strengthening indigenous community health and, ultimately, sovereignty. The seamlessness with which contemporary FN GLBT-TS experience is forged—between the ancestral understandings of status and roles and contemporary ones—is best explained by Anguksuar:

> Some of the qualities that have traditionally been associated with the Gay and Lesbian American Indian people are: generosity, skill in arts and healing, leadership skills, certain abilities in the use of magic, preservation of old knowledge. . . . [T]hese are some of the traditions we live up to in our everyday lives, and for which we consciously and unconsciously strive. As we look at the future, these are some of the things we see, which, as it turns out, are old and were never completely forgotten. (in Roscoe, 1998, p. 111).

African Americans

The cultural heritage of most African Americans is firmly rooted in the African continent. Unfortunately, the collective memory of most African Americans regarding the historical traditions and values of various tribes from which they have descended has been eroded due to slavery and other colonial practices over the years. Today, hundreds of years since the first slave ship landed on the shores of what is now the United States, many African Americans believe that same-sex behavior was not indigenous to ancient

African cultures. Anthropological reports and historical records, however, reveal this belief to be unfounded. For example, in the Horn of Africa, nonmasculine males who were called *londo* by Nuban and *tubele* by the Mesakin could marry men (Katz, 1976). Similar observations exist about same-sex behavior among African women. As an illustration, in the 17th century, a Dutch military attaché observed in the Ndogno kingdom a warrior woman named Nzinga who dressed as a man, ruled as a king rather than a queen, and had a harem of young men dressed as women serving as her wives. Gilbert Herdt (1990) similarly observed other types of institutionalized homosexuality in traditional African cultures. However, as European colonization ensued, narrow definitions of "normal" sexual behaviors slowly replaced "traditional" definitions of same-sex relationships in African societies.

Throughout U.S. history, as African Americans have struggled to overcome the adversities of prejudice and discrimination, homosexual African American men and women have had to contend with an additional struggle. Reports of overt displays of same-sex attractions among African American men and women living in the colonies during the 17th century reveal harsh punishments for public offenses. The judicial penalties were particularly harsh for African American men, and even more so for African American men who were found engaging in same-sex behaviors with White men. This double burden continued into the early 20th century. For example, "the names of Black gays, their feminine aliases and addresses appeared in the press of their arrest, while the names of their White consorts were not given" (Katz, 1976, p. 46). Still, under such conditions, during the early parts of the 20th century, African American homosexual men and women developed ways to affirm their sexual orientations and sexual identity by forming communities that were largely invisible to the public eye. As one eyewitness noted, "I am credibly informed that there is, in the city of Washington, D.C., an annual convocation of Negro men called the drag dance, which is an orgy of lascivious debauchery beyond pen power of description" (as cited in Katz, 1976, pp. 42–43).

By the 1920s, self-identified homosexual or practicing bisexual African American men and women, particularly those who were in the arts and entertainment field, experienced a shift in how they were received by African American and White communities. By the 1920s, it was fashionably chic among upper-class Whites and middle-class African Americans to associate with openly homosexual and bisexual African American men and women (Katz, 1976). Despite their brief moment of acceptance during the Harlem Renaissance, the highly visible community of homosexual and bisexual African American men and women went underground with the advent of the Great Depression and did not resurface until the 1960s.

The '60s, although characterized as an age of civil rights and Black empowerment for African Americans, did not connote liberation for African Americans whose sexual identities and affiliations for intimacy were defined by same-sex behavior. Perhaps the most notable example of the conflicting identities these men and women experienced between their racial identity and validation of their sexuality during this time was the case of Bayard Rustin. Bayard Rustin, an out homosexual and civil rights leader, was prevented from being named director of the 1963 march on Washington because of his sexual orientation. Moreover, according to Hutchinson (2000), a popular African American nationalist magazine frequently referred to Rustin as "the little fairy." These types of antigay statements went unchallenged by the majority of African American leaders during this period

(Hutchinson, 2000). Similarly, during this period, no African American leader emerged to challenge Eldridge Cleaver for attacking James Baldwin's homosexuality in his book *Soul on Ice* (Hutchinson, 2000). Thus, Black nationalism became equated with antigay discourse throughout this period. This discourse was based on the (mis)perception that acknowledging African American homosexuality or embracing African American homosexual leaders would lead to undermining African American unity in fighting against racist oppression. Interestingly, shortly after the civil rights movement, the gay rights movement was spearheaded by several African American transvestites (e.g., Stonewall riots in New York City).

During the decades following the '60s, tensions continued within African American communities regarding sexual orientation, sexual behavior, and group identity commitments (see Lorde, 1984, for an analysis of these tensions). Over the years, this tension has waxed and waned in response to conditions in the larger society. By the 1980s and 1990s, as social attitudes became more relaxed and media portrayals increased, the denial and invisibility of sexual minorities, in particular those who were African American, gave way to visible stereotypes of effeminate African American men through television comedies such as *In Living Color*, the monologues of comedian Eddie Murphy, and the fictional portraits of the urban African American community by young filmmakers like Spike Lee in his movie *School Days*. Such gender-distorted depictions of African American homosexual men did not help reduce the flames that have burned so long in the African American community over the fiery issue of African American homosexuality.

The beginning of the AIDS pandemic in the United States served to magnify the hostile antigay attitudes that had been an undercurrent in the African American community. Early HIV-prevention studies among African Americans exposed the antagonism toward and rejection of African American gay men and women by the general African American community (Icard, Schilling, El-Bassel, & Young, 1992). The AIDS crisis facilitated mobilization of gay and lesbian communities. As White gay men mobilized themselves politically to overcome the threat that HIV/AIDS presented in their community, so too did the African American gay community mobilize. The goal for this mobilization was twofold: (1) to address the threat that AIDS presented to the African American community in general and to the African American gay community in particular; and (2) to counteract the resistance and ineffectiveness of African American churches in fighting the disease and developing support for African American gay men.

African Americans: Culturally Specific Practice Themes. *Multiple generational cohorts and realities.* Henry Louis Gates (1997) stated, "My grandfather was colored, my father is Negro, and I am Black." These labels reflect different social constructions of African American identity at different points in time as defined by the individual, the African American community, and society at large. Gates pointed out that each generation of African Americans has shared distinct psychologies and social concerns. He further noted that across all generations, being African American has always carried the connotation of a "restrictive covenant" in relation to race, racial identity, and racial processes. This restrictive covenant is one in which a person of color could run from or live with but never fully escape. Thus, the significant role that race plays in the lives of gay and lesbian African Americans can never be fully comprehended without recognizing the primacy of skin color in American society and the impact this has on gay and lesbian African

American experience. In response to the interaction between cultural and political processes and corresponding identity imperatives, each generational cohort of African American lesbians and gay men has developed particular coping strategies regarding level of self-disclosure and terminology for self-labeling as both a person of color (e.g., Negro, Black, African American) and a sexual minority (e.g., MSM, straight, bisexual, gay, lesbian, queer). Although generational cohorts might have their unique language, themes, and other sociocultural particulars, there is tremendous within-group diversity; as a result, the self-labeling process needs to be respected and tailored according to the expressed desires of the individual African American client.

From a socioecological perspective, several other important dimensions must be taken into account in providing culturally competent services to African American sexual minorities. Significant ecological factors include the family, religion, school, workplace, the African American gay community, socioeconomic status, and the White gay community, as well as the region of the country where the person resides. The practitioner must attend to the intersection of these ecological factors and individual factors such as personality and coping mechanisms, age, gender, physical attributes, economic status, and level of education.

Role of the family. For all age groups, the African American family has continued to serve over the years as a positive resource. One of the earliest studies of homosexuals to include African Americans reveals that African American gay respondents reported more acceptance and tolerance from their family members than their White counterparts reported (Bell & Weinberg, 1978). Among African Americans, the family is considered to be a site of resistance and support in surviving racist environments and oppression. As a result, strong value for family connectedness and cohesion generally exists according to which family members are accepted and supported regardless of adversity. Although White gays and lesbians may be willing to reject their family of origin for a family of choice that is comprised of a strong gay social support system, African American gays and lesbians are often less eager to do so.

Role of the church. Although the African American family has served as a positive resource, the African American church has continued to function as a major source of strain and conflict with respect to an African American's racial identity, religious identity, and sexual identity. The religious view that same-sex behavior is an abomination has dominated the attitudes of many in the African American community. Thus, although an individual may find tolerance and acceptance within his or her family, the African American church as a whole continues to struggle with embracing gay affirmative attitudes and behaviors. Within African American gay and lesbian communities, African American churches, such as Unity in Los Angeles, have responded to this crisis by developing gay-affirmative sermons and creating safe spaces for African American gays and lesbians to worship freely and openly.

Regional factors. In Philadelphia, the Balls and Houses, as portrayed in the film, *Paris Is Burning*, are strong and thriving. Monthly, as many as 300 African American men and women crowd into a ballroom in a hotel located in Philadelphia. Ballrooms and houses tend to be uniquely an East Coast phenomenon and are rarely seen as a central element to West Coast African American gay life.

Multiple social realities and niches. Another practice issue that has received recent attention is the phenomenon of living "down low" among African American men who engage in same-sex behaviors yet identify themselves as heterosexuals and have women partners for their primary relationships. Research suggests men living on the "down low" do not go to gay bars, may or may not have a boyfriend on the side, are likely to engage in quick sexual encounters (e.g., in restrooms and movie houses), and have a primary partner who is either a wife or a girlfriend. The phenomenon of men on the "down low," as well as the ballroom phenomenon, provides evidence of the need to recognize the multiple social categories and particular niches within which African American sexual minority men and women function. Murray and Roscoe (1998) remind us of the importance of abandoning or at least suspending our Western beliefs and values concerning sexuality, love, and personal relations if we are to understand African American homosexuality. Similarly, responding competently to the cultural factors influencing the lives of African American men and women whose sexuality involves same-sex relations requires suspending conventional beliefs and values regarding sexuality and intimate relations.

Black gay and lesbian community mobilization. The politicization and mobilization of the gay and lesbian African American community inspired many African American gay activists to create a more accurate picture of African American gay men and lesbian women as equally oppressed members of the larger African American community. The visibility of African American gay men and lesbian women was significantly increased in cinema by Marlon Riggs' *Tongues Untied* and in literature by Cornwell's (1983) *Black Lesbian in White America*; Lorde's (1984) *Sister Outsider*; hooks's (1990) *Yearning: Race, Gender, and Cultural Politics*; E. Lynn Harris's (1999) *The Invisible Life*; and Hempill's (1991) *Brother-to-Brother*. More importantly, community mobilization helped to create a voice and vision from which to analyze and deconstruct multiple intersecting oppressed statuses—both within African American communities as well as between African American gay and lesbian communities and White gay and lesbian communities. Consequently, since the 1980s there has been an increase in the recognition of homosexual African American men and women as full members of the African American community. As the attention in the popular media and literature on African American sexual minorities has increased, so too have positive role models emerged. For example, former Seattle city council member Sherry Harris was the first self-identified African American lesbian to be elected to public office. Thus, community mobilization has inspired hope for future generations of African American gay men and lesbians.

Asian Americans

Despite prevailing stereotypes that Asian Americans are more sexually conservative and less open to alternative forms of sexual expression than other racial groups, the history of homosexual behavior in Asia reflects a different picture. Rather than condemning homosexual acts, Asian societies (particularly Chinese, Japanese, Korean, Thai, and Indian) embraced homosexual activities during most of the last millennium.

Asian homosexual relationships were rarely egalitarian; rather, they emphasized the inherent power of age and gender differences. For example, the younger and more effeminate men were the passive recipients of sexual advances by older and often more powerful men. In keeping with age-structured relationships, however, sexual receptivity depended on age. The expectation was that younger men would change positions and become the assertive partner as they became older (Dynes & Donaldson, 1992). At the same time, it was not uncommon for younger, passive partners engaging in homosexual relations with powerful older men to reach levels of influence and power themselves (Leupp, 1995). It is unclear whether age-structured same-gender relations were also found among women. Murray (2000) reported some evidence of female age-stratified homosexuals in the Pacific Islands.

China. In China, recorded cases of homosexual relations date at least to the 6th century BC. Most of the earliest references describe relationships between emperors or other rulers and younger boys employed by the court, suggesting that age-structured relationships were the dominant form of homosexual practice. For instance, the historical text *Han Fei Zi*, written during the Zhou period by Han Fei Tzu, references a relationship between Duke Ling of Wei and his minister Mizi Zia (Watson, 1964). Other writings from the Zhou period also indicate homosexual relationships among the nobility. By the Han period (206 BC to 8 AD.), homosexual acts were so common among the nobility that the topic warranted a special section in the historical text *Shiji*. Although all adult Han emperors enjoyed the favor of young male lovers, the relationship between Emperor Ai (r. 6 BC to 1 AD) and Dong Xian is perhaps the most celebrated. According to the historical text *Han shi* (History of the Han), Emperor Ai cut off his sleeve rather than awaken his young lover. Thus, the term *duanxiu* (cut sleeve) became synonymous with homosexuality in most of East Asia (Van Gulik, 1974). Additionally, the historical text found in China is devoid of negative connotation toward homosexuality, treating it as simply an alternative form of sexual expression.

There is much evidence that following the Han dynasty, the practice of homosexuality spread to the common classes. For example, men of the southern coastal provinces acquired a reputation for homosexual interests during the Tang dynasty by producing many eunuchs for the courts and practicing homosexual marriages (Taisuke, 1970). During this period, it was not uncommon for two families to "arrange" a union between an older male and a younger male with the understanding that the older male would not only provide for the younger male but would later assist the younger male in finding a wife (Leupp, 1995).

By the 12th century, male prostitution was common throughout most of southern China. Although laws were enacted to criminalize this activity, historical evidence suggests that they were only sporadically enforced (Meijer, 1992). Tied intimately to the Beijing opera, male prostitution in China flourished despite governmental sanctions. Court officials often patronized male brothels, and by the Ming period, *actor* and *prostitute* became almost synonymous (Bullough, 1976).

Japan. According to Leupp (1995), homosexual behavior was extremely common during the Tokugawa period (1603–1868) in Japan. Homosexuals were not merely tolerated but positively celebrated in popular art and literature. Additionally, homosexual behavior was institutionally organized in Buddhist monasteries, samurai mansions, and male brothels. During much of Japanese history, homosexuality was framed as one kind of sexual activity that did not necessarily exclude the possibility of opposite-sex sexual activity (McLelland, 2000). Rather than lifelong partnerships, these homosexual relations "most often mirrored the status and power differentials inherent in the greater society," much as they did in China (McLelland, 2000). For example, homosexual relationships among the Samurai class were based on a formalized relationship between the older *nenja*, who loves, and the younger *chigo*, who is loved (Furukawa, 1994). Among the citizenry, relations between masters and their younger apprentices were common and widely accepted (Leupp, 1992). Within Buddhist monasteries, relations between an older monk and a young acolyte were common as well (McLelland, 2000). Within all of these relationships, it was understood that the younger partner was the passive subject of an elder partner's sexual advances and acts (McLelland, 2000).

Homosexuality was especially celebrated within the world of theaters and brothels (McLelland, 2000). The vocabulary of homosexual sex, rather than having pejorative connotations, contained positive tones such as "the beautiful way," or simply "the way of men" (Leupp, 1995). Within these terms, the commonality and the celebratory aspects of homosexual acts are obvious. In fact, McLelland (2000) pointed out, "[I]n the absence of a discourse stigmatizing the same-sex relationships, it was entirely to be expected that older men would establish emotional and sexual bonds with the younger boys who shared their living space."

Korea.   Like its neighbors, Korea also has a long and celebrated history of homosexual behavior. A unique aspect of Korean homosexuality can be seen in the establishment of the *hwarang* (flower boys) during the Shilla dynasty (57 BC to 935 AD). The *hwarang* were a class of aristocratic boys chosen for their beauty, education, and martial prowess for an elite military unit. Although soldiering was their primary role, they also performed ritual dances and recited prayers for the welfare of the state. In addition, members of the *hwarang* unit often acted as concubines to the nobility.

As in China and Japan, actors were often associated with homosexuality. The Korean theater was all male, and troupes lived in homosexual communes where individuals took on gender roles of "butches" and "queens" (Kim, 1992).

India.   The homosexual tradition in India seems to be remarkably different from that of the East Asian countries. The most marked aspect of Indian homosexuality is the existence of the *hijras*, an institutionalized third gender. According to Nanda (1992), the *hijras* of India are a community of emasculated men who dress and live as women. They are unique in that their sexual behavior/identification is not judged as a deviation from a norm but rather as a pseudo-naturally occurring third sex.

The institutionalization of the *hijras* can be traced to the story of King Baria of Gujerat. According to the mythology, Baria was a devote follower of the goddess Bahucharaji who blessed him with a son, Jetho. Although Jetho was born impotent, Baria set him aside for service out of respect for the goddess. The story further explains that Bahucharaji appeared to Jetho in a dream and told him to cut off his genitals and dress himself as a woman (Mehata, 1946). This connection to the goddess Bahucharaji gives the *hijras* a unique position in India, as they are the only caste allowed to bless newborn baby males. Through an elaborate ritual, the *hijras* confer fertility, prosperity, and health on the newborn infant and the infant's family.

Changing Times and Norms.   It was not until the middle of the last millennium that attitudes toward homosexual behavior began to harden in most of Asia. Although historical evidence is still unclear about how such radical shifts occurred from the way that sex and sexuality were viewed in ancient Asia, a number of competing, yet nonexclusive, reasons are provided for the demise of homosexuality. One possible explanation is that homosexuality grew out of favor due to internal forces. For example, following the decline of the Koryo dynasty that was plagued with corruption and political lethargy from the ruling class, rulers of the Chosun dynasty ushered in a series of social, political, and moral ideological shifts based on the Confucian model that led to the hardening of popular attitudes toward homosexuality and other forms of sensuality. A more popular explanation of the demise of homosexual behavior in Asia attributes it to growing foreign (European) influence. Although this explanation is supported by the coincidence in time between extended European contact and the demise of homosexual behavior (Leupp, 1995; Sohng & Icard, 1996), the continuing tolerance of homosexuality in the Philippines—arguably the most heavily Christian influenced nation in Asia—leads us to question the significance of European influences on sexual behavior in Asia. Whatever the reason for the decline, official documentation of homosexuality virtually disappeared from popular and academic text and discourse.

Asian Americans: Culturally Specific Practice Themes. *Contemporary issues for gay Asian American men.* Even when measured by the changing patterns of the American mosaic, gay Asian men occupy a unique space. That they are both gay and Asian, a "double" minority, is not unique in itself. Women of color have occupied this position for centuries. And still others, such as lesbian women of color, have occupied a position of "triple" minority status. Yet unlike other multiply oppressed groups, gay Asian men continue to be invisible both in scholarly and nonacademic writings and popular media. What is known about gay Asian American men comes from the small but growing number of literary and artistic works produced by gay Asian men as well as the literature on HIV/AIDS and the Asian American community. Given that so little has been written about gay Asian Americans, researchers working on ways to prevent the spread of HIV/AIDS within the gay Asian American community have been faced with the daunting task of not only gathering data about HIV/AIDS but also describing this population.

Marginalization in Asian and gay communities. A common theme found in the literature referring to gay Asian men is their marginalization in both the gay and Asian communities. Chay Yew's acclaimed play, *Porcelain*, highlights how both the Chinese and the gay communities deny "ownership" of protagonist John Lee when he is charged with murdering his White lover in a London lavatory. In a particularly biting scene, members of the Chinese community adamantly exclaim, "He is not one of us," only to have members of the gay community also state, "He is not one of us." In fact, Choi and her colleagues (1998) argue that marginalization by both of these communities has led to self-esteem problems for some gay Asian men and may be a major factor contributing to increased rates of unsafe sex and HIV infection among gay Asian men.

In his essay "China Doll," Tony Ayers (1999) discusses feeling outside of the gay mainstream due to his Chinese ethnicity. In addition to discussing the overt forms of racism, such as gay classified ads that specifically state "no fats, femmes, or Asians," and being told by other gay men that they are "not into Asians," Ayers describes the more subtle forms of racism, that of the "rice queens" who desire Asian men purely for the purpose of eroticizing and exoticizing them. Although rice queens may desire Asian men, the cause of the affection is based on the eroticized notion of the Asian "other." Rice queens are often attracted to Asian men based on idealized notions of a passive, docile, and submissive lover, eager to please any White man. Anecdotal evidence suggests that many gay Asian men have internalized these stereotypes. For example, in his article "Using Chopsticks to Eat Steak," Kent Chuang (1999) quotes a young gay Asian man as stating: "There [in Europe] we [Asians] are considered exotic. The Europeans treat us like special people, *like a real woman*. They buy us dinner and drinks and even drive us back to the hotel" (emphasis added). By participating in their own exoticization, gay Asian men further alienate themselves from, and marginalize themselves in, the mainstream gay community.

Asian men themselves have bought into the gay Western notion of what is desirable. Ayers (1999) explains that the "sexually marginalized Asian man who has grown up in the West or is Western in his thinking is often invisible in his own fantasies. [Their] sexual daydreams are populated by handsome Caucasian men with lean, hard Caucasian bodies." In a survey of gay Asian men in San Francisco, Choi and her colleagues (1995) found that nearly 70 percent of gay Asian men indicated a preference for White men. This high percentage is particularly telling given that within gay Asian communities, San Francisco is seen as a mecca for "sticky rice," Asian men who prefer to date other Asian men. If even in this mecca, the vast majority of Asian men prefer to date White men, anecdotal evidence suggests that the percentage is much higher in other locales. More damaging to the gay Asian population is that most of these men seem to be competing for the attention of a limited number of rice queens (Ayers, 1999). This competition hinders the formation of a unified gay Asian community and further acts to splinter those who should be seen as natural allies.

Gay Asian men report feeling inadequate within the larger gay community that stresses and adopts Eurocentric images of physical beauty as the ideal (Ayers, 1999; Choi et al., 1998; Chuang, 1999). Given these feelings of inadequacy, gay Asian men may suffer low levels of self-esteem and actively pursue the company of White men in order to feel accepted by the gay mainstream. The internalization of the White beauty ideal can lead gay Asian men to reject aspects of themselves as Asian and to adopt high levels of internalized colonized attitudes toward themselves as Asian men. For example, Chuang (1999) writes about how he tried desperately to avoid anything related to his Chinese heritage and attempted to transform his "shamefully slim Oriental frame . . . into a more desirable Western body." Other manifestations of attempting to hide their Asian heritage may include bleaching their hair or wearing colored contact lenses.

Role of the family. Although common to all ethnic groups, the fear of rejection from family and friends may be more acute for gay Asians than for other groups. Although some have noted the cultural factors associated with Confucianism and the strong family values associated with Asian Americans, these explanations fall short given that many Asian American communities (particularly Filipino and South Asian) are not rooted in a Confucian ethic. Instead, the compounded feeling of fear may have more to do with their status as racial and ethnic minorities within the United States. For example, Fung (1996) argues that for Asian Americans, "families and [their] ethnic communities are a rare source of affirmation in a racist society." Thus, in coming out, Asian American gays and lesbians risk losing the support of their ethnic communities and facing an inherently racist society on their own. Unlike gay White men, who can find representation and support in the gay community, gay Asian men often do not have the option of finding a new community outside of the ethnic one they would be leaving behind. In fact, there is some evidence that gay Asian men who are less integrated into the Asian American community may be at higher risk for HIV/AIDS due to a lack of available support networks (Choi et al., 1998).

In their study with gay Asian men, Choi and her colleagues (1998) found that gay Asian men often feel that their families would not support their sexual orientation; as a result, gay Asian men tend to remain closeted and do not disclose their sexual orientation to others until a later age than White gay men do. Remaining in the closet carries a heavy burden both physically and psychologically. For example, closeted men may be more likely to engage in unsafe sexual behavior through anonymous sex. In addition, remaining in the closet exerts a psychological stress where gay Asian men are forced to hide their true identity from loved ones, thereby creating deep feelings of inauthenticity with family and ethnic community networks.

Empowerment in redefining self and community. In the absence of a vocabulary to describe their experiences, gay Asian men and women have had to create new words and names to define their identity (Shah, 1998). In fact, within the past few years, a number of gay Asian groups and activists have challenged the Western notions of beauty and questioned the effects of these notions on the gay Asian community. These scholars have rallied against adding gay Asian Americans as simply another ad hoc subject (Takagi, 1996) but have insisted on looking at the intersections of race and sexuality where gay Asian Americans have come to exist. In fact, Eric Reyes (1996) asks, "[W]hich do you really want—rice queen fantasies at your bookstore or freedom rings at the checkout stand of your local Asian market?" In posing this question, Reyes asks us where we should begin to build our home in this place we call America, in the "heterosexual male-dominated America, White gay male-centered Queer America, the marginalized People of Color America, or our often-romanticized Asian America?" It is this continuing attempt to find a gay Asian space that is perhaps at the heart of gay Asian America.

Latino Americans

Latino people are an ethnically diverse population, originating from the Spanish-speaking nations of the Americas, the West Indies, and Spain. In 2002, people of Mexican origin represented nearly two thirds of the total Latino population in the United States, followed by Central and South Americans (14.3 percent), Puerto Ricans (8.6 percent) and Cubans (3.7 percent) (U.S. Bureau of the Census, 2002). Although many may refer to themselves as Latino or Hispanic in the context of U.S. society, individually they usually prefer to be known in terms of their national origin (e.g, as Cubans, Columbians, Chileans, Puerto Ricans, Mexicans, or Chicanos).

Racially, Latinos are also diverse because the nations were formed from the conquest of indigenous people by Spain. People from Africa were later forcefully added, especially in the countries around the Caribbean basin. Unlike the United States, however, racial mixing among indigenous, European, and African people was common. Likewise, Latinos historically measure their degree of Europeanness, and so it is a sort of one-drop rule in reverse. If you have a European parent, you have a claim to Europeanness, which in the United States, often means you think of yourself as "White."

In the 2000 U.S. Census, individuals were asked to indicate their ethnic origin and, in a separate question, their racial category. With respect to race, 48 percent of Latinos indicated they were White, whereas only 2 percent indicated they were Black. Some 6 percent marked two racial categories, often both White and Black, whereas 43 percent chose "other," thereby opting out completely from the standard racial categories used in the United States. According to a Pew Hispanic Center (2004) news release, the choice of a racial category did not "exclusively reflect permanent markers such as skin color or hair texture." Whiteness seems to measure the extent to which Latinos feel a sense of belonging in the United States (Pew Hispanic Center, 2004). The more Latinos were born in the United States, had a good education, were economically secure, participated in civic organizations, and considered themselves Americans, the more they responded that they were "White." Those who think of themselves as racially "other" or "Hispanic Hispanics," as the Pew Hispanic Center calls them, are more likely to be foreign born, less educated, and less likely to think of themselves as Americans. Race is also related to ethnicity among Latinos: Those born in Cuba are more likely to see themselves as White, and the highest percentage of "other" is found among Mexican-born Latinos.

The reader may wonder if Latinos, many of whom have some indigenous parentage, also identify as Native Americans or American Indians. In Latin America, Native Americans or *Indios* are those who have refused to mix and who have retained their native languages and customs. The Latino world retains many such indigenous people. However, once Indios marry out of their tribe, they generally take on a Spanish-speaking ethnic identity. For that reason, the Census Bureau rarely finds Latinos who identify themselves as Native Americans.

Latino people also are diverse along socioeconomic lines. People of Mexican origin in the United States have the lowest proportion of people having graduated from high school or college. Puerto Ricans and Mexicans have the highest levels of unemployment among Latin groups in the United States. Within each of the groups, a lot of economic inequality exists both here and abroad. Among Americans with managerial or professional occupations, 11.3 percent are Latino men and 18.1 percent are Latina women (U.S. Bureau of the Census, 2002).

Given the diversity we have identified, social workers should strive to follow, not lead, in identifying their Latino clients. Social workers should understand that *Latino* and *Hispanic* are terms largely invented in the United States to describe a complex population. We also must realize that the United States constructs racial categories differently than in Spanish-speaking countries.

In addition to ethnicity, race, and class, cultural competence requires that social workers understand the issues surrounding Latino sexuality. This is easier said than done. Cultures have a history and they change depending on external and internal influences. In this section, we will describe traditional Latino norms surrounding sexuality and same-sex relationships and go on to suggest that these traditions are changing as a result of the international gay rights movement.

Same-sex sexual behavior on the Iberian Peninsula was thoroughly suppressed as Catholicism and the Spanish Inquisition took hold in the 15th century (Torres, 2003). Catholic priests traveling with the Conquistadores brought their repressive attitudes to the Americas putting an end to existing indigenous social norms that often accepted same-sex sexual behavior, albeit in forms very different from current ideas about lesbian or gay relationships (see previous discussion of First Nations Peoples). In spite of repression, same-sex sexual behavior and relationships continued to exist as a form of resistance to the repressive norms about sexuality and its expression throughout the Spanish-speaking world.

Traditional Sexuality. Influenced by the Napoleonic code, Latin American legal traditions give a great deal of freedom to the private lives of individuals (Arguelles & Rich, 1989). Nevertheless, those who would openly flaunt their same-sex interests often became targets of social ostracism and even imprisonment (Molloy & McKee Irwin, 1998; Torres & Pertusa, 2003). It is not surprising that discretion in all things sexual became an overriding value. As if to emphasize their underground nature, incipient communities of same-sex–oriented people called themselves *de amibiente* (of the ambience) or *entendido* (in the know).

In addition, people interested in same-sex relationships had to accommodate to the ideals of *familismo*, the centrality of family and kin in Spanish-speaking societies. The expression of sexuality was expected to take place in the context of the private family separate from the public life of middle-class society (Ramos, 1987; Taylor, 1991; Hidalgo, 1995). As a result, men were expected to be *macho*, which meant that in addition to assuming responsibility for the welfare of their family, they had license to exert their sexual prowess with willing "bad" women. Women, on the other hand, were expected to be virgins at marriage, loving mothers, and the emotional center of family life. *Marianismo*, the good and virginal woman who only gives herself to her husband, was often counterposed with the *macho* male role.

By the 20th century, same-sex experiences throughout Latin America reflected these then-emerging traditions. Homosexuality, from the point of view of popular culture, became associated with *travesti*, that is, flamboyant men and cross-dressing women (McKee Irwin, 1998). Their same-sex partners—who lived within the expected social norms—often escaped the label. For instance, men who acted in manly ways, both sexually and socially, could participate in same-sex sexual encounters without being labeled "homosexual." With close friends, they could even brag about homosexual exploits (Lancaster, 1988). Often, such men married and raised children all the while maintaining discretion in their homosexual encounters. Those who could not or would not pass as *macho*, who were effeminate, took the passive or womanly role, were labeled homosexual or *travesti* (transvestite). Effeminate men could also operate within the family system, but it necessitated great discretion and often led to a conspiracy of silence about their sexuality (Carrier, 1989).

It should not surprise that the distinction between the active *macho* and the passive effeminate male could be blurred. Role switching often took place in the coming together of these supposed opposites. Murray (1990) found that on occasion, *macho* men could play the passive role without feeling that their masculinity was threatened. However, conflict over sexuality could also occur when a man who saw himself as *macho* took on the passive role. Zamora-Hernandez and Patterson (1996) conjecture that desire for other men, whether active or passive, had—as in non-Hispanic societies—at least some implications for one's sexual identity.

Curiously, given that single men and women were expected to live in their parents' home till they married, even middle- and upper-class homosexuals who could have afforded to live on their own, did not. Homosexual men and women often preferred to live at home as a way to avoid loneliness in societies that provided little alternative to family living.

Murray (1987) emphasizes that unmarried homosexuals strove very hard to maintain good family relations so as to avoid possible expulsion and loss of the security that family life gave. Given these norms, the notion of long-term relationships with same-sex partners was unlikely. As Murray notes (1990) male same-sex sex in Spanish-speaking nations was pushed "into the streets," into bathrooms, alleys, or parks. The possibility for forming long-term relationships was nearly impossible. Although these circumstances appear harsh, Zamora-Hernandez and Patterson (1996) argue that there were certain advantages to these traditions. Latin homosexual men and women were not cut off from family and society as are contemporary gay men and women living in relatively isolated ghettos in the United States. That many lesbians and gays prefer to live with their families is underscored in a study that found that some 80 percent of a sample of Mexican men who have sex with men either lived at home with family members or, if married, lived with their wives (Carrier, 1976).

Contemporary Sexuality.   Cultural norms and values change due to external influences and internal contradictions. Presently, we find that many Latino traditions are loosening. Latino lesbians and gays have been out and active in the United States since even before Stonewall. Since then, they have continued to be in the forefront in their communities (Roque-Ramirez, n.d.). In addition, the international lesbian and gay movement is having a pronounced and liberating impact. In no small part, these efforts at social action are taking hold because men and women attracted to members of their same sex recognize the intense homophobia in their countries and are being given a way to stop it. Thus, many of the terms used in the past—*de ambiente* and *entendido*—are decreasing in use as *homosexual, gay, and lesbiana* are becoming popular. Words like *orientacion sexual* (sexual orientation) and *minoria sexual* (sexual minority) are also becoming part of everyday Spanish, not just among Hispanic Americans but throughout the Spanish-speaking world. Additionally, the many homosexual organizations that now exist in the Spanish-speaking world are working to, among other things, eliminate from their societies the derogatory words used in the past to ridicule lesbians (*tortillera, marimacho,* and *culera*) and gays (*maricon*). Some of these same words, however, are being reclaimed as "affirming identities" by the more progressive elements in the movement (Torres & Pertusa, 2003, p. 6).

The past 10 years have seen a number of legal advances throughout Latin America and Spain. The Ecuadorian and Chilean Constitutions have been rewritten to decriminalize sex between any two consenting adults. Similar efforts to decriminalize homosexual conduct are being promoted in Mexico, Peru, Costa Rica, and Cuba. Panama has had a gay and lesbian political party, the Association of Panamanian Homosexuals, since 1998. Since 1994, some Mexican presidential candidates have reached out for the lesbian and gay vote. Gay and lesbian pride parades and film festivals have occurred throughout Latin American and Spain since the early 1990s, even in Bolivia, one of the least industrialized of Latin nations. Lesbian and gay–friendly resorts and bed and breakfast accommodations are easily found throughout Spanish America. In 2003, the city of Buenos Aires provided civil union same-sex persons with the right to adopt and raise children. In 2005, the Spanish parliament became the fourth nation to grant marriage equality. Lesbians and gays in Spain now have the right to marry, inherit, and adopt children (Guardian Unlimited, 2005). Even in Cuba, Berkowitz (2001) recounts the celebration of public gay "marriages" in a working-class district in Havana.

These advances should not mask the bitter struggles taking place across the Spanish-speaking world. Conservatives, often supported by the Catholic Church, are fighting back. In spite of the advances made, considerable discrimination still exists even in those countries that have an improved lesbian and gay legal climate. For instance, although laws of domestic violence now cover lesbian and gay couples in Puerto Rico, the gay rights movement is fighting an uphill battle. The commonwealth government voted against marriage equality and has continued to support anti-sodomy laws (Hay Brown, 2003). In spite of a large and increasingly out gay and lesbian population, however, the situation in Cuba continues to be difficult.

Social workers should not see Latino culture as unchanging and tradition bound. Although Latinos have enormous pride in their heritage, this does not mean that they are committed to preserving all aspects of their culture including the repression of same-sex desires. Acculturation and education are likely to be central in understanding Latino attitudes about same-sex sexual relations. Bonilla and Porter (1990) found that Latinos were generally more tolerant than African Americans and just as tolerant as Whites on the morality of homosexuality. Yet, support for civil rights for lesbians and gays was found largely among the more acculturated Latinos, those who have lived in the United States for many years. Similarly, in a survey of 92 self-identified U.S. Latina lesbians, acculturation was a factor in lesbian identity formation. Those with a more committed lesbian identity were significantly more likely to have a higher occupational status, a good education, and a good income. Also, the more exclusively lesbian they were on the Kinsey scale, the more committed they were to a lesbian identity (Alquijay, 1997).

Even as Latino culture changes, traditional elements of personal and sexual identity may persist and create emotional conflict. Involvement in family life is likely to persist as an important value. Although those born in the United States are likely to participate in the lesbian and gay community, there is little evidence that Latin Americans are creating the separate community life so common in the United States (Murray, 1987). Thus, social workers should be prepared to deal with family issues, working to create a more hospitable climate for same-sex–oriented single and coupled sons and daughters. Although this may prove difficult, Marsiglia (1998) notes that many Latino gays and lesbians find supportive families once they come out. Social workers should not assume a monolithically homophobic Latin community.

Latino Americans: Culturally Specific Practice Themes. *Immigration.* Immigration issues play a particularly significant role in the lives of gay and lesbian Latinos. Many reasons for immigration into the United States exist, including persecution in countries of origin. For example, 10,000 to 20,000 of the refugees in the Mariel boat exodus from Cuba were thought to be homosexuals seeking freedom from persecution (Arguelles & Rich, 1989). Central and South Americans were able to immigrate at will up until 1966 when immigration quotas for each country began. Many lesbian and gay Latinos entered as part of this migration even though there were policies that could have excluded them as inverts, deviates, criminals, and people who committed crimes of "moral turpitude" (Eskridge, 2003). By 1976, with the push of the lesbian and gay movement, the Immigration and Naturalization Service began to allow immigration by "practicing sexual deviate[s]" so long as they have not been convicted of "homosexual act[s]" (Eskridge, 2003). Today, in part because of suits by lesbian and gay Latinos (Luibheid, & Cantu, 2003), lesbians and gays can enter through our federal asylum laws (Eskridge, 2003).

Although some immigrating lesbians and gays experience a considerable sense of liberation, all must deal with the social, financial, and emotional losses that go hand in hand with immigration. Immigrants often see the United States as a sexual utopia, but this vision is often shattered by the homophobia and racism experienced by Latinos in the United States (Roque-Ramirez, n.d.). Likewise, even though Latino family life can be oppressive, we should realize that *familismo* is a core cultural value and that family also serves to sustain many lesbians and gays (Ramos, 1987; Taylor, 1991).

Although it is unclear whether Latino lesbian and gay organizations work directly to overcome homophobia in Latino families, it is clear that they work to build community among Latino lesbians, gays, bisexuals and transgender individuals. They also work to end discrimination in the Latino community through organizations like *Entre Hermanos* (2005) and *Llego* (2005).

HIV/AIDS. HIV/AIDS continues to be a major social problem for Latinos. Although only some 14 percent of the U.S. population, including Puerto Rico, they comprised 18 percent of all AIDS cases through 2002 (Center for Disease Control, 2002). By 2001, AIDS was the third leading cause of death for Latino men aged 35–44 and the fourth leading cause of death among Latina women in the same age group. Given the level of homophobia in the community in the United States, a high level of bisexuality exists among Latinos. As previously noted, furtive relations often prevail in same-sex relations involving Latino men who, in spite of maintaining a heterosexual lifestyle, also feel same-sex urges. Thus, it is not surprising that most Hispanic men are infected through sexual contact with other men. Most Hispanic women, on the other hand, are exposed to HIV through heterosexual contact often enough with their bisexual husbands or boyfriends. The situation may be getting worse because Hispanics account for 20 percent of the new AIDS diagnoses since 2001 even as they already account for 20 percent of all people living with AIDS in the United States.

Alcohol and Other Drugs. Given that bars are still a major source of refuge for lesbians and gays, social workers should be prepared to work on drug and alcohol abuse. Alcohol and drug use among gay men tends to follow the same pattern as other populations (Mayers-Sanchez et al., 1993). As they become acculturated, many immigrant men pick up the drinking patterns of American men, moving from more frequent use to normative restrictive use. (Mayers-Sanchez et al., 1993; Amaro et al., 1990) There is evidence that Latina lesbians use alcohol and drugs at a lower rate than do other women (Comas-Diaz & Greene, 1994). This, however, may be an unreliable result given the relative absence of studies with findings on Latina lesbians.

In a study of 35 Latina lesbians, Migdalia Reyes (1998) found that all 35 described themselves as alcoholics, and 20 described themselves as multiple drug users. She reports there is no one reason why Latina lesbians turn to alcohol and drugs. Some 16 of the women began using alcohol and drugs in high school as a result of peer pressure. Family dysfunction including domestic violence and alcoholic parents were also common explanations as were general cultural and neighborhood expectations. Twelve of the women acknowledged having been sexually abused. All 35 women reported experiencing family conflict around general expectations, suggesting that *marianismo* and lesbophobia are important contextual issues in understanding drug and alcohol use.

Public–private dichotomies. As discussed, Latinos have traditionally had to hide their same-sex desires from public and familial scrutiny. This public–private dichotomy causes considerable stress for Latino gays and lesbians. Hidalgo (1995) provides an example of the stress experienced in Latino social service agencies where heterosexuality is the norm. In these agencies, sexuality and sexual identity are often viewed as personal concerns that should be kept separate from the public act of being a staff member. This may work for heterosexuals who can take their sexuality for granted all the while marking their spaces with pictures of husbands, wives, and children. Hidalgo writes of the particular difficulties experienced by Latina lesbians, but the situation is a little different for Latino gay men. Negotiating membership under such circumstances is fraught with peril. To speak up may invite ostracism. To remain quiet is to lead a duplicitous life and, in the end, support heterosexist norms. All too often Latinas and Latinos remain quiet.

Ramos (1987) uses these same ideas in identifying the adjustments Latina lesbians living in the United States must make in negotiating membership across groups. Latinas simultaneously negotiate (1) their cultural roots and the dominant Anglo culture in which they now live and often work (both cultures share heterosexist, patriarchal norms); (2) their marginality, or sense of being "on the other side," in whatever social situation they are interacting in; and (3) their lesbian creativity that provides a unique standpoint and has helped them survive and achieve *contra viento y marea* (against all odds). Social workers can help reframe this public–private conflict as a source of strength, pride, and survival that helps to transcend oppression. As community and family reconcile competing cultural demands in embracing their gay and lesbian family members, community unity in fighting all types of oppression will be strengthened.

SOCIAL WORK PRACTICE WITH GAYS AND LESBIANS OF COLOR: UNIVERSAL CULTURAL COMPETENCE PRACTICE THEMES AND SKILLS

Culturally competent practice implies serving the needs of people in ways that are meaningful and appropriate to them (Pinderhughes, 1989). A key skill is the ability to take the role of others, that is, to see the world from the standpoint of one's clients, and from that position, to work with them and their communities to improve their lives and their social and economic conditions. The concept of cultural competence aids us in this endeavor by teaching us to locate our clients in historical and social space. Culturally competent workers tune into the risks, obstacles, barriers, and limited opportunities their clients endure in the here and now as a result of their group's history in American society. They are sensitive to ongoing issues of prejudice and discrimination, and they avoid working from negative stereotypes. Culturally competent social workers also recognize the strengths and resilience of their oppressed clients and corresponding communities. They understand that their values and worldview have been internalized through centuries of family and community socialization, and that these have enabled survival. Culturally competent social workers build from their clients' aspirations for a better life. In short, to be culturally competent is to accurately empathize with our clients by connecting the present with the past, the personal with the political, and the psychological with the social.

One dilemma in implementing cultural competence is that clients are rarely members of a single group. Even if they were, no group is marked by undifferentiated homogeneity. The concept of cultural competence, rather than simplifying practice, requires us to be sensitive across a complex landscape of social diversity. Diversity exists within diversity. Although clients may be of a particular ethnic or racial group, they can be different with respect to nationality, socioeconomic status, gender status, ability status, sexual orientation, and religious or spiritual preference. Increasingly, they are also of mixed racial and ethnic backgrounds and not infrequently of mixed sexual orientation (i.e., bisexual) or mixed gender (i.e., transgender). Furthermore, there is no such thing as a generic group member. Groups may be understood as a set of endless niches drawn together through simultaneous consensual and coercive processes. Within any one group, clients may be central or marginal, young or old, rich or poor, conservative or liberal, orthodox or progressive, and so on.

Being culturally competent with GALOCs, therefore, means recognizing that they span multiple social categorizes and are embedded in particular niches within them. This fact raises a number of tensions around identity for people of color who are also gay or lesbian. These tensions are exacerbated when class, gender, mixed racial background, and bisexuality are also included, but as stated earlier, that is beyond the scope of this chapter.

Culturally Competent Practice Theme #1: Racial and Sexual Identity Processes

The late 1950s through the 1970s were times of great turbulence and dynamic social change. Social movements began to coalesce, and contemporary identity politics was born. For gays and lesbians, declaring one's sexual identity as an "out of the norm" identity meant declaring separateness from the heterosexual dominant culture and a membership to a boundaried sexual minority grouping. Although much of this identity process involves internal awareness (e.g., realizing sexual affinities), it is the external, group-based sexual identity affiliation that shaped an "identity politic" and, ultimately, the creation of a social movement for gays and lesbians. Chan (1997) notes:

> Much as ethnic minority people of color defined themselves in terms of racial minorities in the 1960s and 1970s, homosexual men and women, by identifying and declaring a sexual minority status, chose to define themselves in a new category as a means of empowerment and group cohesion. To achieve this empowerment, both sexual minorities and racial minorities chose to accentuate, to draw attention to, aspects of their being that previously were viewed as negative and stigmatized (race or homosexuality), and to express pride, not shame at their minority status. (p. 242)

How one negotiates a stigmatized status, how much one internalizes colonizing and oppressive dominant group stereotypes, how much one internalizes positive attitudes about one's group, and how much one externalizes and resists these colonizing attitudes, all interact to form a unique and challenging process of identity attitude development among GALOCs.

There is evidence that a parallel process of racial and sexual orientation identity development exists for oppressed populations where individuals can move from internalized negative attitudes about self in relation to group to an integrated, positive self and group identity (Atkinson, Morten, & Sue, 1983; Helms, 1990; Walters, 1999). For example, the Urban American Indian Identity (UAII) model (Walters, 1995, 1999) consists of four domains (i.e., internalization, marginalization, externalization, and actualization) that "tap into a process of identity development from internalized oppression and self/group deprecation to a positive, integrated self and group identity" (p. 49). Like most racial and ethnic identity models, identity processes are highly contextualized, most likely nonlinear, and multidimensional. For example, the UAII incorporates political, ethnic, racial, cultural, and spiritual identity attitudes within each of the domains; moreover, the context of the person's social environment (e.g., city) and the historical relationship with the dominant society (dominant group environment and institutional responses) are all taken into consideration in forming the self and group identity attitude clusters.

Research on GALOC identity has been sparse and has been conducted primarily on small samples of African Americans (Hendin, 1969; Icard, 1986; Johnson, 1982; Loicano, 1989), Mexican Americans (Espin, 1987; Morales, 1989), Asian Americans (Chan, 1989; Wooden, Kawasaki, & Mayeda, 1983), and American Indians (Walters, 1997) or based on conceptual models on gays and lesbians of color as a group (Morales, 1989; Walters, 1999). Most GALOC identity researchers combine racial or ethnic identity models (e.g., Atkinson, Morten, & Sue, 1983; Parham & Helms, 1985; Phinney, 1990) with Cass's (1984) gay and lesbian identity model. Cass's model contains six stages and begins with the premise that an individual starts with an initial self-awareness of feelings and possibly behaviors associated with being defined as "gay" or "homosexual," and from this awareness, the individual progresses through stages from conflictual feelings to self-acceptance to pride to integration with other aspects of self. Chan (1997) notes that although the model is considered universally applicable, it "presupposes that there are favorable conditions that must be present to allow for the affiliation and identification described to occur" (p. 243). In some gay communities, a GALOC presence is either rendered invisible or highly marginalized, thereby making a positive association with a gay or lesbian identity highly difficult to achieve.

The GALOC identity research describes two orthogonal processes that occur for GALOCs—one in terms of racial identity and one in terms of the acquisition of a gay or lesbian identity. The gay identity models focus on "coming out" as a hallmark of identity acquisition and are self-focused on the realization of being gay or lesbian, whereas the racial identity models are focused on a "coming in" to the deepening understanding of racial community processes and the redefinition of Blackness or Indianness, for example, on identity formation. Morales (1989) proposed a five-state model of GALOC identity that consists of (1) denying conflicts in allegiances, (2) coming out as bisexual versus gay or lesbian, (3) experiencing conflicts in allegiance, (4) establishing priorities in allegiances, and (5) integrating identities. Walters (1999) proposed a GALOC identity matrix model where racial identity attitudes (R) and gay/lesbian identity attitudes (G) are assessed simultaneously to form a 2×2 matrix of potential identity attitude constellations, specifically: combined positive identity attitudes (G+ R+), mixed positive and negative identity attitudes (G+ R– or G– R+), and combined negative identity attitudes (G– R–). Walters (1999) states that the practitioner can utilize this matrix to identify areas of cultural strength and vulnerability in assessing GALOC identity attitudes and designing culturally relevant interventions (usually cognitive restructuring) to address conflicting allegiances associated with imbalance in identity structures.

Paradigm of the GALOC Stress Process. Life stressors can take a variety of forms for GALOCs, including, but not limited to, antigay or antiracial discrimination, hate crimes, historical trauma, daily hassles, and other manifestations of stressors that are externally generated (e.g., racism), which can then lead to the internalization of the stressors (e.g., internalized racism) by those who are members of the targeted group. Germain and Gitterman (1996) point out that life stressors can also take the form of anticipated loss and rejection by significant others and community. The bio-psycho-social-spiritual consequences of these life stressors can become expressed as guilt, helplessness, powerlessness, anxiety, ambivalence, or despair (Germain & Gitterman, 1996).

For GALOCs, the ability to reconcile both psychologically and socially the conflict in allegiances that arises as the result of being a member of (at minimum) two (e.g., gay men of color) or three (e.g., lesbian women of color) oppressed groups is a critical task for GALOCs (Chan, 1989; Greene, 1994; Icard, 1986; Loicano, 1989; Morales, 1989; Walters, 1999). GALOCs participate in multiple disparate social and cultural worlds, including their gay and lesbian community (which may or may not be integrated—it may be segregated and primarily White, or segregated and primarily persons of color, and not necessarily from the same racial or ethnic group), their "home" communities of color, and the dominant culture (i.e., heterosexuals and White Americans). Walking in multiple worlds, crossing boundaries, and at times transgressing normative cultural standards by crossing boundaries involves multiple social roles and expectations and multiple levels of stressors (Walters, 1999). GALOCs experience discrimination within their own culture (heterosexism as a gay man or lesbian); within the gay and lesbian community (racism as a racial minority); and within the dominant group (heterosexism and racism as both a gay male and as an ethnic person, or heterosexism and racism and sexism as an ethnic person, a woman, and a lesbian) (Walters, 1999). Morales (1989) notes that for GALOCs, difficulties in integrating conflicting allegiances can lead to feelings of anxiety, tension, depression, isolation, anger, and difficulties in integrating aspects of self.

In working with GALOC client populations, it is important to incorporate a heuristic model that examines how GALOC identity attitudes buffer the effects of life stressors (e.g., heterosexism, sexism, racism) on the experience and fueling of conflicts in allegiances. Identification of this process in practice will assist social workers in facilitating healthy coping responses to the various demands of their multiple communities.

Culturally Competent Practice Theme #2: Negotiating Conflicting Allegiances

Walters (1999) notes that by their very presence, GALOCs challenge preconceived notions of group membership and norms associated with racial and sexual identity group memberships. Thus, racial membership or sexual orientation membership is socially constructed to force blended individuals to "pick" the "side" they belong to, thereby enforcing an authenticity test and questions of group loyalty (Root, 1996; Walters, 1999). The insistence on singular racial or sexual orientation loyalties is predicated on what Audre Lorde (1984) calls the "homogeneity fallacy." The homogeneity fallacy is the intense press by group members toward within-group homogenization as a way to become unified, as *the* only way to group unity in the fight against racial or sexual oppression. Thus, group unity becomes confounded with group homogeneity (we must all think, look, and act alike to fight the oppressor). Lorde (1984) reminds us of our strength in embracing our diversity and our interlocking oppressions; otherwise, she cautions, we run the risk of marginalizing and oppressing our own community members, which only serves to benefit the oppressors. Lorde (1984) states that the homogeneity fallacy also allows group members who experience one form of oppression as *primary* (e.g., race while a heterosexual) to forget that other group members experience multiple oppressed statuses. The homogeneity fallacy can lead to a colonized mentality where group members assume that individuals who embrace their interlocking oppressions are automatically dangerous to the group's unity and survival and, therefore, cannot be tolerated or must be silenced in order to fight racial oppression. Additionally, as Walters (1999) notes, "[B]ecause of the continuous battle against genocide [and ethnocide], the disavowal to recognize and name the within-group oppressions such as sexism and heterosexism [and racism in the case of White-dominated gay and lesbian communities] becomes the status quo, and in fact, [these oppressions] are sometimes [mis]labeled as 'cultural norms.'"

Racism in the Gay and Lesbian Community. As highlighted by the experiences of the communities of color earlier in this chapter, the institutions (e.g., Human Rights Campaign), businesses (e.g., bars, social clubs), and popular culture (e.g., print media) tend to be White-male dominated (Garnets & Kimmel, 1991). Underrepresentation of GALOCs in White-led gay institutions and businesses as well as the unchecked power and privilege of the White gay and lesbian community have led to racial discrimination and negative social and economic outcomes for GALOCs. Examples of discrimination that GALOCs encounter include "ethnosexual stereotyping" where racism and sexism intersect by objectifying lesbians and gay men according to racial stereotypes (e.g., Asian men as geishas, Asian women as Lotus Blossom Baby or China Doll) (Chan, 1997). Other forms are more insidious, such as being rendered invisible and completely unacknowledged in social or institutional settings (Chan, 1989; Greene, 1993), which then leads to feelings of social isolation and disempowerment. More overt displays of discrimination include being asked to present multiple identifications for admittance to gay or lesbian bars (Icard, 1986) when White counterparts are only asked for one piece of identification.

Although GALOCs may experience a tremendous amount of support from the gay and lesbian community, especially in reference to providing a space for sexual and romantic expression, the supports that are provided are diminished when the stressors associated with racism are introduced. Thus, GALOCs do not have the strength of support in combating heterosexism that is otherwise available to White gays and lesbians. The primary conflict in allegiance that arises as the result of racism in the gay and lesbian community is whether it is worth jeopardizing ethnic community priorities and ties to connect with a community that is fraught with racism. In fact, White gay and lesbian activists are sometimes mystified when GALOCs do not want to fight for gay and lesbian rights (as they are defined by the current social institutions within the White-dominated gay and lesbian community). Moreover, although heterosexism is abundant in communities of color, the potential loss of support from one's ethnic community is quite often perceived as a price too dear to pay when GALOCs seek powerful refuge in the racial community to combat everyday racial oppression.

Heterosexism in Communities of Color. GALOCs also experience rejection, stigmatization, and heterosexism within their communities of color. It is important to note, however, that although the process parallels that of heterosexism for White gays and lesbians, it is not to be mistaken as the same process. Walters (1999) notes that the within-group prejudices must be understood as follows:

> [Within-group prejudices are] [m]anifestations of internalized, colonized processes within a system of White heterosexual institutionalized systems of power. . . . [T]he group that ultimately benefits from within-group oppressions is White heterosexual men and to some degree, heterosexual women. Thus, White gays and lesbians reinforce their power as members of White society by being racist, whereas heterosexuals of color do not benefit communities of color by being heterosexist. (p. 56)

Authenticity tests and tests of group loyalty are often drawn upon when GALOCs openly identify as gay or lesbian. Frequently, GALOCs will face questioning of their community commitments and priorities, and in some cases, they will be assumed to be abandoning the fight against racial oppression. Second, the expectations regarding gender roles in the survival of community and one's race also play a considerable role in creating stressors and conflicts in allegiances. For example, Wong (1992) noted that any deviation in gender roles for Chinese women would be interpreted as a sign of assimilation to "unnatural" power imbalances between men and women. Thus, any deviation from prescribed cultural gender roles is at times interpreted to be an attack on the group's survival. Lesbians of color in particular face considerable stress regarding childbearing and childrearing, as both roles are quite often linked to cultural continuity and survival (Greene, 1993). Heterosexism and sexism work simultaneously to reinforce gender roles and to establish unilateral definitions of group membership and group survival that leave little room for expressions outside of these "controlling images." Thus, the implicit assumption inherent in such imperatives is that being gay or lesbian is a "White thing" or a pathological response to White racism, an unnecessary added burden on an already oppressed status, and that being gay or lesbian is associated with rejection of childbearing or childrearing and an ultimate rejection of ethnic nationalism. For GALOCs, the internalization of such assumptions exacerbates anxiety and feelings of inauthenticity (e.g., not being a "real" Indian or African American).

Functions of Heterosexism, Sexism, and Racism. These controlling images by both racial and sexual minority groups are rooted in racism, sexism, and heterosexism. They function as a form of social control for unilateral oppressed-group conformity and ultimately constrain GALOCs from having the option to experience a full and complete self. More often than not, these images are used to keep the "other" or "nonnormative" self silenced in order to fight the "true" good fight. Conflicts in allegiances arise in response to these stressors. As a result, GALOCs who internalize these group imperatives may not feel like they belong to one group or the other, may feel marginalized within both groups, or may have difficulty in consolidating an identity as a GALOC.

Culturally Competent Practice Theme #3: Acculturative Stress and Value Conflicts

Although past research had focused on assimilationist framing of acculturative processes (e.g., replacing one's culture of origin with new cultural values, norms, behaviors), recent studies reveal that individuals can be both highly acculturated and ethnically identified simultaneously (Hutnik, 1985) and that individuals may orthogonally identify with many different cultures simultaneously (Oetting & Beauvais, 1991). The multidimensionality of acculturative and biculturative processes has only recently been investigated, as have enculturative processes (immersion into culture of origin practice or retraditionalization) (Zimmerman, Washienko, Walter, & Dyer, 1996). However, despite this multidimensionality, many GALOCs and communities of color bear considerable colonial pressure to relinquish ethnic cultural values and replace them with Euro-American cultural values, and, among GALOCs, with White gay and lesbian community values. This acculturative stress is manifest in the White gay and lesbian community as an imperative to "come out" to one's community and family as both a political statement and because it is equated with "psychological health" (Walters, 1999). However, as Walters notes, "coming out" may conflict with cultural values associated with collectivist cultures (e.g., when there is a strong value to not draw attention to one's self above the group collective—which might happen with traditional coming out disclosure models that are currently utilized in White gay and lesbian community settings). The key is to facilitate culturally relevant ways and situational ways to "come out" to self, others, family, and community that can buffer against internalizing heterosexist attitudes.

Another potential stressor is that acculturation levels vary not only within cultural groups but also within families (i.e., intergenerationally). Culturally competent practice with GALOCs should always include an assessment of the individual client's acculturation and enculturation level and corresponding traditional cultural values, as well as an assessment of the family's cultural values, including those of siblings, parents, and grandparents and among other kinship family networks and support networks. Terminology is particularly critical here—both for the GALOC client and his or her family. Reframing and translating behaviors, values, and gender roles can assist familial communication between GALOCs who self-disclose their sexual identity and family support systems. Moreover, practitioners should utilize traditional family healers and helpers in this communication and healing process to assist the GALOC client in achieving a positive and affirmative GALOC identity (Walters, 1999).

Acculturative stress might also affect affiliation and identification of GALOCs with other GALOCs. For example, Walters (1999) notes:

> If an assimilationist ideology is internalized within a particular cultural group and is rooted in heterocentric biases from the dominant society, then the probability for contacting other GALOCS from one's own culture is diminished . . . [and] there is increased chance of isolation from important GALOC cultural supports, within-group GALOC role models, and [identification of] GALOC survival strategies. (p. 67)

Negotiating, framing, and dealing with conflicts in allegiances that arise as a result of these acculturative stressors is a major task for the practitioner working with GALOCs and their families of origin. GALOCs could benefit from developing a bicultural competence repertoire (LaFromboise, 1988) that equips them with ways to successfully negotiate *between*-group conflicting allegiances (i.e., with White gay and lesbian communities) and *within*-group conflicting allegiances (i.e., different acculturation and enculturation levels among family, kin, and ethnic community). Walters (1999) notes: "GALOC bicultural competence would assist GALOCS in integrating positive aspects of both cultures (gay/lesbian and racial/cultural) without losing their own cultural values or internalizing heterosexist biases" (p. 68).

Culturally Competent Practice Theme #4: Immigration Issues

The reason for immigration to the United States may be a critical factor in understanding GALOC conflicts in allegiances and other related concerns. Circumstances under which immigration takes place or refugee flight occurs must be identified during the assessment phase with GALOC clients. Espin (1987) notes that the time and the reasons for immigrating to the United States are critical factors that shape how GALOCs perceive and experience competing community demands. For example, if the reason for immigration to the United States was to find a safe haven for same-sex sexual expression and romantic relationships, perceptions of the immigration experience and expectations might be quite different than for those who immigrated to the United States because they were expulsed from their country due to their sexual orientation (as was seen in the Cuban boat lift in the 1980s). Likewise, immigrating to the United States might be irrespective of sexual orientation issues and instead be linked to economic opportunities or flight from war-torn regions. Either way, immigration processes involve significant losses—loss of community and family of origin ties and loss of land and place. Espin notes that if the immigration is recent, the GALOC might lose significant economic support from his or her family of origin and might become financially dependent on extended family in the United States or other ethnic community members. This interdependence on ethnic community financial and emotional supports during immigration transitions may place the GALOC individual in a difficult position regarding whether to disclose his or her sexual orientation to other family members and whether to connect with a gay or lesbian community.

SOCIAL WORK PRACTICE SKILLS

Empowerment-Oriented Reframing: Micro Practice

Empowerment-oriented reframing is a social work practice skill (Walters, 1999) in which stressors associated with multiply situated identities are historically contextualized and reframed by the social work practitioner as empowering experiences that evolve out of a unique vantage point associated with multiple statuses. This unique vantage point is reframed as a site of strength and resistance rather than as a site of isolation and assimilation. Thus, conflicting allegiances between and within these multiple worlds can be reframed as an opportunity to form a unique vantage point from which stressors can be contextualized, analyzed, and reframed.

The task of the social work practitioner is to assist GALOCs in cognitively reframing marginalizing experiences as "centering" experiences from which the GALOCs can reassess group survival strategies and their unintentional and intentional impingements on their own bio-psycho-social-spiritual-cultural functioning. Specifically, the "border" status of the GALOC experience allows for identification of cognitive interventions that assist GALOC clients in reframing, negotiating, straddling, and ultimately embracing multiple social realities and identities as a source of strength, pride, and empowerment.

Another component of empowerment-oriented reframing entails assisting GALOC clients in developing a border consciousness. Developing a border consciousness is based on the work of Gloria Anzaldua, who suggests that multiple-status individuals are a bridge for different communities. Moreover, this border status can be nurtured by having

GALOCs' feet planted solidly in gay and ethnic as well as ethnic gay communities simultaneously. This border positionality then allows the GALOC to create a border consciousness that buffers against conflicting allegiances and facilitates incorporation of identity affiliations into an integrated GALOC identity (Anzaldua, 1987; Root, 1996; Walters, 1999). Practitioners conversant in empowerment-oriented reframing and developing a border consciousness focus on identifying split-off aspects of self (e.g., by racial identity or gay identity as seen in the GALOC identity matrix model) in context to specific situations and then work toward assisting the client in naming the split-off parts of self, identifying the conflicts in allegiances that are internalized and contribute to this splitting-off of self, and then reframing such splitting as opportunities for sites of resistance to the racism, sexism, and heterosexism that are internalized and embodied in community structures and imperatives (Walters, 1999). Reframing marginalized experiences of self by creating a border consciousness that supports this unique vantage point from which critical analyses of group identity processes and survival strategies are developed will help GALOCs to develop healthy resistance to internalizing oppressions associated with each status.

Other opportunities to employ empowerment-oriented reframing include challenging GALOC notions that one is "stuck" or "caught" between two worlds or communities. Social work practitioners can reframe this positionality not as a problem but rather as an opportunity to have a unique vantage point from which to analyze conflicting allegiances, assumptions of community legitimacy, and within-group authenticity and group loyalty tests. In fact, maintaining and negotiating both insider and outsider positions allows GALOCs to have a positive learning experience and to achieve new insights that can then inform new strategies for strengthening community ties and integrating better their multiply situated identities.

Empowerment-oriented reframing regarding conflicting allegiances in response to group survival processes embedded in oppressive structures calls for the development of cognitive flexibility on the part of the social work practitioner as well as the GALOC client. Cognitive flexibility is the ability to demonstrate emotional, attitudinal, and behavioral flexibility and to tolerate and manage increasing levels of complexity and differentiation regarding intersecting statuses, identity dimensions, and historical processes that influence individual and group behavioral processes (e.g., the ability to integrate racial and sexual orientation categories as salient and noncompetitive at the same time). Cognitive flexibility is a culturally competent practice skill that will assist both social worker and client in contextualizing the fluidity of boundaries between and within communities. Moreover, as Kich (1996) points out, "a person's degree of emotional/cognitive/social flexibility may be understood as a developmental consequence of a healthy adaptation to life" (p. 275).

Empowerment-oriented reframing and associated interventions also include identifying culturally relevant ways in which GALOC clients might "come out" to kin and community networks that do not require a splitting off of gay or lesbian aspects of self (Walters, 1999). Identifying traditional roles and stories associated with gay or lesbian statuses for the client's particular cultural affiliation might facilitate growth in cultural pride and competency as well as contextualize their cognitive constructions of gay or lesbian identities within cultural historical perspectives.

Finally, empowerment-oriented practice skills include identifying gay/lesbian and ethnic/cultural community resiliencies, survival strategies, and individual, familial, and communal strengths. Incorporating a strengths-based approach in both assessment and intervention selection will help practitioners identify reframing opportunities for particular stressors and identify positive coping strategies for further strengthening. Too often, a deficit practice model focusing on negative mental health processes has dominated social work practice approaches. Empowerment-oriented practice skills counter the deficit model approach by focusing on the GALOC's resilience and positive coping. Focusing on resilience assists GALOCs in dealing with colonial and other oppressive processes associated with disparaged statuses (Walters, 1999). Finally, identification of client strengths reinforces client competencies and a positive sense of an integrated GALOC self (Walters, 1997).

Overall, social work practitioners need to tailor their interventions to the developmental needs of the GALOC client. Practitioners should be aware of the interaction between intrapsychic problems and external, systemic problems such as heterosexism and racism that affects individual GALOC functioning as well as community functioning (Walters, 1999). Moreover, historical and current traumas associated with multiply oppressed statuses should be incorporated into any assessment and intervention plan. Ultimately, practitioner effectiveness will depend on the practitioner's ability to differentiate among these systemic and individual-level factors. Walters notes:

> [Becoming competent regarding] [t]he multidimensionality of GALOC experience and the corresponding factors that contribute to identity development; maintenance of within-group heterosexism, racism and sexism; and the resulting conflicts in allegiances assists practitioners and program planners in developing culturally relevant treatment strategies and agency programs. (p. 71)

Meso/Macro Practice and Social Justice

Dispelling stereotypes and providing access to culturally relevant GALOC role models are key to familial and community-level interventions (Walters, 1999). Meso- and macro-level interventions include panel presentations with GALOC role models who should be culturally matched with the community in which the panel is presented. Additionally, GALOC panels in communities of color will help to dispel within-group stereotypes and heterosexist attitudes as well as increase GALOC visibility and decrease denial of GALOC existence within such communities. Moreover, these panels can include heterosexual allies of color, in particular, elders who carry the stories of GALOC traditions or other forms of storytelling that include positive historical GALOC role models in relation to the community. Likewise, panels in White-dominated gay and lesbian communities can be developed to specifically address GALOC issues such as invisibility and racism in gay and lesbian communities; they should also include White gay and lesbian allies who can model antiracist attitudes and behaviors.

Community-level interventions should include mild confrontation of racist and heterosexist community processes and norms. For example, panel discussions and community outreach can help to educate communities regarding the homogeneity fallacy and how when one group intimidates others within their own group, their marginalizing power can ultimately undermine group unity in fighting external oppressive structures. Additionally, community relational competence can be developed to deepen the "community relational space" so that *all* people from within that community can express themselves and so that the community can have a safe space for conflicts to emerge, community tensions to be discussed, and creative community resolutions to be achieved (Kich, 1996).

SUMMARY

Culturally competent social work practice with gays and lesbians of color includes examination of multiple social and private identities, identification of conflicts in allegiances, appraisal of historical and contemporary within- and between-group discriminatory processes and oppressive incidents, and refinement of social work practice skills such as empowerment-oriented reframing and cognitive flexibility. Cultural competence must include a commitment to social justice on behalf of and with GALOC communities and, ultimately, a commitment to dismantling the within- and between-group oppressive hierarchies that keep potential allies from standing in solidarity with GALOC communities. Our social justice orientation in social work practice reminds us that if oppression is allowed to operate in one sphere—whether racial, economic, or gender, to name just a few—then no one is truly free. Culturally competent social work practice embraces a libratory pedagogy that values our differences and embraces the struggle for social and economic justice for all. Audre Lorde (1984) summed up the tasks well:

> The true focus of revolutionary change is never merely the oppressive situations that we seek to escape, but that piece of the oppressor that is planted deep within each of us, and that knows only the oppressors' tactics, the oppressors' relationships. Change means growth, and growth can be painful. But we sharpen self-definition by exposing the self in work and struggles together with those whom we define as different from ourselves, although sharing the same goals. For Black and White, old and young, lesbian and heterosexual women alike, this can mean new paths to survival. (p. 123)

TOOLS FOR STUDENT LEARNING 14.1

Case Examples

You can use the following case examples to facilitate class discussions, role-plays, or for role-plays in dyads or triads or other small breakout groups. In discussing the case examples, be sure to address the following questions:

1. What knowledge do you currently have about this ethnic population? The gay and lesbian community? The ethnic gay and lesbian community particular to this client's ethnic group? What knowledge will you have to seek in order to provide culturally competent services? What individuals, groups, and local and national organizations might you contact and identify as a resource for this client?

2. How did you personally react to this client? Discuss the cultural values, worldviews, and assumptions you currently hold in relation to this population. Discuss how your own multiple status affiliations—oppressed and privileged (e.g., by gender,

race, sexual orientation, etc.)—influence your assessment of this client's presenting concerns. Discuss what you need to challenge yourself on or examine further in order to provide culturally competent services to this client and client population.

3. Are this client's self and group racial identity attitudes positive or negative? Are this client's self and group gay identity attitudes positive or negative? Identify the client's identity matrix: Gay+ Race+, Gay– Race+, or Gay+ Race–. Does the client have high or low levels of internalized racism, heterosexism, sexism? What developmental processes might the client be dealing with as well?

4. What culturally competent skills are necessary for the worker to have in providing services to this client? What are the conflicts in allegiances for this client? How might you use empowerment-oriented reframing for this particular client? What types of meso- or macro-level interventions would benefit this client and client population?

Case #1: Eloise

Eloise has referred herself to you for counseling at a local counseling center. She is a Sansei (third-generation) Japanese woman in her early 20s. Her grandparents were interned at the Manzanar Japanese Internment Camp in the mountains of California during World War II. Eloise's mother was born at the camp. Family members have always been very proud of being Americans and have downplayed their Japanese heritage. An uncle who served with a famous combat team against the Japanese is still viewed as a family hero. Recently, Eloise became aware of the humiliation and economic losses her grandparents suffered during and following internment. Eloise is becoming increasingly angry toward White people and at the same time feels very confused about why her grandparents do not complain about what happened to them.

Recently at college, Eloise met a friend with whom she has grown very close. She is quite concerned because she feels that she has fallen in love with her and is afraid to discuss it with anyone. Her "friend" is a White woman. Eloise states that she feels ambivalence over her friend being White, especially because her friend hangs out with other White lesbians (with whom Eloise does not identify). Eloise states that she does not think she is "that way" and, for her, she just loves the person, not the gender. However, last week, her mother "walked in on her" while she and her friend were kissing. Her mother has refused to talk with her since this incident. Since then, her cousin, the daughter of her mother's sister, has been spreading rumors to their mutual Asian friends on campus that she has that "White problem, you know, being gay." Eloise reports feeling isolated from her Asian support system.

Case #2: Mark and Dewayne

Mark is a 30-year-old White male, and Dewayne is a 28-year-old African American male. Both are coming to see you for help with their communication problems in their relationship. Mark identifies as "out and proud" about his homosexuality. He states that he has been out since he was 19 and very active in gay rights activities since his early 20s. He met Dewayne a little over a year ago at a coffee shop in the local gay community, and he states that they "clicked" right away. They have begun to date seriously in the last few months, but tensions have increased since Dewayne has met all Mark's friends (who are mostly affluent, White men) and his immediate family. Mark reports that he has not met any of Dewayne's friends or his family.

Mark states that he is frustrated that Dewayne is not out at the workplace or with his family. Frequently, Dewayne goes out with his "straight" friends and does not invite Mark. Mark expresses sadness and frustration that Dewayne is ashamed of him. Mark has been encouraging Dewayne to get over his internalized homophobia and come out—finally. Mark has sought support from his White gay male friends, but he is appalled at their comments about his relationship with Dewayne. Mark contextualizes their comments as racist, and he is beginning to question the value of these friendships. Dewayne states that he really cares about Mark but is tired of hanging out with Mark's White friends. Dewayne feels that Mark is pressuring him to come out, and he is not sure he is ready to come out to his family or his straight friends. He does not want to lose Mark, but he does not want to lose his family either. He sometimes feels that Mark "just doesn't get it—especially around the race issue . . . I have way more to lose than he does . . . it's easy for him to come out."

Case #3: Ned

You are interning at a local university counseling center. Ned has been referred to you for academic probation as well as his problems at the dorm. Ned is a 19-year-old male of European and American Indian descent. He was born and raised in Los Angeles and, until this year, has had little to no contact with any Native people other than his family. During the end of the previous school year, which was Ned's freshman year, his drinking dramatically increased, usually with binges on the weekends. He also got into fistfights with others in his dorm. Ned reports that nobody understands him. He states that he used to be happy that he could "pass" as non-Indian because he felt like most of his relatives were "good for nothing." When Ned came on campus last fall, however, he met a Native male and started to hang out at the Native student center with this new buddy. His new Native friend is openly gay, which makes Ned really uncomfortable, especially when he is around other Native men.

Moreover, in the last two months, Ned has begun with this male friend a sexual and romantic relationship, the first one he has ever had. Ned reports feeling confused about his sexual orientation and states he cannot stand the thought of being a "queer." Ned also said that he worries he will not be accepted in the Native community if people there were to find out. His most recent fights have been with White males in the presence of his heterosexual Native male friends. His drinking and fighting have landed him on probation at the university, and he is worried about flunking out of school.

Case #4: Cece

Cece is a 30-year-old, second-generation Cuban woman whose family lives in Miami; she lives on the West Coast. Cece has been "out" in the lesbian community since she was 21 years old and has recently been making friends with other Latina lesbians. Additionally, Cece is in a committed relationship of two years with another Latina woman, Irena, and is employed as an editor for a large publishing company. Cece is upwardly mobile and feels good about her Cuban identity and her bourgeoning connections to a Latina lesbian community.

In the last two months, however, Cece's maternal grandmother and grandfather moved from Miami to her neighborhood. Cece views this as both a blessing and a strain. She visits her grandmother and takes her shopping weekly. Because her grandmother has become acquainted with the local Cuban community, she worries that her grandmother will find out about her sexual orientation from someone else in the community, especially because she dated a well-known lesbian Cuban activist for a while. Moreover, whenever Cece visits with her grandmother, her grandmother constantly asks her about boyfriends, dating, and marriage. In the last week, Cece turned 30, and her grandmother carried on about how old she is getting and how she will "miss the bus" in getting a man. Cece lost her temper with her grandmother and told her she will never have a man and that the "bus" is broken. Cece felt horrible about the outburst, and her grandmother clearly did not understand Cece's reaction.

Cece is not "out" to her family and wants to come out at some point but is unsure when and where. Cece reports that she and her mother are quite close, talking nightly on the phone, yet her mother stopped asking about "boyfriends" about two years ago, and since then, Cece has not mentioned a word to her mother about "dating" anyone. Cece reports she could have continued with never discussing her dating life had her grandmother not moved into town.

Finally, Cece and Irena have been trying to have a baby together. Cece was going through artificial insemination procedures at a local clinic (using frozen sperm from an unknown donor). In the last week, she went to the doctor and found out that she is pregnant. She and Irena are thrilled but very anxious about their families' reactions. Cece says she sought help to figure out "what to do."

PART FOUR

Reflections on Culturally Competent Practice

Part Four includes summary reflections on culturally competent practice that cover the major components of cultural competence; the social context of diversity, racism, sexism, and homophobia; the strivings for social and economic justice; cultural and ethnic diverse groups in need; and reflections that we hope will make you a better person, a more perceptive student, and an effective social worker.

At the November 2005 Cultural Competence and Mental Health Summit XIII in Fresno, California, the theme of the conference was Building Bridges to Recovery and Wellness in our Communities. Since 1992, mental health professionals in California have gathered annually to discuss a wide array of topics ranging from Creating Culturally Blended Communities to Overcoming Health Disparities through Cultural Competency and to focus on such learning vehicles as Hmong Narratives: Narrative as Identity, Treatment, and Renewal. In a workshop that I led called Culturally Competent Intervention Strategies, I asked the question: Where is cultural competence going? Various answers were given but one woman observed: "It's not so much cultural competence that we are concerned about. Rather, it is about delivering culturally effective services to our clients." Perhaps this book will also help you to reflect on the future of cultural competence. What is beyond this present theme and the next horizon in working with cultural and ethnic peoples?

CHAPTER FIFTEEN

Some Reflections on Culturally Competent Practice

DOMAN LUM

This book has taken you on a journey that started with an introduction to cultural competence. We began by giving you a thorough understanding of this concept, particularly how it is defined and implemented in competencies and measurements. We are pleased that the National Association of Social Workers has *Standards for Cultural Competence in Social Work Practice* and that the Council on Social Work Education has specific curriculum standards on diversity, populations-at-risk, and social and economic justice. These criteria have been the guideposts for this text.

Culturally competent practice is emerging as an integral part of social work practice and education. We have sought to present a culturally competent practice model that addresses a number of areas: social context, diverse groups, and social and economic justice. Social context explored the theme of diversity as a person-centered context and the themes of racism, sexism, homophobia, ageism, discrimination, and oppression as environment-centered contexts. Diverse groups focused on First Nations Peoples, African Americans, Latino Americans, Asian Americans, women of color, and gay and lesbian people of color. These groups were ably described by social work education and practice contributors.

The purpose of this closing chapter is to highlight the major themes of this book and to offer some reflections on the present state of cultural competence.

THE MEANING OF CULTURAL COMPETENCE

Cultural competence and *cultural competencies* are defined in specific ways to establish a division of labor between the terms. *Cultural competence* is the subject area that relates to the cultural awareness of the worker and the client and their mutual backgrounds; knowledge acquisition about historical oppression and related theories of understanding the multiple dimensions of the human person; skill development to deal effectively with the needs of the culturally diverse client; and inductive learning, which heuristically processes new information about emerging new populations. *Cultural competencies* involve turning culturally competent areas and concepts into specific and measurable statements. These areas have been addressed in detail to help you with your interpersonal and academic understanding of self, others, and the information needed to become culturally competent. Along the way, we have developed a new section on the ethics of cultural competence.

We hope that you are now more aware of your own sense of culture and identity and that you will be more effective with culturally diverse groups and individuals. We trust that your social work educational experience will contribute to your knowledge about diverse people and help you to develop skills for working with clients in a helping relationship. Finally, we want you to have a methodology of inquiry and investigation so that you can continuously learn and uncover culturally competent knowledge and skills with new clients who will be a part of the American scene.

SOCIAL CONTEXT

Contextual social work practice is concerned with the person and the environmental or situational setting. We have sought to involve you in exploring diversity by introducing related concepts and asking you to apply them to your diverse background. It is hoped that you have gained a new respect for your diversity and the diversity of others and will make this theme a part of your knowledge about a client. You also may have noticed that we tried to offer answers in our discussion of racism, sexism, homophobia, ageism, discrimination, and oppression. We agree that these "isms" will always be with us, but we hope that you now have some coping tools for dealing with them.

The social context chapter was enlivened by the 2000 U.S. Census, which reported on ethnic population trends and growth and on 63 ethnic combination identities of people. The doubling of the number of ethnic and diverse people over a 20-year period is certainly the contextual background for the richness of diversity as well as the problems we have of getting along with each other. Perhaps the tragedies of September 11, 2001, brought us together in a new and transcendent way. They certainly gave us pause to understand the present social context for Americans and all peoples of the world.

GOAL STRIVING

Social and economic justice is the goal striving for the discipline and profession of social work. Social justice governs how social institutions deal fairly or justly with the social needs of people as far as opening access to what is good for individuals and groups. Economic justice encompasses moral principles of how to design economic institutions so that a person can earn a living, enter into social and economic contracts, and exchange goods and services in order to produce an independent material foundation for economic sustenance.

In her chapter in this text on social and economic justice, Van Soest skillfully connects cultural competence to social and economic justice when she argues that the goal of cultural competence is to transform oppressive and unjust systems into nonoppressive and just alternatives. She is thorough in her understanding of the distributive, legal, and commutative types of social justice, and she discusses the ideal social contract versus nonideal racial and gender contracts. The latter explain how and why social injustices exist along race and gender lines. Van Soest also connects social justice and oppression in terms of moral exclusion and balances these themes with a global perspective on human rights and oppression. Using material from the United Nations as her basis, she makes a strong case for social workers becoming involved in this arena through our use of an empowerment process, our sharing of experiences and reactions to injustice and oppression, and our use of positive energy.

THE CULTURAL COMPETENCE FRAMEWORK

The cultural competence framework has been the point of reference for shaping culturally competent themes into a model. The social work cultural competence framework draws on the contributions of the Association for Multicultural Counseling and Development (AMCD) (Sue, Arredondo, & McDavis, 1992). Culturally competent worker characteristics include the following: an awareness of personal assumptions about human behavior, values, biases, preconceived notions, and personal limitations; understanding of the culturally different client without negative judgments; and development and practice of appropriate, relevant, and sensitive intervention strategies and skills in working with culturally different clients. When I wrote this text, I knew that a framework was essential for social workers to understand how cultural competence fitted together.

The social work cultural competence model is for both undergraduate and graduate social work students. It addresses generalist and advanced levels in the areas of cultural awareness, knowledge acquisition, skill development, and inductive learning. The generalist practice level emphasizes beginning professional relationships, knowledge, values, skills, and process stages. The advanced practice level covers breadth and depth of knowledge and skills and advanced content areas. This framework serves as a guide for developing a social work curriculum on cultural competence. The essential elements of the framework are reviewed in the following pages.

Cultural Awareness

The first component of the framework is cultural awareness, which is the gatekeeper of the model. The social worker cannot be effective with diverse clients unless the worker grapples with his or her self-awareness about cultural diversity and his or her awareness of others. This self-awareness arises from past impressions, personal experiences, learned beliefs, stereotypes, and factual realities that are a part of our past. It is very difficult to develop a consciousness about one's own culture, ethnicity, and racism. Moreover, these areas have a strong impact on the professional social worker's attitudes, perceptions, and behavior toward clients in general, and toward the culturally different client in particular.

Achieving cultural awareness is a difficult and time-consuming task. It starts with the social worker's awareness of his or her life experiences as a person related to a culture. Family heritage, family and community events, beliefs, and practices serve as a baseline for an understanding of one's own culture. Next, the worker explores his or her range of contacts with individuals, families, and groups of other cultures and ethnicities to determine his or her perceptions and impressions of various cultural groups. Of particular concern are positive and negative experiences with culturally and ethnically diverse people and events. Often these experiences contribute to the worker's beliefs, feelings, and behaviors and feed into racism, prejudice, and discrimination. The worker must become aware of his or her own racism, prejudice, and discrimination. Racism is emphasized here because of its underlying dynamic in the social history of the United States. We respectfully acknowledge the related issues of sexism, homophobia, ageism, classism, and other -isms that plague our moral fabric. Uncovering, discovering, and dealing with these dynamics is painful, but the worker becomes a more effective helper as a result.

Knowledge Acquisition

Knowledge encompasses a range of information, facts, principles, and social work practice concepts. Knowledge acquisition influences the refinement of theory into a series of systematically arranged principles and categories.

Demographic knowledge provides a baseline of statistical data and alludes to client and problem profiles. Cultural/ethnic demographics report the rapid and steady growth of ethnic/racial populations and the precipitating causes of immigration and birthrate. Critical thinking develops theory and problem analysis and assessment, and applies several principles to culturally diverse practice models. Critical thinking as a part of knowledge building and development is an important tool for social work education.

The history of oppression of African, Latino, and Asian Americans, First Nations Peoples, women of color, and gays and lesbians of color is related to economic and social exploitation; removal from land and/or restriction to geographic ghettos; social and geographic segregation and barriers to equal opportunities; the struggle for civil and human rights; and poverty, family fragmentation, and social dysfunction. Historical knowledge provides the student with a necessary background about what has already happened and helps the student to anticipate better results in the present and future.

Knowledge about cultural values is rooted in ethnic, religious, and generational beliefs, traditions, and practices. A respect for cultural values helps the social worker to better understand the lives and actions of multicultural clients. Among the range of culturally diverse values are family, respect, harmony, spirituality, and cooperation. Values reflect core cultural beliefs, practices, and behaviors that come from ethnic traditions. Culturally competent social workers must understand and respect these cultural values, which are essential to the well-being of people of color.

We have introduced you to a number of emerging theories that we hope you will incorporate into your practice. Social constructionism is an inductive indigenous approach focusing on cultural story or narratives. Identity development looks at the various stages of an individual, family, group, and/or community as we grow and interact with cultural and ethnic issues. Finally, we have included a summary of culturally competent practice that illustrates how social work educators and practitioners are seriously engaged in theory discussion about this concept.

Skill Development

Skill development refers to the acquisition of a helping repertoire that can readily be used at the professional discretion of the worker. Skill is the practical application of cultural awareness and knowledge at the actual helping interface between the social worker and the multicultural client. Whether the worker has a set of culturally sensitive and responsive skills determines whether the worker can be regarded as culturally competent.

We like the Bernard model, which clusters skills groupings. Bernard (1979) identifies three types of skills in the helping relationship: process skills, conceptualization skills, and personalization skills. Process skills refer to therapeutic techniques and strategy; conceptualization skills include deliberate thinking and case analysis abilities; and personalization skills relate to the learning, the observable and subtle behaviors, and the personal growth of the worker.

Contact, problem identification, assessment, intervention, and termination are the five stages (Lum, 2004) that have been identified with the process, conceptualization, and personalization skills they each involve. Contact process skills center on understanding the ethnic community, relationship protocols, professional self-disclosure, and communication style (Lum, 2004). Contact conceptualization skills focus on the words, thoughts, and feelings of the client from an ethnographic point of view. Contact personalization skills involve the subjective feelings and reactions of the worker in the initial sessions.

Problem identification process skills are problem area disclosure, problem orientation perspective, and racial/ethnic theme analysis (Lum, 2004). Problem identification conceptualization skills involve Green's (1999) four principles: the client's definition and understanding of an experience as a problem, the client's semantic evaluation of a problem, indigenous strategies of problem intervention, and culturally based problem resolution. These procedural steps have been helpful in conceptualizing how to lead a client through a problem-solving process. Problem identification personalization skills focus on the worker's own reactions to the problem.

Assessment process skills include psychosocial perspective analysis (assessing socioenvironmental impacts and the psychoindividual reactions), assessment of cultural strengths, and the inclusion of cultural and spiritual assessment (Lum, 2004). Assessment conceptualization skills focus on cultural/ethnic group strengths, use of indigenous sources of help, and a supportive learning approach to assessing clients. Assessment personalization skills evaluate the positive potential of the client, which mobilizes positive resources to support change intervention strategies.

Intervention process skills implement goal setting and agreement, the selection of culturally diverse intervention strategies, and micro/meso/macro levels of intervention (Lum, 2004). We have focused on the empowerment intervention approach. Intervention conceptualization skills involve careful selection of intervention components based on unique cultural factors related to the client, the problem, and the social/cultural environment. Particular micro, meso, and macro dimensions were covered, along with applications to three ethnically diverse groups. The culturally competent worker crafts with the client a responsive and meaningful intervention plan. Intervention personalization skills explore the worker's concerns about client change, client decision making, and the definition of a change procedure.

Termination is a critical transition time for the client. Termination process skills involve destination, or a connection to a support network; recital, or a retrospective analysis of the problem situation; and completion, or goal attainment/outcomes appraisal (Lum, 2004). Termination conceptualization skills entail a follow-up plan and the study of premature and successful terminations. Termination personalization skills help the worker to use short-term treatment with reachable, concrete, and practical goals. The worker relies on referral to appropriate social service resources, indigenous community agencies, and the ethnic church and community.

We have also discussed the importance of the skill of designing service delivery structures of programs, facilities, staff, funding, and administration to serve the needs of the client population in a geographic area. Social service delivery systems are changing as populations in the United States become diversified due to immigration and birthrates. Service delivery will continue to change as series of events or new policies alter program emphases (Iglehart & Becerra, 2000).

Lum (2004) has written about the characteristics of multicultural service delivery: location and nature of services, staffing, community outreach programs, agency setting, and service linkage. Iglehart and Becerra (2000) identified internal and external factors of agency change and service delivery related to funding, external pressure groups, agency and worker leadership, agency ideology and technology, and client inputs. These aspects of service delivery shape agency linkage or interorganizational relations, especially program design and implementation. The ethnic social service agency is the link between mainstream service organizations and ethnic communities and is the key mediator in multicultural service delivery.

Research on cultural skill development uncovers new data on how to work effectively with multicultural clients. For example, the worker–client interpersonal relationship is an essential part of the dynamic process of change. Bordin (1979) explains the importance of initial bonding between the worker and the client. The clinical relationship has developed around the concept of the therapeutic alliance (Frank & Gunderson, 1990) or the working alliance (Horvath & Greenberg, 1994), which has a direct effect on positive outcome (Henggeler et al., 1994). This area of research is an example of how social class, race and ethnicity, and cross-cultural factors add a multicultural dimension to skill development.

Inductive Learning

Inductive learning deals with the question of how a social work professional continues to evaluate his or her multicultural practice and carries out the learning process of exploring new information about this field after graduation. Dean (1994) suggests the importance of reflecting on case studies and conducting qualitative analysis in informal ways with supervisors and staff. Inductive learning is a lifelong process of continuous discovery about the changing nature of multicultural families and communities.

The inductive learning approach has some similarities to participatory action research, which uses reflection, group planning, action, and observation in a group setting. Inductive learning assembles particular facts or individual cases about a subject and draws general conclusions based on findings. The social work student learns about inductive and deductive reasoning in the social work foundation research class. Inductive learning becomes a linkage between what we know in the present and what we may discover in the future about cultural diversity. Social work practitioners (graduates of social work programs) gain new knowledge and skills as they use an open-ended inductive process to uncover new data about multicultural clients.

Inductive social research is an important tool to teach students because it shapes openended questions and allows the data to tell us about clients. One gathers observations and information from a range of cases. Lang (1994, p. 275) talks about the importance of asking, "What do I know from this processing?" and "Therefore, what should I do?"

These questions capture the essence of inductive data gathering and processing, which lead to abstracting or generalizing and, later, conceptualization. This critical mind-set should be taught to social work students in practice-oriented research and research-oriented practice so they will always ask, "What does the data tell us?" As social work students graduate and become professional practitioners, it is incumbent on them to establish a research-oriented line of inquiry that can be applied throughout their social work careers.

A relationship exists between inductive learning and qualitative inductive research. Lang (1994) argues for the needed integration of the data processing of qualitative research and social work practice in order to advance the practitioner as knowledge builder. Her model involves data gathering, data processing and data transformation, and integration of qualitative research and social work practice. Data-gathering strategies consist of firsthand observation and writing down those observations in process-recording descriptions of important client–worker verbal and nonverbal interactions. Data processing consists of abstracting features and characteristics that are primary in the data into categories that can be linked. Data transformation takes these categories and translates them into a framework, model, or paradigm. The product is placed in the context of relevant existing theories about a subject. The generation of new knowledge and skills creates implications for cultural competence.

The integration of qualitative research and social work practice stems from a three-way partnership between social work educators, practitioners, and students. Social work educators are familiar with social work practice literature, course material, and research tools. They are able to conceptualize new material for cultural competence. Social work practitioners have knowledge about past and current clinical cases, notions about clients and their problems, and a repertoire of practical experiences. They are the pragmatic realists of the group. Social work students are learning about social work practice and research and have assignments in these areas. They are motivated, by and large, by the course work and writing and research requirements they must complete to earn their degree. Together, social work educators, practitioners, and students form the basis for focus groups to work on short-term inductive learning and research-oriented practice projects involving cultural diversity. These discussion and work-oriented groups have the potential of identifying baseline data on cultural competence and culturally diverse social work based on culturally oriented research methodologies and resulting in the publication of articles and texts in the field. We hope that inductive learning will be taught and practiced in social work education programs.

DIVERSITY GROUPS

Eleven social work educators contributed original, theme-related chapters on First Nations Peoples, African Americans, Latino Americans, Asian Americans, women of color, and gays and lesbians of color. Although distinctive emphases have been made in the discussion of each group, a number of themes have emerged from the contributors' efforts of writing from a common outline chapter format.

The contributors have enlarged our understanding of *defining cultural competence*. Weaver emphasizes the need to develop knowledge competencies for working with First Nations clients in diversity, history, culture, and contemporary realities of Native people. The social worker's values and attitudes for cultural competence should include helper wellness and self-awareness, humility and willingness to learn, respect and open-mindedness, a nonjudgmental stance, and social justice. For African American clients, according to McRoy, culturally competent workers should commit to diversity, recognize social factors leading to single-parent families, and seek out African American staff. McRoy makes African American client applications to the Cross and colleagues (1989) continuum. Garcia and Zuniga remind us that for Latino American clients, cultural competence means unbiased worker attitudes, particularly toward undocumented people (which is underscored in their chapter).

For Asian Americans and Pacific Islanders, Fong believes that cultural competence involves knowledge of cultural values, indigenous interventions, and Western interventions that support traditional cultural values. The starting point is macro-level societal values and issues and their implications for communities, families, and individuals. For work with women of color, Lie and Lowery emphasize culturally competent practice with regard to the multiple identities (ethnicity, gender, social class, and related areas) and interventions at the multiple levels of micro, meso, and macro systems. Walters, Longres, Han, and Icard point out the multiple dimensions for gay and lesbian of color clients in terms of understanding their history of oppression and exclusion, membership in many groups, racial and sexual identity processes, stress, and the functions of heterosexism, racism, and sexism. Understanding and balancing these issues on behalf of this client group calls for an extra portion of culturally competent wisdom, grace, and skill.

Our understanding of the multiple meanings of cultural competence is broadening to include client and community, worker and staff, values, and multiple identities and interventions beyond our present meanings. That is, a culturally competent worker must have respect for the client and knowledge and skills to deal culturally with the client and the community of which the client is a part; must focus on the worker as a part of a culturally competent and integrated staff; must have appropriate and coherent values that culturally fit the populations served; and must recognize that people have complex and multilayered identities that require micro, meso, and macro multiple interventions. These insights should make us revisit our understanding of cultural competence.

For *understanding diversity* among and between the various groups, Weaver reminds us of the rich and widespread diversity within First Nations Peoples. One must ask to what extent a First Nations Peoples client is culturally affiliated as far as identification is concerned. Culture, spiritual practices, the social environment, and family and community are important areas to explore in building an understanding of diversity. McRoy's view of African American diversity involves explaining 10 ethnic population demographic areas that must be understood by the social worker. For Latino Americans, Garcia and Zuniga portray the richness of diversity as we conduct assessment on language, acculturation, and immigration; planning from an ecological, cultural, and practical perspective; and practice that is family-based, involves crisis intervention, and is support-group oriented. In her portrayal of Asian American diversity, Fong is concerned for a number of emerging groups of Asian American immigrants and refugees, biracial and mixed racial children, adults, and families, including families adopting children from the People's Republic of China.

Lie and Lowery study women of color diversity from the demographics of African American, Hispanic American/Latina, Asian American and Pacific Islander, and First Nations Peoples women. At the same time, a number of contemporary challenges facing women of color make diversity a complex set of issues: health, mental health, behavioral health, political intersectionality, prostitution, reproductive freedom, immigrant women of color, and lesbians of color. Multiple identities linking a number of these variables create interesting combinations for comprehending the diversity of women. Likewise, Walters, Longres, Han, and Icard give us both a historical and a current perspective of gays and lesbians of color in First Nations Peoples, African American, Asian American, and Latino American settings, weaving in ethnic community values and tensions, gay and lesbian community exclusion, and ethnic traditions of acceptance and inclusion.

Inter- and intragroup diversity causes us to realize how similar and how different we are both as members of an ethnic and cultural group and as we relate to other ethnic and cultural peoples. Individuality and uniqueness and difference and distinction are present in a single group, yet we are able to transcend these realities and come together with common concerns, bonding with each other.

Pertaining to *conceptualizing oppression*, all contributors reiterated the major events of historical oppression inflicted upon these groups. We gain an understanding of the particular history of clients who are a part of these groups. The theme of historical trauma helps us to understand the psychohistorical pain of people who still carry these events in their inner selves. That is, ethnic people and groups carry and pass on a sense of collective trauma and pain over what happened to them and their ancestors that affects their individual and group psyches. Colonialization and other forms of oppression require people to revisit these events, re-experience them, and learn new ways through re-education to deal with the trauma and pain. Weaver's sharing of the concept of the Seven Generations provides a historical perspective—for First Nations Peoples' cultures, ancestors seven generations ago were planning for future generations to preserve land, language, and culture. The message is that people today have the same responsibility to ensure that the needs of future generations will be met. McRoy reminds us of the historical background of African Americans: involuntary migration, slavery, segregation, and continued oppression. In numerous ways, racism and oppression are still daily experiences for African Americans.

Garcia and Zuniga offer a multidimensional view of oppression affecting Mexicans, Puerto Ricans, Cubans, and Central Americans and its impact on new geographical settlements in parts of the country where there is limited Latino presence. Likewise, Fong traces the historical oppression of Asian immigrant groups in the United States during the last two centuries, and she traces racist attitudes and behaviors during World War II with Japanese Americans and during the Vietnam War with Amerasian children. She also highlights the past colonialist practices toward Pacific Islanders, particularly Hawaiians, and the current oppression experiences faced by native Hawaiians who are struggling with the issue of sovereignty and the return of their lands.

Our task is to realize that people carry their histories with them and are cautious of how they relate to others, particularly in the helping process. Learning how historical events of oppression affect the client and how these past happenings influence present thoughts, feelings, and behaviors is crucial to our development of cultural competence.

Addressing *cultural awareness* and social service needs, Weaver offers suggestions on how to structure needs assessment, intervention choice, and program design for First Nations Peoples to achieve a cultural fit and connection with a particular client in a particular cultural setting. McRoy offers practical suggestions for working with African American clients in the establishment of relationship building and trust, the use of the strengths perspective in assessment, the use of helping networks and community intervention support, and awareness of spiritual belief systems and the role of the Black church. The strengths approach, in finding positive coping strategies and looking for family strengths, moves away from a pathological, deficit view. Garcia and Zuniga identify a number of areas crucial to fostering Latino American cultural awareness and social service needs: an understanding of Latino American religious trends and family structure and composition, the importance of engaging and including fathers as heads of households, and the use of group services to reach Latino families. Fong surveys the wide array of cultural and service needs of Asian American groups: the elderly, the immigrant, the refugee, the victim of substance abuse and family violence, and gay, lesbian, bisexual, and transgender Asians and Pacific Islanders. Needs and services vary among these different but similar populations. Lie and Lowery point to the high poverty levels of women of color, the effect of poverty on health and mental health, and the availability of health care services and systems for such women to meet their needs.

Cultural awareness areas underscore the need for social services delivery planning to be based on a cultural orientation foundation of particular service intent according to the groups served and for the maintenance of cultural awareness throughout the beginning, middle, and end of the helping process. That is, cultural awareness should permeate how to begin the relationship, how to couch the problem, how to articulate a strengths-based assessment, and how to form an intervention that will encompass the many cultural and social needs of people.

Concerning *knowledge acquisition*, there are so many knowledge areas to become familiar with and master. Weaver underscores the worker's knowledge of Native people's diversity, extended family networks and community ties, historical trauma and grief, distinctiveness of urban and reservation communities, sovereignty issues and policies surrounding the Indian Child Welfare Act and the Indian Health Service, and attitudinal values of the worker toward the client (worker wellness and self-awareness, humility and the willingness to learn, respect and open-mindedness, nonjudgment, and a sense of social justice). McRoy identifies numerous general knowledge areas about African Americans and specific knowledge concerns about a particular African American client. The many knowledge areas include help-seeking behaviors of African Americans, the use of the strengths perspective, and the client's interpersonal style and perceptions of racial identity and relationships.

Garcia and Zuniga are concerned about the acquisition of knowledge about Latino immigrants in terms of their mental health and social/environmental needs. They trace the stages of migration and isolation issues, and their effects on families, particularly children and youth. Fong looks at knowledge theories that may be pertinent to Asians and Pacific Islanders: colonization theory, historical trauma theory, Confucian philosophy, and related areas. She also encourages us to construct new theories that address policy and social change, which will broaden our understanding of family subgroups such as Chinese children abandoned and then adopted from the People's Republic of China, and the various interacting diverse variables that force us to view and understand clients in multidimensional levels.

I encourage you to choose a few of the knowledge concepts that catch your interest and to begin to study and focus on them. Family-related knowledge areas, such as extended family support networks and family structure and dynamics, and immigrant and refugee transitions are areas with overlapping themes that bridge various cultural and ethnic groups.

Focusing on *practice skill development*, Weaver stresses good communication skills, problem solving with clear and practical steps, and good containment skills such as listening and patience as key to working with First Nations Peoples. McRoy pinpoints the development of the therapeutic relationship, communication skills, worker abilities, and Afrocentric practice approaches. Garcia and Zuniga identify relationship protocols (self-disclosure, style of communication), problem identification, and interventions that realize realistic cultural support network approaches. Fong teaches the need to develop indigenous and traditional ways of healing and to match them with Western interventions in a treatment plan that makes sense to the client, as well as with interventions that meet the multiple variable dimensions and needs of the client. Lie and Lowery concentrate on rapport development and engagement; family ethnocultural and related assessment that uncovers multiple layers of the client's behavioral background; and interventions that deal with stress, role changes, coping strategies, reframing, and multiple helping roles.

One must combine traditional social work interventions such as problem solving and empowerment with indigenous approaches that come from the culture itself. The biculturalization and integration of the two offer an opportunity to create interventions that make sense in the cultural context and that are functional and practical for both the worker and the client.

Concerning *inductive learning*, there are many ways to learn from various ethnic groups. Weaver believes in experiential learning opportunities such as spending time in First Nations communities in a classroom context, attending cultural and ethnic activities that are open to the public, and becoming a cross-cultural learner. McRoy suggests the use of gathering clients' life narratives and workers' observations through meaningful questions that generate understanding, and the use of the strengths perspective, which looks for positives. Garcia and Zuniga recommend seeking the consultation of culturally competent Latino workers who have worked with and understand Latino Americans, asking for assistance on a Latino case, and finding the literature and pertinent conferences that will foster inductive learning of this population. Fong is keen on such new inductive learning areas for Asians and Pacific Islanders as new diverse groupings and identities, transitional cultural value conflicts, indigenous strategies, and commonalities and differences within and between groups. Lie and Lowery encourage the use of research to study the individual and collective voices of women of color, particularly on issues related to violence, racism, sexism, poverty, and heterosexism/homophobia.

Inductive learning is a participatory experience of observing, asking questions, and listening as the client and community representatives teach the worker. Asking the client about his or her life story reveals life narrative events that are informative and meaningful for the teller and the listener. Reading helpful books that are recommended by the cultural and ethnic community is another means of learning. As new populations come to America, social workers must practice more inductive learning to uncover and record new information.

Finally, with *social and economic justice*, Weaver identifies a number of concerns for First Nations Peoples: Indian child welfare removal, economic development that offers employment with a future, environmental and health concerns such as the use of Native lands for dumping toxic waste, and indigenous sovereignty. McRoy is concerned about equal access to resources (education and the public schools in the African American community), everyday practices of oppression that become internalized, and strategies of empowerment. Garcia and Zuniga focus on Latino employment exploitation, inequitable educational facility resources, and immigrant exploitation in employment and housing. They suggest the need for empowering clients through community participation in collaborative resource development in the local Latino communities. Fong zeroes in on land rights and welfare reform for Asian and Pacific Islander immigrants as the most important social and economic justice issues for this population. For women of color, Lie and Lowery discuss the following social and economic justice concerns: health coverage, employment, education and training, and safeguards against sexual harassment.

Social and economic justice reveals past and present incidents of injustice and fuels the need to practice and maintain equality for all. We constantly strive for the ideal but struggle with the real. The contributors point out the realities of our imperfections and the need to empower others for access to resources.

SOCIAL WORK AND CULTURAL COMPETENCIES

Preliminary Research Results on Self-Assessment Tests

We have discussed the importance of measuring cultural competencies. You may find useful the following preliminary research results examining cultural competencies described in this text.

This author administered the Social Work Cultural Competencies Self-Assessment Pretest and Posttest to his Social Work 102 Multicultural Theory and Practice undergraduate classes from the Spring 1999 to the Fall 2004 semesters at California State University, Sacramento. A reliability analysis scale (alpha) of the pre- and posttests was established with the reliability coefficients of 388 cases and 44 items of the questionnaire. There was an alpha of .9437 reliability for the pretest and an alpha of .9245 for the posttest. Instrumentation reliability was very high.

The demographics of these 388 undergraduate students revealed the following characteristics:

- Age: ranged from 17 years old to 59 years old with a mean of 26 years
- Gender: 336 females and 52 males
- Ethnicity: 158 European Americans, 55 Asian Americans, 48 Latino Americans, 48 African Americans, 18 Native Americans, 16 Middle Easterners, 6 Jewish Americans, and 25 others (3 unanswered)
- Education: ranged between 12 years and 19 years of school with a mean of 15 years (undergraduate junior year)
- Number of years as a volunteer in social services: ranged from 1 to 5 years with a mean of 1.6 years
- Number of years in social work employment: ranged from 1 to 4 years with a mean of 1.2 years
- Previous diversity courses taken in college: ranged from 1 to 4 courses with a mean of 2.2 courses

Pretest and posttest mean scores for the following areas revealed increases in understanding: (1) cultural awareness pretest score (25.8080) and posttest score (28.6108); (2) knowledge acquisition pretest score (22.4575) and posttest score (31.2487); (3) skill development pretest score (51.2977) and posttest score (75.4472); and (4) inductive learning pretest score (10.2371) and posttest score (11.9588). The category of skill development experienced the most growth (+24.1494), followed by knowledge acquisition (+8.7912), cultural awareness (+2.8028), and inductive learning (+1.7216). The course content was devoted to the skill areas of contact, problem identification, assessment, intervention, and termination along with knowledge concepts. The total pretest cultural competencies mean score was 109.8003, whereas the total posttest cultural competencies score was 147.2655. There was a total increase of +37.4652, which was a high outcome measure for a social work diversity course teaching culturally competent practice.

Paired sample t-tests revealed two-tailed significance of .000 for all pairs of pre- and posttest categories (cultural awareness, knowledge acquisition, skill development, and inductive learning) and for the total pre- and posttest cultural competencies scores.

The companion Social Work Cultural Competencies with Diverse Groups of Color and Social and Economic Justice Pretest and Posttest was administered to the author's Social Work 102 Multicultural Theory and Practice undergraduate classes from Fall 2002 to Fall 2005 semesters at California State University, Sacramento. The demographics of 168 undergraduate students were as follows:

- Age: ranged from 18 years to 55 years with a mean age of 24
- Gender: 142 females, 24 males, 2 missing
- Ethnicity: 59 European Americans, 34 Asian Americans, 22 African Americans, 17 Latino Americans, 15 Middle Easterners, 5 Native Americans, 1 Jewish American, 8 others, and 7 missing
- Years of education: ranged from 12 to 19 years with a mean of 14.81 years

Pretest and posttest mean scores revealed the following increases for six groups and for social and economic justice: (1) First Nations Peoples pretest (18.4524) and posttest (24.3661) with a 5.9136 increase; (2) African Americans pretest (15.9196) and posttest (23.5446) with a 7.6250 increase; (3) Latino Americans pretest (17.7768) and posttest (24.6518) with a 6.8750 increase; (4) Asian Americans pretest (16.4970) and posttest (24.2589) with a 7.7619 increase; (5) Women of Color pretest (14.5000) and posttest (24.1786) with a 9.6785 increase; (6) Gay and Lesbian Persons of Color pretest (16.0000) and posttest (24.2560) with a 8.2559 increase; and (7) Social and Economic Justice pretest (17.2560) and posttest (27.3631) with a 10.1071 increase. The total pretest scores were 116.4018 and the total posttest scores were 172.6190.

Paired samples correlations were conducted on these six groups and subject area and revealed a two-tailed significant difference of .000 for all.

Further follow-up studies in various social work programs in the United States are important to compare results. However, these preliminary findings indicate that the Social Work Cultural Competencies Self-Assessment and the Social Work Cultural Competencies with Diverse Groups of Color and Social and Economic Justice instruments measure positive outcomes in a social work education diversity course.

Self-Assessment Instruments

In Chapter 1, you were asked to complete the Social Work Cultural Competencies Self-Assessment instrument as a pretest that measured your level of cultural competence at the start of a course on culturally diverse social work practice. Now it is important for you to take a posttest to determine the extent of your cultural competence at the end of the course.

The cultural competence areas may have been foreign and unfamiliar to you at the beginning of this book. I hope that the lectures, discussions, exercises, and assignments have contributed to your understanding of cultural competence and cultural competencies and to an enthusiastic passion for culturally diverse social work practice.

As you complete the Social Work Cultural Competencies Self-Assessment instrument (see Tools for Student Learning 15.1) for the second time, compare your levels of competence as indicated by the pretest and the posttest scores. Write a two-page analysis comparing the results of your pretest and posttest. Indicate the particular items where your score shows a significant difference and those where there is no change.

A companion instrument measures your knowledge and understanding of the diverse groups of color and of the social and economic justice issues you have read about and studied in your class. You took the pretest of this instrument in Chapter 1 of this text; now we would like you to take the posttest here. You and your instructor now have two research instruments to measure your learning outcomes based on this text. We hope that they also will be the source of further discussion, research, and inquiry into various aspects of culturally competent practice.

TOOLS FOR STUDENT LEARNING 15.1

Social Work Cultural Competencies Self-Assessment Posttest

Written by Doman Lum, PhD (all rights reserved)

Introduction

This instrument measures your level of cultural competence at the beginning and end of the semester. The results of this self-assessment will be evaluated by your social work instructor. Strict confidentiality is observed regarding the results of this self-assessment.

Rate yourself on your level of competency on a scale of 1–4: 1 = Unlikely; 2 = Not very likely; 3 = Likely; and 4 = Definitely. Circle the appropriate number.

Social Security # (last four digits):   *Course:*   *Instructor:*   *Campus:*

Background Information

1. Age: _____
2. Sex: Male _____   Female _____
3. Ethnicity: (please check all that apply)

   African American _____   Asian American _____   European American _____

   Jewish American _____   Latino American _____   Middle Eastern _____

   First Nations Peoples _____   Other (please specify) _____

4. Years of education (e.g., 12 = high school graduate) (circle correct number)

   12   13   14   15   16   17   18   19   20   21 or more

5. Highest degree earned/major:

6. Years of previous social service volunteer experience:

    None _____   1–3 years _____   4–6 years _____   7–9 years _____   10 years or more _____

7. Years of previous social work employment:

    None _____   1–3 years _____   4–6 years _____   7–9 years _____   10 years or more _____

8. Prior courses on cultural diversity:

    None _____   1 course _____   2 courses _____   3 or more courses _____

Cultural Awareness

1. I am aware of my life experiences as a person related to a culture (e.g., family heritage, household and community events, beliefs, and practices).

    1–Unlikely   *2–Not very likely*   *3–Likely*   *4–Definitely*

2. I have contact with other cultural and ethnic individuals, families, and groups

    1–Unlikely   *2–Not very likely*   *3–Likely*   *4–Definitely*

3. I am aware of positive and negative experiences with cultural and ethnic people and events.

    1–Unlikely   *2–Not very likely*   *3–Likely*   *4–Definitely*

4. I know how to evaluate my cognitive, affective, and behavioral experiences and reactions to racism, prejudice, and discrimination.

    1–Unlikely   *2–Not very likely*   *3–Likely*   *4–Definitely*

5. I have assessed my involvement with cultural and ethnic people of color in childhood, adolescence, young adulthood, and adulthood.

    1–Unlikely   *2–Not very likely*   *3–Likely*   *4–Definitely*

6. I have had or plan to have academic course work, fieldwork experiences, and research projects on culturally diverse clients and groups.

    1–Unlikely   *2–Not very likely*   *3–Likely*   *4–Definitely*

7. I have had or plan to have professional employment experiences with culturally diverse clients and programs.

    1–Unlikely   *2–Not very likely*   *3–Likely*   *4–Definitely*

8. I have assessed or plan to assess my academic and professional work experiences with cultural diversity and culturally diverse clients.

    1–Unlikely   *2–Not very likely*   *3–Likely*   *4–Definitely*

Knowledge Acquisition

9. I understand the following terms: *ethnic minority*, *multiculturalism*, *diversity*, and *people of color*.

    1–Unlikely   *2–Not very likely*   *3–Likely*   *4–Definitely*

10. I have knowledge of demographic profiles of some culturally diverse populations.

    1–Unlikely   *2–Not very likely*   *3–Likely*   *4–Definitely*

11. I have developed a critical thinking perspective on cultural diversity.

    1–Unlikely　　*2–Not very likely*　　*3–Likely*　　*4–Definitely*

12. I understand the history of oppression and multicultural social group history.

    1–Unlikely　　*2–Not very likely*　　*3–Likely*　　*4–Definitely*

13. I know information about men, women, and children of color.

    1–Unlikely　　*2–Not very likely*　　*3–Likely*　　*4–Definitely*

14. I know about culturally diverse values.

    1–Unlikely　　*2–Not very likely*　　*3–Likely*　　*4–Definitely*

15. I know how to apply systems theory and psychosocial theory to multicultural social work.

    1–Unlikely　　*2–Not very likely*　　*3–Likely*　　*4–Definitely*

16. I have knowledge of theories on ethnicity, culture, minority identity, and social class.

    1–Unlikely　　*2–Not very likely*　　*3–Likely*　　*4–Definitely*

17. I know how to draw on a range of social science theory from cross-cultural psychology, multicultural counseling and therapy, and cultural anthropology.

    1–Unlikely　　*2–Not very likely*　　*3–Likely*　　*4–Definitely*

Skill Development

18. I understand how to overcome the resistance and lower the communication barriers of a multicultural client.

    1–Unlikely　　*2–Not very likely*　　*3–Likely*　　*4–Definitely*

19. I know how to obtain personal and family background information from a multicultural client and determine the client's ethnic/community sense of identity.

    1–Unlikely　　*2–Not very likely*　　*3–Likely*　　*4–Definitely*

20. I understand the concepts of ethnic community and practice relationship protocols with a multicultural client.

    1–Unlikely　　*2–Not very likely*　　*3–Likely*　　*4–Definitely*

21. I use professional self-disclosure with a multicultural client.

    1–Unlikely　　*2–Not very likely*　　*3–Likely*　　*4–Definitely*

22. I have a positive and open communication style and use open-ended listening responses.

    1–Unlikely　　*2–Not very likely*　　*3–Likely*　　*4–Definitely*

23. I know how to obtain problem information, facilitate problem area disclosure, and promote problem understanding.

    1–Unlikely　　*2–Not very likely*　　*3–Likely*　　*4–Definitely*

24. I view a problem as an unsatisfied want or an unfulfilled need.

    1–Unlikely　　*2–Not very likely*　　*3–Likely*　　*4–Definitely*

25. I know how to explain problems on micro, meso, and macro levels.

1–Unlikely   *2–Not very likely*   *3–Likely*   *4–Definitely*

26. I know how to explain problem themes (racism, prejudice, discrimination) and expressions (oppression, powerlessness, stereotyping, acculturation, and exploitation).

1–Unlikely   *2–Not very likely*   *3–Likely*   *4–Definitely*

27. I know how to find out about problem details.

1–Unlikely   *2–Not very likely*   *3–Likely*   *4–Definitely*

28. I know how to assess socioenvironmental impacts, psychoindividual reactions, and cultural strengths.

1–Unlikely   *2–Not very likely*   *3–Likely*   *4–Definitely*

29. I know how to assess the biological, psychological, social, cultural, and spiritual dimensions of the multicultural client.

1–Unlikely   *2–Not very likely*   *3–Likely*   *4–Definitely*

30. I know how to establish joint goals and agreements with the client that are culturally acceptable.

1–Unlikely   *2–Not very likely*   *3–Likely*   *4–Definitely*

31. I know how to formulate micro, meso, and macro intervention strategies that address the cultural needs of the client and special needs populations such as immigrants and refugees.

1–Unlikely   *2–Not very likely*   *3–Likely*   *4–Definitely*

32. I know how to initiate termination in a way that links the client to an ethnic community resource, reviews significant progress and growth development, evaluates goal outcomes, and establishes a follow-up strategy.

1–Unlikely   *2–Not very likely*   *3–Likely*   *4–Definitely*

33. I know how to design a service delivery and agency linkage and culturally effective social service programs in ethnic communities.

1–Unlikely   *2–Not very likely*   *3–Likely*   *4–Definitely*

34. I have been involved in services that have been accessible to the ethnic community.

1–Unlikely   *2–Not very likely*   *3–Likely*   *4–Definitely*

35. I have participated in delivering pragmatic and positive services that meet the tangible needs of the ethnic community.

1–Unlikely   *2–Not very likely*   *3–Likely*   *4–Definitely*

36. I have observed the effectiveness of bilingual/bicultural workers who reflect the ethnic composition of the clientele.

1–Unlikely   *2–Not very likely*   *3–Likely*   *4–Definitely*

37. I have participated in community outreach education and prevention that establish visible services, provide culturally sensitive programs, and employ credible staff.

1–Unlikely   *2–Not very likely*   *3–Likely*   *4–Definitely*

38. I have been involved in a service linkage network to related social agencies that ensures rapid referral and program collaboration.

    1–Unlikely   2–Not very likely   3–Likely   4–Definitely

39. I have participated as a staff member in fostering a conducive agency setting with an atmosphere that is friendly and helpful to multicultural clients.

    1–Unlikely   2–Not very likely   3–Likely   4–Definitely

40. I am involved or plan to be involved with cultural skill development research in areas related to cultural empathy, clinical alliance, goal-obtaining styles, achieving styles, practice skills, and outcome research.

    1–Unlikely   2–Not very likely   3–Likely   4–Definitely

Inductive Learning

41. I have participated or plan to participate in a study discussion group with culturally diverse social work educators, practitioners, students, and clients on cultural competency issues, emerging cultural trends, and future directions for multicultural social work.

    1–Unlikely   2–Not very likely   3–Likely   4–Definitely

42. I have found or am seeking new journal articles and textbook material about cultural competence and culturally diverse practice.

    1–Unlikely   2–Not very likely   3–Likely   4–Definitely

43. I have conducted or plan to conduct inductive research on cultural competence and culturally diverse practice, using survey, oral history, and/or participatory observation research methods.

    1–Unlikely   2–Not very likely   3–Likely   4–Definitely

44. I have participated or will participate in the writing of articles and texts on cultural competence and culturally diverse practice.

    1–Unlikely   2–Not very likely   3–Likely   4–Definitely

What are your questions and views on cultural competence and cultural competencies?

What are your reactions to this self-assessment instrument?

Please count your scores on the 44 self-assessment items and rate your level of cultural competence. Circle the appropriate level and write your raw score in one of the following levels:

Level 1: Unlikely (scores 44–77)
Level 2: Not very likely (scores 78–101)
Level 3: Likely (scores 102–135)
Level 4: Definitely (scores 136–176)

Thank you for your cooperation on this self-assessment instrument. You have made a significant contribution to our research on social work cultural competence.

TOOLS FOR STUDENT LEARNING 15.2

Social Work Cultural Competencies with Diverse Groups of Color and Social and Economic Justice Posttest

Written by Doman Lum, PhD (all rights reserved)

Introduction

This instrument measures your level of cultural competence with diverse groups of color and social and economic justice at the beginning and end of the semester. The results of this test will be evaluated by your social work instructor. Strict confidentiality is observed regarding the results of this instrument.

Rate yourself on your level of competence on a scale of 1–4; 1 = Unlikely; 2 = Not very likely; 3 = Likely; and 4 = Definitely. Circle the appropriate number.

Social Security # (last four digits):   *Course:*   *Instructor:*   *Campus:*

First Nations Peoples

1. I know about the diversity of Native nations, which differ in terms of language, religion, social structure, political structure, and many aspects of culture.

   1–Unlikely   *2–Not very likely*   *3–Likely*   *4–Definitely*

2. I understand the concept of Seven Generations, which provides a historical and current perspective on oppression experiences.

   1–Unlikely   *2–Not very likely*   *3–Likely*   *4–Definitely*

3. It is important to choose interventions and design programs that accurately target the needs of First Nations Peoples, which may be different for each community.

   1–Unlikely   *2–Not very likely*   *3–Likely*   *4–Definitely*

4. Knowledge about First Nations Peoples requires an understanding of sovereignty issues and policies that apply to indigenous people.

   1–Unlikely   *2–Not very likely*   *3–Likely*   *4–Definitely*

5. Patience, listening, and silence are important skills to practice when working with First Nations Peoples clients.

   1–Unlikely   *2–Not very likely*   *3–Likely*   *4–Definitely*

6. I know about First Nations community immersion projects to increase inductive learning.

   1–Unlikely   *2–Not very likely*   *3–Likely*   *4–Definitely*

7. The Supreme Court has consistently ruled against the rights of First Nations Peoples.

   1–Unlikely   *2–Not very likely*   *3–Likely*   *4–Definitely*

African Americans

8. Diversity among African Americans involves such factors as physical characteristics, residential patterns, marital status, education, income, age, social class, and employment.

1–Unlikely   *2–Not very likely*   *3–Likely*   *4–Definitely*

9. I understand the unique historical background of African Americans regarding involuntary migration, slavery, segregation, and continued oppression.

1–Unlikely   *2–Not very likely*   *3–Likely*   *4–Definitely*

10. I am able to explain the four stages of the helping process that African American clients may go through with a practitioner.

1–Unlikely   *2–Not very likely*   *3–Likely*   *4–Definitely*

11. I can identify several knowledge areas about the African American population and about the African American client.

1–Unlikely   *2–Not very likely*   *3–Likely*   *4–Definitely*

12. I understand Afrocentric practice approaches, which are based on the Nguzo Saba value system.

1–Unlikely   *2–Not very likely*   *3–Likely*   *4–Definitely*

13. I can explain the inductive learning strengths perspective approach for African American clients.

1–Unlikely   *2–Not very likely*   *3–Likely*   *4–Definitely*

14. I comprehend the internalization of oppression that leads to disempowerment as a starting point for understanding how to achieve social and economic justice.

1–Unlikely   *2–Not very likely*   *3–Likely*   *4–Definitely*

Latino Americans

15. I know the distinctions in Latino diversity pertaining to language differences, immigration history and patterns, and traditional and intergenerational acculturation.

1–Unlikely   *2–Not very likely*   *3–Likely*   *4–Definitely*

16. I understand the historical and current oppression experiences of Mexican, Puerto Rican, Cuban, and Central American Latinos.

1–Unlikely   *2–Not very likely*   *3–Likely*   *4–Definitely*

17. The religion of a Latino client is important because Catholic and Protestant denominations often establish social service outreach resources for the Latino community.

1–Unlikely   *2–Not very likely*   *3–Likely*   *4–Definitely*

18. Knowledge of children and youth from war-torn countries such as El Salvador and Nicaragua indicates that exposure to violence may result in suicidal behaviors, serious antisocial acts, insomnia, and other physical, psychological, and social problems.

1–Unlikely   *2–Not very likely*   *3–Likely*   *4–Definitely*

19. In social work practice with Latinos, it is important to use a "dicho" to create a cultural ambience.

    1–Unlikely   *2–Not very likely*   *3–Likely*   *4–Definitely*

20. It is important to cover legal documentation with Latino clients in order to seek, in an inductive nonthreatening manner, services that will not endanger them.

    1–Unlikely   *2–Not very likely*   *3–Likely*   *4–Definitely*

21. I understand the dynamics of Latino immigrant exploitation in employment and housing as issues of social and economic justice.

    1–Unlikely   *2–Not very likely*   *3–Likely*   *4–Definitely*

Asian Americans

22. I know about the diversity between Asians and Pacific Islanders, among different ethnic groups of Asian Americans, and between Asian immigrants and refugees.

    1–Unlikely   *2–Not very likely*   *3–Likely*   *4–Definitely*

23. I am aware of the discriminatory experiences of Asian immigrants, the racist attitudes and behaviors toward American-born Asians, and the colonialist practices toward Pacific Islanders, particularly Native Hawaiians.

    1–Unlikely   *2–Not very likely*   *3–Likely*   *4–Definitely*

24. I understand the broad and varied social service needs of specific Asian American and Pacific Islander groups.

    1–Unlikely   *2–Not very likely*   *3–Likely*   *4–Definitely*

25. I know that Asian American and Pacific Islander knowledge acquisition consists of knowing the ethnic culture and using the cultural values to explain ways of thinking and behaving.

    1–Unlikely   *2–Not very likely*   *3–Likely*   *4–Definitely*

26. I understand that in developing treatment planning with Asians and Pacific Islanders, traditional ways of healing should be matched with Western interventions, and the Western interventions should be evaluated to determine whether they foster the cultural values of the ethnic community.

    1–Unlikely   *2–Not very likely*   *3–Likely*   *4–Definitely*

27. I am aware of the need to discuss Asian Americans and Pacific Islanders by life-span development, gender, and sexual orientation issues and needs in order to create an intersection of inductive learning themes.

    1–Unlikely   *2–Not very likely*   *3–Likely*   *4–Definitely*

28. I understand the social and economic issues of land rights and welfare reform for Asian and Pacific Islander immigrants.

    1–Unlikely   *2–Not very likely*   *3–Likely*   *4–Definitely*

Women of Color

29. I can explain several of the multiple identifying characteristics of diversity among the 42 million women of color in the United States.

    1–Unlikely   *2–Not very likely*   *3–Likely*   *4–Definitely*

30. I am able to explain the meanings of structural intersectionality and political intersectionality and relate these concepts to oppression among women of color.

    1–Unlikely   *2–Not very likely*   *3–Likely*   *4–Definitely*

31. I am aware of the specific health and mental health needs of women of color.

    1–Unlikely   *2–Not very likely*   *3–Likely*   *4–Definitely*

32. I am knowledgeable of the issues facing immigrant women of color.

    1–Unlikely   *2–Not very likely*   *3–Likely*   *4–Definitely*

33. I know the principles related to the practice skills of rapport development/engagement, assessment, and intervention pertaining to women of color.

    1–Unlikely   *2–Not very likely*   *3–Likely*   *4–Definitely*

34. I have a strong notion of new inductive learning areas about women of color.

    1–Unlikely   *2–Not very likely*   *3–Likely*   *4–Definitely*

35. I understand the areas for advocating social and economic justice for women of color.

    1–Unlikely   *2–Not very likely*   *3–Likely*   *4–Definitely*

Gay and Lesbian Persons of Color

36. I understand the different meanings of the terms *sexual orientation* and *homosexual*.

    1–Unlikely   *2–Not very likely*   *3–Likely*   *4–Definitely*

37. I am aware of the issues of gays and lesbians of color in terms of their negotiating and reconciling competing demands from the dominant society, their own ethnic/racial community, and the gay and lesbian community.

    1–Unlikely   *2–Not very likely*   *3–Likely*   *4–Definitely*

38. I can explain the meaning of women–men, men–women, and two-spirited people from a First Nations perspective.

    1–Unlikely   *2–Not very likely*   *3–Likely*   *4–Definitely*

39. I understand the effects of HIV/AIDS on the African American community in general and on the African American gay and lesbian community in particular.

    1–Unlikely   *2–Not very likely*   *3–Likely*   *4–Definitely*

40. I am aware of the dilemmas that many gay Asian men face in their ethnic community and the larger gay community.

    1–Unlikely   *2–Not very likely*   *3–Likely*   *4–Definitely*

41. I am aware that in some instances Latino men can engage in same-sex sexual behavior without threatening their heterosexual masculine identity.

    1–Unlikely   *2–Not very likely*   *3–Likely*   *4–Definitely*

42. I understand the gay and lesbian of color sense of bicultural competence that integrates positive aspects of gay/lesbian and racial/cultural perspectives without losing cultural values or internalizing heterosexist biases.

    1–Unlikely   *2–Not very likely*   *3–Likely*   *4–Definitely*

Social and Economic Justice

43. I understand the relationship between cultural diversity and social justice in terms of historical and ongoing oppression and privilege that different social identity groups experience in our society.

   1–Unlikely   *2–Not very likely*   *3–Likely*   *4–Definitely*

44. I understand the meaning of economic class as a prime indicator of oppression and the creation of a class system based on difference as a function of oppression.

   1–Unlikely   *2–Not very likely*   *3–Likely*   *4–Definitely*

45. I can explain the concept and perspectives of distributive justice and their implications for social and economic justice.

   1–Unlikely   *2–Not very likely*   *3–Likely*   *4–Definitely*

46. I can connect the concepts of moral exclusion and fairness.

   1–Unlikely   *2–Not very likely*   *3–Likely*   *4–Definitely*

47. I understand the human rights and oppression concepts of the United Nations Universal Declaration of Human Rights.

   1–Unlikely   *2–Not very likely*   *3–Likely*   *4–Definitely*

48. I am aware of the United Nations materials on human rights for social work.

   1–Unlikely   *2–Not very likely*   *3–Likely*   *4–Definitely*

49. I understand the meaning of and the connection between empowerment and social and economic justice.

   1–Unlikely   *2–Not very likely*   *3–Likely*   *4–Definitely*

50. I understand how the grieving cycle is related to how a person feels about oppression and injustice.

   1–Unlikely   *2–Not very likely*   *3–Likely*   *4–Definitely*

Please count your scores on the 50 items and rate your level of cultural competence. Circle the appropriate level and write your raw score in one of the following levels.

Level 1: Unlikely (scores 50–89)
Level 2: Not very likely (scores 90–129)
Level 3: Likely (scores 130–169)
Level 4: Definitely (scores 170–200)

Thank you for your cooperation on this self-assessment instrument. You have made a significant contribution to our research on social work cultural competence.

CLOSING THOUGHTS

As social work education and culturally diverse social work practice actively engage in a host of efforts during the 21st century, cultural competence has been an emerging topic that can catalyze new growth and development in curriculum. It is a topic taught in medical schools, graduate programs in psychology, social work, nursing, education, and related disciplines; mandated in the mental health and health care programs of such states as California, New Jersey, New York, and South Carolina; and fostered on the federal level through the National Center for Cultural Competence. In many ways throughout the helping professions, cultural competence is being promoted as essential for working with client populations.

Cultural competence is clearly mandated in the National Association of Social Workers Code of Ethics and the Standards for Cultural Competence in Social Work Practice. Cultural competence points toward the future of social work education and practice: outcome-based knowledge and skills, measurement accountability, and mastery of culturally competent practice with people. The basic concepts of ethnic-sensitive, culturally aware, and culturally diverse social work practice have been clearly articulated and accepted by the social work education and practice communities.

It is now time to move ahead with cultural competence, which fits into the profession's emphasis on competency-based practice. As a social work educator, I have had and will continue to have the good fortune to teach and write about cultural competence in the 20th and 21st centuries. If you have any thoughts on culturally competent practice, please email me: lumd@csus.edu. I look forward to the future as I interact with my social work education colleagues and students about this vital area of cultural competence.

References

CHAPTER 1

Adams, D. (2005). Cultural competency now law in New Jersey. http://www.ama-assn.org/amednews/2005/04/25/prl20425.htm

American Psychological Association (APA). (1993). Guidelines for providers of psychological services to ethnic, linguistic, and culturally diverse populations. *American Psychologist, 48*, 45–48.

American Psychological Association (APA), Educational and Training Committee of Division 17. (1980, September). *Cross-cultural competencies: A position paper.* Paper presented at the annual meeting of the American Psychological Association, Montreal, Canada.

A rapid move to diversity. (2001, March 13). *Sacramento Bee,* p. A.

BlueCross BlueShield of Florida. (2004, December 27). Diversity program. http://www.bcbsfl.com/index.cfm?secion=&fuseaction=Careers.diversityProgram

Bureau of Primary Health Care Project. (2005). http://gucchd.georgetown.edu/nccc/nccc.html

California Social Work Education Center (CalSWEC) at the University of California at Berkeley. (2005, March). *CalSWEC II mental health initiative mental health competencies foundation year and advanced/specialization year: A competency-based curriculum in community mental health for graduate social work students.* Berkeley, CA: Author.

Casas, J. M., Ponterotto, J. G., & Gutierrez, J. M. (1986). An ethical indictment of counseling research and training: The cross-cultural perspective. *Journal of Counseling and Development, 64,* 467–349.

Center on an Aging Society, Georgetown University. (2004). *Cultural competence in health care: Is it important for people with chronic conditions?* Issue brief, No.5, February 2004, pp. 1–13. http://ihcrp.georgetown.edu/agingsociety/pubhtml/cultural/cultural.html

Children and Youth with Special Health Needs. (2005). http://gucchd.georgetown.edu/nccc/nccc4.html

Constantine, M. G.. & Sue, D. W. (Eds.) (2005a). *Strategies for building multicultural competence in mental health and educational settings.* Hoboken, NJ: John Wiley & Sons.

Constantine, M. G. & Sue, D. W. (2005b). The American Psychological Association's guidelines on multicultural education, training, research, practice, and organizational psychology: Initial development and summary. In M. G. Constantine & D. W. Sue (Eds.), *Strategies for building multicultural competence in mental health and educational settings* (pp. 3–15). Hoboken, NJ: John Wiley & Sons.

Council on Social Work Education (CSWE), Commission on Accreditation. (2003). *Site visitors training manual.* Alexandria, VA: Author.

Cross, T. L., Bazron, B. J., Dennis, K. W., & Isaacs, M. R. (1989). *Toward a culturally competent system of care.* Washington, DC: Georgetown University Child Development Center.

Delgado, M., Jones, K., & Rohani, M. (2005). *Social work practice with refugee and immigrant youth in the United States.* Boston: Allyn & Bacon Pearson Education.

Devore, W., & Schlesinger, E. G. (1981). *Ethnic-sensitive social work practice.* St. Louis, MO: Mosby.

Draguns, J. G. (1996). Humanly universal and culturally distinctive: Charting the course of cultural counseling. In P. B. Pedersen, J. G. Draguns, W. J. Lonner, & J. F. Trible (Eds.), *Counseling across cultures* (pp. 1–20). Thousand Oaks, CA: Sage.

Fong, R. (Ed.). (2004). *Culturally competent practice with immigrant and refugee children and families.* New York: Guilford Press.

Fong, R., & Furuto, S. (Eds.). (2001). *Culturally competent practice: Skills, interventions, and evaluations.* Boston: Allyn & Bacon.

Galan, F. J. (1992). Experiential focusing with Mexican-American males with bicultural identity problems. In K. Corcoran (Ed.), *Structuring change: Effective practice for common client problems* (pp. 234–254). Chicago: Lyceum Books.

Gordon, M. M. (1978). *Human nature, class, and ethnicity.* New York: Oxford University Press.

Green, J. W., & Associates. (1982). *Cultural awareness in the human services.* Englewood Cliffs, NJ: Prentice-Hall.

Green, R. G., et al. (2005). The multicultural counseling inventory: A measure for evaluating social work student and practitioner self-perceptions of their multicultural competencies. *Journal of Social Work Education, 41,* 191–208.

Greene, B., & Hucles-Sanchez, J. (1994). Diversity: Advancing an inclusive feminist psychology. In J. Worell & N. Johnson (Eds.), *Feminist visions: New directions in education and training for feminist psychology practice* (pp. 173–202). Washington, DC: American Psychological Association Press.

Hall, E. (1976). *Beyond culture.* Garden City, NY: Anchor Press/Doubleday.

Harvard Medical School. (2005). Highlighting cultural competence education at the AAMC annual meeting. *Mentations News from the Office of Diversity and Community Partnership at Harvard Medical School News from our Colleagues, 20,* Winter 2005.

Hepworth, D. H., Rooney, R. H., & Larsen, J. A. (1997). *Direct social work practice: Theory and skills.* Pacific Grove, CA: Brooks/Cole.

Higginbotham, H. N., West, S., & Forsyth, D. (1988). *Psychotherapy and behavior change: Social, cultural and methodological perspectives.* New York: Pergamon Press.

Hodge, D. R. (2004). Spirituality and people with mental illness: Developing spiritual competency in assessment and intervention, *Families in Society, 85,* 36–44.

Hodge, J. L., Struckmann, D. K., & Trost, L. D. (1975). *Cultural bases of racism and group oppression.* Berkeley, CA: Two Riders Press.

Ibrahim, F. A., & Arredondo, P. M. (1986). Ethical standards for cross-cultural counseling: Counselor preparation, practice, assessment, and research. *Journal of Counseling and Development, 64,* 349–352.

James, R. K., & Gilliland, B. E. (2005). *Crisis intervention strategies.* Belmont, CA: Thomson Brooks/Cole.

Jenkins, Y. M. (2001). The Stone Center theoretical approach revisited: Applications for African American women. In L. C. Jackson & B. Greene (Eds.), *Psychotherapy with African American women: Innovations in psychodynamic perspectives and practice* (pp. 62–81). New York: Guilford Press.

Jenkins, Y. M., De La Cancela, V., & Chin, J. L. (1993). Historical overviews: Three sociopolitical perspectives. In J. L. Chin, V. De La Cancela, & Y. M. Jenkins, *Diversity in psychotherapy: The politics of race, ethnicity, and gender* (p. 34). Westport, CT: Praeger.

Kaiser Permanente. (December 2004). Diversity and inclusion. http://www.kaiserpermanentejobs.org/workinghere/diversity.asp

LaFromboise, T., Coleman, H. L. K., & Gerton, J. (1993). Psychological impact of biculturalism: Evidence and theory. *Psychological Bulletin, 114,* 395–412.

Leigh, J. W. (1998). *Communicating for cultural competence*. Boston: Allyn & Bacon.

Lum, D. (1996). *Social work practice and people of color: A process-stage approach* (3rd ed.). Pacific Grove, CA: Brooks/Cole.

Lum, D. (1999). *Culturally competent practice: A framework for growth and action*. Pacific Grove, CA: Brooks/Cole.

Lum, D., & Lu, Y. E. (1997, March). *Developing cultural competency within a culturally sensitive environment*. Paper presented at the Council on Social Work Education annual program meeting, Chicago, Illinois.

Manoleas, P. (1994). An outcome approach to assessing the cultural competence of MSW students. *Journal of Multicultural Social Work, 3*, 43–57.

Miley, K. K., O'Melia, M., & DuBois, B. I. (1998). *Generalist social work practice: An empowering approach*. Boston: Allyn and Bacon.

National Association of Social Workers (NASW). (1996). *NASW code of ethics*. Washington, DC: Author.

National Association of Social Workers (NASW). (2001). *NASW Standards for Cultural Competence in Social Work Practice*. http://www.naswdc.org/pubs/standards/cultural.htm

National Center for Cultural Competence. (2005). http://gucchd.georgetown.edu/nccc/pa.html

Nebraska Prevention. (n.d.). Cultural competency/ethics of prevention. http://www.nebraskaprevention.gov/CCEP.htm. Citing Leppien-Christensen, J. K., http://jkrislc.freeservers.com/

Nybell, L. M., & Gray, S. S. (2004). Race, place, space: Meanings of cultural competence in three child welfare agencies. *Social Work, 49*, 17–26.

Office of Multicultural Services, South Carolina Department of Mental Health. (2005). Cultural competence plan 2003–2005. http://www.state.sc.us/dmh/cultural_competence/cultural_plan.htm

Oregon Department of Education. (May 2004). *Resources on cultural competency*. http://www.ode.state.or.us/opportunities/grants/saelp/resrcescultcomp.aspx

Organizational self-assessment. (2005). http://gucchd.georgetown.edu/nccc/orgselfassess.html

Orlandi, M. A. (1992). The challenge of evaluating community-based prevention programs: A cross-cultural perspective. In M. A. Orlandi, R. Weston, & L. G. Epstein (Eds.), *Cultural competence for evaluators: A guide for alcohol and other drug abuse prevention practitioners working with ethnic/racial communities* (pp. 1–22). Rockville, MD: U.S. Department of Health and Human Services, Office for Substance Abuse Prevention.

Orlandi, M. A., Weston, R., & Epstein, L. G. (Eds.). (1992). *Cultural competence for evaluators: A guide for alcohol and other drug abuse prevention practitioners working with ethnic/racial communities*. Rockville, MD: U.S. Department of Health and Human Services, Office for Substance Abuse Prevention.

Paasche-Orlow, M. (2004). The ethics of cultural competence. *Academic Medicine, 79*, 347–350.

Pantoja, A., & Perry, W. (1976). Social work in a culturally pluralistic society: An alternative paradigm. In M. Sotomayor (Ed.), *Cross-cultural perspectives in social work practice and education* (pp. 79–94). Houston, TX: University of Houston, Graduate School of Social Work.

Pinderhughes, E. (1989). *Understanding race, ethnicity, and power: The key to efficacy in clinical practice*. New York: Free Press.

Ponterotto, J. G., Casas, J. M., Suzuki, L. A., & Alexander, C. M. (Eds.). (1995). *Handbook of multicultural counseling*. Thousand Oaks, CA: Sage.

Pope-Davis, D. B., & Coleman, H. L. K. (Eds.). (1997). *Multicultural counseling competencies: Assessment, education and training, and supervision*. Thousand Oaks, CA: Sage.

Pope-Davis, D. B., & Dings, J. G. (1995). The assessment of multicultural counseling competencies. In J. G. Ponterotto, J. M. Casas, L. A. Suzuki, & C. M. Alexander (Eds.), *Handbook of multicultural counseling* (pp. 287–311). Thousand Oaks, CA: Sage.

Ridley, C. R. (2005). *Overcoming unintentional racism in counseling and therapy: A practitioner's guide to intentional intervention.* Thousand Oaks, CA: Sage Publications.

Ridley, C. R., & Lingle, D. W. (1996). Cultural empathy in multicultural counseling: A multidimensional process model. In P. B. Pedersen, J. G. Draguns, W. J. Lonner, & J. E. Trimble (Eds.), *Counseling across cultures* (pp. 21–46). Thousand Oaks, CA: Sage.

Schriver, J. M. (2001). *Human behavior and the social environment: Shifting paradigms in essential knowledge for social work practice.* Boston: Allyn & Bacon.

Solomon, B. B. (1976). *Black empowerment: Social work in oppressed communities.* New York: Columbia University Press.

Straussner, S. L. A. (2001). Ethnocultural issues in substance abuse treatment. In S. L. A. Straussner (Ed.), *Ethnocultural factors in substance abuse treatment* (pp. 3–28). New York: Guilford Press.

Substance Abuse and Mental Health Services Administration. (1997a). *Cultural competence guidelines in managed care mental health services for Asian and Pacific Islander populations.* The Asian and Pacific Islander American Task Force: The Western Interstate Commission for Higher Education Mental Health Program.

Substance Abuse and Mental Health Services Administration. (1997b). *Cultural competence guidelines for Native American populations.* Native American Managed Care Panel: The Western Interstate Commission for Higher Education.

Sudden Infant Death Syndrome (SIDS)/Other Infant Death (ID) Project. (2005). http://gucchd.georgetown.edu/nccc/nccc5.html

Sue, D. W., Arredondo, P., & McDavis, R. J. (1992). Multicultural counseling competencies and standards: A call to the profession. *Journal of Counseling and Development, 70,* 477–486.

Sue, D. W., Arredondo, P., & McDavis, R. J. (1995). Multicultural counseling competencies and standards: A call to the profession, Appendix III. In J. G. Ponterotto, J. M. Casas, L. A. Suzuki, & C. M. Alexander (Eds.), *Handbook of multicultural counseling* (pp. 624–640). Thousand Oaks, CA: Sage.

Sue, D. W., Carter, R. T., Casas, J. M., et al. (1998). *Multicultural counseling competencies: Individual and organizational development.* Thousand Oaks, CA: Sage.

Sue, D. W., Ivey, A. E., & Pedersen, P. B. (Eds.). (1996). *A theory of multicultural counseling and therapy.* Pacific Grove, CA: Brooks/Cole.

Sue, D. W., & Sue, D. (2003). *Counseling the culturally diverse: Theory and practice.* New York: John Wiley & Sons.

Teasley, M. L. (2005). Perceived levels of cultural competence through social work education and professional development for urban school social workers. *Journal of Social Work Education, 41,* 85–98.

U.S. Census Bureau. (2004). Interim projection of the U. S. population by age, sex, race, and Hispanic origin: Summary methodology and assumptions. http://www.census.gov/ipc/www/usinterimproj/idbsummeth.html

Van Den Bergh, N., & Crisp, C. (2004). Defining culturally competent practice with sexual minorities: Implications for social work education and practice. *Journal of Social Work Education, 40,* 221–238.

Van Hook, M., & Aguilar, M. (2001). Health, religion, and spirituality. In M. Van Hook, B. Hugen, & M. Aguilar (Eds.), *Spirituality within religious traditions in social work practice* (pp. 273–289). Pacific Grove, CA: Brooks/Cole.

Zayas, L. H., Evans, M. E., Mejia, L., & Rodriguez, O. (1997). Cultural-competency training for staff serving Hispanic families with a child in psychiatric crisis. *Families in Society, 78,* 405–412.

CHAPTER 2

Andersen, M. L., & Collins, P. H. (1998). *Race, class and gender: Anthology.* Belmont, CA: Wadsworth Publishing Company.

Appleby, G. A. (2001). Dynamics of oppression and discrimination. In G. A. Appleby, E. Colon, & J. Hamilon, (Eds.), *Diversity, oppression, and social functioning: Person-in-environment assessment and intervention* (pp. 36–52). Boston: Allyn & Bacon.

Appleby, G. A., & Anastas, J. W. (1998). *Not just a passing phase: Social work with gay, lesbian, and bisexual people.* New York: Columbia University Press.

Armour, M. P., Bain, B., & Rubio, R. (2004). An evaluation study of diversity training for field instructors: A collaborative approach to enhancing cultural competence. *Journal of Social Work Education, 40,* 27–37.

Ashford, J. B., LeCroy, C. W., & Lortie, K. L. (2001). *Human behavior in the social environment: A multidimensional perspective.* Pacific Grove, CA: Brooks/Cole.

Bonacich, E., & Goodman, R. F. (1972). *Deadlock in school desegregation: A case study of Inglewood, California.* New York: Praeger.

Bradshaw, C. K. (1994). Asian and Asian American women: Historical and political considerations in psychotherapy. In L. Comas-Diaz & B. Greene (Eds.). *Women of color: Integrating ethnic and gender identities in psychotherapy* (pp. 72–113). New York: Guilford.

Butler, R. N. (1969). Ageism: Another form of bigotry. *The Gerontologist, 9,* 243–246.

Carter, R. T., & Jones, J. M. (1996). Racism and white racial identity merging realities. In B. P. Bowser & R. G. Hunt (Eds.), *Impacts of racism on white Americans.* Thousand Oaks, CA: Sage.

Cohen, E., & Goode, T. D. (1999). *Policy brief 1: Rationale for cultural competence in primary health care.* Georgetown University Child Development Center, National Center for Cultural Competence.

Collins, P. H. (1990). *Black feminist thought: Knowledge, consciousness, and the politics of empowerment.* Boston: Unwin Hyman.

Comas-Diaz, L. (1994). An integrative approach. In L. Comas-Diaz & B. Greene (Eds.), *Women of color: Integrating ethnic and gender identities in psychotherapy* (pp. 287–318). New York: Guilford.

Council on Social Work Education (CSWE), Commission on Accreditation. (2002). *Educational policy and accreditation standards.* Alexandria, VA: Author.

Crenshaw, K. W. (1994). Mapping the margins: Intersectionality, identity politics, and violence against women of color. In M. A. Fineman & R. Mykitiuk (Eds.), *The public nature of private violence: The discovery of domestic abuse* (pp. 93–118). New York: Routledge.

Daniel, J. H. (2000). The courage to hear: African American women's memories of racial trauma. In L. C. Jackson & B. Greene (Eds.), *Psychotherapy with African American women: Innovations in psychodynamic perspectives and practice* (pp. 126–144). New York: Guilford.

Deaux, K., Dane, F. C., & Wrightsman, L. S. (1993). *Social psychology in the 90s.* Pacific Grove, CA: Brooks/Cole.

Du Bois, W. E. B. (1903/1969). *The souls of Black folks.* New York: New American Library.

Fain, M. J. (2005). *Cultural competency for the older adult.* http://www.eddev.arizona.edu/courses/sbs/yl/docs/Cultural Competency.pdf

Freire, P. (1970). *Pedagogy of the oppressed.* New York: Herder & Herder.

Friedman, M. B. (2004). Focus on geriatric mental health: Testimony regarding the New York State Office of Mental Health's 5-Year Plan, June 4, 2004. http://mhawestchester.org/advocates/tfriedman60404.asp

Garcia, B., & Van Soest, D. (2000). Facilitating learning on diversity: Challenges to the professor. *Journal of Ethnic & Cultural Diversity in Social Work, 9*(1/2), 21–39.

Gil, D. G. (1998). *Confronting injustice and oppression: Concepts and strategies for social workers.* New York: Columbia University Press.

Greene, B. (1994a). Lesbian and gay sexual orientations: Implications for clinical training, practice, and research. In B. Greene & G. M. Herek (Eds.), *Lesbian and gay psychology: Theory, research, and clinical applications* (pp. 1–24). Thousand Oaks, CA: Sage.

Greene, B. (1994b). Lesbian women of color: Triple jeopardy. In L. Comas-Diaz & B. Greene (Eds.), *Women of color: Integrating ethnic and gender identities in psychotherapy* (pp. 389–427). New York: Guilford.

Greene, B. (2000). African American lesbian and bisexual women in feminist-psychodynamic psychotherapies: Surviving and thriving between a rock and a hard place. In L. C. Jackson & B. Greene (Eds.), *Psychotherapy with African American women: Innovations in psychodynamic perspectives and practice* (pp. 82–125). New York: Guilford.

Greene, R. R., Watkins, M., McNutt, J., & Lopez, L. (1998). Diversity defined. In R. R. Greene & M. Watkins (Eds.), *Serving diverse constituencies: Applying the ecological perspective.* New York: Aldine De Gruyter.

Gutierrez, L. M., & Lewis, E. A. (1999). *Empowering women of color.* New York: Columbia University Press.

Keenan, E. K. (2004). From sociocultural categories to socially located relations: Using critical theory in social work practice. *Families in Society, 85,* 539–548.

Jones, J. M. & Carter, R. T. (1996). Racism and white racial identity: Merging realities. In B. P. Bowser & R. G. Hunt (Eds.), *Impacts of racism on white Americans* (2nd ed), (pp 1–23). Thousand Oaks, CA: Sage.

Kemp, S. P., Whittaker, J. K., & Tracy, E. M. (2002). Contextual social work practice. In M. O'Melia & K. K. Miley (Eds.), *Pathways to power: Readings in contextual social work practice* (pp. 15–34). Boston: Allyn & Bacon.

Longres, J. F. (1995). *Human behavior in the social environment.* Itasca, IL: F. E. Peacock.

Mahoney, M. R. (1994). Victimization or oppression? Women's lives, violence, and agency. In M. A. Fineman & R. Mykitiuk (Eds.), *The public nature of private violence: The discovery of domestic abuse* (pp. 59–92). New York: Routledge.

McAleavy, T. M. (2002, January 21). Race colors views of job fairness. *Sacramento Bee,* pp. E1, E4.

Messinger, L. (2004). Out in the field: Gay and lesbian social work students' experiences in field placement. *Journal of Social Work Education, 40,* 187–204.

Murphy, B. C., & Dillon, C. (1998). *Interviewing in action: Process and practice.* Pacific Grove, CA: Brooks/Cole.

Pence, E. (n.d.) *Power and control wheel.* Duluth, MN: Domestic Abuse Intervention Project.

Ragg,, D. M. (2001). *Building effective helping skills: The foundation of generalist practice.* Boston: Allyn & Bacon.

Reed,, B. G., Newman, P. A., Suarez, Z. E., & Lewis, E. A. (1997). Interpersonal practice beyond diversity and toward social justice: The importance of critical consciousness. In C. D. Garvin & B. A. Seabury (Eds.), *Interpersonal practice in social work: Promoting competence and social injustice* (pp. 44–77). Boston: Allyn & Bacon.

Reid, P. T. (2000). Foreword. In L. C. Jackson & B. Greene (Eds.), *Psychotherapy with African American women: Innovations in psychodynamic perspectives and practice* (pp. xiii–xv). New York: Guilford.

Ridley, C. R. (2005). *Overcoming unintentional racism in counseling and therapy: A practitioner's guide to intentional intervention.* Thousand Oaks, CA: Sage Publications.

Rose, S. M. (1990). Advocacy/empowerment: An approach to clinical practice for social work. *Journal of Sociology and Social Welfare, 17*(2): 41–52.

Schriver, J. M. (2001). *Human behavior and the social environment: Shifting paradigms in essential knowledge for social work practice.* Boston: Allyn & Bacon.

Spencer, M., Lewis, E., & Gutierrez, L. (2000). Multicultural perspectives on direct practice in social work. In P. Allen-Meares & C. Garvin (Eds.), *The handbook of social work direct practice* (pp. 131–149). Thousand Oaks, CA: Sage.

Stockard, J., & Johnson, M. M. (1992). *Sex and gender in society.* Englewood Cliffs, NJ: Prentice-Hall.

Sue, D. W. (2006). *Multicultural social work practice.* Hoboken, NJ: John Wiley & Sons.

Tully, C. T. (2000). *Lesbians, gays and the empowerment perspective.* New York: Columbia University Press.

Van Den Bergh, N., & Crisp, C. (2004). Defining culturally competent practice with sexual minorities: Implications for social work education and practice. *Journal of Social Work Education, 40,* 221–238.

Weinberg, G. (1972). *Society and the healthy homosexual.* New York: St. Martin's Press.

Wilgoren, J. (2001, September 16). A new breed: Hijackers had reason to live. *Sacramento Bee*, pp. A1, A21.

Worden, B. (2001). Women and sexist oppression. In G. A. Appleby, E. Colon, & J. Hamilton (Eds.), *Diversity, oppression, and social functioning: Person-in-environment assessment and intervention*. Boston: Allyn & Bacon.

Young, I. M. (1990). *Justice and the politics of difference*. Princeton, NJ: Princeton University Press.

CHAPTER 3

Barker, R. L. (2003). *The social work dictionary* (5th ed.). Washington, DC: NASW Press.

Beverly, D. P., & McSweeney, E. A. (1987). *Social welfare and social justice*. Englewood Cliffs, NJ: Prentice-Hall.

Bulhan, H. A. (1985). *Frantz Fanon and the psychology of oppression*. New York: Plenum.

Callahan, S. (1982, November 19). Peace-making strategies for inertia. *National Catholic Reporter*, 1.

Conrad, A. P. (1988). The role of field instructors in the transmission of social justice values. *Journal of Teaching in Social Work, 2*(2), 63–82.

Council on Social Work Education (CSWE). (1992). *Curriculum policy statements for baccalaureate degree and master's degree programs in social work education*. Alexandria, VA: Author.

Council on Social Work Education (CSWE). (2002). *Educational policy and accreditation standards*. Alexandria, VA: Author.

Cross, T. L., Bazron, B. J., Dennis, K. W., & Isaacs, M. R. (1989). *Towards a culturally competent system of care*. Washington, DC: Georgetown University Child Development Center.

Derman-Sparks, L., & Brunson Phillips, C. (1997). *Teaching/learning anti-racism: A developmental approach*. New York: Teachers College Press, Columbia University.

Ferguson, M. (1980). *The aquarian conspiracy*. Los Angeles: J. P. Tarcher.

Flynn, J. P. (1995). Social justice in social agencies. In R. L. Edwards (Ed.-in-Chief), *Encyclopedia of social work* (19th ed.) (pp. 2173–2179). Washington, DC: NASW Press.

GATT and NAFTA: How trade agreements can change your life. (n.d.). San Francisco, CA: Global Exchange.

Gil, D. (1998). *Confronting injustice and oppression: Concepts and strategies for social workers*. New York: Columbia University.

Giroux, H. A. (2000). Racial politics, pedagogy, and the crisis of representation in academic multiculturalism. *Social Identities, 6*(4), 493–510.

Goldberg, D. T. (1993). *Racist culture*. Cambridge, MA: Basil Blackwell.

International Federation of Social Workers (IFSW). (1994). *International declaration of ethical principles of social work*. Oslo, Norway: Author.

Kubler-Ross, E. (1975). *Death: The final stage of growth*. Englewood Cliffs, NJ: Prentice-Hall.

Lum, D. (1999). *Culturally competent practice: A framework for growth and action*. Belmont, CA: Wadsworth.

Macy, J. R. (1983). *Despair and personal power in the nuclear age*. Philadelphia: New Society.

Marris, P. (1974). *Loss and change*. London: Routledge & Kegan Paul.

Mill, J. S. (1863). On the connection between justice and utility. In *Utilitarianism*, Chapter V, as reprinted in J. P. Sterba (1992), *Justice: Alternative political perspectives* (pp. 171–184). Belmont, CA: Wadsworth.

Mills, K. W. (1997). *The racial contract*. Ithaca, NY: Cornell.

National Association of Social Workers (NASW). (1996a). *Code of ethics*. Washington, DC: Author.

National Association of Social Workers (NASW). (1996b). *The violence and development project: Expanding capacities for community building and global learning* (preliminary funding proposal by the National Association of Social Workers in collaboration with the Council on Social Work Education and the Benton Foundation). Washington, DC: Author.

Nozick, R. (1974). *Anarchy, state, and utopia*. New York: Basic Books.

Opotow, S. (1990). Moral exclusion and injustice: An introduction. *Journal of Social Issues, 46*(1), 1–20.

Pateman, C. (1988). *The sexual contract.* Stanford, CA: Stanford University Press.

Pinderhughes, E. (1989). *Understanding race, ethnicity, and power.* New York: Free Press.

Rawls, J. (1971). *A theory of justice.* Cambridge, MA: Harvard University Press.

Reisch, M. (2002, July/Aug). Defining social justice in a socially unjust world. *Families in society,* 83(4), 343–354.

Reisch, M., & Taylor, C. T. (1983). Ethical guidelines for cutback management: A preliminary approach. *Administration in Social Work,* 7(3/4), 59–72.

Sterba, J. P. (Ed.) (1992). *Justice: Alternative political perspectives.* Belmont, CA: Wadsworth.

United Nations. (1987). *Human rights: Questions and answers.* New York: Author.

United Nations. (1992). *Teaching and learning about human rights: A manual for schools of social work and the social work profession.* New York: Author.

Van Voorhis, R. M. (1998). Culturally relevant practice: A framework for teaching the psychosocial dynamics of oppression. *Journal of Social Work Education,* 34(1), 121–133.

van Wormer, K. (2004). *Confronting oppression, restoring justice: From policy analysis to social action.* Alexandria, VA: Council on Social Work Education.

Wakefield, J. C. (1988, June). Psychotherapy, distributive justice, and social work. Part I: Distributive justice as a conceptual framework for social work. *Social Service Review,* 187–210.

Wronka, J. (1998). *Human rights and social policy in the 21st century.* Lanham, MD: University Press of America.

Young, I. M. (1990). *Justice and the politics of difference.* Princeton, NJ: Princeton University Press.

CHAPTER 4

Alter, C., & Egan, M. (1997). Logic modeling: A tool for teaching practice evaluation. *Journal of Social Work Education,* 33(1), 75–84.

Arredondo, P., et al. (1996). *Operationalization of the multicultural counseling competencies.* Washington, DC: Association for Multicultural Counseling and Development.

Congress, E. P. (Ed.). (1997). *Multicultural perspectives in working with families.* New York: Springer.

Council on Social Work Education (CSWE), Commission on Accreditation. (1992). *Handbook of accreditation standards and procedures* (4th ed.). Alexandria, VA: Author.

Council on Social Work Education (CSWE), Commission on Accreditation. (2002). *Educational policy and accreditation standards.* Alexandria, VA: Author.

Cross, T. L., Bazron, B. J., Dennis, K. W., & Isaacs, M. R. (1989). *Towards a culturally competent system of care.* Washington, DC: CASSP Technical Assistance Center.

Devore, W., & Schlesinger, E. G. (1999). *Ethnic-sensitive social work practice.* New York: Allyn & Bacon.

Flexner, A. (1961). Is social work a profession? In R. E. Pumphrey & M. W. Pumphrey (Eds.), *The heritage of American social work: Readings in its philosophical and institutional development* (pp. 301–307). New York: Columbia University Press.

Green, J. W. (1999). *Cultural awareness in the human services: A multi-ethnic approach.* Boston: Allyn & Bacon.

Hills, H. I., & Strozier, A. L. (1992). Multicultural training in APA approved counseling psychology programs: A survey. *Professional Psychology: Research and Practice,* 23, 43–51.

Kurfiss, J. G. (1989). Helping faculty foster students' critical thinking in the disciplines. In A. F. Lucas (Ed.), *New directions for teaching and learning* (No. 37). San Francisco: Jossey-Bass.

Lu, F. G., Lim, R. F., & Mezzich, J. E. (1995). Issues in the assessment and diagnosis of culturally diverse individuals. In J. Oldham & M. Riba (Eds.), *Review of psychiatry* (Vol. 14, pp. 477–510). Washington, DC: American Psychiatric Association Press.

Lum, D. (1986). *Social work practice and people of color: A process-stage approach.* Monterey, CA: Brooks/Cole.

Lum, D. (2000). *Social work practice and people of color: A process-stage approach* (4th ed.). Pacific Grove, CA: Brooks/Cole.

McFadden, J., & Wilson, T. (1977). *Non-white academic training with counselor education rehabilitation counseling and student personnel programs.* Unpublished research.

Pedersen, P. (1991). Multiculturalism as a fourth force in counseling. *Journal of Counseling and Development, 70*(1), 5–25.

Ponterotto, J., & Casas, M. (1991). *Handbook of racial/ethnic minority counseling research.* Springfield, IL: Charles C. Thomas.

Pope-Davis, D. B., & Dings, J. G. (1995). The assessment of multicultural counseling competencies. In J. G. Ponterotto, J. M. Casas, L. A. Suzuki, & C. M. Alexander (Eds.), *Handbook of multicultural counseling* (pp. 287–311). Thousand Oaks, CA: Sage.

Reid, W. J. (1978). *The task-centered system.* New York: Columbia University Press.

Smith, T. B., Richards, P. S., Granley, H. M., & Obiakor, F. (2004). Practicing multiculturalism: An introduction. In T. B. Smith (Ed.), *Practicing multiculturalism: Affirming diversity in counseling and psychology* (pp. 3–16). Boston: Allyn & Bacon/Pearson Education.

Sue, D. W. (2001). Multidimensional facets of cultural competence. *The Counseling Psychologist, 29*, 790–821.

Sue, D. W., Arredondo, P., & McDavis, R. J. (1992). Multicultural counseling competencies and standards: A call to the profession. *Journal of Counseling and Development, 70*, 477–486.

Sue, D. W., Arredondo, P., & McDavis, R. J. (1995). Multicultural counseling competencies and standards: A call to the profession, Appendix III. In J. G. Ponterotto, J. M. Casas, L. A. Suzuki, & C. M. Alexander (Eds.), *Handbook of multicultural counseling* (pp. 624–640). Thousand Oaks, CA: Sage.

Sue, D. W., & Sue, D. (1990). *Counseling the culturally different: Theory and practice.* New York: John Wiley.

Van Den Bergh, N., & Crisp, C. (2004). Defining culturally competent practice with sexual minorities: Implications for social work education and practice. *Journal of Social Work Education, 40*, 221–238.

CHAPTER 5

Bankston, C. L., & Zhou, M. (1995). Effects of minority-language literacy on academic achievement of Vietnamese youths in New Orleans. *Sociology of Education, 68*, 1–17.

Bourguignon, E. (1979). *Psychological anthropology.* New York: Holt, Rinehart, & Winston.

Carter, R. T., & Qureshi, A. (1995). A typology of philosophical assumptions in multicultural counseling and training. In J. G. Ponterotto, J. M. Casas, L. A. Suzuki, & C. M. Alexander (Eds.), *Handbook of multicultural counseling* (pp. 239–262). Thousand Oaks, CA: Sage.

Council on Social Work Education (CSWE), Commission on Accreditation. (1992). *Handbook of accreditation standards and procedures* (4th ed.). Alexandria, VA: Author.

Council on Social Work Education (CSWE), Commission on Accreditation. (2002). *Educational policy and accreditation standards.* Alexandria, VA: Author.

Delgado, M., Jones, K., & Rohani, M. (2005). *Social work practice with refugee and immigrant youth in the United States.* Boston: Allyn & Bacon/Pearson Education.

Giordano, J., & McGoldrick, M. (1996). European families: An overview. In M. McGoldrick, J. Giordano, & J. K. Pearce (Eds.), *Ethnicity and family therapy* (pp. 427–441). New York: Guilford.

Goldstein, H. (1983). Starting where the client is. *Social Casework, 64*, 267–275.

Green, J. W. (1995). *Cultural awareness in the human services: A multi-ethnic approach.* Boston: Allyn & Bacon.

Green, J. W. (1999). *Cultural awareness in the human services: A multi-ethnic approach.* Boston: Allyn & Bacon.

Gushue, G. V., Greenan, D. E., & Brazaitis, S. J. (2005). Using the multicultural guidelines in couples and family counseling. In M. G. Constantine & D. W. Sue (Eds.), *Strategies for building multicultural competence in mental health and educational settings* (pp. 56–72). Hoboken, NJ: John Wiley & Sons.

Hardy, K. V., & Laszloffy, T. A. (1995). The cultural genogram: Key to training culturally competent family therapists. *Journal of Marital and Family Therapy, 21,* 227–237.

Kadushin, A., & Kadushin, G. (1997). *The social work interview: A guide for human service professionals.* New York: Columbia University Press.

Leigh, J., & Green, J. (1989). Teaching ethnographic methods to social service workers. *Practicing Anthropology, 11,* 8–10.

Lum, D. (2004). *Social work practice and people of color: A process-stage approach.* Belmont, CA: Brooks/Cole-Thomson Learning.

McGoldrick, M., & Giordano, J. (1996). Overview: Ethnicity and family therapy. In M. McGoldrick, J. Giordano, & J. K. Pearce (Eds.), *Ethnicity and family therapy* (pp. 1–27). New York: Guilford.

Muslim refugees in the United States. (n.d.) Muslim refugee populations and special concerns. http://www.culturalorientation. net/muslims/mc4.html

Perez, R. M., Fukuyama, M. A., & Coleman, N. C. (2005). Using the multicultural guidelines in college counseling centers. In M. G. Constantine & D. W. Sue (Eds.), *Strategies for building multicultural competence in mental health and educational settings* (pp. 160–179) Hoboken, NJ: John Wiley & Sons.

Pope, R. L. (1993). An analysis of multiracial change efforts in student affairs (Doctoral dissertation, University of Massachusetts at Amherst, 1982). *Dissertation Abstracts International, 53–10,* 3457A.

Portes, A., & Hao, L. (2002). The price of uniformity: Language, family and personal adjustment in the immigrant second generation. *Ethnic and Racial Studies, 25,* 889–912.

Portes, A., & Rumbaut, R. (2001). *Legacies: The story of the immigrant second generation.* Berkeley: University of California Press.

Potocky-Tripodi, M. (2002). *Best practices for social work with refugees and immigrants.* New York: Columbia University Press.

Reynolds, A. L. (1995). Challenges and strategies for teaching multicultural counseling courses. In J. G. Ponterotto, J. M. Casas, L. A. Suzuki, & C. M. Alexander (Eds.), *Handbook of multicultural counseling* (pp. 312–330). Thousand Oaks, CA: Sage.

Ridley, C. R. (2005). *Overcoming unintentional racism in counseling and therapy: A practitioner's guide to intentional intervention.* Thousand Oaks, CA: Sage Publications.

Sanday, P. R. (1976). *Anthropology and the public interest.* New York: Academic Press.

School district shuffles bosses: Board changes job of 25 administrators. (1997, May 13). *Sacramento Bee,* pp. B1, B4.

Segal, U. A. (2002). *A framework for immigration: Asians in the United States.* New York: Columbia University Press.

Thornton, S., & Garrett, K. J. (1995). Ethnography as a bridge to multicultural practice. *Journal of Social Work Education, 31,* 67–74.

Van Den Bergh, N., & Crisp, C. (2004). Defining culturally competent practice with sexual minorities: Implications for social work education and practice. *Journal of Social Work Education, 40,* 221–238.

Yan, M. C., & Wong, Y. L. R. (2005). Rethinking self-awareness in cultural competence: Toward a dialogic self in cross-cultural social work. *Families in Society, 86,* 181–188.

CHAPTER 6

Acevedo, G., & Morales, J. (2001). Assessment with Latino/Hispanic communities and organizations. In R. Fong & S. B.C.L. Furuto (Eds.), *Culturally competent practice: Skills, interventions, and evaluations* (pp. 147–162). Boston: Allyn & Bacon.

Aguilar, M. A., & Williams, L. P. (1993). Factors contributing to the success and achievements of minority women. *Affilia, 8*(4), 410–424.

American FactFinder. (2000). Profile of general demographic characteristics: 2000 (DP-1). http://www.factfinder.census.gov

Anderson, H., & Goolishian, H. (1992). The client is the expert: A not-knowing approach to therapy. In S. McNamee & K. J. Gergen

(Eds.), *Therapy as social construction* (pp. 25–39). London: Sage.

Brown, E. F., & Gundersen, B. N. (2001). Organization and community intervention with American Indian tribal communities. In R. Fong & S. B. C. L. Furuto (Eds.), *Culturally competent practice: Skills, interventions, and evaluations* (pp. 299–312). Boston: Allyn & Bacon.

Brown, L. S. (1990). The meaning of a multicultural perspective for theory-building in feminist therapy. In L. S. Brown & M. P. P. Root (Eds.), *Diversity and complexity in feminist therapy* (pp. 1–21). New York: Haworth.

Browne, C., & Mills, C. (2001). Theoretical frameworks: Ecological model, strengths perspective, and empowerment theory. In R. Fong & S. B.C.L. Furuto (Eds.), *Culturally competent practice: Skills, interventions, and evaluations* (pp. 10–32). Boston: Allyn & Bacon.

Collins, P. H. (1990). *Black feminist thought.* Boston: Unwin Hyman.

Comas-Diaz, L., & Greene, B. (Eds.). (1994). *Women of color: Integrating ethnic and gender identities in psychotherapy.* New York: Guilford.

Congress, E. P., & Kung, W. W. (2005). Using the culturagram to assess and empower culturally diverse families. In E. P. Congress & M. J. Gonzalez (Eds.) *Multicultural perspectives in working with families* (pp. 3–21). New York: Springer Publishing Company.

Daly, A. (2001). A heuristic perspective of strengths when intervening with an African American community. In R. Fong & S. B.C.L. Furuto (Eds.), *Culturally competent practice: Skills, interventions, and evaluations* (pp. 241–254). Boston: Allyn & Bacon.

Davis, E. (2001). Evaluation skills with African American individuals and families: Three approaches. In R. Fong & S. B.C.L. Furuto (Eds.), *Culturally competent practice: Skills, interventions, and evaluations* (pp. 343–354). Boston: Allyn & Bacon.

Devore, W., & Schlesinger, E. G. (1999). *Ethnic-sensitive social work practice.* New York: Allyn & Bacon.

Dressel, P. L. (1994). . . . And we keep on building prisons: Racism, poverty and challenges to the welfare state. *Journal of Sociology and Social Welfare, 21,* 7–30.

Epston, D., White, M., & Murray, K. (1992). A proposal for a re-authoring therapy: Rose's revisioning of her life and a commentary. In S. McNamee & K. J. Gergen (Eds.), *Therapy as social construction* (pp. 96–115). London: Sage.

Fong, R. (2001). Culturally competent social work practice: Past and present. In R. Fong & S. B.C.L. Furuto (Eds.), *Culturally competent practice: Skills, interventions, and evaluations* (pp. 1–9). Boston: Allyn & Bacon.

Fong, R., Boyd, T., & Browne, C. (1999). The Gandhi technique: A biculturalization approach for empowering Asian and Pacific Islander families. *Journal of Multicultural Social Work, 7,* 95–110.

Fong, R., & Furuto, S. B.C.L. (Eds.). (2001a). *Culturally competent practice: Skills, interventions, and evaluations.* Boston: Allyn & Bacon.

Fong, R., & Furuto, S. B.C.L. (2001b). Future directions for culturally competent social work practice. In R. Fong & S. B.C.L. Furuto (Eds.), *Culturally competent practice: Skills, interventions, and evaluations* (pp. 454–458). Boston: Allyn & Bacon.

Froggeri, L. (1992). Therapeutic process as the social construction of change. In S. McNamee & K. J. Gergen (Eds.), *Therapy as social construction* (pp. 40–53). London: Sage.

Furuto, S. B.C.L., Nicolas, R. J., Kim, G. E., & Fiaui, L. M. (2001). Interventions with Kanaka Maoli, Chamorro, and Samoan communities. In R. Fong & S. B.C.L. Furuto (Eds.), *Culturally competent practice: Skills, interventions, and evaluations* (pp. 327–342). Boston: Allyn & Bacon.

Geertz, C. (1973). *The interpretation of cultures.* New York: Basic Books.

Gelman, C. R. (2004). Empirically-based principles for culturally competent practice with Latinos. *Journal of Ethnic & Cultural Diversity in Social Work, 13,* 83–108.

Gergen, K. J. (1985). The social constructionist movement in modern psychology. *American Psychologist, 40,* 266–275.

Gergen, K. J., & Davis, K. E. (1985). *The social construction of the person.* New York: Springer-Verlag.

Gilbert, D. J., & Franklin, C. (2001). Developing culturally sensitive practice evaluation skills with Native American individuals and families. In R. Fong & S. B.C.L. Furuto (Eds.), *Culturally competent practice: Skills, interventions, and evaluations* (pp. 396–411). Boston: Allyn & Bacon.

GlenMaye, L. (1998). Empowerment of women. In L. M. Gutierrez, R. J. Parsons, & E. O. Cox (Eds.), *Empowerment in social work practice: A sourcebook* (pp. 29–51). Pacific Grove, CA: Brooks/Cole.

Goldstein, H. (1986). Toward the integration of theory and practice: A humanistic approach. *Social Work, 3,* 352–357.

Gordon, M. M. (1978). *Human nature, class, and ethnicity.* New York: Oxford University Press.

Grant, D. (2001). Evaluation skills with African American organizations and communities. In R. Fong & S. B.C.L. Furuto (Eds.), *Culturally competent practice: Skills, interventions, and evaluations* (pp. 355–369). Boston: Allyn & Bacon.

Green, J. W. (1999). *Cultural awareness in the human services: A multi-ethnic approach.* Boston: Allyn & Bacon.

Greene, B. (1994). Diversity and difference: Race and feminist psychotherapy. In M. P. Mirkin (Ed.), *Women in context: Toward a feminist reconstruction of psychotherapy* (pp. 333–351). New York: Guilford.

Gutierrez, L. (1992). Empowering clients in the twenty-first century: The role of human service organizations. In Y. Hasenfeld (Ed.), *Human service organizations as complex organizations* (pp. 320–338). Newbury Park, CA: Sage.

Gutierrez, L., & Nagda, B. A. (1996). The multicultural imperative in human services organizations: Issues for the twenty-first century. In P. R. Raffoul & C. A. McNeece (Eds.), *Future issues for social work practice* (pp. 203–213). Boston: Allyn & Bacon.

Helms, J. E. (1990). An overview of black racial identity theory. In J. E. Helms (Ed.), *Black and white racial identity: Theory, research, and practice* (pp. 9–33). New York: Greenwood.

Holland, T. P., Gallant, J. P., & Colosetti, S. (1994). Assessment of teaching a constructivist approach to social work practice. *Arete, 18,* 45–60.

Holmes, G. E. (1992). Social work research and the empowerment paradigm. In D. Saleebey (Ed.), *The strengths perspective in social work practice* (pp. 158–168). White Plains, NY: Longman.

Iglehart, A. P., & Becerra, R. M. (1995). *Social services and the ethnic community.* Boston: Allyn & Bacon.

Kanuha, V. K. (2001). Individual and family intervention skills with Asian and Pacific Island American lesbians and gay men. In R. Fong & S. B.C.L. Furuto (Eds.), *Culturally competent practice: Skills, interventions, and evaluations* (pp. 313–326). Boston: Allyn & Bacon.

Kliman, J. (1994). The interweaving of gender, class, and race in family therapy. In M. P. Mirkin (Ed.), *Women in context: Toward a feminist reconstruction of psychotherapy* (pp. 25–47). New York: Guilford.

Kopacsi, R., & Faulkner, A. O. (1988). The papers that might be: The unity of white and black feminist. *Affilia, 3*(3), 33–50.

Korber, D. (2001, March 30). Census finds majority of none. *Sacramento Bee,* pp. A1, A28.

Leigh, J. W. (1998). *Communicating for cultural competence.* Boston: Allyn & Bacon.

Leung, P., & Cheung, M. (2001). Competencies in practice evaluations with Asian American individuals and families. In R. Fong & S. B.C.L. Furuto (Eds.), *Culturally competent practice: Skills, interventions, and evaluations* (pp. 426–437). Boston: Allyn & Bacon.

Lewis, L. G. (2001). Program evaluation with Native American/American Indian organizations. In R. Fong & S. B.C.L. Furuto (Eds.), *Culturally competent practice: Skills, interventions, and evaluations* (pp. 412–425). Boston: Allyn & Bacon.

Lum, D. (2004). *Social work practice and people of color: A process-stage approach* (5th ed.). Belmont, CA: Brooks/Cole–Thomson Learning.

Manning, M. C., Cornelius, L. J., & Okundaye, J. N. (2004). Empowering African Americans through social work practice: Integrating an Afrocentric perspective, ego psychology, and spirituality. *Families in Society, 85*, 229–235.

McNamee, S., & Gergen, K. J. (Eds.). (1992). *Therapy as social construction.* London: Sage.

Mirkin, M. P. (Ed.). (1994). *Women in context: Toward a feminist reconstruction of psychotherapy.* New York: Guilford.

Morris, J. K. (1993). Interacting oppressions: Teaching social work content on women of color. *Journal of Social Work Education, 29*(1), 99–110.

Morton, G., & Atkinson, D. R. (1983). Minority identity development and preference for counselor race. *Journal of Negro Education, 52*(2), 156–161.

MSNBC. (2001a). Census shows narrower gender gap. *Census 2000—The changing face of America,* 1–3. http://www.msnbc.com/news/626462.asp

MSNBC. (2001b). Fewer working moms with infants. *Census 2000—The changing face of America,* 1–3. http://www.msnbc.com/news/644425.asp

MSNBC. (2001c). More Americans living to age 100. *Census 2000—The changing face of America,* 1–4. http://www.msnbc.com/news/637212.asp

MSNBC. (2001d). Several generations under one roof. *Census 2000—The changing face of America,* 1–3. http://www.msnbc.com/news/625336.asp

Mumm, A. M., & Kerstling, R. C. (1997). Teaching critical thinking in social work practice courses. *Journal of Social Work Education, 33*, 75–84.

Muslim refugees in the United States. (n.d.). Muslim refugee populations and special concerns. http://www.culturalorientation.net/muslims/mc4.html

Norton, D. G. (1993). Diversity, early socialization, and temporal development: The dual perspective revisited. *Social Work, 38*(1), 82–90.

Ozawa, M. (1986). Nonwhites and the demographic imperative in social welfare spending. *Social Work, 31*, 440–445.

Paniagua, F. A. (2005). *Assessing and treating culturally diverse clients: A practical guide.* Thousand Oaks, CA: Sage Publications.

Parker, I., & Shotter, J. (Eds.). (1990). *Reconstructing social psychology.* London: Routledge.

Paul, R. (1992). Critical thinking: What, why, and how. *New Directions for Community Colleges, 77*, 3–24.

Pieper, M. H. (1994). Science, not scientism: The robustness of naturalistic clinical research. In E. Sherman & W. J. Reid (Eds.), *Qualitative research in social work* (pp. 71–88). New York: Columbia University Press.

Ponterotto, J. G. (1997). Multicultural counseling training: A competency model and national survey. In D. B. Pope-Davis & H. L. K. Coleman (Eds.), *Multicultural counseling competencies: Assessment, education and training, and supervision* (pp. 11–130). Thousand Oaks, CA: Sage.

Puig, M. (2001). Organizations and community intervention skills with Hispanic Americans. In R. Fong & S. B.C.L. Furuto (Eds.), *Culturally competent practice: Skills, interventions, and evaluations* (pp. 269–284). Boston: Allyn & Bacon.

Radtke, H. L., & Stam, H. J. (Eds.). (1994). *Power/gender: Social relations in theory and practice.* Thousand Oaks, CA: Sage.

Renzetti, C. M., & Curran, D. J. (1995). *Women, men, and society.* Boston: Allyn & Bacon.

Ridley, C. R., Espelage, D. L., & Rubinstein, K. J. (1997). Course development in multicultural counseling. In D. B. Pope-Davis & H. L. K. Coleman (Eds.), *Multicultural counseling competencies: Assessment, education and training, and supervision* (pp. 131–158). Thousand Oaks, CA: Sage.

Romanyshyn, R. D. (1982). *Psychological life: From science to metaphor.* Austin: University of Texas Press.

Rosenblum, K. E., & Travis, T. C. (Eds.). (2000). *The meaning of difference: American constructions of race, sex and gender, social class, and sexual orientation.* Boston: McGraw-Hill.

Sacks, O. (1987). *The man who mistook his wife for a hat and other clinical tales*. New York: Harper & Row.

Sarri, R. (1986). Organizational and policy practice in social work: Challenges for the future. *Urban and Social Change Review, 19*, 14–19.

Simon, B. L. (1994). *The empowerment tradition in American social work*. New York: Columbia University Press.

Sivan, E. (1986). Motivation in social constructivist theory. *Educational Psychologist, 2*, 209–233.

Song, Y. I. (1995). *A women-centered perspective on Korean American women today*. Paper presented at the second joint symposium of Korean social worker educators in the United States and Korea, Soong-Sil University, Seoul, Korea.

Takaki, R. (1990). *Iron cages: Race and culture in 19th century America*. New York: Oxford University Press.

Tanemura Morelli, P. T., & Spencer, M. S. (2000). Use and support of multicultural and antiracist education: Research-informed interdisciplinary social work practice. *Journal of Social Work, 45*(2), 166–175.

Van Den Bergh, N., & Crisp, C. (2004). Defining culturally competent practice with sexual minorities: Implications for social work education and practice. *Journal of Social Work Education, 40*, 221–238.

Weaver, H. N. (2001). Organization and community assessment with First Nations People. In R. Fong & S. B.C.L. Furuto (Eds.), *Culturally competent practice: Skills, interventions, and evaluations* (pp. 178–195). Boston: Allyn & Bacon.

Weaver, H. N. (2004). The elements of cultural competence: Applications with Natve American clients. *Journal of Ethnic & Cultural Diversity in Social Work, 13*, 19–35.

Westbrooks, K. L., & Starks, S. H. (2001). Strengths perspective inherent in cultural empowerment: A tool for assessment with African American individuals and families. In R. Fong & S. B.C.L. Furuto (Eds.), *Culturally competent practice: Skills, interventions, and evaluations* (pp. 101–118). Boston: Allyn & Bacon.

Westphal, D. (2001, March 13). Giant leap in U.S. diversity. *Sacramento Bee*, pp. Al, A18.

Williams, L. (1990). The challenge of education to social work: The case of minority children. *Social Work, 35*, 236–242.

CHAPTER 7

Acevedo, G., & Morales, J. (2001). Assessment with Latino/Hispanic communities and organizations. In R. Fong & S. B.C.L. Furuto (Eds.), *Culturally competent practice: Skills, interventions, and evaluations* (pp. 147–162). Boston: Allyn & Bacon.

Amato-von Hemert, K. (1994). Should social work education address religious issues? Yes! *Journal of Social Work Education, 30*(1), 7–11, 16, 17.

American Psychiatric Association (APA). (1994). *Diagnostic and statistical manual of mental disorders* (4th ed.). Washington, DC: Author.

Barnes, A., & Ephross, P. H. (1995). The impact of hate crimes on victims: Emotional and behavioral responses to attacks. *Social Work, 39*, 247–251.

Beach, M. C., et al. (2005, April). Cultural competence: A systematic review of health care provider educational interventions. *Medical Care, 43(4):* 356–373.

Bergin, A. E., & Garfield, S. L. (1996). *Handbook of psychotherapy and behavior change*. New York: John Wiley.

Bernard, J. M. (1979). Supervisor training: A discrimination model. *Counselor Education and Supervision, 19*, 60–68.

Boehm, A., & Staples, L. H. (2004). Empowerment: The point of view of consumers. *Families in Society, 85*, 270–280.

Bordin, E. S. (1979). The generalizability of the psychoanalytic concept of the working alliance. *Psychotherapy: Theory, Research, and Practice, 16*, 252–260.

Bricker-Jenkins, M. (1997). Hidden treasures: Unlocking strengths in the public social services. In D. Saleebey (Ed.), *The strengths perspective in social work practice* (pp. 133–150). New York: Longman.

Browne, C., & Mills, C. (2001). Theoretical frameworks: Ecological model, strengths perspective, and empowerment theory. In R. Fong & S. B.C.L. Furuto (Eds.), *Culturally competent practice: Skills, interventions and evaluations* (pp. 10–32). Boston: Allyn & Bacon.

Chen, S., Sullivan, N. Y., Lu, Y. E., & Shibusawa, T. (2003). Asian American and mental health services: A study of utlization patterns in the 1990s. *Journal of Ethnic & Cultural Diversity in Social Work, 12*, 19–42.

Clark, J. (1994). Should social work education address religious issues? No! *Journal of Social Work Education, 30*(1), 11–16.

Comas-Diaz, L. (1994). An integrative approach. In L. Comas-Diaz & B. Greene (Eds.), *Women of color: Integrating ethnic and gender identities in psychotherapy* (pp. 287–318). New York: Guilford.

Cowger, C. D. (1994). Assessing client strengths: Clinical assessment for client empowerment. *Social Work, 39*, 262–268.

Cox, C. B., & Ephross, P. H. (1998). *Ethnicity and social work practice.* New York: Oxford University Press.

Dana, R. H. (1993). *Multicultural assessment perspectives for professional psychology.* Boston: Allyn & Bacon.

Docherty, J. P., & Fiester, S. J. (1985). The therapeutic alliance and compliance with psychopharmacology. In R. E. Hales & A. F. Frank (Eds.), *Psychiatry Update, 4*, 607–632.

Dore, M. M., & Alexander, L. B. (1996). Preserving families at risk of child abuse and neglect: The role of the helping alliance. *Child Abuse and Neglect, 20*(4), 349–361.

Dupree, D., Spencer, M. B., & Bell, S. (1997). African American children. In G. Johnson-Powell and J. Yamamoto (Eds.), *Transcultural child development: Psychological assessment and treatment* (pp. 237–268). New York: John Wiley.

Eaton, T. T., Abeles, N., & Gotfreund, M. J. (1988). Therapeutic alliance and outcome: Impact of treatment length and pretreatment symptomatology. *Psychotherapy, 25*, 536–542.

Eisenthal, S., Emery, R., Lazare, A., & Udin, H. (1979). Adherence and the negotiated

approach. *Archives of General Psychiatry, 36*, 393–398.

Fassinger, R. E., & Richie, B. S. (1997). Sex matters: Gender and sexual orientation in training for multicultural counseling competency. In D. B. Pope-Davis & H. L. K. Coleman (Eds.), *Multicultural counseling competencies: Assessment, education and training, and supervision* (pp. 83–110). Thousand Oaks, CA: Sage.

Fong, R. (2004). Overview of immigrant and refugee children and families. In R. Fong (Ed.), *Culturally competent practice with immigrant and refugee children and families* (pp. 1–18). New York: Guilford Press.

Fong, R., & Furuto, S. B.C.L. (2001). *Culturally competent practice: Skills, interventions, and evaluations.* Boston: Allyn & Bacon.

Fortune, A. E. (1987). Grief only? Client and social worker reactions to termination. *Clinical Social Work Journal, 15*, 159–171.

Fortune, A. E., Pearlingi, B., & Rochelle, C. D. (1992). Reactions to termination of individual treatment. *Social Work, 37*, 171–178.

Frank, A. F., & Gunderson, J. G. (1990). The role of the therapeutic alliance in the treatment of schizophrenia. *Archives of General Psychiatry, 47*, 228–236.

Franklin, A. J. (1993, July/August). The invisibility syndrome. *Family Therapy Networker,* 33–39.

Gibson, C. M. (1993). Empowerment theory and practice: With adolescents of color in the child welfare system. *Families in Society, 74*, 387–396.

Giordano, J., & Giordano, M. A. (1995). Ethnic dimensions in family therapy. In R. Mikesell, D. Lusterman, & S. McDaniel (Eds.), *Integrating family therapy.* Washington, DC: American Psychological Association.

GLSEN (Gay, Lesbian, and Straight Education Network). (2001, January 2). Building culturally competent organizations. http://www.lgbthistorymonth.org/cgi-bin/iowa/all/news/record/339.html

Grant, D. (2001). Evaluation skills with African American organizations and communities, In R. Fong & S. B.C.L. Furuto (Eds.), *Culturally competent practice: Skills, interventions, and evaluations* (pp. 355–369). Boston: Allyn & Bacon.

Green, J. W. (1995). *Cultural awareness in the human services: A multi-ethnic approach.* Boston: Allyn & Bacon.

Greene, G. J., Lee, M. Y., & Hoffpauir, S. (2005). The language of empowerment and strengths in clinical social work: A constructivist perspective. *Families in Society, 86,* 267–277.

Gutierrez, L. M. (1990). Working with women of color: An empowerment perspective. *Social Work, 35,* 149–153.

Helms, J. E., & Richardson, T. Q. (1997). How "multiculturalism" obscures race and culture as differential aspects of counseling competency. In D. B. Pope-Davis & H. L. K. Coleman (Eds.), *Multicultural counseling competencies: Assessment, education and training, and supervision* (pp. 60–79). Thousand Oaks, CA: Sage.

Henggeler, S. W., Schoenwald, S. K., Pickrel, S. G., Rowland, M. D., & Santos, A. B. (1994). The contribution of treatment outcome research to the reform of children's mental health services: Multisystem therapy as an example. *Journal of Mental Health Administration, 21,* 229–239.

Hepworth, D. H., Rooney, R. H., & Larsen, J. A. (2002). *Direct social work practice: Theory and skills* (5th ed.). Pacific Grove, CA: Brooks/Cole.

Hines, P. M., & Boyd-Franklin, N. (1996). African American families. In M. McGoldrick, J. Giordano, & J. K. Pearce (Eds.), *Ethnicity and family therapy* (pp. 66–84). New York: Guilford.

Horvath, A. O., & Greenberg, L. S. (Eds.). (1994). *The working alliance: Theory, research, and practice.* New York: John Wiley.

Iglehart, A. P., & Becerra, R. M. (2000). *Social services and the ethnic community.* Prospect Heights, IL: Waveland Press.

Kadushin, A., & Kadushin, G. (1997). *The social work interview: A guide for human service professionals.* New York: Columbia University Press.

Kochman, T. (1981). *Black and white styles in conflicts.* Chicago: University of Chicago Press.

Kumabe, K., Nishida, C., & Hepworth, D. (1985). *Bridging ethnocultural diversity in social work and health.* Honolulu: University of Hawaii Press.

Lefley, H. P., & Pedersen, P. B. (1986). *Crosscultural training for mental health professionals.* Springfield, IL: Charles C. Thomas.

Leigh, J. W. (1984). *Empowerment strategies for work with multi-ethnic populations.* Paper presented at the Council on Social Work Education Annual Program Meeting, Detroit, Michigan.

Lipman-Blumen, J., Handley-Isaksen, A., & Leavitt, H. J. (1983). Achieving styles in men and women: A model, an instrument, and some findings. In J. Spence (Ed.), *Achievement and achievement motives.* San Francisco: Freeman & Company.

Longres, J. F. (1991). Toward a status model of ethnic sensitive practice. *Journal of Multicultural Social Work, 1,* 41–56.

Lu, Y. E., DuBray, W. H., Chen, S., & Ahn, J. H. (2000). Culture and clinical social work: American Indian vs. European American achieving styles. An unpublished paper.

Lu, Y. E., Lum, D., & Chen, S. (2001). Cultural competency and achieving styles in clinical social work: A conceptual and empirical exploration. *Journal of Ethnic and Cultural Diversity in Social Work, 9*(3–4), 1–32.

Lu, Y. E., Organista, K., Manzo, S., Jr., Wong, L., & Phung, J. (2002). Exploring dimensions of culturally sensitive clinical styles with Latinos. *Journal of Ethnic and Cultural Diversity in Social Work, 10*(2), in press.

Luborsky, L. (1975). Helping alliance in psychotherapy. In J. L. Claghorn (Ed.), *Successful psychotherapy* (pp. 92–116). New York: Brunner/Mazel.

Lum, D. (1996). *Social work practice and people of color: A process-stage approach.* Pacific Grove, CA: Brooks/Cole.

Lum, D. (2000). *Social work practice and people of color: A process-stage approach* (4th ed.). Pacific Grove, CA: Brooks/Cole.

Manning, M. (2001). Culturally competent assessment of African American communities and organizations. In R. Fong & S. B.C.L. Furuto (Eds.), *Culturally competent practice: Skills, interventions, and evaluations* (pp. 119–131). Boston: Allyn & Bacon.

Manning, M. C., Cornelius, L. J., & Okundaye, J. N. (2004). Empowering African Americans through social work practice: Integrating an Afrocentric perspective, ego psychology, and spirituality. *Families in Society, 85*, 229–235.

Mayer, J., & Timms, W. (1969). Clash in perspective between worker and client. *Social Casework, 50*, 32–40.

Muslim refugees in the United States (n.d.). Muslim refugee populations and special concerns. http://www.culturalorientation.net/muslims/mc4.html

Negroni-Rodriguez, L. K., & Morales, J. (2001). Individual and family assessment skills with Latinio/Hispanic Americans. In R. Fong & S. B.C.L. Furuto (Eds.), *Culturally competent practice: Skills, interventions, and evaluations* (pp. 132–146). Boston: Allyn & Bacon.

Paniagua, F. A. (2005). *Assessing and treating culturally diverse clients: A practical guide.* Thousand Oaks, CA: Sage Publications.

Pinderhughes, E. (1989). *Understanding race, ethnicity, and power: The key to efficacy in clinical practice.* New York: Free Press.

Potocky-Tripodi, M. (2002). *Best practices for social work with refugees and immigrants.* New York: Columbia University Press.

Proctor, E. K., & Davis, L. E. (1994). The challenge of racial difference: Skills for clinical practice. *Social Work, 39*, 314–323.

The question of race in America. (1997, June 15). *Sacramento Bee*, p. Forum 4.

Raue, P. J., & Goldfried, M. R. (1994). The therapeutic alliance in cognitive-behavior therapy. In A. O. Horvath & L. S. Greenberg (Eds.), *The working alliance: Theory, research and practice* (pp. 131–152). New York: John Wiley.

Reid, W. J. (1978). *The task-centered system.* New York: Columbia University Press.

Reynolds, A. L., & Pope, R. L. (1991). The complexities of diversity: Exploring multiple oppressions. *Journal of Counseling and Development, 70*, 174–180.

Ridley, C. R., Espelage, D. L., & Rubinstein, K. J. (1997). Course development in

multicultural counseling. In D. B. Pope-Davis & H. L. K. Coleman (Eds.), *Multicultural counseling competencies: Assessment, education and training, and supervision* (pp. 131–158). Thousand Oaks, CA: Sage.

Saleebey, D. (Ed.). (2002). *The strengths perspective in social work practice.* Boston: Allyn & Bacon.

Schriver, J. M. (2001). *Human behavior and the social environment: Shifting paradigms in essential knowledge for social work practice.* Boston: Allyn & Bacon.

Sobeck, J. L., Chapleski, E. E., & Fisher, C. (2003). Conducting research with American Indians: A case study of motives, methods, and results. *Journal of Ethnic & Cultural Diversity in Social Work, 12*, 69–84.

Solomon, B. (1976). *Black empowerment: Social work in oppressed communities.* New York: Columbia University Press.

Spence, J. T. (1985). Achievement American style: The rewards and costs of individualism. *American Psychologist, 40*(12), 1285–1295.

Stanhope, V., Solomon, P., Pernell-Arnold, A., Sands, R. G., & Bourjolly, J. N. (2005, Winter). Evaluating cultural competence among behavioral health professionals. *Psychiatric Rehabilitation Journal, 28*(3), 225–233.

Tsui, P., & Schultz, G. L. (1985). Failure of rapport: Why psychotherapeutic engagement fails in the treatment of Asian clients. *American Journal of Orthopsychiatry, 55*, 561–569.

Vasquez, M. J. T. (2005). Independent practice settings and the multicultural guidelines In M. G. Constantine & D. W. Sue (Eds.), *Strategies for building multicultural competence in mental health and educational settings* (pp. 91–108). Hoboken, NJ: John Wiley & Sons.

Waldinger, R. J., & Frank, A. F. (1989). Clinicians' experiences in combining medication and psychotherapy in the treatment of borderline patients. *Hospital and Community Psychiatry, 40*, 712–718.

Wallace, S. (1990). The no-care zone: Availability, accessibility, acceptability in community-based long-term care. *Gerontologist, 30*, 254–261.

Weaver, H. N. (2001). Organization and community assessment with First Nations People. In R. Fong & S. B.C.L. Furuto (Eds.), *Culturally competent practice: Skills, interventions, and evaluations* (pp. 178–195). Boston: Allyn & Bacon.

Yellow Horse Brave Heart, M. (2001). Culturally and historically congruent clinical social work assessment with Native clients. In R. Fong & S. B.C.L. Furuto (Eds.), *Culturally competent practice: Skills, interventions, and evaluations* (pp. 163–177). Boston: Allyn & Bacon.

CHAPTER 8

Bein, A. (1994). *Early termination of outpatient counseling among Hispanics.* Unpublished doctoral dissertation, University of Illinois at Chicago.

Bein, A., Torres, S., & Kurilla, V. (2000). Service delivery issues in early termination of Latino clients. *Journal of Human Behavior in the Social Environment, 3*(2), 43–59.

Dean, R. G. (1994). Commentary: A practitioner's perspective on qualitative case evaluation methods. In E. Sherman & W. J. Reid (Eds.), *Qualitative research in social work* (pp. 279–284). New York: Columbia University Press.

De Jong, P., & Miller, S. (1995). How to interview for client strengths. *Social Work, 40,* 729–736.

Delgado, M. (1997). Strengths-based practice with Puerto Rican adolescents: Lessons from a substance abuse prevention project. *Social Work in Education, 19,* 101–112.

Devore, W., & Schlesinger, E. G. (1999). *Ethnic-sensitive social work practice.* Boston: Allyn & Bacon.

Epstein, L. (1992). *Brief treatment and a new look at the task-centered approach.* New York: Macmillan.

Fortune, A. E. (1994). Commentary: Ethnography in social work. In E. Sherman & W. J. Reid (Eds.), *Qualitative research in social work* (pp. 63–67). New York: Columbia University Press.

Garcia, E., & Dyer, L. (1996). *Exploring issues of academic success among Latino students and families.* Unpublished master's thesis, California State University, Sacramento.

Gilgun, J. F. (1994). Hand into glove: The grounded theory approach and social work practice research. In E. Sherman & W. J. Reid (Eds.), *Qualitative research in social work* (pp. 115–125). New York: Columbia University Press.

Glaser, B. G., & Strauss, A. L. (1967). *The discovery of grounded theory: Strategies for qualitative research.* New York: Aldine de Gruyter.

Gould, K. (1999). The misconstructing of multiculturalism: The Stanford debate and social work. *Social Work, 40*(2), 198–205.

Green J., & Sherr, L. (1989). Dying, bereavement and loss. In J. Green & A. McCreaner (Eds.), *Counseling in HIV infection and AIDS* (pp. 207–223). Oxford: Blackwell Scientific Publications.

Green, J. W. (1995). *Cultural awareness in the human services.* Boston: Allyn & Bacon.

Hardcastle, D. A., Wenocur, S., & Powers, R. (1997). *Community practice: Theories and skills for social workers.* New York: Oxford University Press.

Hartman, A. (1994). Setting the theme: Many ways of knowing. In E. Sherman & W. J. Reid (Eds.), *Qualitative research in social work* (pp. 459–463). New York: Columbia University Press.

Lang, N. C. (1994). Integrating the data processing of qualitative research and social work practice to advance the practitioner as knowledge builder: Tools for knowing and doing. In E. Sherman & W. J. Reid (Eds.), *Qualitative research in social work* (pp. 265–278). New York: Columbia University Press.

Leigh, J. (1983). The black experience with health care delivery systems: A focus on the practitioners. In A. E. Johnson (Ed.), *The black experience: Considerations for health and human services* (pp. 115–129). Davis, CA: International Dialogue Press.

Lum, D. (2000). *Social work practice and people of color: A process-stage approach* (4th ed.). Pacific Grove, CA: Brooks/Cole.

Mizrahi, T., & Abramson, J. S. (1994). Collaboration between social workers and physicians: An emerging typology. In E. Sherman & W. J. Reid (Eds.), *Qualitative research in social work* (pp. 135–151). New York: Columbia University Press.

Mokuau, N. (1985). Counseling Pacific Islander–Americans. In P. Pedersen (Ed.), *Handbook of cross-cultural counseling and therapy*. Westport, CT: Greenwood.

Monette, D. R., Sullivan, T. J., & De Jong, C. R. (1994). *Applied social research: Tool for the human services*. Fort Worth, TX: Harcourt Brace.

Moore, K. (1998). *Patterns of inductive reasoning: Developing critical thinking skills* (4th ed.). Dubuque, IA: Kendall/Hunt.

National Association of Social Workers (NASW). (2001). *Standards for cultural competence in social work practice*. http://www.naswdc.org/pubs/standards/cultural.htm

Patton, M. (1990). *Qualitative evaluation and research methods* (2nd ed.). Newbury Park, CA: Sage.

The question of race in America. (1997, June 15). *Sacramento Bee*, p. Forum 4.

Rodwell, M. (1998). *Social work constructivist research*. New York: Garland.

Root, M. P. (Ed.). (1992). *Racially mixed people in America*. Newbury Park, CA: Sage.

Rothman, J. (1999). *The self-awareness workbook for social workers*. Needham, MA: Allyn & Bacon.

Rubin, A., & Babbie, E. (2005). *Research methods for social work* (5th ed.). Belmont, CA: Brooks/Cole.

Saleeby, D. S. (Ed.). (2000). *The strengths perspective in social work practice*. Boston: Allyn & Bacon.

Sherman, E., & Reid, W. J. (Eds.). (1994). *Qualitative research in social work*. New York: Columbia University Press.

Stern, S. B. (1994). Commentary: Wanted! Social work practice evaluation and research—All methods considered. In E. Sherman & W. J. Reid (Eds.), *Qualitative research in social work* (pp. 285–290). New York: Columbia University Press.

Strauss, A., & Corbin, J. (1990). *Basics of qualitative research: Grounded theory procedures and techniques*. Newbury Park, CA: Sage.

Weick, A. (1992). Building a strengths perspective for social work. In D. Saleebey (Ed.), *The strengths perspective in social work practice* (pp. 18–26). New York: Longman.

Yegidis, B., Weinbach, R., & Morrison-Rodriguez, B. (1999). *Research methods for social workers* (3rd ed.). Boston: Allyn & Bacon.

Yuen, F. K. O. (1999). Family health and cultural diversity. In J. T. Pardeck & F. K. O. Yuen (Eds.), *Family health: A holistic approach to social work practice* (pp. 101–113). Westport, CT: Auburn House.

Yuen, F. K. O. (2003). Critical concerns for family health practice. In F. K. O. Yuen, G. Skibinski, & J. T. Pardeck. *Family health social work practice: A knowledge and skills casebook*. Binghamton, NY: Haworth.

CHAPTER 9

Abe-Kim, J. S., & Takeuchi, D. T. (1996). Cultural competence and quality of care: Issues for mental health service delivery in managed care. *Clinical Psychology: Science and Practice, 3*(4), 273–295.

Angell, G. B., Kurz, B. J., & Gottfried, G. M. (1997). Suicide and North American Indians: A social constructavist perspective. *Journal of Multicultural Social Work, 6*(3/4), 1–25.

Bachman, R. (1992). *Death and violence on the reservation*. New York: Auburn House.

Barsh, R. L. (1996). The Indian Child Welfare Act of 1978: A critical analysis. In J. R. Wunder, *Recent legal issues for American Indians, 1968 to the present* (pp. 219–268). New York: Garland.

Brave Heart-Jordan, M., & DeBruyn, L. (1995). So she may walk in balance: Integrating the impact of historical trauma in the treatment of American Indian women. In J. Adelman & G. Enguidanos (Eds.), *Racism in the lives of women: Testimony, theory, and guides to antiracist practice* (pp. 345–368). New York: Haworth.

Churchill, W., & Morris, G. T. (1992). Key Indian laws and cases. In M. A. Jaimes (Ed.), *The state of Native America: Genocide, colonization, and resistance* (pp. 13–21). Boston: South End Press.

Claymore, B. J., & Taylor, M. A. (1989). AIDS—Tribal nations face the newest communicable disease: An Aberdeen area perspective. *American Indian Culture and Research Journal, 13*(3/4), 21–31.

Coleman, H. L. K. (1998). General and multicultural counseling competency: Apples and oranges? *Journal of Multicultural Counseling and Development, 26,* 147–156.

Council on Social Work Education (CSWE). (2000). *Educational policy and accreditation standards* (first draft). Alexandria, VA: Author. http://www.cswe.org/accreditation.htm

DeGraw, R. G. (1989). The Navajo cultural immersion project. In P. S. Denise & I. M. Harris (Eds.), *Experiential education for community development* (pp. 223–231). New York: Greenwood.

Good Tracks, J. G. (1973, November). Native American non-interference. *Social Work,* 30–35.

Green, J. W. (1999). *Cultural awareness in the human services: A multi-ethnic approach.* Boston: Allyn & Bacon.

Gurnee, C. G., Vigil, D. E., Krill-Smith, S., & Crowley, T. J. (1990). Substance abuse among American Indians in an urban treatment program. *American Indian and Alaska Native Mental Health Research, 3*(3), 17–26.

Jaimes, M. A. (Ed.). (1992). *The state of Native America: Genocide, colonization, and resistance.* Boston: South End Press.

Kramer, B. J. (1992). Health and aging of urban American Indians. *The Western Journal of Medicine, 157*(3), 281–286.

Kramer, J. B. (1992). Serving American Indian elderly in cities: An invisible minority. *Aging, 363/364,* 48–52.

MacEachron, A. E., Gustavsson, N. S., Cross, S., & Lewis, A. (1996). The effectiveness of the Indian Child Welfare Act of 1978. *Social Service Review, 70*(3), 451–463.

Mannes, M. (1995). Factors and events leading to the passage of the Indian Child Welfare Act. *Child Welfare, 74*(1), 264–282.

Mason, J. L., Benjamin, M. P., & Lewis, S. (1996). The cultural competence model:

Implications for child and family mental health services. In C. A. Heflinger & C. T. Nixon (Eds.), *Families and the mental health system for children and adolescents* (pp. 165–190). Thousand Oaks, CA: Sage.

Mitchell, J. (1991). The Mohawks in high steel. In E. Wilson (Ed.), *Apologies to the Iroquois* (pp. 1–36). Syracuse, NY: Syracuse University Press.

Mitka, M. (2002). Two new projects to help Native Americans end substance abuse and domestic violence. *Journal of the American Medical Association, 288*(15), 1834–1835.

Moran, J. R. (1999). Preventing alcohol use among urban American Indian youth: The Seventh Generation program. *Journal of Human Behavior in the Social Environment, 2*(1/2), 51–67.

Morrisette, P. J. (1994). The holocaust of First Nation people: Residual effects on parenting and treatment implications. *Contemporary Family Therapy, 16*(5), 381–392.

Napoli, M. (2002). Native wellness for the new millennium: The impact of gaming. *Journal of Sociology and Social Welfare, 29*(1), 17–34.

National Association of Social Workers (NASW). (1999). *Code of ethics of the National Association of Social Workers.* Washington, DC: Author.

National Indian Gaming Association. (2005). http://www.indiangaming.org

Native American Leadership Commission on Health and AIDS. (1994). *A Native American leadership response to HIV and AIDS.* New York: American Indian Community House.

Oetting, E. R., & Beauvais, F. (1991). Orthogonal cultural identification theory: The cultural identification of minority adolescents. *The International Journal of the Addictions, 25*(5A & 6A), 655–685.

Ogunwole, S. (2002). *The American Indian and Alaska Native Population: 2000.* Washington DC: U.S. Census Bureau.

Parker, L., Jamous, M., Marek, R., & Camacho, C. (1991). Traditions and innovations: A community-based approach to substance abuse prevention. *Rhode Island Medical Journal, 74,* 281–286.

Red Horse, J. (1978). Family behavior of urban American Indians. *Social Casework, 59*(2), 67–72.

Robbins, R. L. (1992). Self-determination and subordination: The past, present, and future of American Indian governance. In M. A. Jaimes (Ed.), *The state of Native America: Genocide, colonization, and resistance* (pp. 87–121). Boston: South End Press.

Ronnau, J. P. (1994). Teaching cultural competence: Practical ideas for social work educators. *Journal of Multicultural Social Work, 3*(1), 29–42.

Schafer, J. R., & McIlwaine, B. D. (1992). Investigating child sexual abuse in the American Indian community. *American Indian Quarterly, 16*(2), 157–167.

Schinke, S. P., Tepavac, L., & Cole, K. (2000). Preventing substance use among Native American youth: Three-year results. *Addictive Behaviors, 25*(3), 387–397.

Shulman, L. (1999). *The skills of helping individuals, families, groups, and communities.* Itasca, IL: F. E. Peacock.

Sowers-Hoag, K. M., & Sandau-Beckler, P. (1996). Educating for cultural competence in the generalist curriculum. *Journal of Multicultural Social Work, 4*(3), 37–56.

Stiffarm, L. A., & Lane, P., Jr. (1992). The demography of Native North America: A question of American Indian survival. In M. A. Jaimes (Ed.), *The state of Native America: Genocide, colonization, and resistance* (pp. 23–25). Boston: South End Press.

Sue, D. W., et al. (1998). *Multicultural counseling competencies: Individual and organizational development.* Thousand Oaks, CA: Sage.

Thomason, T. C. (2000). Issues in the treatment of Native Americans with alcohol problems. *Journal of Multicultural Counseling and Development, 28*(4), 243–252.

Unclaimed Assets.com. (2005). Unclaimed individual Indian monies and tribal trust accounts. http://www.unclaimedassets.com/US2.htm

U.S. Department of the Interior. (2005). Historical accounting for individual Indian monies: A progress report. http://www.doi.gov

U.S. Bureau of the Census. (1993). *We the . . . first Americans.* Washington, DC: Author.

Voss, R. W., Douville, V., Little Soldier, A., & Twiss, G. (1999). Tribal and shamanic-based social work practice: A Lakota perspective. *Social Work, 44*(3), 228–241.

Walters, K. L. (1999). Urban American Indian identity attitudes and acculturation styles. *Journal of Human Behavior in the Social Environment, 2*(1/2), 163–178.

Wares, D. M., Wedel, K. R., Rosenthal, J. A., & Dobrec, A. (1994). Indian child welfare: A multicultural challenge. *Journal of Multicultural Social Work, 3*(3), 1–15.

Waters, M. C. (1990). *Ethnic options: Choosing identities in America.* Berkeley: University of California Press.

Weaver, H. N. (1996). Social work with American Indian youth using the orthogonal model of cultural identification. *Families in Society: The Journal of Contemporary Human Services, 77*(2), 98–107.

Weaver, H. N. (1999a). Assessing the needs of Native American communities: A Northeastern example. *Evaluation and Program Planning: An International Journal, 22*(2), 155–161.

Weaver, H. N. (1999b). Indigenous people and the social work profession: Defining culturally competent services. *Social Work, 44*(3), 217–225.

Weaver, H. N. (2000). Activism and American Indian issues: Opportunities and roles for social workers. *Journal of Progressive Human Services, 11*(1), 3–22.

Weaver, H. N. (2001), Native Americans and substance abuse. In S. L. A. Straussner (Ed.), *Ethnocultural factors in substance abuse treatment* (pp. 77–96). New York: Guilford Press.

Weaver, H. N., & White, B. J. (1997). The Native American family circle: Roots of resiliency. *Journal of Family Social Work, 2*(1), 67–79.

Weaver, H. N., & White, B. J. (1999). Protecting the future of indigenous children and nations: An examination of the Indian Child Welfare Act. *Journal of Health and Social Policy, 10*(4), 35–50.

Westerfelt, A., & Yellow Bird, M. (1999). Homeless and indigenous in Minneapolis. *Journal of Human Behavior in the Social Environment, 2*(1/2), 145–162.

CHAPTER 10

African Americans: Cultural diversity curriculum for social workers and health practitioners. (1998). Center for Social Work Research, University of Texas at Austin.

Akbar, N. (1984). Africentric social sciences for human liberation. *Journal of Black Studies, 14,* 395–414.

Alter, J. (1997, December 8). The long shadow of slavery. *Newsweek,* pp. 58–63.

The American Black family: Looking back. (1987). *American Visions, 2*(6), 26–27.

Annie E Casey Foundation. (2003). *Kids count pocket guide: African-American children.*

Beedon, L., & Wu, K. (2004, September). African Americans age 65 and older: Their sources of income. AARP Public Policy Institute.

Bell, P., & Evans, J. (1981). *Counseling the Black client: Alcohol use and abuse in Black America.* Center City, MN: Hazelden.

Bennett, C. E., & Debanos, K. A. (1998). The Black population. In *The official statistics.* Washington, DC: U.S. Census Bureau.

Bennett, C. I. (1986). *Comprehensive multicultural education: Theory and practice.* Boston: Allyn & Bacon.

Bennett, L., Jr. (1982). *Before the Mayflower: A history of Black America* (5th ed.). Chicago: Johnson.

Billingsley, A. (1968). *Black families in White America.* Englewood Cliffs, NJ: Prentice-Hall.

Billingsley, A. (1992). *Climbing Jacob's ladder: The enduring legacy of African American families.* New York: Simon & Schuster.

Bond, S., & Cash, T. F. (1992). Black beauty: Skin color and body images among African-American college women. *Journal of Applied Social Psychology, 22,* 874–888.

Burbridge, L. C. (1995). Policy implications of a decline in marriage among African Americans. In M. B. Tucker & C. Mitchell-Kernan (Eds.), *The decline in marriage among African Americans: Causes, consequences, and policy implications* (pp. 323–344). New York: Russell Sage.

Chatters, L. M., Taylor, R. J., & Neighbors, H. (1989). Size of informal helper network mobilized during a serious personal problem among Black Americans. *Journal of Marriage and the Family, 51,* 667–676.

Comer, J. P., & Poussaint, A. F. (1975). *Black child care: How to bring up a healthy Black child in America: A guide to emotional and psychological development.* New York: Pocket Books.

Cose, E. (1999). The good news about Black America. *Newsweek,* pp. 28–40.

Crawley, B., & Freeman, E. (1992). Themes in the life views of older and younger African American males. *Journal of African American Male Studies, 1*(1), 15–29.

Crawley, B. H. (1996). Effective programs and services for African American families and children: An African centered perspective. In S. L. Logan (Ed.), *The Black family: Strengths, self-help, and positive change* (pp. 112–130). Boulder, CO: Westview Press.

Cross, T. L., Bazron, B. J., Dennis, K. W., & Isaacs, M. R. (1989). *Towards a culturally competent system of care.* Washington, DC: Georgetown University Child Development Center.

Daly, A., Jennings, J., Beckett, J., & Leashore, B. (1995). Effective coping strategies of African Americans. *Social Work, 40,* 240–248.

Dana, R. H. (1993). *Multicultural assessment perspectives for professional psychology.* Boston: Allyn & Bacon.

Devore, W., & Schlesinger, E. G. (1996). *Ethnic-sensitive social work practice.* New York: Allyn & Bacon.

Diller, J. V. (1999). Working with African American clients: An interview with Jimmie Turner. In *Cultural diversity: A primer for the human services* (pp. 174–188). Toronto: Wadsworth.

Drake, S., & Cayton, H. R. (1962). *Black metropolis: A study of Negro life in a northern city.* New York: Harper & Row.

Du Bois, W. E. B. (1903). *The souls of Black folk.* Chicago: McClurg.

Dungee-Anderson, D., & Beckett, J. O. (1995). A process model for multicultural social work practice. *Families in Society: The Journal of Contemporary Human Services, 76*(8), 459–468.

Everett, J. E., Chipungu, S. S., & Leashore, B. R. (Eds.). (1991). *Child welfare: An Africentric perspective.* New Brunswick, NJ: Rutgers University Press.

Feagan, J., & Sikes, M. (1994). *Living with racism: The Black middle-class experience.* Boston: Beacon Press.

Freeman, E. M. (1990). Theoretical perspectives for practice with Black families. In S. Logan, E. Freeman, & R. G. McRoy (Eds.), *Social work practice with Black families: A culturally specific perspective* (pp. 38–52). White Plains, NY: Longman.

Gary, L. E. (1985). Correlates of depressive symptoms among a select population of Black men. *American Journal of Public Health, 75,* 1220–1222.

Grace, C. A. (1992). Practical considerations for program professionals and evaluators working with African-American communities. In M. A. Orlandi (Ed.), *Cultural competence for evaluators: A guide for alcohol and other drug abuse prevention practitioners working with ethnic/racial communities* (pp. 55–74). Rockville, MD: U.S. Department of Health and Human Services, Office for Substance Abuse Prevention.

Grier, W. H., & Cobbs, P. M. (1968). *Black rage.* New York: Basic Books.

Harper, B. C. O. (1990). Blacks and the health care delivery system: Challenges and prospects. In S. Logan, E. Freeman, & R. G. McRoy (Eds.), *Social work practice with Black families* (pp. 239–256). White Plains, NY: Longman.

Harrison, D. D. (2000). "Wild women don't have the blues": Blues from the Black woman's perspective. In F. W. Hayes, III (Ed.), *A turbulent voyage: Readings in African American studies* (3rd ed.). San Diego: Collegiate Press.

Hill, R. (1972). *The strengths of Black families.* New York: National Urban League.

Hill, R. (1978). *The illusion of black progress.* Washington, DC: National Urban League, Research Department.

Hill, R. (1987). The black middle class defined. *Ebony, 42*(10), 30–32.

Jaynes, G. D., & Williams, R. M. (Eds.). (1989). *A common destiny: Blacks and American society.* Washington, DC: National Academy Press.

Jewell, K. S. (1988). *Survival of the Black family: The institutional impact of U.S. social policy.* New York: Praeger.

Jones, D. L. (1983). African-American clients: Clinical practice issues. In F. J. Turner (Ed.), *Differential diagnosis and treatment in social work* (pp. 565–578). New York: Free Press.

Kantrowitz, B., & Wingert, P. (2001, May 28). Unmarried, with children. *Newsweek, 137*(2), 46–54.

Keith, V. M., & Herring, C. (1991). Skin tone and stratification in the Black community. *American Journal of Sociology, 97*(3), 760–778.

Klonoff, E., & Landrine, H. (2000). Revising and improving the African American acculturation scale. *Journal of Black Psychology, 26*(2), 235–261.

LaFromboise, T., Coleman, H. L. K., & Gerton, J. (1993). Psychological impact of biculturalism: Evidence and theory. *Psychological Bulletin, 114,* 395–412.

Landrine, H., & Klonoff, E. (1994). The African American acculturation scale: Development, reliability, and validity. *Journal of Black Psychology, 20*(2), 104–127.

Logan, S. (Ed.). (1996). Epilogue: Understanding help-seeking behavior and empowerment issues for Black families. In S. L. Logan (Ed.), *Black family strengths, self help and positive change* (pp. 193–206). Boulder, CO: Westview Press.

Logan, S. M. L. (1990). Black families: Race, ethnicity, culture, social class, and gender issues. In S. Logan, E. Freeman, & R. G. McRoy (Eds.), *Social work practice with Black families: A culturally specific perspective* (pp. 18–37). White Plains, NY: Longman.

Lum, D. (1999). *Culturally competent practice: A framework for growth and action.* Pacific Grove, CA: Brooks/Cole.

Lum, D. (2000). *Social work practice and people of color: A process-stage approach.* Pacific Grove, CA: Brooks/Cole.

Mays, V., Chatters, L., Cochran, S., & Mackness, J. (1998, Spring). African

American families in diversity: Gay men and lesbians as participants in family networks. *Journal of Comparative Family Studies, 29*(1), 73–88.

McIntosh, P. (1992). White privilege and male privilege: A personal account of coming to see correspondences through work in women's studies. In M. L. Anderson & P. H. Collins (Eds.), *Race, class and gender: An anthology* (pp. 70–81). Belmont, CA: Wadsworth.

McKinnon, J. (2003): *The Black population in the United States: March 2002.* U.S. Census Bureau, Current Population Reports, Series P20–541. Washington, DC.

McRoy, R. (1999). *Preserving African American culture: Perspectives on transracial placements.* Los Angeles: Institute for Black Parenting.

McRoy, R., & Grape, H. (1999). Skin color in transracial and inracial adoptions. *Child Welfare, 78*(5), 673–692.

McRoy, R. G. (1990). A historical overview of Black families. In S. Logan, E. Freeman, & R. G. McRoy (Eds.), *Social work practice with Black families: A culturally specific perspective* (pp. 3–17). White Plains, NY: Longman.

McRoy, R. G. (Ed.). (1998). *Cultural diversity curriculum*. Final report to Texas Department of Health.

Miley, K. K., O'Melia, M., & DuBois, B. I. (1995). *Generalist social work practice: An empowering approach.* Boston: Allyn & Bacon.

Moynihan, D. P. (1965). *The Negro family: The case for national action.* Washington, DC: Government Printing Office.

Myrdal, G. (1962). *An American dilemma: The Negro problem and modern democracy.* New York: Harper & Row.

Neal, A. M., & Wilson, M. L. (1989). The role of skin color and features in the Black community: Implications for Black women and therapy. *Clinical Psychology Review, 9,* 323–333.

Neighbors, H. W., & Jackson, J. S. (1984). The use of informed help: Four patterns of illness behavior in the Black community. *American Journal of Community Psychology, 12*(5), 551–565.

Neighbors, H. W., & Taylor, R. J. (1985). The use of social service agencies by Black Americans. *Social Service Review, 59,* 259–268.

Oliver, W. (1989). Black males and social problems. *Journal of Black Studies, 20*(1), 15–39.

Oppression: Cultural diversity curriculum for social workers and health practitioners. (1998). Center for Social Work Research, University of Texas at Austin.

Oyebade, B. (1990). African studies and the Afrocentric paradigm: A critique. *Journal of Black Studies, 21*(2), 233–238.

Pinderhughes, E. (1989). *Understanding race, ethnicity, and power: The key to efficacy in clinical practice.* New York: Free Press.

Robinson, J. T. (1989). Clinical treatment of Black families: Issues and strategies. *Social Work, 34,* 323–329.

Russell, K., Wilson, M., & Hall, R. (1992). *The color complex: The politics of skin color among African Americans.* Garden City, NY: Anchor.

Ryan, W. (1976). *Blaming the victim* (Rev. ed.). New York: Vintage Books.

Saldana, D. (2001). *Cultural competency: A practical guide for mental health service providers.* Hogg Foundation for Mental Health, University of Texas at Austin.

Sanders-Thompson, V. L. (1994). Socialization to race and its relationship to racial identification among African Americans. *Journal of Black Psychology, 20*(2), 175–188.

Schiele, J. (1996). Afrocentricity: An emerging paradigm in social work practice. *Social Work, 41*(3), 284–295.

Staub, E. (1987, August). *Moral exclusion and extreme destructiveness: Personal goal theory, differential evaluation, moral equilibration and steps along the continuum of destruction.* Paper presented at the American Psychological Association Meeting, New York.

Sudarkasa, N. (1993). Female-headed African American households: Some neglected dimensions. In H. P. McAdoo (Ed.), *Family ethnicity: Strength in diversity* (pp. 81–89). Newbury Park, CA: Sage.

U.S. Census Bureau. (1999). *Current population survey, racial statistics branch, population division.* http://www.census.gov/ population/www/socdemo/race/Black99tabs. html

U.S. Census Bureau. (2000a). *Current population survey, racial statistics branch, population division*.http://www.census.gov/population/www/socdemo/race/ppl-142.html

U.S. Census Bureau. (2000b). *Poverty rate lowest in 20 years, household income at record high, Census Bureau reports*. http://www.census.gov/Press-Release/www.2000/cb00-158.html

U.S. Census Bureau. (2002). *Poverty rate rises, household income declines, Census Bureau* Reports. Washington, D.C. US Department of Commerce News, p. 1.

Van Soest, D., & Bryant, S. (1995). Violence reconceptualized for social work: The urban dilemma. *Social Work, 40*(4), 549–558.

What makes you Black? (1983). *Ebony, 38*(3), 115–118.

Wilson, J. (2003). African-born residents of the United States. Migration Information Source. http://www.migrationinformation.org/USfocus/display.cfm

Winkelman, M. (1999). *Ethnic sensitivity in social work*. Dubuque, IA: Eddie Bowers Publishing.

CHAPTER 11

Acuna, R. (1972). *Occupied American: The Chicano's struggle toward liberation*. San Francisco: Canfield Press.

Arroyo, F., & Eth, S. (1985). Children traumatized by Central American warfare. In S. Eth & R. S. Pynoos (Eds.), *Post-traumatic stress disorders in children* (pp. 101–120). Washington, DC: American Psychiatric Press.

Bellisle, M. (1999, May 27). Policy on benefits is praised for clarity. *San Diego Union Tribune*, p. A

Adams, C. (2004). Linguistic differences and culturally relevant interventions for involving monolingual Latino individuals in research efforts. *Journal of Hispanic Higher Education, 3*(4), 382–392.

Adams, E., Cahill, B., & Ackerlind, S. (2005). A qualitative study of Latino lesbian and gay youths' experiences with discrimination and the career development process. *Journal of Vocational Behavior, 66*(2), 199–218.

Alvarez, R. R., Jr. (1986, Spring). The Lemon Grove Incident: The nation's first successful desegregation court case. *Journal of San Diego History, 32*, 116–135.

Anderson, H. & Goolishian, H.A. (1992). The client is the expert: A not knowing approach to therapy. In S. McNamee & K. Gere (Eds.). *Therapy as social construction* (pp. 25–39). Newbury Park, CA: Sage Publications.

Ayalon, L. & Huyck, M. (2001). Latino caregivers of relatives with Alzheimer's disease. *Clinical Gerontologist, 24*(3–4), 93–106.

Benjamin, M. P., & Morgan, P. C. (1989). *Refugee children traumatized by war and violence: The challenge offered to the service delivery systems*. Washington, DC: CASSP Technical Assistance Center, Georgetown University Child Development Center.

Bergman, M. (2004, March 18). *Census Bureau projects tripling of Hispanic & Asian populations by 2050*. Washington, DC: U.S. Census Bureau.

Bernstein, R. (2005, June 9). *Hispanic population passes 40 million* (Census Bureau Report CB05-77). Washington, DC: U.S. Census Bureau.

Bertera, E. (2003). Psychosocial factors and ethnic disparities in diabetes diagnosis and treatment among older adults. *Health and Social Work, 28*(1), 33–42.

Castro, F. (1977). *Level of acculturation and related considerations in psychotherapy with Spanish speaking/surnamed clients*. Spanish Speaking Mental Health Research Center, Occasional Paper Number 3, University of California, Los Angeles.

Clark, J. M., Lasaga, J. L., & Reque, R. S. (1981). The Mariel exodus: An assessment and prospects. In *Council for Inter-American Security: A special report*. Washington, DC.

Coalition for Humane Immigrant Rights of Los Angeles (CHIRLA). (1995). *Hate unleashed: Los Angeles in the aftermath of 1287* (pp. 4–19). Los Angeles: Author.

Cohn, D. (2005, June 9). Hispanic growth surge fueled by births in U.S. *Washington Post*.

Colon, E. (2001). An ethnographic study of six Latino gay and bisexual men. *Journal of*

Gay and Lesbian Social Services: Issues in practice, policy and research, 12(3–4), 77–92.

Colon, J. & Lyke, J. (2003). Comparison of hospice use and demographics among European Americans, African Americans, and Latinos. *American Journal of Hospice and Palliative Care, 20*(3), 182–190.

Comas-Diaz, L., & Greene, B. (1994). *Women of color.* New York: Guilford.

Coon, D. et al. (2004). Well being, appraisal, and coping in Latina and Caucasian female dementia caregivers: Findings from the REACH study. *Aging and Mental Health, 8*(4), 330–345.

Cooper, S. P., et al. (2004). Ethical issues in conducting migrant farmworker studies. *Journal of Immigrant Health 6*(1), 29–39.

Cowan, G., Martinez, L., & Mendiola, S. (1997, November). Predictors of attitudes toward illegal Latino immigrants. *Hispanic Journal of Behavioral Sciences, 19*(4), 403–415.

Cross, T., Bazron, B., Dennis, K., & Isaacs, M. (1989). *Towards a culturally competent system of care.* Washington, DC: CASSP Technical Assistance Center, Georgetown University Child Development Center.

Cruz, J. E. (1998). *Identity and power: Puerto Rican politics and the challenge of ethnicity.* Philadelphia:Temple University Press.

Cuellar, I., Bastida, E. & Braccio, S. (2004). Residency in the United States, subjective well-being, and depression among an older Mexican-Origin sample. *Journal of Aging and Health, 16*(4), 447–466.

De Anda, D. (1984, March/April). Bicultural socialization: Factors affecting the minority experience. *Social Work,* 101–107.

Desjarlais, R., Eisenberg, L., Good, B., & Kleinman, A. (1995). *World mental health.* New York: Oxford University Press.

Diaz, R., Ayala, G. & Bein, E. (2004). Sexual risk as an outcome of social oppression: Data from a probability sample of Latino gay men in three U.S. cities. *Cultural Diversity and Ethnic Minority Psychology, 10*(3), 255–267.

Diaz-Stevens, A. M., & Stevens-Arroyo, A. (1998). *The Latino resurgence in U.S. religion.* Boulder, CO: Westview Press.

Drachman, D. (1992). A stage-of-migration framework for services to immigrant populations. *Social Work, 37,* 68–72.

Engstrom, D. (2000). Hispanic immigration at the new millennium. In P. S. J. Cafferty & D. Engstrom (Eds.), *Hispanics in the United States: An agenda for the 21st century* (pp. 69–96). New Brunswick, NJ: Transaction.

Espino, C., Sanguinette, P., Moreno, F., Diehl, V., & Zea, M. C. (1987, August). Testing of Central American children: Effects of war violence. In L. Comas-Diaz (Chair), *Psychological testing with Hispanics: New research findings.* Symposium for the 95th Annual Convention of the American Psychological Association, New York.

Falicov, C. (1998). *Latino families in therapy: A guide to multicultural practice.* New York: Guilford.

Gallagher-Thompson, D., Coon, D., Solando, N., Ambler, C., Rabinowitz, Y., & Thompson, L. (2003). Change in indices of distress among Latino and Anglo female caregivers of elderly relatives with dementia: Site-specific results from the REACH national collaborative survey. *The Gerontologist, 43*(4), 580–591.

Gelfand, D., Balcazar, H., Parzuchowski, J. & Lenox, S. (2004). Issues in hospice utilization by Mexicans. *The Journal of Applied Gerontology, 23*(1), 3–19.

Goodman, C. & Silverstein, M. (2005). Latina grandmothers raising grandchildren: Acculturation and psychological well-being. *International Journal of Aging and Human Development, 60*(4), 305–316.

Hill, T., Angel, J., Ellison, D. & Angel, R. (2005). Religious attendance and mortality: An 8 year follow-up of older Mexican Americans. *Journals of Gerontology, 60B*(2), S102–S109.

Hutchinson, E. D. (1999). *Dimensions of human behavior.* Thousand Oaks, CA: Pine Forge.

Jacob, A. G. (1994). Social integration of Salvadoran refugees. *Social Work, 39,* 307–312.

Jurkovic, G., Kuperminc, G. Perilla, J., Murphy, A., Ibanez, G. & Casey, S. (2004).

Ecological and ethical perspectives on filial responsibility: Implications for primary prevention with immigrant Latino adolescents. *Journal of Primary Prevention, 25*(1), 81–104.

Kim, H. & Lee, J. (2005). Unequal effects of elders health problems on wealth depletion across race and ethnicity. *Journal of Consumer Affairs, 39*(1), 148–172.

Laird, J. (1998). Theorizing culture: Narrative ideas and practice principles. In McGoldrick, M. (Ed.). *Re-Visioning family therapy.* New York: The Guilford Press.

Lindsay, J. M., & Michaelidis, G. (2001, January 5). A timid silence on America's immigration challenge. *San Diego Union Tribune,* p. B7.

Lum, D. (2000). *Social work practice and people of color: A process-stage approach.* Belmont, CA: Wadsworth.

Maldonado, D. (2000). The changing religious practice of Hispanics. In P. S. J. Cafferty & D. Engstrom (Eds.), *Hispanics in the United States: An agenda for the 21st century.* New Brunswick, NJ: Transaction.

Mancilla, Y. E. (1987). *Exposure to war-related violence and psychosocial competence of adolescent males from El Salvador.* Unpublished manuscript.

Marcos, L. R. (1994). The psychiatric examination across the language barrier. In C. Telles & M. Karno (Eds.), *Latino mental health: Current research and policy perspectives.* Neuropsychiatric Institute, University of California, Los Angeles.

Martin, M. & Lantos, J. (2005). Bioethics meets the barrio: Community-based research involving children. In Kodish, E. (Ed.). *Ethics and research with children: A case-based approach* (pp. 63–76). New York: Oxford University Press.

Minuchin, S. (1974). *Families and family therapy.* Cambridge, MA: Harvard University Press.

Morales, A. (1995). Urban gang violence: A psychosocial crisis. In A. Morales & B. Sheafor, *Social work: A profession of many faces* (pp. 433–463). Boston: Allyn & Bacon.

Morano, C. (2003). The role of appraisal and expressive support in mediating strain and gain in Hisapnic Alzheimer's disease caregivers. *Journal of Ethnic & Cultural Diversity in Social Work, 12*(2), 1–18.

Montijo, J. (1985). Therapeutic relationships with the poor: A Puerto Rican perspective. *Psychotherapy, 22,* 436–440.

NASW (2001). *NASW standards for cultural competence in social work practice.* Washington, DC: Author.

NASW (1996). *Code of Ethics.* Washington, DC: Author.

Negroni-Rodriguez, L., & Morales, J. (2001). Individual and family assessment skills with Latino/Hispanic Americans. In R. Fong & S. Furuto (Eds.), *Culturally competent practice: Skills, interventions, and evaluations* (pp. 132–146). Boston: Allyn & Bacon.

O'Brien, J., & Kollock, P. (2001). *The production of reality: Essays and readings on social interaction.* Thousand Oaks, CA: Pine Forge.

Orlando Sentinel. (2001, June 15). Navy officials, GOP lawmakers fume at Bush Vieques decision. Reprinted in *San Diego Union Tribune,* p. A2.

Parks, C., Hughes, T., & Matthews, A., (2004). Race/Ethnicity and sexual orientation: Intersecting identities. *Cultural Diversity and Ethnic Minority Psychology, 10*(3), 21–254.

Passel, J. (2005, June 14). *Unauthorized migrants: Numbers and characteristics.* Washington, DC: Pew Hispanic Center Report.

Perez Foster, R. M. (1998). The clinician's countertransference. *Clinical Social Work Journal, 26,* 253–276.

Perez Foster, R. M. (2001, April). When immigration is trauma: Guidelines for the individual and family clinician. *American Journal of Orthopsychiatry, 71*(1), 153–170.

Pew Hispanic Center. (2005). *Hispanics: A people in motion.* Washington, DC: Author.

Potocky-Tripodi, M. (1999). Refugee children: How are they faring economically as adults? In P. Ewalt, E. Freeman, A. Fortune, D. Poole, & S. Witkin (Eds.), *Multicultural issues in social work: Practice and research* (pp. 622–633). Washington, DC: NASW.

Puig, M. (2001). Organizations and community intervention skills with Hispanic

Americans. In R. Fong & S. Furuto (Eds.), *Culturally competent practice: Skills, interventions, and evaluations* (pp. 269–284). Boston: Allyn & Bacon.

Radina, E., & Barber, C. (2004). Utilization of formal support services among Hispanic Americans caring for aging parents. *Journal of Gerontological Social Work, 43*(2–3), 5–23.

Randall, H. & Csikai, E. (2003). Issues affecting utilization of hospice services by rural Hispanics. *Journal of Ethnic & Cultural Diversity in Social Work, 12*(2), 79–94.

Ramos, B. (2004). Culture, ethnicity, and caregiver stress among Puerto Ricans. *The Journal of Applied Gerontology, 23*(4), 469–486.

Robison, J., Curry, L., Gruman, C., Covington, T., Gaztambide, S., & Blank, S. (2003). Depression in later life Puerto Rican primary care patients: The role of illness, stress, social integration, and religiosity. *International Psychogeriatrics. 15*(3), 239–251.

Roderick, M. (2000). Hispanics and education. In P. S. J. Cafferty & D. W. Engstrom (Eds.), *Hispanics in the United States: An agenda for the 21st century* (pp. 123–174). New Brunswick, NJ: Transaction.

Rodriguez, G. P. (2004). *Immigration: Its mourning and reformulation of identity implications for clinical practice.* Paper presented at the California Society for Clinical Social Work 33rd Annual Conference, October 29–31, Monterey, California.

Roland, A. (1988). *In search of self in India and Japan: Towards a cross-cultural psychology.* Princeton, NJ: Princeton University.

Rosario, M., Schrimshaw, E. & Hunter, J. (2004). Ethnic/Racial differences in the coming out process of lesbian, gay, and bisexual youths: A comparison of sexual identity development over time. *Cultural Diversity and Ethnic Minority Psychology, 10*(3), 215–228.

Rotstein, A. (2005, September 3). Border deaths hit record pace. *Fresno Bee.*

Saleeby, D. (1997). *The strengths perspective in social work practice* (2nd ed.). New York: Longman.

Salinas, M. E., (2005, August 30). Central American gangs toil in violence. *Fresno Bee,* p. B9.

Szapocznick, J., et al. (1997). The evolution of a structural ecosystemic theory for working with Latino families. In J. Garcia & M. Zea (Eds.), *Psychological interventions and research with Latino populations* (pp. 166–190). Boston: Allyn & Bacon.

Tsui, P., & Schultz, G. L. (1985). Failure of rapport: Why psychotherapeutic engagement fails in the treatment of Asian clients. *American Journal of Orthopsychiatry, 55*(4), 561–569.

U.S. Department of Education, National Center for Education Statistics. (2003). *Digest of Education Statistics,* 2002 (NCES 20003-060).

U.S. Department of Homeland Security. (n.d.). *Immigration and borders: Serving our visitors, securing our borders.* http://www.dhs.gov/dhspublic/theme_home4.jsp

Valle, R., & Bensussen, G. (1980). Hispanic social network, social support, and mental health. In R. Valle & W. Vega (Eds.), *Hispanic natural support systems* (No. 620047). Sacramento: State of California Department of Mental Health.

Valle, R., & Vega, W. (Eds.). (1980). *Hispanic natural support systems* (No. 620047). Sacramento: State of California Department of Mental Health.

Van Soest, D. (1994). Social work education for multicultural practice and social justice advocacy: A field study of how students experience the learning process. *Journal of Multicultural Social Work, 3*(1), 17–24.

Vega, W. A., & Kolody, B. (1980). The meaning of social support and the mediation of stress across cultures. In R. Valle & W. Vega (Eds.), *Hispanic natural support systems* (No. 620047). Sacramento: State of California Department of Mental Health.

Weitzman, P., Chang, G. & Reynoso, H. (2004). Middle-aged and older Latino American women in the patient–doctor interaction. *Journal of Cross Cultural Gerontology, 19*(3), 221–239.

Williams, J., Wyatt, G., Resell, J., Peterson, J., & Asuan-O'Brien, A. (2004). Psychosocial issues among gay and non-gay identifying HIV seropositive African American and Latino men who have sex with men. *Cultural Diversity and Ethnic Minority Psychology, 10*(3), 268–286.

Young, J., Flores, G. & Berman, S. (2004). Providing life-saving care to undocumented children: Controversies and ethical issues. *Pediatrics, 114*(5), 1316–1320.

Zea, M. C., Diehl, V. A., & Porterfield, K. S. (1997). Central American youth exposed to war violence. In J. G. Garcia & M. C. Zea (Eds.), *Psychological interventions and research with Latino populations.* Needham Heights, MA: Allyn & Bacon.

Zuniga, M. E. (1991). "Dichos" as metaphorical tools for resistant Latino clients. *Psychotherapy, 28*(3), 480–483.

Zuniga, M. E. (1992). Families with Latino roots. In E. W. Lynch & M. J. Hanson (Eds.), *Developing cross-cultural competence: A guide for working with young children and their families* (pp. 151–179). Baltimore, MD: Brookes.

Zuniga, M. E. (2001). Latinos: Cultural competence and ethics. In R. Fong & S. Furuto (Eds.), *Culturally competent practice: Skills, interventions, and evaluations* (pp. 47–60). Boston: Allyn & Bacon.

Zuniga, M. E. (2003). Latinos' needs: Flexible and empowering interventions. In L. Gutierrez, M. Zuniga, & D. Lum (Eds.), *Education for multicultural social work practice.* Alexandria, VA: CSWE.

Zunker, C., Rutt, C. & Meza, G. (2005). Perceived health needs of elderly Mexicans living on the U.S.-Mexico border. *Journal of Transcultural Nursing, 16*(1), 50–56.

CHAPTER 12

Appleby, G. (2001). Lesbian, gay, bisexual, and transgender people confront heterocentrism, heterosexism, and homophobia. In G. Appleby, E. Colon, & J. Hamilton (Eds.), *Diversity, oppression, and social functioning: Person-in-environment assessment and intervention* (pp. 145–178). Needham Heights, MA: Allyn & Bacon.

Blaisdell, K., & Mokuau, N. (1991). *Kanaka Maoli:* Indigenous Hawaiians. In N. Mokuau (Ed.), *Handbook of social services for Asian and Pacific Islanders* (pp. 131–154). New York: Greenwood.

Brave Heart, M. Y. H. (2001). Culturally and historically congruent clinical social work interventions with Native clients. In R. Fong & S. Furuto (Eds.), *Culturally competent social work practice: Skills, interventions, and evaluations* (pp. 285–298). Boston: Allyn & Bacon.

Browne, C., & Broderick, A. (1994). Asian and Pacific Island elders: Implications for research and mental health administration. *Social Work, 39*(3), 252–259.

Caplan, N., Choy, M., & Whitmore, J. (1991). *Children of the boat people: A study of educational success.* Ann Arbor: University of Michigan Press.

Chan, S. (1994). The Hmong experience in Asia and the United States. In S. Chan (Ed.), *Hmong means free: Life in Laos and America* (pp. 1–60). Philadelphia: Temple University Press.

Chang, S. (2005, April 14). Grocery giants battle in Atlanta Koreatown. *The Korean Times.* http//times.hankooki.com/page/opinion/200504/kt2005041414154054100.htm

Chow, J. (2001). Assessment of Asian American/Pacific Islander organizations and communities. In R. Fong & S. Furuto (Eds.), *Culturally competent social work practice: Skills, interventions, and evaluations* (pp. 211–224). Boston: Allyn & Bacon.

Chung, D. (1992). The Confucian model of transformation. In S. Furuto, R. Biswas, D. Chung, K. Murase, & F. Ross-Sheriff (Eds.), *Social work with Asian Americans* (pp. 125–142). Beverly Hills, CA: Sage.

Council on Social Work Education (CSWE). (1994). *Handbook of accreditation standards and procedures.* Alexandria, VA: Author.

Cross, T., Bazron, B., Dennis, K., & Issacs, M. (1989). *Towards a culturally competent system of care.* Washington, DC: CASSP Technical Assistance Center, Georgetown University Child Development Center.

Daniel, R. (1992). Beyond black and white: The new multiracial consciousness. In M. Root (Ed.), *Racially mixed people in America* (pp. 333–341). Newbury Park, CA: Sage.

DePoy, E., Hartman, A., & Haslett, D. (1999). Critical action research: A model for knowing. *Social Work, 44*(6), 560–570.

Devore, W., & Schlesinger, E. (1999). *Ethnic sensitive social work practice* (5th ed.). Boston: Allyn & Bacon.

Dhooper, S., & Moore, S. (2001). *Social work practice with culturally diverse people.* Thousand Oaks, CA: Sage.

Ewalt, P., & Mokuau, N. (1995). Self-determination from a Pacific perspective. *Social Work, 40*(2), 168–175.

Fong, R. (1992). History of Asian Americans. In S. Furuto, R. Biswas, D. Chung, K. Murase, & F. Ross-Sheriff (Eds.), *Social work with Asian Americans* (pp. 3–26). Beverly Hills, CA: Sage.

Fong, R. (1997). Child welfare practice with Chinese families: Assessment for immigrants from the People's Republic of China. *Journal of Family Social Work, 2*(1), 33–48.

Fong, R. (2001). Culturally competent social work practice: Past and present. In R. Fong & S. Furuto (Eds.), *Culturally competent practice: Skills, interventions, and evaluation* (pp. 1–9). Boston: Allyn & Bacon.

Fong, R., Boyd, T., & Browne, C. (1999). The Gandhi technique: A biculturalization approach for empowering Asian and Pacific Island families. *Journal of Multicultural Social Work, 7*, 95–110.

Fong, R., & Furuto, S. (Eds.). (2001). *Culturally competent social work practice: Skills, interventions, and evaluations.* Boston: Allyn & Bacon.

Fong, R., & Mokuau, N. (1994). Social work periodical literature review of Asians and Pacific Islanders. *Social Work, 39*(3), 298–312.

Fong, R., & Wang. A. (2001). Adoptive parents and identity development for Chinese infants. In N. Choi (Ed.), *Psychosocial aspects of the Asian-American experience: Diversity within diversity* (pp. 19–33). New York: Haworth.

Fong, R., & Wu, D. (1996). Socialization of Chinese children. *Social Work in Education,18*(2), 71–84.

Furuto, S., San Nichols, R., Kim, G., & Fiaui, L. (2001). Interventions with Kanaka Maoli, Chamorro, and Samoan communities. In R. Fong & S. Furuto (Eds.), *Culturally competent social work practice: Skills, interventions, and evaluations* (pp. 327–342). Boston: Allyn & Bacon.

Galan, F. (2001). Intervention with Mexican American families. In R. Fong & S. Furuto (Eds.), *Culturally competent social work practice: Skills, interventions, and evaluations* (pp. 255–268). Boston: Allyn & Bacon.

Hing, B. (1993). Immigration policy: Making and remaking Asian and Pacific America. In *The state of Asian Pacific America* (pp. 127–140). Los Angeles: LEAP Asian Pacific American Public Policy Institute and UCLA Asian American Studies Center.

Ichioka, Y. (1988). *The Issei: The world of the first generation Japanese immigrants.* New York: Free Press.

Jung, M. (1998). *Chinese American family therapy: A new model for clinicians.* San Francisco, CA: Jossey Bass Publishers.

Kanuha, K. (2001). Individual and family intervention skills with Asian and Pacific Island American lesbian and gay men. In R. Fong & S. Furuto (Eds.), *Culturally competent social work practice: Skills, interventions, and evaluations* (pp. 313–326). Boston: Allyn & Bacon.

Kitano, H., & Nakaoka, S. (2001). Asian Americans in the twentieth century. In N. Choi (Ed.), *Psychosocial aspects of the Asian-American experience: Diversity within diversity* (pp. 7–17). New York: Haworth.

Lee, E. (Ed.). (1997). *Working with Asian Americans: A guide for clinicians.* New York: Guilford.

Lee, J., Lei, A., & Sue, S. (2001). The current state of mental health research on Asian Americans. In N. Choi (Ed.), *Psychosocial aspects of the Asian-American experience: Diversity within diversity* (pp. 159–178). New York: Haworth.

Leigh, J. (1998). *Communicating for cultural competence.* Needham Heights, MA: Allyn & Bacon.

Leung, P., & Cheung, M. (2001). Competencies in practice evaluations with Asian American individuals and families. In R. Fong & S. Furuto (Eds.), *Culturally competent social work practice: Skills, interventions, and evaluations* (pp. 426–437). Boston: Allyn & Bacon.

Lott, J. (1998). *Asian Americans: From racial category to multiple identities.* Walnut Creek, CA: Alta Mira Press.

Lum, D. (1999). *Culturally competent practice: A framework for growth and action.* Pacific Grove, CA: Brooks/Cole.

Lum, D. (2000). *Social work practice and people of color* (4th ed.). Pacific Grove, CA: Brooks/Cole.

Matsuoka, J. (2001). Evaluation and assessment in Hawaiian and Pacific communities. In R. Fong and S. Furuto (Eds.), *Culturally competent practice: Skills, interventions, and evaluations* (pp. 438–453). Boston: Allyn & Bacon.

Merkel-Holguin, L., & Ribich, K. (2001). Family group conferencing. In E. Walton, P. Sandau-Beckler, & M. Mannes (Eds.), *Balancing family-centered services and well-being* (pp. 197–218). New York: Columbia University Press.

Mokuau, N. (Ed.). (1991). *Handbook of social services for Asian and Pacific Islanders.* New York: Greenwood Press.

Mokuau, N. (1999). Substance abuse among Pacific Islanders: Cultural contexts and implications for prevention programs. In B. Yee, N. Mokuau, & S. Kim (Eds.). *Developing cultural competence in Asian-American and Pacific Islander communities: Opportunities in primary health care and substance abuse prevention* (pp. 221–248). Washington, DC: U.S. Department of Health and Human Services, Substance Abuse and Mental Health Services Administration, Center for Substance Abuse Prevention.

Mokuau, N. (2001). *Substance use and family violence among Native Hawaiians: Problems and culturally-based solutions.* Paper presented at the National Institute on Drug Abuse, Differential Drug Use, HIV/AIDS, and Related Health Outcomes among Racial and Ethnic Populations.

Mokuau, N., Lukela, D., Obra, A., & Voeller, M. (1997). *Native Hawaiian spirituality: A perspective on connections.* Honolulu, HI: University of Hawaii School of Social Work and Native Hawaiian Safe and Drug Free Schools and Communities Program at Kamehameha Schools Bishop Estate.

Morelli, P. (2001). Culturally competent assessment of Cambodian American survivors of the killing fields: A tool for social justice. In R. Fong and S. Furuto (Eds.), *Culturally competent social work practice: Skills, interventions, and evaluations* (pp. 196–210). Boston: Allyn & Bacon.

Morton, H. (1996). *Becoming Tongan: An ethnography of childhood.* Honolulu: University of Hawaii Press.

Mui, A. (1996). Depression among elderly Chinese immigrants: An exploratory study. *Social Work, 41,* 633–645.

Mui, A. (2001). Stress, coping, and depression among elderly Korean immigrants. In N. Choi (Ed.), *Psychosocial aspects of the Asian-American experience: Diversity within diversity* (pp. 281–299). New York: Haworth.

Mui, A., & Burnette, D. (1996). Coping resources and self-reported depressive symptoms among frail, older ethnic women. *Journal of Social Service Research. 21*(3), 19–37.

Nagata, D. (2000). World War II internment and the relationships of Nisei women. In J. Chin (Ed.), *Relationships among Asian American women* (pp. 49–70). Washington, DC: American Psychological Association.

Ngo, D., Tran, T., Gibbons, J., & Oliver, J. (2001). Acculturation, premigration, traumatic experiences, and depression among Vietnamese Americans. In N. Choi (Ed.), *Psychosocial aspects of the Asian-American experience: Diversity within diversity* (pp. 225–242). New York: Haworth.

Nishi, S. (1995). Japanese Americans. In P. Min (Ed.), *Asian Americans: Contemporary trends and issues* (pp. 95–133). Thousand Oaks, CA: Sage.

Pennell, J., & Buford, G. (2000). Family group decision-making: Protecting women and children. *Child Welfare, LXXIX*(2), 131–158.

Poon, M. (2000). Inter-racial same sex abuse: The vulnerability of gay men of Asian descent in relationships with Caucasian men. *Journal of Gay and Lesbian Social Services, 11*(4), 39–68.

Reeves, T. & Bennett, C. (2004). *We the people: Asians in the United States.* http://www.census.gov/prod/2004pubs/censr-17.pdf

Ross-Sheriff, F., & Husain, A. (2001). Values and ethics in social work practice with Asian Americans: A South Asian Muslim case example. In R. Fong & S. Furuto (Eds.), *Culturally competent social work practice: Skills, interventions, and evaluations* (pp. 75–88). Boston: Allyn & Bacon.

Ross-Sheriff, F., & Husain, A. (2004). South Asian Muslim children and families. In R. Fong (Ed.), *Culturally competent practice with immigrant and refugee children and families* (pp. 163–182). New York: Guilford Press.

Sanchez-Hucles, J. (1998). Racism: Emotional abusiveness and psychological trauma for ethnic minorities. *Journal of Emotional Abuse, 1*(2), 69–88.

Sanders, D. (1991). Future directions in social services: Asian and Pacific Islander perspectives. In N. Mokuau (Ed.), *Handbook of social services for Asian and Pacific Islanders* (pp. 233–242). New York: Greenwood Press.

Scheinfeld, D., Wallach, B., & Langendorf, T. (1997). *Strengthening refugee families: Designing programs for refugee and other families in need.* Chicago: Lyceum Books.

Schriver, J. (2001). *Human behavior in the social environment* (3rd ed.). Boston: Allyn & Bacon.

Spickard, P., Fong, R., & Ewalt, P. (1995). Undermining the very basis of racism—Its categories. *Social Work, 40*(5), 581–584.

Straussner, S. (Ed.). (2001). *Ethnocultural factors in substance abuse treatment.* New York: Guilford.

Sung, B. (1967). *Mountain of gold.* New York: Macmillan.

Swingle, D. (2000). Immigrants and August 22, 1996: Will the public charge rule clarify program eligibility? *Families in Society, 81*(6), 605–610.

Takaki, R. (1993). *A different mirror.* Boston: Little Brown.

Takamura, J. (1991). Asian and Pacific Islander elderly. In N. Mokuau (Ed.), *Handbook of social services for Asian and Pacific Islanders* (pp. 185–202). New York: Greenwood Press.

Tien, L. (2000). U.S. attitudes toward women of Asian ancestry: Legislative and media perspectives. In J. Chin (Ed.), *Relationships among Asian American women* (pp. 29–48). Washington, DC: American Psychological Association.

Tran, C., & Des Jardins, K. (2000). Domestic violence in Vietnamese refugee and Korean immigrant communities. In J. Chin (Ed.), *Relationships among Asian American women* (pp. 71–100). Washington, DC: American Psychological Association.

Trask, H. (1984–1985). Hawaiians, American colonization, and the quest for independence. In G. Sullivan & G. Gawes (Eds.), *Social process in Hawaii, 31,* 101.

Trueba, H., Jacobs, L., & Kirton, E. (1990). *Cultural conflict and adaptation: The case of Hmong children in American society.* Bristol, PA: Falmer Press.

Uba, L. (1994). *Asian Americans: Personality patterns, identity, and mental health.* New York: Guilford.

Uehara, E., Morelli, P., & Abe-Kim, J. (2001). Somatic complaint and social suffering among survivors of the Cambodian killing fields. In N. Choi (Ed.), *Psychosocial aspects of the Asian-American experience* (pp. 243–262). New York: Haworth.

U.S. Bureau of the Census. (2001). *Overview of race and Hispanic origin census of 2000 brief.* Washington, DC: U.S. Government Printing Office.

U.S. Bureau of the Census. (2004). *We the people: Asians in the United States.* Census 2000 Special Reports. Washington, DC: U.S. Department of Commerce, Economics and Statistics Administration.

U.S. Commission on Civil Rights. (1992). *Civil rights facing Asian Americans in the 1990s.* Washington, DC: U.S. Government Printing Office. http://www.census.gov/prod/2001/pubs/c2kbr01-1.pdf

Weaver, H. N. (2001). Organization and community assessment with First Nations People. In R. Fong & S. B.C.L. Furuto (Eds.), *Culturally competent social work practice: Skills, interventions, and evaluations* (pp. 178–195). Boston: Allyn & Bacon.

Wu, D. (1991). The construction of Chinese and non-Chinese identities. *Daedalus, 120*(2), 159–180.

Yellow Bird, M. (2001). Critical values and First Nations Peoples. In R. Fong & S. Furuto (Eds.), *Culturally competent practice: Skills, interventions, and evaluation* (pp. 61–74). Boston: Allyn & Bacon.

Zhou, M., & Bankston, C. (1998). *Growing up American: How Vietnamese children adapt to life in the United States.* New York: Russell Sage Foundation.

CHAPTER 13

Alexander, P. (1987). Prostitution: A difficult issue for feminists. In F. Delacoste & P. Alexander (Eds.), *Sex work: Writings by women in the sex industry.* San Francisco: Cleis Press.

American Diabetes Association (ADA). (2005). *All about diabetes.* http://www.diabetes.org

American Psychiatric Association (APA). (1994). *Diagnostic and statistical manual of mental health disorders* (4th ed.). Washington, DC: Author.

Aristide, J. B. (2000). *Eyes of the heart: Seeking a path for the poor in the age of globalization.* Monroe, ME: Common Courage Press.

Baines, D. R. (1998). Native American women and healthcare. In E. A. Blechman & K. D. Brownell (Eds.), *Behavioral medicine and women: A comprehensive handbook* (pp. 839–842). New York: Guilford.

Bamberger, M., Blackden, M., Fort, L., & Manoukian, V. (2001). Gender (draft for comments). *Poverty reduction strategy sourcebook.* Washington, DC: The World Bank. http://www.worldbank.org/poverty/strategies/chapters/gender/gender.htm

Brave Heart, M. Y. H. (2001). Clinical social work assessment with native clients. In R. Fong & S. Furuto (Eds.), *Culturally competent practice: Skills, interventions, and evaluations* (pp. 163–177). Boston: Allyn & Bacon.

Brounstein, P. (2001). The nature of the hidden epidemic. *The hidden epidemic: Prevention and intervention of alcohol and medication misuse and abuse among older adults.* First Joint Conference of the American Society of Aging (ASA), the National Council on Aging (NCA), and the U.S. Substance Abuse and Mental Health Services Administration (USSAMHSA), Center for Substance Abuse Prevention (CSAP) PHD880.

Castillo, R. J. (1998). *Meanings of madness.* Pacific Grove, CA: Brooks/Cole.

Cloud, J. (1998, March 23). Sex and the law. *Time,* pp. 48–54.

Collins, P. H. (1986). Learning from the outsider within: The sociological significance of black feminist thought. *Social Problems, 33*(6), 514–532.

Collins, P. H. (1994). Foreword. In M. B. Zinn & B. T. Dill (Eds.), *Women of color in U.S. society* (pp. xi–xv). Philadelphia: Temple University Press.

Crenshaw, K. W. (1994). Mapping the margins: Intersectionality, identity politics, and violence against women of color. In M. A. Finerman and R. Mykitiuk (Eds.), *The public nature of private violence* (pp. 93–118). New York, Routledge.

du Guerny, J., & Sjöberg, E. (1999). Interrelationship between gender relations and the HIV/AIDS epidemic: Some possible considerations for policies and programs. In J. M. Mann, S. Gruskin, M. A. Grodin, & G. J. Annas (Eds.), *Health and human rights: A reader* (pp. 202–226). New York: Routledge.

Espin, O. M. (1997). Crossing borders and boundaries: The life narratives of immigrant lesbians. In B. Greene (Ed.), *Ethnic and cultural diversity among lesbians and gay men* (pp. 191–215). Series: Psychological Perspectives on Lesbians and Gays, vol. 3. Thousand Oaks, CA: Sage.

Essed, P. (1991). *Understanding everyday racism: An interdisciplinary theory.* Newbury Park, CA: Sage.

Essed, P. (1994). Contradictory positions, ambivalent perceptions: A case study of a black woman entrepreneur. *Feminism and Psychology, 4*(1), 99–118.

Federal Interagency Forum on Aging Related Statistics. (2005). *Older Americans 2004:*

Key indicators of well-being. http://www.agingstats.gov/chartbook2004/population.html#Indicatorpercent202

Finn, J. L., Castellanos, R., McOmber, T., & Kahan, K. (2000). Working for equality and economic liberation: Advocacy and education for welfare reform. *Affilia, 15*(2), 294–310.

Foot, D. K., & Stoffman, D. (1996). *Boom, bust, and echo: How to profit from the coming demographic shift.* Toronto: Macfarlane, Walter & Ross.

Friedman, E. (1995). Women's human rights: The emergence of a movement. In J. Peters & A. Wolper (Eds.), *Women's rights, human rights: International feminist perspectives* (pp. 18–35). New York: Routledge.

Gomez, L. E. (1997). *Misconceiving mothers: Legislators, prosecutors, and the politics of prenatal drug exposure.* Philadelphia: Temple University Press.

Gould, K. (2000). Beyond *Jones v. Clinton:* Sexual harassment law and social work. *Social Work, 45*(3), 237–248.

Greene, B. (1994). Lesbian women of color. In L. Comas-Diaz & B. Greene (Eds.), *Women of color: Integrating ethnic and gender identities in psychotherapy* (pp. 389–427). New York: Guilford.

Helstrom, A. W., Coffey, C., & Jorgannathan, P. (1998). Asian American women's health. In E. A. Blechman & K. D. Brownell (Eds.), *Behavioral medicine and women: A comprehensive handbook* (pp. 826–832). New York: Guilford.

hooks, b. (1994). From "Black is a woman's color." In D. Soyini Madison (Ed.), *The woman that I am: The literature and culture of contemporary women of color.* New York: St. Martin's Griffin.

Kanuha, V. (1994). Women of color in battering relationships. In L. Comas-Diaz & B. Greene (Eds.), *Women of color: Integrating ethnic and gender identities in psychotherapy* (pp. 428–454). New York: Guilford.

Lee, E. (1997). Overview: Assessment and treatment. In E. Lee (Ed.), *Working with Asian Americans: A guide for clinicians* (pp. 3–36). New York: Guilford.

Liu, T. (2000). Teaching the differences among women from a historical perspective. In V. L. Ruiz & E. C. DuBois (Eds.), *Unequal sisters: A multicultural reader in U.S. women's history* (pp. 627–638). New York: Routledge.

Lowe, L. (1997). Work, immigration, gender: Asian "American" women. In E. H. Kim, L. V. Villanueva, & Asian Women United of California (Eds.), *Making more waves: New writing by Asian American women.* Boston: Beacon Press.

Mantell, J. E., & Susser, E. S. (1998). HIV prevention among homeless women. In E. A. Blechman & K. D. Brownell (Eds.), *Behavioral medicine and women: A comprehensive handbook* (pp. 203–212). New York: Guilford.

Maypole, D. E. (1987). Sexual harassment at work: A review of research and theory. *Affilia, 2*(1), 24–38.

Mays, V. M., Cochran, S. D., & Sullivan, J. G. (2000). Health care for African American and Hispanic women: Report on perceived health status, access to care and utilization patterns. In C. J. R. Hogue, M. A. Hargraves, & K. S. Collins (Eds.), *Minority health in America: Findings and policy implications from the Commonwealth Fund Minority Health Survey* (pp. 97–123). Baltimore, MD: Johns Hopkins University Press.

McGrath, E., Keita, G. P., Strickland, B. R., & Russo, N. F. (Eds.). (1990). *Women and depression: Risk factors and treatment issues.* Washington, DC: American Psychological Association.

McNair, L. D., & Roberts, G. W. (1998). African American women's health. In E. A. Blechman & K. D. Brownell (Eds.), *Behavioral medicine and women: A comprehensive handbook* (pp. 821–825). New York: Guilford.

Meintjes, G. (1997). Human rights education as empowerment: Reflections on pedagogy. In G. J. Andreopoulos & R. P. Claude (Eds.) *Human rights education for the twenty-first century.* Philadelphia: The University of Pennsylvania Press.

National Association of Social Workers (NASW). (1996). *Code of ethics.* Washington, DC: Author.

National Institute on Aging (2001). Portfolio for progress. *Older Americans 2004: Key indicators of well-being.* U.S. Department of Health and Human Services. http://www.agingstats.gov/chartbook2004/population.html#Indicator%202

National Women's Health Information Center. (2001). *Women of color health data book: Factors affecting the health of women of color— Black Americans.* http://www.4women.gov/owh/pub/woc/black.htm

National Women's Health Information Center. (May 2003a). *Frequently asked questions about health problems in African American women.* http://www.4woman.gov/faq/africanamerican.pdf

National Women's Health Information Center. (May 2003b). *Frequently asked questions about health problems in Asian American/Pacific Islander and Native Hawaiian women.* http://www.4woman.gov/faq/asian_pacific.pdf

National Women's Health Information Center. (May 2003c). *Frequently asked questions about health problems in American Indian/Alaskan Native women.* http://www.4woman.gov/faq/american_indian.pdf

National Women's Health Information Center. (May 2003d). *Frequently asked questions about health problems in Hispanic/Latino women.* http://www.4woman.gov/faq/latina.pdf

National Women's Health Information Center. (May 2003e). *Minority women and mental health.* http://www.4woman.gov/minority/mh.cfm

Negroni-Rodriguez, L. K., & Morales, J. (2001). Individual and family assessment skills with Latino/Hispanic Americans. In R. Fong & S. Furuto (Eds.), *Culturally competent practice: Skills, interventions, and evaluations* (pp. 132–146). Boston: Allyn & Bacon.

Office of Management and Budget. (2000). *Revisions to the standards for the classification of federal data on race and ethnicity.* http://www.whitehouse.gov/WH/EOP/OMB/html/fedreg.html

Office of Refugee Resettlement. (1988). *Report to the Congress: Refugee resettlement program.* Washington, DC: U.S. Government Printing Office.

Office on Women's Health. (2001). *The health of minority women.* http://www.4women.gov/owh/pub/minority/concerns.htm

O'Nell, T. D. (1993). "Feeling worthless": An ethnographic investigation of depression and problem drinking at the Flathead reservation. *Culture, medicine and psychiatry, 16,* 447–469.

Paisano, E. (1995). The American Indian, Eskimo, and Aleut population. In *U.S. Bureau of the Census, Population profile of the United States: 1995.* Current Population Reports, Series P23–189. Washington, DC: U.S. Government Printing Office.

Prostitution Education Network. (2001). *Prostitution in the United States: The statistics.* http://www.bayswan.org/stats.html

Rasche, C. E. (2000). Minority women and domestic violence: The unique dilemmas of battered women of color. In H. M. Eigenberg (Ed.), *Women battering in the United States: Till death us do part* (pp. 86–102). Prospect Heights, IL: Waveland Press.

The Refugee Council U.S.A. (2004). *Interim report of the U.S. Refugee Admissions Program for fiscal years 2004 and 2005,* Washington, DC. http://www.refugeecouncilusa.org/2004RCUSAinterim-w.pdf

The Refugee Council U.S.A. (2005). *Refugee admission figures for September 2005.* Washington, DC. http://www.refugeecouncilusa.org/sept-fy2005.pdf

Ruggiero, L. (1998). Diabetes: Biopsychosocial aspects. In E. A. Blechman & K. D. Brownell (Eds.), *Behavioral medicine and women: A comprehensive handbook* (pp. 615–622). New York: Guilford.

Schutte, O. (2000). Cultural alterity: Cross-cultural communication and feminist theory in north-south contexts. In U. Narayan & S. Harding (Eds.), *Decentering the center: Philosophy for a multicultural, postcolonial, and feminist world* (pp. 47–66). Bloomington: Indiana University Press.

Silko, L. M. (1996). *Yellow Woman and a beauty of the spirit: Essays on Native American life today.* New York: Simon & Schuster.

State of Washington Division of Mental Health. (1987). *Analysis of factors that affect mental health and utilization of mental health services by the refugee population in Washington State.* Olympia, WA: Department of Social and Health Services.

Stout, K. D., & McPhail, B. (1998). *Confronting sexism and violence against women: A challenge for social work.* New York: Longmans.

Sue, D. W., & Sue, D. (1999). *Counseling the culturally different: Theory and practice.* New York: John Wiley.

Tien, L. (1994). Southeast Asian American refugee women. In L. Comas-Diaz & B. Greene (Eds.), *Women of color: Integrating ethnic and gender identities in psychotherapy* (pp. 479–503). New York: Guilford.

Torres, L. (1991). The construction of the self in U.S. Latina autobiographies. In C. T. Mohanty, A. Russo, & L. Torres (Eds.), *Third world women and the politics of feminism* (pp. 271–287). Bloomington: Indiana University Press.

United Nations. (1995). *Women: Looking beyond 2000.* New York: Author.

U.S. Bureau of the Census. (2000a). *Current population survey.* Racial Statistics Branch, Population Division.

U.S. Bureau of the Census. (2000b). *Population profile of the United States, 1999.* Current Population Reports, Series P23-205. Washington, DC: U.S. Government Printing Office.

U.S. Bureau of the Census. (2000c). *Poverty in the United States, 1999.* Current Population Reports, Series P60-210. Washington, DC: U.S. Government Printing Office.

U.S. Bureau of the Census. (2001). *Women in the United States: March 2000.* PP1-121. Detailed Tables and Documentation for P20-524.

U.S. Department of Health and Human Services. (2000). *Mental health: A report of the Surgeon General.* Washington: DC: U.S. Government Printing Office.

U.S. Small Business Administration. (n.d.). *Women.* http://www.sba.gov/financing/special/women.html

Vickers, J. (1991). *Women and the world economic crisis.* London: Zed Books.

Westbrooks, K. L., & Starks, S. H. (2001). Strengths perspective inherent in cultural empowerment: A tool for assessment with African American individuals and families. In R. Fong & S. Furuto (Eds.), *Culturally competent practice: Skills, interventions, and evaluations* (pp. 101–118). Boston: Allyn & Bacon.

Zinn, M. B., & Dill, B. T. (1994). Difference and domination. In M. B. Zinn & B. T. Dill (Eds.), *Women of color in U.S. society* (pp. 3–12). Philadelphia: Temple University Press.

CHAPTER 14

Allman, K. M. (1996). (Un)Natural boundaries: Mixed race, gender, and sexuality. In M. P. P. Root (Ed.), *The multiracial experience: Racial borders as the new frontier* (pp. 275–290). Thousand Oaks, CA: Sage.

Alquijay, M. A. (1997). The relationship among self-esteem, acculturation, and lesbian identity formation. In Beverly Greene (Ed.), *Ethnic and cultural diversity among lesbians and gay men* (pp. 249–265.) Thousand Oaks, CA: Sage Publications.

Amaro, H., Whitaker, R., Coffman, G., & Heeren, T. (1990). Acculturation and marijuana and cocaine use. *American Journal of Public Health, 80,* 54–60.

Anguksuar [Richard LaFortune]. (1997). A postcolonial colonial perspective on Western [mis]conceptions of the cosmos and the restoration of indigenous taxonomies. In S. Jacobs, W. Thomas, & S. Lang (Eds.), *Two-spirit people: Native American gender identity, sexuality, and spirituality* (pp. 217–222). Chicago: University of Illinois.

Anguksuar [Richard LaFortune]. (1990). Vision. In *Twin Cities gay and lesbian celebration 1990 official pride guide* (pp. 58–59). Minneapolis: Twin Cities Lesbian-Gay Pride Committee.

Anzaldua, G. (1987). *Borderlands/LaFrontera: The new Mestiza.* San Francisco: Spinsters/Aunt Lute Foundation.

Arguelles, L., & Rich, H. R. (1989). Homosexuality, homophobia, and revolution: Notes toward an understanding of the Cuban lesbian and gay male experience. In M. B. Duberman, M. Vicinus, & G. Chauncey, Jr. (Eds.), *Hidden from history: Reclaiming the gay and lesbian past* (pp. 441–456). New York: New American Library.

Atkinson, D., Morten, G., & Sue, D. (1983). *Counseling American minorities.* Dubuque, IA: W. C. Brown.

Ayers, T. (1999). China doll: The experience of being a gay Chinese Australian. In P. A. Jackson & G. Sullivan (Eds.), *Multicultural queer: Australian narratives* (pp. 87–98). New York: Haworth.

Bell, A. P., & Weinberg, M. S. (1978). *Homosexualities: A study of diversity among men and women.* New York: Simon & Schuster.

Berrill, K. (1990). Anti-gay violence and victimization in the United States: An overview. *Journal of Interpersonal Violence, 5,* 274–294.

Berkowitz, B. (2001). *Viva gay Cuba.* http://www.workingforchange.com/article.cfm?ItemID=11550

Bonilla, L., & Porter, J. (1990). A comparison of Latino, Black and non-Hispanic White attitudes toward homosexuality. *Hispanic Journal of Behavioral Science, 12,* 437–452.

Broude, G. J., & Greene, S. J. (1976). Crosscultural codes on twenty sexual attitudes and practices. *Ethnology, 15*(4), 419–429.

Brown, J. C. (1989). Lesbian sexuality in medieval and early modern Europe. In M. Vicinus, M. B. Duberman, & G. Chauncey, Jr. (Eds.), *Hidden from history: Reclaiming the gay and lesbian past* (pp. 67–76). New York: New American Library.

Bullough, V. L. (1976). *Sexual variance in society and history.* New York: John Wiley.

Calzavara, L. M., Bullock, S. L., Meyers, T., Marshall, V. W., & Cockerill, R. (1999). Sexual partnering and risk of HIV/STD among Aboriginals. *Canadian Journal of Public Health, 90*(3), 186–191.

Carrier, J. M. (1976). Family attitudes and Mexican male homosexuality. *Urban Life, 5,* 359–375.

Carrier, J. M. (1989). Gay liberation and coming out in Mexico. *Journal of Homosexuality, 17*(3/4), 225–252.

Cass, V. C. (1984). Homosexual identity formation: Testing a theoretical model. *Journal of Sex Research, 20,* 143–167.

Centers for Disease Control (CDC). (1999). *HIV/AIDS surveillance report, 11*(2). Atlanta, GA: National Center for HIV, STD, TB Prevention.

Centers for Disease Control. (2002). *Division of HIV/AIDS: Fact sheets.* http://www.cdc.gov/hiv/pubs/facts/hispanic.htm

Chan, C. S. (1989). Issues of identity development among Asian-American lesbians and gay men. *Journal of Counseling and Development, 68*(1), 16–20.

Chan, C. S. (1997). Don't ask, don't tell, don't know: The formation of a homosexual identity and sexual expression among Asian American lesbians. In B. Greene (Ed.), *Ethnic and cultural diversity among lesbians and gay men: Psychological perspectives on lesbian and gay issues* (Vol. 3, pp. 240–248). Thousand Oaks, CA: Sage.

Choi, K. H., Coates, T. J., Catania, J. A., & Lew, S. (1995). High HIV risk among gay Asian and Pacific Islander men in San Francisco. *AIDS, 9,* 306–307.

Choi, K. H., Yep, G. A., & Kumekawa, E. P. (1998). HIV prevention among Asian and Pacific Islander American men who have sex with men: A critical review of theoretical models and directions for future research. *AIDS Education and Prevention, 10* (Supplement A), 19–30.

Chuang, K. (1999). Using chopsticks to eat steak. In P. A. Jackson & G. Sullivan (Eds.), *Multicultural queer: Australian narratives* (pp. 29–42). New York: Haworth.

Chung, C., Kim, A., Nguyen, Z., & Ordona, T. (1996). In our own way: A roundtable discussion. In R. Leong (Ed.), *Asian American sexualities: Dimensions of the gay and lesbian experience* (pp. 99–101). New York: Routledge.

Comas-Diaz, L., & Greene, B. (1994). Women of color with professional status. In L. Comas-Diaz & B. Greene B (Eds.), *Women of color: Integrating ethnic and gender identities in psychotherapy* (pp. 347–388). New York: Guilford Press.

Cornwell, A. (1983). *Black lesbian in White America.* Tallahassee, FL: Naiad Press.

Deschamps, G. (1998). *We are part of a tradition: A guide on two-spirited people for First Nations communities.* Toronto, Canada: 2-Spirited People of the 1st Nations.

Downing, C. (1989). *Myths and mysteries of same-sex love.* New York: Continuum.

Dynes, W. R., & Donaldson, S. (1992). Asian homosexuality. New York: Garland.

Entre Hermanos, Organizacion LGBT Latina. (2005). http://www.entrehermanos.org/home.html

Eskridge, Jr., W. N. (2003). Immigration, asylum, and deportation law and policy. In *Encyclopedia of lesbian, gay, bisexual, and transgender history in America* (pp. 78–81). New York: Charles Scribner & Sons.

Espin, O. M. (1987). Issues of identity in the psychology of Latina lesbians. In Boston Lesbian Psychologies Collective (Eds.), *Lesbian psychologies: Explorations and challenges* (pp. 35–51). Urbana: University of Illinois Press.

Fung, R. (1996). Looking for my penis. In R. Leong (Ed.), *Asian American sexualities: Dimensions of the gay and lesbian experience* (pp. 181–198). New York: Routledge.

Furukawa, M. (1994). The changing nature of sexuality: The three codes framing homosexuality in modern Japan. *U.S.-Japan Women's Journal English Supplement, 7,* 98–126.

Garnets, L., Herek, G. M., & Levy, B. (1990). Violence and victimization of lesbians and gay men: Mental health consequences. *Journal of Interpersonal Violence, 5,* 366–383.

Garnets, L., & Kimmel, D. (1991). Lesbian and gay male dimensions in the psychological study of human diversity. In J. D. Goodchilds (Ed.), *Psychological perspectives on human diversity: Master lecturers* (pp. 143–189). Washington, DC: American Psychological Association.

Gates, H. L. (1997). *Thirteen different ways of looking at a Black man.* New York: Random House.

Gay and Lesbian Alliance against Defamation. (2005). *Programs and services.* http://www.glaad.org/programs/index.php

Germain, C. B., & Gitterman, A. (1996). *The life model of social work practice: Advances in theory and practice* (2nd ed.). New York: Columbia University Press.

Greenberg, D. F. (1988). *The construction of homosexuality.* Chicago: University of Chicago Press.

Greene, B. (1993). Stereotypes of African American sexuality: A commentary. In S. Rathus, J. Nevid, & L. Rathus-Fichner (Eds.), *Human sexuality in a world of diversity* (p. 257). Boston: Allyn & Bacon.

Greene, B. (1994). Lesbian women of color: Triple jeopardy. In L. Comas-Diaz & B. Greene (Eds.), *Women of color: Integrating ethnic and gender identities in psychotherapy* (pp. 339–427). New York: Guilford.

Greene, B. (1997). *Ethnic and cultural diversity among lesbians and gay men: Psychological perspectives on lesbian and gay issues.* Thousand Oaks, CA: Sage.

Guardian Unlimited, Special Reports. (2005, June 30). *Spain legalizes gay marriage.* http://www.guardian.co.uk/gayrights/story/0,12592,1518144,00.html

Harris, E. L. (1999). *The invisible life.* New York: Anchor Books.

Hay Brown, M. (2003). Gay rights movement struggles in Puerto Rico. *The Morning Call Online.* http://www.mcall.com/news/nationworld/all-gay0603,0,5102554.story

Helms, J. E. (1990). *Black and white racial identity: Theory, research, and practice.* New York: Greenwood Press.

Hempill, E. (1991). *Brother-to-brother: New writings by Black gay men.* Boston: Alyson Publications.

Hidalgo, H. (1995). The norms of conduct in social service agencies: A threat to the mental health of Puerto Rican lesbians. In H. Hidalgo (Ed.), *Lesbians of color: Social and human services* (pp. 23–42). New York: Haworth.

Hendin, J. (1969). *Black suicide.* New York: Basic Books.

Herdt, G. (1989). Gay and lesbian youth, emergent identities, and cultural scenes at home and abroad. *Journal of Homosexuality, 12*(1), 135–151.

Herdt, G. (1990). Developmental discontinuities and sexual orientation across cultures.

In D. P. McWhirter, S. A. Sanders, & J. M. Reinisch (Eds.), *Homosexuality/heterosexuality: Concepts of sexual orientation* (pp. 208–236). New York: Oxford University Press.

hooks, b. (1990). *Yearning: Race, gender, and cultural politics.* Boston: South End Press.

Hutchinson, E. O. (2000). *My gay problem, your Black problem.* http://www.afronet.com/wb/051997-1html

Hutnik, N. (1985). Aspects of identity in a multiethnic society. *New Community, 12,* 298–309.

Icard, L. (1986). Black gay men and conflicting social identities: Sexual orientation versus racial identity. *Journal of Social Work and Human Sexuality, 4,* 83–92.

Icard, L., Schilling, R. F., El-Bassel, N., & Young, D. (1992). Preventing AIDS among Black gay men and Black gay and heterosexual male intravenous drug users. *Journal of Social Work, 37*(5), 440–445.

Jacobs, S., Thomas, W., & Lang, S. (1997). *Two-spirit people: Native American gender identity, sexuality, and spirituality.* Chicago: University of Illinois.

Johnson, J. (1982). *The influence of assimilation on the psychosocial adjustment of black homosexual men.* Unpublished dissertation, California School of Professional Psychology.

Katz, J. (1976). *Gay American history: Lesbians and gay men in the U.S.A.* New York: Crowell.

Kich, G. K. (1996). In the margins of sex and race: Difference, marginality, and flexibility. In M. P. P. Root (Ed.), *The multiracial experience: Racial borders as the new frontier* (pp. 263–274). Thousand Oaks, CA: Sage.

Kim, Y. J. (1992). The Korean namsadang. In W. R. Dynes & S. Donaldson (Eds.), *Asian homosexuality* (pp. 81–88). New York: Garland.

Kinsey, A. C., Pomeroy, W. B., & Martin, C. E. (1948). *Sexual behavior in the human male.* Philadelphia: Saunders.

LaFromboise, T. D. (1988). American Indian mental health policy. *American Psychologist, 43,* 388–397.

Lancaster, R. N. (1988). Subject honor and object shame: The construction of male homosexuality and stigma in Nicaragua. *Ethnology, 27*(2), 111–125.

Lang, S. (1998). *Men as women, women as men: Changing gender in Native American cultures.* Austin: University of Texas Press.

Leong, R. (1996). *Asian American sexualities.* New York: Routledge.

Leupp, G. (1992). Population registers and household records as sources for the study of urban women in Tokugawa Japan. *Gest Library Journal, 5,* 49–86.

Leupp, G. (1995). Male colors: The construction of homosexuality in Tokugawa Japan. Berkeley: University of California Press.

LLego: The National Latina/o Lesbian, Gay, Bisexual, and Transgender Organization. (2005). http://www.llego.org/main_pages/programs.html

Loecker, G., Smith, D. A., Smith, L., & Bunger, P. (1992). HIV associated risk factors: A survey of troubled adolescent population. *South Dakota Journal of Medicine, 45*(4), 91–94.

Loicano, D. K. (1989). Gay identity issues among Black Americans: Racism, homophobia, and the need for validation. *Journal of Counseling and Development, 68,* 21–25.

Lorde, A. (1984). *Sister outsider.* Freedom, CA: The Crossing Press.

Luibheid, E., & Cantu, L. (Eds.). (2005). *Queer migrations: Sexuality, U.S. citizenship, and border crossings.* Minneapolis: University of Minnesota Press.

Mallon, G. (1999). Knowledge for practice with transgendered children. *Journal of Gay and Lesbian Social Services, 10*(4), 1–18.

Marsiglia, F. F. (1998). Homosexuality and Latinos/as: Toward an integration of identities. *Journal of Gay and Lesbian Social Services, 4*(3), 36–50.

Mayers-Sanchez, R., and Kail, B. L. and Watts T. D. (Eds.). (1993). *Hispanic Substance Abuse.* Springfield, Il: Charles C. Thomas.

McLelland, M. J. (2000). *Male homosexuality in modern Japan: Cultural myths and social realities.* Richmond, UK: Curzon.

McKee Irwin, R. (1998). The legend of Jorge Cuesta. In S. Molloy & R. McKee Irwin (Eds.), Hispanisms and homosexuality (pp. 29–53) Durham, NC: Duke University Press.

Mehata, S. (1946). Eunuchs, pavaiyas and hijadas. In *Gujarat ahitya Sabha, Amdavad, Karyavahi 1945–1946* (pp. 3–75). Amedabad, India.

Meijer, M. J. (1992). Homosexual offenses in Ch'ing law. In W. R. Dynes & S. Donaldson (Eds.), *Asian homosexuality* (pp. 109–134). New York: Garland.

Meyers, T., Calzavara, L. M., Cockerill, R., Marshall, V. W., & Bullock, S. L. (1993). *Ontario First Nations AIDS and healthy lifestyle survey.* National AIDS Clearinghouse, Canadian Public Health Association, Ottawa, Ontario.

Molloy, S., & McKee Irwin, R. (Eds.). (1998). *Hispanisms and Homosexuality.* Durham, NC: Duke University Press.

Morales, E. S. (1989). Ethnic minority families and minority gays and lesbians. *Marriage and Family Review, 14,* 217–239.

Murray, S. O. (1987). The family as an obstacle to the growth of a gay subculture in Latin America. In S. O. Murray (Ed.), *Male homosexuality in Central and South America* (pp. 118–129). New York: Gay Academic Union.

Murray, S. O. (1990). Latin America. In W. R. Dynes (Ed.), *Encyclopedia of homosexuality* (Vol. 2, pp. 678–681). New York: Garland Publishing.

Murray, S. O. (2000). *Homosexualities.* Chicago: University of Chicago Press.

Murray, S. O., & Arboleda, G. (1987). Stigma transformation and relexification: "Gay" in Latin America. In S. O. Murray (Ed.), *Male homosexuality in Central and South America* (pp. 130–138). New York: Gay Academic Union.

Murray, S. O., & Roscoe, W. (1998). *Boy wives and female husbands: Studies of African homosexualities.* New York: St. Martin's Press.

Nanda, S. (1992). The hijras of India: A preliminary report. In W. R. Dynes & S. Donaldson (Eds.), *Asian homosexuality* (pp. 135–152). New York: Garland.

Pew Hispanic Center. (2004, December). *News release: Latinos see race as a measure of belonging.* http://pewhispanic.org/newsroom/releases/release.php?ReleaseID=16

Oetting, E. R., & Beauvais, F. (1990–1991). Orthogonal cultural identification theory: The cultural identification of minority adolescents. *International Journal of the Addictions, 25*(5A & 6A), 655–685.

Parham, T., & Helms, J. (1985). Attitudes of racial identity and self-esteem of Black students: An exploratory investigation. *Journal of College Student Personnel, 26,* 143–147.

Phinney, J. (1990). Ethnic identity in adolescents and adults: Review of research. *Psychological Bulletin, 108*(3), 499–514.

Pilkington, N. W., & D'Augelli, A. R. (1995). Victimization of lesbian, gay, and bisexual youth in community settings. *Journal of Community Psychology, 23,* 34–56.

Pinderhughes, E. (1989). *Understanding race, ethnicity, and power: The key to efficacy in clinical practice.* London: Collier Macmillan.

Ramos, J. (1987). *Companeras: Latina Lesbians* (an anthology). New York: Latina Lesbians History Project.

Read, K. E. (1980). *Other voices: The style of a male homosexual tavern.* Novato, CA: Chandler & Sharp.

Reyes, E. E. (1996). Strategies for queer Asian and Pacific Islander spaces. In Russell Leong (Ed.), *Asian American sexualities* (pp. 85–90). New York: Routledge.

Reyes, M. (1998). Latina lesbians and alcohol and other drugs: Social work implications. In M. Delgado (Ed.), *Alcohol use/abuse among Latinos: Issues and examples of culturally competent services* (pp. 179–192). Binghampton, NY: The Hayworth Press.

Root, M. P. P. (1996). *The multiracial experience: Racial borders as the new frontier.* Thousand Oaks, CA: Sage.

Roque Ramírez, H. N. (n.d.). Latina/Latino Americans. In *GLBTQ: Encyclopedia of gay, lesbian, bisexual, transgender and queer culture.* http://www.glbtq.com/social-sciences/latina_latino_americans,3.html

Roscoe, W. (1998). *Changing ones: Third and fourth genders in Native North America.* New York: St. Martin's Press.

Saewyc, E. M., Skay, C. L., Bearinger, L. H., Blum, R. W., & Resnick, M. D. (1998). Sexual orientation, sexual behaviors, and pregnancy among American Indian adolescents. *Journal of Adolescent Health, 23,* 238–247.

Shah, N. (1998). Sexuality, identity, and the uses of history. In D. Eng and A. Y. Hom (Eds.), *Queer in Asian America* (pp. 141–156). Philadelphia: Temple University Press.

Simoni, J. M., Meyers, T., & Walters, K. L. (2001). Heterosexual identity and heterosexism: Recognizing privilege to reduce prejudice. *Journal of Homosexuality, 41*(1), 157–172.

Sohng, S., & Icard, L. D. (1996). A Korean gay man in the United States: Toward a cultural context for social service practice. In J. F. Longres (Ed.), *Men of color: A context for service to homosexually active men* (pp. 115–137). New York: Haworth.

Tafoya, T. (1992). Native gay and lesbian issues: The two-spirited. In Betty Berzon (Ed.), *Positively gay: New approaches to gay and lesbian life* (pp. 253–260). Berkeley, CA: Celestial Arts Publishing.

Tafoya, T., & Rowell, R. (1988). Counseling gay and lesbian Native Americans. In M. Shernoff & W. A. Scott (Eds.), *Sourcebook on lesbian/gay health* (pp. 63–67). Washington, DC: National Lesbian and Gay Foundation.

Tafoya, T., & Wirth, D. A. (1996). Native American two-spirit men. In J. F. Longres (Ed.), *Men of color: A context for service to homosexually active men* (pp. 51–67). New York: Harrington Park Press.

Taisuke, M. (1970). *Chinese eunuchs: The structure of intimate politics.* Rutland, VT: Tuttle.

Takagi, D. Y. (1996). Maiden voyage: Excursion into sexuality and identity politics in Asian America. In R. Leong (Ed.), *Asian American sexualities* (pp. 21–36). New York: Routledge.

Taylor, C. L. (1991). Mexican gaylife in historical perspective. In W. Leyland (Ed.), *Gay roots* (pp. 190–202). San Francisco: Gay Sunshine Press.

Thomas, W. T. (1997). Navajo constructions of gender and sexuality. In S. Jacobs, W. Thomas, & S. Lang (Eds.), *Two-spirit people: Native American gender identity,*

sexuality, and spirituality (pp. 156–173). Chicago: University of Illinois.

Torres, L. (2003). Introduction. In L. Torres and I. Pertusa (Eds.), *Hispanic and U.S. Latina lesbian expression* (pp 1–15) Philadelphia: Temple University Press.

Torres, L., & Pertusa, I. (Eds.). (2003). *Tortilleras: Hispanic and U.S. Latina lesbian expression.* Philadelphia: Temple University Press.

U.S. Bureau of the Census. (1991). *Resident populations distribution for the United States, region, and states by race and Hispanic origin: 1990* (Census Bureau Press Release No. CB91-100). Washington, DC: U.S. Government Printing Office.

U.S. Bureau of the Census. (2002). *Current population reports. The Hispanic population in the United States: March 2002 (P20–545).* Washington DC: Department of Commerce.

Van Gulik, R. (1974). *Sexual life in ancient China.* Leiden, Netherlands: E. J. Brill.

Walters, K. L. (1995). *Urban American Indian identity and psychological wellness.* Unpublished doctoral dissertation, University of California, Los Angeles.

Walters, K. L. (1997). Urban lesbian and gay American Indian identity: Implications for mental health social service delivery. *Journal of Gay and Lesbian Social Services, 6*(2), 43–65.

Walters, K. L. (1999). Negotiating conflicts in allegiances within lesbian and gay communities of color. In G. Mallon (Ed.), *Foundations of social work practice with gay and lesbian persons* (pp. 47–75). New York: Harrington Park Press.

Walters, K. L., & Simoni, J. M. (1993). Lesbian and gay male group identity attitudes and self-esteem: Implications for counseling. *Journal of Counseling Psychology, 40,* 94–99.

Walters, K. L., Simoni, J. M., & Horwath, P. F. (2001). Sexual orientation bias experiences and service needs of gay, lesbian, bisexual, transgendered, and two-spirited American Indians. *Journal of Gay and Lesbian Social Services, 13*(1/2), 133–149.

Watson, B. (1964). *Han Fei Tzu: Basic writings.* New York: Columbia University Press.

Wong, S. C. (1992). Ethnicizing gender, gendering ethnicity. In S. G. Lim and A. Ling (Eds.), *Reading the literatures of Asian America* (pp. 111–129). Philadelphia: Temple University Press.

Wooden, W. S., Kawasaki, H., & Mayeda, R. (1983). Lifestyles and identity maintenance among gay Japanese-American males. *Alternative Lifestyles, 5*, 236–243.

Yue, A. (1999). Interface: Reflections of an ethnic toygirl. In P. A. Jackson & G. Sullivan (Eds.), *Multicultural queer: Australian narratives* (pp. 113–134). New York: Haworth.

Zamora-Hernandez, C. E., & Patterson, D. G. (1996). Homosexually active Latino men: Issues for social work practice. *Journal of Gay and Lesbian Social Services, 5*(2/3), 69–92.

Zimmerman, M. A., Washienko, K. M., Walter, B., & Dyer, S. (1996). The development of a measure of enculturation for Native American youth. *American Journal of Community Psychology, 24*, 295–310.

CHAPTER 15

Bernard, J. M. (1979). Supervisor training: A discrimination model. *Counselor Education and Supervision, 19*, 60–68.

Bordin, E. S. (1979). The generalizability of the psychoanalytic concept of the working alliance. *Psychotherapy: Theory, Research, and Practice, 16*, 252–260.

Cross, T. L., Bazron, B. J., Dennis, K. W., & Isaacs, M. R. (1989). *Toward a culturally competent system of care.* Washington, DC: Georgetown University Child Development Center.

Dean, R. G. (1994). Commentary: A practitioner's perspective on qualitative case evaluation methods. In E. Sherman & W. J. Reid (Eds.), *Qualitative research in social work* (pp. 279–284). New York: Columbia University Press.

Frank, A. F., & Gunderson, J. G. (1990). The role of the therapeutic alliance in the treatment of schizophrenia. *Archives of General Psychiatry, 47*, 228–236.

Green, J. W. (1999). *Cultural awareness in the human services: A multi-ethnic approach* (3rd ed.). Boston: Allyn & Bacon.

Henggeler, S. W., Schoenwald, S. K., Pickrel, S. G., Rowland, M. D., & Santos, A. B. (1994). The contribution of treatment outcome research to the reform of children's mental health services: Multisystem therapy as an example. *Journal of Mental Health Administration, 21*, 229–239.

Horvath, A. O., & Greenberg, L. S. (Eds.). (1994). *The working alliance: Theory, research, and practice.* New York: John Wiley.

Iglehart, A. P., & Becerra, R. M. (2000). *Social service and the ethnic community.* Prospect Heights, IL: Waveland Press.

Lang, N. C. (1994). Integrating the data processing of qualitative research and social work practice to advance the practitioner as knowledge builder: Tools for knowing and doing. In E. Sherman & W. J. Reid (Eds.), *Qualitative research in social work* (pp. 265–278). New York: Columbia University Press.

Lum, D. (2004). *Social work practice and people of color: A process-stage approach* (5th ed.). Belmont, CA: Brooks/Cole–Thomson Learning.

Orlandi, M. A. (1992). The challenge of evaluating community-based prevention programs: A cross-cultural perspective. In M. A. Orlandi, R. Weston, & L. G. Epstein (Eds.), *Cultural competence for evaluators: A guide for alcohol and other drug abuse prevention practitioners working with ethnic/racial communities* (pp. 1–22). Rockville, MD: U.S. Department of Health and Human Services, Office for Substance Abuse Prevention.

Orlandi, M. A., Weston, R., & Epstein, L. G. (Eds.). (1992). *Cultural competence for evaluators: A guide for alcohol and other drug abuse prevention practitioners working with ethnic/racial communities.* Rockville, MD: U.S. Department of Health and Human Services, Office for Substance Abuse Prevention.

Sue, D. W., Arredondo, P., & McDavis, R. J. (1992). Multicultural counseling competencies and standards: A call to the profession. *Journal of Counseling and Development, 70*, 477–486.

Index